Diversity and Inclusion in Organizations

A Volume in:
Research in Human Resource Management

Series Editors

Dianna L. Stone
James H. Dulebohn

Research in Human Resource Management

Series Editors

Dianna L. Stone
Universities of New Mexico, Albany, and Virginia Tech

James H. Dulebohn
Michigan State University

Diversity and Inclusion in Organizations

Edited by

Dianna L. Stone
James H. Dulebohn
Kimberly M. Lukaszewski

INFORMATION AGE PUBLISHING, INC.
Charlotte, NC • www.infoagepub.com

Library of Congress Cataloging-In-Publication Data

The CIP data for this book can be found on the Library of Congress website (loc.gov).

Paperback: 978-1-64802-004-9
Hardcover: 978-1-64802-005-6
eBook: 978-1-64802-006-3

Printed in the United States of America

CONTENTS

CHAPTER 1

THE IMPACT OF MULTICULTURALISM ON HUMAN RESOURCE POLICIES AND PRACTICES

Dianna L. Stone, James H. Dulebohn, and
Kimberly M. Lukaszewski

It has been predicted that by the year 2060 ethnic minorities will constitute the ma-jority of the population. One important implication of this change in demographics in our society is that ethnic minorities differ from Anglo-Americans in key cultural values including collectivism, familism, power distance and time orientation. Giv-en these differences in cultural values, current human resource management (HR) policies and practices may be less effective in attracting, motivating, and retaining members of a multicultural than a monocultural workforce. Thus, we have argued that existing HR practices may need to be modified to fit with the cultural values of the new multicultural population. In order to consider the influence of cultural val-ues on changes in HR practices, we describe the average cultural values of four of the major ethnic groups in the US including Hispanics, African-Americans, Asians, and Native Americans. We also discuss how these cultural values might influence changes in several HR practices (e.g., recruitment, selection, compensation). Fi-nally, we provide suggestions for future research and practice on the influence of multiculturalism on HR policies and practices.

Diversity and Inclusion in Organizations, pages 1–31.

In the biological world diversity plays an important role in boosting and increasing the survival rate of ecosystems (Biological Diversity, 2019). For example, a recent meta-analysis on the relation between biodiversity and ecosystem success revealed that the greater the diversity of species the more that an ecosystem will be sustainable, and persevere when confronted with diseases and natural disasters (Balvanera et al., 2006). The diversity of species also prevents the negative effects of inbreeding, and ensures the continued existence of the species. For instance, assume a gardener decided to grow a rose garden, and planted yellow roses. However, soon after she planted them they were besieged by pests (e.g., aphids, mites, caterpillars, nematods), and infected with diseases (e.g., black spot fungus, downey mold). Before she could control these pests and diseases all of the plants died and the garden was completely bare. One way of preventing these problems would have been to plant a variety of companion plants that deter pests, improve soil, and enhance the overall health of roses (Biological Diversity, 2019). Given the importance of a diversity of plants to the health of roses and the garden, the gardener learned that sowing an assortment of plants would have protected the roses, and enabled the garden to thrive throughout the season. As a consequence, including a diversity of species in a biosystem is critical because it increases the strength and endurance of the system, and enables it to survive in the face of threats and diseases (Biological Diversity, 2019).

Similarly, we also believe that diversity has a comparable function in organizations, and helps companies hire people who (a) bring complementary sets of talents and skills to the workforce, (b) develop innovative solutions to problems, (c) create relations with diverse groups of customers, and (d) enable organizations to adapt to changes and threats in the environment. For example, research has shown that employee diversity increases the breadth of individuals' knowledge and skills, allows companies to expand their customer base, and enhances the overall performance of innovative organizations (Cox, 1993; Richard, Bennett, Dwyer, & Chadwick, 2004). Despite the significant benefits of diversity in organizations, there is still a great deal of resistance to diversity, and many companies have not fully included or utilized the talents and skills that people with diverse backgrounds bring to the workforce (Stone & Stone-Romero, 2008).

Although there are a number of advantages of diversity in organizations, it also poses challenges for organizations because current human resource management (HR) policies and practices are largely based on Anglo-American (Anglo) cultural values, and may be less effective with members of multicultural than monocultural groups (Stone & Stone-Romero, 2008). One reason for this is that ethnic group members in our nation often have a very different set of cultural values than Anglos, and contemporary HR practices and reward systems may not reflect the values or appeal to multicultural groups (Stone & Stone-Romero, 2008). Thus, a better understanding is needed of the cultural values of the different ethnic groups in our society so that organizations can align their HR practices with the needs and values of all applicants and employees. Given the growing need to modify

HR practices to fit with the cultural values of an increasingly diverse workforce, the primary purposes of this paper are to: (a) review the research on the cultural values of four major ethnic groups in the US (e.g., Hispanic- Americans, African-Americans; Asian Americans, and Native Americans), (b) consider the degree to which current HR practices will be effective with the cultural values of the new multicultural groups, (c) suggest modifications in HR policies and practices that might meet the needs and values of a diverse workforce, and (d) offer directions for future research and practice on these issues.

INCREASED MULTICULTURAL DIVERSITY IN US

It is clear that the US is becoming much more diverse, and recent estimates indicate that the current population is made up of 60.7% Anglos, and approximately 38.6% ethnic minorities (e.g., 13.4% African-Americans, 1.3% Native Americans, 5.8% Asian-Americans, 18.1% Hispanic-Americans) (US Census Bureau, 2018a). However, the US Census Bureau (2018b) predicts that there will be a critical turning point in the population by the year 2060, and the percentage of Anglos will decrease and ethnic group members will constitute the majority of the population (i.e., 57%). Therefore, in the next few decades there will be major changes in the workforce and the new workforce will have very different cultural values than the current set of employees. Thus, we believe that organizations may have to alter their HR practices to attract, motivate, and retain members of the new multicultural labor force (Stone, Stone-Romero, & Lukaszewski, 2007).

Given the transformation in the population, it is important to understand how these changes will be beneficial for organizations, and prompt modifications in the current HR policies and practices. On average, ethnic minorities have very different cultural value systems than Anglos, and these cultural differences are likely to affect job choice and reward preferences, and the overall success of HR policies and practices (Stone & Stone-Romero, 2008; Triandis, 1994). For example, differences in cultural values have been shown to affect role taking, the desirability of job attributes, reward preferences, the acceptance of feedback, job attitudes, desire for family friendly practices, and the ability to work effectively in teams (Gelfand, Erez, & Aycan, 2007; Stone & Stone-Romero, 2008). Research has also indicated that most US organizations were founded on Anglo cultural values that emphasize independence, competitive achievement, autonomy, egalitarianism, separation of job and job holder, and equity-based views of fairness (Markus & Kitayama, 1991a; Trice & Beyer, 1993). However, the cultural values of the major ethnic minorities in the US are more likely to stress collectivism, familism, different views of power distance, or time orientation than Anglos (Stone & Stone-Romero, 2008; Triandis, 1994). Thus, organizations may have to modify their HR policies and practices in order to attract and retain members of the new multicultural workforce (Stone & Stone-Romero, 2008). It merits noting that in the following sections we refer to Hispanic-Americans as Hispanics, and Asian-Americans as Asians.

Despite the emerging changes in the US workforce, relatively little research has examined the influence of the cultural values of ethnic minority groups on the effectiveness of HR policies and practices (Erez & Earley, 1993; Stone & Stone-Romero, 2008; Thomas & Wise, 1999; Triandis, 1994). There has been an increased interest in the effects of international culture on the success of varying HR policies (e.g., Gelfand, Erez, & Aycan 2007; Schuler & Jackson, 2005), but much less research has been designed to understand the cultural values of domestic diversity groups, and the impact of these values on the success of HR policies and practices (e.g., Stone & Stone-Romero, 2008; Thomas & Wise, 1999). Prior to discussing cultural values of the changing workforce, we believe that it is important to define cultural values and distinguish those values from personality (Parks-Leduc, Feldman, & Bardi, 2015). Triandis and his colleagues defined culture as "shared behavior and shared human-made aspects of the society…that includes 'practices' (the way things are done here) and 'values' (the way things should be done here" (Triandis & Wasti, 2008, p. 1). Personality is typically defined as the characteristic set of behaviors, cognitions, and emotional patterns that evolve from biological and environmental factors (Allport, 1953). Cultural values differ from personality because values include "a right or wrong based judgment" and personality does not emphasize a right or wrong framework (Triandis, 1994). Further, cross-cultural theorists indicate that cultural values influence personality through socialization practices (see Triandis, 1994). For instance, the environment shapes the culture which, in turn, influences child rearing practices, socialization, and individuals' personality (Triandis, 1994).

Given the growing changes in the workforce, we describe the cultural values of four of the major ethnic minority groups in the US (e.g., Hispanics, Native Americans, African-Americans and Asians), and examine how their cultural values might affect their job and reward preferences and the design of HR practices. Whenever possible, we also review the existing research on these issues, and offer directions for future research on the topic.

Cultural Value Differences

Individuals emphasize a variety of different cultural values, but we limit our discussion to four specific values considered in cross-cultural research (Hofstede, 1980; Triandis, 1994). In particular, we consider the terms individualism/collectivism, familism, power distance, and time orientation then describe the extent to which the four major ethnic minority groups in the US endorse these values below.

Collectivism. One of the most important cultural values in a society is individualism/collectivism (Triandis, 1994). Individuals who value collectivism use the group as the unit of analysis in social relationships, and the goals of the group take precedence over those of the individual (Hofstede, 1980). In contrast, individualism is a value having to do with the strength of ties that should exist between individuals. Individualists believe that such ties should be loose, and that individuals should look after themselves and their immediate families (Hofstede, 1980). Collectivist cultures are characterized by values that favor interdependence, security, obedience, duty, in-group harmony, and personalized relationships (Markus & Kitayama, 1991a,b; Triandis, 1994). Individualist cultures often emphasize independence, competitive achievement, autonomy, freedom, and self-reliance (Triandis 1994; Trice & Beyer, 1993). Research has shown that differences in individualism and collectivism cultural values influence individuals' preferences for rewards, work schedules, allocation of outcomes, team orientation, and responses to feedback (Stone-Romero & Stone, 2008).

Familism. Those characterized as high in in terms of familism values place a great deal of emphasis on the family, and have a deep sense of commitment and obligation to their families (McGoldrick, Giordano, & Pearce, 1996; Stone-Romero, Stone, & Salas, 2003). There is also a strong expectation that when a family member is in trouble others will help, and individuals will make every effort to spend time with their families. In contrast to high familism cultures, those who are low in familism (e.g., Anglos) emphasize that work should be the priority in one's life, and people should be willing to sacrifice their family life in the interest of work and achievement (e.g., Lobel & Kossek, 1996). Not surprisingly, the differences in commitment to the family should evoke very different needs, reward preferences, and work-related attitudes and behaviors.

Power Distance. Power distance is a value that reflects the degree to which the less powerful members of a social system (e.g. organization) accept the unequal distribution of power and status among people in the society (Hofstede, 1980). The construct of power distance has also been viewed as a measure of interpersonal power or influence that exists between two individuals. Cultures that are characterized as high-power distance support the notion that some people have more power because of inherited (e.g., status, intelligence) or acquired characteristics (e.g. education) (Marin & Marin, 1991). However, those that are labeled low power distance believe that power should be shared equally among people, and people should have a great deal of freedom and autonomy (Hofstede, 1980). Low power distance cultures emphasize egalitarianism and believe that individuals should have a great deal of personal power. For example, they stress that "people have rights that even kings should respect" (Stone-Romero & Stone, 2008). Given that there are cultural differences in power distance, those ethnic group members who are high in power distance are likely to prefer working in an organization that is characterized by high status, hierarchical structures, authority-based decision making, and dependence on supervisors (Stone et al., 2007). However, those who endorse low power distance should prefer egalitarian organizations, those that use participation in decision making, and jobs that emphasize autonomy and freedom (Stone et al., 2007; Stone-Romero & Stone, 2008).

Time Orientation. Time orientation refers to a culture's views about time, and the degree to which it stresses a past, present, or future time orientation (Bond & Hofstede, 1989; Triandis, 1994). For instance , some cultures (e.g., Anglos) view time as linear and place a great deal of emphasis on efficiency and punctuality which is noted in Benjamin Franklin's quote that "time is money" (Okun, Friend, & Okun, 1999). However, other cultures have a present time orientation (e.g., Hispanics) and view the present as more important than the past or the future (Bond & Hofstede, 1989; Okun et al., 1999; Sue & Morishima, 1982). Still other cultures highlight the importance of the past (e.g., Asians) (Bond & Hofstede, 1989; Sue & Morishima, 1982), or have a circular view of time (e.g., Native Americans) (Fixico, 2003). The cultural differences in time orientation should have important implications for understanding how members of a multicultural workforce will react to reward allocation (e.g., pay raises, promotions) and benefit systems (e.g., retirement programs) in organizations.

In the sections that follow we consider the degree to which members of four different ethnic groups in the US are likely to endorse each of the cultural values described above. However, we want to emphasize that there are often within group differences in cultural values so researchers have argued that inferences based on a person's ethnicity or nationality may result in erroneous assumptions (Betancourt & Lopez, 1993). As a result, we specify that our predictions about the cultural values of members of various ethnic groups are based, *on average,* not absolute levels of a particular cultural value. Stated differently, not all members of an ethnic group may endorse a specific cultural value. It is especially important to understand this issue in the US where some ethnic group members have assimilated to the dominant Anglo culture, and others are bicultural which means that they are comfortable and proficient with their heritage and current culture (Berry, 1997).

Research has shown that members of some ethnic groups have maintained their original culture more than others (Berry, 1997). For instance, Hispanics, Asians, and Native Americans are more likely to maintain their specific heritage or cultural values than Anglos or African-Americans (Huynh, Nguyen, & Benet-Martinez, 2011). Unfortunately, African-Americans have not always retained their original culture because they were stripped of their culture when they were transported to the US as part of the transatlantic slave trade. However, the US culture has incorporated some of their original African-American culture into their beliefs and values (Portes & Rumbaut, 2006).

CULTURAL VALUES OF DIFFERENT US ETHNIC GROUPS

In view of the cultural values described above, we consider the unique sets of cultural values of the four major ethnic minority groups in the US (e.g., Hispanics, African-Americans, Asians, and Native Americans) below. We also highlight the cultural values of the dominant group of Anglos in our nation, and indicate how these values shape current HR policies and practices. To our knowledge, relatively little research in human resource management or organizational behavior has examined the cultural values of domestic ethnic minority group members (Stone & Stone-Romero, 2008; Thomas & Wise, 1999). Most of the existing research on cultural values has stressed international differences in cultural values, and the research on domestic diversity has focused primarily on unfair discrimination faced by these groups (Bell, 2012). Prior to discussing the cultural values of these four ethnic groups, it is important to distinguish between the terms race and ethnicity. Race is typically defined in terms of physical characteristics such as skin color, facial features, and hair type (Betancourt & Lopez, 1993), and the term ethnicity is used to refer to groups that are characterized in terms of a common nationality, culture or language.

Anglo-Americans

At present, Anglo-Americans are the largest ethnic group in the US (about 60%) and their values dominant today's organizational cultures and the design of HR practices. On average, they emphasize cultural values associated with individualism, competitive achievement, autonomy, freedom, egalitarianism, equity or proportionality-based views of fairness, and a future time orientation (Trice & Beyer, 1993). Most of these individuals trace their ancestry to Europe (e.g., United Kingdom, Germany, France, Ireland, Italy), and they started migrating to the US in the 1600s. However, one of the largest migrations was in the early 1900s, and these individuals focused on assimilating to the dominant culture and language in the US (American Ancestors, 2019).

Given that they are the dominant group in our nation, Anglo cultural values have influenced the culture of work organizations, and existing HR policies and practices (Trice & Beyer, 1993). For instance, Anglos emphasis on autonomy, and freedom, and low power distance resulted in the use of participation in decision making in organizations, and the design of jobs that stress autonomy (American Ancestors, 2019). Their focus on individualism, independence, and competitive achievement affected the competitive culture of organizations, and the use of individual merit pay plans (Trice & Beyer, 1993). Their endorsement of a future time orientation also influenced the use of retirement and benefit programs that focus on protecting individuals' future (Trice & Beyer, 1993).

Hispanic-Americans

Hispanics are currently the largest ethnic minority group in the US, and make up approximately 18.1 percent of the population (US Census Bureau, 2018a). The Census Bureau also predicts that they will constitute approximately 33 percent of the population by 2060 (US Census Bureau, 2018b). The term Hispanic can be defined as individuals who are indigenous to the Americas, but trace their ancestry to Spain or the Ibero pennisula (Betancourt & Lopez, 1993; Marin & Marin, 1991). Hispanics in the US trace their ancestry to Colombia, Mexico, Guatemala, Peru, Cuba, etc. It should be noted that Hispanics settled in the area later labeled the US in the 1500s, and populated the region prior to the European migrations of the 1600s.

Research has shown that, on average, Hispanics have a very set different of cultural values than Anglos, and place emphasis on collectivism, familism, high power distance, and a present time orientation (Marin & Marin, 1991; Stone-Romero et al., 2003). For instance, research has revealed that Hispanics are more likely to endorse collectivism or stress the good of the group over the individual more than Anglos (Marin & Marin, 1991; Triandis, 1994). They also place a great deal of emphasis on familism, and they even make sacrifices to attend special events for extended family members (e.g., nephews, nieces) (Gaines et al., 1997; Triandis, 1994). Studies have also shown that they stress high power distance, and defer to those in positions of authority (Marin & Marin, 1991). Hispanics also have a present time orientation and have a much more relaxed view of time than Anglos (Stone-Romero et al., 2003). Apart from these cultural values, Hispanics advocate *personalismo* or preference for personalized rather than distant contact, and they subscribe to a *sympatia* style of communication which stresses harmonious and smooth social relations with others (Velasquez, Arellano, & McNeill, 2004). Finally, they are often more likely to maintain their original cultural heritage and language (i.e., Spanish) than other ethnic groups in the US (Marin & Marin, 1991).

African-Americans

African-Americans make up approximately 13% of the population in the US, and they trace their ancestry to the cultures of Western and Central Africa (Portes & Rumbaut; 2006; US Census Bureau, 2018a). Their culture has also been influenced by their experiences as part of the transatlantic slave trade that occurred between 1600 and 1800s. As slaves they were prevented from practicing their original cultural traditions, but some of their values, ceremonies, and beliefs survived despite these restrictions. As a result, their cultural values today are a blend of Anglo culture, Native American cultures, and their original African cultural background. Not surprisingly, enslaved African-Americans brought their religious views and distinct beliefs to America, and it has helped shape American cultural values and norms.

Research has shown that African-Americans place a great deal of emphasis on collectivism, familism, low power distance, and a present time orientation (e.g., Federico, 2006; Portes & Rumbaut, 2006; Vandello & Cohen, 1999). For instance, Portes and Rumbaut (2006) found that African Americans were more likely to maintain collectivistic values than any other ethnic group. Studies have also indicated that African-Americans scored higher in terms of familism, filial piety, and the primacy of the family relationship than any other group (Gaines et al., 1997; Schwartz et al., 2010). On average, African Americans also endorse a low or moderately low power distance value system (e.g., Gibson, 2008; Swaidan, Rawwas, & Vitell, 2008). In addition, research revealed that they have a present time orientation (de Mooij & Beniflah, 2017), and emphasize a very direct, truthful, and animated communication style (Kochman, 1981). Their conversational style is intense, focuses on the validity of the ideas being discussed, (Kochman, 1981, pp. 30–31), and is characterized by a preference for communicating directly when talking with another person (Kochman, 1981).

Asian-Americans

Asians make up approximately 5.6% of the population of the US and are actually a heterogeneous group of people who trace their origins to East, South, and Southeast Asia (US Census Bureau, 2018b). For example, their ancestors were from a variety of countries including, but not limited to, China, India, Korea, Japan, Vietnam, and the Philippines. Asians started migrating to the US in the 17th century, but there were major restrictions on immigration and their to ability to work until 1965. During this time, they developed a large number of successful small businesses, and own 1.5 million businesses today.

Asian Americans endorse a set of cultural values that is somewhat similar to Hispanics and African Americans. For example, research revealed that they stress collectivism and familism, but they are more likely to emphasize a high-power distance and a past time orientation than other ethnic groups (e.g., Triandis, 1993; Vandello & Cohen, 1999; Xia, Do & Xie, 2013). In particular, research by Vandello and Cohen (1999) found that the correlation between Asians and collectivism values was $r=.54$, and a study by Chang, Natsuaki, and Chen (2013) revealed that the centrality of the family and shared collectivism were major values among Asians and key sources of social support. Other research by Chen and Jeung (2012) indicated that the family was the object of worship, sacrifice, and moral obligation among second generation Chinese Americans.

Apart from these values, studies have shown that Asian Americans are, on average, higher in power distance than Anglos (Xin & Tsui, 1996), and defer to authority and accept power and status differentials (Triandis, 1993; Xin, 2004). However, unlike other ethnic minority groups in the US, they have a past time orientation which means that they are slow to change those things that are tied to the past, and look to the past and elders for inspiration, motivation, hope and guidance (Carter, 1991; Sue & Sue, 1999). Research has also shown that Asians, on average, place more emphasis on education than other ethnic groups, have the highest educational attainment level, and the highest salary levels of any ethnic group (Sue & Sue, 1999). The Asian communication style stresses honor and respect for others, and they place a great deal of emphasis on silence, quietness, and listening to others, and avoid eye contact with others as a sign of respect (Cross-cultural Communications, 2019).

Native Americans

There are approximately 5.2 million Native Americans and Alaskan Natives in the US, and estimates indicate that they have inhabited the land labeled the US for 13,000 to 15,000 years (500 Nations, 2019). Today, most of these individuals are members of over 500 tribes, but it merits emphasis that members of different tribes are not exact replicas of one another (500 Nations, 2019). Further, there has been very little research on Native Americans in Human Resource Management or related fields, but there has been some research in the fields of Sociology and Counseling Psychology (Attneave, 1982; Bennett, 1994). Results of that research, has shown that, on average, they endorse a set of common underlying cultural values including collectivism, familism, high power distance, and a circular time orientation. For instance, research has shown that Native Americans value cooperation. generosity, community, and place the welfare of the group (or tribe) over the individual (Attneave, 1982; Bennett, 1994; Leong, 1991; Yamauchi, 1998).

Native Americans also stress respect for elders, family obligations, and familism as core beliefs (Rodriguez-Galan, 2014). The roles of elders are highly prized, and a sense of kinship often extends to the entire tribe (Weibel-Orlando, 2003). Children are expected to be quiet in the presence of elders to show respect, and this behavior is indicative of familism and high power distance (Finley, 2001). Another index of high power distance is that in most tribes, tribal leaders (e.g., Governor, Counsel of Elders) have the right to make decisions for all tribal members without seeking their approval, and when leaders make decisions tribal members are expected to comply (Weibel-Orlando, 2003).

Native Americans also have a very different view of time than other ethnic groups. Anglos are said to have a linear or monochronic view of time, but Native Americans are said to have a circular time orientation (Carter, 1991). A circular time orientation emphasizes that the universe and all existence and energy has been recurring and will continue to recur in a similar form for an infinite number of times across time and space (Fixico, 2003). When cultures stress a circular time orientation, they are more attuned to event time than clock time, and stress the involvement of people and completion of transactions over adherence to strict schedules (Harris, 1998). Members of Athabaskan tribes (e.g., Apache, Navajos) also believe that it is inappropriate to speak of plans and anticipate the future. For example, the Navajos believe that one should live a long life, and not limit one's potential by setting a specific timeline or plan (Mike, Bidtah & Thomas, 1989). Their belief is if one sets a plan for the future, actions may limit all other possibilities for living one's best life (Mike et al., 1989).

Native Americans also have a very different communication style than Anglos, and focus on silence, quietness, and do not express emotions even when they are upset or angry. In conversations they emphasize listening rather than speaking and express their feelings about someone or something (Rice, 2019).

Taken together, it is clear that the cultural values of the four ethnic minority groups in the US are very different than Anglo values. However, there are some commonalities among the groups, and all four ethnic groups stress collectivism and familism. However, they vary in terms of power distance and time orientation values. Given that members of these groups will be the majority in the population by 2060, we believe that it is important to understand how organizations might design HR practices to attract and retain them. Thus, we consider a model of the influence of cultural values on HR policies and practices in the sections below, and discuss potential modifications in recruitment selection, and compensation practices needed for the changing workforce.

MODEL OF THE INFLUENCE OF CULTURAL VALUES ON HR POLICIES AND PRACTICES

In view of the changing composition workforce, we believe it is important to develop a better understanding of how the cultural values of ethnic minorities will influence the effectiveness of current HR processes and practices in organizations. In 2007, Stone, Stone-Romero, and Lukaszewski developed a model to describe how cultural values affect the design and effectiveness of HR practices. A depiction of the model is noted in Figure 1.1.

The model predicts that societal culture influences the cultures of organizations, HR policies and practices, and cultural values of potential job applicants and job incumbents (Stone et al., 2007). For instance, the dominant culture in the US reflects the Anglo cultural values of standardization, rational decision-making efficiency, individualism, and the separation of the job and job holder (Kossek & Lobel, 1996; Trice & Beyer, 1993). Thus, the cultures of US organizations and the design of HR processes reflect the same values. The Stone et al. (2007)

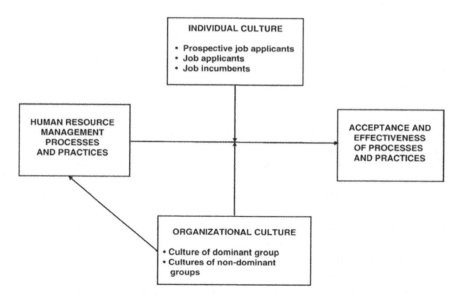

FIGURE 1.1. The influence of culture on the acceptance and effectiveness of human resource management processes and practices

model posits that the use of particular HR practices influences key outcomes in organizations including the attraction, motivation, and retention of organizational members. However, the model predicts that the relation between HR practices and outcomes depends on the cultural values of applicants and job incumbents. It also maintains that the acceptance and effectiveness of HR practices depends on the fit or congruence between the cultural values of individuals and the culture of the organization (Triandis & Wasti, 2008). For instance, merit-based compensation systems designed for individualistic US organizations may be effective with Anglo employees, but may not be as effective with those who have collectivistic values (Joshi & Martocchio, 2008). One reason for this is that individuals who are high in collectivism typically emphasize that group-gains take precedence over individual gains, and merit-based pay plans stress individual and personal gains. As a result, merit-based pay plans may not be motivating for people who have high levels of collectivistic values (e.g., Hispanics, Asians, African-Americans).

As a result, the model suggests that job applicants' and job incumbents' cultural values will influence the extent to which the HR practices are accepted and effective (Stone et al., 2007). Although Stone et al. (2007) considered the effects of a broad range of cultural values on the effectiveness of HR practices, they did not describe how the specific cultural values of ethnic minorities in the US would affect these practices. As a result, we discuss the extent to which the four cultural values highlighted above are likely to shape or modify the design and effectiveness of recruitment, selection, and compensation systems.

Recruitment

The model described above argues that individuals' culture values will have a major impact on desirability of job attributes and reactions to the recruitment process (Stone et al., 2007). Further, organizations that offer applicants the opportunity to express their cultural values should be more likely to attract and retain talented employees than those that do not. Thus, we believe that organizations need to be proactive in developing or altering recruitment processes in order to attract members of the new multicultural workforce.

It merits noting that several studies have examined the relations between Anglo values or personality and job choice preferences (Bretz Ash, & Dreher, 1989; Tom, 1971; Turban & Keon, 1993), and found that individuals are more attracted to organizations when their values or personality fit with the organization's values than when they do not. In particular, results of this research found that individuals who stressed high levels of need for achievement were more likely to prefer jobs in individualistic organizations that used merit-based pay systems than those with low levels of need for achievement (Bretz et al., 1989; Tom, 1971). Findings of other studies revealed that perceptions of person-organization fit were related to the congruence between individuals' personality and the culture of the organization (Chatman, 1989).

Despite these studies, very little research has examined the extent to which the perceived fit between ethnic minorities' cultural values and the culture of organizations influences attraction to organizations (e.g., Harrison & Stone, 2018; Thomas & Wise, 1999). Taken together, results of these studies revealed that the job choice preferences of ethnic minorities (e.g., Hispanics and African-Americans) were positively related to their unique cultural values (e.g., collectivism, familism). Given the lack of research on the effects of cultural values on the job choice preferences of ethnic minorities, we consider these issues in the sections below.

Influence of Cultural Values on Desirability of Job Attributes

We predict that the cultural values of ethnic minority applicants will have a major impact on their preferences for job attributes and individuals' attraction to organizations. Thus, we consider the relations between the four cultural values noted above and preferences for job attributes below.

Collectivism. Research has shown that members of all four ethnic minority groups are, on average, more collective than Anglos (Attneave, 1982; Marin & Marin, 1991; Portes & Rumbaut, 2006; Vandello & Cohen, 1999). Thus, we believe that they should place more emphasis on personal relationships in organizations, and be more likely to underscore the importance of work group welfare than those who are low in collectivism. As a result, we predict that ethnic minorities who are highly collectivistic will be more likely to prefer jobs that (a) offer the opportunities for teamwork, (b) close relations with coworkers and supervisors, and (c) organizations with a diverse workforce than those who are low in terms of this value.

In support of these arguments, research by Thomas and Wise (1999) found that African-Americans preferred organizations that had a diverse workforce to ones that did not. Similarly, a study by Stone et al. (2007) found that Hispanics who were high in terms of collectivism were more likely to choose jobs that had good coworkers and diversity compared to job seekers low in collectivism. Further, research by Gowan (2004) suggested that those who are high in collectivism would prefer jobs that involve quality circles, and autonomous work groups than those who are low in terms of these values. Other researchers also argued that those in highly collective cultures would prefer group-based work, feel socially responsible for ingroup members, and sacrifice their own interests for the group's interests (Ma & Allen, 2009). Kirkman and Shapiro (1997) also argued that companies need to focus on rewards for individual performance in work groups for those who are low rather than high in collectivism.

Even though a number of researchers have argued that those who are high in collectivism may have very different job choice preferences than those who are low in terms of this value (e.g., Gowan, 2004; Thomas & Wise, 1999), there has been relatively little empirical research to examine this prediction. Thus, we believe that additional research is needed to identify the job choice preferences of applicants who are high in collectivism, familism, high in power distance, and those who have varying time orientations. Based on the review noted above, it can also be argued that personalized recruitment practices (e.g., contact with recruiters or current employees) may be more effective with job applicants with collective cultural values than impersonal practices (e-recruitment) members. However, research is needed to examine the degree to which aligning recruitment practices with the cultural values of job applicants influences attraction to organization and the success of recruitment practices.

Familism. Members of ethnic minority groups in the US are, on average, higher in terms of familism than Anglos (e.g., Attneave, 1982; Marin & Marin, 1991; Vandello & Cohen, 1999), and we believe that high levels of familism values should affect preferences for job attributes. For example, we predict that members of ethnic minority groups who are high in familism should prefer jobs that offer (a) family-friendly work policies, (b) flexible work schedules, and (c) time off to spend with their families more than those who are low in familism values.

In support of these arguments, research by Stone et al. (2007) found that Hispanics who were high in familism values were more likely to prefer jobs that offered time off to spend with their families than those who were low in familism. Further research by Casper, Wayne and Manegold (2013) revealed that family and diversity values influenced intentions to pursue jobs with organizations that offered family friendly policies. In addition, results of a study by Fernandez and Fritzsche (2007) indicated that regardless of their ethnicity, most job applicants preferred jobs that offered family-friendly policies. Although there has been some research on the relations between familism values, ethnicity and preference for jobs offering family-work policies, we believe that much more research is needed to examine the job choice preferences of applicants who are high in familism values.

Power Distance. Research has revealed that three of the ethnic groups considered above (e.g., Hispanics, Asians, and Native Americans) are, on average, higher in terms of power distance than Anglos or African-Americans (Attneave, 1982; Marin & Marin, 1991; Vandello & Cohen, 1999). Consistent with the Stone et al., (2007) model we believe that power distance cultural values should influence preferences for job attributes because individuals with these values emphasize interpersonal power, status, hierarchical systems, and unequal distribution of power more than those low in power distance. Thus, we predict that those ethnic minorities who are high in power distance may prefer jobs that stress (a) opportunities for promotion, (b) the status or reputation of the organization, and (c) hierarchical organizations, and (d) authority-oriented supervisors than their counterparts.

There has been very little research on this issue, but a study by Stone-Romero, Isenhour, and Stone (2006) found that Hispanics who emphasized high power distance were more likely to trade off money for working in a high-status organization than those who were low in power distance. Further, Erez and Earley, (1987) argued that those high in power distance would view hierarchical organizations, clearly defined career paths, and autocratic supervisors more favorably than those who are low in power distance. Other research found that those high in power distance were more likely to prefer highly formalized jobs than those low in terms of this value (Lee & Antonakis, 2014). Research by Stone et al. (2006) found that Hispanics who were high in power distance values preferred (a) jobs that offered promotions, and (b) organizations with high status reputations compared to those who were low in these values.

Although there has been some research on the relations between individuals' power distance values and their preferences for certain job attributes, we believe that additional research is needed to identify the job choice preferences of applicants with high levels of power distance.

Time Orientation. The four ethnic minority groups described above have very distinct time orientations. For instance, Hispanics and African-Americans have a present or short-term time orientation, but Asians have a past or long-term orientation. Further, Native Americans have a circular view of time which is also long-term. Based on the model by Stone et al. (2007) we maintain that these different time orientations should influence the attractiveness of various job attributes. For instance, those with a present time orientation may not prefer long-term retirement benefits, but find immediate bonuses and flexible work schedules attractive because they have a present time orientation. Those with a long-term time orientation may prefer (a) rewards for seniority or continuity, and (b) performance appraisals that consider previous and performance over time. In support of these predictions, Ma and Allen (2009) argued that those with a long-term time orientation should be more willing to sacrifice present benefits for future opportunities. In particular, the same authors and others maintained that those with a long-term emphasis on time preferred training opportunities, and placed little priority on pay, benefits, working conditions or flexible scheduling (Elizur, Borg, Hunt, & Beck, 1991; Ma & Allen, 2009). However, those with a short-term time orientation placed more emphasis on bonuses and working hours (Ma & Allen, 2009).

Ma and Allen (2009) also argued that those with a long-term time orientation should be more willing to sacrifice present benefits for future opportunities. However, those with a short-term time orientation placed more emphasis on the present and were more motivated by extrinsic job factors (e.g., pay, status, working hours) than intrinsic ones (e.g., pride in work, meaningfulness of work) (Ma & Allen, 2009).

Even though the arguments about the relations between different time orientations and job choice preferences seem plausible, most of the predictions are not based on empirical research. Thus, we believe that additional research is needed to identify the job choice preferences of applicants with varying time orientations.

Given that the cultural values of the changing workforce will influence attraction to organizations, organizations may have to alter the strategies and outcomes that they use to recruit individuals. For example, they might want to use a variable job attribute and benefit system that will appeal to applicants who vary in cultural values. Professional sports teams have long used variable reward and benefit systems to encourage star athletes to join a particular team (Walters, 2002). These systems would advertise that the organizations offer a variety of jobs including those that involve teamwork as well as those that emphasize individualized work. They could also publicize that jobs offer a broad set of benefits, and employees can choose from flexible work hours, short-term bonuses, training for advancement, or company matching for retirement contributions. Although these ideas may appeal to a wide array of applicants, we believe that research is needed to examine the effectiveness of this strategy.

Recruitment Sources

Organizations use a variety of methods and sources to recruit prospective employees including newspaper ads, employment services, recruiters, web-based recruiting, and social media sites like LinkedIn. Based on the Stone et al. (2007) model, it can be argued that the cultural values of applicants should influence reactions to various recruitment sources and methods, and the overall effectiveness of these methods.

Collectivism. We predict that applicants who are high in collectivism will prefer personal recruitment sources and methods (e.g., meetings with recruiters) to more impersonal methods (e.g., web-based recruiting). The primary reason for this is that those high in collectivism prefer personal relationships with others and emphasize social relations more than those who are low in terms of this value. Thus, we argue that those high in collectivism may react more positively to meeting recruiters or current employees in person than using impersonal web-based recruitment systems. Indirect support for this argument comes from research by McManus and Ferguson (2003). They examined the reactions of ethnic minority group members to e-recruiting and found that some ethnic minorities (e.g., Hispanics) were less likely to use online recruiting than majority group members (e.g., Anglos). Of course, these results may be due to the fact that Hispanics and others who have low socioeconomic status may lack access or the ability to use computers rather than their reactions to the use of the impersonal web-based recruitment (Stone, Krueger, & Takach, 2017). Thus, additional research is needed to examine the relations between individuals' collectivism values and preference for personal rather than impersonal recruitment sources.

Given that some individuals may react negatively to e-recruitment because it does not allow for interactions with members of the organization, some companies (e.g., Cisco) have developed an alternative strategy for increasing contact between applicants and employees. In particular, they offer an opportunity to "make a friend" at Cisco on their website so that applicants can ask questions or learn more about the organization from current employees. Interestingly, recent research revealed that the effectiveness of this strategy may depend on the cultural values of the applicant (Harrison & Stone, 2018), and found that individuals high in collectivism values were more attracted to organizations that offered a chance to make contact with an employee than those who were low in collectivism. These results suggest that individuals' cultural values may also influence reactions to other types of recruitment methods (e.g., use of videoconferencing to contact recruiters, use of webcams to help applicants become familiar with the organization), but little research has examined these relations. As a result, research is needed to examine the extent to which aligning recruitment practices with applicants' cultural values is related to the success of recruitment processes.

Familism, Power Distance, and Time Orientation. As noted above, recruitment sources and practices that are aligned with applicants' cultural values should be more effective attracting individuals than those that are not. For instance, recruiting websites that emphasize that an organization has values that are consistent with the applicants' cultural values should be more likely to attract ethnic minorities than those that do not. For example, websites that stress that the organization offers family friendly policies and flexible hours should be more likely to attract individuals high rather than low in familism, and websites that stress the organization has high status or offers advancement opportunities should be more likely to attract applicants who are high rather than low in power distance. To our knowledge, only one study has examined the extent to which the congruence between cultural values displayed on recruiting websites and applicants' cultural values influenced attraction to organizations (Harrison & Stone, 2018). Results of this study revealed that those high in individualism were more attracted to organizations that offered opportunities for achievement than those low in these values. However, the results did not support the relation between applicants' high levels of collectivism and attraction to organizations that offered opportunities for developing interpersonal relations than those low in terms of this value. Given that relatively little research has examined the relations between applicants' cultural values and their reactions to recruitment sources and practices, we believe that additional research is needed to assess the effectiveness of aligning recruitment practices with applicants' cultural values.

Taken together, the arguments and research in the section noted above suggested that organizations may want to offer variable job attributes and benefit systems in order to attract members of a multicultural workforce. They may also want to use a wide array of strategies to recruit applicants who differ in cultural values. For instance, they may want to use personal meet ups with recruiters or employees to attract those high in collectivism, or web-based recruitment to appeal to those high in individualism or preference for efficiency. However, we believe that research is needed to assess the effectiveness of these strategies for attracting and retaining members of a multicultural workforce.

Influence of Culture on Selection Processes

We believe that the changes in the cultural values of the population should have a key impact on the effectiveness and acceptance of selection practices used in organizations. The current systems used for selection were designed for a relatively homogeneous population of Anglo job applicants, and these systems may result in misleading results for ethnic minority applicants or those with different cultural values. For instance, the difference in applicants' cultural values and backgrounds are likely to influence scores on tests of cognitive ability, results of personality inventories, and ratings of applicants' performance in interviews. Therefore, in the sections that follow we consider the impact of applicants' cultural values on three methods used to select individuals in organizations (e.g., cognitive ability tests, personality inventories, and interviews).

Impact of Culture on Cognitive Ability Test Scores. It has long been argued that culture influences individuals' scores on standardized tests of cognitive ability (Sternberg, Grigorenko, & Kidd, 2005). For example, some researchers found that African-Americans may score one standard deviation lower than Anglos on cognitive ability tests, and Hispanics score one half a standard deviation lower than Anglos on these tests (Herrnstein & Murray, 1994). However, research also revealed that Asians score higher on tests of quantitative ability than Anglos (Herrnstein & Murray, 1994). There has been very little research on the cognitive ability test scores of adult Native Americans, but a review of the research indicated that Native Americans scored 18 points lower than Anglos on tests of overall cognitive ability (Reynolds, 1982). However, they scored higher on tests of visual/spatial ability than Anglos (Reynolds, Willson, & Ramsey, 1999). Other reviews found that Native Americans scored higher on cognitive ability than African-Americans, and Jamaican Americans (Rushton & Jensen, 2005).

These differences in cognitive ability test scores have created a great deal of controversy in Psychology and HRM, and have important implications for designing fair testing systems in organizations (Sternberg et al., 2005). Some researchers have argued that there are genetic or innate differences in cognitive ability which accounts for the differences in tests scores (Jensen, 1969). Others disagreed with this contention, and argued that there are cultural biases in the design of tests, test items, and criterion scores because the tests and criteria are typically developed by Anglos (Sternberg et al., 2005). The same researchers maintained that there are cultural biases in test scores because test-takers vary in terms of socioeconomic status, health, nutrition, quality of education, and English language proficiency (Sternberg et al., 2005). In spite of these arguments, today most researchers agree that differences in cognitive ability test scores are due to the design of tests and differences in the background of test takers rather than genetic differences in cognitive ability (Sternberg et al, 2005).

Regardless of the reasons for differences in test scores, it is important that employment tests be equivalent across test takers if the scores on these tests are used to make critical employment decisions (e.g., hiring, promotion). Thus, a number of researchers (Aguinis & Smith, 2007; Cascio, Outtz, Zedeck, & Goldstein, 1991: Stone-Romero, 2019, personal communication) argued that we need to take steps to reduce cultural biases and ensure that tests predict job performance for all test takers. Results of research on reducing cultural biases in cognitive ability tests have shown that it decreases adverse impact and enhances the diversity of the workforce (Aguinis & Smith, 2007). In view of these results, we believe, as do others (Stone-Romero, personal communication, 2019) that the following steps should be taken to reduce cultural biases in cognitive ability tests.

a. Test items should be analyzed for cultural biases, and all items that are biased toward one group should be eliminated prior to administering tests in the selection process.

b. Selection decision makers should use banding to set cutoff scores for passing tests rather than using top down or one cutoff score. Banding refers to the process of grouping test scores into ranges and treating scores within a particular range as equivalent when making hiring decisions.

The primary assumption behind banding is that small differences in test scores do not translate into meaningful differences in performance on the job. For example, a candidate who scores 94% on a test may not perform better on the job than a candidate who scores 89% because tests are not perfect predictors of job performance and have varying degrees of measurement error. Thus, the differences in scores for applicants who have scores that fall within the same band are not meaningful because they are associated with the same level of job performance. Stated differently, the purpose of testing is to predict job performance, and banding allows decision makers to select applicants who will be able to successfully perform the job. Research has also shown that banding increases fairness for all applicants in the selection process, decreases adverse impact, and enhances diversity of the workforce (Aguinis, Culpepper, & Pierce, 2010; Cascio et al., 1991).

In summary, we believe that changes in the cultural values of applicants are likely to affect the employment testing process, and organizations need to modify tests or change how decision makers use scores on the tests to make hiring decisions. In addition, all tests and test items need to be examined to ensure that they are not culturally biased prior to using them in the selection process. For instance, items should be examined for biases by members of different ethnic minority groups not just Anglo test developers. Although a number of researchers have made the arguments that (a) cognitive ability tests should be examined for biases in test items, and (b) banding should be used to set cutoff scores for passing tests (Aguinis et al., 2010; Cascio et al., 1991; Stone-Romero, personal communication, 2019). To our knowledge no empirical research has examined the effectiveness of the strategies noted above. Therefore, we believe that additional research is needed to examine the processes just noted to reduce biases in cognitive ability tests.

Influence of Cultural Values on Scores Personality Inventories. In view of the relation between personality and cultural values, it can also be argued that applicants' cultural values should influence scores on personality inventories. In support of this argument, Stone-Romero and Thornson (2008) argued that applicants' cultural values are likely to have an impact on their responses to personality inventories, and influence the effectiveness of these inventories in the selection process (Stone- Romero, 2005; Stone-Romero & Thornson, 2008). Others have argued that use of personality inventories in the selection process may have an adverse impact on members of some ethnic minorities (e.g., African–Americans, Hispanic–Americans) (Stone & Stone-Romero, 2008). The primary reason for these arguments is that personality inventories are developed by Anglos and tend to emphasize the cultural values of the dominant Anglo culture (e.g., competitive achievement, extraversion). For instance, research has found that there are positive correlations (albeit low) between personality predictors including conscientiousness, openness to experience, emotional adjustment, extraversion, agreeableness, and job performance (Barrick & Mount, 1991; Tett, Jackson & Rothstein, 1991). However, cultural research has also revealed that some ethnic minority group members in the US (e.g., Asian–Americans, Native-Americans, Hispanic– Americans) are socialized to emphasize cultural values that are different than those in the dominant culture in the country, and may obtain different scores on personality inventories than Anglos (e.g., Asians and Native Americans should be higher in introversion and deference to authority than Anglos). For example, Asians, Native Americans and Hispanics are socialized to stress modesty, quietness, respect for superiors, passivity (rather than proactivity), and indirect communication styles that emphasize agreeableness (Stone & Stone-Romero, 2008). Some of these values are antithetical to Anglo cultural values that emphasize competitive achievement, extraversion, proactivity, openness to experience, and direct communication styles (Stone & Stone-Romero, 2008).

As a consequence, some ethnic minorities may not be hired because their scores on personality inventories are not consistent with dominant Anglo cultural values (e.g., employees should be extraverted, open to experience, proactive, and self-promoting). Further, decision makers may incorrectly infer that applicants from these minority groups lack managerial potential, good interpersonal skills, and are not open to new experiences (Stone-Romero & Thornson, 2008).

In support of these arguments, empirical research by Hough, Oswalt and Ployhart (2001) revealed that there were differences in personality scores between African–Americans and Anglos on emotional adjustment, affiliation, openness to experience, and managerial potential (Stone-Romero & Thornson, 2008). Similarly, research showed that Native-Americans scored lower than Anglos on measures of extraversion, surgency, proactivity, and agreeableness (Hough et al., 2001). Likewise, studies indicated that Asians were less likely to be promoted to managerial positions because they were not perceived to fit the prototype of the ideal leader in US organizations (e.g., extraverted, assertive, risk takers) (Sy et al., 2010). Thus, if organizations use personality inventories to select applicants, members of some ethnic minority groups may be viewed as less qualified for jobs than members of the dominant group. As noted previously, personality and cultural values are distinct constructs, but culture influences socialization practices and the development of personality in a society (Triandis, 1994).

Given that personality inventories are normed on the cultural values of Anglos, we believe that it is important to determine the actual personality traits that are critical to success on the job rather than using a standard set of dimensions (e.g., Big Five Personality Dimensions) to predict job performance. For example, conscientiousness may predict performance of a manager of a software development unit, but extraversion and dominance may not predict job performance on the same job because the manager is supervising highly knowledgeable subordinates. Identifying the personality profile that predicts actual success on the job should decrease any potential adverse impact against ethnic minority groups, and enable organizations to increase the diversity of their workforce. Although these arguments seem plausible, we know of no research that has examined the impact of using standardized personality inventories (Big Five) on the diversity of a workforce. Thus, we believe that additional research is needed to examine the degree to which use of standardized personality dimensions influences the effectiveness of selection procedures.

Influence of Culture on the Employment Interview Process. Consistent with the arguments above, we also believe that the standards set in the employment interview process may be biased by the dominant values in the US culture, and result in the exclusion of ethnic minorities in the hiring process. For instance, the Anglo culture stresses that interviewees should make direct eye contact with interviewers, have a firm handshake, be proactive, extraverted, and engage in impression management during the interview(e.g., self-promotion). However, some ethnic minority cultures (e.g., Asian, Native American) stress that people should be quiet, listen, display modesty, be self-effacing, and avoid eye-contact (Xia et al., 2013). Hispanic culture also emphasizes that job applicants should avoid eye contact and use a *sympatia* or a smoothing rather than a dominant communication style (Marin & Marin, 1999). As a consequence, when interviewees' cultural values and behaviors differ from the dominant culture's prototype of the ideal applicant, they should be rated more negatively in the employment interview than those who values and behavior are similar to the dominant culture. Thus, those with different cultural values may not be hired because their interview performance is different than the ideal prototype of applicants in the dominant culture.

Further, we maintain that organizations should only use criteria that are based on job analysis to evaluate interviewees, and it is not clear that expected interview behaviors (e.g., extraverted communication style, looking at someone directly in the eye, self-promotion) are related to job performance. For example, one major question is " do people who look at interviewers directly or display extraverted communications perform at higher levels on the job than those who do not engage in those behaviors."

If interviewers rate applicants negatively when they do not conform to the prototypical behaviors in a culture, then organizations may fail to hire talented individuals who are qualified for jobs, and reduce the diversity of the workforce. We only know of one study on this issue (Bye, Horverak, Sandal, Sam, & de Vijver, 2014), and the results of this study found that regardless of ethnic background (i.e., immigrants vs. Norwegians) interviewees who were viewed as a poor culture fit were given more negative interview ratings than those who were viewed as a good fit. In particular, the results indicated that applicants who were rated as a low culture fit were rated as less similar, less likeable, and less likely to perform the job well than those who were rated as a high culture fit (Bye et al., 2014).

Given that the cultural background of interviewees is likely to affect their ratings on job interviews, we believe that additional research is needed to examine the extent to which the criteria (based on dominant culture) used to evaluate interviewee performance influences its effectiveness and the diversity of the workforce.

Cultural Influences on Compensation and Benefit Systems

Organizations typically use a variety of rewards and benefits to attract, motivate, retain, and align individuals' behavior with organizational goals (Stone et al., 2007). Models of motivation and reward systems have been shown to be effective in understanding and explaining the motivation and behavior of employees in organizations, but these models are primarily based on Anglo value systems (e.g., individualism, competitive achievement) (Gerhart & Fang, 2015: Joshi & Martocchio, 2008). As a result, the model by Stone et al. (2007) argued that motivational theories and compensation systems may not be as effective in motivating the behavior of workers with cultural values that are different to traditional Anglo values. Thus, a number of researchers argued that individuals' cultural values will influence reward preferences, reactions to reward allocation procedures, and the overall effectiveness of compensation and benefit systems (Gerhart & Fang, 2015: Joshi & Martocchio, 2007; Stone et al., 2007). These researchers also maintained that compensation and reward systems will be much more effective when they are aligned with the cultural values of individuals than when they are not (Joshi & Martocchio, 2008; Stone et al., 2007). In view of these arguments, we consider the influence of cultural values on the effectiveness of incentive and benefit systems below.

The Influence of Culture on Incentive Systems. A number of financial and non-financial reward and incentive systems are used to motivate and retain employees in organizations. As noted above, these reward and incentive systems are typically based on dominant Anglo values, and emphasize individual incentives and allocations based on proportionality or equity (e.g., rewards proportional to performance or contributions) (Stone et al., 2007). However, we believe, as do others (Erez, 1994; Joshi & Martocchio, 2008; Stone et al., 2007), that individuals' evaluations of pay, incentives, and reward allocation systems will be influenced by the degree to which they correspond to their cultural values. For example, if an individual stresses collective cultural values, then rewards based on team performance should be more effective in motivating them than individually-based incentive systems. The primary reason for this is that individuals high in collectivism values typically emphasize the good of the group over the individual. Likewise, if the individual endorses familism values then they may prefer time off to spend with their families to other types of rewards. In support of these arguments, research by Stone, Johnson, Stone-Romero, & Hartman (2006) found that Hispanics' (a) collectivism values were positively related to preferences for good coworkers and working in a diverse organization, (b) familism values were positively related to preferences for personal time off and flexible hours, and (c) level of power distance values was related to preferences for promotion opportunities and working for a high status organizations. Even though there has been some research on the reward preferences of Hispanics, much more research is needed to identify the reward preferences of multicultural group members.

Influence of Cultural Values on Benefits. In addition to pay and incentive systems, organizations typically offer employees a variety of benefits (Joshi & Martocchio, 2008) including (a) insurance programs (e.g., health insurance, retirement benefits), (b) paid time off (e.g., vacations), and (c) accommodation benefits (e.g., flexible work schedules, day care). The model noted by Stone et al., (2007) argued that cultural values will affect (a) individuals' preferences for different types of benefits and (b) the effectiveness of benefit systems for motivating and retaining employees in organizations. For instance, we predict that workers' levels of collectivism or familism values will be positively related to preferences for benefits that offer paid time off, flexible work schedules and family-oriented programs (e.g., day care). One reason for this that employees who have high levels of collectivism and familism should place more emphasis on personal relationships with others and their families than those who have low levels of these values. In support of these arguments, research by Joshi and Martocchio (2008) maintained that employees with high levels of collective values should be more likely to prefer benefits that provide security and support for families than those with low levels of these values. Further, research showed that employees with high levels of individualistic values preferred benefit systems that gives them the freedom to choose the components of their benefits package than those with low levels of these values (Joshi & Martocchio, 2008).

Based on the Stone et al. (2007) model we also predict that individuals' time orientation values will influence workers preferences for benefits. For example, researchers argued that there should be a positive relation between individuals' future time orientation and preference for long term benefits (e.g., retirement programs) (Stone et al., 2006). In contrast, those with a short-term time orientation are likely to prefer immediate benefits (e.g., short term bonuses) to long term benefits (e.g., retirement) (Stone et al., 2006). In view of this, we believe that aligning benefits systems with the cultural values of employees and allowing them to select their specific benefits is likely to enhance their motivation and retention level.

However, research is needed to examine the degree to which aligning benefits with the cultural values of employees influences their effectiveness.

Influence of Cultural Values on Reactions to Reward Allocation Systems. Organizations also use a number of different procedures to allocate outcomes and reward in organizations. For example, some of them distribute rewards equally, others distribute them based on need, and still other distribute rewards based on the norm of equity or proportionality which means that those who perform at the highest levels receive the highest rewards. Based on theories of social justice (Deutsch, 1975), and cultural self-representation (Erez, 1994), the model by Stone et al., (2007) argued that the cultural values of individuals will determine their reactions to reward allocation systems. Given that the Anglo culture stresses equity-based systems, then many US organizations use equity-based reward allocations (e.g., merit-based pay) because they are likely to appeal to members of the Anglo culture (Stone et al., 2007). However, individuals who endorse collective value systems tend to prefer rewards allocated on the basis of equality or need because they place emphasis on the well-being of the group and in-group harmony not individual needs (Deutsch, 1975).

Although there has been little research in the US on cultural differences in reactions to reward allocation systems, there has been international research on this topic in China, India, and Europe (Bond, Leung & Wan, 1982). For example, the study by Bond et al. (1982) found that employees in China (who are, on average, more collectivistic than Americans) were more likely to use equality-based allocation systems than workers in the US (who are, on average, more individualistic). A similar study in India found that individuals in India prefer allocations based on need because they view themselves as highly interdependent and sensitive to the needs of others (Murphy-Berman, Berman, Singh, Pachauri & Kumar, cited in Erez, 1994). It merits noting that India is generally considered a collectivistic country, but some research has shown that Indians vary in individualism and collectivism (Daun, 1996). Further, research in Europe by Thierry (2002) revealed that countries that emphasize individualism often use pay for performance systems more than those that stress collectivism.

Taken together, this research suggests that individuals' cultural values will influence their reactions to and satisfaction with reward allocation systems in organizations. Thus, current merit or equity-based allocations of rewards may be more effective with those who value individualism than those who emphasize collectivism.

CONCLUSION

The US Census Bureau (2018b) has predicted that by the year 2060 ethnic minorities will constitute the majority of the population. One important implication of this change in the demographics of our society is that ethnic minorities differ from Anglos in key cultural values including collectivism, familism, power distance and time orientation. Given these differences in cultural values, current HR policies and practices may be less effective in attracting, motivating, and retaining members of a multicultural than a monocultural workforce. Thus, we argued that existing HR practices may need to be modified to fit with the cultural values of new multicultural population. In order to consider the influence of cultural values on changes in HR practices, we described the average cultural values of four of the major ethnic groups in the US including Hispanics, African-Americans, Asians, and Native Americans. We also discussed how these cultural values might influence changes in several HR practices (e.g., recruitment, selection, compensation). We also provided suggestions for future research and practice on the influence of multiculturalism on HR policies and practices. Our hope is that this article will foster additional research on the relations between individuals' cultural values, and the effectiveness of HR policies and practices. We also hope that the paper will enable organizations to develop new HR practices that attract and retain members of the new diverse workforce.

OVERVIEW OF DIVERSITY AND INCLUSION IN ORGANIZATIONS ISSUE

We have assembled a number of very intriguing articles for this issue of *Research in HRM*. Topics include (a) multiculturalism and HRM, (b) life partners and the promotion of women, (c) stereotypes of ethnic minorities, (d) effect sizes in diversity research, (e) inauthentic experiences of minorities at work, (f) the effectiveness of diversity training, (g) increasing the inclusion of LGBT employees, (h) an ecological model of research on aging, (i) climates for inclusion at work, (j) a measure of responses to perceived discrimination, (k) a model of workplace racial harassment, and (l) a model of factors affecting discrimination against immigrants. We hope that these articles foster additional research on these important issues, and help organizations develop sound diversity policies and practices.

In closing, we want to thank George Johnson for his support in the development of this issue, and want to express our appreciation to Rodger Griffeth for giving us the opportunity to edit *Research in HRM*. We are also grateful to all of the authors who submitted papers, and all of those individuals who provided thoughtful reviews of the manuscripts.

REFERENCES

500 Nations. (2019). *500 Nation Documentary.* Retrieved from: https://documentaryheaven.com/500-nations-the-story-of-native-americans/

Aguinis, H., Culpepper, S. A., & Pierce, C. A. (2010). Revival of test bias research in pre-employment testing. *Journal of Applied Psychology, 95*(4), 648.

Aguinis, H., & Smith, M. A. (2007). Understanding the impact of test validity and bias on selection errors and adverse impact in human resource selection. *Personnel Psychology, 60*(1), 165–199.

Allport, G. W. (1953). The trend in motivational theory. *American Journal of Orthopsychiatry, 23*(1), 107–119.

American Ancestors (2019). *Fact Sheet*. Retrieved from https://www.americanancestors. org/about/press-and-media/fact-sheet

Attneave, C. (1982). American Indians and Alaska Native families: Emigrants in their own homeland. In M. McGoldrick, J. Pearce, & J. Giordano (Eds.), *Ethnicity and family therapy* (pp. 55–83). New York, NY: Guilford Press.

Balvanera, P., Pfisterer, A. B., Buchmann, N., He, J. S., Nakashizuka, T., Raffaelli, D., & Schmid, B. (2006). Quantifying the evidence for biodiversity effects on ecosystem functioning and services. *Ecology letters, 9*(10), 1146–1156.

Barrick, M. R., & Mount, M. K. (1991). The Big Five personality dimensions and job performance: A meta-analysis. *Personnel Psychology, 44*, 1–26.

Bell, M. P. (2012). *Diversity in organizations*. Mason, OH: Cengage.

Bennett, S. (1994). The American Indian: A psychological overview. In W. Lonner & R. Malpass (Eds.), *Psychology and culture* (pp. 35–39). Boston, MA: Allyn & Bacon.

Berry, J. W. (1997). Immigration, acculturation and adaptation. *Applied Psychology, 46*, 5–68.

Betancourt, H., & Lopez, S. 1993. The study of culture, ethnicity, and race in American psychology. *American Psychologist, 48*, 629–637.

Biological Diversity. (2019). *The endangered species act: A wild success*. Retrieved from: https://www.biologicaldiversity.org/campaigns/esa_wild_success/

Bond, M. H., & Hofstede, G. (1989) The cash value of Confucian values. *Human Systems Management, 8*, 195–200.

Bond, M. H., Leung, K., & Wan, K.C. (1982). How does cultural collectivism operate? The impact of task and maintenance contributions on reward distribution. *Journal of Cross-Cultural Psychology, 13*, 186–200.

Bretz, R., Ash, R., & Dreher, G. (1989). Do people make the place? An examination of the attraction–selection–attrition hypothesis. *Personnel Psychology, 42*, 561–581.

Bye, H. H., Horverak, J. G., Sandal, G. M., Sam, D. L., & Van de Vijver, F. J. (2014). Cultural fit and ethnic background in the job interview. *International Journal of Cross-Cultural Management, 14*(1), 7–26.

Carter, R. T. (1991). Cultural values: A review of empirical research and implications for counseling. *Journal of Counseling & Development, 70*, 164–173.

Cascio, W. F., Outtz, J., Zedeck, S., & Goldstein, I. L. (1991). Statistical implications of six methods of test score use in personnel selection. *Human Performance, 4*(4), 233–264.

Casper, W. J., Wayne, J. H., & Manegold, J. G. (2013). Who will we recruit? Target deep and surface level diversity with human resource policy advertising. *Human Resource Management, 52*(3), 311–332.

Chang, J., Natsuaki, M. N., & Chen, C. N. (2013). The importance of family factors and generation status: Mental health service use among Latino and Asian Americans. *Cultural Diversity and Ethnic Minority Psychology, 19*(3), 236.

Chatman, J. A. (1989). Improving interactional organizational research: A model of person-organization fit. *Academy of Management Review, 14*, 333–349.

Chen, C., & Jeung, R. (Eds.). (2012). *Sustaining faith traditions: Race, ethnicity, and religion among the Latino and Asian American second generation*. New York, NY: NYU Press.

Cox, T. (1993). *Cultural diversity in organizations: Theory, research, and practice*. San Francisco, CA: Berrett-Koehler.

Cross-cultural Communications. (2019). Cross-cultural communication: What to expect. Retrieved from https://www.findcourses.co.uk/inspiration/articles/cross-cultural-communication-styles-8888

Daun, A. (1996). *Swedish mentality*. University Park, PA: The Pennsylvania State University Press.

de Mooij, M., & Beniflah, J. (2017). Measuring cross-cultural differences of ethnic groups within nations: Convergence or divergence of cultural values? The case of the United States. *Journal of International Consumer Marketing, 29*(1), 2–10.

Deutsch, M. (1975). Equity, equality, and need: What determines which value will be used as the basis of distributive justice? *Journal of Social Issues, 31*(3), 137–149.

Elizur, D., Borg, I., Hunt, R., & Beck, I. M. (1991). The structure of work values: A cross cultural comparison. *Journal of Organizational Behavior, 12*(1), 21–38.

Erez, M. (1994). Toward a model of cross-cultural industrial and organizational psychology. In H. C. Triandis, M. D. Dunnette, & L. M. Hough (Eds.), *Handbook of industrial and organizational psychology* (Vol. 4, pp. 559–608). Palo Alto, CA: Consulting Psychologists Press.

Erez, M., & Earley, P. C. (1993). *Culture, self-identity, and work*. New York, NY: Oxford University Press.

Federico, C. M. (2006). Race, education, and individualism revisited. *The Journal of Politics, 68*(3), 600–610.

Finley, T. L. (2001). *American Indian culture as a potential intervening factor in Internet acceptance* (unpublished thesis). University of Montana, Bozeman, MT.

Fixico, D. L. (2003). *The American Indian mind in a linear world: Traditional knowledge and American Indian studies*. Oxfordshire, UK: Routledge.

Gaines, S. O., Marelich, W. D., Bledsoe, K. L., Steers, W. N., Henderson, M. C., Granrose, C. S., ... Page, M. S. (1997). Links between race/ethnicity and cultural values as mediated by race/ethnic identity and moderated by gender. *Journal of Personality and Social Psychology, 72,* 1460–1476.

Gelfand, M. J., Erez, M., & Aycan, Z. (2007). Cross-cultural organizational behavior. *Annual Review of Psychology, 58*(20), 1–35.

Gerhart, B., & Fang, M. (2015). Pay, intrinsic motivation, extrinsic motivation, performance, and creativity in the workplace: Revisiting long-held beliefs. *Annual. Review Organizational Psychology. and Organizational. Behavior, 2*(1), 489–521.

Gibson, A. (2008). Cultural value differences and women-owned businesses in the United States: A preliminary exploration. *Journal of Applied Business and Economics, 8,* 23–34.

Gowan, M. A. (2004). Development of the recruitment value proposition for geocentric staffing. *Thunderbird International Business Review, 46*(6), 687–708

Harris, G. (1998). American Indian cultures: A lesson in diversity. In D. E. Battle (Ed.), *Communication disorders in multicultural populations* (2nd ed., pp. 117–156). Boston, MA: Butter-worth-Heinemann.

Harrison, T., & Stone, D. L. (2018). Effects of organizational values and employee contact on e-recruiting. *Journal of Managerial Psychology, 33*(3), 311–324.

Herrnstein, R. J., & Murray, C. (1994). *The bell curve: Intelligence and class structure in American Life*. New York, NY: Free Press.

Hofstede, G. (1980). *Culture's consequences: International differences in work-related values*. Beverly Hills, CA: Sage Publications.

Hough, L. M., Oswalt, F. L., & Ployhart, R. E. (2001). Determinants, detection, and amelioration of adverse impact in personnel selection procedures: Issues, evidence, and lessons learned. *International Journal of Selection and Assessment, 9*, 152–194.

Huynh, Q.- L., Nguyen, A.- M. D., & Benet-Martínez, V. (2011). Bicultural identity integration. In S. J. Schwartz, K. Luyckx, & V. L. Vignoles (Eds.), *Handbook of identity theory and research* (pp. 827–844). New York: Springer.

Jensen, A. R. (1969). How much can we boost IQ and scholastic achievement? *Harvard Educational Review, 39*, 1–123.

Joshi, A., & Martocchio, J. J. (2008). Compensation and reward Systems in a multicultural context. In D.L. Stone & E.F. Stone-Romero (Eds.), *The influence of culture on human resource management processes and practices.* New York, NY: Taylor and Francis.

Kirkman, B. L., & Shapiro, D. L. (1997). The impact of cultural values on employee resistance: Toward a model of globalized self-managing work team effectiveness. *Academy of Management Review, 22*, 730–757.

Kochman, T. (1981). *Black and white styles in conflict.* Chicago, IL: University of Chicago Press.

Kossek, E. E., & Lobel, S. (Eds.). (1996). *Managing diversity: Human resources strategies for transforming the workplace.* Hoboken, NJ: Oxford-Blackwell.

Lee, Y. T., & Antonakis, J. (2014). When preference is not satisfied but the individual is: How power distance moderates person–job fit. *Journal of Management, 40*(3), 641–675.

Leong, F. T. L. (1991) Career development attributes and occupational values of Asian American and White American college students. *The Career Development Quarterly. 39*, 221–230.

Lobel, S. A., & Kossek, E. E. (1996). Human resource strategies to support diversity in work and personal lifestyles: Beyond the "family-friendly" organization. In E. E. Kossek & S. A. Lobel (Eds.), *Managing diversity: Human resource strategies for transforming the workplace* (pp. 221–244). Oxford, UK: Blackwell.

Ma, R., & Allen, D. G. (2009). Recruiting across cultures: A value-based model of recruitment. *Human Resource Management Review, 19*(4), 334–346.

Marin, G., & Marin, B. V. (1991). *Research with Hispanic populations.* Newbury Park, CA: Sage Publications, Inc.

Markus, H. R., & Kitayama, S. (1991a). Culture and the self: Implications for cognition, emotion, and motivation. *Psychological review, 98*(2), 224.

Markus, H. R., & Kitayama, S. (1991b). Cultural variation in self concept. In G. R. Goethals & J. Strauss (Eds.), *Multidisciplinary perspectives on the self* (pp. 18–48). New York, NY: Springer-Verlag

McGoldrick, M., Giordano, J, & Pearce, J. K. (1996). *Ethnicity and family therapy* (2nd ed.). New York, NY: Guildford Press.

McManus, M.A., & Ferguson, M. W. (2003). Biodata, personality, and demographic differences of recruits from threes sources. *International Journal of Selection and Assessment, 11*, 175–183.

Mike, E. H., Bidtah, L., & Thomas, V. (1989). *Cultural conflict.* Central Consolidated Schools District 22, Title VII, Bilingual Education Program.

Okun, B. F., Friend, J., & Okun, M. L. (1999). *Understanding diversity: A learning-as-practice primer.* Pacific Grove, CA: Brooks/Cole.

Parks-Leduc, L., Feldman, G., & Bardi, A. (2015). Personality traits and personal values: A meta-analysis. *Personality and Social Psychology Review, 19*(1), 3–29.

Portes A., & Rumbaut R. G. (2006). *Immigrant America: A portrait* (3rd ed.). Berkeley, CA: University of California Press.

Reynolds, C. R. (1982). The problem of bias in psychological assessment. In C. R. Reynolds & T. B. Gutkin (Eds.), *The handbook of school psychology* (pp. 178–208). New York, NY: Wiley.

Reynolds, C. R., Willson, V. L., & Ramsey, M. (1999). Intellectual differences among Mexican Americans, Papagos and Whites, independent of g. *Personality and Individual Differences, 27*(6), 1181–1187.

Rice, M. (2019). *Differences in communication.* Retrieved from: https://unioncollegenativeamericans.weebly.com/cultural-differences-in-communication.html

Richard, O. C., Barnett, T., Dwyer, S., & Chadwick, K. (2004). Cultural diversity in management, firm performance, and the moderating role of entrepreneurial orientation dimensions. *Academy of Management Journal, 47*(2), 255–266.

Rodríguez-Galán, M. B. (2014). The ethnography of ethnic minority families and aging: Familism and beyond. In K. E. Whitfield & T. A. Baker (Eds.), *Handbook of minority aging,* (pp. 435–453). New York, NY: Springer.

Rushton, J. P., & Jensen, A. R. (2005). Thirty years of research on race differences in cognitive ability. *Psychology, Public Policy, and Law, 11*(2), 235.

Schuler, R. S., & Jackson, S. E. (2005). A quarter-century review of human resource management in the US: The growth in importance of the international perspective. *Management Revue, 16,* 11–35.

Schwartz, S. J., Weisskirch, R. S., Hurley, E. A., Zamboanga, B. L., Park, I. J., Kim, S. Y., ... & Greene, A. D. (2010). Communalism, familism, and filial piety: Are they birds of a collectivist feather? *Cultural Diversity and Ethnic Minority Psychology, 16*(4), 548–560.

Sternberg, R. J., Grigorenko, E. L., & Kidd, K. K. (2005). Intelligence, race, and genetics. *American Psychologist, 60*(1), 46.

Stone, D. L., Johnson, R. D., Stone-Romero, E. F., & Hartman, M. (2006). A comparative study of Hispanic-American and Anglo-American cultural values and job choice preferences. *Management Research, 4,* 8–21.

Stone, D. L., Krueger, D., & Takach, S. (2017). Social issues associated with the Internet at work. In G. Hertel, D. Stone, R. Johnson, & J. Passmore (Eds.), *The handbook of the psychology of the Internet at work* (pp. 423–448). San Francisco, CA: Wiley-Blackwell.

Stone, D. L., & Stone-Romero, E. F. (Eds.) (2008). *The Influence of Culture on Human Resource Processes and Practices.* New York: Taylor and Francis.

Stone, D. L., Stone-Romero, E. F., & Lukaszewski, K. M. (2007). The impact of cultural values on the acceptance and effectiveness of human resource management policies and practices. *Human Resource Management Review, 17*(2), 152–165.

Stone-Romero, E. F. (2005). The effects of eHR system characteristics and culture on system acceptance and effectiveness. In H. G. Gueutal & D. L. Stone (Eds.). *The brave new world of eHR* (pp. 226—254). San Francisco, CA: Jossey-Bass.

Stone-Romero, E. F., Isenhour, L. C., & Stone, D. L. (2006). *The relations among cultural values, ethnicity, and job choice trade-off preferences* (unpublished manuscript). University of Central Florida, Orlando, FL.

Stone-Romero, E. F., Stone, D. L., & Salas, E. (2003). The influence of culture on role conceptions and role behavior in organizations. *Applied Psychology, 52*(3), 328–362.

Stone-Romero, E. F., & Thornson, C. A. (2008). Culture and human resource management practices: Personnel selection based on personality measures. In D. L. Stone & E. F. Stone-Romero (Eds.), *The influence of culture on human resource management processes and practices* (pp. 85–114). New York, NY: Lawrence Erlbaum Associates.

Sue, S., & Morishima, J. K. (1982). *The mental health of Asian Americans: Contemporary issues in identifying and treating mental problems.* San Francisco, CA: Jossey-Bass.

Sue, D. W., & Sue, D. (1999). *Counseling the culturally different: Theory and practice* (3rd ed.). Hoboken, NJ: John Wiley & Sons Inc.

Swaidan, Z., Rawwas, M. Y., & Vitell, S. J. (2008). Culture and moral ideologies of African Americans. *Journal of Marketing Theory and Practice, 16*(2), 127–137.

Sy, T., Shore, L. M., Strauss, J., Shore, T. H., Tram, S., Whiteley, P., & Ikeda-Miromacho, (2010). Leadership perceptions as a function of race-occupation fit: The case of Asian-Americans. *Journal of Applied Psychology (Italics), 95*(5), 902–919.

Tett, R. P., Jackson, D. N., & Rothstein, M. (1991). Personality measures as predictors of job performance: a meta-analytic review. *Personnel psychology, 44*(4), 703–742.

Thomas, K. M., & Wise, P. G. (1999). Organizational attractiveness and individual differences: are diverse applicants attracted by different factors? *Journal of Business and Psychology, 13*(3), 375–390.

Tom, V. R. (1971). The role of personality and organizational images in the recruiting process. *Organizational Behavior and Human Performance, 6*(5), 573–592.

Triandis, H. C. (1993). Collectivism and individualism as cultural syndromes. *Cross-cultural Research, 27*(3/4), 155–180.

Triandis, H. C. (1994). *Culture and social behavior.* New York, NY: McGraw-Hill.

Triandis, H., & Wasti, S. (2008). Culture. In D. L. Stone & E. F. Stone-Romero (Eds.), *The influence of culture on human resources management processes and practices* (pp. 1–24). New York, NY: Psychology Press.

Trice, H. M., & Beyer, J. M. (1993). *The cultures of work organizations.* Englewood, NJ: Prentice-Hall, Inc.

Turban, D. B., & Keon, T. L. (1993). Organizational attractiveness: An interactionist perspective. *Journal of Applied Psychology, 78*(2), 184–193.

US Census Bureau (2018a). *Population estimates.* Retrieved from: https://www.census.gov/quickfacts/fact/table/US/PST045218

US Census Bureau (2018b). *US demographic turning points for the United States: Population projections for 2020 to 2060.* Retrieved from: https://census.gov/content/dam/Census/library/publications/2018/demo/P25_1144.pdf

Vandello, J. A., & Cohen, D. (1999). Patterns of individualism and collectivism across the United States. *Journal of Personality and Social Psychology, 77*(2), 279.

Velasquez, R. J., Arellano, L. M., & McNeill, B. W. (2004). Culturally competent assessment of Chicana/os with the Minnesota Multiphasic Personality Inventory-2. In R. J. Velasquez, L. M. Arellano, & B. W. McNeill (Eds.), *The handbook of Chicana/o psychology and mental health* (pp. 171–192). Mahwah, NJ: Lawrence Erlbaum Associates

Walters, C. (2002). *Do variable-compensation plans for employees really work?* Retrieved from: http://www.hrworks-inc.com/article/do-variable-compensation-plans-employees-really-work

Weibel-Orlando, J. (2003). Elderhood in contemporary Lakota society. In J. F. Gubrium & J. A. Holstein (Eds.), *Ways of aging* (pp. 36–57). Malden, MA: Blackwell.

Xia, Y. R., Do, K. A., & Xie, X. (2013). *The adjustment of Asian American families to the US context: The ecology of strengths and stress.* Retrieved May 5, 2015 from http:// digitalcommons.unl.edu/famconfacpub/80

Xin, K. R. (2004). Asian American managers: An impression gap? *Journal of Applied Behavioral Science, 40,* 160–181.

Xin, K. R., & Tsui, A. S. (1996). Different strokes for different folks? Influence tactics by Asian-American and Caucasian-American managers. *The Leadership Quarterly, 7*(1), 109–132.

Yamauchi, L. A. (1998). Individualism, collectivism, and cultural compatibility: Implications for counselors and teachers. *The Journal of Humanistic Education and Development, 36*(4), 189–198.

CHAPTER 2

WOMEN REACHING THE SENIOR EXECUTIVE SUITE

A Framework of Life Partner Advocacy and Power

George F. Dreher, Aarti Ramaswami, and
Thomas W. Dougherty

This work focuses on extra-organizational processes that consider the extent to which a life partner can act as a career catalyst (or inhibitor) during the final rounds of the competition to reach the C-suite. Our objective has been to contribute to the theoretical underpinning needed to address the contention that there is a strong association between the type of life partner one has at mid-career and ultimate career attainment. We have presented a framework for describing the domain of possible partner types, proposed linkages between these partner types and reaching the C-suite, and proposed how gender affects these linkages and processes. We contend that it will be through building better theory regarding the extra-organizational circumstances surrounding the careers of high potential managerial and professional talent that needed progress will be made in understanding why there is little gender diversity in top-management teams.

I truly believe that the single most important career decision that a woman makes is whether she will have a life partner and who that partner is
—*Sandberg (2013, p. 110)*.

Diversity and Inclusion in Organizations, pages 33–58.
Copyright © 2020 by Information Age Publishing
All rights of reproduction in any form reserved.

What would be the most advantageous personal situation for a high-potential woman to be in at mid-career if she aspires to be a senior manager? For example, would it be most advantageous to have a high earning partner who possesses considerable social capital who can serve as a career coach and mentor? Or would it be best to have no partner at all, or to have a stay-at-home partner who has very limited career aspirations? Women continue to be very underrepresented at the highest levels of multinational enterprises (MNEs). As of January, 2020, there were only 29 Fortune 500 companies lead by female CEOs (Catalyst, 2020). Given this state of affairs, one would expect that Sandberg's claim in the above quote regarding the centrality of marriage markets or the role a life partner plays in the career attainment process would have been fully addressed in the diversity literature devoted to the "glass-ceiling" and career success. However, a review of this literature suggests that this is not the case. While current theory about career attainment has become increasingly complex and sophisticated, it has predominantly focused on human capital development, temperament and motivational states, the acquisition of social capital, mentoring and sponsorship, or bias, barriers, and discrimination in the workplace (Galunic, Ertug, & Gargiulo, 2012; Hamori, 2014; Judge, Cable, Boudreau, & Bretz, 1995; Ramaswami, Dreher, Bretz, & Wiethoff, 2010; Seibert, Kraimer, & Linden, 2001; Slaughter, 2015). This focus continues to be the norm, as illustrated by a recent special issue of the ILRR (2017), an issue devoted to gender inequality in the workplace. Not one of the eight articles considered whether extra-organizational processes may help account for gender inequality. The focus was exclusively on independent variables that pertain to organizational structures and workforce management practices. Thus, while current popular wisdom may hold that Sandberg's (2013) claim is valid, the career success and diversity literatures offer little in the way of evidence-based support for the view that the most important career choice a person makes is whom to choose as a life partner.

This lack of extra-organizational explanations for gender inequality in the workplace is problematic for a couple of reasons. First, a focus on only intra-organizational factors offers a limited view of the variables relevant to understanding men's and women's career attainment. By ignoring extra-organizational factors, we fail to consider the full range of explanations for why so few women reach the C-suite (i.e., the group of officers of a business organization who have the word "chief" in their titles, including the chief executive officer, the chief financial officer, and the chief operating officer) in MNEs. Considering extra-organizational factors allows us to shift the focus from organizational cultural and structural barriers, or individual ability and willingness, to a set of variables related to an individual's personal relational context that influences the opportunity and the resources needed to compete at the highest organizational levels. The importance of this personal relational context is beginning to be recognized by economists studying the marriage markets of high potential managerial and professional talent (Bursztyn, Fujiwara, & Pallais, forthcoming). Here, researchers have learned that very early, even while attending elite MBA programs, single women avoided signaling traits that would advantage them in the labor market but disadvantage them in the marriage market. New ideas and theories also are emerging in the dual-career couples literature. For example, Petriglieri and Obodaru (2019) used the findings from their qualitative study of 50 dual-career couples to formulate a theory of how partners shape the development of each other's professional identities.

Also, while progress has been made developing models about the work-family interface (Kossek & Lambert, 2005; Poelmans, 2005; Powell, 2011; Powell & Greenhaus, 2010; Tharenou, 1999; Wayne, Butts, Casper, & Allen, 2017), this body of research does not explicitly address the career attainment process among those competing for senior executive roles and associate it with a life-partner typology. Furthermore, in the most thorough and integrated treatment to date of theories and empirical findings related to the family-work interface, there is virtually no discussion of this interface from the perspective of high potential women competing for positions as senior managers (Allen & Eby, 2016). As will be developed throughout this discussion, it is during this final round of the career tournament that a life partner may play a particularly decisive role.

Thus, in order to build better theory about the career competition that begins at mid-career and that accounts for who does and does not reach senior management in large MNEs, we propose a typology of partners, linkages between these partner types and reaching the C-suite, and also how gender dynamics in heterosexual couples affects and moderates these linkages and processes. Our objective is to help provide the theoretical underpinning needed to address Sandberg's (2013) contention that there is a strong association between the type of life partner one chooses and reaching the C-suite, and that these choices are particularly important to women. This work will focus on extra-organizational processes that consider the extent to which a life partner can act as a career advocate and/or as one who inhibits career advancement. In doing so, we rely on and broaden a theory from the past—family power theory (Rodman, 1972), a theory closely aligned with social exchange models of behavior (Cropanzano & Mitchell, 2005; Kelley & Thibaut, 1978). We also draw on and attempt to integrate a variety of other theories and models to more fully understand how a life partner can serve as a career advocate. The ultimate objective is to use this integrated analysis of extra-organizational processes to improve current models of managerial career attainment and our understanding of why so few women reach the C-suite. It is this type of integrative framework that Jaskiewicz, Combs, Shanine, and Kacmar (2017) recently called for in their review of the family science literature.

Our concern is for individuals, especially women, who at mid-career still aspire to the C-suite in MNEs. Our framework will be best used to understand heterosexual partner selection and transition processes that apply to aspirational managerial and professional talent—talent that is often represented by individuals who complete undergraduate degrees in business, engineering, and science, and individuals who complete graduate degrees in business and law. We also focus on heterosexual cohabitating couples because research suggests that earning power dynamics and gender norms play out differently in heterosexual couples compared to same-sex couples (Weisshaar, 2014). Furthermore, our work draws not only from the careers literature, but also from the marriage market literature. This literature clearly suggests that marriage markets are highly segmented and very sensitive to demographic parameters (Becker, 1991; Carbone & Cahn, 2014; Smith & Hamon, 2012; Winton, 1995).

In what follows, we will be drawing from a number of theoretical perspectives. The perspectives we rely on the most include the following: The first is family development theory (Aldous, 1978; White, 1991). This focuses on how families go through transitions and how family development is reciprocal (i.e., changes in the circumstances of one partner influence the behavior of the other). The second is social exchange theory (Kelley & Thibaut, 1978). This, and its derivative, family power theory (Rodman, 1972), will be central to the model depicted in Figure 2.1. Also, we draw from the work of Mainiero and Sullivan, and their "kaleidoscope" model of careers (2005), from Greenhaus and Powell's (2006) theory of work-family enrichment, and from Petriglieri and Obodaru's (2019) theory of "secure-base relationships."

For many partnerships, an initial state of career parity (designated as T_1) will be the norm. But, as suggested by the life stage models of Super (1957) and Levinson (1978), this state of parity will give way to movement (by mid-career) into one

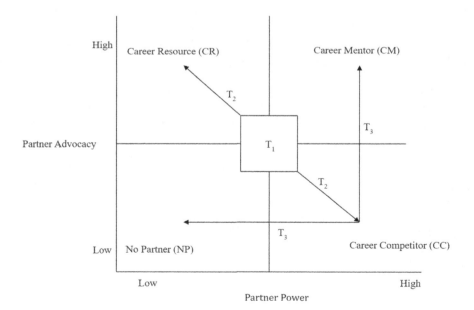

FIGURE 2.1.   A Typology of Partner Types

of the four quadrants depicted in the figure. Others will begin relationships with partners already established as one of the types depicted, while others will find themselves without partners. Once this descriptive space is defined, we will then develop propositions about the career consequences associated with being in a relationship (at mid-career) with each type of partner depicted in Figure 2.1.

A TYPOLOGY FOR UNDERSTANDING PARTNER TYPES

To initiate the presentation, consider the two axes shown in the Figure. The X-axis (Partner Power) considers a partner's competitiveness in a relationship from multiple perspectives or dimensions, with each associated with relative career dominance versus deference. While the level of partner power will likely be in a state of change early in a career, by mid-career one partner in a dual career couple will begin to see his or her career as taking precedence over the career of a lower status partner. Over time, if the divergence in career paths continues, the lower status partner will typically begin to defer his or her career in order to promote their partner's career. The X-axis captures the essence of Rodman's (1972) theory of family power. It focuses on a partner's relative contribution to total family income. Using social exchange theory as the fundamental underpinning (Blau, 1964; Thibaut & Kelley, 1959), family power theory posits that there will be a variety of career-oriented costs incurred from forming a committed relationship with a person who commands the relative salary advantage in the relationship. Few have used this family power perspective to empirically study the career attainment process (see Stroh, Brett, & Reilly, 1992 for an exception), but Rodman (1972) built a formal theory devoted to financial resources and marital power, and Gergen, Greenberg, and Willis (1980) further refined these ideas.

Perhaps the most important career-oriented cost that is incurred from having a partner who commands the relative salary advantage is related to geographical mobility. In contemporary labor markets, the path to senior management often requires the willingness to accept expatriate assignments or to relocate domestically in order to develop global and cross-functional skill sets (Dreher & Cox, 2000; Dreher, Lee, & Clerkin, 2010; Ramaswami, Carter, & Dreher, 2016). An illustration comes from the career path of Marillyn Hewson (eCelebrityFacts, 2017), the first female CEO of Lockheed Martin. She initiated her career in 1983 as a senior industrial engineer working on military aircraft in Marietta, Georgia. She then moved to Fort Worth, Texas in 1995 to become director of material systems and advanced sourcing. Over the years, her jobs also included running Lockheed's systems integration business in Owego, New York, managing corporate internal audits in Bethesda, Maryland, and then returning to Fort Worth to manage Lockheed's aeronautics business. She also managed the Company's electronic systems business, a unit with employees in the United States, Canada, Australia, and the United Kingdom. This career path to the C-Suite required that she move eight times over a 19-year period, moves that included her husband and two children. As the career or personal needs of a life partner increasingly interfere with accepting expatriate assignments or domestic assignments requiring geographical relocation, this partner will increasingly become more of a career competitor. Furthermore, it is this need to develop global and cross-functional skills that makes the competition to reach the C-suite in MNEs fundamentally different from career competitions taking place at lower organizational levels or within different business contexts.

Now consider the Y-axis (Partner Advocacy). One of the basic assumptions of social exchange theory is that social relationships are characterized by interdependence and reciprocity (Smith & Hamon, 2012, pp. 251–252). This means that, in order to maintain a stable relationship, the partner who is creating career costs and liabilities for the other partner must reciprocate in some way. This type of recipro-cation can take many forms (see Blau, 1964 and Nye, 1978 for early perspectives). But the more recent perspective developed by Greenhaus and Powell (2006), in their theory of work-family enrichment, will be used as a basis for characterizing the Y-axis. According to Greenhaus and Powell, there are five dimensions or themes related to how a person can enrich the career prospects of their partner. For our purposes, we focus on such things as a) providing financial resources which can be used to purchase career-enabling domestic services (Greenhaus and Powell's *material resources* dimension); b) affection, social acceptance, respect, prestige, and status (*psychological resources* dimension), c) information and ca-reer guidance (*skills and perspective* dimension); d) the opportunity to relocate and work long hours (*flexibility* dimension); and e) linkages to social networks (*social-capital resources* dimension).

In addition to the X-axis (Partner Power) and Y-axis (Partner Advocacy), the other feature of the framework is its temporal nature, here represented by three time periods (T_1, T_2, and T_3). As previously noted, T_1 is characterized as a time of relative partner parity. During the last stages of receiving a formal education and soon after completing a terminal degree, many people will form partnerships with significant others. For individuals in this managerial/professional marriage mar-ket, these partnerships are typically formed between people who are very similar in terms of educational attainment and career-oriented values (Carbone & Cahn, 2014). One major caveat is that there seems to be a universal preference (in het-erosexual couples) for an age gap of about three to four years, in favor of men (Hakim, 2000, p. 197). This age gap can provide an early advantage in cultural and economic capital to the male partner. There is also evidence for a gender-identity based aversion to a woman earning more than her male partner, thus leading to an early family power advantage favoring men (Bertrand, Kamenica, & Pan, 2015).

But family development theory (Smith & Hamon, 2012, pp. 69–91) has as a basic tenet the notion that families change over time, and many of these changes can be associated with workplace outcomes. Changes in the experienced out-comes of one partner will, in turn, influence the life and career trajectories of the other partner. That is, a basic assumption of family development theory is that de-velopment is reciprocal (Smith & Hamon, 2012, p. 71). While some couples may begin a relationship where the career of each is equally emphasized, with rare exceptions we see this as being a relatively unstable state of affairs (thus, we do not formalize this relationship as a partner type in the proposed framework). Change can come in a variety of forms, and here we are most interested in change to the relative level of career success and advancement experienced by each member of the partnership. Even after an initial period of partner parity, one partner's career attainment prospects will likely begin to outpace those of his/her partner. This will then initiate a movement (depicted as T_2 in the framework) where couples will begin to differentiate themselves by transitioning into more extreme positions within the four quadrants depicted in Figure 1.

Social exchange theory "focuses on the dynamics of relationships and how they are formed, maintained, and dissolved" (Smith & Hamon, 2012, p. 251). According to social exchange theory and family development theory, early career success, relative to that of a partner's, will influence one's own career choices. One way to reciprocate for the growing level of family income and security at-tributable to the early career success of one partner is for the other partner to begin scaling back his or her own career and providing additional career support to the lead careerist. This could be in the form of working fewer hours or pursuing posi-tions that allow for a greater degree of flexibility and work-life balance. Thus, for members of our population of interest (individuals who aspire to executive posi-tions in MNEs) who are experiencing accelerating levels of early career success, we would expect their partners to begin transitioning into the low power/high ad-vocacy cell of the figure. This phenomenon of opting out or scaling back a career also is more likely to be observed among women (Stone, 2007). That is, we would expect that among male members of our population of interest, the T_2 movement of their (female) partners into the low power/high advocacy cell would be more likely than among the female members of our population of interest.

Considering individuals who find their early career prospects growing at a rate below that of their partners, they may find themselves in the untenable position of experiencing a partner's transition into the high power/low advocacy cell of the figure. That is, because of their partners' increased contribution to family income and security, those partners may begin to see their career choices as deserving a new level of preference. We note that, in the long term, this will likely be untenable to a person who stills aspires to the C-suite, and therefore time 3 (T_3) transitions into relationships with high power/high advocacy partner types (or transitioning out of relations entirely) are anticipated. That is, over time, they may choose to end a rela-tionship or require their partner to reciprocate by providing additional resources in terms of career guidance and access to networks of influential associates.

While the nature of partner relationships may undergo considerable change and adjustment early in a career, this pace of change is expected to slow, and more stable relationship patterns are expected to emerge as it becomes clear that a per-son will or will not become a viable candidate for senior management roles. It is to these more stable mid-career partner types that we now turn our attention, with full descriptions and formal propositions about the career consequences of each.

THE CAREER CONSEQUENCES OF PARTNER TYPE

Partner as Career Competitor (CC)

Our first partner type, the "Career Competitor (CC)," resides in the high partner power/low partner advocacy cell of the proposed framework. In addition to the use of family power theory in the characterization of this partner type, we also draw on the work of Sullivan and Mainiero (2006) and the recent work of Petriglieri and Obodaru (2019). Sullivan and Mainiero (2006) base their ideas on two in-depth qualitative studies where their interviews of 12 men and 40 women (representing a wide range of professional occupations) revealed two distinctive career patterns; one was labeled the alpha pattern, the other was labeled the beta pattern. The CC partner takes on many of the characteristics of the alpha pattern. This is a partner who believes that his or her career is the lead career in the relationship and behaves accordingly. They actively pursue "career challenges as an important, all encompassing, parameter of their lives (Sullivan & Mainiero, 2006, p. 247)." They are a member of what Petriglieri and Obodaru (2019) label a bidirectional couple. These couples experience "the relationship between their professional identities as conflictual (p. 15)" These researchers define interpersonal identity conflict "as occurring when members of the couple come to regard the development of one partner's professional identity as an infringement on the development of the other's (p. 15)."

This partner type will have typically experienced more rapid early career and salary progression than their partner. From a neoclassic market model perspective (Becker, 1974; Mincer, 1978), the increased financial and social capital that accompanies this early career advancement will prioritize this partner's career over the other's career. The key idea here is that partners will maximize overall family well-being. By doing so, this often means that one partner will be expected to forgo career opportunities that are optimal from a personal calculation. Perhaps the most fundamental problem associated with being in a relationship with a partner in this cell is the inability to freely relocate for a better job (Bielby & Bielby, 1992). In fact, Mincer (1978) has developed a parsimonious model of family migration. As summarized by Bielby and Bielby, Mincer argues that "if the utility being maximized were family income, the family would relocate if the husband's gain in earnings in the new location exceeded the absolute value of the wife's loss (net of the cost of the move)" (1992, p. 1242). Of course, the long-term view of a partner who is behind in the early career rounds of the competition may disagree with this short-term calculation, and this person may argue that to maximize long-term family gain both partners may need to forego short-term private gains.

The Mincer (1978) model has received considerable empirical support, with the typical finding being that, on average, men's earnings increase after geographical relocation to a new job, while their female partners' earnings decline or increase at a lower rate. For Mincer (1978), this differential male/female rate of return is not the result of men being better able to impose their private interests, but simply captures the biases built into the structure of the labor market. This same pattern of results has been observed in more recent studies of the financial returns associated with changing employers; and these studies have been conducted while focusing on populations of highly educated managers and professionals (Brett & Stroh, 1997; Dreher & Cox, 2000; Dreher, Lee, & Clerkin, 2011).

Understanding the career consequences associated with maintaining a relationship with a career competitor also can be analyzed using social exchange theory (Emerson, 1976; England, 1989). According to Bielby and Bielby, in contrast to neoclassical explanations, "social exchange theory invokes the notion of *power* as the mechanism through which decisions are made. That is, the spouse in command of the most resources is able to impose outcomes that further her or his own goals to the detriment of the partner's" (1992, p. 1244). As applied to career attainment and reaching the C-suite, we anticipate that CCs, more so than any of the other partner types, would be able to devote more time and attention to their personal career goals and objectives, thus giving them the advantage in the final rounds of the career tournament. This advantage results from being able to make the most of career opportunities and developmental experiences required of the successful executive (McCall, 1998). At the core of these experiences are challenging assignments that place individuals in ambiguous situations that require learning to manage unfamiliar functions, businesses, and people (McCall, 1998, p. 71). This often requires changing jobs, employers, geographical locations, and working long hours. It will be difficult in a dual-career couple for both partners to avail themselves of these opportunities; thus, accommodating the career demands of a CC will come at a cost to the secondary partner.

Finally, a partner's cultural orientation can exacerbate the negative career costs associated with a partner's salary advantage and need to be geographically mobile. Here, for partners who have been exposed to societal values that are aligned with preferences for hierarchy, status, and achievement, relative early career success will more likely lead those partners to believe that their career is the lead career in the relationship.

It is this set of costs and associated career consequences that lead to our first formal research proposition.

Proposition 1: Forming and maintaining a personal partnership with a career competitor produces two partner-related forces working against the likelihood of one's reaching the C-suite (a high level of partner power and a low level of partner advocacy). Compared to all other partner types, forming and maintaining a personal partnership with a career competitor will reduce the likelihood of reaching the C-suite.

As noted earlier, given that our central interest is why so few women reach senior executive positions in MNEs, we will emphasize the moderating role of gender within the context of our framework throughout the remainder of the discussion. One of the earliest discussions about how gender relates to the making of economic decisions within households headed by heterosexual couples is that of

Hood (1983). According to Hood, a partner's bargaining power is shaped by "the mutually recognized right or authority to exercise power in a given area" (1983, p. 7). Thus, gender identity norms are seen to play an important role in understanding how relative income within households influences marriage satisfaction, the likelihood of divorce, and the division of home production (Bertrand et al., 2015). According to Akerlof and Kranton (2000, 2010), identity is all about belonging to a social category and a shared view about how one in the category is supposed to behave. One of the most intriguing findings from this literature is that there seems to be an aversion or unease associated with being in relationships in which the female partner earns more than the male partner (Bertrand et al., 2015). This assertion is supported by survey and opinion-oriented data and by the observation that frequency distributions of the share of income earned by female partners show discontinuous declines at the point the female partner begins to earn more than the male partner (US Bureau of Labor Statistics, 2011).

A violation of this gender identity norm can lead to outcomes that run counter to classic social exchange explanations about the division of labor within households. For example, Bertrand et al. (2015) found that the gender gap in home production, or how much more time the female partner spends on domestic (non-job related) tasks than her male partner, is larger in couples where the female partner has more family power (i.e., she earns more than her male partner). For Bertrand et al. (2015, p. 573) this suggests that a "threatening wife takes on a greater share of housework so as to assuage the husband's unease with the situation." This process of assuaging the male partner's feelings of unease means that men in life partnerships with career competitors will not likely experience the full force of the negative career consequences being proposed here. These differential consequences are addressed in Proposition 2, the first of a series that will address the moderating role of gender in the proposed framework.

> **Proposition 2:** The negative association between forming and maintaining a partnership with a career competitor and subsequent career attainment will be moderated by gender, such that the negative effects will be less pronounced among male contenders for C-suite positions than among female contenders.

Partner as Career Mentor (CM)

In some ways, this partner type resembles a member of what Petriglieri and Obodaru (2019) label a bidirectional secure-base couple. Here, without considering the family power perspective and the relative pay level of each, these couples experience a form of professional-identity symmetry and regard "the development of one partner's professional identity as benefiting the development of the other's (p. 10)." But research suggests that it very difficult for couples to sustain two C-suite directed careers, and that eventually the person with the higher level of family power will see his or her career as taking precedence, or being the lead career in the relationship (Blair-Loy, 2003, Stone, 2007). Their partner will be asked to defer his or her career in order to promote the career of the partner who has been particularly successful early in their career, whose career progress requires geographical mobility, and/or who is culturally disposed to hierarchical and power-oriented privilege. We also contend that in order to maintain stability in the relationship, the partner who creates career costs for the other partner must reciprocate in some way. One way for this partner to reciprocate is to fulfill the role we have labeled in the figure as the "Career Mentor." This partner's career does take precedence, but he or she also serves as a valuable resource for the "deferring" spouse and contributes to his or her career attainment.

This powerful partner seeks to leverage his or her considerable experience and insights to provide mentoring, coaching, and sponsorship to the deferring spouse (their protégé) and may take advantage of existing social networks to enhance the spouse's social capital. Admittedly, the deferring spouse's career progress is likely to be slowed down or even derailed in certain ways, especially in terms of constraints on opportunities and career mobility. However, the career mentor can also offer valuable developmental experiences that serve as a positive force to enhance the deferring spouse's success.

The career mentor can provide valuable social support to help the spouse cope with the stressful demands and subsequent strains of a challenging and demanding managerial career (see Viswesvaran, Sanchez, & Fisher, 1999). But, perhaps more importantly, this partner is in a unique position to provide significant assistance as a mentor, coach, and sponsor. Mentoring refers to various kinds of developmental assistance provided by a mentor to a (usually) less experienced mentee (Kram, 1985). A powerful partner can offer what are labelled as psychosocial mentoring functions including acceptance and confirmation, counseling, friendship, and role modeling to enhance the spouse's growth, identity, and self-worth (Ragins, 1997; Ragins & Kram, 2007, p. 5). Moreover, a capable and experienced partner may be uniquely qualified to provide *career mentoring* behaviors helping the spouse to "learn the ropes" and achieve hierarchical advancement. These career mentoring functions include behaviors such as coaching, sponsorship for key opportunities and roles, providing exposure and visibility to powerful others, and even protection from potentially harmful situations or people (Ragins & Kram, 2007). We note that the mentoring provided by this type of partner appears to be aligned with Sandberg's (2013) advice about making one's partner a "real partner," that is, a 50–50 partner fully supportive of one's own career. In addition, there is evidence that mentoring functions are often provided by persons located outside one's own work unit or organization (Wanberg, Welsh, & Hezlett, 2003), which is often the case with one's partner.

Taking a somewhat broader perspective on relationships, the partner who serves as a coach and sponsor may also provide a valuable enhancement to the spouse's *social capital*. Social capital refers to the goodwill engendered by networks of social relationships that can be mobilized to promote various actions. Social capital has been found to influence career success and compensation and to assist workers in finding jobs, among other outcomes (Adler & Kwon, 2002). Of particular relevance is the theoretical approach to social capital known as weak tie theory (Granovetter, 1973). It appears that in social networks, both strong ties (frequent, emotionally intense) to others and weak ties (not intense, infrequent, including a narrower group) produce career benefits. For example, strong ties have been found to be valuable for providing useful information from others and for social support. Weak ties may be especially valuable for attaining social resources overall and for making high-status contacts (Seibert et al., 2001). Thus, considering the development of weak ties with others, one's spouse can provide valuable social network resources, whether he or she is located within the same organization or even in a different industry. In summary, a highly successful partner who serves as a career coach and sponsor can connect one's spouse with an active social network—in essence a network of mentors—producing social resources that promote the spouse's career advancement.

Thus, having a high achieving partner who is willing to act as a broker within powerful networks, act as a mentor, understand career-oriented problems and stressors, and provide abundant support, should be advantageous when competing in the senior management career tournament.

> **Proposition 3:** Forming and maintaining a personal partnership with a career mentor produces forces working both for and against the likelihood of one's reaching the C-suite, with favorable career consequences compared to individuals in relationships with career competitors and individuals with no partners.

We also expect to see sex differences in the efficacy for one's career advancement of having a partner who is a career mentor. As noted, there is an aversion or unease associated with being in relationships in which the female partner earns more than the male partner (Bertrand et al., 2015). This discomfort, or even resentment, may also be experienced by male managers when their higher earning female partner attempts to serve as a coach and sponsor. That is, the male spouses (particularly if they are from certain cultural backgrounds) may have difficulty asking for or even accepting career assistance and advice from their female partners. However, for women in a relationship with a career mentor, there may be a relative advantage. This is because these male partners will typically be older, and their more extensive work experience will result in providing higher quality mentoring, coaching, role modeling, and career advice. And male executives' better access to various power resources, and also to powerful social networks to which women may not have access, could be especially potent for assisting their female spouses in striving for career advancement (Ramaswami et al., 2010).

> **Proposition 4:** The positive career consequences associated with forming and maintaining a partnership with a career mentor will be moderated by gender, such that the positive effects will be more pronounced for women striving to reach the C-suite than for their male counterparts.

Partner as Career Resource (CR)

As noted earlier, one way to reciprocate for the growing level of family income and security attributable to the early career success of one partner is for the other partner to begin scaling back his or her own career and providing additional career support to the lead careerist. This partner could dial back a career in the form of working fewer hours or pursuing positions that allow for a greater degree of flexibility and work-life balance. This represents the second career pattern identified by Sullivan and Mainiero (2006), the beta career pattern. These partners have "factored in the needs of their children, spouses, aging parents, friends, and even coworkers and clients—as part of the total gestalt of their careers (Mainiero & Sullivan, 2005, p. 111)." This type of partner may choose to gravitate to part-time work, allowing significant additional time for supporting the more career-oriented spouse, the family and the household. Another approach might be taking early retirement or retiring as soon as normal retirement options become available, thus enhancing the prominence and priority given to the partner's career. Still another example might be transitioning to new full-time work, but in a setting providing a maximum of work flexibility and/or a minimum of highly-challenging work demands. In a sense, scaled-back partners impose fewer mobility restrictions as they are not career competitors. This type of partner can use a variety of mechanisms for providing an enhanced support system to assist one's spouse in taking full advantage of opportunities for career achievement, mobility, and ultimately success in reaching the C-Suite.

A key contribution here is the enhanced capacity for providing *social support*, which we briefly mentioned earlier. Social support is information that leads a person to believe that he or she is cared for, esteemed, and valued and belongs to a network of communication and mutual obligation (Cobb, 1976). This support has also been defined more broadly as "the availability of helping relationships and the quality of those relationships" (Leavy, 1983, p. 5). Social support, as provided by family and friends in addition to coworkers and supervisors, has received much attention in the scholarly literature on stress and coping. There is considerable evidence that social support plays a beneficial role in one's experience of a variety of stressful demands and the resultant strains (see Viswesvaran et al., 1999). Researchers have theorized about and studied numerous specific alternative mechanisms by which social support operates, with some mixed results. However, there is clear evidence that social support can directly diminish one's experience of stressful demands, and also "buffer" the effect of stressors on the subsequent experienced suffering or strain (Viswesvaran et al., 1999). Although all spouses would be expected to provide support, a partner who had previously experienced the demands of corporate life, would have an enhanced capacity to serve as a key source of social support to help his or her spouse cope with the demands of an executive career, in part because of a unique understanding of the demands placed upon someone striving to succeed in such a setting. As a related but distinctive resource, this partner type also could provide mentoring support to his or her spouse. Of particular note, would be the ability to provide *psychosocial* mentoring that enhances the partner's professional and personal growth, identity, self-worth, and self-efficacy (Ragins & Kram, 2007, p. 5). These kinds of mentoring assistance have been shown to be directly linked to a variety of positive personal outcomes, in addition to objective career outcomes (Dougherty & Dreher, 2007).

Because of the extra availability of time and a flexible schedule, an income, and knowledge of the workplace, the partner type we have discussed thus far has the potential to enrich their partner's career across all five of the dimensions proposed in Greenhaus and Powell's (2006) theory of work-family enrichment. However, another variant of the CR type is the so called "stay-at-home" partner. A stay-at-home partner is someone who is unemployed and has chosen to give up or postpone career aspirations in order to take care of the household. In the context of our framework, a stay-at-home partner is likely to be beneficial for the working partner given that the former takes care of household activities, responsibilities, and so on, saving the physical and mental resources of the working partner to invest such surplus of energies in work and in the building human capital. Specialization benefits from marriage allow a couple to maximize the return they receive from work and non-work activities (Becker, 1991). However, given that work in the labor market is typically valued more than work at home, specialization becomes a source of additional inequality between partners (Solaz, 2005), thus further enhancing the decision-making and bargaining power of the employed partner. Nevertheless, a stay-at-home partner can provide a level of support not attainable via paid social services. This type of support includes the ability to engage in conferences with children's teachers and to provide very personal and specialized care to elderly parents, including the parents of the working partner (Carbone & Cahn, 2014).

But a stay-at-home partner also can enable the career of the other partner in very direct and job-related ways. As popularized in Whyte's (1956) classic book, *The Organization Man*, the stay-at-home partner can do such things as entertain the working partner's clients and colleagues, function in direct staff-support roles by organizing schedules and making business travel arrangements, or even by engaging in the work itself (e.g., editing the working partner's memos and reports). Even though, because of one's lack of ongoing participation in the paid workforce, the stay-at-home partner might not be able to provide the career support and coaching of certain other partner types, these direct ways of enabling the working partner's career can make the stay-at-home partner equally beneficial. Thus, whether we consider the stay-at-home variant of the CR or the scaled-back variant, we offer our next formal proposition:

Proposition 5: Forming and maintaining a personal partnership with a partner classified as a career resource (CR) produces two forces working to increase the likelihood of one's reaching the C-suite (a low level of partner power and a high level of partner advocacy). This increased likelihood of reaching the C-suite will be most pronounced when compared to those with partners of the career competitor (CC) type, but an advantage will be maintained when compared to those with partners in all other cells of the framework.

Once again, the expected strength of this advantage may be influenced by gender. Because of sex role socialization, male partners of this type may not be as potent a household resource to female breadwinners, who, regardless of their employment status, tend to contribute disproportionately to childcare and household maintenance (Sullivan, 2000). Furthermore, men and women behave in line with the social roles they occupy. We have scripts about how men and women should behave, and these are normatively reinforced through socialization since childhood (Eagly, Wood, & Johanessen-Schmidt, 2004; Tracy & Rivera, 2010). Men who have female partners at home conform the best to social expectations of gender roles and are likely to be perceived as more stable and responsible (Pfeffer & Ross, 1982; Tharenou, 1999). Also, in line with human capital theory and wife-as-resource theory, these men have more resources to invest in their jobs and careers, making them more productive (Tharenou, 1999). In addition to that, Tharenou (1999) posits, that traditional fathers (men who have stay-at-home wives) are perceived to have more financial need than single or married men without children, and to be more serious about work, leading organizations to boost their advancement (Kelly & Grant, 2012). For men, marriage is positively related to earnings as these qualities are in line with being an "ideal worker," signaling stability (Kelly & Grant, 2012). Furthermore, married men with working wives earn less than married men with stay-at-home wives (Blackaby, Carlin, & Murphy, 1998), suggesting a premium associated with traditional marriages for men. Additionally, marriage and children generally pose barriers to career progress due to inequitable distribution of household work between married men and married women (Bertrand et al., 2015; Ragins & Sundstrom, 1989; Tharenou 1999). While the number of couples consisting of female breadwinners and male stay-at-home partners is increasing, there are unique challenges specific to this group of male primary caretakers (Dunn, Rochlen, & O'Brien, 2013; Wang, Parker, & Taylor, 2013) given the sex role socialization of men and women that very likely influences the work lives of female breadwinners (Eagly et al., 2004). Therefore, stay-at-home male partners are not likely to be as resourceful to women breadwinners as stay-at-home female partners are to male breadwinners. Women continue to perform a disproportionate amount of childcare and household work, regardless of their employment status (Bertrand et al., 2015; Sullivan, 2000) depleting their resources for work related activities. This mix of differential benefits leads to our next proposition

Proposition 6: The positive career consequences associated with forming and maintaining a partnership with a CR will be moderated by gender, such that the positive effects will be more pronounced among male contenders for C-suite positions than among female contenders.

No Partner (NP)

Being in the no-partner cell (no career competition) produces forces working both for and against the likelihood of one's reaching the C-suite (no partner competition/no partner advocacy). These individuals are those who have never been married or are currently not in a committed relationship (including the divorced or widowed). On first pass, it might seem that having no partner could be a privilege. Such individuals (if not having dependent children or custody constraints) have no immediate social or family obligations or requirements to yolk their careers with another's aspirations and abilities, thereby enabling them to be more mobile and to "job shop." However, being single may very well present its own set of problems. Research suggests that single individuals are subject to cultural biases and discrimination detrimental to their career attainment and to reaching the C-suite.

Signaling theory would suggest that, given the lack of full information about an employee, organizational decision makers rely on observable qualities of individuals to make judgments of their suitability for managerial positions (Spence, 1973). Such observable qualities include demographic characteristics (e.g., sex) and social relations (e.g., family status) among others. Despite the increasing number of adults choosing to be single, cultural norms place a high value on marriage and married couples. Marital status signals to employers that important fundamental desirable properties are present in the individual (Kelly & Grant, 2012; Tharenou, 1999). Society's uncritical acceptance of the "ideology of marriage and family"—which upholds marriage as the most important peer relationship, a milestone signaling maturity, and something that people want and expect to have in order to lead a meaningful life—has marginalized singles as a stigmatized group given their non-conformance to societal norms governing adult behavior (DePaulo & Morris 2005; Morris, Sinclair, & DePaulo, 2007). Singles are therefore potential targets for biases, stereotyping, prejudice, and discrimination. For example, as noted earlier, married men are considered to be more productive and effort-oriented than single men (Blackaby et al., 1998). Singles are assumed to be less responsible, less mature, and more delinquent than married individuals (Morris et al., 2007). Given the above characteristics attributed to single individuals, we offer the following proposition:

Proposition 7: Given the additional negative consequences attributable to cultural bias, having no partner will produce a career advantage over only one other partner type depicted in Figure 1. Here the advantage goes only in the comparison with the person who has established a relationship with a career competitor (CC).

The negative effects of being single on career advancement are more nuanced when considering the consequences for men versus women. While both men and women benefit from a marriage premium within their sexes, research further suggests that there could be differential career outcomes for men versus women because of their "single" status.

Comparing various family statuses among men alone, research suggests that married men earn more than unmarried men, even after controlling for level of education, experience, and other observable characteristics (Allegretto & Arthur, 2001; Gupta, Smith, & Stratton, 2007; Maasoumi, Millimet, & Sarkar, 2009), and in some cases, enjoy a marriage premium of 15% higher wages, when comparing married heterosexuals and unmarried cohabiting heterosexuals (Allegretto & Arthur, 2001). As noted before, single, childless men are expected to advance at slower rates than married men because their single status signals lower stability, responsibility, and need for financial resources (Pfeffer & Ross, 1982; Tharenou, 1999).

Managerial advancement also is more adversely affected when men are single than when women are single (Tharenou, 1999). While some research suggests that married women without children reported the highest hourly wages compared to women who were never married (with or without children) and women who were divorced (with or without children) after controlling for human capital variables, number of children, and race/ethnicity (Budig & England, 2001), other studies and perspectives lead us to expect single women to advance faster in their careers than married women. According to conformance to social expectations theory (Landau & Arthur, 1992; Tharenou 1999), the primary role of the married woman, especially mothers, is to take care of the household, and not engage in market activities, let alone seize advancement opportunities. The wife-as-resource view also suggests that married women are likely to provide career enhancing resources for their working husbands, reducing the married woman's focus on her job and commitment to career, leading to lower productivity and advancement. The childless single woman, on the other hand, is not encumbered by a partner in the same way as a married woman. Furthermore, based on distributive justice theory, Tharenou (1999) notes that career resources such as pay and advancement opportunities are distributed based on need (Pfeffer & Ross, 1982). Following this logic, married men, especially those with children, are likely to advance more than both married men without children and single men. On the other hand, single women are likely to advance more than married women (with or without children) because single women are likely to have more time for energy-intensive jobs than married women, are likely to have fewer employment disruptions than married women and are more likely than married women to be perceived as having financial need because such resources are presumed to be provided by married women's husbands. Thus, we offer our final gender-as moderator proposition.

Proposition 8: The career advantage of having no partner (NP) over a person in a relationship with a career competitor (CC) will be moderated by gender such that the advantage will be more pronounced among women than among men.

Gender and Cell Placement

Finally, now that we have defined the qualities of and the career consequences associated with the various partner types, we will offer two additional gender-related propositions. These propositions relate to how gender affects placement in the framework. Recall the discussion about the accumulation of early-career human and social capital and a central finding from the marriage market literature (Carbone & Cahn, 2014). This finding is that there is a universal preference, found in virtually all cultures, for women to prefer male partners who are three to four years older than they are (or for men to prefer female partners who are younger than they are). It follows, then, that this will normally give the male partner superiority (early after the formation of the relationship) in cultural and economic capital as they will have had longer to accrue these resources. Add to this the evidence for a gender-identity based aversion to a woman earning more than her male partner (Bertrand et al., 2015). Taken together, these two cultural forces suggest that women will be more likely than men to have partners who contribute more to total household income than themselves. This means that women will be more likely than their male counterparts to transition into and form relationships with career competitors (CC)—the partner type associated with the greatest negative career consequences for reaching the C-suite.

Related to the cultural and social processes just discussed, there is reason to believe that a heterosexual woman who aspires to the C-suite will have more difficulty than her male counterpart in finding a partner who will be willing to scale back his career or to leave the labor market entirely. This is because, while both the careers of men and women can be penalized for prioritizing family over career, the penalties are greatest among men (Butler & Skattebo, 2004; Rudman & Mescher, 2013). There also is evidence that stay-at-home fathers experience a higher degree of social isolation and negative reactions from others than do stay-at-home mothers (Rochlen, McKelley, & Whittaker, 2010). This means that women will be less likely than their male counterparts to transition into the cell with the greatest positive career consequences for reaching the C-suite, this being the cell containing partners who provide career resources and partners who do not act as career competitors.

> **Proposition 9:** Gender will have a direct effect upon cell placement, such that women will be more likely than men to be in relationships with career competitors, and less likely to be in relationships with either stay-at-home partners or scaled-back partners; with the consequences being negative for the career prospects of women.

These effects may be diminished or exacerbated depending on the cultural context experienced during a person's developmental years, or the cultural context of a person's home country. While we acknowledge that there can be intra-country variation in cultural values (Au, 1999), individuals exposed to the same shared values at a societal level will likely express these values in a wide range of personal and workplace situations. As an illustration, developmental years spent in more egalitarian societies such as Norway or Sweden will likely shape how one engages in marriage market decision making and subsequent relational attitudes with their partners, and this shaping process will likely differ from the process experienced in a less egalitarian country like India. This is because Norway and Sweden are characterized as being high on gender egalitarianism, and low on power distance and masculinity, while India is characterized as being low on gender egalitarianism, and high on both other dimensions, dimensions that relate to hierarchy, status, and achievement. Experienced gender inequality in one's home country should help account for decisions partners make about family power and career planning. Also, in addition to being high on both power distance and masculinity, countries like India rank near the bottom on the World Economic Forum's (2016) measure of gender-based economic opportunity, while countries like Norway and Sweden rank near the top. This suggests that placement and transitions in the framework will be influenced not only by gender, but also by the cultural context of the individual's home country. This leads to our final proposition.

Proposition 10: Gender will interact with cultural context when accounting for cell placement such that its effects will be most pronounced among those from home countries characterized by low (compared to those characterized by high) gender-based economic opportunity.

DISCUSSION

Theoretical Contributions

We believe this type of theory building and the subsequent empirical examination we hope it stimulates will contribute to building better models of the career attainment process. Following Sandberg (2013), partner selection (e.g., choosing a life partner who is either a career resource or a career competitor) should be central to being competitive in the tournament to reach senior management. While ideas about partner type and selection have the potential to greatly influence how one approaches a career and personal life, there is surprisingly little evidence or academic literature in support of this way of thinking. By this we mean both a theoretical literature that develops even a basic typology of partner types, or an empirical literature that offers some degree of sampling or statistical control. Our intention here has been to initiate a theory building process that will lead to a framework/typology of partner types and to a better understanding of the relative influence of partner selection on the career attainment process. To accomplish our objective, we have drawn on a variety of related theoretical perspectives, with a heavy reliance on social exchange theory (Kelley & Thibaut, 1978) and its derivative, family power theory (Rodman, 1972). We also have drawn on ideas from family development theory (Aldous, 1978; White, 1991), the marriage market literature (Becker, 1991; Carbone & Cahn, 2014; Smith & Hamon, 2012; Winton, 1995), Greenhaus and Powell's theory of work-family enrichment (2006), and the work of Sullivan and Mainiero (2006). The further development of this typology of partner types and the measures that allow for the categorization of individuals within this framework should be the first priority for future researchers interested in this topic. This work needs to be completed before we can move on to answering foundational questions about the most advantageous personal situation to be in at mid-career for a person who still aspires to compete for senior management positions in MNEs.

The theoretical contributions surrounding this effort are twofold. First, we note that organizational researchers have developed increasingly comprehensive models of career success, but these models have tended to focus on investments in human capital, individual differences in temperament and motivational attributes, sponsorship and mentoring, the accumulation of social capital, and bias and discrimination in the workplace (e.g., Dreher & Ash, 1990; Eagly & Karau, 2002; Heilman, 2012; Judge et al., 1995; Kirchmeyer, 1998; Seibert et al., 2001). While family power is only one component of a general model of how gender affects reaching the C-suite, with a few noteworthy exceptions (e.g., Stroh et al., 1992), the class of variables discussed by Sandberg (2013) has been ignored in the career success literature. We see our fuller expression of family power theory as contributing to the improvement of comprehensive models of the career attainment process. Along with existing explanations for gender-based career discrepancies, it is particularly central to understanding the glass ceiling phenomenon and the lack of gender-based diversity in the C-suite.

A related second contribution is our attempt to broaden family power theory by considering a more complex characterization of power and contribution within family units. We use the traditional view—that the family member who provides the most in terms of financial resources will also have increased bargaining power over career-related decision making—to underpin the framework, but also consider other factors that lead to one partner's career being given preference over the career of the other. We also add a second major dimension to the analysis in order to provide a more complete portrayal of partner selection and retention processes and how these processes affect career success and attainment. This dimension is less about financial resources and geographical mobility (and the role they play in creating career competitors) and more about other ways a person can enable and support a partner's career. This has led to a proposed typology of partner types and propositions about how establishing and maintaining a committed relationship with a life partner at mid-career can affect the final round of the career tournament.

Limitations and Future Research Needs

Boundary Conditions and Moderators. As previously noted, our framework and propositions only address the career competition that begins at mid-career and that accounts for who does and does not reach senior management in large multinational enterprises (MNEs). But in addition to limiting career stage and managerial population generalizability, the framework and propositions are likely to be sensitive to a number of unexamined moderator variables. Among them are the moderating effects of dependents (caregiving responsibilities for children and/or relatives), social and cultural values and norms, and sexual orientation. While beyond the scope of our initial treatment of this topic, each of these moderator classes is deserving of extensive theoretical and empirical attention.

Recursive Processes and Causation. Studying the linkages between partner type at mid-career and subsequently reaching senior management will ultimately require longitudinal research designs. This is because the process of choosing and maintaining a relationship with a life partner and mid-career levels of job success and attainment (likely predictors of reaching the C-suite) are likely to be part of a recursive process (a supportive partner leads to mid-career success—mid-career success changes the trajectory of that partner's career focus), a process that makes it particularly difficult to make cause-and-effect statements when using cross-sectional data. To understand the effects of partner type at mid-career on reaching the C-suite, one must be able to partial out the effects of mid-career success. One methodological alternative that may prove useful is a retrospective, biographical approach. Here, late-career respondents could be asked to provide biographical histories about their attainment and success at mid-career, the degree to which their life partners were either career competitors or career enablers at mid-career, and their eventual level of later-career attainment.

Measurement Requirements. Testing the proposed model presents a number of measurement challenges, most notably the categorization of partners into the types depicted in Figure 1. The model's X-axis is the more manageable of the two because it follows traditional family power theory (Rodman, 1972), where a partner's power and degree of career competitiveness is largely determined by his or her relative contribution to total family income. But the X-axis may also require a measurement approach that incorporates a partner's need to be geographically mobile, and their cultural grounding and views related to status, power distance, and gender egalitarianism.

The Y-axis is more complex, taking into account the variety of ways one partner can enable the career of the significant other. This can take the form of entertaining a partner's clients, being willing to relocate to enable a partner to take on challenging new job assignments, allowing one's partner to work long hours, taking on a disproportionate share of childcare responsibilities, providing access to important professional networks, and being a career coach and sponsor. Appropriate construct validity studies will be needed to properly scale this dimension.

But a third challenge will be to properly capture the temporal nature of forming and maintaining a relationship with a life partner. Relationships form and dissolve, and for a partnership to meaningfully influence one's career attainment and success it must be sustained for a reasonably long period of time and sustained during the critical mid-career years. A good example of this challenge comes when examining what appears to be a relatively simple classification exercise, that being the identification of a person who has no partner at mid-career. Having never had a partner is very different from being recently widowed, or recently divorced, or being divorced for many years and still living with (or living apart from) dependent children. It may well be that for many divorced and currently single people, having dependent children poses the same mobility restrictions as maintaining a personal partnership with a partner classified as a career competitor. The other three partner types depicted in our framework will likely also pose measurement challenges that will need to be carefully resolved.

CONCLUSION

Building upon and integrating a variety of theoretical perspectives, we have proposed a typology of partner types that considers the extent to which life partners act as career competitors and/or career enablers for mid-career aspirational managers and professionals. In addition, we have considered how gender informs our understanding of how partner selection affects career attainment and ultimately how it can affect the diversity of top management teams. We believe this type of theory building and the subsequent empirical examination we hope it stimulates will contribute to building better models of the career attainment process and serve to provide individuals, who have the ability and drive to compete for C-Suite positions, with a realistic assessment of what will be required to be successful. Given the centrality of gender in understanding the strength of the proposed effects of partner type on career attainment and its centrality in understanding placement in the typology itself, this blending of the diversity and marriage market literatures seems in order.

REFERENCES

Adler, P. S., & Kwon, S. W. (2002). Social capital: Prospects for a new concept. *Academy of Management Review, 27,* 17–40.

Akerlof, G., & Kranton, R. E. (2000). Economics and identity. *The Quarterly Journal of Economics, 115,* 715–753.

Akerlof, G., & Kranton, R. E. (2010). Identity economics. *The Economists' Voice, 7,* 2010-06-11.

Aldous, J. (1978). *Family careers: Developmental change in families.* New York, NY: Wiley.

Allegretto, S. A., & Arthur, M. M. (2001). An empirical analysis of homosexual/heterosexual male earnings differentials: Unmarried and unequal? *Industrial and Labor Relations Review, 54,* 631–646.

Allen, T. D., & Eby, L. (2016). *The Oxford handbook of work and family.* Oxford, NY: Oxford University Press.

Au, K. Y. (1999). Intra-cultural variation: Evidence and implications for international business. *Journal of International Business Studies, 30,* 799–812.

Becker, G. S. (1974). A theory of social interactions. *Journal of Political Economy, 82,* 1063–1093.

Becker, G. S. (1991). *A treatise on the family.* Cambridge, MA: Harvard University Press.

Bertrand, M., Kamenica, E., & Pan, J. (2015). Gender identity and relative income within households. *The Quarterly Journal of Economics, 130,* 571–614.

Bielby, W. T., & Bielby, D. D. (1992). I will follow him: Family ties, gender-role beliefs, and reluctance to relocate for a better job. *American Journal of Sociology, 97,* 1241–1267.

Blackaby, D. H., Carlin, P. S., & Murphy, P. D. (1998). What a difference a wife makes: The effect of women's hours of work on husband's hourly earnings. *Bulletin of Economic Research, 50,* 1–18.

Blair-Loy, M. (2003). *Competing devotions: Career and family among women executives.* Cambridge, MA: Harvard University Press.

Blau, P. (1964). *Exchange and power in social life.* New York, NY: John Wiley.

Brett, J. M., & Stroh, L. K. (1997). Jumping ship: Who benefits from an external labor market career strategy. *Journal of Applied Psychology, 82,* 331–341.

Budig, M. T., & England, P. (2001). The wage penalty for motherhood. *American Sociological Review, 66,* 204–225.

Bursztyn, L., Fujiwara, T., & Pallais, A. (2017). 'Acting wife': Marriage market incentives and labor market investments. *American Economic Review, 107,* 3288–3319.

Butler, A., & Skattebo, A. (2004). What is acceptable for women may not be for men: The effects of family conflicts with work on performance ratings. *Journal of Occupational Psychology, 77,* 553–564.

Carbone, J., & Cahn, N. (2014). *Marriage markets: How inequality is remaking the American family.* New York, NY: Oxford University Press.

Catalyst. (2018). *Women CEOs of the S&P 500.* New York, NY: Catalyst. Retrieved from: http://www.catalyst.org/knowledge/women-ceos-sp-500

Cobb, S. (1976). Social support as a moderator of life stress. *Psychosomatic Medicine, 38,* 300–314.

Cropanzano, R., & Mitchell, M. S. (2005). Social exchange theory: An interdisciplinary review. *Journal of Management, 31,* 874–899.

DePaulo, B. M., & Morris, W. L. (2005). Singles in society and in science. *Psychological Inquiry, 16,* 57–83.

Dougherty, T. W., & Dreher, G. F. (2007). Mentoring and career outcomes: Conceptual and methodological issues in an emerging literature. In B. R. Ragins & K. E. Kram (Eds.), *The handbook of mentoring at work* (pp. 51–93). Los Angeles, CA: Sage.

Dreher, G. F., & Ash, R. A. (1990). A comparative study of mentoring among men and women in managerial, professional, and technical positions. *Journal of Applied Psychology, 75,* 539–546.

Dreher, G. F., & Cox, T. H. (2000). Labor market mobility and cash compensation: The moderating effects of race and gender. *Academy of Management Journal, 43,* 890–900.

Dreher, G. F., Lee, J., & Clerkin, T. A. (2011). Mobility and cash compensation: The moderating effects of gender, race, and executive search firms. *Journal of Management, 37,* 651–681.

Dunn, M. G., Rochlen, A. B., & O'Brien, K. M. (2013). Employee, mother, and partner: An exploratory investigation of working women with stay-at-home fathers. *Journal of Career Development, 40,* 3–22.

Eagly, A. H., & Karau, S. J. (2002). Role congruity theory of prejudice toward female leaders. *Psychological Review, 109,* 573–598.

Eagly, A. H., Wood, W., & Johannesen-Schmidt, M. C. (2004). Social role theory of sex differences and similarities: Implications for the partner preferences of women and men. In A. H. Eagly, A. E. Beall, & R. J. Sternberg, *The Psychology of gender* (pp. 269–295). New York, NY: Guilford.

eCelebrityFacts. (2017). Accessed on 14 July 2017. www.ecelebrityfacts.com/ceo-maril-lyn-hewson-many-hats-lockheed-martin

Emerson, R. (1976). Social exchange theory. In A. Inkeles, J. Coleman, & N. Smelser. *Annual Review of Sociology, 2*, 335–362. Palo Alto, CA: Annual Reviews.

England, P. (1989). A feminist critique of rational choice theories: Implications for sociology. *The American Sociologist, 20*, 14–28.

Galunic, C., Ertug, G., & Gargiulo, M. (2012). The positive externalities of social capital: Benefits from senior brokers. *Academy of Management Journal, 55*, 1213–1231.

Gergen, K. J., Greenberg, M. S., & Willis, R. H. (1980). *Social exchange: Advances in theory and research*. New York, NY: Plenum Press.

Granovetter, M. S. (19730. The strength of weak ties. *American Journal of Sociology, 6*, 1360–1380.

Greenhaus, J. H., & Powell, G. N. (2006). When work and families are allies: A theory of work-family enrichment. *Academy of Management Review, 31*, 72–92.

Gupta, N. D., Smith, N., & Stratton, L. S. (2007) Is marriage poisonous? Are relationships taxing? An analysis of the male marital wage differential in Denmark. *Southern Economic Journal, 74*, 412–433.

Hakim, C. (2000). *Work-life choices in the 21st century: Preference theory*. New York, NY: Oxford University Press.

Hamori, M. (2014). Executive career success in search-firm mediated moves across employers. *The International Journal of Human Resource Management, 25*, 390–411.

Heilman, M. E. (2012). Gender stereotypes and workplace bias. *Research in Organizational Behavior, 32*, 113–135.

Hood, J. C. (1983). *Becoming a two-job family*. New York, NY: Praeger.

ILRR. (2017). Special issue on inequality in the workplace. *Industrial and Labor Relations Review, 70* (1).

Jaskiewicz, P., Combs, J. G., Shanine, K. K., & Kacmar, K. M. (2017). Introducing the family: A review of family science with implications for management research. *The Academy of Management Annals, 11*, 309–341.

Judge, T. A., Cable, D. M., Boudreau, J. W., & Bretz, R. D. (1995). An empirical investigation of the predictors of career success. *Personnel Psychology, 48*, 485–519.

Kelly, K., & Grant, L. (2012). Penalties and premiums: The impact of gender, marriage, and parenthood on faculty salaries in science, engineering and mathematics (SEM) and non-SEM fields. *Social Studies of Science, 42*, 869–896.

Kelley, H. H., & Thibaut, J. W. (1978). *Interpersonal relations: A theory of interdependence*. New York, NY: Wiley.

Kirschmeyer, C. (1998). Determinants of managerial career success: Evidence and explanation of male/female differences. *Journal of Management, 6*, 673–692.

Kossek, E. E., & Lambert, S. J. (Eds). (2005). *Work and life integration: Organizational, cultural, and individual perspectives*. Mahwah, NJ: Erlbaum.

Kram, K. E. (1985). *Mentoring at work: Developmental relationships in organizational life*. Glenview, IL: Scott, Foresman.

Landau, J., & Arthur, M. B. (1992). The relationship of marital status, spouse's career status, and gender to salary level. *Sex Roles, 27*, 665–681.

Leavy, R. L. (1983). Social support and psychological disorder: A review. *Journal of Community Psychology, 11*, 3–21.

Levinson, D. (1978). *The seasons of a man's life*. New York, NY: Alfred A. Knopf.

Maasoumi, E., Millimet, D. L., & Sarkar, D. (2009). Who benefits from marriage? *Oxford Bulletin of Economics and Statistics, 71,* 1–34.

Mainiero, L., & Sullivan, S. E. (2005). Kaleidoscope careers: An alternative explanation for the "opt-out" revolution. *Academy of Management Executive, 19,* 106–123.

McCall, M. W. (1998). *High flyers: Developing the next generation of leaders.* Boston, MA: Harvard Business School Press.

Mincer, J. (1978). Family migration decisions. *Journal of Political Economy, 86,* 749–743.

Morris, W. L., Sinclair, S., & DePaulo, B. M. (2007). No shelter for singles: The perceived legitimacy of marital status discrimination. *Group Processes & Intergroup Relations, 10,* 457–470.

Nye, I. (1978). Is choice and exchange the key? *Journal of Marriage and the Family, 40,* 219–233.

Petriglieri, J. L., & Obodaru, O. (2019). Secure-base relationships as drivers of professional identity development in dual-career couples. *Administrative Science Quarterly, 64,* 694–736. doi: 10.1177/0001839218783174

Pfeffer, J. P., & Ross, J. (1982). The effects of marriage and a working wife on occupational and wage attainment. *Administrative Science Quarterly, 27,* 66–80.

Poelmans, S. A. (2005). The decision process theory of work and family. In E. E. Kossek and S. J. Lambert (Eds.), *Work and life integration: Organizational, cultural, and individual perspectives* (pp. 263–285). Mahwah, NJ: Erlbaum.

Powell, G. N. (2011). *Women & men in management.* Los Angeles, CA: Sage.

Powell, G. N., & Greenhaus, J. H. (2010). Sex, gender, and decisions at the family-work interface. *Journal of Management, 36,* 1011–1039.

Ragins, B. R. (1997). Diversified mentoring relationships in organizations: A power perspective. *Academy of Management Review, 22,* 482–521.

Ragins, B. R., & Kram, K. E. (2007). The roots and meaning of mentoring. In B. R. Ragins & K. E. Kram (Eds.), *The handbook of mentoring at work* (pp. 3–15). Los Angeles, CA: Sage.

Ragins, B. R. & Sundstrom, E. (1989). Gender and power in organizations: A longitudinal perspective. *Psychological Bulletin, 105,* 51–88.

Ramaswami, A., Carter, N. M., & Dreher, G. F. (2016). Expatriation and career success: A human capital perspective. *Human Relations, 69,* 1959–1987.

Ramaswami, A., Dreher, G. F., Bretz, R., & Wiethoff, C. (2010). Gender, mentoring and career success: The importance of organizational context. *Personnel Psychology, 63,* 385–405.

Rochlen, A., McKelley, R., & Whittaker, T. (2010). Stay-at-home fathers' reasons for entering the role and stigma experiences: A preliminary report. *Psychology of Men & Masculinity, 11,* 279–285.

Rodman, H. (1972). Marital power and the theory of resources in cultural context. *Journal of Comparative Family Studies, 3,* 50–69.

Rudman, L. A., & Mescher, K. (2013). Penalizing men who request a family leave: Is flexibility stigma a femininity stigma? *Journal of Social Issues, 69,* 322–340.

Sandberg, S. (2013). *Lean in: Women, work, and the will to lead.* New York, NY: Alfred A. Knopf.

Seibert, S. E., Kraimer, M. L., & Liden, R. C. (2001). A social capital theory of career success. *Academy of Management Journal, 44,* 219–237.

Slaughter, A. (2015). *Unfinished business: Women Men Work Family*. New York, NY: Random House.

Smith, S. R., & Hamon, R. R., (2012). *Exploring family theories*. New York, NY: Oxford University Press

Solaz, A. (2005). Division of domestic work: Is there adjustment between partners when one is unemployed? *Review of Economics of the Household, 3*, 387–4135.

Spence M. (1973). Job market signaling. *Quarterly Journal of Economics, 87*, 355–374.

Stone, P. (2007). *Opting out? Why women really quit careers and head home*. Berkeley, CA: University of California Press.

Stroh, L. K., Brett, J. M., & Reilly, A. H. (1992). All the right stuff: Comparison of female and male career patterns. *Journal of Applied Psychology, 77*, 251–260.

Sullivan, S. E., & Mainiero, L. A. (2006). The changing nature of gender roles, alpha/beta careers and work-life issues: Theory-driven implications for human resource management. *Career Development International, 12*, 238–263.

Sullivan, O. (2000). The division of domestic labor: Twenty years of change? *Sociology, 34*, 437–456.

Super, D. 1957. *Psychology of careers*. New York, NY: Harper & Brothers.

Tharenou, P. (1999). Is there a link between family structures and women's and men's career advancement? *Journal of Organizational Behavior, 20*, 837–863.

Thibaut, J. W., & Kelley, H. H. (1959). *The social psychology of groups*. New York, NY: Wiley.

Tracy, S. J., & Rivera, K. D. (2010). Endorsing equity and applauding stay-at- home moms: How male voices on work- life reveal aversive sexism and flickers of transformation. *Management Communication Quarterly, 24*, 3–43.

US Bureau of Labor Statistics. (2011). Table 25 Wives who earn more than their husbands, 1987–2009, from the *Annual Social and Economic Supplements, 1988–2010, Current Population Survey*. Accessed on 15 March 2017 from https://www.bls.gov/cps/wlf-table25-2011.pdf.

Viswesvaran, C., Sanchez, J. I., & Fisher, J. (1999). The role of social support in the process of work stress: A meta-analysis. *Journal of Vocational Behavior, 54*, 314–344.

Wanberg, C. R., Welsh, E. T., & Hezlett, S. A. (2003). Mentoring research: A review and dynamic process model. *Research in Personnel and Human Resources Management, 22*, 39–124.

Wang, W., Parker, K., & Taylor, P. (2013). *Breadwinner moms*. Accessed on 15 March 2017 from http://www.pewsocialtrends.org/2013/05/29/breadwinner-moms/

Wayne, J. H., Butts, M., Casper, W. J., & Allen, T. D. (2017). Understanding balance: An examination of multiple meanings of work-family balance and their relations to employee attitudes and performance. *Personnel Psychology, 70*, 167–210.

Weisshaar, K. (2014). Earnings equality and relationship stability for same-sex and heterosexual couples. *Social Forces, 931*, 93–123.

White, J. M. (1991). *Dynamics of family development: A theoretical perspective*. New York, NY: Guilford.

Whyte, W. (1956). *The organization man*. New York, NY: Doubleday.

Winton, C. (1995). *Frameworks for studying families*. Guilford, CT: Duskin.

World Economic Forum. (2016). *The global gender gap report*. Accessed on 14 June 2017 from https://www.weforum.org/reports/the-global-gender-gap-report-2016

CHAPTER 3

STEREOTYPES OF ETHNIC GROUPS IN TERMS OF ATTRIBUTES RELEVANT TO WORK ORGANIZATIONS

An Experimental Study

Eugene F. Stone-Romero, Dianna L. Stone,
Mark Hartman, and Megumi Hosoda

Our experimental study considered work-relevant stereotypes of six ethnic groups (i.e., Anglo American, Native American, African American, Mexican American, Chinese American, East Indian American). Members of these groups were rated in terms of such attributes as status, reliability, emotional adjustment, skill, and cognitive ability. The same attributes were assessed with respect to two views or perspectives: (a) subjects' own views or (b) their beliefs about the views of others. Results showed ethnic group differences on numerous attributes. Anglo Americans, Chinese Americans, Native Americans, and East Indian Americans were viewed most positively, whereas African Americans and Mexican Americans were viewed most negatively. In addition, there were numerous (Bonferroni adjusted) statistically significant pairwise differences between ethnic groups on various attributes. Finally,

Diversity and Inclusion in Organizations, pages 59–84.

59

own views were more positive than the views of others. Implications of these findings are considered for human resource management (HRM) policies and practices.

In spite of the fact that there has been progress in race relations in the U.S. in the past several decades, members of various ethnic minority groups continue to face unfair discrimination in a wide variety of settings, including schools, housing, and work organizations (organizations hereinafter). In addition, research shows that older (traditional) forms of *overt racism* have been replaced by *modern or symbolic racism* (Eberhart & Fiske, 1996; McConahay & Hough, 1976; Sears & Kinder, 1971; Sears & McConahay, 1973), defined as "the expression of abstract ideological symbols and symbolic behaviors of the feeling that blacks [and other minorities] are violating cherished values and making illegitimate demands for changes in the racial status quo" (McConahay & Hough, 1976, p. 38). As noted by Ebehart and Fiske, modern racists believe that "Blacks are unfairly pushing themselves into places where they are not wanted and gaining underserved attention and status (p. 375). Underlying both traditional and modern racism are stereotype-based views about members of various ethnic groups (e.g., Arabs, African Americans, Mexican Americans, and Native Americans). Regrettably, coincidental with the rise in political power of Donald J. Trump and his supporters (e.g., the alt-Right, the Aryan Nation, the Christian Identity Movement, the Council of Conservative Citizens, the Ku Klux Klan, the National Alliance, the National Socialist Movement, the Skinheads, and the Stormfront) members of various hate groups feel emboldened to openly express hatred toward various ethnic minorities (Southern Poverty Law Center, 2018). Frequently their expressions of hate are buttressed by their stereotypical beliefs about minorities. Not only do members of various hate groups express negative views about ethnic minorities, but they also denigrate immigrants, Jews, gays, lesbians, and members of many other target groups.

Stereotypes and Stereotyping

Since the introduction of the stereotype concept in the social science literature (Lippmann, 1922) it has been defined in a number of ways. However, there appears to general agreement that *stereotypes* are sets of beliefs about targets, including members of social (e.g., ethnic) groups (Ashmore & Del Boca, 1981; Bodenhausen & Wyer, 1985; Campbell, 1967; Gardner, 1994; Hamilton, 1981; Jussim, Coleman, & Lerch, 1987; Macrae, Stangor, & Hewstone, 1996). As noted by Stangor and Schaller (1996), a basic assumption of the social cognitive view of stereotypes is that "over time, people develop beliefs about the important social groups in their environment, and this knowledge influences their responses toward subsequently encountered individual members of those groups" (p. 5).

It merits adding that stereotypes can be of two basic types: *Individual stereotypes* are beliefs that an individual holds about characteristics of group members, whereas *consensual stereotypes* are beliefs about group member characteristics that individuals tend to hold in common. Although research on stereotypes may deal with either of these types, it typically is concerned with the latter (Gardner, 1994).

Stereotypes serve a number of functions for observers (e.g., people who make HRM decisions), one of which is lessening the cognitive demands that are needed to make inferences about targets (Devine, 1989; Gilbert & Hixon, 1991; Hamilton, 1981; Macrae et al., 1996; McCauley, Stitt & Segal, 1980). More specifically, rather than having to attend to a large number of the attributes of a target (e.g., a job applicant or incumbent), an observer (a) categorizes him or her on the basis of one or more salient attributes (e.g., ethnic group membership) and (b) generates inferences about him or her on the basis of stereotypical beliefs about the attributes of the prototypical member of the target's group or category. It merits noting that although the categorization of targets may be natural and adaptive, it is not the only option available to observers; that is, they can think of each person as a unique individual (Fiske, 1989). However, this involves the expenditure of cognitive resources and observers tend to be effort minimizers. Thus, unless there is a pressing need to obtain individuating information about targets, observers tend to base initial views about them on stereotypes. In organizational contexts individuating information includes information about such attributes of targets as their educational attainment, college major, job-related licenses, certifications, and work experience.

Stereotypes of Ethnic Minority Group Members. A considerable body of research shows that stereotypes of members of various ethnic groups (e.g., African Americans, Mexican Americans) tend to be negative, affecting both (a) their employment opportunities, i.e., access discrimination, and (b) the way they are treated as employees, i.e., treatment discrimination (Stone, Stone, & Dipboye, 1992; Stone-Romero & Stone, 2007). For example, Ilgen and Youtz (1986) argued that bias in performance appraisals occurs mainly because of the stereotyping of members of minority groups. In addition, stigma-based models (e.g., Stone et al., 1992; Stone-Romero & Stone, 2007) posit that observers' cognitive and emotional reactions to targets are a function of the discrepancy between their actual and virtual social identities (Goffman, 1963). A target's *actual social identity* (ASI) reflects the way he or she is actually perceived (or is capable of being perceived) by an observer. In contrast, a target's *virtual social identity* (VSI) reflects what is expected of the target in terms of such attributes as ethnicity, abilities, appearance, attitudes, values, and personality. It represents the ideal incumbent in a given social role.

A target is stigmatized or marked to the degree that there is a negative discrepancy between his or her or her ASI and VSI. That is, the target is stigmatized when an observer believes that he or she falls short of what the observer views as an ideal individual in a particular context (e.g., the job selection process).

It merits noting that the ASI of a target may be a function of numerous factors. However, in an observer's early encounters with the target, stereotype-based inferences typically play a key role in the way that he or she is perceived (e.g., Macrae et al., 1996); that is, the ASI of the target is often stereotype-based. In addition, as research on stereotypes shows, observers tend to base inferences about targets on the groups to which they belong (e.g., Mexican American, male, middle-aged, homosexual). In addition, organizational research indicates that data that are inconsistent with stereotypes about minorities are often ignored in making decisions (e.g., hiring) about a target (Morrison & Von Glinow, 1990).

Stereotypes may have a number of other destructive influences in organizational settings, including (a) lessening support for equal employment opportunities and multiculturalism (e.g., Link & Oldendick, 1996), (b) supporting beliefs and ideologies that justify unfair discrimination against minority group members (Sigelman & Tuch, 1997), (c) legitimizing existing social and power relations within social systems (Augoustinos & Walker, 1998), and (d) serving as "political weapons" that are used to subjugate and dominate ethnic minorities (Oakes, Haslam, & Turner, 1994; Wetherell & Potter, 1992). Thus, stereotypes may have very important negative effects on HRM policies and practices.

Research on Stereotypes

There is a considerable body of research on stereotypes (e.g., Macrae et al., 1996) that dates back to the seminal work of Katz and Braly (1933, 1935). It shows marked differences in the stereotypical beliefs that individuals have about the attributes of race- and nationality-based groups (Blair, Judd, & Fallman, 2004; Branscombe & Smith, 1990; Brigham, 1971, 1972a,b, 1973; CrosbyBromley, & Saxe, 1980; Dovidio, Evans, & Tyler, 1986; Gardner, Kirby, Gorospe, & Willamin, 1972; Gilbert, Carr-Ruffino, Ivancevich, & Lowns-Jackson, 2003; Hamilton, 1981; Katz & Braly, 1933, 1935; Kirby & Gardner, 1972; Kreuger, 1996; Levine, Carmines, & Sniderman, 1999; Powell, 1992; Thorndike, 1977). For example, research reviewed by Dovidio, Brigham, Johnson, and Gaertner (1996) showed that as of 1933, White college students viewed (a) "negroes" (sic.) or Blacks as superstitious, lazy, happy-go-lucky, ignorant, musical, and ostentatious, and (b) Whites as industrious, intelligent, materialistic, ambitious, and progressive. By 1993, relatively large percentages of White college student respondents described (a) Whites as materialistic, ambitious, progressive, pleasure loving, individualistic, and conservative, and (b) Blacks as very religious, aggressive, and straightforward. It is important to note that these findings need to be qualified in two ways. First, because the research was conducted using college student respondents, its results may not reflect the views of people in the general population of the United States. Second, whereas White students may have been quite willing to express highly negative views of Blacks in 1933, by 1993 motives to respond in a socially desirable manner may have tempered their responses to measures of stereotypes.

Ethnic Stereotypes in Organizational Contexts. Although there is a large body of literature on stereotypes, extant research has limited applicability to the employment context; that is, it typically focuses on attributes of targets that are *not* closely linked to attributes or characteristics that are important to observers in organizations (e.g., HRM specialists, managers). However, there are some notable exceptions to this (e.g., Hammer, Kim, Baird, & Bigoness, 1974; Morrison & Von Glinow, 1980; Powell, 1992; Tomakiewicz & Brenner, 1996; Tomakiewicz, Brenner, & Adeyeui-Bello, 1998). For example, a recent experimental study (Rosette, Leonardelli, & Phillips, 2008) showed that (a) prototypes of business leaders (i.e., the VSIs of leaders) were perceived to be more linked to being White (Anglo American) than Black (African American) and (b) evaluations of leader performance were race-based. For example, relative to Black targets, White targets were viewed as having greater leadership potential and as being more effective leaders. In addition, results of an experimental, scenario-based study using undergraduate student participants showed that hypothetical African American males were rated more negatively in terms of competence and seriousness about work than (a) African American females or (b) Asian American males or females.

An experimental study by Hamner et al. (1974) provided evidence consistent with the operation of stereotypes in the performance evaluation context. Participants were randomly assigned to conditions in which (a) race and sex of a performer were manipulated and (b) participants rated the performance of a target worker. The objective performance of the target was equal across conditions. In addition to other findings, the results showed that the high performing White target was rated more positively than the high-performance Black target. The findings are consistent with the operation of race-based stereotypes and biases.

A study by Tomakiewicz et al. (1998) considered the degree of correspondence between descriptions of (a) managers and Whites, and (b) managers and Blacks. Results showed that there was a higher degree of correspondence between the former than the latter pairs of descriptions. The authors concluded that the results were consistent with negative stereotypes of Blacks; that is the Black stereotype did not correspond with that of a manager.

Overall, the results of the just-described studies show that there are negative stereotypes of members of various ethnic minority groups and that the stereotypes have implications for the way that they are treated in organizations. However, the same studies do not provide evidence on the *relative* standing of multiple ethnic minority groups on attributes that are relevant to the world of work. Thus a major objective of the present study was to furnish it.

The stereotype research also is limited in terms of the target groups considered by it. For example, the major focus of the Katz and Braly (1933, 1935) studies was nationality-based stereotypes. Although these are important in societal terms, in organizational contexts they are not as important as stereotypes that may be of value in terms of the way that targets (e.g., job applicants or incumbents) are viewed by observers (e.g., HRM decision makers). Thus, the present study considered stereotypes of ethnic groups that are likely to be encountered and possibly stigmatized by individuals responsible for making HRM decisions about hiring, job placement, promotion, etc. More specifically, it dealt with stereotypes of Anglo Americans, East Indian Americans, Chinese Americans, Mexican Americans, African Americans, and Native Americans (e.g., members of such tribes as Apache, Cherokee, and Navajo). These target groups are important for at least three reasons. First, most decision makers in organizations are Anglo American. Thus, prototypes (ASIs) of Anglo Americans are often used as the standard against which members of other ethnic groups are compared (Stone-Romero & Stone, 2007). Second, research shows that the percentages of members of several ethnic groups (e.g., African Americans, Mexican Americans) are increasing in organizational contexts. In addition, there is widespread concern about the number of Mexican Americans who hold jobs in U.S. organizations, despite the fact that they may be either U.S. citizens or legal residents. Third, there is virtually no quantitative research on work-related stereotypes of Native Americans (Mihesuah, 2009). However, many qualitative studies show that such stereotypes tend to be quite negative. Fourth, recent public statements of President Trump are racist and cast members of ethnic minority groups in a very negative light (National Public Radio, 2018; New York Times, 2018). Among the examples of this are the following: (a) He said that 15,000 recent immigrants from Haiti all have AIDS and that 40,000 Nigerians, once seeing the United States, would never "go back to their huts" in Africa. (b) He called Puerto Ricans who criticized his administration's response to Hurricane Maria "politically motivated ingrates." (c) He referred to a Hispanic Miss Universe as "Miss Housekeeping." (d) In talking about immigrants from Haiti and African countries, he asked, "Why are we having all these people from shithole countries come here?" (e) He often describes African-Americans as unpatriotic, ungrateful, and disrespectful. These are but a few of Trump's bigoted comments. Unfortunately, they all serve to reinforce negative stereotypes of members of ethnic minority groups.

Stereotypes About Other Target Groups in Organizations. A considerable body of research shows that relative to stereotypes of females, those of males are much more consistent with the manager prototype. What's more, many studies demonstrate that physically attractive targets are regarded more positively in organizational roles than unattractive targets (Hosoda, Stone-Romero, & Coats, 2006; Stone et al., 1992). Moreover, numerous studies indicate that disabled individuals are viewed more negatively than individuals without disabilities (Colella & Stone, 2005; Stone & Colella, 1996; Stone et al., 1992). What's more, individuals who are overweight or obese are typically stereotyped as unhealthy, lazy, incompetent, emotionally unstable, and lacking in terms of motivation, conscientiousness, and personal hygiene (Krueger, Stone, & Stone-Romero, 2014; Roehling, Choi, & Roehling, in press). Furthermore, research by Hosoda and Stone-Romero (2010) showed that people with foreign accents were viewed more negatively than those without such accents. In addition, results of an experimental study by Hosoda, Nguyen, and Stone-Romero (2012) indicated that compared to an applicant with an American-English accent, one with a Mexican-American accent was viewed as less suitable for a managerial position. Finally, results of research by Stone, Lukaszewski, Krueger, and Canedo (in press) revealed that immigrants are often stereotyped as untrustworthy, lazy, incompetent, violent, and dangerous criminals. Overall, the findings of these and other studies demonstrate the highly corrosive effects of stereotypes and stereotyping.

Measurement of Stereotypes

There is a large body of theory and research on the measurement of stereotypes (e.g., Brigham, 1972b; Gardner, Kirby, Gorospe, & Willamin, 1972; Gardner, Lalonde, Nero, & Young, 1988; Kirby & Gardner, 1972; Levine et al., 1999; Neimann et al., 1994; Rudman & Ashmore, 2007; Rudman, Greenwald, Mellot, & Schwartz, 1999; Wittenbrink, Judd, & Park, 1997). It indicates that stereotypes may be assessed (measured) at either the individual or consensual level (Ashmore & Del Boca, 1981; Esses, Haddock, & Zanna, 1993). However, the consensual level appears to be the most common in stereotype research.

Typically, questionnaire measures are used in stereotype research and respondents are asked to indicate their beliefs about the attributes of *typical* members of a target group (Brigham, 1971; McCauley & Stitt, 1978). It is worth adding that conclusions derived from group-level data (i.e., consensual stereotypes) may or may not apply at the individual level (i.e., individual stereotypes). However, research shows that to the extent that an individual subscribes to one aspect of the ethnic stereotype of a group, he or she subscribes to most. In addition, the tendency to stereotype tends to generalizes across ethnic groups (Gardner, 1994).

One strategy for assessing stereotypes is to have members of target groups rated in terms of multiple adjectives (e.g., Gardner et al., 1972). For example, Kirby and Gardner (1972) provided normative data for 209 adjectives that have been used in stereotype research. Each was evaluated in terms of several dimensions (e.g., familiarity, imagery, evaluation, and social desirability).

Levine et al. (1999) conducted a large-scale study in which participants expressed their beliefs about the extent to which most Blacks possessed various attributes, in terms of such adjectives as dependable, friendly, irresponsible, and violent. Preliminary results of the study showed support for a two-factor view of the beliefs (positive and negative). However, additional analyses suggested that positive versus negative beliefs vary along a single bipolar continuum.

This use of adjectives for assessing stereotypes of ethnic groups in the present study has multiple advantages. One is that it is relatively easy for respondents to provide such ratings. Another is that it allows for the collection of data on a large number of rated attributes. Thus, we used an adjective-based questionnaire in the present study (see subsection on Measures).

The typical strategy for measuring stereotypes is for research participants to rate members of target groups in terms of multiple attributes or rating dimensions. However, measuring stereotypes in this manner may lead to biased results. The reason for this is that individuals may be reluctant to endorse negative views of minority group members if they believe that doing so may lead them to be labeled as bigoted, biased or prejudiced. Stated somewhat differently, individuals' responses to questionnaire items may motivated by such self-presentation tendencies as impression management and socially desirable responding (Brigham, 1973; Crosby et al., 1980). In this regard, the study by Kirby and Gardner (1972) showed that there were marked social desirability differences among the 209 adjectives rated by subjects.

In the present study it was not possible to control for social desirability statistically. However, in order to deal with the just-noted response bias tendencies, our study assessed stereotypes in two ways. More specifically, participants were randomly assigned to conditions in which they were asked to complete measures of the attributes of target group members in terms of either (a) their *own views* or (b) their beliefs about *others' views* (others' views hereinafter). The latter strategy is projective: Because most individuals do not know how others view members of various social groups, they tend to project their own beliefs on to others (Kreuger, 1996). Moreover, because participants were randomly assigned to treatment conditions, social desirability was controlled by experimental design.

Previous research has measured stereotypes from various perspectives (e.g., Brigham, 1973; Kreuger, 1996; Rettew, Billman, & Davis, 1993). For example, Hort, Fagot, and Leinbach (1990) asked participants to rate men and women from an individual perspective and from a societal perspective (i.e., as society sees them). In addition, Esses et al. (1993) asked individuals to list and rate attributes they would use to describe other group members and to provide consensual stereotypes by listing characteristics that people attribute to group members. Devine (1989) employed a similar procedure, i.e., assessing cultural stereotypes. Thus, there is a solid basis for measuring stereotypes from both peoples' own views and the views of others.

Purposes of Present Study

In view of the above, the present study had two major purposes. The first was to assess consensual stereotypes of members of six ethnic groups, i.e., Anglo American, Native American, African American, Mexican American, Chinese American, and East Indian American. The second was to determine if reports of individual's own views of group members differed from their beliefs about others' views.

On the basis of previous research on stereotypes and possible social desirability biases in self-report measures, we tested two major hypotheses: First, we posited that stereotypes of the ethnic groups would differ from one another (H_1). For example, based on extant research we expected the stereotypes of both Mexican Americans and African Americans to be more negative than those of the other ethnic groups (e.g., Anglo Americans, Chinese Americans). Second, we hypothesized that own views of minority ethnic groups would be more positive than others' views (H_2).

METHOD

Participants

Data were collected from 282 undergraduate and graduate students at a major state university in the southeastern region of the U.S. They had an average age of 23.5 years ($SD = 6.80$). Most of the participants (44.2%) had a psychology major and were female (68.5%). In terms of ethnicity, 61.9% were White, 9.2% were African American, 10.7% were Hispanic American, 11.3% were Asian American, and the remainder had other ethnicities (e.g., Native American).

Experimental Design

Participants were assigned to one of six conditions in a 2×6 randomized experimental design. It dealt with (a) ethnicity of target group (Anglo American, American Indian, African American, Mexican American, Chinese American, and East Indian American) and (b) elicited view (own versus others'). Hereinafter these conditions are referred to as ethnic group and view.

Measures

Views about members of the target groups (i.e., stereotypes) were measured with a semantic differential that had 100 bipolar, trait descriptive adjective pairs separated by seven equally spaced line segments.

In contrast to the types of items found in many stereotype measures, most items in the semantic differential used in the present study focused on attributes relevant to organizations. In the interest of reliability, sets of bipolar adjectives were used to index nine *a priori* attributes. *Skill* ($\alpha = .75$) was assessed with three items (e.g., skilled-unskilled and capable-incompetent). *Cognitive ability* ($\alpha = .85$) was measured with three items (e.g., smart-dumb and intelligent-stupid). *Collective* ($\alpha = .81$) was assessed with two items (i.e., group minded-individualistic and individualistic-group oriented). *Emotional adjustment* ($\alpha = .86$; adjustment hereinafter) was indexed with seven items (e.g., anxious-calm and stable-volatile). *Integrity* ($\alpha = .89$), was assessed with seven items (e.g., dishonest-honest and ethical-corrupt). *Social skill* ($\alpha = .90$) was measured with six items (e.g., quarrelsome-agreeable and cooperative-rebellious). *Reliability* ($\alpha = .86$) was indexed with seven items (e.g., dependable-unreliable and careful-careless). *Expressive* ($\alpha = .76$) was measured with three items (e.g., shy-outgoing and flashy-plain). Finally, *status* ($\alpha = .83$) was assessed with seven items (e.g., worthy-unworthy and admired-disrespected.)

Participants also were asked to respond to items in a demographic questionnaire that dealt with such variables as age, sex, college major, class standing, and ethnicity. It was completed after the semantic differential.

Procedure

Data were collected from participants in classroom settings. In turn, they were (a) asked to read and sign an informed consent form, (b) provided with instructions on responding to items in the semantic differential measure, (c) instructed to read the instructions for the version of the semantic differential that corresponded to their experimental condition, (d) asked to respond to the items in the semantic differential, (e) asked to complete a demographic form, and (f) debriefed about the general purpose of the study.

Analyses

The study's data were analyzed with a 2×6 MANOVA that assessed the effects of the independent variables of view and ethnic group. It was followed up by within attribute Bonferroni adjusted pairwise comparisons of the ratings.

RESULTS

The MANOVA showed effects for both (a) target ethnicity, Wilk's $\Lambda = .259$, $F(45, 1197.46) = 9.701$, $p < .000$ and (b) views, Wilk's $\Lambda = .938$, $F(9, 267) = 1.954$, $p < .000$. Table 3.1 shows the relevant results. Means, standard deviations, and standardized (Z) scores for the 12 conditions are shown in Table 3.2. Note that the Z scores are per-condition specific. For example, the Z row in the Adjustment, Own view in Table 3.2 shows standardized scores for the six ethnic groups based upon the grand mean and standard deviation data for the groups. Thus, for example, the -0.40 for African American indicates that relative to the mean and standard deviation for individuals in all ethnic groups, the African American group was viewed as being .40 standard deviations below the mean.

Ethnicity Effect

Not only did the MANOVA show an ethnicity effect, but univariate tests showed that the ethnic groups differed from one another on all measured attributes. Overall, therefore, these results provide considerable support for Hypothesis 1.

TABLE 3.1. Multivariate Analysis of Variance Results: Wilk's Λ Criterion

Effect	Value	F	Hypothesis df	Error df	p
Intercept	.011	2747.07	9	267.00	.000
View	.938	1.95	9	267.00	.045
Ethnic group	.249	9.70	45	1197.46	.000

TABLE 3.2. Descriptive Statistics for Measured Variables by Ethnic Group and View Experimental Conditions

Variable			African American	Native American	Anglo American	Chinese American	East Indian American	Mexican American
					Ethnic group			
Adjustment	Own view	M	30.92	30.54	32.24	37.54	35.33	29.38
		SD	6.86	5.60	5.54	4.80	4.92	5.41
		Z	-0.40	0.27	-0.18	0.67	0.32	-0.65
	Others' view	M	26.91	32.39	30.43	38.05	32.86	27.50
		SD	7.27	5.62	4.72	4.17	4.81	4.97
		Z	-.69	0.16	-0.15	1.03	0.23	-0.60
Cognitive ability	Own view	M	14.04	15.52	14.36	16.62	16.25	11.77
		SD	3.01	3.54	2.97	2.68	2.40	2.42
		Z	-0.21	0.24	-0.11	0.58	0.47	-0.91
	Others' view	M	11.83	14.65	13.74	17.09	13.95	10.95
		SD	3.59	2.35	2.34	2.33	2.48	1.50
		Z	-0.60	0.29	0.00	1.06	0.07	-088
Collective	Own view	M	9.56	10.00	7.88	9.15	10.17	9.69
		SD	2.58	2.71	3.00	3.36	2.91	2.74
		Z	0.05	0.20	-0.52	-0.08	0.26	0.10
	Others' view	M	9.87	11.87	6.61	8.68	9.82	9.95
		SD	2.85	2.85	3.22	3.61	3.28	2.11
		Z	0.13	0.74	-0.87	-0.24	0.11	0.15

(continues)

TABLE 3.2. Continued

Variable			African American	Native American	Anglo American	Chinese American	East Indian American	Mexican American
					Ethnic group			
Expressive	Own view	M	10.04	7.22	8.56	5.65	6.21	9.19
		SD	2.17	2.13	1.19	2.02	1.84	2.67
		Z	0.86	-0.24	0.28	-0.85	-0.63	0.53
	Others' view	M	10.13	6.39	9.30	4.50	6.64	9.45
		SD	2.62	2.61	1.87	1.68	1.76	1.93
		Z	0.82	-0.46	0.54	-1.11	-0.37	0.59
Integrity	Own view	M	33.68	35.74	30.44	37.62	37.08	29.81
		SD	6.61	6.35	6.30	5.28	6.19	6.16
		Z	-0.05	0.25	-0.53	0.53	0.45	-0.62
	Others' view	M	28.17	34.43	29.26	37.68	33.50	27.50
		SD	8.08	5.71	6.39	5.23	4.97	5.16
		Z	-0.52	0.38	-0.36	0.84	0.24	-0.61
Reliability	Own view	M	30.68	34.00	31.20	39.23	34.50	26.81
		SD	6.56	6.00	5.34	8.64	5.37	6.01
		Z	-0.27	0.17	-0.20	0.87	0.24	-0.79
	Others' view	M	26.39	31.96	31.00	38.05	31.73	25.85
		SD	8.39	6.42	5.33	6.48	5.30	3.30
		Z	-0.62	0.15	0.02	0.99	0.12	-0.70
Skill	Own	M	15.28	15.61	14.96	16.85	16.67	12.04

Measure	Statistic	1	2	3	4	5	6
(Own view)	SD	3.05	2.73	3.01	2.81	1.95	3.45
	Z	0.02	0.12	-0.08	0.50	0.45	-0.97
Others' view	M	13.00	15.87	15.09	17.18	14.41	11.50
	SD	3.55	2.47	2.23	2.08	2.52	2.42
	Z	-0.50	0.42	0.17	0.83	-0.05	-0.97
Social skills — Own view	M	26.04	29.09	26.48	30.27	28.38	25.08
	SD	5.59	6.09	4.45	5.24	6.31	4.87
	Z	-0.26	0.28	-0.19	0.48	0.15	-0.43
Others' view	M	22.74	26.57	26.87	30.82	26.73	23.95
	SD	7.64	6.17	4.68	4.67	4.72	5.23
	Z	-0.58	0.05	0.10	0.74	0.07	-0.38
Status — Own view	M	31.20	32.13	33.40	34.62	32.71	25.50
	SD	6.43	4.82	5.51	5.82	5.91	6.06
	Z	-0.06	0.09	0.29	0.48	0.18	-0.94
Others' view	M	27.57	29.13	33.57	34.36	30.23	23.95
	SD	7.25	6.29	5.58	3.69	5.28	4.24
	Z	-0.36	-0.12	0.57	0.69	0.05	-0.92

Note: M = mean, SD = standard deviation, and Z = Within condition standardized score.

As can be seen in the Table 3.2, and consistent with Hypothesis 1, views of Mexican Americans and African Americans were more negative than those of the other ethnic groups (i.e., Anglo Americans, Native Americans, East Indian Americans, and Chinese Americans). In general, the results revealed that means on the measured attributes were (a) most positive for Chinese Americans, East Indian Americans, and Native Americans, and (b) most negative for African Americans and Mexican Americans. With regards to the latter two groups the results in Table 2 show that Z scores for Mexican Americans were relatively negative on such dimensions as Adjustment Own ($Z = -0.65$), Cognitive Ability Own ($Z = -0.91$), Reliability Own ($Z = -0.79$), and Status Own ($Z = -0.94$). In addition, for African Americans the Z scores were relatively low on such dimensions as Adjustment Others' ($Z = -0.69$), Reliability Others' ($Z = -0.62$), Skill Others' ($Z = -0.50$), and Social Skills Others' ($Z = -0.58$).

Interestingly, the Z scores on selected attributes for some non-Anglo-American ethnic groups were considerably higher than they were for Anglo Americans. For example, (a) for Adjustment Others' the Z for Chinese Americans was 1.03 and -0.15 for Anglo Americans, and (b) for Cognitive Ability Others' the Z for Chinese Americans was 1.06 and 0.00 for Anglo Americans.

Detailed Results for Ethnic Group Conditions

Results of univariate, *Bonferroni adjusted* comparisons of pairs of ethnic groups revealed statistically significant differences ($p < .05$ or below) for all measured variables. The findings are as follows:

Status. Bonferroni adjusted tests of differences between ethnic group means on *status* showed that: (a) Anglo Americans were viewed more positively than Mexican Americans; (b) African Americans were rated less positively than Anglo Americans, and Chinese Americans, but more positively than Mexican Americans; (c) Native Americans were viewed more positively than Mexican Americans, but less positively than Chinese Americans; (d) Mexican Americans were rated less positively than Anglo Americans, African Americans, Native Americans, East Indian Americans, and Chinese Americans; (e) East Indian Americans were looked upon more favorably than Mexican Americans, and (f) Chinese Americans were rated more positively than African Americans, Native Americans, and Mexican Americans.

Reliability. For the *reliability* criterion, Bonferroni adjusted tests of differences between ethnic group means revealed that: (a) African Americans were regarded less positively than Native Americans, East Indian Americans, and Chinese Americans; (b) Native Americans were viewed more positively than African Americans, Mexican Americans, but less favorably than Chinese Americans; (c) Mexican Americans were looked upon more negatively than Anglo Americans, Native Americans, East Indian Americans, and Chinese Americans; (d) East Indian Americans were viewed more positively than African Americans, Mexican Americans, but less positively than Chinese Americans; and (e) Chinese Americans were rated more positively than Anglo Americans, African Americans, Native Americans, Mexican Americans, and East Indian Americans.

Emotional Adjustment. Bonferroni adjusted tests of differences between ethnic group means on *emotional adjustment* showed that: (a) Anglo Americans were viewed less positively than Chinese Americans; (b) African Americans were rated less favorably than Native Americans, and Chinese Americans, and East Indian Americans; (c) Native Americans were regarded more positively than African Americans, Mexican Americans, but less positively than Chinese Americans; (d) Mexican Americans were viewed less positively than Native Americans, East Indian Americans, and Chinese Americans; (e) East Indian Americans were rated more positively than African Americans, and Mexican Americans, but less favorably than Native Americans; and (f) Chinese Americans were looked upon more positively than Anglo Americans, African Americans, Native Americans, Mexican Americans, and East Indian Americans.

Skilled. For the *skilled* criterion, Bonferroni adjusted tests of differences between ethnic group means revealed that: (a) Anglo Americans were viewed more positively than Mexican Americans, but less favorably than Chinese Americans; (b) African Americans were rated less positively than Native Americans, Chinese Americans, and East Indian Americans, but more positively than Mexican Americans; (b) Native Americans were looked upon more positively than Mexican Americans; (c) Mexican Americans were rated more negatively than Anglo Americans, African Americans, Native Americans, East Indian Americans, and Chinese Americans; (d) East Indian Americans were viewed more positively than Mexican Americans, and more negatively than Chinese Americans; and (e) Chinese Americans were rated more positively than Anglo Americans, African Americans, and Mexican Americans;

Cognitive Ability. Bonferroni adjusted tests of differences between ethnic group means on *cognitive ability* showed that: (a) Anglo Americans were viewed more positively then Mexican Americans, but less favorably than East Indian Americans and Chinese Americans; (b) African Americans were rated less positively than Native Americans, East Indian Americans, and Chinese Americans; (c) Native Americans were looked upon more favorably than African Americans and Mexican Americans, but less favorably than Chinese Americans; (d) Mexican Americans were rated less positively than Anglo Americans, Native Americans, East Indian Americans, and Chinese Americans; (e) East Indian Americans were viewed more positively than African Americans, Mexican Americans, but less favorably than Chinese Americans; and (f) Chinese Americans were rated more positively than Anglo Americans, African Americans, Native Americans, Mexican Americans, but less favorably than East Indian Americans.

Social Skills. Bonferroni adjusted tests of differences between ethnic group means on *social skills* revealed that: (a) Anglo Americans were viewed more negatively than Chinese Americans; (b) African Americans were rated less positively than Native Americans and Chinese Americans; (c) Native Americans were looked upon more favorably than African Americans; (d) Mexican Americans were seen more negatively than Native Americans, and Chinese Americans; and (e) Chinese Americans were viewed more favorably than Anglo Americans, African Americans, and Mexican Americans.

Collective. Bonferroni adjusted tests of differences between ethnic group means on *collective* showed that: (a) Anglo Americans were regarded as less collective than African Americans, Native Americans, Mexican Americans, and East Indian Americans; (b) African Americans were viewed as more collective than Anglo Americans; (c) Native Americans were rated as more collective than Anglo Americans, and Chinese Americans; (d) Mexican Americans were seen as more collective than Anglo Americans; (e) East Indian Americans were looked upon as more collective than Anglo Americans; and (f) Chinese Americans were regarded to be less collective than Native Americans.

Integrity. Bonferroni adjusted tests of differences between ethnic group means on *integrity* showed that: (a) Anglo Americans were viewed as having less integrity than Native Americans, East Indian Americans, and Chinese Americans; (b) African Americans were rated below Native Americans, East Indian Americans, and Chinese Americans; (c) Native Americans were looked upon more favorably than Anglo Americans, African Americans, and Mexican Americans; (d) Mexican Americans were rated below Native Americans, East Indian Americans, and Chinese Americans; (e) East Indian Americans were viewed more positively than Anglo Americans, African Americans, and Mexican Americans, but less positively than Chinese Americans; and (f) Chinese Americans were rated more favorably than Anglo Americans, African Americans, and Mexican Americans.

Expressive. Bonferroni adjusted tests of differences between ethnic group means on *expressive* showed that: (a) Anglo Americans were rated above Native Americans, East Indian Americans, and Chinese Americans, but lower than Mexican Americans; (b) African Americans were regarded as more so than Native Americans, East Indian Americans, and Chinese Americans; (c) Native Americans were seen as less so than Anglo Americans, African Americans, Mexican Americans, but more so than Chinese Americans; (d) Mexican Americans were rated higher than Native Americans, East Indian Americans, and Chinese Americans; (e) East Indian Americans were regarded as less so than Anglo Americans, African Americans, Native Americans, Mexican Americans, but more so than Chinese Americans; and (f) Chinese Americans were rated below Anglo Americans, African Americans, Native Americans, Mexican Americans, and East Indian Americans.

View Effects

Consistent with Hypothesis 2, the MANOVA revealed a statistically significant effect for the view manipulation. The means in Table 2 show that own views were more positive than others' views.

Detailed Results for View Conditions

There were statistically significant ($p < .03$), Bonferroni adjusted univariate effects for all of the measured variables. More specifically, the mean for own view was greater (i.e., more positive) than that for other's view for skill, cognitive ability, collective, emotional adjustment, integrity, social skills, reliability, expressiveness, and status.

DISCUSSION

Results of the present study provided clear support for both of its hypotheses. More specifically, they showed that (a) ethnic groups differed from one another on the measured attributes and (b) own views were more positive than others' views. These findings are of considerable interest for the reasons considered below.

Ethnicity Effect

Overall, the effects of ethnicity on the measures attributes are consistent with the findings of a number of stereotype studies (e.g., Timberlake & Williams, 2012) in that they showed that Anglo Americans are viewed more positively than several other selected ethnic groups (e.g., African Americans and Mexican Americans). In addition, stereotypes of three other ethnic groups (i.e., Native Americans, Chinese Americans, and East Indian Americans) were not only more favorable than those of Mexican Americans and African Americans, but they were also more positive than those of Anglo Americans with respect to several attributes.

Stereotypes of Native Americans. As noted above, there is virtually no quantitative research on stereotypes of Native Americans, especially as they pertain to organizations. Results of the present study showed that members of this group had relatively positive stereotypes. More specifically, ratings of this group were more positive on several of the measured attributes than were those of African Americans and Mexican Americans. What's more, as the results in Table 2 indicate, ratings of Native Americans were considerably higher than those of Anglo Americans on the attributes of Collective, Integrity, Reliability, and Social Skills. These findings are important because many publications on Native Americans (Bird, 1999; Church, 1976; Fitzgerald, 2014; Kilpatrick, 1999; Mihesuah, 1996) typically cast them in a very negative light. For example, Kilpatrick (1999) noted that Native Americans have often been depicted in films as unintelligent savages. In addition, Mihesuah (1996) catalogs a large number of negative stereotypes that have been applied to Native Americans, including that they (a) were conquered because they are inferior, (b) are warlike and treacherous, (c) have no religion, (d) live in tipis, wear braids, and ride horses, (e) get a "free ride" from the US government, (f) are incapable of competing in school, (g) have a tendency toward alcoholism, and (h) are stoic and lack a sense of humor. Interestingly, Bird (1999) wrote that although many non-Native Americans have never encountered a Native American, stereotypes about them are often unreal and dehumanizing.

Stereotypes of African Americans and Mexican Americans. Results of the present study revealed that stereotypes of African Americans and Mexican Americans were typically considerably more negative than those of Anglo Americans, Chinese Americans, and East Indian Americans. These findings are not surprising given the long-standing patterns of racism in the United States. Unfortunately, the highly negative characterizations of African Americans and Mexican Americans groups by Trump and his supporters do nothing to change this very deplorable situation.

Applicability to organizations. In contrast to most other studies of stereotypes, the attributes that were considered by the present study are of considerable relevance to organizations. More specifically, they focused on dimensions that have implications for inferences about a target's ability to perform (e.g., cognitive ability, skill), get along with co-workers (e.g., social skill, collective), and behave ethically (i.e., integrity). A focus on these dimensions is important because they are of considerable relevance to the inferences that HRM decision makers (e.g., interviewers, managers) make about targets (e.g., job applicants and/or incumbents). For example, in a selection context a decision maker is likely to consider a number of questions when interviewing a job applicant or viewing his or her application, including: (a) Does the applicant have the cognitive ability needed to succeed on the job? (b) Does the applicant have the skills and abilities needed for job success? (c) Will the applicant be dependable? (d) Is the applicant well-adjusted (psychologically)? (e) Will the applicant get along with his or her co-workers? In the absence of individuating information on these attributes, inferences about an applicant are likely to be influenced by stereotypes. To the degree that they are, members of several ethnic groups (e.g., Mexican Americans, African Americans) are likely to be viewed in relatively negative terms by decision makers, whereas members of other ethnic groups are likely to be perceived more positively by HRM decision makers.

It deserves noting that individuals differ in their propensity to use stereotypes as a basis for making inferences about others (Banaji & Greenwald, 1994; Devine, 1989). For example, the more egalitarian a decision maker the lower the odds that he or she will base inferences about targets on stereotypes. In addition, the lower the level of a decision maker's prejudice, the lower the probability that he or she will make stereotype-based inferences about targets.

VIEW EFFECT

Results of the MANOVA showed that ratings of the attributes of targets were influenced by the view considered by the participants. More specifically, ratings based on own views were more positive than ratings based on others' views. One very plausible explanation of this finding is social desirability-based responding. More specifically, in order to reduce the chances of being regarded as prejudiced, participants rated members of several minority groups (e.g., African American, Mexican American) more positively in the own view condition than the others' view condition. It is noteworthy that the view manipulation had an effect on ratings even though all participants completed their ratings anonymously. This suggests the power that impression management motives may have in research that is based on self-reports. In addition, it is consistent with the results of numerous other studies that have shown differences between obtrusive and unobtrusive measures of racism (Crosby et al, 1980).

Potential Limitations of Study

Three potential limitations of the present study deserve mention. First, because of the fact that the overall sample size was 282, the statistical power of some analyses was limited. More specifically, not all pairwise comparisons of ethnic group means on the measured attributes were statistically significant. Thus, in order to increase power, future studies can employ such strategies as increasing overall sample size and/or decreasing the number of ethnic groups that are rated.

A second potential limitation is the nature of the present study's sample. As noted above, it consisted of students at a large southeastern university. These individuals may have had more negative views about members of some ethnic groups (e.g., African Americans, Mexican Americans) than individuals in other regions of the U.S. (e.g., the northeast, the southwest). However, because of their age and the fact that they were college students, their views may have been more positive than those of typical residents of rural areas in the southeastern U.S. Thus, research is needed that uses samples that are more heterogeneous than those of the present study.

Third, and finally, participants rated targets on the basis of their own or others' views about the "typical" member of a given ethnic group. As such, their ratings were not specific to any given job. Thus, research is needed in which stereotype data are obtained for the typical job applicant or incumbent for a specific job (e.g., automobile mechanic, accountant, software engineer, police officer). Stereotypes of individuals in given ethnic groups may, for example, vary as a function of the title of the job for which they are applying (Jones, 1991).

Conclusions and Implications for Practice

In order to provide individuals with equal employment opportunities it is critical that HRM decision makers base inferences about others (e.g., job applicants, job incumbents) on valid information about their attributes as opposed to stereotypes. Unfortunately, as the present study and many others have shown, stereotypes often have an important role in shaping views about others. Thus, it is vital that organizations establish policies and procedures that lessen the impact of stereotypes on HRM-related decisions (Stone-Romero & Stone, 2007). A number of strategies may be used for doing so. They are listed below. Note that in the material that follows we refer to HRM decision makers as observers and members of stereotyped groups as targets.

Provide Individuating Information. Reliance on stereotypes may be reduced by providing observers with individuating information about targets. This should lead to the controlled (as opposed to automatic) processing of information about the targets (Devine, 1989). To the degree that observers attend to and rely on such information, stereotypes will have a reduced impact on inferences made about targets. Thus, organizations should structure decision-making tasks in ways that reduce the odds of stereotype-based inferences. For example, not only should observers be provided with individuating information about targets, but they should be given ample time to consider it and training on its value in decision making (Gilbert & Hixon, 1991).

Removing Information Leading to Stereotyping. Stereotyping in recruiting and selection may be reduced by removing information about stigmatizing attributes of targets (e.g., race, sex, age) from materials considered by observers (e.g., recruiters). For example, during the process of evaluating the suitability of job applicants, resumes can be "sanitized" by removing information about such attributes as their race, sex, and age.

Promoting Intergroup Contact. Stereotyping also may be reduced by fostering increased intergroup contact between observers and targets who are members of groups that have negative stereotypes (Hewstone & Brown, 1986; Miller & Brewer, 1984, 1988; Stangor & Schaller, 1996). It deserves adding that for such contact to reduce the operation of stereotypes the contact must result in positive outcomes for the observers (Brewer & Miller, 1984, 1988).

Changing Organizational Cultures. Organizational culture serves to determine a number of important variables including the degree to which diversity is valued (Stone-Romero & Stone, 2007). Thus, promoting a diversity supportive culture may serve to reduce the tendency for observers to view ethnic minority targets negatively. Unfortunately, organizational cultures are very resistant to change. Moreover, change is unlikely to occur in the absence of changes in organizational policies and procedures. Thus, for example, research shows that high-tech companies in the US have very few upper-level workers who are members of various minority groups (e.g., Cook & Glass, 2014; Morrison & Von Glinow, 1990; Thomas & Gabarro, 1999).

Providing Training on Stereotyping. The reliance on stereotypes in decision making may be lessened by providing observers with training on the negative effects of stereotyping on members of target groups. For example, they can be given evidence that (a) ethnic minority and non-minority applicants for a job have similar scores on pre-employment tests, and (b) that stereotyping has the potential to harm members of ethnic minority groups (e.g., unfairly bar them from being hired).

Research suggests that confronting observers with information about their tendencies to negatively stereotype members of target groups at one point in time leads observers to experience self-dissatisfaction when the information conflicts with their views of the self (e.g., being egalitarian and unbiased). This self-dissatisfaction should lead the observers to exhibit less stereotype biased evaluations of members of target groups at a subsequent point in time. The findings of three experimental studies by Czopp, Montieth, and Mark (2006) provide support for these predictions. However, research is needed to determine if the confrontation strategy will reduce stereotype-based biases in organizational contexts. One caveat is that organizations may not allow for its use. Even if they did, the effects of the effects of the strategy may not persist over extended time periods (e.g., several months).

Having Observers Attend to Individual Attributes. One more strategy is to have observers review the qualifications of each rate on each attribute being considered and then make an overall evaluation, as opposed to simply making an overall evaluation. This should reduce the degree to which an overall evaluation will be biased by stereotypes.

Recategorizing Targets. Stereotyping is typically the result of observers categorizing targets (e.g., minority, female, old, lesbian, disabled). Thus, it may be reduced by strategies that lead to their recategorization (Dovidio & Gaertner, 1993). For example, observers can be shown that there are many dimensions along which the observers and targets are similar.

Target-Based Strategies. The above-noted strategies for reducing stereotype-based responding to targets are observer-centered. However, targets can employ a number of approaches to foster the same objective, including (a) encouraging observers to categorize them as in-group members, (b) pointing out that targets and observers have shared objectives that can be pursued by joint action, and (c) priming shared values among observers. Eberhart and Fiske (1996) explicate these and other target-based strategies.

To the degree that the above-noted strategies succeed, stereotypes should have a reduced role in HRM-related decisions. In addition, the outcomes experienced by members of negatively stereotyped groups will be based upon factors that are relevant to the decisions being made as opposed to invalid stereotypes.

One of Dr. Martin Luther King's dreams was that his "little children will one day live in a nation where they will not be judged by the color of their skin, but by the content of their character." In order for that dream to be realized, it is vital that inferences about people be based on their actual attributes as opposed to the stereotypes associated with the categories to which observers assign them.

REFERENCES

Ashmore, R. D., & Del Boca, F. K. (1981). Conceptual approaches to stereotypes and stereotyping. In D. L. Hamilton (Ed.), *Cognitive processes in stereotyping and intergroup behavior* (pp. 1–36). Hillsdale, NJ: Lawrence Erlbaum Associates.

Augoustinos, M., & Walker, I. (1998). The construction of stereotypes within social psychology. *Theory and Psychology, 8*, 629–652.

Banaji, M. R., & Greewald, A. G. (1994). Implicit stereotyping and prejudice. In M. P. Zanna & J. M. Olson (Eds.), *The psychology of prejudice: The Ontario Symposium, Volume 7* (pp. 55–76). Hillsdale, NJ: Lawrence Erlbaum Associates.

Bird, S. S. (1999). Gendered construction of the American Indian in popular media. *Journal of Communication, 49*(3), 61–83.

Blair, I. V., Judd, C. M., & Fallman, J. L. (2004). The automaticity of race and Afrocentric facial features in social judgments. *Journal of Personality and Social Psychology, 87*, 763–778.

Bodenhausen, G. V., & Wyer, R. S. (1985). Effects of stereotypes in decision making and information-processing strategies. *Journal of Personality and Social Psychology, 48*, 267–282.

Branscombe, N. R., & Smith, E. R. (1990). Gender and racial stereotypes in impression formation and social decision-making processes. *Sex Roles, 22*, 627–647.

Brewer, M. B., & Miller, N. 1984. Beyond the contact hypothesis: Theoretical perspectives on desegregation. In N. Miller & M. B. Brewer (Eds.), *Groups in contact: The psychology of desegregation* (pp. 281–302). Orlando, FL: Academic Press.

Brewer, M. B., & Miller, N. 1988. Contact and cooperation: When do they work? In P. Katz & D. Taylor (Eds.), *Eliminating racism: Means and consequences* (pp. 315–326). New York, NY: Plenum Press.

Brigham, J. C. (1971). Racial stereotypes, attitudes, and evaluations of and behavioral intentions toward Negroes and whites. *Sociometry, 34*, 360–380.

Brigham, J. C. (1972a). Ethnic stereotypes. *Psychological Bulletin, 76*, 15–38.

Brigham, J. C. (1972b). Racial stereotypes: Measurement variables and the stereotype-attitude relationship. *Journal of Applied Social Psychology, 2*, 63–76.

Brigham, J. C. (1973). Ethnic stereotypes and attitudes: A different mode of analysis. *Journal of Personality, 41*, 206–223.

Campbell, D. T. (1967). Stereotypes and the perception of group differences. *American Psychologist, 22*, 817–829.

Church, A. G. (1976). Academic achievement, IQ, level of occupational plan, and ethnic stereotypes for Anglos and Navahos in a multi-ethnic high school. *Southern Journal of Educational Research, 10*(3), 184–201.

Colella, A., & Stone, D. L. (2005). Workplace discrimination toward persons with disabilities: A call for some new research directions. In R. L. Dipboye, & A. Colella (Eds.), *Discrimination at work: The psychological and organizational bases* (pp. 227–253). Mahwah, NJ: Lawrence Erlbaum Associates.

Cook, A., & Glass, C. (2014). Above the glass ceiling: When are women and minorities promoted to CEO? *Strategic Management Journal, 35*, 1080–1089.

Crosby, F., Bromley, S., & Saxe, L. (1980). Recent unobtrusive studies of Black and White discrimination and prejudice: A literature review. *Psychological Bulletin, 87*, 546–563.

Czopp, A. M., Monteith, M. J., & Mark, A. Y. (2006). Standing up for a change: Reducing bias through interpersonal confrontation. *Journal of Personality and Social Psychology, 90*, 784–803.

Devine, P. G. (1989). Stereotypes and prejudice: Their automatic and controlled components. *Journal of Personality and Social Psychology, 56*, 5–18.

Dovidio, J. F., & Gaertner, S. L. 1993. Stereotypes and evaluative intergroup bias. In D. M. Mackie & D. L. Hamilton (Eds.), *Affect, cognition, and stereotyping: Interactive processes in group perception* (pp. 167–193). San Diego, CA: Academic Press.

Dovidio, J. F., Brigham, J. C., Johnson, B. T., & Gaertner, S. L. (1996). Stereotyping, prejudice, and discrimination: Another look. In C. N. Macrae, C. Stangor, & M. Hewstone (Eds.), *Stereotypes and stereotyping* (pp. 276–319). New York, NY: Guilford Press.

Dovidio, J. F., Evans, N., & Tyler, R. B. (1986). Racial stereotypes: The contents of their cognitive representations. *Journal of Experimental Social Psychology, 22*, 22–37.

Eberhart, J. L., & Fiske, S. T. (1996). Motivating individuals to change: What is a target to do? In C. N. Macrae, C. Stagnor, & M. Hewstone, (1996). *Stereotypes & stereotyping* (pp. 369–415). New York, NY: Guilford Press.

Esses, V. M., Haddock, G., & Zanna, M. P. (1993). Values, stereotypes, and emotions as determinants of intergroup attitudes. In Mackie, D. M., & Hamilton, D. L. (Eds), *Affect, cognition, and stereotyping* (pp. 137–166). New York, NY: Academic Press.

Fiske, S. T. (1989). Examining the role of intent: Toward understanding its role in stereotyping and prejudice. In J. S. Uleman & J. A. Bargh (Eds.), *Unintended thought* (pp. 253–283). New York, NY: Guilford Press.

Fitzgerald, M. R. (2014). *Native Americans on Network TV: Stereotypes, myths, and the "good Indian."* Lanham, MD: Rowman & Littlefield.

Gardner, R. C. (1994). Prejudice and stereotypes—General observations. In M. P. Zanna & J. M. Olson (Eds). *The psychology of prejudice: The Ontario Symposium, Volume 7* (pp. 1–54). Hillsdale, NJ: Lawrence Erlbaum Associates.

Gardner, R. C., Kirby, D. M., Gorospe, F. H., & Willamin, A. C. (1972). Ethnic stereotypes: An alternative assessment technique, the stereotype differential. *Journal of Social Psychology, 87*, 259–267.

Gardner, R. C., Lalonde, R. N., Nero, A. M., & Young, M. Y. (1988). Ethnic stereotypes: Implications of measurement strategy. *Social Cognition, 6*, 40–60.

Gilbert, D. T. & Hixon, J. G. (1991). The trouble of thinking: Activation and application of stereotypic beliefs. *Journal of Personality and Social Psychology, 60*, 509–517.

Gilbert, J., Carr-Ruffino, N., Ivancevich, J. M., & Lownes-Jackson, M. (2003). An empirical examination of inter-ethnic stereotypes: Comparing Asian American and African American employees. *Public Personnel Management, 32*, 251–266.

Goffman, E. (1963). *Stigma: Notes on the management of spoiled identity*. Englewood, NJ: Prentice Hall.

Hamilton, D. L., (1981). *Stereotyping and intergroup behavior: Some thoughts on the cognitive approach*. Hillsdale, NJ: Lawrence Erlbaum Associates.

Hamner, W. C., Kim, J. S., Baird, L., & Bigoness, W. J. (1974). Race and sex as determinants of ratings by potential employers in a simulated work-sampling task. *Journal of Applied Psychology, 59*, 705–711.

Hewstone, M., & Brown, R. (1986). Contact is not enough: An intergroup perspective on the "Contact Hypothesis." In M. Hewstone & R. J. Brown (Eds.), *Contact and conflict in intergroup encounters* (pp. 1–44). London: Blackwell.

Hort, B. E., Fagot, B. I., & Leinbach, M. D. (1990). Are people's notions of maleness more stereotypically framed than their notions of femaleness? *Sex Roles, 23*, 197–212.

Hosoda, M., & Stone-Romero, E. F. (2010). The effects of foreign accents on employment-related decisions. *Journal of Managerial Psychology, 25, 113–132.*

Hosoda, M., Nguyen, L. T., & Stone-Romero, E. F. (2012). The effect of Hispanic accents on employment decisions. *Journal of Managerial Psychology, 27, 347–364.*

Hosoda, M., Stone-Romero, E, F., & Goats, G. (2006). The effects of physical attractiveness on job-related outcomes: A meta-analysis of experimental studies. *Personnel Psychology, 56,* 431–462.

Ilgen, D. R., & Youtz, M. A. (1986). Factors affecting the evaluation and development of minorities in organizations. *Research in Personnel and Human Resources Management, 4,* 307–337.

Jones, M. (1991). Stereotyping Hispanics and Whites: Perceived differences in social roles as a determinant of ethnic stereotypes. *Journal of Social Psychology, 131,* 469–476.

Jussim, L., Coleman, L. M., & Lerch, L. (1987). The nature of stereotypes: A comparison and integration of three theories. *Journal of Personality and Social Psychology, 52,* 536–546.

Katz, D., & Braly, K. (1933). Racial stereotypes of one hundred college students. *Journal of Abnormal and Social Psychology, 28,* 280–290.

Katz, D., & Braly, K. W. (1935). Racial prejudice and racial stereotypes. *Journal of Abnormal and Social Psychology, 30,* 175–193.

Kilpatrick, J. (1999). *Celluloid Indians: Native Americans and film.* Lincoln, NE: University of Nebraska Press.

Kirby, D. M., & Gardner, R. C. (1972). Ethnic stereotypes: Norms on 208 words typically used in their assessment. *Canadian Journal of Psychology/Revue, 26,* 140–154.

Krueger, D. C., Stone, D. L., & Stone-Romero, E. F. (2014) Applicant, rater, and job factors related to weight-based bias. *Journal of Managerial Psychology, 29,*164–186.

Krueger, J. (1996). Personal beliefs and cultural stereotypes about racial characteristics. *Journal of Personality and Social Psychology, 71,* 536–548.

Levine, J., Carmines, E. G., & Sniderman, P. M. (1999). The empirical dimensionality of racial stereotypes. *Public Opinion Quarterly, 63,* 371–384.

Link, M. W., & Oldendick, R. W. (1996). Social construction and White attitudes toward equal opportunity and multiculturalism. *The Journal of Politics, 58,* 149–168.

Lippman, W. (1922). *Public opinion.* New York, NY: MacMillan Co.

Macrae, C. N., Stagnor, C., & Hewstone, M. (1996). *Stereotypes & stereotyping.* New York, NY: Guilford Press.

McConahay, J. B., & Hough, J. J. Jr. (1976). Symbolic racism. *Journal of Social Issues, 32,* 23–45.

McCauley, C., & Stitt, C. L. (1978). An individual and quantitative measure of stereotypes. *Journal of Personality and Social Psychology, 36,* 929–940.

McCauley, C., Stitt, C. L., & Segal, M. Stereotyping: From prejudice to prediction. *Psychological Bulletin, 87,* 195–208.

Mihesuah, D. A. (2009). *American Indians: Stereotypes and realities.* Atlanta, GA: Clarity Press.

Miller, N., & Brewer, M. B. (1984). *Groups in contact: The psychology of desegregation.* New York, NY: Academic Press.

Miller, N., & Brewer, M. B. (1988). Contact and cooperation. In P. A. Katz & D. A. Taylor (Eds.), *Eliminating racism. Perspectives in social psychology (A series of texts and monographs).* Boston, MA: Springer.

Morrison, A. M., & von Glinow, M. A. (1990). Women and minorities in management. *American Psychologist, 45,* 200–208.

Niemann, Y. F., Jennings, L., Rozelle, R. M., Baxter, J. C., et al. (1994). Use of free responses and cluster analysis to determine stereotypes of eight groups. *Personality and Social Psychology Bulletin, 20*, 379–390.

National Public Radio (2018). *'Low IQ,' 'SPECTACULAR,' 'Dog': How Trump Tweets About African-Americans.* Retrieved from: https://www.npr.org/2018/09/10/645594393/low-iq-spectacular-dog-how-trump-tweets-about-african-americans.

New York Times. (2018). Donald Trump's Racism: The Definitive List. Retrieved from: https://www.nytimes.com/interactive/2018/01/15/opinion/leonhardt-trump-racist.html

Oakes, P. J., Haslam, S. A., & Turner, J. C. (1994). *Stereotyping and social reality.* Malden, MA: Blackwell Publishing.

Powell, G. N. (1992). The good manager: Business students' stereotypes of Japanese managers versus stereotypes of American managers. *Group & Organization Management, 17*, 44–56.

Rettew, D. C., Billman, D., & Davis, R. A. (1993). Inaccurate perceptions of the amount others stereotype: Estimates about stereotypes of one's own group and other groups. *Basic and Applied Social Psychology, 14*, 121–142.

Roehling, M. V., Choi, M. G., & Roehling, P. V. (2019). Weight discrimination in the workplace: Current knowledge and future research needs. In D. L. Stone & J. H. Dulebohn (Eds.), *Research in human resource management* (pp. 97–137). Charlotte, NC: Information Age.

Rosette, A. S., Leonardelli, G. J., & Phillips, K. W. (2008). The White standard: Racial bias in leader categorization. *Journal of Applied Psychology, 93*, 758–777.

Rudman, L. A., & Ashmore, R. D. (2007). Discrimination and the implicit association test. *Group Processes & Intergroup Relations, 10*, 359–372.

Rudman, L. A., Greenwald, A. G., Mellott, D. S., & Schwartz, J. L. K. (1999). Measuring the automatic components of prejudice: Flexibility and generality of the Implicit Association Test. *Social Cognition, 17*, 437–465.

Sears, D. O., & Kinder, D. R. (1971). Racial tensions and voting in Los Angeles. In W. Z. Hirsch (Ed.). *Los Angeles: Visibility and prospects for metropolitan leadership* (pp. 51–88). New York, NY: Prager.

Sears, D. O., & McConahay, J. B. (1973). *The politics of violence: The new urban blacks and the Watts riot.* Boston, MA: Houghton Mifflin.

Sigelman, L., & Tuch, S. A. (1997). Metastereotypes: Blacks' perceptions of White's' stereotypes of Blacks. *Public Opinion Quarterly, 61*, 87–101.

Southern Poverty Law Center. *Hate groups in the U.S.* Retrieved from: https://www.splcenter.org/hate-map

Stangor, C., & Schaller, M. (1996). Stereotypes as individual and collective representations. In C. N. Macrae, C. Stangor, & M. Hewstone (Eds.), *Stereotypes and stereotyping* (pp. 3–40). New York, NY: Guilford Press.

Stone, D. L., & Colella, A. (1996). A model of factors affecting the treatment of disabled individuals in organizations. *Academy of Management Review, 21*, 352–401.

Stone, D. L., Lukaszewski, K. M., Krueger, D. C., & Canedo, J. (in press). Influence of immigrants' attributes on unfair discrimination in organizations. In A. Georgiadou, M. Gonzalez-Perez, & M. Olivas-Lujan (Eds.), *Diversity in diversity management.* Bingley, West Yorkshire: England.

84 • STONE-ROMERO, STONE, HARTMAN, & HOSODA

Stone, E. F., Stone, D. L., & Dipboye, R. L. (1992). Stigmas in organizations: Race, handicaps, and physical attractiveness. In K. Kelley (Ed.), *Issues, theory, and research in industrial/organizational psychology* (pp. 385–457). Amsterdam, Netherlands: Elsevier Science Publishers.

Stone-Romero, E. F., & Stone, D. L. (2007). Cognitive, affective, and cultural influences on stigmatization: Impact on human resource management processes and practices. In J. J. Martocchio (Ed.), *Research in personnel and human resources management, 26,* (pp. 111–161). Amsterdam, Netherlands: Elsevier JAI.

Thomas, D. A., & Gabarro, J. J. (1999). *Breaking through: The making of minority executives in corporate America.* Boston, MA: Harvard Business School Press.

Thorndike, R. L. (1977). Content and evaluation in ethnic stereotypes. *Journal of Psychology: Interdisciplinary and Applied, 96,* 131–140.

Timberlake, M., & Williams, T. R. (2012). Stereotypes of US immigrants from global regions. *Social Science Quarterly, 93,* 867–890.

Tomkiewicz, J., & Brenner, O. C. (1996). The relationship between race (Hispanic) stereotypes and requisite management characteristics. *Journal of Social Behavior & Personality, 11,* 511–520.

Tomkiewicz, J., Brenner, O. C., & Adeyemi-Bello, T. (1998). The impact of perceptions and stereotypes on the managerial mobility of African Americans. *Journal of Social Psychology, 138,* 88–92.

Wetherell, M., & Jonathan Potter, J. (1992). *Mapping the language of racism: Discourse and the legitimation of exploitation.* New York, NY: Columbia University Press.

Wittenbrink, B., Judd, C. M., & Park, B. (1997). Evidence for racial prejudice at the implicit level and its relationship with questionnaire measures. *Journal of Personality and Social Psychology, 72,* 262–274.

CHAPTER 4

EFFECT SIZES AND THE TRANSLATION FROM DIVERSITY RESEARCH TO HUMAN RESOURCE MANAGEMENT

Abby Corrington, David Lane,
Rachel Trump-Steele, and Mikki Hebl

The current paper calls human resource (HR) professionals' attention to the role that effect sizes play in diversity research, with a particular focus on measurement and interpretation. We understand that a great deal of research is fraught with limitations, and researchers make choices accordingly. Furthermore, we know that research reporting is often guided by standard practices. In this article, however, we focus on moving away from standard practices and toward best practices in diversity research. In this way, researchers might do a better job reporting and interpreting effect sizes in terms of their actual real-world impact, which in turn would maximize the utility that HR practitioners take away from diversity research. Our recommendations for diversity researchers, and researchers more generally, focus on three principles: use scaled rather than scale-free measures, report confidence intervals around scaled and scale-free effect sizes, and carefully consider context. We discuss the particular implications for HR management and also recommend future research in this area.

Diversity and Inclusion in Organizations, pages 85–101.
Copyright © 2020 by Information Age Publishing

Diversity research has never been more important. There is a current socio-political upheaval occurring in modern-day society related to diversity issues, such as race, immigration, and religion (Balz, 2017). In 2018 there were 76,418 charges from members of protected classes (e.g., women, disabled, racial and ethnic minorities, religious affiliation) filed with the United States Equal Employment Opportunity Commission (see US EEOC, 2018). And, there is ongoing public debate regarding the efficacy of many diversity-related initiatives, such as diversity training (Lindsey, King, Membere, & Cheung, 2018). As a result of these issues, as well as changing demographics that reveal more diversity than ever before, Human Resource (hereinafter referred to as HR) professionals would benefit by being able to determine what diversity factors are and are not important to and effective for optimizing organizational-related outcomes.

Given that HR professionals are responsible for enacting diversity-related policies, it is critical that diversity researchers carefully present their research and that HR practitioners understand their impact. For example, after two Black men were arrested at a Philadelphia Starbucks in April 2018, more than 8,000 Starbucks locations across the nation were closed for a day-long company-wide racial bias education training (Calfas, 2018). For that time period, Starbucks was dependent on the expertise of HR professionals, who were presumably using evidence-based practices that have been demonstrated by diversity researchers. Starbucks is not the only organization that assumes a clear translation from diversity research to effective HR management.

As with many fields of research, diversity research is characterized by areas of disagreement. For example, some research has found that diversity leads to greater conflict (e.g., Olson, Parayitam, & Bao, 2007), yet other research has found that it leads to greater innovation (e.g., Talke, Solomo, & Kock, 2011). Additional articles claim that diversity training does not work (Dobbin & Kalev, 2016), while others claim that it does (Lindsey et al., 2018). There are a number of reasons why there are contradictions in such research findings, including different methodologies (see Stone, Hosoda, Lukaszewski, & Phillips, 2008), different sample sizes, and the fact that things sometimes simply do not having a significant effect or large effect size. In the current research, we focus on one of these reasons—effect sizes—in much more detail. Effect sizes may be erroneously interpreted by HR professionals. The reasons for this are numerous, but throughout this paper, we argue that one of the most deleterious outcomes is that effects commonly found in diversity research may be routinely dismissed and deemed unimportant because they are "small" by conventional rules of thumb. The problem with this logic is that findings that have small effect sizes in diversity research may have substantial practical significance.

The current paper draws focused attention on effect sizes, which are inherent in most studies done on diversity-related phenomena, by examining the reporting, magnitude, impact, and implications of effect sizes in diversity research. In the sections that follow, we begin by providing a brief overview of the importance of effect sizes generally, enumerating the benefits previous research has identified. Then, we present a series of diversity-related studies that have been published, offering various interpretations based on the effect sizes found. Next, we make three major recommendations: 1) use scaled measures of effect size, 2) report confidence intervals around effect sizes, and 3) carefully consider context. Finally, we present implications and future directions in HR management and diversity research.

THE IMPORTANCE OF EFFECT SIZES

Pierce, Block, and Aguinis (2004) suggest that effect sizes have strong implications for theory development, meta-analytic reviews, and intervention programs. Such consequences may be particularly profound when considering the impact of social disparities. For instance, if HR professionals interpret what is conventionally considered to be a small effect size as indicating that gender has little importance, they might mistakenly conclude that the development and testing of a theory of gender differences is not justified or worthwhile, or erroneously fail to recommend treatment or intervention programs that would actually be beneficial. In other words, a lack of attention due to misguided interpretations of effect size could have far-reaching consequences by inhibiting both academic and practical social progress.

The importance of estimating effect size in psychological research has been recognized for many decades. For example, Hayes (1963) was an early advocate of effect size estimation in general and of the omega square statistic in particular. Subsequently, Cohen (1990) stated that "[t]he primary product of a research inquiry is one or more measures of effect size" (p. 1310). Prentice and Miller (1992) cited several benefits of effect size estimation: (a) they show the size of an effect on a continuous scale, (b) they provide conventions as to what is a sizable effect, (c) they provide indications of the strength of an effect, (d) they can be measured within the vast majority of studies, (e) they can be used to compare phenomena across multiple studies and/or in meta-analyses (see also Baguley, 2009; Rosenthal & Rubin, 2003), and (f) they can be used to assess how many subjects are needed for a study. Notably, the APA Task Force on Statistical Inference made the strong recommendation that researchers should "always report effect size measures for primary outcomes" (Wilkinson et al., 1999, p. 599).

EFFECT SIZES IN DIVERSITY RESEARCH

Over the past twenty years, diversity scholars have conducted an abundance of research that shows evidence of bias (e.g., Hebl, Foster, Mannix, & Dovidio, 2002; Madera & Hebl, 2013; Madera, King, & Hebl, 2013). Many of these studies have effect sizes that appear small based on the measure of effect size employed; however, despite their apparent small magnitude, we argue that they can still be practically important. We base this conclusion on two arguments. First, when we consider processes such as selection with a low selection ratio, these small amounts of bias at the micro level can have a substantial influence at the macro level. Second, these effects have been found in "thin slices" of interactions (Ambady & Rosenthal, 1993) that likely occur repeatedly, thus culminating in a great impact for those individuals who experience this continuous bias. In the three diversity-related research studies that follow, our goal is to highlight how effect sizes that are considered only small to medium by conventional rules of thumb may have substantial practical significance.

First, in one study assessing the impact of goal setting during diversity training on attitudes and behaviors toward LGBT people, students who underwent diversity training as part of their orientation to the university either set goals (related to LGBT-supportive behaviors) or did not (Madera et al., 2013). Students ($N = 158$) who set goals were more likely to engage in LGBT-supportive behaviors ($M = 40.44$, $SD = 10.43$) eight months after the diversity training than students who did not set goals ($M = 36.42$, $SD = 10.17$). In terms of a standardized effect size, the difference corresponds to Cohen's $d = 0.39$, 95% CI: [0.07, 0.70], which would suggest a relatively small effect size (Cohen, 1988). Alternatively, these results could be considered in terms of a non-standardized effect size, showing that those who set goals, on average, engaged in 4.02 more LGBT-supportive behaviors with a 95% CI of somewhere between 0.78 and 7.26 additional engaged-in behaviors. The practical implications of engaging in more behaviors has the potential to be profound when one considers that perhaps these four additional behaviors involved an ally standing up for an LGBT person, learning more about LGBT issues that otherwise never would have been learned, giving support to someone who may be stressed and/or suicidal, and/or deciding to refrain from teasing someone. We have no idea about the impact such behaviors can have, but they might be immense—much more immense than a small effect size would portend.

In a second study assessing the impact of staffing policies on bias against stigmatized individuals, participants ($N = 87$) interviewing a Black interviewee ironically created more social distance (i.e., set their chairs farther away from the Black interviewee) when they were instructed to use an identity-blind policy ($M = 43.79$, $SD = 4.52$) compared to when they were instructed to use an identity-conscious policy ($M = 41.25$, $SD = 4.92$; Madera & Hebl, 2013). In terms of a standardized effect size, the difference corresponds to Cohen's $d = 0.54$, 95% CI: [0.10, 0.96]. However, stating this difference in terms of a non-standardized effect size, on average, participants in the identity-blind condition set their chairs 2.54 inches farther away from the interviewee compared to those in the identity-conscious condition, 95% CI: [0.51, 4.57]. Again, this practical difference may have significant practical impacts. For instance, Sorokowska et al. (2017) reports on the specific interpersonal differences that people prefer to maintain across 42 different countries. People in the U.S. maintain relatively closer (when compared with other people from other countries) social, personal, and intimate partner distances, and violations from this distance—in the range of 2 to 3 inches—may lead people to perceive varying levels of interest, dominance, kinship, and other attitudes (see Hall, 1966).

In a third study exploring the effect of job applicants' ($N = 84$) sexual orientation on interpersonal displays of bias, employers spoke fewer words to gay applicants ($M = 169.45$, $SD = 111.05$) compared to straight applicants ($M = 257.18$, $SD = 210.08$; Hebl et al., 2002). In terms of a standardized effect size, this difference corresponds to Cohen's $d = 0.79$, 95% CI: [0.34, 1.23], which is a medium effect size. However, stating this difference in terms of a non-standardized effect size, 87.73 fewer words were spoken to gay than straight applicants, 95% CI: [39.51, 135.95]. Although the effect size portrays this difference as medium in magnitude, the impact of speaking 87 more words to someone in an interview setting is potentially profound. That is, employers spoke only 66% as much to gay than assumed heterosexual applicants. In such an abbreviated timeframe, not only are employers not able to ask as many questions and find out as much about the applicant, but they are also not able to maximally use the interaction for a recruiting tool. There is simply 34% of the interaction that is not getting transmitted.

In sum, we hope that HR professionals appreciate the fact that effect sizes that appear small may nonetheless have the potential to have profound and widespread practical implications. Our review of three relevant studies demonstrates this, even in the context of our own research. We next move to considering ways in which HR professionals should approach effect size measures with three major recommendations in mind: 1) use scaled measures of effect size, 2) report confidence intervals around effect sizes, and 3) carefully consider context.

USE SCALED RATHER THAN SCALE-FREE MEASURES WHEN MEANINGFUL

Researchers can report effect sizes in a way that is either a) scaled, as in the original scale of measurement, or b) scale-free, as in standardized measures and estimates of variance explained. Examples of the former include mean differences, differences in proportions, odds ratios, and b weights in regression. Examples of the latter include Cohen's d, ω^2, percent of variance explained, r, and β weights in regression. We strongly recommend that HR professionals use scaled rather than scale-free measures whenever the variables are assessed in inherently meaningful units, such as dollars, percent correct, and time to complete a task (Baguley, 2009; Bridgeman, Burton, & Cline, 2008; Pek & Flora, 2018; Wilkinson et al., 1999).

There are several reasons to use scaled rather than scale-free measures. First, they are almost universally easier to interpret. Recall the three studies discussed earlier (Hebl et al., 2002; Madera & Hebl, 2013; Madera et al., 2013). In these studies, the results were easily interpretable because they were based on scaled measures, such as the difference in the number of words (87.73) participants spoke to non-stigmatized compared to stigmatized individuals or the difference in the number of inches (2.54 inches) identity-blind participants created between themselves and stigmatized individuals compared to identity-conscious participants. The magnitudes of these differences are substantially more apparent than the magnitude of differences in means (e.g., 1.4) on Likert-type scales used in most diversity research (including these three studies).

In regression, an effect can be measured in terms of the raw score (scaled) coefficient, b, or the standardized (scale-free) coefficient, β. As in the case of differences between means, a scaled coefficient has a more direct interpretation but is only meaningful when the scales are inherently meaningful. As stated by Bridgeman, Burton, and Cline (2008):

> ... the focus is on how much performance improves on the criterion for a given improvement on the predictor, holding other variables constant. This is exactly the information provided by the unstandardized regression weight. Note that it is only the unstandardized weights that are directly interpretable on the original score scale; standardized weights have no straightforward interpretation on the original scale. (p. 2).

Consider how scale-free measures might be relatively uninformative in the context of a recent study by Nittrouer and colleagues (2018). The authors investigated gender differences in a faculty member's odds of being invited to give a colloquium at prestigious universities. If the authors had used a scale-free measure, they might have reported the percent of variance explained by gender and pitted this against the effects of academic rank, field of study, and all unmeasured variables. Our reanalysis of these data shows that only 1% of the variance is explained by gender, and this could have been used and reported as their scale-free measure of effect size. However, this measure would not have been informative because the effect of gender should have the same interpretation regardless of differences due to academic rank, field of study, and unmeasured variables. Instead, the authors more aptly used a scaled measure. With this, the key result that they were able to report was that, even after controlling for academic rank and field of study, the odds of a man being invited to give a colloquium was 1.2 times higher than the odds for a woman. This gender difference is easily interpreted and speaks for itself. And the practical importance is obvious.

Another reason that scaled effect sizes are preferable is that, unlike scale-free measures, they are not affected by the variability of the independent variable or the reliability of the dependent variable. It is widely known that the variability of an independent or predictor variable has a large effect on scale-free measures of effect size (Sackett & Yang, 2000). Indeed, it is likely that every introductory-level statistics book covers the impact of a restricted range on the size of a correlation. In short, if the variance of the predictor variable in the sample is less than the variability in the population to which it is applicable, then the correlation will be underestimated. Similarly, if the variability is greater than the target population, then the correlation will be overestimated.

This phenomenon is subtler in experimental research in which there is no clear reference population. Consider a hypothetical experiment assessing the efficacy of a program to decrease biases in recruiters' review of job applications. In experiments of this kind, the researcher chooses the levels of the independent variable. For example, an experimenter could choose the training times to range from one to five hours or from one to 100 hours. The unstandardized measure, b, would represent the decrease in biases associated with an hour of training. Assuming linearity, b would be the same for the two ranges of training time. In contrast, scale-free measures such as β, ω^2, and η^2 would be much larger in the design with the larger range of training hours than with the smaller range. This point is additionally made by Dooling and Danks (1975).

REPORT CONFIDENCE INTERVALS AROUND SCALED AND SCALE-FREE EFFECT SIZES

A second-best practice for diversity researchers is to use confidence intervals on effect sizes (Capraro, 2005; Pek & Flora, 2018; Wilkinson et al., 1999). Specifically, Wilkinson et al. (1999) recommend, "[i]nterval estimates should be given for any effect sizes involving principal outcomes. Provide intervals for correlations and other coefficients of association or variation whenever possible" (p. 599). Reporting confidence intervals around effect sizes is particularly important because doing so provides a better understanding of the potential practical importance of "small" effect sizes. Because confidence intervals around effect sizes tend to be extremely large, the actual effect size may be much larger or smaller than what is reported. Because the interpretation of confidence intervals is not as straightforward as one might think, and there is evidence that they are misunderstood by a considerable proportion of researchers (Belia, Fidler, Williams, & Cumming, 2005; Hoekstra, Morey, Rouder, & Wagenmakers, 2014), we begin with a short discussion of the meaning of a confidence interval.

To simplify the discussion, we consider the 95% confidence interval on the mean, probably the simplest confidence interval used in psychological research. Let us assume that our sample mean is 50 and our interval extends from 40 to 60. The formally correct interpretation of this confidence interval is that it was created using a procedure that would contain the population mean 95% of the time. One common fallacy is that the 95% confidence interval has a .95 probability of containing the population mean. That is, the probability that the population mean is somewhere between 40 and 60 is .95. Although this makes intuitive sense, it is not correct and the proper interpretation is more complex.

Confidence intervals allow researchers to assess the level of uncertainty associated with an effect size estimate. Consider a study in which working men, on average, take fewer personal days to spend with their sick children than do working women, and that the mean difference is 8 days per year. We might wonder how sure the researchers are that the mean difference is close to 8 years. Could it be 7 years? 12 years? The difference would be interpreted very differently if the confidence interval extended from -1 to 41 than if it extended from 7 to 10. This information regarding the uncertainty of the estimate is exceptionally important because they demonstrate the certainty of the effect.

The use of confidence intervals is especially important in diversity research. When research findings have practical value, HR professionals want to gain a sense of how large the effect is, not just whether or not there is an effect. Of particular interest, in most cases, is the lower bound of the confidence interval because it determines whether a confident conclusion that an effect is of practical importance is justified. If a lower bound is sufficiently above 0, then the conclusion that the effect is practically important is justified. The following two examples demonstrate how the use of confidence intervals can allow HR professionals to conclude that an effect is or is not large enough to be practically important.

First, Kling, Hyde, Showers, and Buswell (1999) meta-analyzed gender differences in self-esteem. The 95% confidence interval on Cohen's d for self-esteem ranged from 0.19 to 0.22. Because the lower bound of the confidence interval is sufficiently above 0, the conclusion that the effect is large enough to be practically important is justified. On the other hand, Batz-Barbarich, Tay, Kuykendall, and Cheung (2018) meta-analyzed gender differences in life satisfaction and job satisfaction. The 95% confidence interval on Cohen's d for life satisfaction ranged from −0.02 to 0.01, and for job satisfaction, from −0.06 to 0.01. Because the lower bounds of both confidence intervals are both very small (and even the upper bounds of the confidence intervals are very small) the conclusion that the effect is *not* large enough to be practically important is justified.

Although confidence intervals on scaled measures are often reported, confidence intervals on scale-free measures are relatively rare (unless, as shown above, they are reported in the context of a meta-analysis). So, why are researchers (and admittedly, occasionally some of the authors of this very paper) not reporting confidence intervals on standardized effect size measures? We propose two main reasons. First, it has not been a standard practice. We reviewed all 2018 issues of *Journal of Management*. Of the 28 articles that reported standardized effect sizes, none of them included confidence intervals on standardized effect sizes. Although in recent years, some journals such as *Psychological Science*, are requiring authors to include confidence intervals, the instructions to authors do not explicitly state that this applies to standardized effect size measures. In two recent issues of *Psychological Science* (September and October 2018), just under half of the articles (7 out of 16; note that one is a meta-analysis) that report standardized effect sizes also report confidence intervals around those effect sizes. This trend suggests that although some authors have interpreted the "confidence intervals" instruction in the author guidelines as applying to standardized effect sizes, it has not yet been adopted as common practice by all authors.

Second, researchers may prefer not to emphasize the uncertainty of their findings, a practice that is even less helpful for translation to HR management. Diversity researchers who provide estimates of scale-free effect sizes have even less certainty about their true value, and their associated confidence intervals are greater than those for scaled estimates. This is the case because to estimate a scale-free measure, such as Cohen's *d*, it is necessary to estimate the scaled effect size as well as the standard deviation. Because there is uncertainty about both estimates, the uncertainty of a scale-free statistic—which depends on both estimates—is considerable. Accordingly, Simonsohn (2014) argued that with fewer than 1,000 observations, estimations of standardized effect sizes reveal very little about the size of effects. Typically, a meta-analysis is required to achieve a sufficient sample size. Because confidence intervals on scale-free measures are typically very large, researchers may be reluctant to report them. It is understandable that a researcher would not wish to include information that most articles in a given area exclude. However, it is up to the reviewers, readers, and HR professionals to realize that confidence intervals are often wide and that researchers should not necessarily be penalized for that.

In sum, we highly recommend the use of confidence intervals and believe this is a renewed wave that will continue trending in future research both on diversity and more generally. We particularly think they are important to use in diversity research because confidence intervals not only show whether there is an effect but also whether the effect is practically important.

CONSIDER THE CONTEXT CAREFULLY

The meaning of a measure of effect size cannot be properly interpreted without a careful consideration of the context in which it applies. The very same effect size may be very important in one context yet of trivial importance in another (see also Plonsky & Oswald, 2014). One factor that greatly affects the interpretation of a small effect is whether the extremes of a distribution or the middle of a distribution is of primary concern. For example, consider a performance rating scale in which, due to bias, there is a gender difference such that the male mean is 50 and the female mean is 49. Further assume that the standard deviation is 10 and the ratings are normally distributed for each gender. By standard rules of thumb, this would be properly interpreted as a very small effect because it explains only 0.25% of the variance and has a corresponding value of Cohen's *d* of 0.1. In most contexts, this would be a reasonable interpretation. For instance, if a rating of 37 were required to be eligible for a permanent job, then 90.3% of male employees and 88.5% and females would be eligible. This means that the ratio of men to women eligible for a permanent job is 1.02:1, a far cry from adverse impact ratio of 1.25:1 as defined by the 4/5ths rule. However, if we consider a context in which the selection ratio is much smaller, such as promotion to senior management, a smaller proportion of employees would be eligible. For example, if only those scoring over 70 are eligible, then 2.28% of men, but only 1.79% of women, would be eligible. This would make the ratio of eligible men to eligible women 1.27:1, which would be indicative of adverse impact as defined by the 4/5ths rule.

If the bias were slightly greater such that the female mean was 48, then Cohen's *d* would be 0.20 and 1.0% of the variance would be explained. With this small effect (as conventionally defined), the ratios of men to women eligible for a permanent job would be 1.64:1 and 1.79:1 for cutoffs of 70 and 75, respectively. It is likely that the selection ratio for many types of promotions, including promotion to senior management, would be even lower, further increasing the ratio of eligible men to women.

We understand that promotion decisions within organizations are significantly more complex than we have presented in this example; however, the focal idea remains—a small bias will have a large effect any time a small, elite group is selected out of a much larger group. More generally, the interpretation of an effects size statistic should depend on the context in which it is to be applied. Even an effect with a Cohen's d of 0.1 and explaining 0.25% of the variance can have a meaningful impact in some contexts.

Researchers often have interpreted what they consider "minor" gender differences as having no practical impact. For example, Swim, Borgida, Maruyama, and Myers (1989) conducted a meta-analysis examining studies that use basic renditions of paradigms in which participants respond to articles written by a man (e.g., John McKay) or a woman (e.g., Joan McKay). Swim et al. (1989) found effect sizes ranging from -.05 to -.08 and suggested that "the average ratings between differences in men and women is negligible" (p. 409). Similarly, Landy (2008) claimed that gender biases in performance ratings, which he cites as ranging from 0.05 to 0.10 standard deviations, are "exceedingly small" (p. 384). We counter that, as shown in the examples above and by several researchers (e.g., Eagly, 1995; Martell, Lane, & Emrich, 1996; Greenwald, Banaji, & Nosek, 2015), these "small" effect sizes have the potential to produce powerful real-world consequences, especially when the selection ratio is extremely small (see also Agars, 2004).

Another example of an apparently unimportant effect that could make a practical difference was performed by Smith and Plant (1982) on gender differences in the job satisfaction of university professors. Their primary finding was that male professors were significantly more satisfied than female professors with two aspects of their jobs: supervision and co-workers. The authors report ω^2 values (a standardized or scale-free measure of effect size) of .04 for each of these outcomes and go on to conclude that "little or no meaningfulness can be attached" to these findings (pp. 250–251). We argue, however, that these results could have rather substantial practical meaningfulness. Making the simplifying assumption that university professors scoring in the bottom 5% of these two measures of job satisfaction quit, the proportion of female professors who quit would be approximately twice as high as the proportion of male professors who quit. We acknowledge that this simplifying assumption is just that—an assumption. Data on rates of university professor turnover based on these two job satisfaction variables do not exist, so we offer a hypothetical, but reasonable, scenario to illustrate the *potential* practical impact of the difference on these two metrics. Thus, an apparently small effect can result in a very large gender disparity.

An important issue in diversity-related research concerns the relation of the implicit association test (IAT) and behaviors. In a meta-analysis, Oswald, Mitchell, Blanton, Jaccard, and Tetlock (2013) found only a very small overall effect of IAT on behaviors, perception, preferences, response time, and brain activity. The meta-analytically estimated population correlation, ρ, was .14, with a 95% confidence interval ranging from .10 to .19. In a commentary, Greenwald et al. (2015) gave an example of when this "small effect" would have a meaningful impact. Specifically, the authors argued that the data on police stopping shows that if the police force fell one standard deviation below the mean on the IAT, the small effect size estimated by Oswald et al. (2013) would result in a Black-White stop difference as large as 9,976 stops or 5.7%. Oswald, Mitchell, Blanton, Jaccard, and Tetlock (2015) claimed that the data were not sufficient to support Greenwald et al.'s (2015) claim. We do not take sides in this paper as to whether the data support Greenwald et al.'s (2015) conclusion. Rather, we present their argument as a clear illustration of the idea that, when considered in terms of real-world impact, small standardized effects can result in real practical significance in the proper context.

The critical importance of considering the context when interpreting effect sizes is obvious in a real-life medical example in which a study was halted when the results indicated a meaningful real-life outcome, even though the percentage of variance explained was very low. In 1987, the Steering Committee of the Physicians' Health Study Research Group conducted a medical trial exploring the effects of aspirin on heart attacks (Rosenthal, 1990). Interestingly, researchers ended the study early (an uncommon decision at the time) based on the finding that 0.94% of participants in the aspirin condition had heart attacks, compared to 1.71% of participants in the placebo condition—even though the percentage of variance explained was only 0.11%.

An extension of the idea that context is important when interpreting effect sizes is that effects should be considered cumulatively (e.g., women in leadership—Agars, 2004; gender differences—Eagly, 1995; medicine—Rosenthal, 1990). In one of the most illustrative examples to date, Abelson (1985) discussed cumulative effects in sports. In considering the effect of skill (batting average) on the likelihood of a batter getting a hit in a single at-bat, the proportion of variance accounted for by batting average is about 0.003. Based on traditional rules of thumb, this effect would be regarded as negligible. Paradoxically, however, it is undeniable that baseball teams composed of players with higher batting averages are more successful than teams composed of players with lower batting averages. How can these two seemingly divergent findings be explained? Abelson (1985) argues that the influence of skill must be assessed over several events, such as total games won, at-bats over the course of a baseball season, and runs scored by the team, rather than based on a single at-bat. Stated differently, the cumulative impact of skill on baseball team performance is more informative than any single at-bat. More generally speaking, the impact of diversity-related effects (e.g., bias related to gender, race, religion) may not be seen until they are examined aggregately and over time.

IMPLICATIONS AND FUTURE DIRECTIONS FOR HR MANAGEMENT AND DIVERSITY RESEARCH

As we have discussed in previous sections, diversity researchers should a) use scaled rather than scale-free measures, b) report confidence intervals around scaled and scale-free effect sizes, and c) carefully consider context when conducting studies and reporting findings. In addition to these three recommendations, there are a number of implications and future directions we suggest for how effect sizes should be interpreted as they move from diversity research to HR practice.

Future research attention might be placed on additional ways to resolve the seeming contradiction that occurs when effect sizes are small, but the practical implications (or compounding of them) may be substantial. One research strategy is to conduct more field studies in which the practical implications are clearer. For instance, diversity researchers might conduct more studies outside the lab and partner with organizations or institutions in order to observe firsthand the organizational impacts that result from practices. This is particularly important when, by conventional rules of thumb, the results would otherwise be considered small. Field research, of course, is fraught with complications because it risks putting organizations in jeopardy if certain practices, policies, strategies, or interventions are found to be unfair. Thus, although research in field settings and organizations is ideal, access is often a barrier. However, the incentives to conduct field research far outweigh the deterrents because, as Stone et al. (2008) assert, the use of organizational data has the added benefits of reducing social desirability response biases and demand artifacts, while simultaneously improving the mundane realism of research and increasing the extent to which samples are representative of the working populations in organizations.

We hope that one of the primary benefits of this paper is to inform HR professionals about the limitations of relying upon past understanding and practices associated with effect sizes. We hope that HR professionals pay attention to effect sizes but that they are not limited by them, understanding that small effect sizes do not necessarily diminish the potential importance of a study's findings. That is, past research that has reported results with small effect sizes may have inadvertently been dismissed by both diversity researchers and HR professionals when such studies may actually have provided answers or provided preliminary findings that future research could draw upon and extend. We caution against the logic that because an effect size is small in magnitude, it is not worth further pursuing. This type of thinking may have closed doors on some really important findings in diversity research, when in reality, pursuing them might have been the right thing to do and moved the field forward in terms of practical implications.

Finally, HR professionals might want to revisit how we became so dependent on scale-free effect sizes as a measure of importance. Given that findings can be extremely practically important, yet appear small based on the measure of effect size employed, developing norms for reporting other measures that allow for consideration of practical implications may serve the field of diversity research well.

Although we advocate for the use of scaled effect sizes, we recognize that much—and perhaps most—psychological research is conducted using measures, such as Likert-type scales, for which units are not closely linked to practically meaningful effects. As a result, diversity researchers typically have little choice but to use scale-free measures of effect size. As such, we briefly segue into recommending what diversity researchers should do if they must use scale-free measures.

First, when research calls for the computation of an effect size of a standardized difference between two independent group means, Hedges' g (Hedges, 1981) is preferred to Cohen's d, as the latter is a biased estimate (although with 20 or more observations per group, the difference between Hedges' g and Cohen's d is negligible; Goulet-Pelletier & Cousineau, 2018). Second, when calculating an effect size of a standardized difference between two related pairs means, we recommend using the variance between subjects in the measurement of effect size (Goulet-Pelletier & Cousineau, 2018). Third, when computing the percent of variance explained in analysis of variance, we recommend the use of ω^2 rather than η^2, as the latter is positively biased (meaning that it tends to overestimate the percent of variance explained). One benefit of both partial η^2 and partial ω^2 statistics is that they ignore the variance explained by factors other than the factor of interest. Regardless of which is reported, it is important for diversity researchers to specify which version of proportion of variance explained is used.

CONCLUSION

In this paper, we were interested in focusing on how diversity researchers and HR professionals might better engage in best practices related to their reporting and interpreting of effect sizes.[1] It is unlikely that any diversity researcher gets all of this right all of the time. In fact, we fail, too, in some of the most common best practices. But our hope in writing this paper is to clarify what common versus best practices are. We have argued that we should not eschew findings simply because they appear weak according to arbitrary rules of thumb regarding what constitutes a sizeable effect, for they may be very large in practical value. We have argued that researchers should use scaled rather than scale-free measures when practical, report confidence intervals around scaled and scale-free effect sizes, and carefully consider the context surrounding effect sizes. In reeling from the crisis of confidence that squarely hit psychology (see Schmidt & Oh, 2016), and as our field continues to reward skeptics (and diversity research may be a particular target; King et al., 2018), we hope that more care is taken to better understand what effect sizes do tell us but also what they might not be telling us.

NOTE

1. Although we focus on the measurement and interpretation of effect sizes in diversity research in this manuscript, the issues we discuss are relevant to other research areas as well.

REFERENCES

Abelson, R. P. (1985). A variance explanation paradox: When a little is a lot. *Psychological Bulletin, 97*, 129–133. Retrieved from: https://doi.org/10.1037//0033-2909.97.1.129

Agars, M. D. (2004). Reconsidering the impact of gender stereotypes on the advancement of women in organizations. *Psychology of Women Quarterly, 28*(2), 103–111. Retrieved from: https://doi.org/10.1111/j.1471-6402.2004.00127.x

Ambady, N., & Rosenthal, R. (1993). Half a minute: Predicting teacher evaluations from thin slices of nonverbal behavior and physical attractiveness. *Journal of Personality and Social Psychology, 64*(3), 431–441. Retrieved from: http://dx.doi.org/10.1037/0022-3514.64.3.431

Baguley, T. (2009). Standardized or simple effect size: What should be reported? *British Journal of Psychology, 100*(3), 603–617. Retrieved from: https://doi.org/10.1348/000712608X377117

Balz, D. (2017). How attitudes about immigration, race, and religion contributed to Trump victory. *The Washington Post.* Retrieved from https://www.washingtonpost.com/politics/how-attitudes-about-immigration-race-and-religion-contributed-to-trump-victory/2017/06/13/6c2c1892-506f-11e7-b064-828ba60fbb98_story.html?noredirect=on&utm_term=.451e0102103a

Batz-Barbarich, C., Tay, L., Kuykendall, L., & Cheung, H. K. (2018). A meta-analysis of gender differences in subjective well-being: Estimating effect sizes and associations with gender inequality. *Psychological Science, 29*(9), 1491–1503. Retrieved from: https://doi.org/10.1177/0956797618774796

Belia, S., Fidler, F., Williams, J., & Cumming, G. (2005). Researchers misunderstand confidence intervals and standard error bars. *Psychological Methods, 10*(4), 389–396. Retrieved from: https://doi.org/10.1037/1082-989X.10.4.389

Bridgeman, B., Burton, N., & Cline, F. (2008). *Understanding what the numbers mean: A straightforward approach to GRE validity.* ETS GRE Board Research Report No. 04-03. Retrieved from: https://doi.org/10.1002/j.2333-8504.2008.tb02132.x

Calfas, J. (2018). Was Starbucks' racial bias training effective? Here's what these employees thought. *TIME.* Retrieved from http://time.com/5294343/starbucks-employees-racial-bias-training/

Capraro, M. M. (2005). An introduction to confidence intervals for both statistical estimates and effect sizes. *Research in the Schools, 12*(2), 22–33.

Cohen, J. (1988). *Statistical power analysis for the behavioral sciences* (2nd ed.). Hillsdale, NJ: Lawrence Erlbaum Associates.

Cohen, J. (1990). Things I have learned (so far). *The American Psychologist, 45*(12), 1304–1312. Retrieved from: https://doi.org/10.1037/0003-066X.45.12.1304

Dobbin, F., & Kalev, A. (2016). Why diversity programs fail. *Harvard Business Review.* Retrieved from https://hbr.org/2016/07/why-diversity-programs-fail

Dooling, D. J., & Danks, J. H. (1975). Going beyond tests of significance: Is psychology ready? *Bulletin of the Psychonomic Society, 5*(1), 15–17. Retrieved from: https://doi.org/10.3758/BF03336685

Eagly, A. H. (1995). The science and politics of comparing women and men. *American Psychologist, 50*(3), 145–158. Retrieved from: https://doi.org/10.1037/0003-066X.50.3.145

Goulet-Pelletier, J. C., & Cousineau, D. (2018). A review of effect sizes and their confidence intervals, Part I: The Cohen's *d* family. *Quantitative Methods for Psychology, 14*(4), 242–265. Retrieved from: https://doi.org/10.20982/tqmp.14.4.p242

Greenwald, A. G., Banaji, M. R., & Nosek, B. A. (2015). Statistically small effects of the Implicit Association Test can have societally large effects. *Journal of Personality and Social Psychology, 108*, 553–561. Retrieved from: https://doi.org/10.1037/pspa0000016

Hall, E. T. (1966). *The hidden dimension.* New York, NY: Doubleday.

Hayes, W. L. (1963). *Statistics for psychologists.* New York, NY: Holt, Rinehart & Winston.

Hebl, M. R., Foster, J. B., Mannix, L. M., & Dovidio, J. F. (2002). Formal and interpersonal discrimination: A field study of bias toward homosexual applicants. *Personality and Social Psychology Bulletin, 28*(6), 815–825. Retrieved from: https://doi.org/10.1177/0146167202289010

Hedges, L. V. (1981). Distribution theory for Glass's estimator of effect size and related estimators. *Journal of Educational Statistics, 6*(2), 107–128. Retrieved from: https://doi.org/10.3102/10769986006002107

Hoekstra, R., Morey, R. D., Rouder, J. N., & Wagenmakers, E.-J. (2014). Robust misinterpretation of confidence intervals. *Psychonomic Bulletin & Review, 21*(5), 1157–1164. Retrieved from: https://doi.org/10.3758/s13423-013-0572-3

Kling, K. C., Hyde, J. S., Showers, C. J., & Buswell, B. N. (1999). Gender differences in self-esteem: A meta-analysis. *Psychological Bulletin, 125*(4), 470–500. Retrieved from: https://doi.org/10.1037/0033-2909.125.4.470

Landy, F. J. (2008). Stereotypes, bias, and personnel decisions: Strange and stranger. *Industrial and Organizational Psychology, 1*(04), 379–392. Retrieved from: https://doi.org/10.1111/j.1754-9434.2008.00071.x

Lindsey, A., King, E., Membere, A., & Cheung, H. K. (2018). Two types of diversity training that really work. *Harvard Business Review.* Retrieved from https://hbr.org/2017/07/two-types-of-diversity-training-that-really-work

Madera, J., & Hebl, M. (2013). "Don't stigmatize": The ironic effects of equal opportunity guidelines in interviews. *Basic and Applied Social Psychology, 35*(1), 123–130. Retrieved from: https://doi.org/10.1080/01973533.2012.746601

Madera, J., King, E., & Hebl, M. (2013). Enhancing the effects of sexual orientation diversity training: The effects of setting goals and training mentors on attitudes and behaviors. *Journal of Business and Psychology, 28*(1), 79–91. Retrieved from: https://doi.org/10.1007/s10869-012-9264-7

Martell, R. F., Lane, D. M., & Emrich, C. (1996). Male-female differences: A computer simulation. *American Psychologist, 51*(2), 157–158. Retrieved from: https://doi.org/10.1037/0003-066X.51.2.157

Nittrouer, C. L., Hebl, M., Ashburn-Nardo, L., Trump-Steele, R. C. E., Lane, D., & Valian, V. V. (2018). Gender disparities in colloquium speakers at top universities. *Proceed-

ings of the National Academy of Sciences, 115(1), 104–108. Retrieved from: https://doi.org/10.1073/pnas.1708414115

Olson, B. J., Parayitam, S., & Yongjian Bao. (2007). Strategic decision making: The effects of cognitive diversity, conflict, and trust on decision outcomes. *Journal of Management, 33*(2), 196–222. Retrieved from: https://doi.org/10.1177/0149206306298657

Oswald, F. L., Mitchell, G., Blanton, H., Jaccard, J., & Tetlock, P. E. (2013). Predicting ethnic and racial discrimination: A meta-analysis of IAT criterion studies. *Journal of Personality and Social Psychology, 105*(2), 171–192. Retrieved from: https://doi.org/10.1037/a0032734

Oswald, F. L., Mitchell, G., Blanton, H., Jaccard, J., & Tetlock, P. E. (2015). Using the IAT to predict ethnic and racial discrimination: Small effect sizes of unknown societal significance. *Journal of Personality and Social Psychology, 108*(4), 562–571. Retrieved from: https://doi.org/10.1037/pspa0000023

Pek, J., & Flora, D. B. (2018). Reporting effect sizes in original psychological research: A discussion and tutorial. *Psychological Methods, 23*(2), 208–225. Retrieved from: https://doi.org/10.1037/met0000126

Pierce, C. A., Block, R. A., & Aguinis, H. (2004). Cautionary note on reporting eta-squared values from multifactor ANOVA designs. *Educational and Psychological Measurement, 64*(6), 916–924. Retrieved from: https://doi.org/10.1177/0013164404264848

Plonsky, L., & Oswald, F. L. (2014). How big is "big"? Interpreting effect sizes in L2 research. *Language Learning, 64*(4), 878–912. Retrieved from: https://doi.org/10.1111/lang.12079

Prentice, D. A., & Miller, D. T. (1992). When small effects are impressive. *Psychological Bulletin, 112*(1), 160–164. Retrieved from: https://doi.org/10.1037//0033-2909.112.1.160

Rosenthal, R. (1990). How are we doing in soft psychology? *American Psychologist, 45*(6), 775–777. Retrieved from: https://doi.org/10.1037/0003-066X.45.6.775

Rosenthal, R., & Rubin, D. B. (2003). r equivalent: A simple effect size indicator. *Psychological Methods, 8*(4), 492–496. Retrieved from: https://doi.org/10.1037/1082-989X.8.4.492

Sackett, P. R., & Yang, H. (2000). Correction for range restriction: An expanded typology. *Journal of Applied Psychology, 85*(1), 112–118. Retrieved from: https://doi.org/10.1037/0021-9010.85.1.112

Schmidt, F. L., & Oh, I.-S. (2016). The crisis of confidence in research findings in psychology: Is lack of replication the real problem? Or is it something else? *Archives of Scientific Psychology, 4*(1), 32–37. Retrieved from: https://doi.org/10.1037/arc0000029

Simonsohn, U. (2014). *We cannot afford to study effect size in the lab.* Retrieved March 29, 2019, from http://datacolada.org/20

Smith, D. B., & Plant, W. T. (1982). Sex differences in the job satisfaction of university professors. *Journal of Applied Psychology, 67*(2), 249–251. Retrieved from: https://doi.org/10.1037/0021-9010.67.2.249

Sorokowska, A., Sorokowski, P., Hilpert, P., Cantarero, K., Frackowiak, T., Ahmadi, K., ... Pierce, J. D. (2017). Preferred interpersonal distances: A global comparison. *Journal of Cross-Cultural Psychology, 48*(4), 577–592. Retrieved from: https://doi.org/10.1177/0022022117698039

Stone, D. L., Hosoda, M., Lukaszewski, K. M., & Phillips, T. N. (2008). Methodological problems associated with research on unfair discrimination against racial minorities.

Human Resource Management Review, 18(4), 243–258. Retrieved from: https://doi.org/10.1016/j.hrmr.2008.06.001

Swim, J. K., Borgida, E., Maruyama, G., & Myers, D. G. (1989). Joan McKay versus John McKay: Do gender stereotypes bias evaluations? *Psychological Bulletin, 97*, 409–429. Retrieved from: https://doi.org/10.1037/0033-2909.105.3.409

Talke, K., Salomo, S., & Kock, A. (2011). Top management team diversity and strategic innovation orientation: The relationship and consequences for innovativeness and performance. *Journal of Product Innovation Management, 28*(6), 819–832. Retrieved from: https://doi.org/10.1111/j.1540-5885.2011.00851.x

United States Equal Opportunity Employment Commission (US EEOC). (2018). *Fiscal year 2018 performance and accountability report.* Retrieved from: https://www.eeoc.gov/eeoc/plan/upload/2018par.pdf

Wilkinson, L., & the Task Force on Statistical Inference. (1999). Statistical methods in psychology journals: Guidelines and explanations. *American Psychologist, 54*, 549–604. Retrieved from: https://doi.org/10.1037//0003-066X.54.8.594

CHAPTER 5

AUTHENTICALLY DIFFERENT

Authenticity as a Diversity Management Issue

Jennifer L. Wessel, Sara E. Barth, and
Courtney M. Bryant

Minority and marginalized employees at work frequently need to hide their true selves to fit in with a majority-defined workplace culture. We focus here on inauthentic experiences at work that are commonly experienced by minority employees, including: hiding or downplaying their collective social identities, having more superficial coworker relationships, and having their opinions and experiences suppressed. After presenting a brief overview of research on authenticity in organizations, we present a model that outlines general and specific constraints that lead to inauthentic experiences for minority employees and the work-related outcomes associated with those experiences. In the final section of the paper, we present recommendations that integrate authenticity and diversity management with the aim of benefitting both organizations and employees.

The idea of being your authentic self has gained popularity recently in both organizations (Helgeson, 2015; Kabir, 2018) and in academic research (Caza, Moss, & Vough, 2018; Emmerich & Rigotti, 2017; Taris & Van den Bosch, 2018), yet it is rarely discussed in academic organizational/ Human Resources (HR) literature as a diversity management issue. When it is discussed as such an issue, extant work tends to focus on one specific type of inauthentic experience: the downplay-

Diversity and Inclusion in Organizations, pages 103–135.

ing or hiding of the minority identity itself (Martinez, Sawyer, Thoroughgood, Ruggs, & Smith, 2017; Riggle, Rostosky, Black, & Rosenkrantz, 2017). Indeed, the experience of marginalization includes feeling one has to be inauthentic about one's minority identity, but also includes other inauthentic experiences such as feeling one's authentic voice is being silenced and feeling isolated from authentic relationships. Overall, it could be argued that one of the central indignities faced by minority employees at work is the need to hide their true selves to fit in with a majority-defined workplace culture. We aim here to shed light on the need to focus on minority authenticity and show that effective diversity management needs to be integrated with effective "authenticity management."

This manuscript includes three sections. The first section will include a brief overview of research on authenticity in organizations, including clarification on what it means to be authentic at work and the proposed benefits of workplace authenticity. The second section will focus on our main argument—that authenticity is a uniquely important issue for minority employees who face profound obstacles to being their true selves at work. We will focus on three *inauthentic experiences* that minority employees commonly face: 1) downplaying/ hiding collective identities at work, 2) having more superficial work relationships, and 3) lacking voice in the organization. In the final section of the paper, we will present recommendations that integrate authenticity and diversity management with the aim of benefitting both organizations and employees. It is important to note that in this paper we use the term *minority employees* as shorthand for a category of workers that are in the numerical minority in society and/or are in the minority in their given workplace context and are thus stigmatized in that context (Crocker, Major, & Steele, 1998). We include research focused on the workplace experiences of individuals from a variety of identities including racial minorities, women in male-dominant contexts (such as leadership positions), LGBT individuals, individuals with a disability, etc.

We see our contribution as threefold. First, we aim to highlight the inauthentic experiences unique to minority employees, including those relevant to their collective identities, relationships, and individual voice. Second, we delineate the general and minority-specific workplace constraints that lead to these inauthentic experiences and subsequent negative outcomes. Lastly, we propose several recommendations that integrate positive diversity management with positive "authenticity management."

Background on Authenticity

Authenticity has existentialist philosophical roots (Golomb, 1995), but has entered the HR and other organizational research literatures in several ways. In line with the widely-used psychological definition of authentic behavior as *acting in accordance with one's true-felt self* (e.g., Goldman & Kernis, 2002; Schlegel, Hicks, Arndt, & King, 2009), several studies have examined the general degree to which one feels authentic at work and/or can express their opinions and values at work (Cable, Gino, & Staats, 2013; Sheldon, Ryan, Rawsthorne, & Ilardi, 1997; van den Bosch & Taris, 2014; Wood, Linley, Maltby, Baliousis, & Joseph, 2008). Authentic behavior at work has also been discussed specifically in terms of work-related relationships, such as being an authentic leader (e.g., Ilies, Morgeson, & Nahrgang, 2005) and having a more authentic mentoring relationship (e.g., Ragins, 2016). Additionally, authenticity has also been discussed in the diversity literature in terms of the extent to which individuals suppress their minority identities at work (e.g., transgender identity, Martinez et al; 2017; sexual minority identity, Riggle et al., 2017; Black identity, Sue, Capodilupo, & Holder, 2008). In this paper we take a more holistic and inclusive approach to authenticity by focusing on *inauthentic experiences* of minority employees, defined as *experiences at work in which one's self-relevant expressions fail to reflect one's true self.* Self-relevant expressions at work include how one expresses/ discusses their minority identity at work but also include other expressions, such as what one discusses at work and social exchanges between coworkers.

Inauthentic experiences have been linked to negative repercussions for minority and majority employees alike, such as lower well-being (Frable, Platt, & Hoey, 1998; Pachankis, 2007; Wood et al., 2008) and lower job satisfaction (e.g., Cable et al., 2013; Ellis & Riggle, 1996; van den Bosch & Taris, 2014). These negative outcomes are explained by violations of basic psychological needs such as self-verification (Swann, 1987) and self-determination (Deci & Ryan, 1995). For minority employees, the need to constantly manage an inauthentic impression at work (Roberts, 2005; Smart & Wegner, 2000;) and the disconnect between their public and private lives (Ragins, 2008) will exacerbate the identity-based stress they experience due to their outsider status and experiences of discrimination (Harrell, 2000; Meyer, 2003).

MODEL OF INAUTHENTIC EXPERIENCES
FOR MINORITY EMPLOYEES

We will briefly overview our model of inauthentic expression for minority employees (see Figure 5.1) before discussing each section in detail. This model positions inauthentic experiences as mediators between constraining environmental conditions and work-related outcomes. Although certain variables might co-occur, we do not depict all potential correlations in this model, but rather only the hypothesized causal relationships. Specifically, our model outlines how different constraints affect the extent to which minority employees experience authenticity at work, which in turn, affect work-related outcomes. The model identifies two general environmental constraints that affect experienced authenticity for all employees (and thus minority employees as well): autonomy and psychological safety. We then turn our focus to three constraining conditions that result in minority employees specifically experiencing more inauthentic experiences at work, including: fear of stigmatization, informal power, and formal power. We hypothesize that greater fear of stigmatization and lower power (both informal and for-

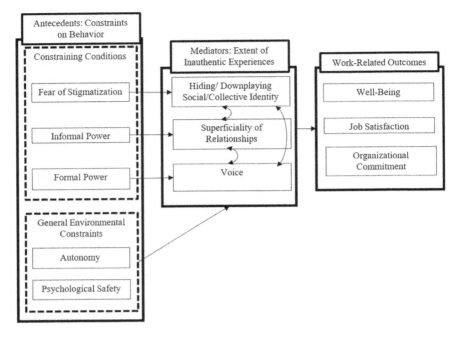

FIGURE 5.1.   Model of Inauthentic Experiences for Minority Employees

mal) increase the likelihood of minority employees having inauthentic experiences at work, including: hiding/downplaying their collective identity, having a greater number of superficial relationships at work, and having less voice at work. Lastly, we argue that minority inauthentic experiences have negative effects for minority employees on several job-relevant outcomes.

Inauthentic Experiences

We specifically chose to highlight three inauthentic experiences (i.e., hiding/downplaying one's collective identity, developing more superficial relationships, and having a general lack of voice) that 1) are more frequently experienced by or exclusive to minority employees and 2) cover inauthentic experiences tied to an individual's entire self (collective, relational, and individual; respectively). Focusing on the former point, although individuals might downplay or hide non-stigmatized majority identities for various reasons (e.g., downplaying Christianity because it is deemed inappropriate to discuss at work; Lyons, Wessel, Ghumman, Ryan, & Kim, 2014), hiding or downplaying a collective identity is more likely to be a daily occurrence for individuals with minority identities due to the potential risks involved with making that identity more salient to others and the benefits of being seen as similar to the majority (Ragins, 2008; Roberts, 2005). Examples ranging from Black professionals actively trying to distance themselves from negative stereotypes (Sue et al., 2008) to female lawyers acting purposefully more masculine or feminine as a tactic for being valued at work (Ely, 1995) to sexual minority employees actively hiding their sexual orientation from others to avoid discrimination (Ragins, Singh, & Cornwell, 2007) illustrate the difference in experiences that come from having a collective identity that requires conscious effort to "fit the mold," compared to one that naturally assimilates to a majority-dominant work environment (e.g., White, heterosexual, male).

Minority employees are also more likely to have more relationships at work that are superficial and lack the "openness, sincerity, and truthfulness" associated with relational authenticity (Kernis & Goldman, 2006, p. 300). As with hiding/downplaying identities, the experience of having superficial work relationships is not unique to minority employee populations, but we argue the general lack of integration into informal networks at work (Ibarra, 1995; Kulkarni, 2012; Mehra, Kilduff, & Brass, 1998; Sloan, Newhouse, & Thompson, 2013) increases the likelihood that minority employees will have more superficial relationships at work, compared to majority employees.

Minority employees are also less likely to feel they have a voice at work. Lack of voice, or organizational silence, is an inauthentic experience defined by the inability to "contribute freely to organizational discourse" (Bowen & Blackmon, 2003, p. 1394). As with the other two inauthentic experiences outlined above, employees with majority identities can also experience a lack of voice, particularly if they do not have a lot of formal power in the organization (Kraus, Chen, & Keltner, 2011). However, minority employees tend to have less formal power in organizations overall (Cox, 2001; Shore, Chung-Herrera, Dean, Ehrhart, Jung, Randel, Singh, 2009) and thus have a unique barrier to voice (Bell, Özbilgin, Beauregard, & Sürgevil, 2011; Bowen & Blackmon, 2003; Syed, 2014).

On the latter point, authenticity has often been discussed differently in the diversity literature than it has in the general authenticity literature. Diversity research concerning authenticity tends to focus on the extent to which minority employees have to "cover" their collective identity in majority spaces (Riggle et al., 2017; Yoshino & Smith, 2013), whereas general authenticity research tends to focus on expressing one's opinions/values at work, both as an individual (e.g., Goldman & Kernis, 2002; Wood et al., 2008) and in one's work relationships (e.g., Ilies et al., 2005). We view expressing one's collective identity, maintaining authentic work relationships, and expressing one's authentic individual voice as all critical to understanding the experiences of minority employees at work and thus include each of them in our model of inauthentic experiences for minorities at work.

Our model hypothesizes that these three inauthentic experiences mediate relationships between specific constraints (fear of stigmatization, informal power, formal power) and work-related outcomes. Hiding or downplaying a collective identity often stems from fear of being stigmatized by others (Roberts, 2005). In turn, hiding or downplaying a collective identity leads to a conflict between one's own identity and one's understanding of their organization, resulting in negative attitudes toward the organization itself (Bowen & Blackmon, 2003; Madera, King, & Hebl, 2012; Martinez et al., 2017). The lack of integration into informal networks experienced by minority employees (Combs, 2003; Cox & Nkomo, 1990; Kanter, 1977; Walton & Cohen, 2007) puts them at greater risk of relationships that are characterized by lower intimacy and support (Bell & Nkomo, 2001; Ibarra, 1995; Sloan et al., 2013). In turn, having more superficial relationships leads to negative workplace outcomes such as a lower sense of well-being and more negative job-related attitudes (Barak & Levin, 2002; Blancero & Delcampo, 2005). Lastly, the low formal power that minority employees often experience in organizations can make employees reluctant to speak up (Milliken, Morrison, & Hewlin, 2003; Pinder & Harlos, 2001). That lack of voice can subsequently lead to negative well-being and job-related attitudes (e.g., Morrison & Milliken, 2000; Rusbult, Farrell, Rogers, & Mainous, 1988). Overall, it is our contention that authenticity is a major barrier to full inclusion in the workplace for minority employees and a key explanatory mechanism of the relationships between constraining conditions and work-related outcomes.

Constraints on Authentic Behavior

As we are focused on inauthentic experiences, our antecedents are focused on those that constrain behavior, in general or for the minority specifically. Inauthentic behavior is often discussed as "constrained" behavior that fails to reflect the true self (Goldman & Kernis, 2002; Harter, 2002; Schlegel et al., 2009; Sheldon et al., 1997; Wood et al., 2008), and as such, it is important to understand various constraints felt by minority employees that then lead to inauthentic experiences. We begin by briefly discussing characteristics of the work environment that constrain behavior in general, thus increasing the likelihood of inauthentic experiences for majority and minority employees alike. Then we move our focus to the constraining conditions more specifically felt by minority employees and argue how those conditions directly lead to particular inauthentic experiences.

General Environmental Constraints

Although we are focusing specifically on the inauthentic experiences of minority/marginalized employees, there are broader environmental constraints that affect employee authenticity in general. In the following section, we focus on autonomy and psychological safety, two environmental characteristics that, when absent or low, constrain authenticity for both minority and majority employees.

Autonomy. Autonomy is viewed as a fundamental driver of authenticity (Deci & Ryan, 2000; Heppner, Kernis, Nezlek, Foster, Lakey, & Goldman, 2008). Low autonomy workplaces are characterized by rigid scripts on how to behave at work and can be either formal or informal. For example, certain organizations have emotional display rules (i.e., specifications on how to behave, like "service with smile"; Diefendorff & Richard, 2003; Grandey & Brauburger, 2002) which are often seen as formal requirements (Diefendorff, Richard, & Croyle, 2006). Jobs can also differ in how much discretion the employee has in carrying out the duties of their job in general, with individuals in low-autonomy jobs feeling like they have little personal control over how they perform their work role (Gellatly & Irving, 2001; Hackman & Oldham, 1976).

Beyond formal rules and requirements, organizations also differ in their informal climates for personal autonomy, including organizations that focus on building organizational identity to the exclusion of individual identity (Cable et al., 2013) and organizations where there are strong norms to behave in certain ways (e.g., a strong impression management culture, Harris, Gallagher, & Rossi, 2013). Formal and informal restrictions on personal autonomy lead to inauthentic expressions of self, such as faked emotional displays, less organizational voice in general, and overall concealment of one's "true self" (Brotheridge & Grandey, 2002; Brotheridge & Lee, 2003; Cable et al., 2013; Gosserand & Diefendorff, 2005; Ng & Feldman, 2012).

Psychological Safety. Psychological safety, or the experience of feeling that one will not be punished for taking an interpersonal risk (Edmonson & Lei, 2014; Kahn, 1990), is another foundational element in creating authenticity in the workplace. Employees in work environments high in psychological safety are less focused on their own self-protection (Schein, 1993), freeing them to be more open with others. Additionally, work groups high in psychological safety are characterized by interpersonal trust and mutual respect (Edmondson, 1999), which are associated with a greater degree of openness in relationships (Gardner, Avolio, Luthans, May, & Walumbwa, 2005). On the other hand, when employees do not feel that they are psychologically safe they feel that they must protect themselves and will not take risks in order to avoid damage to their image (Edmondson & Lei, 2014), which ultimately inhibits authentic expression.

Low psychological safety has been linked to inauthentic behaviors such as sharing less information and knowledge amongst coworkers (Collins & Smith, 2006; Siemsen, Roth, Balasubramanian, & Anand, 2009) and speaking up less at work (Detert & Burris, 2007; Detert & Treviño, 2010: Liang, Farh, &Farh, 2012). Overall, minority employees have more inauthentic experiences in work environments that are low in autonomy and low in psychological safety, due to the constraints these characteristics place on all employees in that environment:

Hypothesis 1: Employees in workplaces with low autonomy and low psychological safety will have more inauthentic experiences, compared to workplaces with high autonomy and high psychological safety.

Constraining Conditions for Minority Employees

Now we turn our focus to constraining conditions that characterize the experiences many minorities face in their workplace and uniquely affect their ability to be authentic at work. Specifically, we argue that fear of stigmatization and low relative power (both formal and informal) constrain minority employees in their ability to be authentic. These constraining conditions lead to inauthentic experiences that are uniquely prevalent for minority employees, including: hiding/ downplaying their collective identities, engaging in more superficial relationships, and being silenced at work. It is important to note that there are other negative conditions experienced by minority employees, such as cultural bias of majority employees and intergroup conflict (Cox, 2001; Kanter, 1977), however, we focused on those antecedents that we view as having the most direct constraints on authentic behavior.

Fear of Stigmatization. Minority individuals often anticipate discrimination and commonly experience fear of encountering prejudice or confirming other people's prejudice (Kanter, 1977; Steele, Spencer, & Aronson, 2002). In Kanter's seminal work on tokenism, she discusses how token employees (i.e., employees who are in the severe minority in a given organization) feel highly visible due to their minority status and fear being stereotyped, resulting in changes to their behavior in order to avoid being stereotyped. Steele's work on stereotype and social identity threat outlines how individuals will experience threat when the environment signals their identity is devalued and activates associated stereotypes, which in turn alters their subsequent behaviors in efforts to avoid negative stereotyping (Steele et al., 2002). Indeed, minority individuals often become hyper-aware of their own behaviors in high-threat contexts (Johns & Schmader, 2010; Schmader, Forbes, Zhang, & Mendes, 2009) and will engage in more conscious monitoring of their own behavior due to experienced stereotype and social identity threat (Beilock, Rydell, & McConnell, 2007; Forbes, Schmader, & Allen, 2008).

One of the ways minority employees cope with anticipated stigmatization is by trying to proactively manage it (Miller & Kaiser, 2001), including through hiding or downplaying their identities. Roberts (2005) discussed how minority employees engage in social identity-based impression management strategies in order to avoid stereotyping and prejudice, including deemphasizing their collective identity and emphasizing similarity to the majority identity. Related research highlights how some employees will hide their sexual orientation in order to avoid negative outcomes such as discrimination or isolation (Anderson, Croteau, Chung, & DiStefano, 2001; Chaudoir & Fisher, 2010; Ragins, 2008). A form of hiding or downplaying can also be avoidance, such as when individuals with visible disabilities avoid discussing their disabilities in order to avoid potential discrimination (Jans, Kaye, & Jones, 2012).

These identity management behaviors may help avoid discrimination or improve interpersonal interactions, but come at a cost of feeling inauthentic. For example, racial minority employees who are more socially engaging in an effort to put interaction partners at ease end up feeling inauthentic afterwards (Shelton, Richeson, Salvatore, & Trawlater, 2005). Though not specifically labeled as inauthenticity, Ragins (2008) outlines how minority employees who perceive risks to disclosing an invisible identity (e.g., sexual orientation), and thus conceal that identity at work, end up feeling "psychological incongruence" between their public and private lives (p. 209). Overall, the constant monitoring of one's professional image to counteract stereotypes (Roberts, 2005) or the vigilant concealment of one's identity altogether (Smart & Wegner, 1999) constitute inauthentic experiences that can be linked to fear of being stigmatized:

Hypothesis 2: Individuals who fear being stigmatized will be more likely to engage in hiding or downplaying the collective identities associated with that fear than those individuals who do not fear being stigmatized.

Informal Power. Informal power, also known as informal integration, refers to access to and inclusion in informal social networks and activities with coworkers (Chrobot-Mason & Aramovich, 2013; Cox, 2001). Employees who are in the demographic minority are at a greater risk to being socially isolated at work (Combs, 2003; Cox & Nkomo, 1990; Kanter, 1977; Walton & Cohen, 2007), due to both employee preferences for homophilous friend groups when in the minority, as well being excluded and/or stigmatized by majority employees (Kulik, Bainbridge, & Cregan, 2008; Mehra et al., 1998). Although the majority of this research has focused on racial minorities and women, it has also been suggested that other minority employees, such as individuals with disabilities (Kulkarni, 2012) and sexual minorities (O'Ryan & McFarland, 2010) also experience barriers to social inclusion at work. Minority employees tend to have smaller networks in general that are characterized by lower intimacy and support (Bell & Nkomo, 2001; Ibarra, 1995; Sloan et al., 2013). Although there is evidence to suggest that minority employees receive an equitable amount of career and psychosocial support from mentors (Eby, Allen, Evans, Ng, & Dubois, 2008), minority employees do experience certain barriers to accessing a mentoring relationship, such as in-group preferences (Hu, Thomas, & Lance, 2008) and a lack of minority mentors who can be of benefit by sharing experiences of being in the minority (Zambrana, Ray, Espino, Cohen, & Eliason, 2015).

This lack of integration into the organization's social networks increases the likelihood that minority employees will have more superficial, inauthentic relationships with others in the workplace. Several studies have linked relational integration and closeness with relational authenticity. Specifically, coworker friendships that include emotional support have been linked to more open communication within the relationship (Gordon & Hartman, 2009) and relational security has been related to greater authentic expression within relationships (Gillath, Sesko, Shaver, & Chun, 2010).

Minority employees may also engage in socialization activities to increase their access to or inclusion in social networks, but that can still lead to more superficial relationships. Traditional impression management strategies are performed by many employees with the goal of creating a positive image with important others at work (Jones & Pitman, 1982; Roberts, 2005). Yet, Roberts (2005) emphasizes that "impression management is especially important for people whose salient social identities differ from the majority of their colleagues," given their lack of incorporation into core social networks (p. 701). Two oft-used impression management techniques, self-promotion and ingratiation, involve several behaviors that can be inauthentic: opinion conformity, using flattery or praise, embracing values with which one does not agree, highlighting others' accomplishments, or even body language to act in a way that is preferred by a target (Bolino, Long, & Turnley, 2016; Hewlin, 2003; Jones & Pittman, 1982; Tal-Or, 2010). Researchers have also found that employees indirectly engage in impression management by forming relationships with others that are doing well with the sole purpose of self-promotion (rather than genuine connection; Long, Baer, Colquitt, Outlaw, & Dhensa-Kahlon, 2015). To the degree that impression management is inauthentic, having low informal power makes it more likely that minority employees will engage in behaviors that create superficial relationships. Overall, we argue that a greater number of minority employees' relationships will lack the typical preconditions for authenticity within a relationship, such as feelings of closeness and support or genuine connection (rather than impression management), which will then lead to a greater number of superficial relationships for those individuals at work:

> **Hypothesis 3:** Individuals who have less informal power at work will be more likely to have superficial workplace relationships than those individuals who have more informal power.

Formal Power. Formal, or structural, power refers to integration into an organization's hierarchy (Cox, 2001). There is overwhelming evidence demonstrating that employees in the minority have less formal power as compared to employees in the majority. For example, although women hold almost 52 percent of all professional-level jobs (Bureau of Labor Statistics, 2018) they hold only 25 percent of executive- and senior-level manager positions, 20 percent of seats on boards, and 6 percent of top CEO positions (Catalyst, 2018). Furthermore, women of color held only 3.8% of board seats in 2016 for the Fortune 500 (Alliance for Board Diversity/ Deloitte, 2017). In 2011, African American men made up only 5.3% of Fortune 500 boards, Latino men made up only 2.4%, and Asian men made up only 2.0%. It is also difficult to name more than a few LGB executives across all major U.S. organizations; Tim Cook of Apple, Inc., Claudia Brind-Woody of IBM. All of these statistics demonstrate that even though the U.S. is more demographically diverse than ever, formal power within organizations is not equitably distributed.

Employees with relatively low formal power may not want to jeopardize the relationships that they have with more powerful employees, leading them to be reluctant to speak up and engage in voice (Milliken et al., 2003; Pinder & Harlos,

2001). Further, those who have formal power may not welcome or elicit voice from low-power employees (Milliken et al., 2003), due to overconfidence in their own abilities (Morrison & Rothman, 2009; See, Morrison, Rothman, & Soll, 2011). When interacting with high-power individuals, those with relatively lower power are also more likely to follow emotional display rules and reign in the expression of certain emotions (Morris & Feldman, 1996). Specifically for minority employees, Bowen and Blackmon (2003) argue that they often experience a 'spiral of silence' in which they become less and less willing to express their opinions as the dominant opinion reinforces itself and becomes more powerful. It has also been suggested that employees who are demographically dissimilar from their coworkers are less likely to deviate from organizational norms in order to increase their chances of acquiring resources and avoiding negative consequences (Hewlin, 2003; Liao, Joshi, & Chuang, 2004), creating a situation where minority employees may feel constrained from authentic expression of their voice in general.

In terms of specific types of voice, when minority employees voice their concerns about prejudiced comments or actions, they are at higher risk of being met with hostility (Czopp & Monteith, 2003), viewed as a "complainer" (Kaiser & Miller, 2001), and viewed less favorably in general (ibid; Schultz & Maddox, 2013), compared to majority employees. Thus, real costs to speaking up can make minority employees particularly fearful of engaging in this type of voice. For example, Yoshino and Smith (2013) quote two employees discussing their reluctance to speak up at work concerning prejudice: an Asian employee states, "… I would never correct people if they make jokes or comments about Asian stereotypes," and an LGBT employee states, "I didn't feel I could protest when the person put in charge of diversity for our group was in fact an extremely vocal homophobe," (p 9). Sue and colleagues, who conducted an investigation of the life experiences of Black Americans, quote an individual describing the consequences of dealing with microaggressions: "you can't really say what's on your mind, or you have to filter it through so many lenses 'til it comes out sounding acceptable to whoever's listening," (p. 334, Sue et al. 2008). Overall, we argue low formal power increases the likelihood that minority employees will suppress their own authentic voice in order to hold onto the limited resources that they have:

> **Hypothesis 4:** Individuals who have less formal power at work will be less likely to express their authentic voice in their organization than those individuals who have more formal power.

Inter-relationships between Inauthentic Experiences

Although our model makes direct links between specific constraining conditions and specific inauthentic experiences (e.g., fear of stigmatization and hiding/downplaying collective identities), we are not suggesting that each constraining condition has no effect on the other two inauthentic experiences that were not directly linked to it. For example, fear of stigmatization can be associated with more superficial relationships and lack of voice, but we argue that that is due to the relationship barriers (Chaudoir & Fisher, 2010) and "spirals of silence" (Bowen & Blackmon, 2003) that stem from hiding one's identity, respectively. Likewise, lack of informal power can affect both hiding/downplaying collective identities and lack of voice through superficial and unsupportive relationships that reduce the likelihood of discussing one's collective identities (King, Mohr, Peddie, Jones, & Kendra, 2017; Wessel, 2017) or speaking one's mind (Milliken et al., 2003). Lastly, we argue that lack of formal power increases hiding/downplaying behaviors by increasing the likelihood that one will not speak up on identity-related concerns (Bell et al., 2011) and increases the number of superficial relationships by decreasing the likelihood that one will be open in relationships with more powerful people (Kraus et al., 2011).

Outcomes of Inauthentic Experiences

We posit that inauthentic experiences decrease psychological well-being and positive attitudes toward work by failing to meet basic psychological needs. Namely, most individuals want to be able to determine their own outcomes in life (i.e., self-determination, Deci & Ryan, 1995) and feel like others see them as they see themselves are viewed inaccurately by others (Swann, 1987). Fulfilling these goals via behaving authentically thus improves an individual's feelings of self-worth (Goldman & Kernis, 2002). In general, being less authentic has been linked to lower well-being (including affective well-being, stress, and burnout), both in and outside of the workplace (Goldman & Kernis, 2002; Grandey, Foo, Groth, & Goodwin, 2012; Kernis & Goldman, 2006; Sheldon et al., 1997; Wood et al., 2008), as well as more negative job-related attitudes (Cable et al., 2013; Metin, Taris, Peeters, van Beek, & van den Bosch, 2016).

Specific to the inauthentic experiences we highlight in our model, the act of concealing or downplaying one's identities involves constant self-monitoring (Smart & Wegner, 1999) and feelings of loss of collective identity (Jackson, Thoits, & Taylor, 1995; Sue et al., 2008), resulting in poorer psychological functioning (Chaudoir & Fisher, 2010; Griffith & Hebl, 2002, Roberts, 2005; Sue et al., 2008). Further, hiding/downplaying one's identity may cause the individual to experience conflict between their own identity and their understanding of their organization, resulting in negative attitudes toward the organization itself, such as lower job satisfaction and lower organizational commitment (Bowen & Blackmon, 2003; Madera, King, & Hebl, 2012; Martinez et al., 2017). When minority employees have more superficial relationships due to their isolation or exclusion, they are deprived of a large network of individuals who can help them cope with negative experiences related to being in the minority (Miller & Kaiser, 2001). Social isolation for minority employees has been linked to both a lower sense of well-being and more negative job-related attitudes (Barak & Levin, 2002; Blancero & Delcampo, 2005). Lastly, having a lack of voice at work has been associated with greater stress (Morrison & Milliken, 2000; Perlow & Repenning, 2009) and lower job-related attitudes (Rusbult et al. 1988, Withey & Cooper 1989). Specific to minority employees, Morrison and Milliken (2000) propose that the effect leadership has on organizational silence will be exacerbated when employees are demographically dissimilar from them, leading to more negative outcomes for those minority employees. Overall, we posit that the inauthentic experiences we outlined will have a negative effect on several work-related outcomes:

Hypothesis 5: The extent to which an individual has inauthentic experiences at work will negatively affect well-being, job satisfaction, and organizational commitment.

Overall, these proposed relationships provide several fruitful avenues for future research. First, although research has begun to explore the link between being in the minority and experiencing inauthenticity (e.g., Schmader & Sedikides, 2018), there has been less attention paid to specific types of inauthentic experiences that minority employees face. Quantifying those constructs and examining their antecedents and outcomes will add to our understanding of minority employee experiences. Second, there has not been a direct examination of the links between specific constraints (e.g., fear of stigmatization) and specific inauthentic experiences (e.g., hiding/downplaying identity). Specifying these relationships will improve our understanding of the process of experiencing inauthenticity at work. Lastly, much attention has been paid to minority/majority disparities in organizational and HR outcomes (see Colella, Hebl, & King, 2017 for an overview), but specific inauthentic experiences have not been tested as explanatory mechanisms of those disparities. Understanding the extent to which minority disparities in authenticity explain disparities in other workplace outcomes (e.g., job satisfaction, stress) will provide opportunities to develop interventions to reduce inequalities.

RECOMMENDATIONS

In this section we discuss common principles derived from both diversity management and authenticity literatures. Based on our model, we highlight ways in which authenticity- and diversity-related issues are overlooked in those principles, respectively. We then offer recommendations that integrate "authenticity management" with diversity management, or vice versa. These principles, issues, and recommendations are outlined in Table 5.1.

Principle: Promote a bias-free environment through a commitment to standardized formal policies and employee expectations

Diversity research often suggests promoting a bias-free environment through the standardization and enforcement of formal policies, procedures, and employee expectations (e.g., Lindsey, King, McCausland, Jones, & Dunleavy, 2013; Ryan & Wessel, 2008; Shen, Chanda, D'netto, & Monga, 2009; Stone-Romero & Stone, 2008). Standardizing policies related to the recruitment and selection process,

TABLE 5.1.   Proposed Integrative Recommendations for Promoting Inclusive Authenticity

	Principles	Issues/Limitations	Recommendations
Diversity Management Principles	Promote a bias-free environment through a commitment to standardized formal policies and employee expectations	Standardized policies may encourage inauthentic behaviors for particular groups	Formal policies and employee expectations should be examined to see if standardized criteria have differential effects on particular groups in terms of self-expression, and should be revised accordingly
		Formal policies will not be successful in creating a positive diversity climate without addressing inequities in authentic voice	Managers must allow for, seek out, and amplify marginalized voices
	Develop mentoring and networking programs targeting minority employees	Mentoring/networking initiatives will be less successful if minority mentees cannot be authentic	Rather than solely focusing on networking, social support, and instrumental needs, organizations should incorporate promoting authenticity into the mentoring and networking programs
Authenticity Management Principles	Promote a positive "authenticity climate" in which individuals feel open to express themselves	There are differences in the perceived risk to being authentic for majority and minority employees	Providing and supporting Employee Resource Groups (ERGs) can provide spaces where minority employees can feel most welcome to be authentic
	Encourage leaders to be authentic	Minority employees may benefit less from authentic leadership if the relationship is more superficial	Having representation at the top levels of the organization will help encourage minority follower authenticity

performance evaluations, and employee appearance or behavior is thought to help eliminate biases by presenting more objective, rather than subjective standards, allowing all employees an equal opportunity for success (Graves & Powell, 2008; Kossek, Lobel, & Brown, 2006; Mitchell, Koen, & Moore, 2013; Reskin & McBrier, 2000; Riger, 1991; Triana, Garcia, & Colella, 2010).

Issue: Standardized policies may encourage inauthentic behaviors for particular groups

Although implementing standards and reducing subjectivity that could adversely affect minority employees is a key aspect of diversity management, it is essential that organizational leaders go the extra step and ask themselves: *whose standards are they?* Standards that are created by majority group members without taking into account the diverse pool of employees affected by them may inadvertently reflect the dominant culture to the exclusion of other cultures (Stone-Romero & Stone, 2008), encouraging inauthenticity in minority employees via assimilation (Cox, 2001). For example, organizations often impose dress code policies that are designed to present a uniform image to external agents (Hay & Middlemiss, 2002; Warhaust & Nickson, 2007). Although standardized dress codes seem fair on face value, these standards can be wrought with Eurocentric and heterosexual beauty standards that adversely affect minority populations by limiting the expression of their minority identities (Rossette & Dumas, 2007; Taylor, Burke, Wheatley, & Sompayrac, 2011). For example, a 2014 army regulation included hairstyle standards that disproportionately precluded women of African descent or mixed race from wearing their hair in a style that felt authentic to them in order to assimilate to Eurocentric standards (Carroll & Millham, 2014; Rosado, 2003; Rosette & Dumas, 2007). This regulation required these minority employees to downplay their collective identity and assimilate to the majority.

Further, certain selection or promotion criteria may be standardized, but nonetheless disproportionately affect how minority employees express their collective identities. For example, the "think manager, think male" finding suggests that individuals tend to associate the criteria needed to be a successful manager (particularly in male-dominated industries) with characteristics more associated with being male (Duehr & Bono, 2006; Eagly & Karau, 2002; Wessel, Hagiwara, Ryan, & Kermond, 2015). This association can make women being evaluated for leadership positions feel that they need to behave in a stereotypically masculine way to be accepted and promoted (Ellemers, Rink, Derks, & Ryan, 2012; Ely, 1995), even if masculine behavior does not feel authentic to them. Individuals with disabilities are also less likely to be associated with these types of agentic terms, such as "individualistic" and "assertive" (Stone & Colella, 1996), potentially causing those individuals to fight that stereotype by behaving in overly agentic ways, even in cases where that does not fit their true sense of self. Overall, promoting standardized practices and policies may inadvertently damage the well-being of minority employees by pressuring them to express their collective identities in a way that fits in with the majority.

Recommendation 1: Formal policies and employee expectations should be examined for any differential effects of standardized criteria on minority employee self-expression and revised accordingly

We suggest organizations evaluate their formal procedures and policies for adverse effects on minority employees and refine their standards accordingly. In general, when organizations have a diverse body of people making decisions, those decisions tend to be more equitable for minority employees (Cook & Glass, 2015; Stainbeck & Kwon, 2012), suggesting that one way in which to avoid implementing standards that systematically target one group's ability to be authentic is to seek out and listen to multiple perspectives when crafting standards (Kamenou & Fearfull, 2006; Shen et al., 2009). For example, Chevron and Ernst & Young paid attention to the needs of their transgender employees and added gender transitioning guidelines to their standard dress codes, thus creating procedures that take into account the specific circumstances of their transgender employees (Taylor et al., 2011). This also requires being open to altering policies after receiving feedback about adverse effects. Following the above example of the 2014 army grooming regulations, the U.S. military listened to the grievances of service members and lawmakers and agreed to review and change the policies in the new regulation regarding hairstyles (Joachim, 2014). The new rules allowed African-American women service members to maintain their jobs without restrictions on their authentic self-expression. Including the voices of minority populations both in the creation of new policies and in the revision of existing policies are key steps in creating inclusive organizations where employees are free to be themselves.

We also suggest organizations attempt to identify any subtle cues in policies and procedures that signal a code of conduct that requires inauthenticity for certain groups of employees. In developing personnel practices, for example, it is important for organizations to recognize that the ways in which they communicate to their employees send coded messages as to expected behavior. Gaucher and colleagues (2011) found that job advertisements that used masculine-associated wording (like *adventurous, assertive, dominant*) signaled to women that they would not belong at that organization, regardless of their own qualifications. Organizations can also make sure their signals promote authenticity, rather than exclusion. For example, pro-LGBT policies and practices, such as including sexual orientation in the company's nondiscrimination policy and explicitly welcoming same-sex partners to company social events, have been linked to greater employee sexual orientation disclosure (Griffith & Hebl, 2002; Ragins & Cornwell, 2001; Wessel, 2017), suggesting a link between organizational signals of acceptance and authentic expression of minority identities. By taking the extra step to examine selection criteria, performance evaluation standards, and other organizational practices for these types of inadvertent signals, organizations will be able to be more inclusive in their standards of desirable behavior, thus lessening the likelihood that minority employees will feel they have to downplay or hide their collective identities at work.

Issue: Formal standardized policies will not be successful in creating a positive diversity climate without addressing inequities in authentic voice

Standardized organizational approaches to managing diversity, such as "color-blind" approaches, can result in the silencing of minority employees. Color-blind philosophies are based on the idea of seeing all people the same and not focusing on the uniqueness of individuals (Ely & Thomas, 2001; Markus, Steele, & Steele, 2002; Plaut, Thomas, & Goren, 2009). Although "treating everyone the same" seems like a goal consistent with good diversity management, the colorblind approach has been shown to reduce the likelihood of identifying and reporting racial discrimination and leads to the justification of group-based inequality by denying the unique experiential reality of minority employees (Apfelbaum, Pauker, Sommer, & Ambady, 2010; Knowles, Lowery, Hogan, & Chow, 2009; Liberman, 2013).

Beyond color-blind approaches, other standardized policies or procedures may not account for the issues minority employees have with being empowered to speak up to the organization. As stated earlier, minority individuals are uniquely vulnerable to backlash from reporting prejudice or discrimination (Czopp & Monteith, 2003; Kaiser & Miller, 2001; Schultz & Maddox, 2013), meaning that having formalized policies for reporting these types of workplace violations will not be enough to elicit voice if the targets of said mistreatment are fearful of the consequences of speaking up. In summary, organizations can have standardized and formalized procedures for reporting discrimination or harassment but if minority employees are silenced informally or lack the voice to speak up (even through formalized channels), the policies will not work.

Recommendation 2: Managers must seek out marginalized voices and reduce the risk for expressing authentic voice for those individuals

First and foremost, organizations must have safe mechanisms for employees to adequately voice their concerns and experiences that are available to all employees. This requires giving thought to issues of confidentiality and ease of access. For example, an internal investigation of a highly publicized harassment case at *NBC News* found that employees were reticent to file formal complaints, in part, because the Human Resources department had glass-walled offices and employees visiting the offices were easily seen by their coworkers (Grynbaum & Koblin, 2018). As another example, after allegations related to both sexual and racial harassment, *Fox News* began more openly promoting their hotline for reporting misconduct as one remedy for combatting a workplace culture in which many did not speak out (Snider, 2017). In addition to these individual anecdotes, Cortina and Magley (2003) found that low power victims of interpersonal treatment (i.e., those with relatively less power in the organization or compared to the perpetrator) received significantly more retaliation at work for confronting the person who mistreated them. This underlines the importance of having clear policies in place to protect individuals who need to speak out, particularly those with the least formal power.

Beyond creating clear mechanisms for reporting misconduct, we argue that to truly empower individuals to speak up and out against identity-based concerns such as prejudice and discrimination, organizations must do more than *allow* for employee voice. Organizations must *elicit* and *amplify* voice. Given the barriers to minority voice that we previously outlined, we recommend that organizations actively seek out minority voices in workplace conversations and amplify their opinions and experiences, creating a culture of voice. For example, women on the staff in President Obama's administration ensured that their voices were acknowledged by male staff by using amplification strategies such as repeating other women's ideas and verbally crediting the women who initially voiced the idea (Hatch, 2016). This example supports Miller and Kaiser's (2001) coping with stigmatization model, which suggests that collective action can help individuals cope with identity-based mistreatment based and gain more power as a group.

However, we are not suggesting that minority employees are solely responsible for empowering their own voices. In general, employee silence is associated with the perception that speaking up will lead to negative outcomes from those in power and will not lead to anything constructive (Milliken, Morrison, & Hewlin, 2003). Indeed, managers tend to view employees who speak up in ways that challenge the status quo as less loyal, more threatening, and poorer performers (Burris, 2012). However, research suggests that managers who listen to their employees, express interest in their employees' ideas, and show a willingness to take action based on employee ideas or opinions increase employee feelings of psychological safety and subsequent use of voice (Detert & Burris, 2007). Overall, we suggest that organizations show a clear path for formally voicing complaints and for more general voice within the workplace, as well as train managers and other organizational leaders to actively express interest in their employees' opinions and experiences.

Principle: Develop mentoring and networking programs targeting minority employees

Mentoring and networking programs targeting minorities have been put forth as important interventions for improving the career trajectories of minority employees (Blood, Ullrich, Hirshfeld-Becker, Seely, Connelly, Warfield, & Emans, 2012; Dunham, Weathers, Hoo, & Heintz, 2012; Giscombe, 2017; Murrell & Blake-Beard, 2017). Mentoring has been shown to have positive effects on careers (Eby et al., 2008; Kammeyer-Mueller, & Judge, 2008) by providing both social and career–related resources. However, mentoring may not succeed in building strong relationships and advancing careers in the workplace if the relationship is not authentic.

Issue: Mentoring or networking initiatives will be less successful if minority mentees cannot be authentic

As stated earlier, minority employees are often more isolated in their organizations (Combs, 2003; Cox & Nkomo, 1990; Kanter, 1977; Kulkarni, 2012; O'Ryan & McFarland, 2010; Walton & Cohen, 2007), meaning that mentoring initiatives should be particularly useful to this population as a means for gaining informal and formal power. However, even if power is increased for minority employees, we argue other constraints will still lead to more superficial relationships with mentors and peers if not counteracted. Specifically, minority employees will continue to feel isolated from coworkers and mentors if they feel they cannot discuss their collective identities at work due to fear of stigmatization.

Recommendation 3: Organizations and mentors should incorporate authenticity goals into mentoring relationships and programs

The mentoring research traditionally focuses on psychosocial support and career-focused support (Kram, 1983), but rarely discusses the role of authenticity (see Ragins, 2016 for an exception). Being more open about oneself has been associated with better mentoring outcomes (Blickle, Schneider, Perrewé, Blass, & Ferris, 2008; Wanberg, Welsh, & Kammeyer-Mueller, 2007), as it strengthens the relationship between mentor and mentee (Ghosh, 2014). Ragins (2016) discusses the importance of "relational mentoring," which differs from traditional ideas of mentorship by emphasizing relational processes such as building trust, mutual disclosure, and relational authenticity.

We suggest that organizations encourage their mentors to engage in relational mentoring (that includes relational authenticity) and provide training for how to do so. Ragins (2016) offers several suggestions for creating an authentic mentoring relationship via a relational mentoring approach, including signaling one's willingness to listen and sharing one's own emotions, opinions and experiences. Although relational mentoring is a newer concept in the literature, there is empirical support for a link between mentoring relationships high in relational qualities and better outcomes for mentees, such as higher self-esteem and less loneliness (Liang, Tracy, Taylor, & Williams, 2002). Importantly, minority mentees should not be punished for being inauthentic. Encouraging mentors to engage in a mentoring style that elicits open exchange should help minority mentees overcome barriers to being themselves within their mentoring relationships.

Principle: Promote a positive "authenticity climate" in which individuals feel open to express themselves

Many organizations are now encouraging their employees to "bring their whole selves to work" (Brooks, 2013; Douglas, 2013) and intentionally building a climate where their employees feel free to be themselves. In research, Grandey and colleagues (2012) focused on organizational climates that promote emotional authenticity (i.e., climates where one feels free to express one's authentic emotions) and found that health care providers experienced less burnout due to patient interactions when their work unit had a high climate for emotional authenticity. Similarly, Porke and Seo (2017) proposed that organizational climates that allow for experiential authenticity (focusing on emotions) will benefit in terms of employee performance across several domains (i.e., relationships, productivity, creativity, reliability). Overall, both organizations and researchers have shown support for the idea of creating work climates that accommodate authentic self-expression.

Issue: Minority employees experience greater obstacles to authenticity, compared to majority employees

As our model posits, fear of discrimination and lack of power create a situation where minority employees are less likely to authentically express themselves at work. Thus, a positive climate for authenticity may not be sufficient for encouraging authentic self-expression for minority employees without addressing these obstacles.

Recommendation 4: Organizations should provide and support employee resource groups or other spaces that promote authentic expression for minority employees

Employee Resource Groups (ERGs; also called affinity groups, employee networks, employee forums, etc.) are employee-led groups typically based on a specific identity (e.g. women, LGBT, Generation Z) where members collectively work towards group-level or organizational goals (Kaplan, Sabin, & Smaller-Swift, 2009; Welbourne, Rolf, & Schlachter, 2017). ERGs are meant to foster diversity and inclusion, innovation, information sharing, social and professional support, and advocacy (Kravitz, 2008; McGrath & Sparks, 2005; Welbourne et al., 2017). Although there is a dearth of research connecting ERGs to individual outcomes, there is some evidence that these groups can empower minority employees through increased voice and collective action (Briscoe & Saffod, 2010; Colgan & McKearney, 2012). Because members of ERGs all identify as the same identity of interest, ERGs provide a space that does not pose unequal risks to authenticity. ERGs are also typically horizontal rather than hierarchical, eliminating the power dynamics that could create within-group risks to being authentic (Welborne et al., 2016). The space that ERGs provide can be a starting point for marginalized employees to be open about their collective identities, forge authentic relationships, and use their authentic voice. As one example, Ford's network for Gay, Lesbian or Bisexual Employees (GLOBE) has made it a goal of theirs to contribute to the authenticity of their corporate environment (Catalyst, 2012). They were instrumental in shaping domestic partner benefits for employees and increasing cultural competence around diversity that advanced inclusion across the company (Morgan, 2015). This type of collective voice removes barriers of formal and informal power and provides safe channels for marginalized employees to express themselves and their viewpoints.

Organizational leaders can also provide forums or discussion series where minority employees feel safe to discuss tough issues related to their identities authentically. CEOs at companies such as PriceWaterhouseCooper and U.S. Bank have engaged their workforces in such activities, providing a space for authentic discourse around identity-related issues (e.g., race, privilege) that unearthed both tensions and subsequent healing (McCluney, Roberts, & Wooten, 2017; McGirt, 2016). Just as a space to discuss emotional hardships improved the work lives of health care employees (Grandey et al., 2012), we posit that the creation of a space that is intentionally designed for authentic expression about issues affecting minority employees will help buffer concerns minority employees have about voicing their authentic opinions and create a more positive work environment.

Principle: Encourage leaders to be authentic

One of the proposed benefits of authentic leadership is positive behavioral modeling (Illies et al., 2005), in which leader demonstrations of authenticity are thought to establish organizational norms that positively affect employees. Indeed, research supports a positive relationship between authentic leaders and follower outcomes such as basic needs satisfaction (Leroy, Ansel, Gardner, & Sels, 2015), affective commitment (Kiersh & Byrne, 2015), turnover intentions (ibid), job satisfaction (Wong & Laschinger, 2013), and performance (ibid).

Issue: Minority employees will benefit less from authentic leadership if the relationship is more superficial

In order for authentic leaders to positively affect their followers, the leader-follower relationship must be active and genuine on both sides (Leroy et al., 2015). Followers must acknowledge that the leader is authentic and be open to an authentic relationship with the leader (Eagly, 2005), otherwise they are less likely to receive the benefits of having an authentic leader. Given the increased potential risk to being authentic for minority followers, we argue that leaders in the majority demonstrating authentic behavior may not signal safety for minority employees, thus not eliciting the positive outcomes typically associated with authentic leadership.

Recommendation 5: Organizations should have diverse representation at the top levels of the organization to help increase the benefits of authentic leadership for all

We argue that having more authentic leaders from traditionally underrepresented groups will help encourage authenticity amongst minority employees. Minority employees will benefit from being able to share identity-related experiences with more senior employees (Zambrana et al., 2015), decreasing the fear of stigmatization associated with their identities. For example, lesbian, gay, and bisexual (LGB) employees who have LGB supervisors are less likely to fear disclosing their sexual orientation at work than those who do not (Ragins, Singh, & Cornwell, 2007). Minority leaders are also more likely to speak out on issues related to discrimination (Bell & Nkomo, 2001), and tend to be more supportive of diversity-related initiatives (Kalev, Dobbin, & Kelly, 2006; Raeburn, 2004), increasing the safety and acceptance felt by minority employees. Overall, we argue that the presence of authentic minority leaders signals to minority employees that they can express their true-felt experiences and be supported by someone with structural power.

CONCLUSION

Researchers and practitioners alike have espoused the benefits of authentic self-expression at work and the costs of inauthenticity. Being authentic, by definition, will entail a different experience for each and every employee and comes with a different set of risks. Particularly for minority employees, authentic self-expression is constrained by specific conditions that uniquely affect those who differ from the majority culture. However, organizations can help increase authenticity and inclusion simultaneously through evidence-based interventions that are grounded in both authenticity and diversity management literatures.

ACKNOWLEDGEMENT

Ms. Bryant's contribution is based upon work supported by the National Science Foundation Graduate Research Fellowship Program under Grant No. (DGE-1848739). Any opinions, findings, and conclusions or recommendations expressed in this material are those of the author(s) and do not necessarily reflect the views of the National Science Foundation.

REFERENCES

Alliance for Board Diversity/Deloitte. (2017). *Missing pieces report: The 2016 board diversity census of women and minorities on Fortune 500 boards.* Alliance for Board Diversity. Retrieved from https://www2.deloitte.com/us/en/pages/center-for-board-effectiveness/articles/board-diversity-census-missing-pieces.html

Anderson, M. Z., Croteau, J. M., Chung, Y. B., & DiStefano, T. M. (2001). Developing an assessment of sexual identity management for lesbian and gay workers. *Journal of Career Assessment, 9*(3), 243–260.

Apfelbaum, E. P., Pauker, K., Sommers, S. R., & Ambady, N. (2010). In blind pursuit of racial equality? *Psychological Science, 21,* 1587–1592.

Barak, M. E. M., & Levin, A. (2002). Outside of the corporate mainstream and excluded from the work community: A study of diversity, job satisfaction and well-being. *Community, Work & Family, 5*(2), 133–157.

Beilock, S. L., Rydell, R. J., & McConnell, A. R. (2007). Stereotype threat and working memory: mechanisms, alleviation, and spillover. *Journal of Experimental Psychology: General, 136*(2), 256–276.

Bell, E. L. E., & Nkomo, S. M. (2001). *Our separate ways: Black and White women and the struggle for professional identity.* Boston, MA: Harvard Business School Press.

Bell, M. P., Özbilgin, M. F., Beauregard, T. A., & Sürgevil, O. (2011). Voice, silence, and diversity in 21st century organizations: Strategies for inclusion of gay, lesbian, bisexual, and transgender employees. *Human Resource Management, 50*(1), 131–146.

Blancero, D. M., & DelCampo, R. G. (2005). Hispanics in the workplace: Experiences with mentoring and networking. *Employment Relations Today, 32*(2), 31–38.

Blickle, G., Schneider, P. B., Perrewé, P. L., Blass, F. R., & Ferris, G. R. (2008). The roles of self-disclosure, modesty, and self-monitoring in the mentoring relationship: A longitudinal multi-source investigation. *The Career Development International, 13*(3), 224–240.

Blood, E. A., Ullrich, N. J., Hirshfeld-Becker, D., Seely, E. W., Connelly, M. T., Warfield, C. A., & Emans, S. J. (2012). Academic women faculty: Are they finding the mentoring they need? *Journal of Women›s Health, 21*(11), 1201–1208.

Bolino, M., Long, D., & Turnley, W. (2016). Impression management in organizations: Critical questions, answers, and areas for future research. *Annual Review of Organizational Psychology and Organizational Behavior, 3*, 377–406.

Bowen, F., & Blackmon, K. (2003). Spirals of silence: The dynamic effects of diversity on organizational voice. *Journal of Management Studies, 40*(6), 1393–1417.

Briscoe, F. & Safford, S. (2010). Employee affinity groups: Their evolution from social movement vehicles to employer strategies. *Perspectives on Work, 14*(1), 42–45.

Brooks, C. (2013). Corner office: Diversity means bringing 'whole self' to work. *Roger Crockett.* Retrieved From: http://rocrockett.com/2013/09/corner-office-diversity-means-bringing-whole-self-to-work/.

Brotheridge, C. M., & Lee, R. T. (2003). Development and validation of the emotional labour scale. *Journal of Occupational and Organizational Psychology, 76*(3), 365–379.

Brotheridge, C., & Grandey, A. (2002). Emotional labor and burnout: Comparing two perspectives of "people work." *Journal of Vocational Behavior, 60*, 17–39.

Bureau of Labor Statistics. (2018). *Employed persons by detailed occupation, sex, race, and Hispanic or Latino ethnicity.* Retrieved from: http://www.bls.gov/cps/cpsaat11.htm.

Burris, E. R. (2012). The risks and rewards of speaking up: Managerial responses to employee voice. *Academy of Management Journal, 55*(4), 851–875.

Cable, D. M., Gino, F., & Staats, B. R. (2013). Breaking them in or eliciting their best? Reframing socialization around newcomers' authentic self-expression. *Administrative Science Quarterly, 58*(1), 1–36.

Carroll, C., & Millham, M. (2014). Black congresswomen ask Hagel to review hairstyle guidance. *Stars and Stripes, Online.* Retrieved from: https://www.stripes.com/news/army/black-congresswomen-ask-hagel-to-review-hairstyle-guidance-1.277405

Catalyst (June 1, 2012). *Case Study: Ford Motor Company—GLOBE: Fostering LGBT inclusion, valuing diversity, and empowering authenticity.* Retrieved from: https://www.catalyst.org/research/ford-motor-company-globe-fostering-lgbt-inclusion-valuing-diversity-and-empowering-authenticity/

Catalyst. (June 1, 2018). *Pyramid: Women in S&P 500 Companies.* Retrieved from: https://www.catalyst.org/knowledge/women-sp-500-companies.

Caza, B. B., Moss, S., & Vough, H. (2017). From synchronizing to harmonizing: The process of authenticating multiple work identities. *Administrative Science Quarterly, 63*(4), 703–745.

Chaudoir, S. R., & Fisher, J. D. (2010). The disclosure processes model: Understanding disclosure decision making and postdisclosure outcomes among people living with a concealable stigmatized identity. *Psychological Bulletin, 136*(2), 236.

Chrobot-Mason, D., & Aramovich, N. P. (2013). The psychological benefits of creating an affirming climate for workplace diversity. *Group & Organization Management, 38*(6), 659–689.

Colella, A., Hebl, M., & King, E. (2017). One hundred years of discrimination research in the *Journal of Applied Psychology*: A sobering synopsis. *Journal of Applied Psychology, 102*(3), 500–513.

Colgan, F., & McKearney, A. (2012). Visibility and voice in organisations: Lesbian, gay, bisexual, and transgendered employee networks. *Equality, Diversity and Inclusion: An International Journal, 31*(4), 359–378.

Collins, C. J., & Smith, K. G. (2006). Knowledge exchange and combination: The role of human resource practices in the performance of high-technology firms. *Academy of Management Journal, 49*(3), 544–560.

Combs, G. M. (2003). The duality of race and gender for managerial African American women: Implications of informal social networks on career advancement. *Human Resource Development Review, 2*(4), 385–405.

Cortina, L. M., & Magley, V. J. (2003). Raising voice, risking retaliation: Events following interpersonal mistreatment in the workplace. *Journal of Occupational Health Psychology, 8*(4), 247–265.

Cox Jr, T. (2001). The multicultural organization. In M. H. Albrecht (Ed.), *International HRM: Managing diversity in the workplace* (pp. 245–260). Oxford, UK: Blackwell Publishers Ltd.

Cox Jr, T., & Nkomo, S. M. (1990). Invisible men and women: A status report on race as a variable in organization behavior research. *Journal of Organizational Behavior, 11*(6), 419–431.

Crocker, J., Major, B., & Steele, C. (1998). Social Stigma. In D. T. Gilbert, & S. T. Fiske (Eds.), *The handbook of social psychology* (Vol. 2, pp. 504–553). New York, NY: McGraw-Hill.

Czopp, A. M., & Monteith, M. J. (2003). Confronting prejudice (literally): Reactions to confrontations of racial and gender bias. *Personality and Social Psychology Bulletin, 29*(4), 532–544.

Deci, E. L., & Ryan, R. M. (1995). Human autonomy: The basis for true self-esteem. In M. H. Kernis (Ed.), *Plenum series in social/clinical psychology. Efficacy, agency, and self-esteem* (pp. 31–49). New York, NY, US: Plenum Press.

Deci, E. L., & Ryan, R. M. (2000). The" what" and" why" of goal pursuits: Human needs and the self-determination of behavior. *Psychological Inquiry, 11*(4), 227–268.

Detert, J. R., & Burris, E. R. (2007). Leadership behavior and employee voice: Is the door really open? *Academy of Management Journal, 50*(4), 869–884.

Detert, J. R., & Treviño, L. K. (2010). Speaking up to higher-ups: How supervisors and skip-level leaders influence employee voice. *Organization Science, 21*(1), 249–270.

Diefendorff, J. M., & Richard, E. M. (2003). Antecedents and consequences of emotional display rule perceptions. *Journal of Applied Psychology, 88*(2), 284–294.

Diefendorff, J. M., Richard, E. M., & Croyle, M. H. (2006). Are emotional display rules formal job requirements? Examination of employee and supervisor perceptions. *Journal of Occupational and Organizational Psychology, 79*(2), 273–298.

Douglas, D. (2013). The freedom to be your whole self at work. *Top Golf.* Retrieved from: http://topgolf.com/blog/post/2013/07/the-freedom-to-be-your-whole-self-at-work/

Duehr, E. E., & Bono, J. E. (2006). Men, women, and managers: Are stereotypes finally changing? *Personnel Psychology, 59*, 815–846.

Dunham C. C., Weathers, L. H., Hoo, K., & Heintz, C. (2012). I just need someone who knows the ropes: Mentoring and female faculty in science and engineering. *Journal of Women and Minorities in Science and Engineering, 18*(1), 79–96.

Eagly, A. H. (2005). Achieving relational authenticity in leadership: Does gender matter? *The Leadership Quarterly, 16*(3), 459–474.

Eagly, A. H., & Karau, S. J. (2002). Role congruity theory of prejudice toward female leaders. *Psychological Review, 109*(3), 573–598.

Eby, L. T., Allen, T. D., Evans, S. C., Ng, T., & DuBois, D. L. (2008). Does mentoring matter? A multidisciplinary meta-analysis comparing mentored and non-mentored individuals. *Journal of Vocational Behavior, 72*(2), 254–267.

Edmondson, A. (1999). Psychological safety and learning behavior in work teams. *Administrative Science Quarterly, 44*(2), 350–383.

Edmondson, A. C., & Lei, Z. (2014). Psychological safety: The history, renaissance, and future of an interpersonal construct. *Annual Review of Organizational Psychology and Organizational Behavior, 1*(1), 23–43.

Ellemers, N., Rink, F., Derks, B., & Ryan, M. K. (2012). Women in high places: When and why promoting women into top positions can harm them individually or as a group (and how to prevent this). *Research in Organizational Behavior, 32,* 163–187.

Ellis, A. L., & Riggle, E. D. (1996). The relation of job satisfaction and degree of openness about one's sexual orientation for lesbians and gay men. *Journal of Homosexuality, 30*(2), 75–85.

Ely, R. J. (1995). The power in demography: Women's social constructions of gender identity at work. *Academy of Management Journal, 38*(3), 589–634.

Ely, R. J., & Thomas, D. A. (2001). Cultural diversity at work: The effects of diversity perspectives on work group processes and outcomes. *Administrative Science Quarterly, 46*(2), 229–273.

Emmerich, A. I., & Rigotti, T. (2017). Reciprocal relations between work-related authenticity and intrinsic motivation, work ability and depressivity: A two-wave study. *Frontiers in Psychology, 8,* 1–12.

Forbes, C. E., Schmader, T., & Allen, J. J. (2008). The role of devaluing and discounting in performance monitoring: A neurophysiological study of minorities under threat. *Social Cognitive and Affective Neuroscience, 3*(3), 253–261.

Frable, D. E., Platt, L., & Hoey, S. (1998). Concealable stigmas and positive self-perceptions: feeling better around similar others. *Journal of Personality and Social Psychology, 74*(4), 909–922.

Gardner, W. L., Avolio, B. J., Luthans, F., May, D. R., & Walumbwa, F. (2005). "Can you see the real me?" A self-based model of authentic leader and follower development. *The Leadership Quarterly, 16*(3), 343–372.

Gaucher, D., Friesen, J., & Kay, A. C. (2011). Evidence that gendered wording in job advertisements exists and sustains gender inequality. *Journal of Personality and Social Psychology, 101*(1), 109–128.

Gellatly, I. R., & Irving, P. G. (2001). Personality, autonomy, and contextual performance of managers. *Human Performance, 14*(3), 231–245.

Ghosh, R. (2014). Antecedents of mentoring support: A meta-analysis of individual, relational, and structural or organizational factors. *Journal of Vocational Behavior, 84*(3), 367–384.

Gillath, O., Sesko, A. K., Shaver, P. R., & Chun, D. S. (2010). Attachment, authenticity, and honesty: Dispositional and experimentally induced security can reduce self- and other-deception. *Journal of Personality and Social Psychology, 98,* 841–855.

Giscombe, K. (2017). Creating effective formal mentoring programs for women of color. In A. J. Murrell, S. Blake-Beard (Eds.), *Mentoring diverse leaders: Creating change for people, processes, and paradigms* (pp. 145–157). New York, NY: Routledge/ Taylor & Francis Group.

Goldman, B. M., & Kernis, M. H. (2002). The role of authenticity in healthy psychological functioning and subjective well-being. *Annals of the American Psychotherapy Association, 5*(6), 18–20.

Golomb, J. (1995). *In search of authenticity.* London, UK: Routledge

Gordon, J., & Hartman, R. L. (2009). Affinity-seeking strategies and open communication in peer workplace relationships. *Atlantic Journal of Communication, 17*(3), 115–125.

Gosserand, R. H., & Diefendorff, J. M. (2005). Emotional display rules and emotional labor: the moderating role of commitment. *Journal of Applied Psychology, 90*(6), 1256–1264.

Grandey, A., Foo, S. C., Groth, M., & Goodwin, R. E. (2012). Free to be you and me: A climate of authenticity alleviates burnout from emotional labor. *Journal of Occupational Health Psychology, 17*(1), 1–14.

Grandey, A. A., & Brauburger, A. (2002). The Emotion regulation behind the customer service smile. In R. Lord & R. Klimoski & R. Kanfer (Eds.), *Emotions in the workplace: Understanding the structure and role of emotions in organizational behavior* (pp. 260–294). San Francisco, CA: Jossey-Bass.

Graves, L. M., & Powell, G. N. (2008). Sex and race discrimination in personnel decisions. In Susan Cartwright and Cary L. Cooper (Eds.) *Oxford handbook of personnel psychology* (pp. 438–463). Oxford,UK: Oxford University Press.

Griffith, K. H., & Hebl, M. R. (2002). The disclosure dilemma for gay men and lesbians: "Coming out" at work. *Journal of Applied Psychology, 87*(6), 1191–1199.

Grynbaum, M. M., & Koblin, J. (2018). NBC investigation finds no wrongdoing in handling of Matt Lauer case. *The New York Times, Online.* Retrieved from https://www. nytimes.com/2018/05/09/business/media/matt-lauer-nbc-investigation.html.

Hackman, J. R., & Oldham, G. R. (1976). Motivation through the design of work: Test of a theory. *Organizational Behavior and Human Performance, 16*(2), 250–279.

Harrell, S. P. (2000). A multidimensional conceptualization of racism-related stress: Implications for the well-being of people of color. *American Journal of Orthopsychiatry, 70*, 42–57.

Harris, K. J., Gallagher, V. C., & Rossi, A. M. (2013). Impression management (IM) behaviors, IM culture, and job outcomes. *Journal of Managerial Issues, 25*(2), 154–171.

Harter, S. 2002. Authenticity. In C. R. Snyder & S. J. Lopez (Eds.), *The handbook of positive psychology* (pp, 382–394). New York, NY: Oxford University Press.

Hatch, J. (2016, September 15). How the women on Obama's staff made sure their voices were heard. *Huffpost.* Retrieved from: https://www.huffingtonpost.com/ entry/how-the-women-on-obamas-staff-made-sure-their-voices-were-heard_ us_57d94d9fe4b0aa4b722d79fe.

Hay, O., & Middlemiss, S. (2002). Fashion victims, dress to conform to the norm or else? Comparative analysis of legal protection against employers' dress codes in the United Kingdom and United States. *International Journal of Discrimination and the Law, 6*(1), 69–102.

Helgeson, H. (2015, January 5). 7 Steps to a healthy, authentic, company culture. *CNN. com.* Retrieved from: https://www.cnn.com/2014/09/11/business/7-steps/index. html.

Heppner, W. L., Kernis, M. H., Nezlek, J. B., Foster, J., Lakey, C. E., & Goldman, B. M. (2008). Within-person relationships among daily self-esteem, need satisfaction, and authenticity. *Psychological Science, 19*(11), 1140–1145.

Hewlin, P. F. (2003). And the award for best actor goes to…: Facades of conformity in organizational settings. *Academy of Management Review, 28*(4), 633–642.

Hu, C., Thomas, K. M., & Lance, C. E. (2008). Intentions to initiate mentoring relationships: Understanding the impact of race, proactivity, feelings of deprivation, and relationship roles. *The Journal of Social Psychology, 148*(6), 727–744.

Ibarra, H. (1995). Race, opportunity, and diversity of social circles in managerial networks. *Academy of Management Journal, 38*(3), 673–703.

Ilies, R., Morgeson, F. P., & Nahrgang, J. D. (2005). Authentic leadership and eudaemonic well-being: Understanding leader–follower outcomes. *The Leadership Quarterly, 16*(3), 373–394.

Jackson, P. B., Thoits, P. A., & Taylor, H. F. (1995). Composition of the workplace and psychological well-being: The effects of tokenism on America's Black elite. *Social Forces, 74*(2), 543–557.

Jans, L. H., Kaye, H. S., & Jones, E. C. (2012). Getting hired: Successfully employed people with disabilities offer advice on disclosure, interviewing, and job search. *Journal of Occupational Rehabilitation, 22*(2), 155–165.

Joachim, D. (2014). Military to ease hairstyle rules after outcry from Black recruits. *The New York Times, Online.* Retrieved from https://www.nytimes.com/2014/08 /15/us/military-hairstyle-rules-dreadlocks-cornrows.html.

Johns, M., & Schmader, T. (2010). Meta-cognitive regulation as a reaction to the uncertainty of stereotype threat. In R. M. Arkin, K. C. Oleson, & P. J. Carroll (Eds.), *The uncertain self: A handbook of perspectives from social and personality psychology* (pp. 176–192). Mahwah, NJ: Lawrence Erlbaum.

Jones, E. E., & Pittman, T. S. (1982). Toward a general theory of strategic self-presentation. In J. Suls (Ed.), *Psychological perspectives on the self* (pp. 101–108). Hillsdale, N\J: Lawrence Erlbaum Associates.

Kabir, H. (2018, August 6). 3 ways of enhancing women's authenticity and success at work. *Forbes.* Retrieved from: https://www.forbes.com/sites/womensmedia/2018/08/06/3-ways-of-enhancing-womens-authenticity-and-success-at-work/#4db38f1e2dd5.

Kahn, W. A. (1990). Psychological conditions of personal engagement and disengagement at work. *Academy of Management Journal, 33*(4), 692–724.

Kaiser, C. R., & Miller, C. T. (2001). Stop complaining! The social costs of making attributions to discrimination. *Personality and Social Psychology Bulletin, 27*(2), 254–263.

Kalev, A. & Dobbin, F. & Kelly, E. (2006). Best practices or best guesses? Assessing the efficacy of corporate affirmative action and diversity policies. *American Sociological Review, 71,* 589–617.

Kamenou, N., & Fearfull, A. (2006). Ethnic minority women: A lost voice in HRM. *Human Resource Management Journal, 16*(2), 154–172.

Kammeyer-Mueller, J., & Judge, T. A. (2008). A quantitative review of mentoring research: Test of a model. *Journal of Vocational Behavior, 72*(3), 269–283.

Kanter, R. M. (1977). Some effects of proportions on group life: Skewed sex ratios and responses to token women. *American Journal of Sociology, 82*(5), 965–990.

Kaplan, M. M., Sabin, E., & Smaller-Swift, S. (2009). *The catalyst guide to employee resource groups* (vol. 1): *Introduction to ERGS.* New York, NY: Catalyst. Retrieved from https://www.catalyst.org/research/the-catalyst-guide-to-employee-resource-groups-1-introduction-to-ergs/

Kernis, M. H., & Goldman, B. M. (2006). A multicomponent conceptualization of authenticity: Theory and research. *Advances in Experimental Social Psychology, 38,* 283–357.

Kiersch, C. E., & Byrne, Z. S. (2015). Is being authentic being fair? Multilevel examination of authentic leadership, justice, and employee outcomes. *Journal of Leadership & Organizational Studies, 22*(3), 292–303.

King, E. B., Mohr, J. J., Peddie, C. I., Jones, K. P., & Kendra, M. (2017). Predictors of identity management: An exploratory experience-sampling study of lesbian, gay, and bisexual workers. *Journal of Management, 43*(2), 476–502.

Kossek, E. E., Lobel, S., & Brown, J. (2006). Human resource strategies to manage workforce diversity: Examining "the business case." In A. M. Konrad, P. Prasad, & J. K. Pringle (Eds.), *Handbook of workplace diversity* (pp 53–74). Thousand Oaks, CA: Sage.

Knowles, E. D., Lowery, B. S., Hogan, C. M., & Chow, R. M. (2009). On the malleability of ideology: Motivated construals of color blindness. *Journal of Personality and Social Psychology , 96,* 857–869.

Kram, K. E. (1983). Phases of the mentor relationship. *Academy of Management Journal, 26*(4), 608–625.

Kraus, M. W., Chen, S., & Keltner, D. (2011). The power to be me: Power elevates self-concept consistency and authenticity. *Journal of Experimental Social Psychology, 47*(5), 974–980.

Kravitz, D. A. (2008). The diversity-validity dilemma: beyond selection—The role of affirmative action. *Personnel Psychology, 61*(1), 173–193.

Kulik, C. T., & Bainbridge, H. T. (2006) HR and the line: The distribution of HR activities in Australian organisations. *Asia Pacific Journal of Human Resources, 44,* 240–256.

Kulik, C. T., Bainbridge, H. T., & Cregan, C. (2008). Known by the company we keep: Stigma-by-association effects in the workplace. *Academy of Management Review, 33*(1), 216–230.

Kulkarni, M. (2012). Social networks and career advancement of people with disabilities. *Human Resource Development Review, 11*(2), 138–155.

Leroy, H., Anseel, F., Gardner, W. L., & Sels, L. (2015). Authentic leadership, authentic followership, basic need satisfaction, and work role performance: A cross-level study. *Journal of Management, 41*(6), 1677–1697.

Liang, J., Farh, C. I., & Farh, J. L. (2012). Psychological antecedents of promotive and prohibitive voice: A two-wave examination. *Academy of Management Journal, 55*(1), 71–92.

Liang, B., Tracy, A. J., Taylor, C. A., & Williams, L. M. (2002). Mentoring college-age women: A relational approach. *American Journal of Community Psychology, 30*(2), 271–288.

Liao, H., Joshi, A., & Chuang, A. (2004). Sticking out like a sore thumb: Employee dissimilarity and deviance at work. *Personnel Psychology, 57*(4), 969–1000.

Liberman, B. E. (2013). Eliminating discrimination in organizations: The role of organizational strategy for diversity management. *Industrial and Organizational Psychology: Perspectives on Science and Practice, 6*(4), 466–471.

Lindsey, A., King, E., McCausland, T., Jones, K., & Dunleavy, E. (2013). What we know and don't: Eradicating employment discrimination 50 years after the Civil Rights Act. *Industrial and Organizational Psychology, 6*(4), 391–413.

Long, D. M., Baer, M. D., Colquitt, J. A., Outlaw, R., & Dhensa-Kahlon, R. K. (2015). What will the boss think? the impression management implications of supportive relationships with star and project peers. *Personnel Psychology, 68*(3), 463–498.

Lyons, B., Wessel, J., Ghumman, S., Ryan, A. M., & Kim, S. (2014). Applying models of employee identity management across cultures: Christianity in the USA and South Korea. *Journal of Organizational Behavior, 35*(5), 678–704.

Madera, J. M., King, E. B., & Hebl, M. R. (2012). Bringing social identity to work: The influence of manifestation and suppression on perceived discrimination, job satisfaction, and turnover intentions. *Cultural Diversity and Ethnic Minority Psychology, 18*(2), 165.

Markus, H. R., Steele, C. M., & Steele, D. M. (2002). Color blindness as a barrier to inclusion: Assimilation and nonimmigrant minorities. In R. A. Shweder, M. Minow & H. R. Markus (Eds.), *Engaging cultural differences: The multicultural challenge in liberal democracies; engaging cultural differences: The multicultural challenge in liberal democracies* (pp. 453–472). New York, NY: Russell Sage Foundation.

Martinez, L. R., Sawyer, K. B., Thoroughgood, C. N., Ruggs, E. N., & Smith, N. A. (2017). The importance of being "me": The relation between authentic identity expression and transgender employees' work-related attitudes and experiences. *Journal of Applied Psychology, 102*(2), 215–226.

McCluney, C. L., Roberts, L. M., & Wooten, L. (2017). It takes courage: lessons learned from Starbucks #RaceTogether campaign. In R. Koonce, P. Robinson, & B. Vogel (Eds.), *Developing Leaders for Positive Organizing.* Bingley, UK: Emerald Publishing Group.

McGirt, E. (2016). Top diversity exec tells how he creates a 'safe space' at work. *Fortune, Online.* Retrieved from http://fortune.com/2016/09/13/diversity-safe-spaces-workplace/

McGrath, R., & Sparks, W. L. (2005). The importance of building social capital. *Quality Control and Applied Statistics, 50*(4), 45–49.

Mehra, A., Kilduff, M., & Brass, D. J. (1998). At the margins: A distinctiveness approach to the social identity and social networks of underrepresented groups. *Academy of Management Journal, 41*(4), 441–452.

Metin, U. B., Taris, T. W., Peeters, M. C., van Beek, I., & van den Bosch, R. (2016). Authenticity at work—A job-demands resources perspective. *Journal of Managerial Psychology, 31*(2), 483–499.

Meyer, I. H. (2003). Prejudice, social stress, and mental health in lesbian, gay, and bisexual populations: Conceptual issues and research evidence. *Psychological Bulletin, 129*, 674–697.

Miller, C. T., & Kaiser, C. R. (2001). A theoretical perspective on coping with stigma. *Journal of Social Issues, 57*(1), 73–92.

Milliken, F. J., Morrison, E. W., & Hewlin, P. F. (2003). An exploratory study of employee silence: Issues that employees don't communicate upward and why. *Journal of Management Studies, 40*(6), 1453–1476.

Mitchell, M. S., Koen Jr., C. M., & Moore, T. W. (2013). Dress codes and appearance policies: Challenges under federal legislation, Part 1Title VII of the Civil Rights Act and religion. *The Health Care Manager, 32*(4), 294–302.

Morgan, C. (2015). Busting myths about ERGs, One resource at a time. *Catalyst*. Retrieved from: http://www.catalyst.org/zing/busting-myths-about-ergs-one-resource-time.

Morris, J. A., & Feldman, D. C. (1996). The dimensions, antecedents and consequences of emotional labor. *Academy of Management Review, 21,* 986–1010.

Morrison, E. W., & Milliken, F. J. (2000). Organizational silence: A barrier to change and development in a pluralistic world. *Academy of Management Review, 25*(4), 706–725.

Morrison, E. W., & Rothman, N. B. (2009). Silence and the dynamics of power. *Voice and Silence in Organizations, 6,* 111–134.

Murrell, A. J., & Blake-Beard, S. (2017). *Mentoring diverse leaders: Creating change for people, processes, and paradigms.* New York, NY: Routledge/Taylor & Francis Group.

Ng, T. W., & Feldman, D. C. (2012). Employee voice behavior: A meta-analytic test of the conservation of resources framework. *Journal of Organizational Behavior, 33*(2), 216–234.

O'Ryan, L. W., & McFarland, W. P. (2010). A phenomenological exploration of the experiences of dual-career lesbian and gay couples. *Journal of Counseling & Development, 88*(1), 71–79.

Pachankis, J. E. (2007). The psychological implications of concealing a stigma: a cognitive-affective-behavioral model. *Psychological Bulletin, 133*(2), 328–345.

Park, J. Y., Wessel, J. L., & Huth, M. L. (April, 2017). *Authentic expression of key self-aspects: A scale validation study.* A poster presented at the 32nd Annual Conference for the Society of Industrial and Organizational Psychology (SIOP), Orlando, FL.

Perlow, L. A., & Repenning, N. P. (2009). The dynamics of silencing conflict. *Research in Organizational Behavior, 29,* 195–223.

Pinder, C. C., & Harlos, K. P. (2001). Employee silence: Quiescence and acquiescence as responses to perceived injustice. *Research in Personnel and Human Resources Management, 20,* 331–369.

Plaut, V. C., Thomas, K. M., & Goren, M. J. (2009). Is multiculturalism or color blindness better for minorities? *Psychological Science, 20*(4), 444–446.

Porke, M. R., & Seo, M. (2017). The role of affect climate in organizational effectiveness. *The Academy of Management Review, 42*(2), 334–360.

Raeburn, N. C. (2004). *Changing corporate america from inside out: Lesbian and gay workplace rights.* Minneapolis, MN: University of Minnesota Press.

Ragins, B. R. (2008). Disclosure disconnects: Antecedents and consequences of disclosing invisible stigmas across life domains. *Academy of Management Review, 33*(1), 194–215.

Ragins, B. R. (2016). From the ordinary to the extraordinary: High-quality mentoring relationships at work. *Organizational Dynamics, 45*(3), 228–244.

Ragins, B. R., & Cornwell, J. M. (2001). Pink triangles: antecedents and consequences of perceived workplace discrimination against gay and lesbian employees. *Journal of Applied Psychology, 86*(6), 1244–1261.

Ragins, B. R., Singh, R., & Cornwell, J. M. (2007). Making the invisible visible: Fear and disclosure of sexual orientation at work. *Journal of Applied Psychology, 92*(4), 1103–1118.

Reskin, B. F., & McBrier, D. B. (2000). Why not ascription? Organizations' employment of male and female managers. *American Sociological Review, 65*(2), 210–233.

Riger, S. (1991). Gender dilemmas in sexual harassment policies and procedures. *American Psychologist, 46*(5), 497–505.

Riggle, E. D. B., Rostosky, S. S., Black, W. W., & Rosenkrantz, D. E. (2017). Outness, concealment, and authenticity: Associations with LGB individuals' psychological distress and well-being. *Psychology of Sexual Orientation and Gender Diversity, 4*(1), 54–62.

Roberts, L. M. (2005). Changing faces: Professional image construction in diverse organizational settings. *Academy of Management Review, 30*(4), 685–711.

Rosado, S. D. (2003), No nubian knots or nappy locks: Discussing the politics of hair among women of African decent in the diaspora. A report on research in progress. *Transforming Anthropology, 11*, 60–63.

Rosette, A. S., & Dumas, T. D. (2007). The hair dilemma: Conform to mainstream expectations or emphasize racial identity. *Duke Journal of Gender Law & Policy, 14*, 407–421.

Rusbult, C. E., Farrell, D., Rogers, G., & Mainous III, A. G. (1988). Impact of exchange variables on exit, voice, loyalty, and neglect: An integrative model of responses to declining job satisfaction. *Academy of Management Journal, 31*(3), 599–627.

Ryan, A. M., & Wessel, J. L. (2008). Fairness in selection and recruitment: A stigma theory perspective In S. Cartwright & C. L. Cooper (Eds.), *Oxford handbook of personnel psychology* (pp. 517–542). Oxford, UK: Oxford University Press.

Schein, E. H. (1993). On dialogue, culture, and organizational learning. *Organizational Dynamics, 22*(2), 40–51.

Schlegel, R. J., Hicks, J. A., Arndt, J., & King, L. A. (2009). Thine own self: True self-concept accessibility and meaning in life. *Journal of Personality and Social Psychology, 96*(2), 473–490.

Schmader, T., Forbes, C. E., Zhang, S., & Mendes, W. B. (2009). A metacognitive perspective on the cognitive deficits experienced in intellectually threatening environments. *Personality and Social Psychology Bulletin, 35*(5), 584–596.

Schmader, T., & Sedikides, C. (2018). State authenticity as fit to environment: The implications of social identity for fit, authenticity, and self-segregation. *Personality and Social Psychology Review, 22*(3) 228–259.

Schultz, J. R., & Maddox, K. B. (2013). Shooting the messenger to spite the message? Exploring reactions to claims of racial bias. *Personality and Social Psychology Bulletin, 39*(3), 346–358.

See, K. E., Morrison, E. W., Rothman, N. B., & Soll, J. B. (2011). The detrimental effects of power on confidence, advice taking, and accuracy. *Organizational Behavior and Human Decision Processes, 116*(2), 272–285.

Sheldon, K. M., Ryan, R. M., Rawsthorne, L. J., & Ilardi, B. (1997). Trait self and true self: Cross-role variation in the Big-Five personality traits and its relations with psychological authenticity and subjective well-being. *Journal of Personality and Social Psychology, 73*(6), 1380–1393.

Shelton, J. N., Richeson, J. A., Salvatore, J., & Trawalter, S. (2005). Ironic effects of racial bias during interracial interactions. *Psychological Science, 16*(5), 397–402.

Shen, J., Chanda, A., D'netto, B., & Monga, M. (2009). Managing diversity through human resource management: An international perspective and conceptual framework. *The International Journal of Human Resource Management, 20*(2), 235–251.

Shore, L. M., Chung-Herrera, B. G., Dean, M. A., Ehrhart, K. H., Jung, D. I., Randel, A. E., & Singh, G. (2009). Diversity in organizations: Where are we now and where are we going? *Human Resource Management Review, 19*(2), 117–133.

Siemsen, E., Roth, A. V., Balasubramanian, S., & Anand, G. (2009). The influence of psychological safety and confidence in knowledge on employee knowledge sharing. *Manufacturing & Service Operations Management, 11*(3), 429–447.

Sloan, M. M., Newhouse, R. J. E., & Thompson, A. B. (2013). Counting on coworkers: Race, social support, and emotional experiences on the job. *Social Psychology Quarterly, 76*(4), 343–372.

Smart, L., & Wegner, D. M. (1999). Covering up what can't be seen: Concealable stigma and mental control. *Journal of Personality and Social Psychology, 77*(3), 474–486.

Smart, L., & Wegner, D. M. (2000). The hidden costs of hidden stigma. In T. F. Heatherton, R. E. Kleck, M. R. Hebl, & J. G. Hull (Eds., pp. 220–242), *The social psychology of stigma*. London, UK: The Guilford Press.

Snider, M. (2017). Sexual harassment at Fox News: Murdochs overhaul culture with eyes on Sky. *USA Today, Online*. Retrieved from https://www.usatoday.com/story/money/business/2017/07/17/sexual-harassment-fox-news-murdochs-overhaul-culture-eyes-sky/460303001/

Stainback, K., & Kwon, S. (2012). Female leaders, organizational power, and sex segregation. *The Annals of the American Academy of Political and Social Science, 639*(1), 217–235.

Steele, C. M., Spencer, S. J., & Aronson, J. (2002). Contending with group image: The psychology of stereotype and social identity threat. *Advances in Experimental Social Psychology, 34*, 379–440.

Stone, D. L., & Colella, A. (1996). A model of factors affecting the treatment of disabled individuals in organizations. *The Academy of Management Review 21*(2), 352–401

Stone-Romero, E., & Stone, D. L. (2008). Culture and human resource management: Prospects for the future. In D. L. Stone, & E. F. Stone-Romero (Eds.), *The influence of culture on human resource management processes and practices* (pp. 307–312) New York, NY: Psychology Press.

Sue, D. W., Capodilupo, C. M., & Holder, A. (2008). Racial microaggressions in the life experience of Black Americans. *Professional Psychology: Research and Practice, 39*(3), 329–336.

Swann, W. B. (1987). Identity negotiation: where two roads meet. *Journal of Personality and Social Psychology, 53*(6), 1038.

Syed, J. (2014). Diversity management and missing voices. In A. Wilkinson, J. Donaghey, T. Dundon, & R. Freeman (Eds.), *Handbook of research on employee voice,* (pp. 421–438). Cheltenham, UK: Edward Elgar.

Tal-Or, N. (2010). Indirect ingratiation: Pleasing people by associating them with successful others and by praising their associates. *Human Communication Research, 36*(2), 163–189.

Taris, T., & Van den Bosch, R. (2018). Authenticity at work: Its relations with worker motivation and well-being. *Frontiers in Communication, 3*, 1–11.

Taylor, S., Burke, L. A., Wheatley, K., & Sompayrac, J. (2011). Effectively facilitating gender transition in the workplace. *Employee Responsibilities and Rights Journal, 23*(2), 101–116.

Triana, M. D. C., García, M. F., & Colella, A. (2010). Managing diversity: How organizational efforts to support diversity moderate the effects of perceived racial discrimination on affective commitment. *Personnel Psychology, 63*(4), 817–843.

van den Bosch, R., & Taris, T. W. (2014). The authentic worker's well-being and performance: The relationship between authenticity at work, well-being, and work outcomes. *The Journal of Psychology, 148*(6), 659–681.

Walton, G. M., & Cohen, G. L. (2007). A question of belonging: race, social fit, and achievement. *Journal of Personality and Social Psychology, 92*(1), 82–96.

Wanberg, C. R., Welsh, E. T., & Kammeyer-Mueller, J. (2007). Protégé and mentor self-disclosure: Levels and outcomes within formal mentoring dyads in a corporate context. *Journal of Vocational Behavior, 70*(2), 398–412.

Warhurst, C., & Nickson, D. (2007). Employee experience of aesthetic labour in retail and hospitality. *Work, Employment and Society, 21*(1), 103–120.

Welbourne, T. M., Rolf, S., & Schlachter, S. (2017). The case for employee resource groups: A review and social identity theory-based research agenda. *Personnel Review, 46*(8), 1816–1834.

Wessel, J. L. (2017). The importance of allies and allied organizations: Sexual orientation disclosure and concealment at work. *Journal of Social Issues, 73*(2), 240–254.

Wessel, J. L., Hagiwara, N., Ryan, A. M., & Kermond, C. M. Y. (2015). Should women applicants "man up" for traditionally masculine fields? Effectiveness of two verbal identity management strategies. *Psychology of Women Quarterly, 39*(2), 243–255.

Withey, M. J., & Cooper, W. H. (1989). Predicting exit, voice, loyalty, and neglect. *Administrative Science Quarterly, 34*(4), 521–539.

Wong, C. A., & Laschinger, H. K. S. (2013). Authentic leadership, performance, and job satisfaction: The mediating role of empowerment. *Journal of Advanced Nursing, 69*(4), 947–959.

Wood, A. M., Linley, P. A., Maltby, J., Baliousis, M., & Joseph, S. (2008). The authentic personality: A theoretical and empirical conceptualization and the development of the Authenticity Scale. *Journal of Counseling Psychology, 55*(3), 385.

Yoshino, K., & Smith, C. (2013). *Uncovering talent: A new model of inclusion.* The Leadership Center for Inclusion Deloitte University.

Zambrana, R. E., Ray, R., Espino, M. M., Castro, C., Douthirt Cohen, B., & Eliason, J. (2015). Don't leave us behind" The importance of mentoring for underrepresented minority faculty. *American Educational Research Journal, 52*(1), 40–72.

CHAPTER 6

DIVERSITY TRAINING EFFECTIVENESS

Affective Mechanisms, Motivational Drivers, Individual Difference Moderators, and Contextual Boundary Conditions

Alex Lindsey, Eden King, and Brittney Amber

Most organizations rely on diversity training to effectively leverage an ever-diversifying workforce. As a result, critical questions have emerged regarding if diversity training works, and if so, for whom, how, when, and why it works. Despite somewhat discouraging and inconsistent findings in this domain, no overarching theoretical framework exists to guide the science or practice of diversity training. Accordingly, the purpose of this paper is to develop a comprehensive model and testable hypotheses of diversity training effectiveness. Specifically, this model considers emotions and motivations as key, yet generally ignored, mediators in the process by which diversity training affects diversity-related attitudes, behaviors, and cognitions. This model also considers more traditional diversity training variables such as training focus, trainee characteristics, training type, and training approach as moderators of diversity training effectiveness. Finally, we consider the temporal ordering in which specific proximal and distal diversity training outcomes will be affected. This model will guide future empirical research in the diversity training lit-

Diversity and Inclusion in Organizations, pages 137–164.

erature by explaining for whom, how, when, and why diversity training works when it is indeed effective. This model will also offer guidance to practitioners regarding how to effectively leverage diversity training exercises, what outcomes should be measured, when those outcomes should be measured, and what contextual and individual difference variables need to be in place for diversity training to be as effective as it possibly can be.

Organizations are increasingly depending on employees to effectively interact with people who are different from themselves. Indeed, diversity in the US workplace has steadily increased over the past 50 years, and this increase is expected to continue in the future (Toosie, 2006). The most common response by organizations to this substantial change has been to institute diversity training programs in the workplace. Approximately two thirds of human resource managers report using diversity training in their organizations (Esen, 2005). However, critical yet unanswered questions have emerged regarding if diversity training works, and if so, for whom, how, when, and why it works. A seminal review paper revealed that diversity training had only small to moderate effects on trainees' immediate attitudes and that other potentially meaningful outcomes of diversity training were not frequently measured (Kulik & Roberson, 2008a). Another review suggested that the most common approaches to diversity training might not be effective in accomplishing their goals (Bezrukova, Jehn, & Spell, 2012). These reviews are corroborated by a longitudinal analysis showing that diversity training often produces null or negative effects (Kalev, Dobbin, & Kelly, 2006), and a recent comprehensive meta-analysis showing that diversity training often has small effects that decay over time (Bezrukova, Spell, Perry, & Jehn, 2016). Other recent research has demonstrated that diversity training methods, if not framed appropriately, can actually lead to increases in both implicit and explicit expressions of prejudice via backlash (Legault, Gutsell, & Inzlicht, 2011). Furthermore, work has also indicated that awareness training aimed at informing people of the prevalence of stereotyping often leads to a counterproductive increase in prejudice and discrimination (Duguid & Thomas-Hunt, 2014). Despite these discouraging findings, no overarching theoretical framework exists to guide the science or practice of diversity training. This is troubling, as companies spend billions of dollars every year on diversity and inclusion initiatives (Lipman, 2018), but often lack even basic policies regarding diversity, devoted staff and budgets for training, or plans to measure the impact of training (Wilkie, 2014). Additionally, it may not be sufficient or even appropriate to simply apply classic training models to diversity training research given that diversity training is more emotionally and politically charged and that outcomes of diversity training extend beyond cognitive outcomes like knowledge gained and skills learned. For organizations to effectively manage their diverse workforce and create a more inclusive workplace, we need to know more about how to successfully conduct and leverage diversity training by building more consensus around what drives diversity training effectiveness.

Accordingly, the purpose of this paper is to develop a comprehensive model of diversity training effectiveness (see Figure 6.1), including testable hypotheses to inspire future research. Specifically, this model considers emotions and motivations as key, yet generally ignored, mediators in the process by which diversity training affects diversity-related attitudes, behaviors, and cognitions. This represents the first integration of emotions into the process by which diversity training produces its desirable (or in some cases, undesirable) effects. Thus, this work will guide our understanding of the explanatory mechanisms behind diversity training effectiveness while also unveiling proximal outcomes of effective diversity training programs.

This model also considers more traditional diversity training variables such as training focus (inclusive vs. group-specific), trainee characteristics (trait empathy and social dominance orientation), training type (awareness-based vs. behavior-based), and training approach (stand-alone vs. integrated) as moderators of diversity training effectiveness. Given that previous research findings with regard to diversity training effectiveness have been mixed, this search for moderators is of academic and practical importance. Indeed, diversity training scholars and practitioners need to have a firm understanding of contextual and individual difference variables that may alter training effectiveness.

Finally, we consider the temporal ordering in which specific proximal and distal diversity training outcomes will be affected. Specifically, we stipulate the causal ordering in which proximal and distal outcomes are affected. Additionally, we argue that while behavior-based training may first produce a change in diversity-related behaviors before later impacting attitudes via cognitive dissonance (Festinger, 1957), the opposite temporal ordering may be true of awareness-based training exercises. In terms of theoretical contribution, this model will guide future empirical research in the diversity training literature by explaining for whom, how, when, and why diversity training works when it is indeed effective. In terms of practical contribution, this model will offer guidance to practitioners regarding how to effectively leverage diversity training exercises, what outcomes should be measured, when those outcomes should be measured, and what contextual and individual difference variables need to be in place for diversity training to be as effective as it possibly can be. In turn, effective diversity training can be an important tool that improves critical human resource outcomes, such as selecting, retaining, and promoting diverse employees, creating more effective teams, and reducing prejudice and discrimination in the workplace.

Diversity Training

Training in organizations is broadly used to enhance employees' skills and capabilities, improve team effectiveness, and provide organizations a competitive advantage (Bell, Tannenbaum, Ford, Noe, & Kraiger, 2017; Goldstein, 1980). As the US workforce becomes increasingly more diverse, organizations have turned to training efforts to manage diversity. Diversity training can be defined as "a

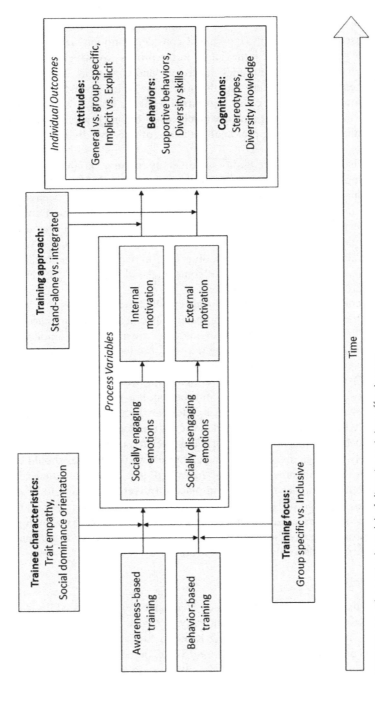

FIGURE 6.1. Theoretical model of diversity training effectiveness.

distinct set of programs aimed at facilitating positive intergroup interactions, reducing prejudice and discrimination, and enhancing the skills, knowledge, and motivation of people to interact with diverse others" (Bezrukova et al., 2012, p. 208). Importantly, diversity training differs from more traditional workplace training in that it deals with subjective and emotionally-laden topics, such as one's presumably engrained attitudes about stigmatized groups (Hanover & Cellar, 1998). Indeed, while attitudinal outcomes are considered in more traditional training programs, cognitive outcomes and skill development tend to receive more emphasis in standard training programs. On the other hand, because attitudes toward outgroups and diversity more generally are likely developed prior to training, diversity trainers need to focus on more affective outcomes such as attitudes and emotions, and training sessions tend to be more emotionally and politically charged as a result (Paluck, 2006). This is likely part of the reason that diversity training can sometimes result in backlash, where individuals react against the training, producing the opposite of desired training effects (see Legault et al., 2011). Diversity trainers hope to avoid such backlash, and instead pursue goals such as compliance, harmony, and (most desirably) inclusion (Rossett & Bickham, 1994). Importantly, meeting these goals is thought to benefit not only stigmatized individuals but also non-stigmatized others and organizational entities by improving work attitudes and social climates, increasing creativity and innovation, and reducing the negative consequences of discrimination such as employee turnover and lawsuits (Bezrukova et al., 2012; Simons, 1992). In sum, the most important objective of diversity training is for groups of diverse individuals to learn how to work together effectively, which may increase overall success for stigmatized and non-stigmatized individuals, as well as organizations as a whole (Bezrukova et al., 2012).

Individual Diversity Training Outcomes

As mentioned previously, findings have been somewhat mixed regarding the effectiveness of various diversity training initiatives, specifically at impacting individuals' attitudes, behaviors, and cognitions (Bezrukova et al., 2016). One factor that may be able to account for these inconsistencies is the type of outcome criterion chosen to indicate program success. Indeed, in the training literature there are several outcomes to examine when determining the success or failure of a given program. Kirkpatrick's (1994) commonly used typology of training outcomes includes reaction (i.e., how trainees felt about the training and its value overall), learning (i.e., knowledge acquired, skills improved, or attitudes changed), behavior (i.e., transfer of training to job-relevant behavior), and results (i.e., organization-level indicators of training success). Kulik and Roberson's (2008a) review of diversity education, as well as other reviews and meta-analyses (Bezrukova et al., 2012, 2016), similarly looks at the impact of diversity training for three main outcomes: (1) diversity knowledge, (2) diversity attitudes, and (3) diversity skills and behaviors. Our model of diversity training effectiveness focuses on learning outcomes at the individual level of analysis while conceptualizing these outcomes in a similar fashion as Kraiger and colleagues (1993) and Kulik and Roberson (2008a). These learning outcomes include the distal outcomes of diversity knowledge, diversity attitudes, and diversity skills and behaviors, but also include affective and motivational outcomes (Kraiger et al., 1993), which will be considered as more proximal outcomes and mediators of diversity training effectiveness. As Goldstein (1980) noted, "the objectives of instructional programs reflect numerous goals ranging from trainee progress to organizational goals." Thus, we find it important to measure these proximal and distal outcomes for individuals before assessing how these outcomes translate into organizational goals. Too often diversity training programs are categorized as failures because of how they are evaluated, and so we believe that far more care and attention should be placed on how training is evaluated, starting at the individual level. As can be seen in our model (Figure 6.1), we consider three key outcomes that should be evaluated in diversity training, including knowledge, attitudes, and behaviors.

Diversity Knowledge. Diversity knowledge is a cognitive outcome of diversity training that simply refers to gaining information that one did not know before training about groups that are different from one's own. This can include gaining knowledge of another group's experiences, customs, communication styles, or perceptions that are different from one's ingroup (Thomas, 2005). This outcome usually focuses on changes in an individual's awareness of differences or perceived learning following training. However, it can also focus on understanding the biases that lead to prejudice and discrimination or an understanding of general organizational policies related to diversity initiatives (Kulik & Roberson, 2008a). Change in diversity knowledge is typically measured using the Multicultural Awareness-Knowledge-Skills Survey (D'Andrea, Daniels, & Heck, 1991), which contains a knowledge subscale focusing specifically on diversity knowledge gained by individuals during training (Kulik & Roberson, 2008a).

It appears that diversity programs in organizations are reasonably effective when diversity knowledge is viewed as the main outcome of interest. Kulik and Roberson (2008a) found that 75% of their reviewed assessments of diversity training programs in organizations showed a positive effect of diversity training on diversity knowledge. Additionally, at least some of these knowledge gains persisted over time in studies that utilized a follow-up outcome survey (Kulik & Roberson, 2008a). A recent meta-analysis also confirms this finding, showing that cognitive learning showed the strongest effect size compared to behavioral and affective learning, and that cognitive knowledge was most likely to persist over time after diversity training (Bezrukova et al., 2016). While it is an impressive finding that these effects can persist several months after even a very short training session, it could be argued that we need to focus on more consequential outcomes of diversity training. This is a reasonable call for a shift in focus because a self-assessment of diversity knowledge is particularly vulnerable to social desirability, especially when assessed immediately after diversity training programs, which usually have fairly transparent objectives. It is with this thought in mind that we now turn our attention to the outcome of diversity attitudes.

Diversity Attitudes. In traditional training models, attitudes that may be measured include how trainees felt about the training, the value of the training, and satisfaction (Kirkpatrick, 1994). However, in diversity training, outcome measures regarding attitudes are expanded to include other relevant criteria. Diversity attitudes consist of general attitudes towards diversity and the value of diversity in the workplace as well as specific attitudes directed at different minority groups (e.g., Blacks, gays and lesbians; Kulik & Roberson, 2008a). Attitudes towards specific groups can be measured using both explicit and implicit measures. Some explicit measures assess so called "old-fashioned" forms of prejudice by asking about blatant forms of prejudice against various groups. Such measures are rarely used today due to their high likelihood of producing socially desirable responding. An example of a more modern version of an explicit measure is the Modern Racism Scale (McConahay, 1986), which poses more subtle questions about attitudes towards African Americans. Due to the extreme likelihood of presenting socially desirable responses on explicit measures of prejudice, many researchers have begun using more implicit measures, namely the Implicit Association Test (Greenwald, McGhee, & Schwartz, 1998).

The Implicit Association Test utilizes response latencies and paired stimuli in order to reveal implicit biases or preferences that an individual possesses for one group over another. For example, being able to pair "good" with "White" stimuli faster than one could pair "good" with "Black" stimuli would reveal an automatic preference for Whites over Blacks, and the degree of this preference would be larger or smaller depending on the relative latency of the responses to the two groups. While a detailed account of the Implicit Association Test's reliability, validity, and other psychometric properties is beyond the scope of this paper, suffice it to say that the use of this measure has been met with considerable controversy in both the fields of social and industrial/ organizational psychology (e.g., Blanton et al., 2009). However, a recent meta-analysis provided support for the incremental and predictive validity of both implicit and explicit measures of prejudice (Greenwald, Poehlman, Uhlmann, Banaji, 2009). Thus, it would appear that continuing to use both explicit and implicit attitude measures as outcome variables when evaluating diversity training interventions is both necessary and appropriate to provide evidence of this important outcome of diversity training programs.

Diversity attitudes have been cited as being the most common outcome measured when assessing the effectiveness of diversity training programs, but the results obtained when using this outcome measure are somewhat mixed (Kulik & Roberson, 2008a). Additionally, when compared to other outcomes like reactions, behavioral learning, and cognitive learning, a meta-analysis shows the weakest overall effect size for affective learning/attitudes (Bezrukova et al., 2016). When studies utilize general attitudes towards diversity and its importance as their outcome measure they generally report positive effects (e.g., Ellis & Sonnenfeld,

1994). Additionally, there is evidence to support that this positive effect can persist over time (DeMeuse & Hostager, O'Neill, 2006). However, the effect of diversity training on attitudes towards specific minority groups is less clear. There is evidence to support that diversity training can have a positive effect on racial attitudes (Hill & Augoustinos, 2001) and attitudes towards homosexual individuals (Lindsey, King, Hebl & Levine, 2015), but evidence supporting positive effects of diversity on attitudes toward other minority groups (e.g., women) is lacking (Kulik & Roberson, 2008a). These differential findings are not as surprising when interpreted in light of empirical evidence showing that diversity training participants (especially men) respond more negatively to diversity training programs framed with specific goals (i.e., focused on reducing prejudice against one specific minority group) when compared to training programs framed with more general goals (i.e., promoting diversity and its importance more generally in the workplace; Holladay, Knight, Paige, & Quiñones, 2003).

Diversity Skill and Behaviors. Diversity skill is a critical diversity training outcome, which can be broadly defined as the behavior needed to effectively and ethically work with individuals who are not a member of one's ingroup (Avery & Thomas, 2004). This outcome is potentially the most important outcome to measure when assessing the effectiveness of any diversity training program; employees would need to possess these skills or gain them from training in order to effectively work with people from different backgrounds in the workplace. In other words, trainees need to gain these skills in order for researchers to see any sort of behavioral outcomes from diversity training. In spite of this, diversity skills and behavioral outcomes have received less attention in the evaluation of diversity training programs than both diversity attitudes and diversity knowledge outcomes (Kulik & Roberson, 2008a).

One problem that has arisen in studies that use this outcome to assess the effectiveness of diversity training programs is that few studies use objective behavioral outcomes (e.g., actually displaying a learned skill in the work setting). Rather, many studies have settled for using a self-report measure that asks participants to assess what skills they learned from the training (e.g., DeMeuse et al., 2006). This method could be viewed as biased in that the goals of diversity training programs tend to be transparent to participants, which could lead them to respond in a socially desirable way to the self-assessing outcome measures. Indeed, studies using the skills subscale of the Multicultural Awareness-Knowledge-Skills Survey (D'Andrea et al., 1991) as a self-assessing measure of diversity skill acquisition consistently show positive effects of diversity training of self-rated skill improvement, but the results are somewhat mixed in the few cases that objective behavioral criteria are used (Kulik & Roberson, 2008a). Supportive behaviors for a variety of minority groups can also be measured directly. For instance, Madera, King, and Hebl (2013) developed a scale of self-reported supportive behaviors toward LGB individuals (e.g., "Been to a social or community event supporting gay and lesbian individuals") that could easily be adapted for a wide range of stigmatized populations. While such scales are relatively new to the literature, we would argue that these objective indicators of supportive behaviors should be focused on more explicitly in future diversity training work.

One reassuring piece of evidence for diversity training promoting diversity skills and behaviors in the workplace is some work done by Roberson, Kulik, and Pepper (2002) that revealed that the focus of the diversity training program can have an effect on objective behavioral outcomes. In this study the researchers were able to show that when the focus of diversity training was to learn diversity skills (instead of just to gain diversity awareness), the training was much more effective in producing objective diversity skills behaviors (measured by responses to critical incidents that could very well occur in the workplace). While this study does provide support for the idea that diversity training can have a positive effect on diversity behaviors and discrimination outcomes, much more work needs to be done to replicate this result and show that diversity training truly does teach people the skills they need to work with others from different backgrounds.

Training Type

In our model of diversity training effectiveness, we begin by specifying the type of training used (see the leftmost side of Figure 6.1). In line with previous research (see Bezrukova et al., 2012), we conceptualize and compare two distinct types of diversity training: awareness training and behavior-based training (Kulik & Roberson, 2008b). Awareness training typically emphasizes understanding the experiences of diverse groups of individuals and seeks to promote training participants' self-awareness of issues important to diversity such as cognitive and attitudinal biases that may affect how a member of an outgroup is perceived (Probst, 2003). Importantly, this training generally seeks to change cognitions, emotions, and attitudes in diversity training participants (Bezrukova et al., 2012). Behavior-based training seeks to have training participants monitor their own actions so that the can behave and react appropriately in socially sensitive situations. For instance, some behavior-based diversity training exercises might seek to encourage employees to confront prejudice when they hear inappropriate racial jokes in the workplace (Ashburn-Nardo, Morris, & Goodwin, 2008; Hanover & Cellar, 1998). Such training exercises may be more beneficial to the extent that minorities are actually present in the training environment (see Parker, Moore, & Neimeyer, 1998). Behavior-based training exercises can also be aimed at developing skills within oneself when interacting with diverse others (Armour, Bain, & Rubio, 2004). For instance, cultural sensitivity training might teach individuals to better deal with socially disengaging feelings such as frustration and confusion when interacting with individuals from various outgroups (Majumdar, Keystone, & Cuttress, 1999). Importantly, the goals of this training type include changing behaviors to improve interactions between fellow employees and customers (Hanover & Cellar, 1998).

While awareness training and behavior-based training can be used separately, they can also be used in conjunction with one another. Indeed, a common assumption made by diversity trainers is that if an initiative targets both awareness and behaviors it may be more beneficial than diversity training that only targets one or the other (Griffiths, 2005). Perhaps an even more important assumption is that diversity training will be more effective to the extent that training type and training goals are aligned (Roberson et al., 2003). For instance, one study showed self-reported behavioral changes in response to behavior-based diversity training (Armour et al., 2004), but programs that measure behaviors after conducting awareness-based training may not be deemed to be as effective (Roberson et al., 2002). Bezrukova et al.'s (2016) meta-analysis shows a strong effect-size for awareness-based training impacting cognitive learning, as well as when both awareness and behavior-based training are used. However, for affective attitudes as well as behavioral learning, awareness-based training alone is less effective. Thus, it is important to match the diversity training exercise with the outcome that it is most likely to affect. This is indeed a hallmark of good training evaluation (Goldstein, 1950; Noe 2010).

Which Outcomes are Affected? In a qualitative review of the effects of diversity training on relevant training outcomes, Kulik and Roberson (2008a) concluded that while diversity training is generally effective in terms of improving overall attitudes toward diversity, effects are far more variable when it comes to attitudes toward specific stigmatized groups. Similarly, the authors conclude that while trainees generally perceive themselves as having higher skill levels for interacting with diverse populations after training has taken place, there has not been overwhelming evidence that diversity training exercises actually improve behaviors toward stigmatized groups (Kulik & Roberson, 2008a). Given that the goal of diversity training initiatives is to improve diversity-related attitudes and behaviors in an effort to help dissimilar individuals work harmoniously with one another (Bezrukova et al., 2012), these inconsistent findings are somewhat troubling for diversity training science and practice.

We would argue that one potential explanation for these inconsistent findings is that the outcomes measured after diversity training are not always (or even often) the outcomes that are most likely to be affected by the training method in question. With this in mind, it is not surprising that general attitudes and perceived diversity skill have received the most support as outcomes of diversity training, given that most training exercises err on the side of inclusion and focus on diversity as a general topic of interest (e.g., in lectures), as opposed to focusing on specific stigmatized groups and using more targeted exercises (Bezrukova et al., 2012). The training literature generally agrees that establishing multiple outcome criteria is important, specifically ones that reflect "instructional objectives and organizational goals" (Goldstein, 1980, p. 240).

When are Outcomes Affected? Another factor to consider when discussing the outcomes of diversity training exercises is the order in which these outcomes are affected. The role of time and the order in which outcomes are affected has been all but ignored in the diversity training literature thus far, but some empirical work has guided our thoughts on this issue. For instance, as mentioned earlier, a study by Madera and colleagues (2013) revealed that diversity-related goal setting first had an effect on behaviors, before showing a positive impact on attitudes months later. The authors explained this finding using cognitive dissonance theory (Festinger, 1957), which states that when attitudes and behaviors are not concordant, individuals seek to change one or the other in order to reduce this dissonance over time. Thus, it stands to reason that behavior-based diversity training might first produce a change in diversity-related behaviors (e.g., we would not expect a trainee to create a goal that explicitly focuses on their diversity-related attitudes) before having its effect on attitudes and cognitions via dissonance at a later point in time.

This ordering may be reversed when considering how awareness-based diversity training exercise has its positive effects. Indeed, awareness-based exercises such as perspective taking may be better positioned to first impact attitudes rather than behaviors. We say this because attitudes toward stigmatized groups are particularly emotion-laden (Jackson, 1999), and awareness-based training exercises are designed to appeal to these emotions through the promotion of empathy. It is difficult for trainees to hold a negative attitude about a group while also feeling empathy for them. Thus, we expect that awareness-based training exercises will first have their impact on attitudes before then also improving behaviors over time.

Hypothesis 1: Awareness-based training more readily produces change in cognitions and attitudes, whereas behavior-based more readily produce change in behaviors.

Explanatory Mechanisms of Diversity Training Effectiveness

In his seminal work on training in organizations, Goldstein (1980) emphasizes Campbell's (1974) conclusion that "our evaluation efforts have emphasized outcome and ignored process measures. Thus, evaluation efforts have missed the richness of detail concerning how events occurred and even what went wrong" (p. 241). As mentioned previously, Kraiger and colleagues' (1993) conceptualization of training learning outcomes includes not only attitudes, behaviors, and cognitions, but also emotions and motivations experienced as a result of the training. Accordingly, this paper proposes that affect (i.e., socially engaging/disengaging emotions) and motivation (i.e., internal/external motivation to respond without prejudice) are important, proximal outcomes of diversity training that may serve as important mediators when evaluating the effectiveness of training strategies. In

Figure 1 we call these process variables and place them at the center of our model. Although these variables have not been integrated specifically in the diversity training domain previously, work from Batson and colleagues' (1983) has provided some theoretical guidance as to what to expect regarding the relationship between these variables and how they might transmit diversity training effectiveness. Specifically, this work argues (and empirically supports the notion) that empathy (a socially engaging emotion) gives rise to an altruistic motivation to help, whereas personal distress (which may be indicated by socially disengaging emotions) gives rise to an egoistic motivation to help. In terms of the model we are justifying, altruistic motivation to help is most similar to an internal motivation to respond without prejudice, whereas egoistic motivation is more similar to an external motivation to respond without prejudice. These constructs, their relationships with one another, and their relationships with diversity training outcomes are the focus of the following sections.

Socially Engaging/Disengaging Emotions. Emotions have been a startling and nearly complete omission from the diversity training literature thus far. This is somewhat surprising, given that the outcomes of diversity training fairly emotion-laden (Jackson, 1999), and given that emotions experienced during or immediately after the training may be able to explain the backlash effects that sometimes occur (e.g., Legault et al., 2011). This is also surprising given that emotions are thought to aid us in simplifying complex social situations such as interacting with diverse others. Indeed, previous research has demonstrated that individuals use the affect they are experiencing as a heuristic cue when responding to influence attempts (Forgas, 1995). Additionally, other work has shown that public vs. private compliance varies depending on the emotional reaction one has to an influence attempt (Whatley, Webster, Smith, & Rhodes, 1999).

A useful framework for thinking about emotions as they might be relevant in diversity training comes to us from cross-cultural psychology, where researchers distinguish between socially engaging and socially disengaging emotions. Socially engaging emotions include discrete emotions such as empathy, sympathy, guilt, and shame, while socially disengaging emotions include discrete emotions such as pride, self-esteem, and frustration (Kitayama, Mesquita, & Karasawa, 2006). Importantly, this conceptualization goes beyond the valence (i.e., positive vs. negative affect) of an emotion to consider the core relational theme or appraisal surrounding this emotion (Lazarus, 1999). Indeed, emotions such as pride, friendly feelings, anger, and guilt all have meaningful themes or appraisals associated with them that go beyond simple positive or negative evaluations. These themes guide the individual in understanding their relationships with others around them (Kitayama, Karasawa, & Mesquita, 2004). For example, although pride and friendliness are both considered to be positive emotions, they are associated with very different relational themes; namely, personal achievement for pride and social harmony for friendliness. Similarly, although anger and guilt are similar in terms of their unpleasantness, they are associated with vastly different relational themes, such as goal interference and failure of repayment. Thus, experiencing anger implies that the person is appraising the situation as one that prevents goals from being achieved, whereas experiencing guilt implies that the person is appraising a situation as one in which he/she has failed to repay a given obligation (Kitayama et al., 2006).

Independence and interdependence are two major sets of social objectives and associated ideals that are present in all cultures. The idea is that some themes, such as social harmony and failed repayment, are most likely to be experienced by the interdependent self which seeks harmonious relationships. Themes that are derived from social interdependence are referred to as socially engaging. In contrast, themes such as personal achievement and unfair infringement on personal goals are most likely to be experienced by the independent self that seeks to pursue individual goals and desires. Themes that are derived from such social independence are referred to as socially disengaging (Kitayama et al., 2006). Empirical work has supported the notion that there exists a social orientation dimension when it comes to measuring emotions. Thus, emotions that are both positive (e.g., friendliness, respect) and negative (e.g., guilt and shame) in valence have been shown to comprise the engagement end of the social orientation spectrum, while the disengagement end was defined by a different set of both positive (e.g., pride, feeling superior) and negative (e.g., anger and frustration) emotions (Kitayama, Markus, & Kurokawa, 2000). These findings suggest that people are able to categorize emotions in terms of both pleasantness and social orientation (Kitayama et al., 2006). Thus, it stands to reason that diversity initiatives may be more effective to the extent that they engender more socially orienting (i.e., engaging) emotions.

While diversity training scholars have yet to incorporate this framework into their studies, empathy is a socially engaging emotion that has received both theoretical and empirical attention. Empathy is an "other-focused" emotion that allows one to acknowledge, understand, and show concern for how someone else is feeling (Batson et al., 1995). Thus, empathy seems to fit well into socially engaging end of the social orientation dimension of emotional experience. Importantly, empathy has been conceptualized as both a trait- and a state-level variable (Van Lange, 2008), with state empathy being our focus for now. State empathy can be defined as "an affective sate that is elicited by the observation or imagination of another person's affective state" (De Vignemont & Singer, 2006, p. 435). Thus, state empathy is an emotional reaction that could be triggered by various environmental stimuli, including diversity training exercises, while trait empathy may affect an individual's level of receptivity to such an exercise before training begins. More recently, researchers have begun discussing empathy not as a discrete emotion, but as an "emotional process with substantial implications for moral behavior" (Tangney, Stuewig, & Mashek, 2007, p. 362). Accordingly, empathy, along with other socially engaging vs. disengaging emotions, experienced during and/or immediately after training, is a key explanatory mechanism in my model of diversity training effectiveness, which has several outcomes with moral implications. In line with Batson and colleagues' (1983) work, we predict that socially engaging emotions will give rise to an altruistic motivation to change (i.e., an internal motivation to respond without prejudice), while socially disengaging emotions will give rise to an egoistic motivation to change (i.e., an external motivation to respond without prejudice).

Previous empirical work has shown that diversity training can lead to an increase in state empathy (Madera et al., 2011), which in turn had a beneficial effect on diversity related attitudes. Other diversity training work has also provided indirect support some of the other socially engaging emotions as mediators of diversity training effectiveness. For instance, Pendry, Driscoll, and Field (2007) reviewed and categorized a variety of diversity training strategies while indicating that some of the more effective strategies (e.g., the walking through white privilege exercises; McIntosh, 1988) are designed specifically to induce guilt in training participants. These findings and approaches make sense when interpreted in light of cognitive dissonance theory (Festinger, 1957), which states that psychological discomfort is likely to be experienced when attitudes, behaviors, and cognitions are not concordant with one another. Thus, becoming aware of the needs and experiences of diverse populations could lead to psychological discomfort if the trainee has negative diversity-related attitudes, cognitions, or past behaviors, which should theoretically motivate them to improve these diversity-related outcomes to reduce dissonance. Although motivational variables and socially engaging/disengaging emotions have not been measured and accounted for in concert with one another in a diversity training context, we would argue that motivation to respond without prejudice is the unmeasured mediator from this previous work that can account for the relationship between empathy and more distal diversity training outcomes. Accordingly, socially engaging/disengaging emotions are the proposed transmitters (i.e., mediators) and more proximal outcomes of these diversity training effects.

Hypothesis 2: Diversity training is more effective to the extent that it engenders socially engaging, as opposed to socially disengaging, emotions.

Hypothesis 3: Socially engaging emotions are more positively associated with internal motivation to respond without prejudice when compared to external motivation to respond without prejudice.

Hypothesis 4: Socially disengaging emotions are more positively associated with external motivation to respond without prejudice when compared to internal motivation to respond without prejudice.

Hypothesis 5: Socially engaging/disengaging emotions partially mediate the relationship between diversity training exercises and motivation to respond without prejudice.

Motivation. If the overarching goal of diversity training programs is to get people who are meaningfully different from each other to have more supportive attitudes and behaviors toward one another, a more proximal outcome might be to change motivations to have such attitudes and engage in such behaviors in the first place. In classic training research, trainee motivation is considered an important personal characteristic in determining transfer of training. Although some training scholars consider motivation to be an important input in determine training effectiveness (Colquitt, LePine, & Noe, 2000), Kraiger and colleagues (1993) list motivation as an important affective learning outcome of training exercises, which maps on well with the way that diversity trainers typically think about motivational constructs. Indeed, improving individuals' motivation to successfully interact with differing others is actually listed as a goal outcome in the definition of diversity training provided by Bezrukova and colleagues (2012). Internal motivation to respond without prejudice can be defined as responding without prejudice due to one's own egalitarian beliefs and values (Plant & Devine, 1998). On the other hand, external motivation to respond without prejudice can be defined as responding without prejudice due to external constraints such as laws and norms preventing the expression of prejudice (Plant & Devine, 1998).

Promoting external motivation to respond without prejudice has actually been shown to increase expressions of prejudice (e.g., Legault et al., 2011), and thus may not be as effective in terms of promoting diversity-related outcomes when compared to internal motivation to respond without prejudice. Such findings are in line with the idea that external motivators are seen as controlling (Deci, Koestner, & Ryan, 1999), thus providing less motivation to change. Such findings can also be explained by psychological reactance theory (Brehm, 1966), which states that when people perceive threats to their control of their own lives, they may react by trying to reassert that control. This attempt to reassert control could cause them to change attitudes and/or behaviors in the opposite direction that was originally intended by the diversity training initiative.

An individual who participates in a diversity training initiative aimed at getting them to react positively to a given stigmatized group should theoretically be motivated to respond without prejudice. Indeed, previous research has shown that participative goal setting (a behavior-based diversity training strategy) can lead to an increase in intrinsic motivation to accomplish those goals (Harackiewicz & Elliot, 1993). Thus, we would hope to extend these findings to a diversity training context. In turn, this internal motivation to respond without prejudice should improve diversity-related attitudes and behaviors by motivating people to respond to stigmatized individuals positively based on their own egalitarian beliefs. Indeed, internal motivation to respond without prejudice has been shown to be predictive of positive diversity-related attitudes in previous research (e.g., Ratcliff, Lassiter, Markman, & Snyder, 2006).

This role of internal motivation to respond without prejudice in influencing diversity training effectiveness has received some preliminary empirical support.

For instance, one study of diversity training programs among health care professionals found that the training successfully altered not only attitudes and behaviors, but also improved the motivation of the participants to take action regarding diversity after the study (Celik, Abma, Klinge, & Widdershoven, 2012). Additionally, another study showed beneficial effects of perspective taking on group-specific diversity training outcomes, with internal motivation to respond without prejudice serving as an explanatory mechanism for these effects (Lindsey et al., 2015). We would also expect a variety of diversity training initiatives to be effective in promoting external motivation to respond without prejudice, as having a diversity initiative in the first place signals that the organization values diversity and wants its employees to respond without prejudice. However, based on previous research (Legault et al., 2011), we would not expect this external motivation to respond without prejudice to be as strongly associated with more distal diversity training outcomes such as diversity-related attitudes, behaviors, and cognitions.

Hypothesis 6: Internal motivation to suppress prejudice will have a more positive impact on diversity training attitudes, behaviors, and cognitions when compared to external motivation to suppress prejudice.

Hypothesis 7: Internal (to a greater extent than external) motivation to respond without prejudice partially mediates the relationship between socially engaging emotions and diversity-related attitudes, behaviors, and cognitions.

Hypothesis 8: External (to a greater extent than internal) motivation to respond without prejudice partially mediates the relationship between socially disengaging emotions and diversity-related attitudes, behaviors, and cognitions.

Moderators of Diversity Training Effectiveness

Given inconsistent findings regarding diversity training effectiveness, the search for substantive moderators is of great theoretical and practical importance. Accordingly, we examine several important moderators related to training context, training design, and trainee characteristics (Baldwin & Ford, 1988; Bezrukova et al., 2012; Blume et al., 2010). While the context of training in terms of academic vs. organizational settings has been considered extensively by previous work (Kulik & Roberson, 2008a), we build on this work by also considering the important training context variable of training approach (stand-alone vs. integrated with other diversity initiatives; Bezrukova et al., 2012). Additionally, we consider the important training design variable of training focus (group-specific vs. inclusive; Roberson et al., 2003). Finally, we consider important trainee characteristics such as trait empathy (Knafo et al., 2008) and social dominance orientation (Pratto et al., 1994) that may alter the effectiveness of diversity training for certain types of individuals. Thus, our comprehensive model (see Figure 6.1) integrates several critical components of diversity training that have previously been discussed separately or completely ignored in this literature, which will help build consensus around when, for whom, and under what conditions diversity training is effective.

Training Focus. One element of training design that is important to discuss for this theoretical model is the focus of training. We conceptualize and distinguish between two forms of training focus: group-specific and inclusive. Indeed, training focus can range from addressing prejudice and discrimination toward a specific stigmatized group (e.g., LGBT populations) to taking a more inclusive focus that spans across multiple groups, with the goal of promoting acceptance of diverse characteristics of all employees, regardless of race, gender, or any one potentially stigmatizing characteristic (Roberson, et al., 2003; Stewart, Crary, & Humberd, 2008). Below, we highlight potential advantages and drawbacks of each training focus.

There are a few reasons why diversity trainers may prefer a more inclusive training focus. First, managers have been shown to perceive diversity training as more effective when it encompasses a broad range of individual differences as opposed to focusing only on racial and gender differences (Rynes & Rosen, 1995). Additionally, some researchers have suggested that the group-specific focus may not be as effective because it limits the conversation to specific stigmatized groups as opposed to expanding trainees' perspectives about diversity beyond consideration of any one group (see Thomas, 1991). Indeed, a popular argument for favoring an inclusive focus as opposed to a group-specific focus is that an inclusive focus is less likely to produce backlash by highlighting intergroup differences and tensions (Bezrukova et al., 2012, 2016). For instance, Chavez and Weisinger (2008) developed a diversity training model that shifts the focus of diversity training from group differences to the unique experiences of individuals more generally. They believe that focusing on the unique experiences of individuals more generally could prevent an "us versus them" mentality which could cause backlash against various diversity initiatives. Similarly, other researchers have suggested focusing on similarities and inclusiveness rather than highlighting group differences to avoid diversity training resistance (Thomas, Tran, & Dawson, 2010).

Despite the aforementioned arguments to the contrary, there are several reasons to believe that it may be beneficial to include in diversity training a more focused effort pertaining to certain marginalized groups. First, research has been inconsistent when investigating the effectiveness of inclusive vs. group-specific diversity training initiatives. For example, one experiment assigned workers to register for a diversity training course that was either inclusive or focused on a more specific group difference (Holladay et al., 2003). Although the researchers hypothesized that participants would be more receptive to diversity training with an inclusive focus than to diversity training with a specific focus on certain groups, the researchers did not find any differences in the extent to which participants felt the training would be relevant to their organization, the extent to which they felt the training would transfer to their job, or the extent to which they expected to experience backlash to the training (Holladay et al., 2003). Furthermore, other researchers have effectively demonstrated that group-specific diversity training can indeed be effective at reducing automatic stereotyping against a specific stigmatized group (e.g., Stewart, Latu, Kawakami, & Myers, 2010). A recent meta-analysis also shows similar effect-sizes for one group-specific, multiple group-specific, and inclusive training focuses (Bezrukova et al., 2016).

One potential explanation for these inconsistent findings relates to the specificity of the outcomes that are measured. Indeed, just as training focus can be inclusive or group-specific, training outcomes can be measured to focus on specific groups or focus on attitudes, behaviors, cognitions, and motivations related to diversity in a more holistic manner. In a qualitative review of the effects of diversity training on relevant training outcomes, Kulik and Roberson (2008a) concluded that while diversity training is generally effective in terms of improving overall attitudes toward diversity, effects are far more variable when it comes to attitudes toward specific stigmatized groups. Similarly, the authors conclude that while trainees generally perceive themselves as having higher skill levels for interacting with diverse populations after training has taken place, there has not been overwhelming evidence that diversity training exercises actually improve behaviors toward specific stigmatized groups (Kulik & Roberson, 2008a). One explanation for these findings is that the outcomes measured after diversity training are not always (or even often) the outcomes that are most likely to be affected by the training method in question. With this in mind, it is not surprising that general attitudes and perceived diversity skill have received the most support as outcomes of diversity training, given that most training exercises err on the side of inclusion and focus on diversity as a general topic of interest (e.g., in lectures), as opposed to focusing on specific stigmatized groups and using more targeted exercises (Bezrukova et al., 2012). On the other hand, more group-specific training exercises may be able to produce changes in more specific outcomes of interest (such as attitude and behavior change toward a given stigmatized group, as well as the more proximal outcomes related to empathy and motivation). This line of thinking is corroborated by the classic compatibility principle (Fishbein & Ajzen, 1974), which states that there should be an alignment in the level of specificity of predictor and criterion constructs in order to maximize predictive power. Additionally, general best practices in training, including the notion that outcomes should to be "relevant, reliable, discriminative, and practical" (Noe, 2010, p. 227) should be applied to diversity training as well. Accordingly, while inclusive diversity training may be best positioned to affect general diversity training outcomes, group-specific diversity training may be best positioned to affect more specific diversity training outcomes. More formally, we present the following hypothesis:

Hypothesis 9: An inclusive diversity training focus yields more positive outcomes for general attitudes and behaviors toward diversity, whereas a group-specific focus yields more positive outcomes for specific attitudes and behaviors toward a given stigmatized group.

Trainee Characteristics. Another question this paper will address is whether individual differences may alter the effectiveness of various diversity training initiatives. This search for moderators is important, given that previous studies regarding diversity training exercises have yielded mixed results, with some studies showing positive, some showing negative, and still other studies showing null effects (Kulik & Roberson, 2008a). Training research more broadly has found relationships between certain trainee characteristics and training effectiveness. Specifically, cognitive ability and conscientiousness have been found as the strongest individual difference predictors for transfer of training (Ford et al., 2018). Other individual differences have been identified as an important factor to consider in the general training literature. For instance, one study found that individual differences such as goal orientation and learning self-efficacy predicted training performance (Brown, 2006). Additionally, meta-analytic evidence has indicated that trainee characteristics such as conscientiousness and locus of control are important to consider for the success of training participants (Colquitt et al., 2000). Finally, considering trainee characteristics could serve as a needs analysis of sorts in the diversity training realm, helping trainers to identify not only who is in the most need of training but also which exercises may be most appropriate for specific individuals.

Indeed, needs analysis has been identified as an important part of the training process (Brown & Sitzmann, 2011; Goldstein, 1980; Noe, 2010), though it is often ignored in the training literature. For instance, a meta-analysis revealed that as low as 6% of training studies conducted a needs analysis before training was designed (Arthur et al., 2003). Similarly, diversity training researchers have largely ignored trainee characteristics as an important input variable that can alter training effectiveness. Indeed, a recent review revealed that only five studies have been conducted examining the effects of trainee characteristics other than demographics (see Bezrukova et al., 2012). Beginning with the work of Cronbach & Snow (1977), there is a long history of aptitude by treatment interactions in the effectiveness of employee training, with the idea being that certain training exercises are more beneficial for certain individuals based on trainee characteristics. Although this work has yet to be applied to diversity training, research and theory on empathy and social dominance orientation provide some direction as to which types of individuals may be more responsive diversity training initiatives.

Empathy. Empathy is an "other-focused" emotion that allows one to acknowledge, understand, and show concern for how someone else is feeling (Batson et al., 1995). While we focused on state empathy previously, here we will focus on trait empathy as a potential individual difference moderator of diversity training stand and respond sympathetically to others' emotions and experiences (Knafo et al., 2008). State empathy is a socially engaging emotional reaction that could be triggered by various environmental stimuli, including diversity training exercises (making it a potentially proximal outcome of these exercises) while trait empathy may affect an individual's level of receptivity to such an exercise before training begins.

Indeed, trait empathy has been repeatedly and convincingly shown to negatively relate to expressions of prejudice (see Bäckström & Björklund, 2007). Thus, people low in trait empathy tend to express more prejudice when compared to those who are higher in trait empathy. In terms of the model we are justifying, it stands to reason that highly empathetic people may be relatively aware of and attuned to the needs of diverse populations. These people would not necessarily stand to benefit from a diversity training exercise because their tendency to be aware of others' needs should lead them to respond without prejudice, even in lieu of an empathy-inducing intervention. On the other hand, individuals who are low in trait empathy may need to be prompted by diversity training to enhance understanding and awareness of the experiences of populations. Thus, we reason that individuals who are low in dispositional empathy stand to benefit the most from diversity training aimed at improving diversity-related attitudes and behaviors. This notion has received some preliminary support from an experiment showing that perspective taking was more effective for those low in trait empathy as compared to those who were high on this trait (Lindsey et al., 2015). Additionally, previous work has shown that taking the perspective of others can lead to an increase in *state* empathy (Madera et al., 2011), which should be more beneficial for those low in dispositional empathy than those who are high on this trait.

Hypothesis 10: Trainee trait empathy moderates the effectiveness of diversity training programs, such that training is more beneficial for those lower in empathy when compared to those higher in empathy.

Hypothesis 11: Trainee trait empathy moderates the relationship between training exercise and socially engaging emotions, such that the relationship is more positive for those low on trait empathy compared to those who are high on trait empathy.

Social Dominance Orientation. Social dominance theory (Sidanius, 1993; Sidanius & Pratto, 1999) is grounded in the notion that societies are typically organized in group-based social hierarchies. This theory points us to another individual difference trainee characteristic that likely influences the effectiveness of diversity training initiatives. Specifically, this theory suggests that intergroup conflict represents a manifestation of group-based hierarchies. Group-based beliefs (such as ideologies involving meritocracies and group dominance) legitimize prejudiced attitudes and discriminatory treatment, serving to perpetuate social inequalities over time. This theory also states that individuals vary in the degree to effectiveness. Trait empathy refers to stable and dispositional tendencies to under-which they endorse hierarchical ideologies. Indeed, social dominance orientation (SDO) is defined as "a general attitudinal orientation toward intergroup relations, reflecting whether one generally prefers such relations to be equal, versus hierarchical" (Pratto et al., 1994, p. 742).

SDO has been shown to be negatively related to other variables presumably important to consider in diversity training such as empathy, tolerance, and altruism (Pratto et al., 1994). Additionally, this individual difference has also been shown to be distinguishable from related variables such as conservatism and authoritarianism (Pratto et al., 1994). Perhaps most importantly, SDO is associated with attitudes and behaviors regarding workplace diversity. For example, one study showed that White applicants who were high in SDO viewed diverse organizations as less attractive when compared to those who were low in SDO (Umphress, Smith-Crowe, Brief, Dietz, & Watkins, 2007). Additionally, another study showed that individuals who were higher in SDO expressed more negative attitudes toward low status group members based on race and gender when compared to individuals lower in SDO (Umphress, Simmons, Boswell, & Triana, 2008). These findings serve to demonstrate that SDO is inversely associated with positive diversity-related attitudes, and lead us to reason that trainees who are lower in SDO may be more responsive to diversity training initiatives when compared to those who are higher in SDO. As mentioned previously, high SDO individuals prefer social hierarchies and use group-based beliefs to legitimize prejudice and discrimination toward outgroups. Thus, a diversity training exercise may serve to increase the salience of a high social dominance orientation, which may result in null (or even negative) effects on diversity training outcomes. Indeed, it stands to reason the individuals high in SDO may be more likely to respond to diversity training initiative with socially disengaging (as opposed to engaging) emotions, thus hindering the effectiveness of the training overall. More formally, we present the following hypotheses:

Hypothesis 12: Trainee social dominance orientation moderates the effectiveness of diversity training programs, such that training is more effective for those lower in SDO when compared to those higher in SDO.

Hypothesis 13: Trainee social dominance orientation moderates the relationship between training exercise and socially engaging/disengaging emotions, such that training engenders more socially engaging emotions for those low on SDO, and more socially disengaging emotions for those high on SDO.

Training Approach. Another way that diversity training initiatives can be distinguished is whether they are stand-alone programs or integrated into a larger diversity mission (Bezrukova et al., 2012; Flynn, 1998). In many organizations, diversity training only occurs as a one-time initiative and focuses on compliance and legal issues, leading some scholars to call this a "check-off-the-box" approach that simply shows that employees have participated in some form of diversity training (Anand & Winters, 2008; Curtis, Dreachslin, & Sinioris, 2007). Luckily, this is not the case in all organizations. Indeed, in some organizations, diversity training initiatives take a much broader approach in which employees might participate in a variety of training exercises throughout their tenure at an organization (Bendick, Egan, & Lofhjelm, 2001). Although this approach is often used in educational and university settings, some organizations have also begun to adopt this more curriculum-based approach which emphasizes the importance of diversity in multiple work domains (Murphy, Park, & Lonsdale, 2006).

Not surprisingly, many scholars have argued that any one diversity training session by itself will probably not accomplish much (e.g., Bendick et al., 2001). Rather, the assumption is that a larger culture change, guided by multiple diversity initiatives, is needed to actually make an organization more inclusive and accepting of diversity over time. The idea here is that a broader range of diversity training initiatives (as opposed to one-time training) communicates to employees that the organization is committed to supporting diversity in the workplace, thus making training initiatives more effective in terms of improving diversity-related outcomes (Curtis et al., 2007). Such integrated approaches to diversity training have even been given broad umbrella terms such as "diversity management" and emphasize the importance of overarching diversity-related organizational goals as opposed to the completion of a one-shot diversity training session (Ivancevich & Gilbert, 2000; Thomas, 1991).

Importantly, empirical work has supported the notion that an integrated approach to diversity training may be more effective when compared to a stand-alone approach (Bendick et al., 2001; Naff & Kellough, 2003). For example, one study compared isolated diversity training vs. training that was complemented by other initiatives and found that the integrated approach was perceived as more effective by diversity trainers themselves (Bendick et al., 2001). Additionally, in their comprehensive review of diversity training initiatives, Bezrukova and colleagues (2012) conclude that "the literature suggests that the impact of diversity training is related to its integration in other organizational initiatives or signals from top management that it is a priority for the organization or college and not just 'window-dressing.'" (Bezrukova et al., 2012, p. 215). Indeed, a recent meta-analysis confirms this notion, finding a stronger effect size for integrated approaches compared to stand-alone approaches for behavioral, affective, and cognitive learning outcomes (Bezrukova et al., 2016). Accordingly, we present the following hypothesis:

Hypothesis 14: Training approach moderates the relationship between internal/external motivation to suppress prejudice and diversity training outcomes, such that the relationship is more positive under an integrated approach when compared to a stand-alone approach.

CONCLUSION

Diversity training is a critical tool for organizations which can be used to impact employees' cognitive, behavioral, and affective learning. Beyond this, diversity training is also key to impacting and creating change at many levels of analysis, including the individual and interpersonal level, the group and intergroup level, as well as the organizational level (Ferdman & Brody, 1996). Effective diversity training can be a critical tool that improves necessary human resource outcomes, like reducing prejudice and discrimination, selecting, retaining, and promoting diverse employees, helping employees work better together, and creating more effective teams.

In this paper we developed an omnibus model of diversity training effectiveness. It is our hope that this paper will provide much needed theoretical guidance to researchers in addition to providing practical recommendations to practitioners implementing diversity initiatives in their organizations. In evaluating this model, it is important that analysts move beyond lab studies using student samples and simple survey study designs in order to uncover truths about the processes and contexts that give rise to diversity training effectiveness. Indeed, we recommend pursuing longitudinal field experiments in which researchers conduct diversity training initiatives in actual organizations before measuring the dependent variables proposed in the model at multiple time points thereafter. In designing these field experiments, we recommend that researchers maintain flexibility to design the training interventions as to maintain scientific rigor while also making sure all training conditions are practically appropriate. For instance, when utilizing a control group, instead of having this group receive no training (a condition which many organizations are unlikely to buy into) researchers could instead provide basic training (e.g., a lecture about the modern forms of discrimination an bias) alone for this group while exploring if activities designed to promote socially engaging emotions (see Pendry, Driscoll, & Field, 2007 for an excellent review of such activities) provide incremental value above and beyond basic training sessions. If rigorous studies such as these are conducted, we have confidence that the proposed model will help us to truly uncover for whom, how, when, and why diversity training works.

REFERENCES

Anand, R., & Winters, M. (2008). A retrospective view of corporate diversity training from 1964 to the present. *Academy of Management Learning and Education, 7,* 356–372.

Armour, M. P., Bain, B., & Rubio, R. (2004). Special section: Field education in social work. An evaluation study of diversity training for field instructors: A collaborative approach to enhancing cultural competence. *Journal of Social Work Education, 40,* 27–38.

Arthur, W., Jr., Bennett, W. Jr., Edens, P. S., & Bell, S. T. (2003). Effectiveness of training in organizations: A meta-analysis of design and evaluation features. *Journal of Applied Psychology, 88*, 234–245.

Ashburn-Nardo, L., Morris, K. A., & Goodwin, S. A. (2008). The confronting prejudiced responses (CPR) model: Applying CPR in organizations. *Academy of Management: Learning and Education, 7*, 332–342.

Avery, D. R., & Thomas, K. M. (2004). Blending content and contact: The roles of diversity curriculum and campus heterogeneity in fostering diversity management competency. *Academy of Management Learning & Education, 3*, 380–396.

Bäckström, M., & Björklund, F. (2007). Structural modeling of generalized prejudice. *Journal of Individual Differences, 28*, 10–17.

Baldwin, T. T., & Ford, J. K. (1988). Transfer of training: A review and direction for future research. *Personnel Psychology, 41*, 63–105.

Batson, C. D., Batson, J. G., Todd, R. M., Brummett, B. H., Shaw, L. L., & Aldeguer, C. M. R. (1995). Empathy and the collective good: Caring for one of the others in a social dilemma. *Journal of Personality and Social Psychology, 68*, 619–631.

Batson, C. D., O'Quin, K., Fultz, J., Vanderplas, M., & Isen, A. M. (1983). Influence of self-reported distress and empathy on egoistic versus altruistic motivation to help. *Journal of Personality and Social Psychology, 45*, 706.

Bell, B. S., Tannenbaum, S. I., Ford, J. K., Noe, R. A., & Kraiger, K. (2017). 100 years of training and development research: What we know and where we should go. *Journal of Applied Psychology, 102*(3), 305–323.

Bendick, M., Egan, M. L., & Lofhjelm, S. (2001). Workplace diversity training: From anti-discriminatory compliance to organizational development. *Human Resource Planning, 24*, 10–25.

Bezrukova, K., Jehn, K. A., & Spell, C. S. (2012). Reviewing diversity training: Where we have been and where we should go. *Academy of Management Learning & Education, 11*, 207–227.

Bezrukova, K., Spell, C. S., Perry, J. L., & Jehn, K. A. (2016). A meta-analytical integration of over 40 years of research on diversity training evaluation. *Psychological Bulletin, 142*(11), 1227–1274.

Blanton, H., Jaccard, J., Klick, J., Mellers, B., Mitchell, G., & Tetlock, P. E. (2009). Strong claims and weak evidence: Reassessing the predictive validity of the IAT. *Journal of Applied Psychology, 94*, 567–582.

Blume, B. D., Ford, J. K., Baldwin, T. T., & Huang, J. L. (2010). Transfer of training: A meta-analytic review. *Journal of Management, 36*, 1065–1105.

Brehm, J. W. (1966). *A theory of psychological reactance.* New York, NY: Academic Press.

Brown, K. G. (2006). Using computers to deliver training: which employees learn and why? *Personnel Psychology, 54*, 271–296.

Brown, K. G., & Stitzman, T. (2011). Training and employee development for improved performance. In S. Zedick (Ed.), *APA handbook of industrial and organizational psychology* (pp. 469–503). Washington, DC: APA.

Campbell, D. T. (1974). *Qualitative knowing in action research.* Paper presented at 82nd Annual Meeting of the American Psychological Association, New Orleans, LA.

Celik, H., Abma, T. A., Klinge, I., & Widdershoven, G. A. (2012). Process evaluation of a diversity training program: The value of a mixed method strategy. *Evaluation and Program Planning, 35*, 54–65.

Chavez, C. I., & Weisinger, J. Y. (2008). Beyond diversity training: A social infusion for cultural inclusion. *Human Resource Management, 47*(2), 331–350.

Colquitt, J. A., LePine, J. A., & Noe, R. A. (2000). Toward an integrative theory of training motivation: A meta-analytic path analysis of 20 years of research. *Journal of Applied Psychology, 85,* 678–707.

Cronbach, L. J., & Snow, R. E. (1977). *Aptitudes and instructional methods: A handbook for research on interactions.* New York, NY: Irvington Publishers.

Curtis, E. F., Dreachslin, J. L., & Sinioris, M. (2007). Diversity and cultural competence training in health care organizations: Hallmarks of success. *Health Care Management Review, 26,* 255–262.

D'Andrea, M., Daniels, J., & Heck, R. (1991). Evaluating the impact of multicultural counseling training. *Journal of Counseling and Development, 70,* 143–150.

De Vignemont, F., & Singer, T. (2006). The empathic brain: How, when and why? *Trends in Cognitive Science, 10,* 435–441.

Deci, E. L., Koestner, R., & Ryan, R. M. (1999). A meta-analytic review of experiments examining the effects of extrinsic rewards on intrinsic motivation. *Psychological Bulletin, 125,* 627–668.

DeMeuse, K. P., Hostager, T. J., & O'Neill, K. S. (2006). A longitudinal evaluation of senior managers' perceptions and attitudes of a workplace diversity training program. *Human Resource Planning, 30,* 38–46.

Duguid, M. M., & Thomas-Hunt, M. C. (2014). Condoning stereotyping? How awareness of stereotyping prevalence impacts expression of stereotypes. *Journal of Applied Psychology, 100,* 343–359.

Ellis, C., & Sonnenfeld, J. A. (1994). Diverse approaches to managing diversity. *Human Resource Management, 33,* 79–109.

Esen, E. (2005). *2005 Workplace diversity practices: Survey report.* Alexandria, VA: Society for Human Resource Management.

Ferdman, B. M., & Brody, S. E. (1996). Models of diversity training. In D. Landis & R. S. Bhagat (Eds.), *Handbook of Intercultural Training, 2nd Edition* (pp. 282–303). Thousand Oaks, CA: Sage.

Festinger, L. (1957). *A theory of cognitive dissonance.* Stanford, CA. Stanford University Press.

Fishbein, M., & Ajzen, I. (1974). Attitudes towards objects as predictors of single and multiple behavioral criteria. *Psychological review, 81*(1), 59–74.

Flynn, G. (1998). The harsh reality of diversity programs. *Workforce, 77,* 26–30.

Ford, J. K., Baldwin, T. T., & Prasad, J. (2018). Transfer of training: The known and the unknown. *Annual Review of Organizational Psychology and Organizational Behavior, 5,* 201–225.

Forgas, J. P. (1995). Mood and judgment: the affect infusion model (AIM). *Psychological Bulletin, 117,* 39.

Goldstein, I. L. (1980). Training in organizations. *Annual Review of Psychology, 31,* 229–272.

Greenwald, A. G., McGhee, D. E., & Schwartz, J. K. L. (1998). Measuring individual differences in implicit cognition: The implicit association test. *Journal of Personality and Social Psychology, 74,* 1464–1480.

Greenwald, A. G., Poehlman, T. A., Uhlmann, E., & Banaji, M. R. (2009). Understanding and using the Implicit Association Test: III. Meta-analysis of predictive validity. *Journal of Personality and Social Psychology, 97,* 17–41.

Griffiths, J. (2005). Awareness training needs practical follow-up work. *People Management, 11,* 17.

Hanover, J., & Cellar, D. (1998). Environmental factors and the effectiveness of workforce diversity training. *Human Resource Development Quarterly, 9,* 105–124.

Harackiewicz, J. M., & Elliot, A. J. (1993). Achievement goals and intrinsic motivation. *Journal of Personality and Social Psychology, 65,* 904—915.

Hill, M. E., & Augoustinos, M. (2001). Stereotype change and prejudice reduction: Short- and long-term evaluation of a cross-cultural awareness programme. *Journal of Community and Applied Social Psychology, 11,* 243–262.

Holladay, C. L., Knight, J. L., Paige, D. L., & Quiñones, M. A. (2003). The influence of framing on attitudes toward diversity training. *Human Resource Development Quarterly, 14,* 245–264.

Ivancevich, J. M., & Gilbert, J. A. (2000). Diversity management: Time for a new approach. *Public Personnel Management, 29,* 75–92.

Jackson, L. C. (1999). Ethnocultural resistance to multicultural training: Students and faculty. *Cultural Diversity and Ethnic Minority Psychology, 5,* 27–36.

Kalev, A., Dobbin, F., & Kelly, E. (2006). Best practices or best guesses? Assessing the efficacy of corporate affirmative action and diversity policies. *American Sociological Review, 71*(4), 589–617.

Kirkpatrick, D. L. (1994). *Evaluating training programs: The four levels.* San Francisco, CA: Berrett-Koehler.

Kitayama, S., Karasawa, M., & Mesquita, B. (2004). Collective and personal processes in regulating emotions: Emotion and self in Japan and the U.S. In P. Philippot & R. S. Feldman (Eds.), *The regulation of emotion* (pp. 251–273). Hillsdale, NJ: Erlbaum.

Kitayama, S., Markus, H. R., & Kurokawa, M. (2000). Culture, emotion, and well-being: Good feelings in Japan and the United States. *Cognition & Emotion, 14,* 93–124.

Kitayama, S., Mesquita, B., & Karasawa, M. (2006). Cultural affordances and emotional experience: Socially engaging and disengaging emotions in Japan and the United States. *Journal of Personality and Social Psychology, 91*(5), 890–903.

Knafo, A., Zahn-Waxler, C., Van Hulle, C., Robinson, J. L., & Rhee, S. H. (2008). The developmental origins of a disposition toward empathy: Genetic and environmental contributions. *Emotion, 8*(6), 737–752.

Kulik, C. T., & Roberson, L. (2008a). Common goals and golden opportunities: Evaluation of diversity education in academic and organizational settings. *Academy of Management Learning & Education, 7,* 309–331.

Kulik, C. T., & Roberson, L. (2008b). Diversity initiative effectiveness: What organizations can (and cannot) expect from diversity recruitment, diversity training, and formal mentoring programs. In A. Brief, (Ed.), *Diversity at work* (pp. 265–317). London, UK: Cambridge Press.

Kraiger, K., Ford, J. K., & Salas, E. (1993). Application of cognitive, skill-based, and affective theories of learning outcomes to new methods of training evaluation. *Journal of Applied Psychology, 78,* 311–328.

Lazarus, R. S. (1999). *Stress and emotion: A new synthesis.* New York, NY: Springer Publishing Company.

Legault, L., Gutsell, J. N., & Inzlicht, M. (2011). Ironic effects of antiprejudice messages: How motivational interventions can reduce (but also increase) prejudice. *Psychological Science, 22*(12), 1472–1477.

Lindsey, A., King, E., Hebl, M., & Levine, N. (2015). The impact of method, motivation, and empathy on diversity training effectiveness. *Journal of Business and Psychology, 30*, 605–617.

Lipman, J. (2018, January 25). How diversity training infuriates men and fails women. *Time Magazine*. Retrieved from https://time.com/5118035/diversity-training-infuriates-men-fails-women/

Madera, J. M., King, E. B., & Hebl, M. R. (2013). Enhancing the effects of sexual orientation diversity training: The effects of setting goals and training mentors on attitudes and behaviors. *Journal of Business and Psychology, 28*, 79–91.

Madera, J. M., Neal, J. A., & Dawson, M. (2011). A strategy for diversity training focusing on empathy in the workplace. *Journal of Hospitality & Tourism Research, 35*, 469–487.

Majumdar, B., Keystone, J. S., & Cuttress, L. A. (1999). Cultural sensitivity training among foreign medical graduates. *Medical Education, 33*, 177–184.

McConahay, J. B. (1986). Modern racism, ambivalence, and the Modern Racism Scale. In J. F. Dovidio & S. L. Gaertner (Eds.), *Prejudice, discrimination, and racism* (pp. 91–125). Orlando, FL: Academic Press.

Murphy, M., Park, J., & Lonsdale, N. (2006). Marriage and family therapy students' change in multicultural counseling competencies after a diversity course. *Contemporary Family Therapy: An International Journal, 28*, 303–311.

Naff, K., & Kellough, E. (2003). Ensuring employment equity: Are federal diversity programs making a difference? *International Journal of Public Administration, 26*, 1307–1336.

Noe, R. A. (2010). *Employee training and development* (5th ed.). New York, NY: McGraw-Hill/Irwin.

Paluck, E. L. (2006). Diversity training and intergroup contact: A call to action research. *Journal of Social Issues, 62*, 577–595.

Parker, W. M., Moore, M. A., & Neimeyer, G. J. (1998). Altering white racial identity and interracial comfort through multicultural training. *Journal of Counseling and Development, 76*, 302–310.

Pendry, L. F., Driscoll, D. M., & Field, S. C. (2007). Diversity training: Putting theory into practice. *Journal of Occupational and Organizational Psychology, 80*, 27–50.

Plant, E. A., & Devine, P. G. (1998). Internal and external motivation to respond without prejudice. *Journal of Personality and Social Psychology, 75*, 811–832.

Pratto, F., Sidanius, J., Stallworth, L. M., & Malle, B. F. (1994). Social dominance orientation: A personality variable predicting social and political attitudes. *Journal of Personality and Social Psychology, 67*, 741–763.

Probst, T. M. (2003). Changing attitudes over time: Assessing the effectiveness of a workplace diversity course. *Teaching of Psychology, 30*, 236–239.

Ratcliff, J. J., Lassiter, G. D., Markman, K. D., & Snyder, C. J. (2006). Gender differences in attitudes toward gay men and lesbians: The role of motivation to respond without prejudice. *Personality and Social Psychology Bulletin, 32*, 1325–1338.

Roberson, L., Kulik, C. T., & Pepper, M. B. (2002). Assessing instructor cultural competence in the classroom: An instrument and a development process. *Journal of Management Education, 26,* 40–55.

Roberson, L., Kulik, C. T., & Pepper, M. B. (2003). Using needs assessment to resolve controversies in diversity training design. *Group and Organization Management, 28,* 148–174.

Rossett, A., & Bickham, T. (1994). Diversity training: Hope, faith and cynicism. *Training, 31,* 40–46.

Rynes, S., & Rosen, B. (1995). A field survey of factors affecting the adoption and perceived success of diversity training. *Personnel Psychology, 48,* 247–270.

Sidanius, J. (1993). The psychology of group conflict and the dynamics of oppression: A social dominance perspective. In S. Iyengar & W. McGuire (Eds.), *Explorations in political psychology* (pp. 183–219). Durham, NC: Duke University Press.

Sidanius, J., & Pratto, F. (1999). *Social dominance: An intergroup theory of social hierarchy and oppression.* New York, NY: Cambridge University Press.

Simons, G. F. (1992). *The questions of diversity: Assessment tools for organizations and individuals.* Amherst, MA: ODT, Inc.

Stewart, T. L., Latu, I. M., Kawakami, K., & Myers, A. C. (2010). Consider the situation: Reducing automatic stereotyping through situational attribution training. *Journal of Experimental Social Psychology, 46,* 221–225.

Tangney, J. P., Stuewig, J., & Mashek, D. J. (2007). Moral emotions and moral behavior. *Annual Review of Psychology, 58,* 345–372.

Thomas, K. M. (2005). *Diversity dynamics in the workplace.* Belmont, CA: Thomson Wadsworth.

Thomas, K. M., Tran, N. M., & Dawson, B. L. (2010). An inclusive strategy of teaching diversity. *Advances in Developing Human Resources, 12,* 295–311.

Thomas, R. R. (1991). *Beyond race and gender: Unleashing the power of your total workforce by managing diversity.* New York, NY: American Management Association.

Toosie, M. (2006). A new look at long term labor force projections to 2050. *Monthly Labor Review, 129*(November), 19–39.

Umphress, E., Simmons, A., Boswell, W., & Triana, M. (2008) Managing discrimination in selection: The impact of directives from an authority and social dominance orientation. *Journal of Applied Psychology, 93,* 982–993.

Umphress, E. E., Smith-Crowe, K., Brief, A. P., Dietz, J., & Watkins, M. B. (2007). When birds of a feather flock together and when they do not: Status composition, social dominance orientation, and organizational attractiveness. *Journal of Applied Psychology, 92,* 396–409.

Van Lange, P. A. M. (2008). Does empathy trigger only altruistic motivation? How about selflessness or justice? *Emotion, 8,* 766–774.

Whatley, M. A., Webster, J. M., Smith, R. H., & Rhodes, A. (1999). The effect of a favor on public and private compliance: How internalized is the norm of reciprocity? *Basic and Applied Social Psychology, 21,* 251–259.

Wilkie, D. (2014, April 8). Many companies lack diversity training, budget, metrics. *Society for Human Resource Management.* Retrieved from www.shrm.org.

CHAPTER 7

IN PURSUIT OF INCLUSIVITY

A Review of Human Resource Management Research and Practices Involving LGBT Employees[1]

Patrick J. Rosopa, Jamie M. Fynes,
Katherine B. D'Souza, and Phoebe Xoxakos

Diversity and inclusion have become increasingly important topics in human resource management, organizational behavior, and related fields. As organizations
become increasingly diverse, however, there is the potential for discrimination
against minority groups including employees who identify as lesbian, gay, bisexual,
and transgender (LGBT). The present article reviews extant research on the issues
that LGBT employees face in the workplace. The issues are organized around the
general stages of the employment process, including recruitment and selection,
training and policies, and promotion and termination. We highlight how LGBT individuals can be negatively affected at every stage of the employment process. The intersection of LGBT employees and legal issues in the workplace are also discussed.
We conclude with some best-practices in human resource management and note
future research opportunities.

[1] This material is based upon work supported by the National Science Foundation under Grant No.
1629934.

165

Diversity and inclusion have become increasingly important topics in human resource management, organizational behavior, and related fields (HRM; Robinson & Dechant, 1997). As organizations become increasingly diverse, however, there is the potential for discrimination against minority groups including sexual minorities, racial minorities, women, and individuals with disabilities. For example, a meta-analysis on prejudice and discrimination in the workplace found that racism was associated with discriminatory selection and performance evaluation, and opposition to diversity-supportive policies (Jones, Sabat, King, Ahmad, McCausland, & Chen, 2017). Another study found that discriminatory practices were associated with greater psychological distress among women of color (Velez, Cox, Polihronakis, & Moradi, 2018). Additionally, individuals with physical, behavioral, neurological, and sensory impairments experience discrimination in the workplace, especially regarding reasonable accommodation (Graham, McMahon, Kim, Simpson, & McMahon, 2019). Because discrimination in the workplace can be pervasive, achieving a fair and equitable workplace for all employees and transforming workplace cultures and practices has become vital to organizations. As one salient example, by recognizing lesbian, gay, bisexual, and transgender (LGBT) rights, more inclusive organizations can leverage the value of a more diverse workforce (Köllen, 2016b; Riley, 2008). The focus of the present paper is on LGBT employees.

It is not uncommon for individuals who identify as transgender to be grouped together with individuals who identify as lesbian, gay, or bisexual. However, gender identity and sexual orientation are two distinct constructs. According to VandenBos (2007), gender identity is defined as "a recognition that one is male or female and the internalization of this knowledge into one's self concept. This sense of maleness or femaleness typically results from a combination of biological and... environmental effects of family and cultural attitudes" (p. 401). Thus, gender identity is an individual's perception of one's gender, which may or may not correspond with one's biological sex at birth. A person may identify as female, male, trans-male, trans-female, or transgender.

Alternatively, sexual orientation is defined as, "one's enduring sexual attraction to male partners, female partners, or both. Sexual orientation may be heterosexual...gay...lesbian, or bisexual" (VandenBos, 2007, p. 847). Salomaa and Matsick (2018) add that sexual orientation can be fluid and that there are several types: bisexual, heterosexual, homosexual, lesbian, and pansexual. VandenBos (2007), defines pansexualism as, "the view that all human behavior is motivated by the sexual drive" (p. 666). In that, one's sexual drive is not restricted based on gender identity or sexual orientation. The distinction between gender identity and sexual orientation is important because those who identify as transgender may have different experiences in the workplace than those who identify as lesbian, gay, or bisexual. As a result, different approaches may need to be taken to address prejudice and discrimination in the workplace.

In the present article, we use the terms LGBT (lesbian, gay, bisexual, and transgender) and LGB (lesbian, gay, bisexual). Currently, in popular media, when referring to LGBT individuals, the community is referred to as LGBTQ (lesbian, gay, bisexual, transgender, and queer). However, there is limited research on individuals who identify as queer in the workplace. Thus, the present article examines individuals who identify as LGBT or LGB. As we cite existing research, we present the terminology used by the original researchers, and use the terms LGBT and LGB to clarify as needed.

Regrettably, LGBT workers face challenges at all stages of employment (King & Cortina, 2010). For example, one U.S. national survey conducted in 2008 found that 42% of LGBT-identified respondents had experienced some form of employment discrimination because of their sexual orientation during their lives, with 27% of respondents having experienced discrimination sometime within the previous five years (Sears & Mallory, 2014). Similarly, a national survey conducted in 2013 found that 21% of LGBT-identified respondents reported being treated unfairly in the workplace, specifically in hiring, pay, or promotions (Sears & Mallory, 2014). Moreover, 58% of LGBT respondents on a 2009 survey reported hearing derogatory remarks about sexual orientation and gender identity in their workplaces (Sears & Mallory, 2014). From these reports, it can be concluded that gender identity- and sexual orientation-based discrimination are an ongoing problem in organizations.

LGBT individuals face additional workplace issues that can make their experiences more complicated than their heterosexual counterparts. These issues can be better understood, in part, through a discussion of the minority stress model (Meyer, 2003). Minority stress can be viewed as excess stress that minority groups, such as the LGBT community, experience as a result of their marginalized status (Meyer, 2003). This excess stress can make LGBT individuals more vulnerable to mental health issues. Specifically, stigma, prejudice, and discrimination create a hostile and stressful social environment that can trigger or cause mental health problems (Meyer, 2003). Other types of minority stress that LGBT individuals can experience in the workplace consist of expectations of rejection, hiding and concealing one's sexual orientation or gender identity, and internalized homophobia (Meyer, 2003). Concealing one's identification requires considerable vigilance, which can be mentally and emotionally taxing, especially in the workplace (Meyer, 2003).

Microaggressions, "short, everyday verbal, behavioral, and environmental slights, often automatic and unconscious, aimed at a minority population" (Wegner & Wright, 2016, p. 300), can contribute to minority stress in the workplace. Therefore, any group that is marginalized, including the LGBT community, can be the target of microaggressions. Sexual orientation microaggressions include oversexualization, homophobia, assumed deviance, second-class citizenship, assumptions about gay culture, and heterosexist language and terminology (Sue, 2010; Wegner & Wright, 2016). Bisexual individuals may also experience identification-related microaggressions such as dismissal of their identification, pressure to change to the orientation that coincides with the type of relationship they are in, and accusations of hypersexuality (Bostwick & Hequembourg, 2014). These microaggressions can impact employees whether they disclose their orientation or identity.

The present article is organized around various themes, including gender identity and sexual orientation. In addition, within each theme, we will discuss various stages of the employment process, such as recruitment and selection, training and policies, and promotion and termination and how LGBT individuals can be affected by discrimination in each phase of the employment process. Then, the intersection of LGBT employees and legal issues in the workplace will be discussed. Lastly, we discuss best-practices in HRM and note future research opportunities.

CAREER DEVELOPMENT AND MANAGING ONE'S SEXUAL ORIENTATION AND GENDER IDENTITY

Given their minority status, LGBT employees may have unique career development needs, which can be influenced by how they manage their sexual orientation or gender identity in the workplace. Indeed, there are many factors that can influence the decision to disclose one's sexual orientation or gender identity at work. Part of this involves the ways in which LGBT individuals respond to heterosexism at work and how they navigate their relationships with coworkers. Note that heterosexism refers to a system of beliefs that denigrates and discriminates against non-heterosexual individuals (Ragins, Cornwell, & Miller, 2003). Thus, targets of heterosexism include LGBT individuals. Because sexual orientation and gender identity are separate constructs, managing one's sexual orientation in the workplace is different from managing one's gender identity. Therefore, although there are some similarities, identity management for LGB individuals and identity management for transgender individuals are discussed separately.

Sexual Orientation

Sexual orientation is, for the most part, an invisible identity; other employees may only know another employee's sexual orientation if one reveals it. According to Reed and Leuty (2015), identity management is described as the following, "In an effort to balance the potential benefits and costs of revealing a stigmatized identity, decisions are made on what to reveal and what to conceal, when, and to whom" (p. 985). Even in states where discrimination on the basis of sexual orientation is illegal, some individuals may conceal their sexual orientation and "pass" as heterosexual in order to avoid potential negative repercussions of identifying as LGB (Shippee, 2011). Aside from passing, there are other identity management strategies that sexual orientation minorities might use in the workplace (King et al., 2017) including covering, being implicitly out, and being explicitly out (Griffin, 1992). Passing is an active concealment technique where an LGB individual behaves in a way to appear heterosexual. Covering is a concealment technique where an individual actively censors the personal information they share that could reveal one's sexual orientation. Implicitly out behaviors imply a person's sexual orientation, but do not reveal it directly, like wearing or displaying symbols associated with the LGB community. Explicitly out behaviors involve actively and freely sharing information about sexual orientation. Passing and covering are used to conceal sexual orientation, while implicitly and explicitly out behaviors are meant to reveal sexual orientation. These less subtle strategies may have unfortunate consequences. Specifically, disclosing one's sexual orientation can make one susceptible to discrimination (Riggle, Rotosky, Black, & Rosenkrantz, 2017).

A workplace culture has the potential to determine whether individuals feel comfortable enough to reveal their sexual orientation. For example, the greater the presence of heterosexism in a workplace, the less likely it is that an LGB worker will disclose their sexual orientation (Lipka, 2010; Reed & Leuty, 2015). Occupations such as sports, law enforcement, and elementary education, which have a high degree of heterosexism, may be especially difficult for gay men (Anteby & Anderson, 2014; Chung, Chang, & Rose, 2015). Alternatively, disclosure may be more likely if there are other LGB individuals in the organization, if there are perceived allies in the organization, and if the individual had previous positive disclosure experiences (Ragins, Singh, & Cornwell, 2007; Sabat, Trump, & King, 2014). In addition, LGB workers are more likely to reveal their sexual orientation to women than men (King et al., 2017).

Personality has also been supported as an influential factor in one's decision to disclose at work. Specifically, individuals who are more extraverted are more likely to be explicitly out and less likely to have internalized heterosexism (Reed & Leuty, 2015). Even if one has strong personality traits that can influence the disclosure of one's sexual orientation, there are still other factors that can inhibit disclosure.

The fear of the consequences of disclosure can be greater than the actual consequences (Ragins et al., 2007). However, this fear alone can significantly influence job attitudes, create psychological strain, and reduce job satisfaction and organizational commitment (Ragins et al., 2007). Yet, research in athletics and organizations has shown that there can be beneficial effects of coming out and revealing a stigmatized identity. Some benefits include increased comradery amongst team members, improved psychological well-being, and a sense of authenticity (Fynes & Fisher, 2016; Lipka, 2010; Reed & Leuty, 2015). Unfortunately, both being "out" and "closeted" (not being "out") have been associated with an increase in depressive symptoms, which can be a result of increased susceptibility to minority stress and discrimination (Riggle et al., 2017). Further, concealment of one's sexual orientation can negatively impact psychological well-being (Riggle et al., 2017). Although choosing to conceal or disclose one's sexual orientation may impact the ways in which sexual orientation minorities interact with coworkers, in the long run, revealing rather than concealing one's identity can serve to improve intrapersonal and workplace outcomes (Sabat et al., 2017).

Gender Identity: Transgender Employees

Transgender employees are more likely to disclose their stigmatized status if they perceive that they will be supported by the organization, if being transgender is important to their overall identity, and if they are "out" to those outside the workplace (Law, Martinez, Ruggs, Hebl, & Akers, 2011). Like LGB individuals, transgender individuals may become vulnerable to discrimination if they choose to reveal their stigmatized identity. Transgender individuals are often grouped with those who identify as LGB; however, LGB are sexual orientations and transgender refers to a gender identity (Discont, Russell, & Sawyer, 2016). It is recommended that this distinction is made when discussing LGBT-related workplace issues because sexual orientation minorities and transgender minorities can have different experiences. Although there may be overlap between the issues and barriers faced by sexual orientation minorities and transgender minorities, the latter also encounters unique issues in the workplace.

One unique issue can be determining which bathroom to use. Bathroom usage is a hot topic that has gained national attention over the past few years. Some transgender individuals prefer to use the bathroom that corresponds to their gender identity, which has come with both support and backlash from various groups. Dislike of and misperceptions about transgender people may be partly responsible for the passage of anti-trans legislation such as the now-repealed "Bathroom Bill" in North Carolina. This bill prohibited individuals who identify with a gender that does not match their biological sex at birth from using the bathroom that corresponds to their gender identity (Sawyer, Thai, Martinez, Smith, & Discont, 2016). The bathroom controversy manifests itself in the workplace when transgender individuals are not permitted to use their preferred bathroom, when coworkers have an issue with transgender individuals' bathroom use, and when transgender individuals avoid going to the bathroom (Occupational Safety and Health Administration, 2016). According to OSHA (2016), the latter can negatively impact that individual's mental and physical health.

RECRUITMENT AND SELECTION

For most job applicants, the recruitment process is the first glance potential employees have of an organization's image and values. If individuals perceive that the organization is a place where discrimination and prejudice exists, individuals could be wary of the organization's culture or form incorrect judgements about the organization, resulting in a decision to not apply for employment. If interviewers and recruiters are actually biased against LGBT individuals, LGBT applicants face potential discrimination when being considered for the position.

Recruitment

Organizations may want to investigate how to best attract and retain LGBT employees due to the diverse perspectives they can bring to organizations. Lindsey, King, McCausland, Jones, and Dunleavy (2013) recommend that organizations attempt to attract more diverse employees through targeted recruitment, authentic commitment, explicit communications of diversity-related recruitment efforts, and facilitation of the application process by ensuring application materials are accessible.

State and local nondiscrimination policies can also play a key role in recruiting diverse employees. For example, when a transgender nondiscrimination ordinance was passed in Charlotte, NC, the state legislature passed House Bill 2 in March 2016 to effectively overturn the local ordinance, which had allowed transgender individuals to use the bathrooms of their choice (Parks & Parrish, 2017). In the aftermath of the contentious political debate surrounding the bill and local ordinance, Elon University, located in North Carolina, sent a survey to students who had chosen not to enroll. Out of the surveyed students, 17% reported that the state law had affected their decision-making process (Parks & Parrish, 2017), which suggests that people do take state and local laws and ordinances into account when deciding on organization affiliation.

It should be noted that some occupations are also considered more "gay-friendly" than other occupations, which could affect the ability of some organizations to recruit sexual minorities (Ueno, Pena-Talamantes, & Roach, 2013). For example, as noted by Ueno and colleagues (2013), sexual minority women are overrepresented in craft, operative, and service jobs and underrepresented in managerial, administrative support, and sales jobs, compared to heterosexual women. Meanwhile, sexual minority men are overrepresented in professional, technical, administrative support, and sales positions and underrepresented in managerial, operative, and craft positions. It could be that some of these occupations are considered more suitable for and friendly to certain sexual minorities. Therefore, if organizations do not attempt to recruit sexual minorities, they may not apply for positions that are not perceived as sexual-minority-friendly.

Selection

Research has shown that sexual minorities and heterosexuals differ in their level of success in educational and earnings attainment, and part of this difference may be due to bias in the selection process (Ueno et al., 2013). Specifically, if interviewers and recruiters are biased against LGBT individuals, they may not be selected due to their stigmatized status. Indeed, it is still legal in many U.S. states to treat employees differently in terms of compensation, promotion, hiring, and termination, based on sexual orientation and/or gender identity (Mishel, 2016). Previous research has shown that heterosexual applicants are more desirable than LGBT applicants and may also be more likely to be invited back for a second interview (Drydakis, 2015; Everly, Unzueta, & Shih, 2016; Mishel, 2016; Tilcsik, 2011). For example, Mishel (2016) found that, for a fictitious woman who submitted résumés to 800 jobs online, the résumé that included a secretarial position in a LGBT student organization received 30% fewer callbacks than the control, which did not contain LGBT information. In a field study, Drydakis (2015) found that the probability of receiving an invitation for an interview for gay or lesbian applicants (signaled by the student unions they participated in), was lower than that of their heterosexual counterparts. Additionally, Drydakis (2015) found that the sexual minority applicants received invitations to interview with firms that paid lower salaries than the firms that invited heterosexual applicants to interview.

As noted by King and Cortina (2010), LGBT individuals earn substantially less money than heterosexual individuals. Mize (2016) examined labor market outcomes separately for gay men, lesbian women, and bisexual individuals and found that bisexual workers faced acute disadvantages in the labor market, including a wage gap that could not be explained by differences in human capital (i.e., education, occupational choice). This wage gap could be partially contributing to the differences in occupational status achieved by sexual minorities versus heterosexuals (Ueno et al., 2013).

Occupational status, which refers to the standard of living based on a person's occupation, is generally measured through educational qualifications and earnings (Ueno et al., 2013). Sexual minorities seem to lack representation across several major occupational categories, compared to heterosexuals (Ueno et al., 2013). These differences have been attributed to several factors, including varying levels of discrimination against sexual minorities in selection, dependent on occupation.

Much of the literature concerning discrimination against sexual minorities seems to have found that the levels and rates of discrimination depend upon the occupation in question (Rule, Bjornsdottir, Tskhay, & Ambady, 2016; Ueno et al., 2013). Additionally, much of this difference seems to be explained by whether the occupation is considered more agentic (i.e., assertive, dominant, achieving, need for status) or communal (i.e., sensitive, desirous of harmony, agreeable; Pyatt, 2014; Rule et al., 2016; Wilson, 2016). Agentic qualities are more readily associated with men, while communal qualities are more readily associated with women, but the reverse of this relationship seems to be true with sexual orientation minorities. For example, Pyatt (2014) found that lesbian job applicants were considered to have more agentic qualities than heterosexual women, heterosexual men, and gay men, and agentic ratings were a significant predictor of both hiring decisions and salary recommendations. Despite this predictive relationship, however, there were no differences in hiring or salary recommendations across the four groups studied. Rule et al. (2016) found that without any mention of target sexuality, people tend to rate gay men as more likely to be successful than heterosexual men in obtaining a nursing job in the next six months. Further, heterosexual men were considered more likely to be successful than gay men in obtaining an engineering job in the next six months. Rule et al. (2016) suggested these results may be due to the perception that nursing jobs are more communal and engineering jobs are more agentic.

Similarly, Wilson (2016) compared hiring ratings and salary recommendations between transgender and cisgender applicants (here, cisgender describes someone whose gender identity matches their birth sex), and found that transgender versus cisgender identity did not appear to influence hiring ratings or salary recommendations when participants viewed résumés for an executive position, though cisgender females were perceived as significantly more communal than transgender females. Related research has found other interesting patterns. For example, in terms of earnings, sexual minority women tend to earn more than heterosexual women, but sexual minority men tend to lag behind heterosexual men in earnings (Mize, 2016; Ueno, et al., 2013). Moreover, the results of the Pyatt (2014) and Wilson (2016) studies, which found no differences in hiring and salary recommendations between sexual minority groups and the majority, may be due to demand characteristics and social desirability effects (Shadish, Cook, & Campbell, 2002).

It is important to note that, although sexual orientation is generally considered a perceptually ambiguous characteristic, meaning it is not as visually salient as other identities, sexual orientation is still correctly perceived at a rate better than chance (Rule et al., 2016). This phenomenon could potentially affect the hiring and selection process. Using a sample of working adults with previous hiring experience, Rule et al. (2016) found that participants preferred homosexual men as English teachers and heterosexual men as math teachers, when they were told that the men in the pictures were upcoming graduates seeking teaching positions. In addition, Rule et al. (2016) found that people preferred the images of heterosexual men over the images of homosexual men when they were asked who they would prefer to medically treat a loved one, and this pattern applied to selecting both surgeons and pediatricians, even though pediatricians were selected as a more communal occupation. This research suggests that there is evidence for discrimination against sexual orientation minorities in the hiring process, particularly for occupations that are considered more agentic.

However, not all research has found consistent evidence for discrimination against sexual minorities in selection and hiring. For example, Bailey, Wallace, and Wright (2013) found no significant differences between homosexual versus heterosexual internet applicants in being contacted by potential employers. Mishel (2016) suggested that these results could be attributed to the fact that Bailey et al. (2013) only sent résumés to employers in large metropolitan cities, which tend to have thriving LGBT communities. Interestingly, Mishel (2016) also studied larger, more LGBT-friendly metropolises (e.g., New York and Washington, D. C.) and found that LGBT-identified women were called back significantly less than heterosexual-identified women.

POST-HIRING

Even if LGBT individuals do not experience bias in the selection process, they may still face difficulties and discrimination after they are hired. These difficulties may occur during LGBT employees' interactions with their coworkers. In addition, these issues can affect opportunities for advancement and possibly result in termination.

Workplace Dynamics

Some individuals may not come out to their coworkers due to the fear of rejection, which can be stressful (Meyer, 2003). In an effort to conceal their sexual orientation, some LGB individuals might even avoid engaging in informal conversations with colleagues. As a result, important relationships, particularly those involving trust between coworkers, may never be truly established. This is one example of how navigating one's sexual orientation identity in the workplace can impact relationships with colleagues. Further, even if one is "out" to colleagues, the interactions among them may still be different compared to the interactions among heterosexual employees.

For example, LGB employees can face a double-standard when it comes to sharing information with their coworkers (Human Rights Campaign, 2014). Many non-work-related conversations that occur between coworkers revolve around social relationships and significant others. The Human Rights Campaign (HRC, 2014) found that 70% of non-LGB employees believe that sexual orientation should not be discussed at work, but many of them do not realize that heterosexual is a sexual orientation. Although most non-LGB employees believe that LGB employees should not have to hide who they are at work, more than half are not comfortable hearing about LGB employees' personal relationships (HRC, 2014). Because opposite-sex relationships are deemed the norm, consistent with heterosexism, any amount of sharing by a homosexual man or woman, even when on a similar level to that of a heterosexual man or woman, may be viewed as oversharing (HRC, 2014). Therefore, many LGB individuals may not share at all or even disclose their sexual orientation. According to the HRC (2014), 38% of LGB employees chose not to disclose their sexual orientation because they did not want to make others uncomfortable, potentially indicating internalized homophobia. Transgender employees, another stigmatized group, may face similar issues when managing their gender identity.

Promotion

Another potential issue that LGBT employees may encounter in the workplace is the lack of advancement opportunities. Lewis and Pitts (2015) found that LGBT federal service workers are less satisfied with their treatment than non-LGBT workers. Specifically, 34% of LGBT workers were not satisfied with advancement opportunities. In general, LGBT federal service workers reported significantly higher dissatisfaction regarding pay, performance evaluations, and opportunities to advance in the organization. They were also less likely to agree that promotions in their organization were based on merit (Lewis & Pitts, 2015). Similarly, Cech and Pham (2017) discovered that LGBT employees in science, technology, engineering, and mathematics (STEM) organizations reported significantly more negative workplace treatment than their heterosexual colleagues. Specifically, LGBT employees felt significantly less respected by their supervisors, reported less opportunities to improve their skills, reported less access to resources, and had more negative performance evaluations, all of which can impede promotional opportunities. Sexual minority women in STEM may especially be subject to unfair treatment because of their sexual orientation and gender (Cech & Pham, 2017). Some of these factors, especially performance evaluations, can be particularly influential when evaluating individuals for upper-level management positions.

There are many other factors that can stymie the promotion of LGBT employees such as a lack of networking opportunities (Workplace Fairness, 2016). Networking opportunities may be difficult for LGBT employees to attain due to a lack of connections (Parnell, Lease, & Green, 2012). Because many organizations are and can turn into "good ole boys" clubs where positions are attained by knowing someone, it may be difficult for sexual minorities, especially those who are also a racial minority, to gain entry into those clubs (Parnell et al., 2012). Further, sexual minority women can encounter barriers due to sex discrimination, career-child conflict, and choosing to take non-traditional careers (Parnell et al., 2012). High levels of heterosexism and having a low socioeconomic status can also lead to lower chances of attaining decent work, which may inherently have a greater number of opportunities for advancement (Douglass, Velez, Conlin, Duffy, & England, 2017). Douglass et al. (2017) describe decent work as a job or organization that is safe, provides good healthcare and compensation, allows for rest, and embodies pro-family and pro-social values. Moreover, one may choose a career based on whether one's sexual orientation will be accepted, which may or may not be the career that one most desires or that will offer advancement opportunities (McFadden, 2015).

However, LGBT employees may still face barriers even if they are offered an opportunity for advancement. An LGBT employee in a global organization may be offered an opportunity to climb the hierarchy in a company; however, this may require that employee to move to another country or visit for an extended period of time. The employee not only has to consider the typical factors (e.g., housing, transportation, pay, and family) involved in a move to another country, but one must also consider what the climate is like for LGBT individuals (Gedro, Mizzi, Rocco, & van Loo, 2013). Specifically, the employee might want to know if there is any protective legislation, if same-sex marriage is permitted, and the general sentiments towards LGBT individuals and families with same-sex parents (McPhail, McNulty, & Hutchings, 2014). Depending on the circumstances, a sexual orientation minority may have to decline a promotion in another country if it is perceived as uncomfortable or unsafe. Another problem that can stem from an opportunity to go abroad is that an otherwise closeted employee may have to disclose one's sexual orientation to one's supervisor and organization. In this case, the supervisor and organization may feel that this particular employee should not reside in a country due to the present attitudes toward LGBT individuals, which can create what McNulty and Hutchings (2016) call a "glass border." Additionally, it could leave the individual susceptible to prejudice and discrimination, including termination (McNulty & Hutchings, 2016).

Termination

Just as LGBT individuals can face challenges when it comes to promotion opportunities, they can be subject to other potential discriminatory actions such as unjust termination. Bell, Berry, Marquardt, and Green (2013) refer to discriminatory job loss (DJL) as "involuntary separation due to inequitable treatment based on personal factors that are irrelevant to performance" (p. 585). According to this description, one's sexual orientation can be considered a personal factor. Examples of DJL include discriminatory termination, discriminatory layoff, retaliatory termination, and constructive discharge (Bell et al., 2013). The authors suggest that economic conditions, population diversity, the regulatory environment, and organizational diversity climate impact DJL. Further, they claim that DJL can lead to outcomes such as decreased self-esteem, self-efficacy, perceived control, and re-employment quality as well as an increase in unemployment duration.

LGBT individuals, particularly gay men, may be especially vulnerable to DJL in industries that are highly masculinized, such as law enforcement. According to Collins (2016), there are numerous documented cases of law enforcement officers who were fired for being gay. Further, they can be subject to harassment and teasing, among other forms of discrimination. These aforementioned reasons in addition to the possibility of being subject to heavy scrutiny may prevent or inhibit gay law enforcement personnel from coming out to their colleagues. Indeed, in other contexts such as entrepreneurship, it has been found that homosexual entrepreneurs are judged more harshly than their heterosexual counterparts after they fail (Shepherd & Patzelt, 2015). Alternatively, gay law enforcement personnel may choose to come out because they do not want to be outed by someone else (Collins, 2016). If they choose to come out, it could negatively affect chances for promotion within law enforcement or increase the likelihood of being terminated. Although most organizations have policies stating that they do not discriminate against those who identify as LGBT, the extent to which federal and state legislation protects LGBT employees continues to evolve.

LEGAL ISSUES

Currently, there is no federal legislation that protects against discrimination of LGBT individuals in the workplace and very few states provide protection for LGBT employees (Human Rights Campaign, 2016). Researchers have noted that there exists a patchwork of legal protection at the state or city level (Barron & Hebl, 2013; Hebl, Barron, Cox, & Corrington, 2016). Thus, individual organizations can have their own policies regarding LGBT employees, as long as the policies do not violate state laws. As of 2014, 91% of Fortune 500 companies had protections for sexual orientation minorities, and 61% had protections based on gender identity (Human Rights Campaign, 2016). However, company-implemented policies and protections do not always prevent discrimination from occurring, such as being unjustly terminated. In 2016, there was a sexual orientation discrimination case taken up by the EEOC, but it was settled out of court (EEOC, 2016). In EEOC v. Pallet Companies, Inc. (EEOC, 2016), the employee alleged that she consistently endured harassment from her supervisor, which included offensive comments and suggestions that she should "turn back into a woman" and wear dresses. After complaining to management, the employee was terminated in retaliation. IFCO Systems, the umbrella company of Pallet Companies, Inc. was ordered to pay the employee $182,200 with an additional $20,000 being sent to the HRC.

The push for federal protection for LGBT employees is not a recent trend. Activists have attempted to pass versions of the Employment Non-Discrimination Act (ENDA) in the Senate and House of Representatives since the 1970s but have yet to be successful (Gates, 2010). According to the Gay & Lesbian Alliance Against Defamation (GLAAD, 2016), ENDA would provide federal protections for LGBT employees in both organizations with more than fifteen employees and government employers, making it illegal to discriminate based on sexual orientation and gender identity; it would be enforced similar to Title VII in that LGBT individuals would be protected against discriminatory practices in hiring, firing, promoting, harassing, compensating, and other conditions of employment (Gates & Rodgers, 2014; GLAAD, 2016). Further, transgender employees would have the freedom to dress in accordance with the gender they identify with or to which they are transitioning. Essentially, employees can dress as they please, so long as it is in accordance with the organizations' professional standards (e.g., no jeans at work). According to GLAAD (2016), legislation such as ENDA would increase a sense of safety amongst LGBT employees and thus, increase their job satisfaction and productivity. However, this protection would not extend to religious institutions or affiliated organizations (GLAAD, 2016). For this reason, many organizations, such as the American Civil Liberties Union (ACLU) and Lambda Legal rescinded their support of ENDA (Garcia, 2015). The most recent version of ENDA (2013) was passed in the Senate, but the House of Representatives never took it up for a vote; the last action was taken in January 2014.

However, there is a more recent bill, The Equality Act, which was introduced in the House of Representatives in July 2015. The Equality Act is more encompassing than ENDA; it would provide protections for LGBT individuals not only in employment but also in areas such as housing, credit, and public spaces and services by amending current legislation (Human Rights Campaign, 2016). This legislation includes but is not limited to the Civil Rights Act of 1964, the Equal Credit Opportunity Act, and the Fair Housing Act. Further, it would prevent organizations from using the Religious Freedom Restoration Act of 1993 to challenge these protections. The last action that was taken on The Equality Act was in May 2017 when the House of Representatives introduced it. Although what will become of this act remains unclear, an executive order, E.O. 13672, was signed by former President Barack Obama in 2014 to prohibit discrimination based on sexual orientation and gender identity for federal contractors and subcontractors (U.S. Department of Labor, 2016). Although the LGBT community awaits explicit federal protections for all employees, coverage by interpretation under Title VII might offer the best chance of being protected at work.

SOME BEST-PRACTICES IN HUMAN RESOURCE MANAGEMENT

Having reviewed the issues that LGBT individuals face in the workplace, we now turn to some best-practices. In the following sections, we discuss these from the perspective of HRM professionals and for employees in general.

Suggestions for Practitioners

It is important to train managers, supervisors, and others in positions of power to: (a) recruit LGBT individuals (b) select individuals without bias or discrimination, and (c) maintain policies to assist LGBT-related issues. This involves utilizing resources like professional standards, research, and following laws protecting LBGT employees.

Organizations may want to consider a more proactive approach to recruiting more LGBT individuals by working directly with organizations such as the HRC and Out & Equal Workplace Advocates. Human resource practitioners should be aware that enacting affirmative-action policies are generally accepted legal justifications. For example, the Occupational Safety and Health Administration (OSHA, 2016) suggest the best bathroom-use practice for employers is to allow transgender employees to use the bathroom that corresponds with their gender identity. Organizations can communicate their inclusiveness by publishing resolutions condemning any state or local discriminatory policies (Parks & Parrish, 2017). Implementing affirmative action-type practices in favor of LGBT employees has been explored, due to the discrimination often faced by LGBT employees.

This approach has been enacted in some colleges and universities in the U.S. (Brown, 2015). Further, colleges and universities actively recruit sexual minority students. Cegler (2012) found that colleges and universities engage in passive recruitment, such as advertising LGBT-friendly policies and services. In addition, Newhouse (2013) explains that some colleges and universities in the U.S. ask potential students if they identify with the LGBT community on admission applications to help convey an environment of acceptance and inclusiveness. Newhouse (2013) suggests there is potential for other organizations to adopt similar approaches when seeking job applicants, within the bounds of local and national employment laws. Parks and Parrish (2017) found that organizations can recruit potential employees by publishing statements of nondiscrimination based on sexual orientation or gender identity. Lambert (2013) found that having an LGBT-supportive recruitment statement has been related to an overall decrease in job pursuit intentions. However, inclusive recruitment statements may serve as tools that screen out individuals who may not value diversity and inclusion, helping maintain an overall inclusive work environment.

Related to targeted recruitment, Casper, Wayne, and Manegold (2013) suggest appealing to potential employees' self-interests by advertising resources and diversity policies that would benefit them personally. In similar research, Abben (2015) found that when LGBT participants looked at a fictitious company website they perceived greater person-organization fit when the website included a statement about domestic-partnerships being covered under the company benefits or when the website listed community partnerships with LGBT-oriented organizations, compared to a control website that listed neither of these statements. Abben (2015) also asked participants for qualitative responses regarding what they looked for to determine if an organization offered an LGBT-friendly workplace. Some responses included searching for information about EEO and anti-discrimination policies, benefits for domestic-partners, leave for adoptive parents, and in-house resource groups for LGBT employees (Abben, 2015). In addition, some participants noted that the use of gender-neutral language and avoiding terms like "traditional" or "conservative" were advantageous (Abben, 2015). Overall, research suggests that targeted recruitment via websites can have an impact on potential LGBT employees' perceptions of organizations.

Once LBGT individuals are recruited it is important to ensure selection and hiring personnel are trained to treat all applicants fairly and without bias, regardless of their sexual orientation or gender identity. For instance, HRM practitioners should complete implicit bias training among other forms of training to increase awareness of biases and to learn strategies to mitigate implicit bias. Another way to potentially reduce bias in hiring is to hold the interviewer accountable for their decision (Nadler, Lowery, Grebinoski, & Jones, 2014). For example, Nadler et al. (2014) had participants rate a videotaped interview of either a homosexual or heterosexual man and told participants they would have to justify their ratings. Nadler et al. (2014) found that when the justification of the ratings was required, ratings were less likely to be biased toward the heterosexual applicant. These results suggest that holding individuals accountable for their decisions during the selection process of potential employees could reduce adverse impact against sexual minorities.

Lindsey et al. (2013) offers other recommendations for decreasing bias in the selection process. They recommend training human resource personnel and decision makers on how to avoid bias and discrimination in the selection process. For example, employees should receive compliance training to ensure they follow rules and regulations related to non-discriminatory laws and policies. Lindsey et al. (2013) also recommend that selection procedures be designed to decrease bias by emphasizing standardization and consistency while decreasing subjectivity. Further, interviewers should use structured interviews rather than unstructured interviews when interviewing potential employees (Lindsey et al., 2013). Although Lindsey et al. (2013) suggest some unconventional approaches (e.g., eliminating interviews), additional empirical research is needed in this area.

Not only can the recruitment and selection processes be improved to lessen and hopefully eliminate discrimination against LGBT employees, organizations can foster an inclusive environment by simply encouraging open discussion about, and acknowledgement of, gender and LGBT issues. Additionally, organizations should have fair and non-discriminatory policies in place to manage various issues and conflicts that can occur. For example, organizations should know how to respond to an employee who comes "out" as transgender and announces that he or she is going to transition (Collins, McFadden, Rocco, & Mathis, 2015). This transition can impact workplace dynamics and how other employees and managers interact with the employee. Specifically, pronoun use will change, and depending on how coworkers react, he or she may be mocked, excluded from conversations, or intentionally referred to by the incorrect pronoun (Collins et al., 2015; Nadal, Skolnik, & Wong, 2012). Coworker reactions have been shown to predict workplace discrimination against transgender employees who come "out" (Ruggs, Martinez, Hebl, & Law, 2015). However, when reactions from coworkers are positive, job anxiety for transgender employees is likely to decrease (Law et al., 2011). After the transition, other changes may occur with transgender females losing status and transgender males receiving an increase in status, which can be tied to gender bias (Martinez & Smith, 2016). Though this transition may still be controversial, it is important to implement diversity training that includes transgender employees to educate employees at all levels of the organization on how to effectively cope with and react to these situations.

Suggestions for Employees

With the increased awareness of LGBT issues in our modern culture, various attempts have been made to mitigate some issues that members of this community face in the workplace. Many organizations have turned to diversity training programs as a way to create a more open and accepting workplace for all employees. In fact, Köllen (2016a) found that companies in Germany that include sexual orientation as part of their diversity programs were associated with supportive organizational climates for gay men and lesbians.

Lindsey et al. (2015) offer some recommendations on how to effectively implement diversity training promoting LGB inclusion. In their study, Lindsey et al. (2015) examined three different interactive diversity training approaches, including perspective taking, goal setting, and stereotype discrediting. Perspective taking reduces prejudice by requiring individuals to examine what it would be like in "someone else's shoes," specifically a stigmatized group, in diversity training. This breaks down in-group bias and reduces "us versus them" mentality. Goal setting involves trainees setting challenging, but achievable, diversity-related goals involving a specific stigmatized group. Last, stereotype discrediting involves trainees actively discrediting common stereotypes about a stigmatized out-group.

Lindsay et al. (2015) found perspective taking to be the most effective training method for increasing supportive behaviors toward LGB individuals after a time lapse of eight months. Lindsay et al. (2015) suggest that perspective taking may increase trainees' internal motivation to respond to LGB individuals without prejudice. Additionally, Lindsay et al. (2015) found that dispositional empathy moderated the relationship between training method and motivation to respond without prejudice. Individuals who were high in empathy did not experience an increase in internal motivation to respond without prejudice, while those low in empathy did experience this increase. Lindsay et al. (2015) suggested that individuals who are already high in empathy are also high in internal motivation to respond without prejudice, thus, they do not experience the same motivation increase those low in empathy do. The authors suggest that the study be replicated; we suggest the study be replicated with transgender individuals, as they were not included in this study.

In another study looking specifically at diversity training related to sexual minorities, Madera, King, and Hebl (2013) used a goal-setting approach. Madera et al. (2013) found that individuals who developed sexual orientation supportive goals in training reported more supportive behaviors and attitudes toward lesbian women and gay men. Additionally, Madera et al. (2013) found that sexual orientation supportive behaviors mediated the relationship between goal-setting training and attitudes toward sexual orientation minorities. Although data was collected 3 months and 8 months after the training, Madera et al. (2013) found that behaviors and attitudes toward sexual minority individuals were influenced at 8 months, but not at 3 months, suggesting that participants needed time to meet their goals and change their behaviors.

Another study examined the effects of LGBT-oriented diversity training for law enforcement personnel (Israel, Harkness, Delucio, Ledbetter, & Avellar, 2014). Israel et al. (2014) evaluated participants' pre- and post-test knowledge of interpersonal communication apprehension and self-efficacy in working with LGBT individuals and communities. The researchers found significant increases on knowledge and confidence in using LGBT-affirming tactics on the job from pre- to post-test, but no significant differences were found in participants' comfort with working with LGBT individuals. Although this sounds promising, it should be noted that this was a pre- and post-test design without a control group because the training was mandatory, it is difficult to discern if the results found were due to maturation effects, testing effects, or some other factor (Shadish et al., 2002). In addition, the post-test was administered immediately after the training; it is unclear if the training effects persist long-term.

In recent years, there has been an increased interest in implicit bias training (Lindsey & Gilrane, 2016) for employees. There is a need for research in this area with the LGBT community, especially because implicit biases can permeate any occupation and hiring practice. For example, over 80% of medical students reported some implicit bias against sexual orientation minorities and over 45% held explicit biases (Burke et al., 2015). These biases may seriously impact patient care through potential violation of the Hippocratic Oath and subjecting individuals to unjust medical practices. Transcending the medical field, these findings could imply that bias can impact how employees interact with their coworkers, customers, and business partners. Therefore, it is important that researchers continue to study both the effects of implicit bias and ways to reduce it (Lindsey, King, McCausland, Jones, & Dunleavy, 2013).

However, diversity training programs do not come without drawbacks. For example, Duguid and Thomas-Hunt (2015) found that making people more aware of prevalent stereotypes, as is often done in diversity training, actually exacerbates subsequent stereotypic attitudes about and behavior toward out-group members. This is a key finding because some diversity training methods include stereotype discrediting, which involves directly confronting common stereotypes (Lindsey, King, Hebl, & Levine, 2015). However, based on findings of Duguid and Thomas-Hunt (2015), this strategy may be counteractive to enhancing diversity. HRM practitioners should bear in mind findings such as the ones discussed as they design organizational interventions to promote diversity and acceptance.

Backlash from the majority is another consideration that must be taken into account when designing diversity training programs (Bartels et al., 2013). However, one way to attenuate the risk of backlash is to explicitly include the majority group in an organization's diversity approach; this approach is called all-inclusive multiculturalism (Jansen, Otten, & van der Zee, 2015). Jansen and colleagues (2015) found the all-inclusive multicultural approach, compared to a usual diversity approach, led to higher levels of anticipated inclusion for prospective employees with a high need for belonging. In a follow-up study, Jansen et al. (2015), found the all-inclusive multicultural approach also made current organizational members feel more included, regardless of individual levels of need to belong. Additionally, perceived inclusion was positively related to members of the majority's support for diversity efforts. From these results, it can be concluded that all-inclusive multiculturalism may be a more effective approach to organizational diversity, at least with regard to preventing backlash from the majority and increasing majority support for diversity efforts. In this same line of research, Köllen (2016a) conducted a study in Germany and found that organizational practices that lessen the differences between homosexuality and heterosexuality were more strongly related to positive psychological climates than those practices that accentuated the differences. Additionally, Köllen (2016a) found that practices like "Equalization of heterosexual and homosexual partnerships, internal thematization of homosexuality, and gay marketing are associated with positive climate perceptions; LGBT networks and mentoring are not" (p. 1967).

Lindsey et al. (2013) recommend diversity training to increase inclusion in the workplace, which they suggest can aid in nondiscrimination compliance and increase general appreciation for diversity among employees. Parks and Parrish (2017) also note that inclusion-oriented practices must involve ongoing education, specifically in the form of regularly offered and mandatory trainings. Diversity training, in general, addresses issues of identity, power and privilege, stereotyping, conflict management, and inclusive behavior (Ferdman & Sagiv, 2012). Diversity training can also address organizational models and values regarding diversity, accompanied by strategies for change. One recent meta-analysis on diversity training provided evidence that diversity training influences affective-based, cognitive-based, and skill-based trainee outcomes (Kalinoski et al., 2013). Another more recent meta-analysis on diversity training found an overall effect size (Hedges g) for diversity training of 0.38 (Bezrukova, Spell, Perry, & Jehn, 2016). Additionally, these researchers found that diversity training had the largest effect on reactions to training and cognitive learning, and smaller effects on behavioral and affective learning. Diversity training also seemed most effective when it was complemented by other diversity initiatives targeting awareness and skills development.

Conclusion

There are a variety of practices that organizations can utilize to improve the climate for LGBT applicants and employees. Notably, research suggests that organizations may be more likely to benefit when they take a comprehensive and integrative approach that utilizes diversity and equality management systems (DEMS; Konrad, Yang, & Maurer, 2016). DEMS include such initiatives as diversity training, recruitment monitoring, and promoting minorities. In a Canadian study, Konrad and colleagues (2016) found that DEMS were associated with more positive organizational outcomes. Even more tangible outcomes, like an organization's return on assets (i.e., a measure of firm performance assessing how effectively a company uses its assets) were correlated with the presence of DEMS.

FUTURE RESEARCH OPPORTUNITIES

Having reviewed extant research and offered some practical recommendations, there are various research areas to be investigated regarding the experiences of employees belonging to the LGBT community. For example, because there is a need for additional research on transgender employees (McFadden, 2015), the use of longitudinal studies can help better understand transgender employees' experiences with transitioning, how workplace dynamics are impacted by the transition, and how to address conflicts that may arise. Further, organizations should be aware of the differences that might occur when an individual transitions from a woman to a man versus from a man to a woman. There is also limited research on bisexual employees (McFadden, 2015).

Further research is also needed to investigate the impact sexual minority status has on selection and hiring outcomes. Research needs to be conducted on how other factors, like applicant race and sexual minority status, interact with LGBT identity during the selection process (Mishel, 2016). Sawyer, Salter, and Thoroughgood (2013) advocate for such intersectional research. There is a substantial gap in the research about how having both racial minority and sexual minority status can impact employees in the workplace, which is the type of research that is advocated by Sawyer et al. (2013). These two identities could interact and expose employees to even greater discrimination than their counterparts that belong to only one minority status group. Sexual minority status could also interact with disability status, making individuals more vulnerable to workplace prejudice and discrimination. Additionally, although a few occupations in the U.S. (e.g., administrative, clerical, executive) have been examined through resume audit studies, future research should investigate other, specific positions to better understand where and with what positions LGBT individuals are at the highest risk for discrimination.

There are additional opportunities for research related to LGBT workplace issues. First, is the promotion of LGBT inclusivity worth potential backlash? This not only applies to revenue but also to public image. In an effort to promote an inclusive workplace environment, organizations can be involved in community outreach and take steps to ensure that their advertisements appear more diverse. However, some individuals and groups may react negatively to outreach and advertisements that involve, for example, same-sex couples; it might be necessary to examine the demographics and characteristics of those individuals who "boycott" organizations. Some groups will ask their supporters and others to boycott these organizations in retaliation. Does this backlash actually have a significant impact on these organizations? Or, does the promotion of inclusion lead people to offer more support to those organizations, thereby making backlash a non-factor? Similarly, researchers can further examine organizational outcomes before and after implementation of a policy or a diversity and inclusion initiative.

In general, there is a lack of research on how to implement effective diversity training, specifically for sexual orientation and gender identity. This is due, in part, to the fact that most studies on diversity training have focused on visible identities (Kalinoski et al., 2013). For example, out of the 65 studies analyzed in Kalinoski et al.'s (2013) meta-analysis, only four focused on the LGBT community. Therefore, for diversity training to be effective, it should be based on valid empirical research. It is especially important that future research addresses several factors. For example, research could be conducted on who is most resistant to diversity training in terms of personality characteristics. Though not LGBT-specific, research suggests that individuals who have a high social dominance orientation may not benefit from diversity training (Martinez & Smith, 2016). In addition, researchers could examine if it is more beneficial to have a heterosexual, cisgender person delivering the training or if it should be delivered by a member of the LGBT community.

Future research should investigate how the perception of diversity training can be improved. For many people, diversity training carries a negative connotation. However, if it could be linked to tangible consequences, perceptions could change. For example, participation in training and the desired behavioral outcomes of the training could be tied to a rewards system or performance appraisal. Another topic of future research interest may be how to apply newer media (e.g., some forms of web-based instruction, virtual reality, online video-based instruction) to the implementation of diversity training, and how different media may impact the effectiveness of the training (Rupp, Gibbons, & Snyder, 2008). Mindfulness training is another area with potential for future research regarding diversity training (Allen et al., 2015).

CONCLUSION

Throughout this article, we have discussed the intersection between LGBT issues and phases of the employment cycle. Beyond potentially experiencing bias in the recruitment and selection process, members of the LGBT community face unique challenges and bias on the job. They must manage their sexual orientation or gender identity in a way that they feel is safe for them and allows them to avoid negative consequences. These consequences can come in the form of being rejected by coworkers, having less access to promotional opportunities, and being increasingly susceptible to unjust termination. Overall, LGBT individuals can face discrimination at any phase of the employment cycle based on their sexual orientation or gender identity. These issues not only impact personal outcomes but they also impact organizational outcomes. An unwelcoming environment, the presence of minority stress and microaggressions, and a lack of inclusive policies can affect personal outcomes such as health and job attitudes. This can also affect organizational outcomes such as retention, productivity, and organizational attractiveness (Meyer, 2003; Rabelo & Cortina, 2014; Riggle et al., 2017).

However, there are a variety of strategies that have been presented in this article that can be used in all phases of the employment cycle by HRM professionals. These strategies, including diversity training, can help to decrease bias and discrimination, starting with recruitment and selection. The strategies can also promote an LGBT-supportive workplace that will improve the employment of

LGBT employees and make them less susceptible to wrongful termination or rejection for promotion.

It is important that valid, empirical research be distilled and disseminated such that practitioners in HRM can implement best practices in the workplace. These best practices will improve the work lives of LGBT workers and those around them, creating a safe and inclusive environment for everyone. All employees should have equal opportunities regardless of their gender identity or sexual orientation. In pursuing inclusivity (Huffman, Watrous, & King, 2008), organizations have the chance to not only improve the well-being of their employees, but also improve the well-being of the organization.

REFERENCES

Abben, D. R. (2015). *Web-based recruitment: Strategies for attracting LGBT employees* (Master's thesis). DePaul University's College of Science and Health Theses and Dissertations. (Paper 104). Retrieved from: doi: http://via.library.depaul.edu/csh_etd/104.

Allen, T. D., Eby, L. T., Conley, K. M., Williamson, R. L., Mancini, V. S., & Mitchell, M. E. (2015). What do we *really* know about the effects of mindfulness-based training in the workplace? *Industrial and Organizational Psychology, 8*(4), 652–661. doi: https://doi.org/10.1017/iop.2015.95

Anteby, M., & Anderson, C. (2014). The shifting landscape of LGBT organizational research. *Research in Organizational Behavior, 34*, 3–25. Retrieved from: https://dash.harvard.edu/bitstream/handle/1/15217573/anteby,anderson_shifting-landscape-of-LGBT-Org-Research.pdf?sequence=1

Bailey, J., Wallace, M., & Wright, B. (2013). Are gay men and lesbians discriminated against when applying for jobs? A four-city, internet-based field experiment. *Journal of Homosexuality, 60*(6), 873–894. doi: https://doi.org/10.1080/00918369.2013.774860

Barron, L. G., & Hebl, M. (2013). The force of law: The effects of sexual orientation antidiscrimination legislation on interpersonal discrimination in employment. *Psychology, Public Policy, and Law, 19*(2), 191–205. Retrieved from: http://dx.doi.org/10.1037/a0028350

Bartels, L. K., Nadler, J. T., Kufahl, K., & Pyatt, J. (2013). Fifty years after the Civil Rights Act: Diversity-management practices in the field. *Industrial and Organizational Psychology: Perspectives on Science and Practice, 6*(4), 450–457. doi: https://doi.org/10.1111/iops.12083

Bell, M. P., Berry, D. P., Marquardt, D. J., & Green, T. G. (2013). Introducing discriminatory job loss: Antecedents, consequences, and complexities. *Journal of Managerial Psychology, 28*, 584–605. doi: 10.1108/JMP-10-2012-0319

Bezrukova, K., Spell, C. S., Perry, J. L., & Jehn, K. A. (2016). A meta-analytical integration of over 40 years of research on diversity training evaluation. *Psychological Bulletin, 142*(11), 1227–1274. doi: http://dx.doi.org/10.1037/bul0000067

Bostwick, W., & Hequembourg, A. (2014). 'Just a little hint': Bisexual-specific microaggressions and their connection to epistemic injustices. *Culture, Health, & Sexuality, 16*, 488–503. doi: 10.1080/13691058.2014.889754

Brown, H. C., Jr. (2015). A crowded room or the perfect fit? Exploring affirmative action treatment in college and university admissions for self-identified LGBT individuals. *William & Mary Journal of Women and the Law, 21*(3), 602—667. doi: http://scholarship.law.wm.edu/wmjowl/vol21/iss3/3

Burke, S. E., Dovidio, J. F., Przedworski, J. M., Hardeman, R. R., Perry, S. P., Phelan, S. M., ... & van Ryn, M. (2015). Do contact and empathy mitigate bias against gay and lesbian people among heterosexual first-year medical students? A report from the medical student CHANGE study. *Academic Medicine, 90*, 645–651. doi: 10.1097/ACM.0000000000000661

Casper, W. J., Wayne, J. H., & Manegold, J. G. (2013). Who will we recruit? Targeting deep- and surface-level diversity with human resource policy advertising. *Human Resource Management, 52*(3), 311–332. doi: 0.1002/hrm.21530

Cech, E. A., & Pham, M. V. (2017). Queer in STEM organizations: Workplace disadvantages for LGBT employees in STEM related federal agencies. *Social Sciences, 6*, 12. doi: 10.3390/socsci6010012

Cegler, T. D. (2012). Targeted recruitment of GLBT students by colleges and universities. *Journal of College Admission, 215*, 18–23.

Chung, Y. B., Chang, T. K., & Rose, C. S. (2015). Managing and coping with sexual identity at work. *The Psychologist, 28*, 212–215. Retrieved from: https://thepsychologist.bps.org.uk/volume-28/march-2015/managing-and-coping-sexual- identity-work

Collins, J. C. (2016). Retaliatory strike or fired with cause: A case study of gay identity disclosure and law enforcement. *New Horizons in Adult Education & Human Resource Development, 28*, 23–45.

Collins, J. C., McFadden, C., Rocco, T. S., & Mathis, M. K. (2015). The problem of transgender marginalization and exclusion: Critical actions for human resource development. *Human Resource Development Review, 14*(2), 205–226. doi:10.1177/1534484315581755

Discont, S., Russell, C., & Sawyer, K. (2016, January). Conversations with seasoned SIOP members of the LGBTQ community: Thoughts and observations on past, present, and future pursuit of I-O careers. *The Industrial-Organizational Psychologist, 53*, 44–51. Retrieved from: http://www.siop.org/tip/jan16/pdf/LGBTq.pdf

Douglass, R. P., Velez, B. L., Conlin, S. E., Duffy, R. D., & England, J. W. (2017). Examining the psychology of working theory: Decent work among sexual minorities. *Journal of Counseling Psychology, 64*, 550–559. doi: 10.1037/cou0000212

Duguid, M. M., & Thomas-Hunt, M. C. (2015). Condoning stereotyping? How awareness of stereotyping prevalence impacts expression of stereotypes. *Journal of Applied Psychology, 100*(2), 343–359. doi: http://dx.doi.org/10.1037/a0037908

Drydakis, N. (2015). Sexual orientation discrimination in the United Kingdom's labour market: A field experiment. *Human Relations, 68*(11), 1769–1796. doi: 10.1177/0018726715569855

EEOC. (2016). *Fact sheet: Recent EEOC litigation regarding Title VII & LGBT-related discrimination.* Retrieved from https://www.eeoc.gov/eeoc/litigation/selected/LGBT_facts.cfm

The Employment Non-Discrimination Act of 2013. (2013). S. 815, 113th Cong. (introduced in 2013).

Everly, B. A., Unzueta, M. M., & Shih, M. J. (2016). Can being gay provide a boost in the hiring process? Maybe if the boss is female. *Journal of Business and Psychology, 31,* 293–306. doi: 10.1007/s10869-015-9412-y

Ferdman, B. M., & Sagiv, L. (2012). Diversity in organizations and cross-cultural work psychology: What if they were more connected? *Industrial and Organizational Psychology: Perspectives on Science and Practice, 5,* 323–345. doi: 1754-9426/12

Fynes, J. M., & Fisher, L. A. (2016). Is authenticity and integrity possible for sexual minority athletes? Lesbian student-athlete experiences of U.S. NCAA division I sport. *Women in Sport and Physical Activity Journal, 24,* 60–69. doi: 10.1123/wspaj.2014-0055

Garcia, M. (2015). ACLU, NCLR, and more groups drop support of ENDA. Retrieved from: http://www.advocate.com/enda/2014/07/08/breaking-aclu-nclr-and-more-groups-drop- support-enda

Gates, T. G. (2010). The problem, policy, and political streams of the Employment Non-Discrimination Act of 2009: Implications for social work practice. *Journal of Gay & Lesbian Social Services, 22,* 354–369. doi: 10.1080/10538720.2010.486692

Gates, T. G., & Rodgers, C. G. (2014). Repeal of Don't Ask Don't Tell as a "Policy Window": A case for the passage of the Employment Non-Discrimination Act. *International Journal of Discrimination and the Law, 14,* 5–18. doi: 10.1177/1358229113500419

Gedro, J., Mizzi, R. C., Rocco, T. S., & van Loo, J. B. (2013). Going global: Professional mobility and concerns for LGBT workers. *Human Resource Development International, 16,* 282–297. doi: 10.1080/13678868.2013.771869

GLAAD. (2016). *Frequently asked questions about ENDA.* Retrieved from: http://www.glaad.org/enda/faq

Graham, K. M., McMahon, B. T., Kim, J. H., Simpson, P., & McMahon, M. C. (2019). Patterns of workplace discrimination across broad categories of disability. *Rehabilitation Psychology, 64*(2), 194–202. doi: https://doi.org/10.1037/rep0000227

Griffin, P. (1992). From hiding out to coming out: Empowering lesbian and gay educators. In K. M. Harbeck (Ed.), *Coming out of the classroom closet: Gay and lesbian students, teachers and curricula* (pp. 167–196). Binghampton, NY: Haworth Press.

Hebl, M., Barron, L., Cox, C. B., & Corrington, A. R. (2016). The efficacy of sexual orientation anti-discrimination legislation. *Equality, Diversity and Inclusion: An International Journal, 35*(7/8), 449–466. Retrieved from: https://doi.org/10.1108/EDI-07-2016-0060

Huffman, A., Watrous, K., & King, E. B. (2008). Diversity in the workplace: Support for lesbian, gay, and bisexual workers. *Human Resource Management, 47*(2), 237–253. doi: 10.1002/hrm.20210

Human Rights Campaign. (2014). The cost of the closet and the rewards of inclusion. Retrieved from: http://hrc-assets.s3-website-us-east-1.amazonaws.com//files/assets/resources/ Cost_of_the_Closet_May2014.pdf

Human Rights Campaign. (2016). *The Equality Act.* Retrieved from http://www.hrc.org/resources/the-equality-act

Israel, T., Harkness, A., Delucio, K., Ledbetter, J. N., & Avellar, & T. R. (2014). Evaluation of police training on LGBTQ issues: Knowledge, interpersonal apprehension, and self- efficacy. *Journal of Police Criminal Psychology, 29,* 57–67. doi: 10.1007/s11896-013- 9132-z

Jansen, W. S., Otten, S., & van der Zee, K. I. (2015). Being part of diversity: The effects of an all-inclusive multicultural diversity approach on majority members' perceived inclusion and support for organizational diversity efforts. *Group Processes & Intergroup Relations, 18*(6), 817–832. doi: 10.1177/1368430214566892

Jones, K. P., Sabat, I. E., King, E. B., Ahmad, A., McCausland, T. C., & Chen, T. (2017). Isms and schisms: A meta-analysis of the prejudice-discrimination relationship across racism, sexism, and ageism. *Journal of Organizational Behavior, 38*(7), 1076–1110. Doi: https://doi.org/10.1002/job.2187

Kalinoski, Z. T., Steele-Johnson, D., Peyton, E. J., Leas, K. A., Steinke, J., & Bowling, N. A. (2013). A meta-analytic evaluation of diversity training outcomes. *Journal of Organizational Behavior, 34*, 1076–1104. doi: 10.1002/job.1839

King, E. B., & Cortina, J. M. (2010). Stated and unstated barriers and opportunities to creating LGBT-supportive organizations. *Industrial-Organizational Psychology: Perspectives of Science and Practice, 3*, 103–108.

King, E. B., Mohr, J. J., Peddie, C. I., Jones, K. P., & Kendra, M. (2017). Predictors of identity management: An exploratory experience-sampling study of lesbian, gay, and bisexual workers. *Journal of Management, 43*(2), 476–502. doi: 10.1177/0149206314539350

Köllen, T. (2016a) Lessening the difference is more—The relationship between diversity management and the perceived organizational climate for gay men and lesbians. *The International Journal of Human Resource Management, 27*(17), 1967–1996, doi: 10.1080/09585192.2015.1088883

Köllen, T. (Ed.). (2016b). *Sexual orientation and transgender issues in organizations: Global perspectives on LGBT workforce diversity*. New York, NY: Springer.

Konrad, A. M., Yang, Y., & Maurer, C. C. (2016). Antecedents and outcomes of diversity and equality management systems: An integrated institutional agency and strategic human resource management approach. *Human Resource Management, 55*(1), 83–107. doi: 10.1002/hrm.21713

Lambert, J. R. (2013). The impact of gay-friendly recruitment statements and due process employment on a firm's attractiveness as an employer. *Equality, Diversity, and Inclusion: An International Journal, 34*, 510–526. doi: 10.1108/EDI-03-2013-0012

Law, C., L., Martinez, L. R., Ruggs, E. N., Hebl, M. R., & Akers, E. (2011). Transparency in the workplace: How the experiences of transsexual employees can be improved. *Journal of Vocational Behavior, 79*, 710–723.

Lewis, G. B., & Pitts, D. W. (2015). LGBT-heterosexual differences in perceptions of fair treatment in the federal service. *American Review of Public Administration, 47*(5), 574–587. doi: 10.1177/0275074015605378

Lindsey, A. P., & Gilrane, V. L. (Chairs). (2016). *Novel approaches for enhancing diversity training effectiveness in the workplace*. Symposium conducted at the meeting of the Society for Industrial-Organizational Psychology, Anaheim, CA, (2016, April 14–16).

Lindsey, A., King, E., Hebl, M., & Levine, N. (2015). The impact of method, motivation, and empathy on diversity training effectiveness. *Journal of Business Psychology, 30*, 605–617. doi: 10.1007/s10869-014-9384-3

Lindsey, A., King, E., McCausland, T., Jones, K., & Dunleavy, E. (2013). What we know and don't: Eradicating employment discrimination 50 years after the Civil Rights

Act. *Industrial and Organizational Psychology: Perspectives on Science and Practice, 6*, 391–413. doi: 1754-9426/13

Lipka, P. (2010). *Sexual minorities in the workplace: An examination of individual differences that affect responses to workplace heterosexism.* Clemson University.

Madera, J. M., King, E. B., & Hebl, M. R. (2013). Enhancing the effects of sexual orientation diversity training: The effects of setting goals and training mentors on attitudes and behaviors. *Journal of Business Psychology, 28*, 79–91. doi: 10.1007/s10869-012-9264-7

Martinez, L. R., & Smith, N. A. (Chairs). (2016). *What about the T? Transgender workplace research.* Symposium conducted at the meeting of the Society for Industrial-Organizational Psychology, Anaheim, CA, (2016, April 14–16.

McFadden, C. (2015). Lesbian, gay, bisexual, and transgender careers and human resource development: A systematic literature review. *Human Resource Development Review, 14*(2), 125–162. doi: 10.1177/1534484314549456

McNulty, Y., & Hutchings, K. (2016). Looking for global talent in all the right places: A critical literature review of non-traditional expatriates. *The International Journal of Human Resource Management, 27*, 699–728. doi: 10.1080/09585192.2016.1148756

McPhail, R., McNulty, Y., & Hutchings, K. (2014). Lesbian and gay expatriation: Opportunities, barriers and challenges for global mobility. *The International Journal of Human Resource Management, 27*, 382–406. doi: 10.1080/09585192.2014.941903

Meyer, I. H. (2003). Prejudice, social stress, and mental health in lesbian, gay, and bisexual populations: Conceptual issues and research evidence. *Psychological Bulletin, 129*, 674- 697. doi: 10.1037/0033-2909.129.5.674

Mishel, E. (2016). Discrimination against queer women in the U.S. workforce: A resume audit study. *Socius: Sociological Research for a Dynamic World, 2*, 1–13. doi: 10.1177/2378023115621316

Mize, T. D. (2016). Sexual orientation in the labor market. *American Sociological Review, 81*(6), 1132–1160. doi: 0.1177/0003122416674025

Nadal, K. L., Skolnik, A., & Wong, Y. (2012). Interpersonal and systemic microaggressions toward transgender people: Implications for counseling. *Journal of LGBT Issues in Counseling, 6*, 55–82. doi:10.1080/15538605.2012.648583

Nadler, J. T., Lowery, M. R., Grebinoski, J., & Jones, R. G. (2016). Aversive discrimination in employment interviews: Reducing effects of sexual orientation bias with accountability. *Psychology of Sexual Orientation and Gender Diversity, 1*(4), 480–488. doi: http://dx.doi.org/10.1037/sgd0000079

Newhouse, M. R. (2013, Summer). Remembering the "T" in LGBT: Recruiting and supporting transgender students. *Journal of College Admission, 220*, 22–27. doi: www.nacacnet.org.

OSHA. (2016). *Best practices: A guide to restroom access for transgender workers.* Retrieved from: https://www.osha.gov/Publications/OSHA3795.pdf

Parks, R., & Parrish, J. (2017). HB2: The effects of polarizing legislation on recruitment practices. *Recruiting and Retaining Adult Learners, 19*(8), 6–7. doi: 10.1002/nsr

Parnell, M. K., Lease, S. H., & Green, M. L. (2012). Perceived career barriers for gay, lesbian, and bisexual individuals. *Journal of Career Development, 39*, 248–268. doi: 10.1177/0894845310386730

Pyatt, J. L. (2014). *Reactions to homosexual job applicants: Implications of gender and sexual orientation on hiring decisions, salary appointment, agency, and communality* (Master's thesis). Retrieved from ProQuest, LLC. (UMI 1561076)

Rabelo, V. C., & Cortina, L. M. (2014). Two sides of the same coin: Gender harassment and heterosexist harassment in LGBQ work lives. *Law and Human Behavior, 38*(4), 378–391. doi:10.1037/lhb0000087

Ragins, B. R., Cornwell, J. M., & Miller, J. S. (2003). Heterosexism in the workplace: Do race and gender matter? *Group & Organization Management, 28(1),* 45–74. doi: 10.1177/1059601102250018

Ragins, B. R., Singh, R., & Cornwell, J. M. (2007). Making the invisible visible: Fear and disclosure of sexual orientation at work. *Journal of Applied Psychology, 92,* 1103–1118. doi: 10.1037/0021-9010.92.4.1103

Reed, L., & Leuty, M. E. (2015): The role of individual differences and situational variables in the use of workplace sexual identity management strategies. *Journal of Homosexuality, 63,* 985–1017. doi: 10.1080/00918369.2015.1117900

Riggle, E. D., Rostosky, S. S., Black, W. W., & Rosenkrantz, D. E. (2017). Outness, concealment, and authenticity: Associations with LGB individuals' psychological distress and well-being. *Psychology of Sexual Orientation and Gender Diversity, 4,* 54–62. doi: 10.1037/sgd0000202

Riley, D. M. (2008). LGBT-friendly workplaces in engineering. *Leadership and Management in Engineering, 8*(1)*,* 19–23.

Robinson, G., & Dechant, K. (1997). Building a business case for diversity. *Academy of Management Executive, 11,* 21–31.

Ruggs, E. N., Martinez, L., Law, C., & Hebl, M. (2015). Workplace trans-actions: How organizations, coworkers, and individual openness influence perceived gender identity discrimination psychology of sexual orientation and gender diversity. *Psychology of Sexual Orientation and Gender Diversity, 1,* 1–9. Retrieved from: http://dx.doi.org/10.1037/sgd0000112

Rule, N. O., Bjornsdottir, R. T., Tskhay, K. O., & Ambady, N. (2016). *Journal of Applied Psychology, 101*(12), 1687–1704. doi: http://dx.doi.org/10.1037/apl0000148

Rupp, D. E., Gibbons, A. M., & Snyder, L. A. (2008). The role of technology in enabling third- generation training and development. *Industrial and Organizational Psychology, 1,* 496–500. doi: 1754-9426/08

Sabat, I. E., Lindsey, A. P., King, E. B., Ahmad, A. S., Membere, A., & Arena, D. F. (2017). How prior knowledge of LGB identities alters the effects of workplace disclosure. *Journal of Vocational Behavior, 103,* 56–70.

Sabat, I., Trump, R., & King, E. (2014). Individual, interpersonal, and contextual factors relating to disclosure decisions of lesbian, gay, and bisexual individuals. *Psychology of Sexual Orientation and Gender Diversity, 1,* 431–440. doi: 10.1037/sgd0000061

Salomaa, A. C., & Matsick, J. L. (2018). Carving sexuality at its joints: Defining sexual orientation in research and clinical practice. *Psychological Assessment.* Retrieved from: http://dx.doi.org/10.1037/pas0000656

Sawyer, K., Salter, N., & Thoroughgood, C. (2013). Studying individual identities is good, but examining intersectionality is better. *Industrial and Organizational Psychology: Perspectives on Science and Practice, 6,* 80–84. doi: 10.1111/iops.12012

Sawyer, K. B., Thai, J. L., Martinez, L. R., Smith, N. A., & Discont, S. (2016, July). Trans issues in the workplace 101. *The Industrial-Organizational Psychologist.* Retrieved from http://www.siop.org/tip/july16/LGBT.aspx

Sears, B., & Mallory, C. (2014). Employment discrimination against LGBT people: Existence and impact. In C. M. Duffy & D. M. Visconti (Eds.), *Gender identity and sexual orientation discrimination in the workplace: A practical guide* (pp. 40-2–40-19). Arlington, VA: Bloomberg BNA.

Shadish, W. R., Cook, T. D., & Campbell, D. T. (2002). *Experimental and quasi-experimental designs for generalized causal inference.* Boston, MA: Houghton Mifflin.

Shepherd, D. A., & Patzelt, H. (2015). Harsh evaluations of entrepreneurs who fail: The roles of sexual orientation, use of environmentally friendly technologies, and observers' perspective taking. *Journal of Management Studies, 52,* 253–284. doi: 10.1111/joms.12103

Shippee, N. D. (2011). Gay, straight, and who I am: Interpreting passing within the frames for everyday life. *Deviant Behavior, 32,* 115–157. doi:10.1080/01639621003748514

Sue, D. W. (2010). Sexual orientation microaggressions and heterosexism. In D. W. Sue (Ed.), *Microaggressions in everyday life: Race, gender, and sexual orientation* (pp. 184–206). Hoboken, NJ: Wiley.

Tilcsik, A. (2011). Pride and prejudice: Employment discrimination against openly gay men in the United States. *American Journal of Sociology, 117,* 586–626. doi: 10.1086/661653

Ueno, K., Peña-Talamantes, A. E., & Roach, T. A. (2013). Sexual orientation and occupational attainment. *Work and Occupations, 40*(1), 3–36. doi: 10.1177/0730888412460532.

U.S. Department of Labor. (2016). Amended regulations: Executive Order 11246 prohibiting discrimination based on sexual orientation and gender identity. Retrieved from: https://www.dol.gov/ofccp/LGBT.htmlF

VandenBos, G. R. (Ed.). (2007) *APA dictionary of psychology.* Washington, DC: American Psychological Association.

Velez, B. L., Cox, R., Jr., Polihronakis, C. J., & Moradi, B. (2018). Discrimination, work outcomes, and mental health among women of color: The protective role of womanist attitudes. *Journal of Counseling Psychology, 65*(2), 178–193. doi: https://doi.org/10.1037/cou0000274

Wegner, R., & Wright, A. J. (2016). A psychometric evaluation of the homonegative microaggressions scale. *Journal of Gay & Lesbian Mental Health, 20,* 299–318. doi: 10.1080/19359705.2016.1177627

Wilson, D. J. (2016). *Reactions to transgender job applicants: Implications of gender orientation on hiring decisions, salary recommendation, agency, and communality* (Master's thesis). ProQuest, LLC. (ProQuest Number: 10159235). Retrieved from: https://search-proquest-com.libproxy.clemson.edu/pqdtglobal/docview/1840802741/FAADDE1DFCC74BD9PQ/1?accountid=6167

Workplace Fairness. (2016). *Sexual orientation discrimination.* Retrieved from: https://www.workplacefairness.org/sexual-orientation-discrimination

CHAPTER 8

AN ECOLOGICAL SYSTEMS FRAMEWORK FOR WORK AND AGING

Justin Marcus, Cort W. Rudolph, and Hannes Zacher

We introduce a novel ecological systems framework to guide research and practice on work and aging. This framework delineates societal, organizational, individual, and temporal factors relevant to the study of work and aging. Specifically, the various potential influences of societal, institutional, and cultural factors, as well as normative organizational factors, and individual differences in demography on age-related work outcomes are described. Importantly, the role of time in the interplay between these various macro, meso, and micro systems on age-related work outcomes is considered. To advance this framework, potential theoretical models, directions for future research, and workforce implications for work and aging are discussed.

Population and workforce aging are global phenomena that are accompanied by significant challenges but also opportunities in most countries around the world (Chand & Tung, 2014; Roberts, 2011; Rudolph, Marcus & Zacher, 2019). The coming decades will be characterized by increasingly older and more age diverse workforces (Hertel & Zacher, 2018) both in developed (Albright, 2012; Skirbekk, Loichinger, & Barakat, 2012) and in developing countries (James, 2011; Peng,

Diversity and Inclusion in Organizations, pages 193–222.
Copyright © 2020 by Information Age Publishing
All rights of reproduction in any form reserved.

2011). The aging of the workforce has until recently been a phenomenon primarily affecting developed economies, with a median age above 40, and adults aged 65+ comprising over 15% of those populations (Chand & Tung, 2014). This trend is expected to exacerbate, whereby upwards of 30% of the populations of the majority of developed economies are expected to be aged 65+ by mid-century (UNDESA, 2015). Almost all developing nations outside of sub-Saharan Africa are similarly expected to experience significant population aging in the coming decades (UNDESA, 2015). Indeed, it is estimated that over 60% of people aged 65+ now live in developing countries (Phillips & Siu, 2012), with a projected increase to 80% by 2050 (United Nations, 2013).

It is thus clear that 21st century workforce aging is a global phenomenon that will considerably impact people, organizations, and countries across the globe. In particular, rapid population aging in the world's most advanced economies, such as Germany and Japan, is expected to result in a shortage of workers in those countries. Given this projected shortage of workers in developed nations (and to an extent even developing nations outside sub-Saharan Africa), there is a growing need to retain and utilize the skills and abilities of older workers.

Compounding this issue is the existence of age bias and age discrimination at work. Here, age bias refers broadly to cognitions, emotions, and behaviors toward individuals on the basis of age, whereas age discrimination more narrowly refers to discriminatory behaviors on the basis of age (Finkelstein, Hanrahan, & Thomas, 2019; Marcus, 2017). Age bias and age discrimination potentially affect both younger and older workers (Finkelstein et al., 2019). Nevertheless, stereotypes and beliefs about older workers are overall more negative and more persistent (Webster, Thoroughgood, & Sawyer, 2019), and age discrimination against older workers has been found to exist among all age groups (Axt, Ebersole, & Nosek, 2014). Existing theoretical models to explain age bias at work have commensurately adopted such an older-typed lens, with most existing theories focusing on age discrimination against older workers (see Truxillo, Finkelstein, Pytlovany, & Jenkins, 2016). As reviewed by Truxillo et al. (2016), these theoretical approaches have alternatively focused on the content and/or process of stereotypes toward older workers (Fiske, Cuddy, Glick, & Xu, 2002; Greenwald & Banaji, 1995), relative age distributions in organizations (Tsui, Egan, & O'Reilly, 1992), demographic faultlines at the intersection of age (Lau & Murnigham, 2005), and job contextual factors that magnify the salience of old age (Lawrence, 1988; Perry & Finkelstein, 1999; Shore & Goldberg, 2005; Spence, 1973).

All of these above-mentioned theories tend to focus on micro individual or meso organizational factors related to the work experiences of older and younger workers. Missing from the conversation, however, is the fact that individuals and organizations are themselves embedded within larger societal environments; missing also is the crucial interplay of all of these levels (societal, organizational, and individual) with time, for work experiences are in fact lived through the course of one's career and do not only occur at a single snapshot in time. Existing theoretical frameworks have tended to shy away from a multilevel view. To date, most research on work and aging has been conducted in North America, Western Europe, and Australia, with less focus on cross-cultural and cross-national influences (North & Fiske, 2015).

We address these gaps by considering the broader organizational and societal factors that may influence work outcomes for employed adults across the lifespan and among different types of older workers (e.g., older men and women) across the globe. Our conceptual framework is depicted graphically in Figure 8.1. The figure displays an interrelated set of nested circles, with lower levels of analyses embedded within higher-order circles. The outermost circle represents the societal level, which includes both institutional and societal cultural factors that may influence relations between age and work outcomes. The next highest level, organizational, is embedded within the larger societal circle, denoting that organizations are themselves situated within particular societal environments. Organizational level factors impacting relations between age and work outcomes include those related to the job and work context. The lowest level of analysis and

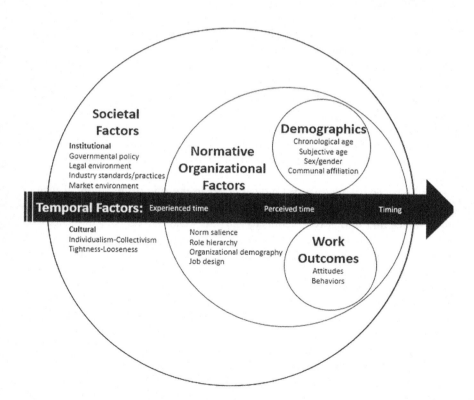

FIGURE 8.1.   An Ecological Systems Framework for Work and Aging

correspondingly smallest circle, embedded within the organizational circle, represents the individual. At the individual level, we specifically consider the role of demographic factors in relations between age and work outcomes, including the main tripartite of surface demographic characteristics including age, sex/gender, and communal affiliation (see Marcus & Fritzsche, 2015; Schneider, 2004, for more on the tripartite division of demographic subgroups). Because work outcomes are most closely associated with individuals, this last circle is depicted as being closest to said outcomes. A temporal factor depicted by a straight-line cuts across all three circles, denoting that societies, organizations, and the individuals that inhabit them are themselves subject to change and evolution across historical time. Finally, and in line with the extant literature, we broadly define the domain of work outcomes to include all cognitions, emotions, and behaviors (see Bal, Reiss, Rudolph, & Baltes, 2011; Finkelstein et al., 2019; Posthuma & Campion, 2009; Zacher, Esser, Bohlmann, & Rudolph, 2018).

The framework as depicted in Figure 8.1 draws upon longstanding traditions of ecological (e.g., Bronfenbrenner, 1979) and systems theories (Ford & Lerner, 1992) of human development, which each explain how individuals' experiences and behaviors are shaped by different contexts at different levels of analysis. From an ecological systems view, individual differences and ontogenetic (i.e., intraindividual) changes associated within aging are optimally understood when macro (e.g., societal cultures, institutional norms), micro/meso (i.e., associative links between the individual and the organization or family), and chronological (i.e., temporal) influences are considered in tandem (see Rudolph, 2016). More specifically, our framework delineates the influences of societal, organizational, and demographic factors on aging in the work context. In order to not limit the scope of the review, worker outcomes are defined broadly to include both job attitudes (e.g., job engagement, job satisfaction), and behaviors (e.g., career-change, retirement decisions).

At the societal level, we distinguish between the role of institutional factors (e.g., governmental policy, industry standards and practices) and particular cultural values and norms (e.g., collectivism) as broad macro-level influences on individuals' behavior at work (see Aycan et al., 2000). At the organizational level, we delineate specific influences of normative, culture-setting organizational practices (see Ashforth & Mael, 1989) that may also impact said relations. At the individual level, we consider how demography may shape the subjective experiences of societal and organizational factors for adults across their lifespan.

Importantly, we consider each of these three sources of influence as they temporally occur across the lifespan for individuals, both younger and older. Accordingly, our model also posits the influence of time, which exerts influences both across and within these different levels of analysis. Such influences directly impact upon the worker, but also with regard to the ways by which such ecological influences may unfold as workers' careers play out over the course of time. Accordingly, we first introduce theory related to the ecological systems framework, summarize the extant research at each level of this ecological system (i.e., societal, organizational, individual), and then posit joint influences of ecology and time on workers of varying ages. Throughout these discussions, we advance both propositions and research questions, with propositions offered where theory and evidence are substantial enough to posit specific directional differences, and research questions posed for more nascent and emerging areas of research in work and aging. To guide the reader, we summarize available theoretical frameworks, possible future research directions, and potential workforce implications in Table 8.1.

The Lifespan Developmental Perspective in Ecological Context

The lifespan perspective emphasizes that individuals' development is influenced by, and interacts with, their sociocultural and historical contexts (Baltes, 1987; Baltes, Reese, & Lipsitt, 1980). From an ecological systems perspective (Bronfenbrenner, 1979), individuals interact with five environmental contexts, including the chronosystem, microsystem, mesosystem, exosystem, and macrosystem; these interactions in turn shape individuals' experiences and behaviors. It is beyond the scope of the present discussion to delineate all of Bronfenbrenner's (1979) ecological contexts; the macrosystem is most currently pertinent. The macrosystem refers to the overarching societal environment in which someone is embedded. The societal environment entails, for instance, individual socioeconomic status (how rich or poor one is), gender (one's biological sex and one's gender identity/expression), tribe (one's race, ethnicity, religion, nationality, and color), and socioeconomic development (whether one lives in a developed, developing, or less developed country). Moreover, the macrosystem includes societal culture (e.g., the extent to which one's society is collectivistic or individualistic) and organizational culture (e.g., the extent to which one's workplace or work team is collectivistic or individualistic; see also Chao & Moon, 2005, for a theoretical review on links between demography and culture).

Bronfenbrenner's (1979) ecological systems theory speaks to the importance of societal, contextual, and cultural influences on the aging process. From a developmental systems perspective, not only does the macrosystemic context shape individual characteristics over time, but individual decisions and actions themselves may also shape the macrosystemic context. As an example, motivational changes at the individual level, such as the motivation to work longer and past traditional retirement ages, in the aggregate, may lead to sociocultural (e.g., attitudes toward older workers) and economic changes (e.g., greater flexibility of businesses to accommodate older workers). The lifespan developmental perspective thus provides a theoretical basis to study individuals' experiences and behavior over time and embedded within multiple layers of context (Baltes, 1987; Baltes, Lindenberger, & Staudinger, 2006). Lifespan researchers not only focus on normative developmental trajectories, but also on how personal and idiosyncratic factors

TABLE 8.1. Potential Theoretical Avenues, Workforce Implications, and Future Research Directions Related to Various Ecological Factors

Ecological Factors	Available Theoretical Frameworks	Future Workforce Implications	Future Research Directions
Societal Institutional	Relational demography theory Socioemotional Selectivity Theory Protean and boundaryless careers Age meta-stereotypes	1. Mean workforce ages will shift upwards in aging societies 2. Retirement at later ages 3. Potential increases in self-employment at later ages 4. Revision of retirement benefits packages 5. Workers increasingly moving across occupational and organizational boundaries	1. Relative age discrimination against older workers from older/younger societies and industries or occupations 2. Predictors and consequences of later retirement ages 3. Predictors and consequences of self-employment among older workers 4. Intersection of age and career change on work experiences of older and younger workers
Societal Cultural	Cultural Anchors of Ageism	1. Cross-cultural differences in age discrimination across societies and organizations 2. Cross-national differences in economic considerations related to retirement	1. Differences in age-based work experiences between collectivistic-tight and individualistic-loose societal and organizational cultures 2. Differences in retirement decision-making between collectivistic-tight and individualistic-loose societal and organizational cultures

Meso	Tightness-looseness Age-graded career norms Social Identity Theory Age-inclusive HR practices Lifespan perspective on job design	1. Differential barriers to occupational mobility and advancement across organizations and occupations 2. Differences in workforce age homogeneity across organizations and occupations 3. Differential levels of age-inclusiveness across organizational HR systems	1. Organizational and industrial cultural effects on age-inclusiveness and age discrimination 2. Best practices regarding job design and HR systems to promote age-inclusiveness and maximize favorable work outcomes in an age-diverse workforce
Micro	Subjective age theory Relational demography theory Intersectional Salience of Ageism	1. Individual differences in retirement decision-making 2. Individual differences in experienced age discrimination 3. Male-female and majority-minority group differences in age-related work outcomes	1. Objective vs. subjective age conceptualizations as predictors of age-related work outcomes 2. Intersections of age, gender and communal affiliation on age-related work outcomes
Temporal	Socioemotional Selectivity Theory Motivational Theory of Lifespan Development	1. Goals shift in meaning with advancing age; Older adults prioritize social goals, whereas younger adults prioritize instrumental goals. 2. The timing of lifespan events matters for goal choice and striving processes.	1. Exploring chronological and subjective age-conditional influences on goal choice, resource allocation, and success. 2. Understanding the interplay between national and/or institutional norms, the timing of career goals, and ultimate goal success.

(e.g., demography) and contexts (e.g., culture) may modify these developmental trajectories.

Development is embedded in a historical and sociocultural context; development in turn is shaped by the interaction of normative and non-normative, as well as person and contextual influences. Importantly, changes in the historical and sociocultural context may interact (Baltes, 1987). For instance, although the proportion of older workers has historically been increasing across industries, some jobs and industries (e.g., social media, internet technology) remain demographically younger than others (e.g., higher education/academia). Thus, workforce aging may be more pronounced in some types of jobs and industries than others, with the consequence that organizations across distinct industries may adopt distinct policies and approaches toward work and retirement, given distinct age-bound demographic pressures. Illustratively, a recent news article highlighted the plights and pitfalls resultant of age bias faced by workers aged 40+ and working in the tech sector in Silicon Valley, where beliefs regarding the inadaptability of older workers abound (Bowles, 2019). In this sense, the processes of aging at work and retirement are influenced by the macrosystemic context in which they occur (e.g., the "Silicon Valley culture"). Various societal (macro), organizational (meso), and individual (micro) factors may influence age-related trajectories of psychological and behavioral outcomes, and differentially across one's span of a life or career.

Ecological Effects on Aspects of Work and Aging

Macro Effects—Institutional. Institutional-level macro effects of the ecological environment include governmental policies, such as the setting of the retirement age, the legal environment such as laws surrounding the minimum/maximum age of work in particular industries or occupations, industry standards and practices, and the market environment (i.e., economic boom-bust periods). Although research on the effects of such institutional practices on age-related work outcomes is scarce (Marcus, 2017), we focus here on two particular issues that have received some attention in the literature, including increases in the retirement age, and the growing proliferation of protean and boundaryless careers.

First, in response to decreases in fertility levels and the consequent aging of the population in developed (e.g., Western Europe, Australia, Japan) and even developing (e.g., China, Russia, Turkey; Chand & Tung, 2014; He, Goodkind, & Kowal, 2016) economies, governmental policy-makers have been gradually raising the age of retirement. Some examples include Russia, where the government recently raised the retirement age to 65 (Ostroukh & Nikolskaya, 2018), and public debate in the UK and Japan suggesting raising of the retirement age to 75 (Hurst, 2017; Swinford, 2016). Coupled with already aging populations, this trend toward longer working lives will ultimately increase the average age composition of the workforce. From a relational demography perspective, whereby "old age" is defined not chronologically but relative to the worker population (i.e., normative age; Kooij, de Lange, Janssen, & Dikkers, 2008), the net result will be that the normative worker will become increasingly "older." That is, it may be expected that, in aging societies at least, the average worker age will shift upwards such that what once would have been considered "older workers" a generation ago will come to occupy the distributional middle. Correspondingly, normative ages of retirement, and employment re-entry/self-employment of older workers may also increase (Ainsworth, 2015; Peiro, Tordero, & Potocnik, 2013).

Hypothesis 1a: As workforces become increasingly older on average, normative definitions of older workers will correspondingly become increasingly older.

Hypothesis 1b: As workforces become increasingly older on average, normative ages of retirement will correspondingly become increasingly older.

Hypothesis 1c: As workforces become increasingly older on average, the average age of workers re-entering the workforce or entering self-employment will become increasingly higher.

Workers aged 50+ have historically been conceptualized as the typical "older worker" age group in psychological research (Ashbaugh & Fay, 1987; Finkelstein, Ryan, & King, 2013). However, given the above-noted demographic shifts, this might no longer be the case in the coming decades, and will likely have consequences for research in various aspects of work and aging (see Table 8.1). Using a relational demography framework (Tsui et al., 1992; Kooij et al., 2008), research could investigate whether workers aged 50+ experience similar effects of age discrimination in societies, industries, and occupations where workers of such ages are more normative compared to those working in societies and/or occupations populated by workers of relatively younger ages.

Hypothesis 2a: Normative differences in the average worker age will be related to age-based stereotypes, prejudice, and unfair discrimination at the institutional (societal, industrial, or occupational) level, such that institutions typified by a lower normative worker age may be expected to exhibit a greater incidence of age bias against older workers.

Research could also utilize such a relational demography perspective to investigate individual differences in predictors and consequences of retiring at later ages (i.e., continued salaried work at later ages), and of self-employment among older workers (i.e., entrepreneurial and/or "gig" work at later ages). That is, differences resultant of institutional norms in worker ages may consequently result in different work and retirement patterns in later life across institutions because of different social pressures created by being either in line or out of step with the normative workforce age. Viewed from a social identity of the organization perspective (Ashforth & Mael, 1989), whereby people compare themselves to relevant others in order to make social comparisons, individuals working in an institution that is typically younger (e.g., a tech worker in Silicon Valley) may feel more "social pressure" to retire and stay retired at a given retirement age; vice versa for individuals in institutions surrounded by fellow older workers (e.g., academia).

> **Hypothesis 2b:** Differences in institutionally normative worker age will be related to retirement, job re-entry, and self-employment patterns at the institutional (societal, industrial, or occupational) level such that institutions typified by a higher normative worker age may be expected to experience greater incidences of post-retirement job re-entry and self-employment, and overall later ages of retirement.

Second, whereby it was once standard practice to advance one's career hierarchically across the ranks of a single organization, the modern career is typified by significantly more career mobility across both careers and organizations. Modern careers are viewed as cyclical, lateral, and individualistic, unfolding across multiple employment settings within and across industries, and whereby work becomes protean and boundaryless, transportable across geographic and structural boundaries (Arthur & Rousseau, 1996; Mirvis & Hall, 1996). Thus, 21st century careers are played out globally and across traditional organizational and career-delimited boundaries (Baruch & Reis, 2016). These macro-systemic changes in career trajectories will also likely have consequences for research and practice in work and aging.

From a research standpoint, the confluence of age and career-change remains a nascent area. Some experimental evidence exists to suggest that older workers are more likely to face age discrimination at work relative to younger workers when making between- as opposed to within-career transitions (Fritzsche & Marcus, 2013). This result finds confluence with studies investigating age-graded career norms, whereby workers perceived as being behind schedule (in less senior positions relative to their age) experience negative age bias at work, whereas workers perceived as being ahead of schedule (in more senior positions relative to their age) experience positive age bias at work (Lawrence, 1988; Shore & Goldberg, 2005).

> **Hypothesis 3a:** Older workers starting jobs different from their previous jobs (between-career transitions) will experience more age bias at work relative to younger workers vis-à-vis older workers starting jobs similar to their previous jobs.

A prototype-matching process has been theorized to account for the above-reviewed disparity, whereby negative stereotypes of old age such as inadaptability and incompetence (Ng & Feldman, 2012) imply that older workers will not be able to make successful career transitions into jobs that are different from their previous jobs (i.e., that may require training). One promising avenue of research in this regard is the notion of age meta-stereotypes. Whereas stereotypes are defined as beliefs about the characteristics or attributes of certain groups, meta-stereotypes refer to beliefs regarding how other groups stereotype one's focal group (Finkelstein et al., 2013). Meta-stereotypes have been found to be overall more negative than stereotypes; people expect other groups to view them more negatively than they actually do (Finkelstein et al., 2013). Deeper examination of such stereotypical and meta-stereotypical processes may thus shed light on the psychological consequences of switching careers in later life. Toward this end, Finkelstein, King, and Voyles (2015) suggest that age meta-stereotypes will most likely be activated in contexts that magnify age salience, such as between-career transitions (for older workers). In turn, more negative work attitudinal outcomes may be expected to result as a function of greater age meta-stereotype activation.

Hypothesis 3b: Older workers making between-career transitions are more likely to endorse negative meta-stereotypes of their age group than older workers making within-career transitions.

Hypothesis 3c: Age meta-stereotypes will mediate the moderated relations between worker age, career-transition type, and work outcomes such that the interactive effect of worker age and career-transition type on work outcomes will be mediated by age meta-stereotypes.

Relatedly, the trends reviewed above regarding shifting career trajectories and retirement patterns also may hold consequence for the stereotyping of older workers. People choose to retire or remain in the workforce for various reasons, such as economic necessity or debilitating health conditions. Such an individual-choice driven retirement decision is different from mandated retirement at particular (older) ages. One implication of a mandated retirement policy is that one is deemed to be no longer "suitable to work" past a particular age by virtue of policy. Therefore, mandatory retirement may lead to or perpetuate negative stereotypes of older workers such as incompetence in terms of cognitive, physical, and memory capacity (Cuddy & Fiske, 2002; Ng & Feldman, 2012), contribute to stereotype threat (Lamont, Swift, & Abrams, 2015), and result in greater age meta-stereotyping among older workers (Finkelstein et al., 2015).

Hypothesis 4a: Mandatory retirement policies will be positively related to negative age stereotyping against older workers.

Hypothesis 4b: Mandatory retirement policies will be positively related to negative age meta-stereotyping by older workers.

Hypothesis 4c: Mandatory retirement policies will be positively related to the likelihood of stereotype threat among older workers.

From a practical standpoint, as summarized in Table 1, traditional organizational pension fund systems, tied to years of service to a specific organization, might be forced to change and become transportable given the new career trajectory (Baruch & Reis, 2016). Indeed, such a shift from defined benefit to defined contribution plans has long since begun and is only gaining momentum. For example, in the US and beginning in the 1980s, a burgeoning share of both private-

and public-sector organizations have been shifting to 401K and 403B defined contribution-style retirement plans (Dulebohn, Murray, & Sun, 2000).

Given the above-reviewed changes in career trajectories and retirement ages, organizational prescriptions and proscriptions regarding hiring workers of "a certain age" may accordingly need to be revised or even abandoned. Organizational reward and promotion systems may have to change and become more merit- as opposed to loyalty-based (years of service) schemes given an increasingly mobile workforce (Baruch & Reis, 2016). Correspondingly, given both an abundance of older workers and an abundance of negative age-based stereotypes and meta-stereotypes against older workers, organizations will increasingly be required to facilitate the acceptance and inclusion of older workers. Toward this end, Boehm, Kunze, and Bruch (2014) recommend a number of age-inclusive human resource practices that organizations can implement. These include the implementation of age-neutral recruiting activities, equal access to training and further education for all age groups, equal opportunities for promotion career progress irrespective of one's age, training and education for managers on how to deal with the needs of an age-diverse workforce, and the active promotion of an overall age-friendly organizational culture (Rudolph & Zacher, in press).

Macro Effects—Cultural. Culture has been theorized to act as a macro-systemic boundary condition, whereby the effects of age on outcomes are either magnified or attenuated depending upon specific cultural characteristics of the society or organization at hand (Posthuma & Guerrero, 2013). However, research on the confluence of age and culture is mixed. On the one hand, proponents of the view that age bias has evolutionary roots and cuts across cultures (Fiske, Cuddy, & Glick, 2007; Kurzban & Leary, 2001) point to evidence that all age groups have been found to exhibit negative bias towards older adults (Axt et al., 2014), and that stereotypes of older adults in the pre-Industrial society of Ottoman Anatolia mirror those found in contemporary Western samples (Marcus & Sabuncu, 2016). Most recently, a meta-analysis studying relations between age discrimination and societal cultures found that samples in both Western and Eastern societal cultures report prejudice and unfair discrimination against older adults (North & Fiske, 2015). Conversely, proponents of the sociocultural view of age bias (Nelson, 2005) point to positive views of older adults held by Eastern societies where norms of filial piety are strong (Palmore & Maeda, 1985). Supporting research from the literature on the social psychology of stigma also indicates Western and individualistic societies to hold more unfairly discriminatory attitudes and cognitions toward older adults because of the prototype of the ideal worker being young and able-bodied in Western society (Stone-Romero & Stone, 2007).

These just-noted and mixed findings may be a function of three related issues. First, "culture" is too often confounded with country. Over 80% of cross-cultural variance has been found to reside within and not between countries (Taras, Steel, & Kirkman, 2016), with the implication that demographic subgroups and organizations or industries/occupations may be more construct valid conveyors of culture than whole nations (see also Triandis, 1995). Second, from a construct validity perspective, it is illegitimate to make inferences about a particular individual's cultural values based upon her nation of origin because this practice confounds the societal and individual levels of the construct (Betancourt & Lopez, 1993). Research on the confluence of age and culture thus needs to further move in the direction of examining individual cultural value differences, as opposed to crude differences between societal (country) collectives; there is indeed a dearth of such research in the broader cross-cultural management literature (Kirkman, Lowe, & Gibson, 2017). Third, extant research has too narrowly focused only on individualism-collectivism; more nuanced and multidimensional inspection may be needed to examine links between culture and prejudice.

One theoretical framework that holds promise here and that specifically focuses on the confluence of age and culture is the Cultural Anchors of Ageism (CAA; Marcus & Fritzsche, 2016). The CAA is multi-level, including organizational- and individual-level differences, and draws upon multiple cultural dimensions to examine relations between culture and age bias. Drawing upon social identity theory (Brewer, 1991; Turner, 1985), the CAA posits that psychological dimensions of culture relating to the formation and permeability of in- and out-groups are most relevant to age-based outcomes, collectivism and tightness. Collectivism focuses on the role of individuals and groups in social relationships and deals with the an relative permeability of group boundaries, whereby cultures with relatively impermeable in-groups are more likely to exhibit tendencies toward prejudice and discrimination (Fiske, 2000). Tightness focuses on the relative importance of rules vs. relationships in behavioral control and deals with the degree to which deviances from group norms are permissible, whereby cultures with relatively greater norm impermissibility are more likely to exhibit tendencies toward prejudice and discrimination (Gelfand, Nishii, & Raver, 2006). Thus, societal and organizational cultures that are *both* collectivistic (strict in- and out-group distinctions) and tight (deviances from group norms are sanctioned) are theorized to be typified by the most age bias; vice versa for individualistic-loose societal and organizational cultures (Marcus & Fritzsche, 2016). Blending an ecological perspective with this prior theorizing by Marcus and Fritzsche (2016), we may construe that collectivistic-tight societies will be typified by more age biased institutional practices (e.g., more discriminatory laws on the basis of age; more discriminatory governmental or organizational policies on the basis of age).

Hypothesis 5a: Collectivistic-tight societies will have a greater incidence of age biased institutional practices.

Hypothesis 5b: Collectivistic-tight organizations will have a greater incidence of age biased institutional practices.

At the individual level, persons holding values most closely aligned with collectivism and tightness are theorized to be more likely to exhibit age bias (Marcus

& Fritzsche, 2016). Because there are interactive effects across levels of culture (Marcus & Le, 2013), such persons that themselves are embedded in collectivistic and tight societal or organizational cultures are theorized to be the most likely to exhibit age bias.

Hypothesis 5c: Individuals holding values most closely aligned with both collectivism and tightness will be more likely to endorse age biased institutional practices.

Hypothesis 5d: Individuals holding values most closely aligned with both collectivism and tightness and who are themselves embedded within collectivistic-tight societal or organizational cultural contexts will be the most likely to endorse age biased institutional practices.

Meso Effects. Because organizations may themselves be viewed as microcosms of societal systems, overall societal effects may be expected to either be emphasized or attenuated, depending upon particularities of organizational context and culture. Here, we focus on four specific aspects of organizational context and culture that best lend themselves theoretically and empirically to the current discussion, including norm salience, role hierarchy, organizational (relational) demography, and the design of the job. These four factors represent job and organizational context variables that have received theoretical and empirical support for understanding links between work and aging (for reviews, see Posthuma & Campion, 2019; Finkelstein et al., 2019; Zacher et al., 2019).

Organizations, like societies, may also alternatively be tighter or looser. Organizations differ on the extent to which they emphasize rules and predictability (e.g., McDonalds, UPS) vs. flexibility and experimentation (e.g., Apple, Facebook), whereby the former are typified by stronger organizational cultures and more salient organizational norms. Organizations with strong norms have stronger socialization and training processes, with higher socially shared cognition and greater behavioral similarity among members (Gelfand et al., 2006). Accordingly, tighter organizations, characterized by systems of greater norm salience, espousing stronger social norms and exhibiting less behavioral latitude around said norms, may be construed as more likely to endorse age-biased values and practices.

Hypothesis 6a: Stereotyping, prejudice, and unfair discrimination based upon age will be higher in organizational cultures with greater norm salience.

Similarly, some organizations have more clearly defined role hierarchies compared to others. Military organizations, for example, have clearly defined ranks based upon both merit and seniority, and do not easily allow "upstarts" to hurdle through the ranks. Likewise, there is a clear role hierarchy amongst the ranks of research-oriented academicians, ranging from Assistant to Full Professors; most universities require considerable contributions to the field, along with other seniority-associated indices for promotion to the rank of Full Professor. Such role hierarchies may also be construed as a form of norm salience, but signified via rank hierarchies (see Lawrence, 1988).

Hypothesis 6b: Stereotyping, prejudice, and unfair discrimination based upon age will be higher in organizational cultures with greater role hierarchies.

In essence, the above lines of reasoning surrounding both organizational norm salience and role hierarchies are manifestations of the larger theories of relational demography and organizational social identity theory, whereby individuals dissimilar to organizational others are posited to be more likely to experience negative work consequences (Ashforth & Mael, 1989). Meso (organizational) cultures manifested in the form of norm salience and role hierarchies thus may be seen to reinforce the role of ontogenetic processes related to work, such that the worker composition of such organizations may itself change.

Hypothesis 7a: Age diversity in organizations will be negatively associated with norm salience.

Hypothesis 7b: Age diversity in organizations will be negatively associated with role hierarchy.

Practically speaking, organizations with strong norm salience regarding the typical worker age may come to be defined by average worker ages reflecting those organizational cultures. For example, organizations with cultures prioritizing young age-stereotypical qualities in hiring new employees, such as being "dynamic," "adaptable," or "energetic" (Finkelstein et al., 2013) may come to be populated by younger workers. Strong age-based role hierarchies may propagate loyalty and length of service-based promotion systems over merit-based promotion systems, thus leading to relatively higher average ages among the managerial ranks. Thus, as summarized in Table 1, differences in organizational and even occupational cultures may create differential types or amounts of hurdles regarding career and job mobility for non-normatively aged workers, with organizations characterized by non-inclusive age norms coming to be characterized by workforce age homogeneity.

Finally, the design of the job itself represents a meso-systemic influence on work and aging. One particular conceptualization of age-related job design that has been the focus of recent scholarship is the role of age-inclusive human resource (HR) practices. Here, age-inclusive HR practices are defined as organizational practices that foster worker motivation and effort, knowledge, skill, and ability acquisition, and opportunities for learning and development, irrespective of worker age (Boehm et al., 2014). For example, organizations can offer on-the-job training for all workers in order to increase worker knowledge and skill acquisition, or provide job mentoring or shadowing upon initial recruitment in the execution of complex or highly technical jobs (Boehm et al., 2014). Organizations implementing such age-inclusive HR practices have shown greater social cohesion, reduced collective turnover intentions, and enhanced firm performance (Boehm et al., 2014). Additionally, cross-societal research from both the United Kingdom and Hong Kong has demonstrated that HR policies supportive of older workers have positive influences on personnel views toward older workers (Chiu, Chan, Snape, & Redman, 2001). Indeed, the importance of enabling an age-inclusive organizational environment has been posited to be essential for older worker career mobility (Baruch & Reis, 2016).

One promising framework to further investigate the confluence of HR practices and age is the lifespan perspective on job design by Truxillo, Cadiz, Rineer, Zaniboni, and Fraccaroli (2012). Taking a lifespan developmental perspective on work and aging via the conceptual lenses of selection-optimization-compensation (Baltes & Baltes, 1990) and socioemotional selectivity theories (Carstensen, 2006; Carstensen, Isaacowitz, & Charles, 1999), Truxillo et al. (2012) posit that chronological age will interact with the task (e.g., task variety), knowledge (e.g., job complexity), and social (e.g., task interdependence) characteristics of the job to predict worker attitudes and behaviors. The specific directionalities in turn are posited to depend on the nature of the job characteristic in question. For example, Truxillo et al. (2012) theorize that while older workers may benefit from job autonomy more than younger workers because the latter may need more direction as a result of relative inexperience, younger workers may benefit more than older workers from task variety because of the association between old age and fluid intelligence. Overall, Truxillo et al. (2012) posit that job characteristics that optimize physical and professional capacities that an individual may hold given said individual's age will be most beneficial in terms of work outcomes. Blending an ecological perspective with prior theorizing by Truxillo et al. (2012), we may construe that organizational cultures typified by a greater diversity of job social, task, and knowledge characteristics will overall have more age inclusive organizational climates and fewer age biased institutional practices. That is, given that different aspects of job social, task, and knowledge characteristics are associated with more or less beneficial for workers of different ages (Truxillo et al., 2012), organizations that enable job structures that are able to cater to the psychosocial needs of workers at both ends of the spectrum on age would ultimately be the most age inclusive organizations.

> **Hypothesis 8a:** More variance in job task characteristics will predict more inclusive age climates, fewer incidences of age biased institutional practices, and more work engagement of younger and older workers.

> **Hypothesis 8b:** More variance in job knowledge characteristics will predict more inclusive age climates, fewer incidences of age biased institutional practices, and more work engagement of younger and older workers.

> **Hypothesis 8c:** More variance in social job characteristics will predict more inclusive age climates, fewer incidences of age biased institutional practices, and more work engagement of younger and older workers.

Micro Effects—Subjective Age. Whereas chronological age is objective, subjective age refers to psychosocial dimensions of age such as lifespan age (e.g., the number of children one has), organizational age (e.g., the number of years worked in the current job or organization), functional age (e.g., one's physical health status), and psychological age (e.g., how old one subjectively "feels'" Kooij et al., 2008; Zacher et al., 2019). There is a lack of research on social or identity-based facets of age such as social age or normative age (see Kooij et al., 2008, for a review). Age is understood to include both objective chronological and subjective psychological aspects (Staudinger, 2015). Traditionally, the concept of "subjective age" has been fuzzier, with researchers (e.g., Barak, Mathur, Lee, & Zhang, 2001) generally conceptualizing the construct as how old one "feels." Recent scholarship, however, suggests that this broad "feel old" construct does not possess incremental validity over chronological age and core self-evaluations in the prediction of work and life outcomes (Zacher & Rudolph, in press). Based upon this, we would strongly suggest to researchers that it is important to test the unique influence of subjective age incremental to core self-evaluations. Nevertheless, it has been theorized that more nuanced measures of subjective age, rooted in the social identity and self-categorization processes, may be worthy of investigation (Zacher et al., 2019).

Hypothesis 9: Age group identification is a better predictor of work outcomes than subjective age, after accounting for core self-evaluations.

As summarized in Table 1, from a workforce implications standpoint, individuals who are psychologically younger than their age may choose to retire later; individuals who "look" or "act" subjectively older than their chronological age may experience more age discrimination than their younger-countenanced counterparts. Much research is needed to better understand the potentially different consequences of chronological, objective age and psychological, subjective age on age-related work outcomes. Recent advances on theory related to subjective vs. objective age (Zacher & Rudolph, 2019; Zacher et al., 2019) represent useful guides for research on these issues.

Micro Effects—Intersectionality. There have been recent calls to advance the study of diversity and work outcomes by considering the intersectional perspective (Jones et al., 2017). At the micro level, it is a given that "older" and "younger" workers are not unitarily binary categories, whereby individuals are simultaneously older/younger and also male/female, or from majority or minority groups such as black vs. white Americans. Here, we may draw upon theory in areas such as intersectionality and double jeopardy/advantage to explain effects of simultaneously occurring demographical characteristics within individuals. Rooted in the multiple identity perspective, these theories imply a power imbalance based upon joint demographic roles. For example, older white males are viewed as "leaders" but older white females as "grandmothers" (Marcus & Fritzsche, 2015). The intersectional view on age postulates that individuals may be conceptualized as qualitatively distinct demographic subgroups bounded by the tripartite of age, gender, and communal affiliation, with different sets of stereotypes and resultant consequences derived as a function of one's idiosyncratic combination of multiple group memberships (Marcus & Fritzsche, 2015; Ozbilgin, Beauregard, Tatli, & Bell, 2011). This perspective has a long history in the multiple category tradition, for example regarding studies on double jeopardy and/or double advantage showing dual effects of both race and sex on outcomes for female workers (Berdahl & Moore, 2006).

Overall, theory on the intersection of age with other major surface demographic characteristics including gender and communal affiliation indicates that older workers of different demographic subcategories will experience qualitatively different work outcomes, depending upon the particular constellation of characteristics at hand (Marcus & Fritzsche, 2015). Because age-based stereotypes of women are more negative than those of men (Hummert, 1990; Marcus & Sabuncu, 2016), researchers have theorized that older and younger females are expected to derive worse work outcomes (e.g., more unfair discrimination, more negative age stereotyping, reduced psychological well-being) relative to their male counterparts (Marcus & Fritzsche, 2015). The interactive effects of age and communal affiliation on work outcomes are less clear because no such published empirical research yet exists. However, borrowing from the double jeopardy and feminist theory literature (c.f., Berdahl & Moore, 2006; Hosoda, Stone, & Stone-Romero, 2003; Purdie-Vaughns & Eibach, 2008; Sesko & Biernat, 2010), Marcus and Fritzsche (2015) theorized older minority group members (both female and male) were expected to derive better work outcomes than their majority member counterparts; vice versa for younger minority group members. Viewed from an ecological perspective, we may thus expect that age biased societal and organizational practices will likely result in more deleterious work outcomes for women, and younger minority members, but result in more beneficial work outcomes for older minority group members.

Hypothesis 10a: Age biased societal and organizational practices will result in the most negative and least positive work outcomes for older females in general.

Hypothesis 10b: Age biased societal and organizational practices will result in the most negative and least positive work outcomes for younger minority group members, both male and female.

Hypothesis 10c: Age biased societal and organizational practices will result in the least negative and most positive work outcomes for older minority group members, both male and female.

As with the former ecological factors, the micro-systemic demographic factors, although remaining under-researched, have potential to influence a wide array of outcomes relevant to work and aging (see Table 8.1). For example, because females are more so burdened with familial responsibilities such as child or eldercare, older female workers may be likely to prioritize different aspects of an organization's benefits program as compared to males, such as flexible work-hours in lieu of pecuniary incentives; older female workers may have different timelines and trajectories for retirement given similar work-life balance issues.

Temporal Factors: An Integrative Mechanism Across Ecological Systems

Our ecological model of work and aging posits a fourth system of temporal factors that serves as an integration mechanism across the macro-, meso-, and micro-systems described above. In line with the work of Bronfenbrenner (1979), we term this system the chronosystem, and consider its influence across three conceptualizations of time: experienced time, perceived time, and timing of events. This broad view of time allows our model to account for various temporal factors that occur across the lifespan, including transitions and shifts (e.g., from school to career; from career to retirement), as well as the experience of socio-historical contexts that may exert influence upon a person. It is important to consider time within an ecological systems framework for a number of reasons. For example, goals are time-bound insomuch as they are framed against deadlines which can be abstracted temporally. As such, understanding and appropriately theorizing the role of time is important for theorizing about self-regulatory processes, broadly defined. Moreover, the process of aging is determined by the experience of time, as ontogenesis is necessarily temporally bound.

Experienced Time. First, we explore several ways in which experienced time interacts with macro- and meso-systems to influence the experience of working. As suggested, experienced time is often taken as a proxy for the process of aging. Regarding macro-systems, it has long been documented that the experience of aging at work varies by country and culture (Rudolph et al., 2019). For example, the decisions to extend one's working life or to work after retirement from one's career job are dependent on the interplay between retirement reforms and a country's other social policies (Henkens et al., 2018).

Considering also intersections between experienced time and meso-systems, the process of aging at work is influenced by organizational factors. To this end, Zacher (2015) speaks about the role of organizational systems for supporting successful aging at work (i.e., maintaining or improving work outcomes with age). Moreover, the action regulation across the adult lifespan (ARAL; Zacher, Hacker, & Frese, 2016) meta-theory is a good embodiment of these principles, wherein principles of work design derived from the traditions of action regulation theory are specifically tied to the process of successful aging.

Beyond studying aging as a developmental process, careers are also a developmental process that unfolds over time (e.g., Super, 1992). Indeed, there are temporal forces at play that influence career paths grounded in both macro- and micro-systems. For example, there are macro-systemic influences on career entry, such as differences in educational systems, required military service, or other factors that occur at the national level. Moreover, societal norms regarding work-related practices such as childcare and eldercare can influence career progression. To some extent, this is also legislated (e.g., in countries where there are specific provisions of maternal/paternal leave), but with notable country-to-country variability.

Career experiences are also more likely to vary as a function of meso-systemic factors, particularly those tied to normative organizational factors. One normative factor that distinguishes organizations is their support of learning and development (Schein, 1996). For example, some organizations place a heavy emphasis on continual education and career development (i.e., so-called "learning organizations"). Moreover, some industries and professions require continual updating of training via requirements for continuing professional educations (e.g., for licensure maintenance requirements). Despite these observations, less research focuses on the relative influence or assumed benefit of career-long learning for later life work outcomes (e.g., those associated with long term employability, retirement decision making, etc.).

Hypothesis 11a: Age is negatively related to perceived remaining time in the work context.

Perceived Time. The idea of perceived time describes a variety of psychologically-constructed notions about temporal processes, and their influence on affective, behavioral, and/or cognitive processes (e.g., "temporal focus"; see Shipp, Edwards, & Lambert, 2009). One particularly relevant perceived time construct, future time perspective, has both a rich theoretical tradition (Henry, Zacher, & Desmette, 2017) and a volume of empirical research that supports linkages to important work outcomes and more general life outcomes (see Kooij, Kanfer, Betts, & Rudolph, 2018; Rudolph, Kooij, Rauvola, & Zacher, 2018).

At the macro-systemic level, research suggests that future time perspective may interact with cultural contexts in a variety complex ways. For example, Fung, Lai, and Ng (2001) investigated preferences for social interactions using an age-matched sample of Chinese individuals, residing in either Taiwan or mainland China. The results of this study suggested that Chinese individuals who lived in mainland China (where life expectancies are relatively shorter) preferred social interactions with emotionally close social partners more so than Chinese individuals living in Taiwan (i.e., where life expectancies are relatively longer; on average seven years higher than mainland China). This study concluded that even naturalistically limited future time perspective, in terms of shorter life expectancies, can have important influences on social behaviors (i.e., preferences for familiar social partners).

Research also points to meso-systemic variation in time perspectives. For example, there is evidence that time perspective varies across industries and jobs (e.g., Zhang, Wang, & Pierce, 2014). Scholars have posited that both temporal career dynamics and core features of job designs concurrently play an important role in codetermining employees' reactions to and influence upon their work environments (e.g., Fried, Grant, Levi, Hadani, & Slowik, 2007).

Finally, in addition to evidence of macro- and meso-level influence of perceived time, there is also evidence for micro-systemic influences of perceived time that can be derived from within-person studies of time perspective. For example, Weikamp and Goritz (2015) investigated changes in occupational future time perspective across four years, finding that people perceive losses in their remaining occupational time and remaining occupational opportunities over time. Highlighting the complexities of these temporal influences, experienced time (i.e., chronological age) was also found to moderate the observed decrease in perceived remaining time over time, such that relatively younger people perceived that their remaining time decreased faster than did relatively older people.

Hypothesis 11b: Perceived remaining time explains associations between worker age and work-related behavior and outcomes.

Timing. We refer to the final temporal component of the chronosystem as timing. Here, timing can refer to a variety of temporally-bound factors related to events, development, or conditions that exist across either macro-, meso-, or micro-systems. Timing can refer to discrete events or temporal fluctuations. For example, the implementation of changes in industry standards and practices represent discrete events that influence the process of working, and can serve to shift the way in which employees engage in their job tasks. Also, dynamics in market environments, unemployment rates, or political climates represent temporal fluctuations. One relevant macro-systemic example of timing-related influences on work behaviors is the development of new technologies, which may represent significant age barriers to adoption and implementation (e.g., Czaja et al., 2006). Also at the macro level, research suggests that variability in economic conditions may have distinct implications for behavior. For example, contemporaneous unemployment rates have been linked to differences in both narcissism (e.g., Bianchi, 2014) and job satisfaction (e.g., Bianchi, 2013).

At the meso-systemic level, timing factors related to organizational events have particular implications for workers across the lifespan (Axelrad, Sabbath, & Hawkins, 2018). For example, job loss can be particularly damning to older workers (see Kanfer & Bufton, 2018, for a review). Organizational downsizing has been tied to worker-wellbeing outcomes, including addictive behaviors, although patterns seem to be age graded, such that "surviving" organizational downsizing is associated with excessive alcohol use among younger, but not older workers. (e.g., Frone, 2018). At the micro-level, choices related to timing have broad implications on career development, particularly school-to-work transitions. Research suggests negative wellbeing consequences of delayed school-to-work transition (Schulenberg, Bryant, & O'Malley, 2004), including higher risks of depression (Nurmi & Salmela-Aro, 2002).

Hypothesis 11c: Life stage moderates the effects of work events on work behavior and work outcomes, such that older and younger workers differ in the reactions to these events due to age-related changes in individual and contextual characteristics.

DISCUSSION

Based on the observation that population and workforce aging are global phenomena that impact individuals, organizations, and societies in many countries and cultures around the globe, we proposed an ecological systems framework for research on work and aging. In doing so, we integrated two complementary meta-theories, that is, Bronfenbrenner's ecological systems approach, and the lifespan developmental perspective. On the one hand, the ecological systems approach focuses not only on various levels of context, but also takes temporal factors (i.e., chronosystem) into account. The lifespan perspective, on the other hand, not only focuses on intraindividual development, but also acknowledges the importance of context. Our framework suggests that various factors at the macro-, meso-, and micro-levels interact in influencing both younger, mid-career, and older workers' experiences and behavior at work. Moreover, we postulated temporal factors to be integrative mechanisms across these levels. While we highlighted selected theoretical and empirical works that address some assumptions of our framework, we also emphasized that more research is needed to gain a comprehensive understanding of work and aging through an ecological systems lens. The goal of this final section of our paper is to summarize and integrate these suggestions for future theory development and empirical research based on our framework.

Macro-Level Institutional and Cultural Factors

Most research on work and aging focuses on associations between (perceived) work and/or organizational characteristics and workers' experiences and behavior. In contrast, the influence of broader institutional and cultural issues, such as changes in retirement age and careers, as well as effects of culture have been largely neglected. Where research does exist, the potential effects of the above-reviewed macro-systemic influences of culture on work-related ontogenetic processes have not been well-studied, with the vast majority of research on these phenomena originating from individualistic-loose "Western" societal cultures (Posthuma & Guerrero, 2013). Nevertheless, these influences potentially may exhibit significant effects on aspects of work and aging as reviewed earlier (see Table 8.1). Of course, cross-cultural research on work and aging may be very resource-intensive, but work on aging demonstrates that this approach is important to distinguish universal (etic) from context-dependent (emic) age-related processes (e.g., Fang, Gong, Lu, & Fung, 2017). The CAA (Marcus & Fritzsche, 2016) provides a useful base for future such research and could be extended to include effects of culture on broader diversity outcomes.

Meso-Level Organizational Factors

At the organizational level, we discussed factors such as organizational (relational) demography, job design, norm salience, and role hierarchy. While organizational demography and job design have received quite a bit of attention in research on work and aging (e.g., Pelled & Xin, 2000; Zacher & Schmitt, 2016), researchers in this area could incorporate insights from the fields of social psychology and sociology in terms of social roles, hierarchies, and norms into their theorizing. For instance, research is emerging on aging and work-family balance, suggesting that organizational norms play an important role in younger and older workers' ability and motivation to balance tasks in work and family domains (e.g., Allen & Shockley, 2012; Huffman, Culbertson, Henning, & Goh, 2013).

Micro-Level Individual Factors

Researchers have argued that age is not only a chronological index, but also has psychological and social facets (Staudinger, 2015). However, in research on aging and work it is still relatively uncommon to examine whether alternative age conceptualizations such as "physical age" or "psychological age" explain workers' experiences and behavior above and beyond chronological age and established personality traits (e.g., core self-evaluations, including dispositional measures of locus of control, neuroticism, self-efficacy, and self-esteem; Zacher & Rudolph, in press). Even less common is research on the intersectionality of age with other demographic characteristics, such as gender (Jones et al., 2017).

Temporal Factors

Our framework posits that various temporal factors that reside within a broader chronosystem serve as integrative mechanisms that bridge these various ecological systems. While research on perceived time (e.g., temporal focus, occupational future time perspective) has rapidly grown over the past decade, we need to learn more about people's experiences of time as well as the importance of timing. For instance, how do younger, mid-career, and older workers react to and cope with unexpected yet significant work events (e.g., job loss) or life events (e.g., accidents)? Research could integrate the theory of discontinuous career transitions (Haynie & Shepherd, 2011) with the lifespan perspective to gain a better understand of age differences in such transitions.

CONCLUSION

In sum, our ecological systems framework contributes to the literature on work and aging by integrating individual age-related processes and outcomes with factors at multiple contextual levels. We hope that our ideas serve to inspire future researchers to adopt a broader cross-level and cross-systematic perspective on the study of aging and work. We believe that our integration of an ecological perspective with the traditions of lifespan developmental psychology offers a promising start to a more contextually informed body of knowledge regarding the work and aging process.

REFERENCES

Ainsworth, S. (2015). Aging entrepreneurs and volunteers: Transition in late career. In P. M. Bal, D. T. A. M. Kooij, & D. Rousseau (Eds.), *Aging workers and the employee-employer relationship* (pp. 243–260). New York, NY: Springer.

Albright, V. A. (2012). Workforce demographics in the United States: Occupational trends, work rates, and retirement projections in the United States. In J. W. Hedge & W. C. Borman (Eds.), *The Oxford handbook of work and aging* (pp. 33–59). New York, NY: Oxford University Press.

Allen, T. D., & Shockley, K. M. (2012). Older workers and work-family issues. In J. W. Hedge & W. C. Borman (Eds.), *The Oxford handbook of work and aging* (pp. 520–537). New York, NY: Oxford University Press.

Arthur, M. B., & Rousseau, D. M. (1996). Introduction: The boundaryless career as a new employment principle. In M. B. Arthur & D. M. Rousseau (Eds.), *The boundaryless career: A new employment principle for a new organizational era* (pp. 3–20). New York, NY: Oxford.

Ashbaugh, D. L., & Fay, C. H. (1987). The threshold for aging in the workplace. *Research on Aging, 9*, 417–427.

Ashforth, B. E., & Mael, F. (1989). Social identity theory and the organization. *Academy of Management Review, 14*, 20–39.

Axelrad, H., Sabbath, E. L., & Hawkins, S. S. (2018). The 2008–2009 Great Recession and employment outcomes among older workers. *European Journal of Ageing, 15*, 35–45.

Axt, J. R., Ebersole, C. R., & Nosek, B. A. (2014). The rules of implicit evaluation by race, religion, and age. *Psychological Science, 25*, 1804–1815.

Aycan, Z., Kanungo, R. N., Mendonca, M., Yu, K., Deller, J., Stahl, G., & Kurshid, A. (2000). Impact of culture on human resource management practices: A 10-country study. *Applied Psychology: An International Review, 49*, 192–221.

Bal, A. C., Reiss, A. E. B., Rudolph, C. W., & Baltes, B. B. (2011). Examining positive and negative perceptions of older workers: A meta-analysis. *The Journals of Gerontology, Series B: Psychological Sciences and Social Sciences, 66*, 687–698.

Becker, E. (1975). *The denial of death.* New York, NY: Free Press.

Baltes, P. B. (1987). Theoretical propositions of life-span developmental psychology: On the dynamics between growth and decline. *Developmental Psychology, 23*, 611–626.

Baltes, P. B., & Baltes, M. M. (1990). Psychological perspectives on successful aging: The model of selective compensation with optimization. In P. B. Baltes & M. M. Baltes (Eds.), *Successful aging: Perspectives from the behavioral sciences* (pp. 1–34). New York, NY: Cambridge University Press.

Baltes, P. B., Lindenberger, U., & Staudinger, U. M. (2006). Lifespan theory in developmental psychology. In W. Damon & R. M. Lerner (Eds.), *Handbook of child psychology: Vol. 1. Theoretical models of human development* (6th ed., pp. 569–664). New York, NY: Wiley.

Baltes, P. B., Reese, H. W., & Lipsitt, L. P. (1980). Life-span developmental psychology. *Annual Review of Psychology, 31,* 65–110.

Barak, B., Mathur, A., Lee, K., & Zhang, Y. (2001). Perceptions of age–identity: A cross-cultural inner-age exploration. *Psychology and Marketing, 18,* 1003–1029.

Baruch, Y., & Reis, C. (2016). How global are boundaryless careers and how boundaryless are global careers? Challenges and a theoretical perspective. *Thunderbird International Business Review, 58,* 13–27.

Berdahl, J. L., & Moore, C. (2006). Workplace harassment: Double jeopardy for minority women. *Journal of Applied Psychology, 91,* 426–436.

Betancourt, H., & Lopez, S. R. (1993). The study of culture, ethnicity, and race in American psychology. *American Psychologist, 6,* 629–637.

Bianchi, E. C. (2013). The bright side of bad times: The affective advantages of entering the workforce in a recession. *Administrative Science Quarterly, 58,* 587–623.

Bianchi, E. C. (2014). Entering adulthood in a recession tempers later narcissism. *Psychological Science, 25,* 1429–1437.

Boehm, S. A., Kunze, F., & Bruch, H. (2014). Spotlight on age diversity climate: The impact of age-inclusive HR practices on firm-level outcomes. *Personnel Psychology, 67,* 667–704.

Bowles, N. (2019, March 4). A new luxury retreat caters to elderly workers in tech (ages 30 and up). *The New York Times.* Retrieved March 13, 2019 from: https://www.nytimes.com/2019/03/04/technology/modern-elder-resort-silicon-valley-ageism.html

Brewer, M. B. (1991). The social self: On being the same and different at the same time. *Personality and Social Psychology Bulletin, 17,* 475–482.

Bronfenbrenner, U. (1979). *The ecology of human development: Experiments by nature and design.* Cambridge, MA: Harvard University Press.

Carstensen, L. L. (2006). The influence of a sense of time on human development. *Science, 312,* 1913–1915.

Carstensen, L. L., Isaacowitz, D. M., & Charles, S. T. (1999). Taking time seriously: A theory of socioemotional selectivity. *American Psychologist, 54,* 165–181.

Chand, M., & Tung, R. L. (2014). The aging of the world's population and its effects on global business. *Academy of Management Perspectives, 28,* 409–429.

Chiu, W. C. K., Chan, A. W., Snape, E., & Redman, T. (2001). Age stereotypes and discriminatory attitudes towards older workers: An East–West comparison. *Human Relations, 54,* 629–661.

Cuddy, A. J. C., & Fiske, S. T. (2002). Doddering but dear: Process, content, and function in stereotyping of older persons. In T. D. Nelson (Ed.), *Ageism: Stereotyping and prejudice toward older persons* (pp. 3–26). Cambridge, MA: MIT.

Czaja, S. J., Charness, N., Fisk, A. D., Hertzog, C., Nair, S. N., Rogers, W. A., & Sharit, J. (2006). Factors predicting the use of technology: Findings from the Center for Research and Education on Aging and Technology Enhancement (CREATE). *Psychology and Aging, 21,* 333–352.

Dulebohn, J. H., Murray, B., & Sun, M. (2000). Selection among employer-sponsored pension plans: The role of individual differences. *Personnel Psychology, 53,* 405–432.

Fang, Y., Gong, X., Lu, M., & Fung, H. H. (2017). Cross-Cultural Aging. In N. A. Pachana (Ed.), *Encyclopedia of geropsychology* (pp. 1–10). New York, NY: Springer Reference.

Finkelstein, L. M., Hanrahan, E. A., & Thomas, C. L. (2019). An expanded view of age bias in the workplace. In K. S. Shultz, & Adams, G. A. (Eds.), *Aging and work in the 21st century* (2nd ed., pp. 59–101). New York, NY: Taylor & Francis.

Finkelstein, L. M., King, E. B., & Voyles, E. C. (2015). Age meta-stereotypes and cross-age workplace interactions: A meta view of age stereotypes at work. *Work, Aging, and Retirement, 1,* 26–40.

Finkelstein, L. M., Ryan, K. M., & King, E. B. (2013). What do the young (old) people think of me? Content and accuracy of age-based metastereotypes. *European Journal of Work and Organizational Psychology, 21,* 1–25.

Fiske, S. T. (2000). Stereotyping, discrimination, and prejudice at the seam between the centuries: Evolution, culture, mind, and brain. *European Journal of Social Psychology, 30,* 299–322.

Fiske, S. T., Cuddy, A. J. C., & Glick, P. (2007). Universal dimensions of social cognition: Warmth and competence. *Trends in Cognitive Sciences, 11,* 77–82.

Fiske, S. T., Cuddy, A. J., Glick, P., & Xu, J. (2002). A model of (often mixed) stereotype content: Competence and warmth respectively follow from perceived status and competition. *Journal of Personality and Social Psychology, 82,* 878–902.

Ford, D. H., & Lerner, R. M. (1992). *Developmental systems theory: An integrative approach.* Thousand Oaks, CA: Sage Publications

Fried, Y., Grant, A. M., Levi, A. S., Hadani, M., & Slowik, L. H. (2007). Job design in temporal context: A career dynamics perspective. *Journal of Organizational Behavior, 28,* 911–927.

Fritzsche, B. A., & Marcus, J. (2013). The senior discount: Biases against older career changers. *Journal of Applied Social Psychology, 43,* 350–362.

Frone, M. R. (2018). Organizational downsizing and alcohol use: A national study of US workers during the Great Recession. *Addictive Behaviors, 77,* 107–113.

Gelfand, M. J., Nishii, L. H., & Raver, J. L. (2006). On the nature and importance of cultural tightness–looseness. *Journal of Applied Psychology, 91,* 1225–1244.

Greenwald, A. G., & Banaji, M. R. (1995). Implicit social cognition: Attitudes, self-esteem, and stereotypes. *Psychological Review, 102,* 4–27.

Haynie, J. M., & Shepherd, D. A. (2011). Toward a theory of discontinuous career transition: Investigating career transitions necessitated by traumatic life events. *Journal of Applied Psychology, 96,* 501–524.

He, W., Goodkind, D. E., & Kowal, P. (2016). *An aging world: 2015.* International Population Reports (P95/09-1). Washington, DC: U.S. Government Printing Office.

Henkens, K., van Dalen, H., Ekerdt, D., Hershey, D., Hyde, M., Radl, J., Solinge, H., Wang, M., & Zacher, H. (2018). What we need to know about retirement: Pressing issues for the coming decade. *The Gerontologist, 58,* 805–812.

Henry, H., Zacher, H., & Desmette, D. (2017). Future time perspective in the work context: A systematic review of quantitative studies. *Frontiers in Psychology, 8,* 413.

Hertel, G., & Zacher, H. (2017). Managing the aging workforce. In N. Anderson, D. S. Ones, C. Viswesvaran, & H. K. Sinangil (Eds.), *Handbook of industrial, work, and organizational psychology* (Vol. 2). New York, NY: Sage.

Hosoda, M. Stone, D. L., & Stone-Romero, E. F. (2003). The interactive effects of race, gender, and job type on the suitability ratings and selection decisions. *Journal of Applied Social Psychology, 33,* 145–178.

Huffman, A., Culbertson, S. S., Henning, J. B., & Goh, A. (2013). Work-family conflict across the lifespan. *Journal of Managerial Psychology, 28*, 761–780.

Hummert, M. L. (1990). Multiple stereotypes of elderly and young adults: A comparison of structure and evaluations. *Psychology and Aging, 5*, 182–193.

Hurst, D. (2017, July 18). Japan's doctors propose raising "outdated" retirement age to 75. *The Guardian*. Retrieved August 24, 2018 from: https://www.theguardian.com/world/2017/jul/18/japan-doctors-propose-raising-retirement-age-to-75

James, K. S. (2011). India's demographic change: Opportunities and challenges. *Science, 333*, 576–580.

Jones, K. P., Sabat, I. E., King, E. B., Ahmad, A., McCausland, T. C., & Chen, T. (2017). Isms and schisms: A meta-analysis of the prejudice-discrimination relationship across racism, sexism and ageism. *Journal of Organizational Behavior, 38*, 1087–1110.

Kanfer, R., & Bufton, G. M. (2018). Job loss and job search: A social-cognitive and self-regulation perspective. *The Oxford handbook of job loss and job search* (pp. 143–160). New York, NY: Oxford University Press.

Kirkman, B. L., Lowe, K. B., & Gibson, C. B. (2017). A retrospective on *Culture's Consequences*: The 35-year journey. *Journal of International Business Studies, 48*, 12–29.

Kooij, D., de Lange, A., Jansen, P., & Dikkers, J. (2008). Older workers' motivation to continue to work: Five meanings of age: A conceptual review. *Journal of Managerial Psychology, 23*, 364–394.

Kooij, D. T., Kanfer, R., Betts, M., & Rudolph, C. W. (2018). Future time perspective: A systematic review and meta-analysis. *Journal of Applied Psychology, 103*, 867–893.

Kurzban, R., & Leary, M. R. (2001). Evolutionary origins of stigmatization: The functions of social exclusion. *Psychological Bulletin, 127*, 187–208.

Lamont, R. A., Swift, H. J., & Abrams, D. (2015). A review and meta-analysis of age-based stereotype threat: Negative stereotypes, not facts, do the damage. *Psychology of Aging, 30*, 180–193.

Lau, D., & Murnighan, J. (2005). Interactions within groups and subgroups: The effects of demographic faultlines. *Academy of Management Journal, 48*, 645–659.

Lawrence, B. S. (1988). New wrinkles in the theory of age: Demography, norms, and performance ratings. *Academy of Management Journal, 31*, 309–337.

Marcus, J. (2017). Age discrimination. In N. A. Pachana (Ed.), *Encyclopedia of Geropsychology* (pp. 75–81). New York, NY: Springer Reference.

Marcus, J., & Fritzsche, B. A. (2015). One size doesn't fit all: Toward a theory on the intersectional salience of ageism at work. *Organizational Psychology Review, 5*, 168–188.

Marcus, J., & Fritzsche, B. A. (2016). The cultural anchors of age discrimination in the workplace: A multilevel framework. *Work, Aging, and Retirement, 2*, 217–229.

Marcus, J., & Le, H. (2013). Interactive effects of levels of individualism-collectivism on cooperation: A meta-analysis. *Journal of Organizational Behavior, 34*, 813–834.

Marcus, J., & Sabuncu, N. (2016). "Old oxen cannot plow": Stereotype themes of older adults in Turkish folklore. *The Gerontologist, 56*, 1007–1022.

Mirvis, P. H., & Hall, D. T. (1996). Psychological success and the boundaryless career. In M. B. Arthur & D. M. Rousseau (Eds.), *The boundaryless career: A new employment principle for a new organizational era* (pp. 237–255). New York, NY: Oxford.

Nelson, T. D. (2005). Ageism: Prejudice against our feared future self. *Journal of Social Issues, 61*, 207–221.

Ng, T. W. H., & Feldman, D. C. (2012). Evaluating six common stereotypes about older workers with meta-analytical data. *Personnel Psychology, 65*, 821–858.

North, M. S., & Fiske, S. T. (2015). Modern attitudes toward older adults in the aging world: A cross-cultural meta-analysis. *Psychological Bulletin, 141*, 993–1022.

Nurmi, J. -E., & Salmela-Aro, K. (2002). Goal construction, reconstruction and depressive symptoms in a life-span context: The transition from school to work. *Journal of Personality, 70*, 385–420.

Ostroukh, A., & Nikolskaya, P. (2018, June 14). Russia, on quest for budget savings, to raise retirement age. *Reuters.* Retrieved August 24, 2018 from: https://www.reuters.com/article/us-russia-retirement-medvedev/russia-on-quest-for-budget-savings-to-raise-retirement-age-idUSKBN1JA16P

Ozbilgin, M. F., Beauregard, T. A., Tatli, A., & Bell, M. P. (2011). Work-life diversity and intersectionality: A critical review and research agenda. *International Journal of Management Reviews, 13*, 177–198.

Palmore, E. B., & Maeda, D. (1985). *The honorable elders revised: A revised cross-cultural analysis of aging in Japan.* Durham, NC: Duke University Press.

Pelled, L. H., & Xin, K. R. (2000). Relational demography and relationship quality in two cultures. *Organization Studies, 21*, 1077–1094.

Peng, X. (2011). China's demographic history and future challenges. *Science, 333*, 581–587.

Perry, E. L., & Finkelstein, L. M. (1999). Toward a broader view of age-discrimination in employment-related decisions: A joint consideration of organizational factors and cognitive processes. *Human Resource Management Review, 9*, 21–49.

Phillips, D. R., & Siu, O. (2012). Global aging and aging workers. In J. W. Hedge & W. C. Borman (Eds.), *The Oxford handbook of work and aging* (pp. 11–32). New York, NY: Oxford University Press.

Peiró, J. M., Tordera, N., & Potočnik, K. (2013). Retirement practices in different countries. In M. Wang (Ed.), *The Oxford handbook of retirement* (pp. 510–540). New York, NY: Oxford University Press.

Posthuma, R. A., & Campion, M. A. (2009). Age stereotypes in the workplace: Common stereotypes, moderators, and future research directions. *Journal of Management, 35*, 158–188.

Posthuma, R. A., & Guerrero, L. (2013). Age stereotypes in the workplace: Multidimensionality, cross-cultural applications, and directions for future research. In J. Field, R. J. Burke, & C. L. Cooper (Eds.), *The Sage handbook of aging, work and society* (pp. 250–265). London, UK: Sage.

Purdie-Vaughns, V., & Eibach, R. P. (2008). Intersectional invisibility: The distinctive advantages and disadvantages of multiple subordinate-group identities. *Sex Roles, 59*, 377–391.

Roberts, L. (2011). 9 Billion? *Science, 333*, 540–543.

Rudolph, C. W. (2016). Lifespan developmental perspectives on working: A literature review of motivational theories. *Work, Aging, and Retirement, 2*, 130–158.

Rudolph, C. W., Kooij, D. T., Rauvola, R. S., & Zacher, H. (2018). Occupational future time perspective: A meta-analysis of antecedents and outcomes. *Journal of Organizational Behavior, 39*, 229–248.

Rudolph, C. W., Marcus, J., & Zacher, H. (2019). Global issues in work, aging and retirement. In K. S. Shultz, & Adams, G. A. (Eds.), *Aging and work in the 21st century* (2nd ed., pp. 292–324). New York, NY: Taylor & Francis.

Rudolph, C. W., & Zacher, H. (in press). Managing employees across the working lifespan. In B. J. Hoffman, M. Shoss, & L. Wegman (Eds.), *The Cambridge handbook of the changing nature of work*. Cambridge, UK: Cambridge.

Schein, E. H. (1996). Three cultures of management: The key to organizational learning. *Sloan Management Review, 38,* 9–20.

Schneider, D. J. (2004). *The psychology of stereotyping*. New York, NY: Guilford Press.

Sesko, A. K., & Biernat, M. (2010). Prototypes of race and gender: The invisibility of Black women. *Journal of Experimental Social Psychology, 46,* 356–360.

Shore, L. M., & Goldberg, C. B. (2005). Age discrimination in the workplace. In R. L. Dipboye & A. Colella (Eds.), *Discrimination at work* (pp. 203–226). Mahwah, NJ: Lawrence Erlbaum Associates.

Shipp, A. J., Edwards, J. R., & Lambert, L. S. (2009). Conceptualization and measurement of temporal focus: The subjective experience of the past, present, and future. *Organizational Behavior and Human Decision Processes, 110,* 1–22.

Shulenberg, J. E., Bryant, A. L., & O'Malley, P. M. (2004). Taking hold of some kind of life: How developmental tasks relate to trajectories of well-being during the transition to adulthood. *Development and Psychopathology, 16,* 1119–1140.

Skirbekk, V., Loichinger, E., & Barakat, B. F. (2012). The aging of the workforce in European countries: Demographic trends, retirement projections, and retirement policies. In J. W. Hedge & W. C. Borman (Eds.), *The Oxford handbook of work and aging* (pp. 60–79). New York, NY: Oxford University Press.

Spence, M. (1973). Job market signaling. *The Quarterly Journal of Economics, 87,* 355–374.

Staudinger, U. M. (2015). Images of aging: Outside and inside perspectives. *Annual Review of Gerontology and Geriatrics, 35,* 187–209.

Stone-Romero, E. F., & Stone, D. L. (2007). Cognitive, affective, and cultural influences on stigmatization: Impact on human resource management processes and practices. *Research in Personnel and Human Resources Management, 26,* 117–167.

Super, D. (1992). Toward a comprehensive theory of career development. In D. H. Montross & C. J. Shinkman (Eds.), *Career development: theory and practice* (pp. 35–64). Springfield, IL: Charles C Thomas Publisher.

Swinford, S. (2016, March 2). Work until you're 75—Or even 81—Under Government review of state's pension age. *The Telegraph.* Retrieved August 24, 2018 from: https://www.telegraph.co.uk/news/politics/georgeosborne/12179375/Work-until-youre-75-or-even-81-under-Government-review-of-state-pension-age.html

Taras, V., Steel, B., & Kirkman, B. L. (2016). Does country equate with culture? Beyond geography in the search for cultural boundaries. *Management International Review, 56,* 455–487.

Triandis, H. C. (1995). *Individualism and collectivism*. Boulder, CO: Westview.

Truxillo, D. M., Cadiz, D. M., Rineer, J. R., Zaniboni, S., & Fraccaroli, F. (2012). A lifespan perspective on job design: Fitting the job and the worker to promote job satisfaction, engagement, and performance. *Organizational Psychology Review, 2,* 340–360.

Truxillo, D. M., Finkelstein, L. M., Pytlovany, A., & Jenkins, J. S. (2016). Age discrimination at work: A review of the research and recommendations for the future. In A. J.

Colella & E. B. King (Eds.), *The Oxford handbook of workplace discrimination* (pp. 129–142). New York, NY: Oxford University Press.

Tsui, A. S., Egan, T. D., & O'Reilly III, C. A. (1992). Being different: Relational demography and organizational attachment. *Administrative Science Quarterly, 37,* 549–579.

Turner, J. C. (1985). Social categorization and the self-concept: A social-cognitive theory of group behavior. In E. J. Lawler (Ed.), *Advances in group processes* (vol. 2, pp 77–122). Greenwich, CT: JAI.

UN—United Nations. (2013). *World population ageing 2013.* New York, NY: United Nations. Accessed August 21, 2017 from: http://www.un.org/en/development/desa/population/publications/pdf/ageing/WorldPopulationAgeing2013.pdf

UNDESA—United Nations Department of Economic and Social Affairs. (2015). *World population prospects: The 2015 revision.* New York, NY: United Nations. Accessed February 26, 2019 from: https://www.helpage.org/global-agewatch/population-ageing-data/population-ageing-map/#

Webster, J., Thoroughgood, C., & Sawyer, K. (2019). Diversity issues for an aging workforce: A lifespan intersectionality approach. In K. S. Shultz, & Adams, G. A. (Eds.), *Aging and work in the 21st century* (2nd ed., pp. 34–58). New York, NY: Taylor & Francis.

Weikamp, J. G., & Göritz, A. S. (2015). How stable is occupational future time perspective over time? A six-wave study across 4 years. *Work, Aging, and Retirement, 1,* 369–381.

Zacher, H. (2015). Successful aging at work. *Work, Aging, and Retirement, 1,* 4–25

Zacher, H., Esser, L., Bohlmann, C., & Rudolph, C. W. (2019). Age, social identity and identification, and work outcomes: a conceptual model, literature review, and future research directions. *Work, Aging and Retirement, 5*(1), 24–43. doi:10.1093/workar/way005

Zacher, H., Hacker, W., & Frese, M. (2016). Action regulation across the adult lifespan (ARAL), A metatheory of work and aging. *Work, Aging, and Retirement, 2,* 286–306.

Zacher, H., & Schmitt, A. (2016). Work characteristics and occupational well-being: The role of age. *Frontiers in Psychology, 7,* 1411. doi:10.3389/fpsyg.2016.01411

Zacher, H., & Rudolph, C. W. (2019). Just a mirage: On the incremental predictive validity of subjective age. *Work, Aging and Retirement, 5*(2), 141–162. doi:10.1093/workar/wax031

Zhang, W., Wang, H., & Pearce, C. L. (2014). Consideration for future consequences as an antecedent of transformational leadership behavior: The moderating effects of perceived dynamic work environment. *The Leadership Quarterly, 25,* 329–343.

CHAPTER 9

INCLUSION AT WORK

A Conceptual Model of Factors that Contribute to Climates for Inclusion

Melinda Key-Roberts, Brigid Lynn,
Nathaniel J. Ratcliff, and James M. Nye

Research on inclusion in organizations has yet to identify the primary factors that contribute to the development and maintenance of climates for inclusion. The present research addresses this gap through the development of a comprehensive conceptual model depicting the critical factors that contribute to inclusive climates, and their proposed relationships to each other. Factors were identified through a comprehensive literature review, and affirmed through input from organizational climate, leadership, and inclusion subject matter experts. The final model focuses on behaviors that are malleable, emphasizing the role of leader and group behaviors in shaping climates for inclusion. The importance of top-down cultural change to support the development and maintenance of specific climates is discussed, as are applications of the research at multiple levels (e.g., leader, group, and organizational). This research provides a foundation for future empirical research on the nature of relationships among factors that foster, maintain, and improve a climate for inclusion.

A climate for inclusion emerges when organizational members feel recognized for having a unique identity, integrated into the group, and valued for their contributions to the team (Ferdman, 2014, 2017; Nishii, 2013; Shore et al., 2011).

Diversity and Inclusion in Organizations, pages 223–250.

Inclusive climates have been identified as a way to leverage and reap the benefits of diversity within organizations (Cox & Blake, 1991; Stahl, Mäkelä, Zander, & Maznevski, 2010). Specifically, scholars suggest that climates for inclusion provide a means for diverse voices to be heard and used in decision-making, providing decision makers with access to a larger pool of knowledge, skills, and experiences (Homan, van Knippenberg, van Kleef, & De Dreu, 2007; Mitchell, Boyle, Parker, Giles, & Chiang, 2015; Nishii, 2013; Reagans, Zuckerman, & McEvily, 2004; van Knippenberg, & Schippers, 2007; Williams & O'Reilly, 1998). Furthermore, organizational members in inclusive environments—especially those who belong to historically marginalized groups—report higher feelings of job satisfaction, organizational commitment, and general well-being (Mor Barak et al., 2016; Nishii, 2013). Due to the positive benefits for both organizations and individuals, research on fostering climates for inclusion is an important avenue for organizational researchers to pursue.

Although the importance of inclusion is clear, the factors which contribute to the growth and sustainment of a climate for inclusion have not been thoroughly identified. In general, much of organizational climate research has focused on identifying and measuring climate itself and the outcomes that follow, with less emphasis on the antecedents that cultivate and sustain climate. Thus, not much is known about what precedes the emergence of organizational climate generally (Ehrhart, Schneider, & Macey, 2014), or climate for inclusion specifically (Shore et al., 2011). To advance research on inclusive climates, the goal of the current research is to develop a conceptual model which identifies critical factors that contribute to inclusion, understand how those factors interact to create climate, and guide future research to test the relationships specified within the model.

ORGANIZATIONAL CLIMATE AND INCLUSION

Organizational climate is "the shared meaning organizational members attach to the events, policies, practices, and procedures they experience and the behaviors they see being rewarded, supported, and expected" (Ehrhart et al., 2014, p. 69). Early climate research focused on molar, or generic organizational climates, which describe an overall sense of well-being at an organization. However, the study of molar climates led to inconsistent results and a general lack of theoretical clarity (Schneider, Ehrhart, & Macey, 2013; Schneider, González-Romá, Ostroff, & West, 2017). In 1975, Schneider advanced the field of climate research with the introduction of focused climates (Schneider, 1975). A focused climate communicates a clear message about what is important through the alignment of policies, practices, procedures, and reward systems (Ehrhart et al., 2014). Ongoing research on focused climates—or the study of climates "for" something—yields evidence for relationships to specific outcomes, strengthening the validity of climate research. Additionally, the study of focused climates highlights opportunities to enhance performance by identifying specific organizational practices and behaviors associated with desired outcomes (Ehrhart et al., 2014; Lynn & Ratcliff, 2018; Schneider et al., 2013).

Climate for Inclusion

As previously stated, a climate for inclusion is a type of focused climate where organizational members feel recognized for having a unique identity, integrated into the group, and valued for their contributions to the team (Ferdman, 2014; 2017; Nishii, 2013; Shore et al., 2011). Within such an environment, people of diverse backgrounds are invited to bring their whole self to work as they contribute to the organization's mission (Ferdman, 2017). Thus, inclusion builds on traditional diversity efforts—with their emphasis on representation and equality (Kossek & Zonia, 1993)—to focus on the ability of all group members to be seen, heard, and have their capabilities leveraged.

Grounded in the "integration-and-learning" perspective adopted by Ely and Thomas (2001), inclusive environments value diversity as a resource for learning and adaptive change which, when leveraged, can lead to beneficial outcomes for individuals and organizations. Consistent with our view on inclusion, this perspective "emphasizes the value that people with a variety of differences bring to the organization (Ferdman, 2014), and not just the "rightness" of supporting equal opportunity" (Shore, Cleveland, & Sanchez, 2018, p. 177). In 2011, Shore and colleagues proposed a framework for workgroup inclusion that built on Optimal Distinctiveness Theory (ODT; Brewer, 1991). ODT states that individuals in groups strive to balance their need for belongingness and uniqueness through "an optimal level of inclusion" (Brewer, 1991, p. 477). Inclusion therefore satisfies competing needs to feel accepted by the group (via decision-making participation and information sharing), as well as valued and respected for one's uniqueness (via openness to different approaches, respect for differing cultural perspectives, and opportunity for voice in the workplace; see Boekhorst, 2015; Shore et al., 2011, 2018).

Research has long shown that organizations can implicitly make members, especially those who are also members of historically marginalized groups, feel rejected (e.g., by not sharing information or inviting input; see Morrison & Milliken, 2000). In contrast, inclusive organizations provide opportunities for all group members to be heard and have influence. Thus, an inclusive climate emerges when all employees possess access to need-to-know information (Mor Barak, 2015; Mor Barak & Daya, 2014; Pelled, Eisenheardt, & Xin, 1999), believe that their ideas and perspectives are both influential and actively sought (Mor Barak, 2015; Mor Barak & Daya, 2014; Nishii, 2013; Shore et al., 2018), and are given opportunities to contribute to the work of the group (Ferdman, 2017; U.S. Office of Personnel Management, Office of Diversity and Inclusion, 2011; Shore et al., 2011). Additionally, feeling respected and valued is a theme that runs through most conceptualizations of inclusion (Boekhorst, 2015; Nishii, 2013; Shore et al., 2018).

Drawing on these existing definitions and research, we identified the following definitional elements from the climate for inclusion literature which served as a foundation for the current effort; for the purpose of this research, individuals in an inclusive climate are believed to share perceptions that all group members are: (a) valued, (b) integrated into the team, (c) recognized and leveraged, and (d) enabled to participate to their full potential.

Organizational Climate Antecedents and Existing Models of Inclusion

Existing conceptual models of inclusion antecedents highlight the role of leaders in influencing the development of climates for inclusion. Gotsis and Grimani (2016) posit that servant leaders instill feelings of belongingness and uniqueness among diverse employees by forming strong relationships with followers, building their self-confidence, attending to their needs, and encouraging their development. According to Gotsis and Grimani (2016), this orientation toward service prompts inclusive practices, which activate subordinate perceptions of workgroup inclusion, leading to higher levels of organizational identification, organizational citizenship behaviors (OCBs), and feelings of psychological well-being. Similarly, Boekhorst's (2015) conceptual framework draws on social learning theory to emphasize the power of leader role-modeling in influencing followers and shaping climate. Boekhorst (2015) further explores the positive impact of reinforcing systems and processes on followers' vicarious learning of inclusive behaviors. Specifically, she suggests higher levels of vicarious learning will strengthen the relationship between leader role modeling and a climate for inclusion when (a) organizational reward systems prompt inclusive behaviors; (b) the group is large and diverse resulting in greater opportunity to practice and observe inclusive behaviors; and (c) authentic leaders and followers share goals related to inclusion which encourage inclusive actions by followers. Like Boekhorst (2015), Shore and colleagues (2018) emphasize the importance of an organization-wide commitment to inclusion. According to their model of inclusive organizations, a high commitment to inclusion practices and processes across the organization (i.e., psychological safety; involvement in the work group; feeling respected and valued; influence on decision making; authenticity; and recognizing, honoring, and advancing of diversity) will foster employee perceptions of inclusion, climates for inclusion, and retention and expansion of talent.

Unique Contributions of Present Research

There has been relatively little research on the antecedents that can be purposefully leveraged so as to intentionally activate inclusive climates (Ehrhart et al., 2014; Kuenzi & Schminke, 2009). Building on earlier work, this research adds specificity to existing conceptualizations of inclusion; in particular, we expand on prior identification of actions leaders can engage in to foster inclusive cli-

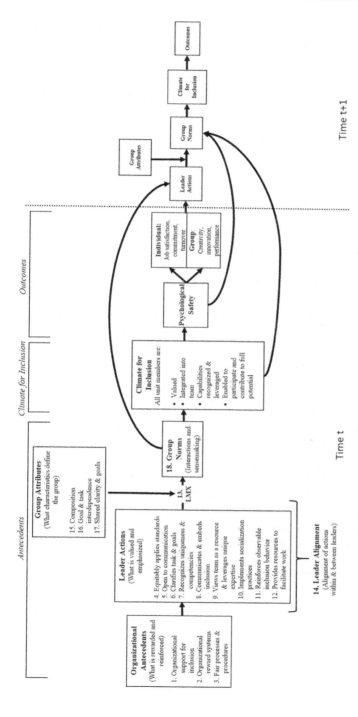

FIGURE 9.1. Climate for Inclusion Conceptual Model. Depicts proposed relationships between antecedents, climate for inclusion, and potential outcomes. Model also depicts proposed recursive relationships as inclusive climates develop over time. Recursive effects on organizational antecedents are not depicted due to their relative permanence compared to other factors.

mates (Boekhorst, 2015; Gotsis & Grimani, 2016) answering calls for specificity in leader behaviors that are interpreted by employees as inclusive (Shore et al., 2018). Our proposed conceptual model also serves a unique purpose by focusing on behaviors and practices that are amenable to change. Thus, the model identifies the key antecedents of a climate for inclusion that can be leveraged to improve outcomes for individuals and organizations. Finally, unlike existing depictions of inclusion, our model illustrates the reciprocity that exists within the organization during the development of organizational climate, emphasizing the co-creation of climate by leaders and followers over time (see Figure 9.1).

A MODEL OF INCLUSIVE CLIMATES

Overview of Conceptual Model

To develop the initial conceptual model, we conducted a large-scale literature review to identify the factors that are most likely to influence a climate for inclusion. Traditional research on diversity, organizational climate and culture, and inclusion were reviewed, as well as literatures that could expand our understanding of inclusion (e.g., ethical leadership). We organized this literature review by creating lines of inquiry (LOIs) based on known categories of organizational climate antecedents: individual, group, leader, and organizational factors[1]. We examined 689 unique articles and identified approximately 70 factors that could potentially relate to a climate for inclusion. Based on input from a preeminent climate expert (Schneider, Personal Communication, July 18–19, 2017), we reduced these factors to a smaller subset of key factors which together inform the development of a climate for inclusion. As part of this process, we evaluated the overlap between factors, considered the degree of correspondence with definitional elements of inclusive climates (e.g., value, integration, recognition of capabilities, and enabled to participate to full potential), and narrowed our focus to observable group-level antecedents. The result was a draft conceptual model that identified 24 factors critical to the development of a climate for inclusion.

This initial model was then subjected to an iterative process of critique and consensus with an additional group of leading organizational climate, leadership, and inclusion experts[2]. The end result is a revised list of 18 key-factors which

---

[1] Although antecedents of climate are generally understudied (Ehrhart et al., 2014; Kuenzi & Schminke, 2009), reviews of the climate literature suggest three general categories of factors that shape focused climates: individual, group, and organizational factors (Kuenzi & Schminke, 2009). Additionally, leaders have been shown to have a strong effect across many climate types, and particular styles of leadership have been linked to the development of specific focused climates (Kuenzi & Schminke, 2009; Schneider et al., 2017, p. 474). Given that leadership is one of the most researched predictors of organizational climate we view it as an additional category of climate antecedent, along with individual, group, and organizational factors.

[2] Subject Matter Experts (SMEs) were selected based on the number of publications in top-tier journals in specified areas, and their ability to demonstrate application of their research findings. The

are organized below by three[3] of the common higher-level antecedent categories: organizational, leader, and group factors. The final conceptual model depicts relationships between antecedents, climate for inclusion, and proposed outcomes. Additionally, it attempts to capture the recursive nature of climate by illustrating changes in climate perceptions across time. Because climate emerges from interactions among factors across multiple organizational levels, it was difficult to draw precise relationships between factors. Given this, we only identify major relationships, and specified pathways need further exploration and validation. It is our intent for the final model to contribute to the limited literature on inclusive climates by generating viable research questions to be tested in future research. Contributions to practice are also anticipated as key-factors were selected, in-part, due to their potential for targeted intervention.

Antecedents

The following sections describe the primary antecedents we classified as contributing to inclusive climates, as well as specific theoretical predictions regarding how those factors interact to manifest a climate for inclusion.

Organizational Antecedents. Organizational antecedents originate from outside the group and are largely beyond the control of group members. These factors indirectly influence organizational climate because they provide a foundational context on which the workgroup operates and functions, and have the power to reinforce or impede a group's efforts to implement inclusive climate practices. Drawing on organizational climate and culture literatures (Ehrhart et al., 2014; Schneider et al., 2013), as well as diversity and inclusion literatures (Boekhorst, 2015; Mello & Rentsch, 2015; Meyer, Shemla, Li, & Wegge, 2015), we identified three primary organizational antecedents of climate for inclusion: (a) organizational support for inclusion (b) organizational reward systems; and (c) fair processes and procedures. These antecedents, as well as their specific effects on inclusive climates, are described below.

Organizational Support for Inclusion. The development of organizational climate necessarily relies on organizational emphasis and support. More specifically, research suggests that the tangible benefits and resources underlying organizational support serve as a foundation for the development of all types of focused climates (Wallace, Popp, & Mondore, 2006, as cited in Ehrhart et al., 2014). In the case of inclusive climates, organizational support may enable group members to share valued aspects of themselves that differ from the dominant culture (Shore et al., 2018). Organizational support may also increase a sense of belongingness

---

iterative analysis by SMEs led to additional model revisions based on the need to prioritize factors which can be used to inform interventions.

[3] In order to create a model to inform interventions, we emphasized antecedents that were most amenable to change. Because many of the individual-level antecedents are relatively resistant to change (e.g. dispositions, see Staw & Ross, 1985), they were removed from the model.

leading to perceptions of insider status, a key aspect of inclusive climates (Stamper & Masterson, 2002, as cited in Shore et al., 2011). Input from organizational climate experts suggests that organizational support, in the form of resources to support inclusion, is particularly important for the development of inclusive climates (Schneider, Personal Communication, July 18–19, 2017; Creary et al., Personal Communication, April 23–24, 2018). Resources such as time allotted to the development of inclusive climates, type of leader selected to shape organizational climate, and leader development support aimed at growing inclusive leaders are foundational to the development of climates for inclusion.

> **Proposition 1:** By providing adequate resources (e.g., time, tools, technology, etc.) dedicated to developing an inclusive climate, and creating systems that enable discussion and decision-making, organizational support can facilitate the emergence of a climate for inclusion.

Organizational Reward Systems. Organizational reward systems include monetary and nonmonetary means of recognizing and promoting certain employee behaviors (Bartol & Srivastava, 2002; Podsakoff, Podsakoff, & Kuskova, 2010, as cited in Boekhorst, 2015). Reward systems elicit inclusive behaviors from employees themselves, while also supporting the vicarious learning of inclusive conduct by group members who observe others being rewarded and punished for their actions (Boekhorst, 2015). Prior research supports the proposed relationship between reward systems and inclusive employee behavior. For example, Ferrin and Dirks (2003) found that reward systems which supported collaborative knowledge sharing resulted in more information sharing among employees. By incentivizing certain leader and group behaviors, reward systems indirectly influence climate, affecting perceptions of what is valued and expected by the organization. According to climate experts, these reward systems are also important to sustaining the effects of inclusive leader training and interventions (Schneider, Personal Communication, July 18–19, 2017; Creary et al., Personal Communication, April 23–24, 2018).

> **Proposition 2:** By rewarding inclusive behaviors, leaders and group members learn what is valued by the organization and shift their behaviors to align with a climate for inclusion.

Fair Processes and Procedures (Standardized for All Group Members). Policies and standard operating procedures that are fairly implemented also contribute to perceptions of inclusion. Specifically, when members perceive all are treated equitably (e.g., members perceive that rewards and promotions are fairly distributed across group members), it signals to employees that groups within the organization have similar social value and are not disproportionally valued as a result of diversity-based status differentials (Nishii, 2013). In her 2013 article, Nishii argued that fair treatment of employees is a foundational requirement for inclusive environments, as the elimination of arbitrary status hierarchies enables employees to fully disclose aspects of their identity and thinking, and facilitates positive interactions across groups within the organization (Nishii, 2013).

Proposition 3: By instituting fair processes and procedures that treat members equitably, arbitrary status hierarchies are mitigated allowing for free participation in the group.

Leader Antecedents and Processes. As noted previously, leaders have a strong influence on the development and maintenance of organizational climates (e.g., Ehrhart et al., 2014; Schein, 2010; Wasserman, Gallegos, & Ferdman, 2008). Forming the central core of groups, leaders drive action within groups (Keltner, Gruenfeld, & Anderson, 2003), influencing group interactions, guiding group problem-solving, and coordinating the collective action of group members (Boehm & Flack, 2010; Keltner, Gruenfeld, Galinsky, & Kraus, 2010; Maner & Mead, 2010; van Vugt, 2006; Zaccaro, Rittman, & Marks, 2001). Leaders shape climate by communicating the importance of specific initiatives through their words and actions. Leaders also serve as gatekeepers for the implementation of policies and procedures by prioritizing particular goals, role modeling expected conduct, and reinforcing desired behaviors via rewards and recognition (e.g., Barling, Loughlin, & Kelloway, 2002; Ehrhart et al., 2014; Hong, Liao, & Jiang, 2013; Schein, 2010; Zohar & Luria, 2005).

Inclusive Actions and Behaviors. The inclusive actions of leaders serve as social cues to the group regarding what behaviors are appropriate within that group (Boekhorst, 2015). Although vicarious learning may occur with or without conscious intent from leaders or followers, effective leaders understand the importance of purposeful role modeling in shaping the team's climate (Boekhorst, 2015). Drawing on research on *inclusive leadership* (e.g., Carmeli, Reiter-Palmon, & Ziv, 2010; Nembhard & Edmondson, 2006), as well as *authentic* (e.g., Kernis & Goldman, 2006; Walumbwa, Avolio, Gardner, Wernsing, & Peterson, 2008), *servant* (e.g., Gotsis & Grimani, 2016; Liden, Wayne, Zhao, & Henderson, 2008; Walumbwa, Hartnell, & Oke, 2010), *ethical* (e.g., Walumbwa et al., 2011; Walumbwa & Schaubroeck, 2009, *mindful* (e.g., Good et al., 2016), *transformational* (e.g., Kearney & Gebert, 2009; Peterson, Walumbwa, Byron, & Myrowitz, 2009), and *culturally-competent* (e.g., Yuengling, Parks, & McDonald, 2011) leadership types, we propose that leaders can promote and maintain an inclusive climate by modeling specific inclusive actions (See Table 9.1). These specific actions extend past research which has generally described inclusive leadership as leaders who are open and accessible, and who value group members by inviting their unique input in group decision-making processes (e.g., Carmeli, et al., 2010; Hannum, McFeeters, & Booysen, 2010; Mor Barak, 2008; Nembhard & Edmondson, 2006).

Proposition 4: Leaders act as the primary gatekeepers and architects of a climate for inclusion. Their decisions to reward inclusive behaviors; enact inclusive policies

TABLE 9.1. Specific Leader Actions Proposed to Influence the Development of Climates for Inclusion

Leader Action	Example
Applying standards equitably across all group members	Treating everyone fairly, without preferential treatment
Showing an openness to communication	Allowing group members to ask questions and provide opposing viewpoints without punishment; proactively encouraging the input of group members, listening, and taking action
Clarifying tasks and goals	Ensuring group members know the task at hand and how it serves a greater purpose for the organization; enabling proactive contributions from group members by providing the "bigger picture"
Recognizing individual uniqueness	Being open to differences; recognizing diverse perspectives
Talking about inclusion	Expressing the importance of inclusion to achieving organizational success
Treating the team as a valuable resource and leveraging unique expertise to accomplish tasks	Utilizing unique differences to accomplish organizational objectives
Articulating and reinforcing socialization practices for inclusion	Establishing processes for integrating new members into the group and setting expectations for how the group functions inclusively
Providing feedback on, and reinforcement of, observable inclusion behaviors	Providing feedback on behaviors that support micro-affirmations, empathy, perspective taking or impede micro-aggressions, incivility inclusion
Providing resources to facilitate work	Allocating resources in alignment with the organization's and leader's espoused inclusive policies

and procedures; allocate resources to support inclusion; and apply standards equitably across group members fosters inclusive climates.

Leader Member Exchange (LMX). An important aspect of inclusive leadership is the quality of exchange between leader and followers, also referred to as leader-member exchange (LMX; see also Graen & Uhl-Bien, 1995). It is through strong exchange relationships that leaders and followers build emotional bonds, and the leader learns the needs, desires, abilities, and potential of their followers (Bambale, 2014; Kearney & Gebert, 2009). Past research suggests that strong LMX is necessary for employee-perceived organizational inclusion. Specifically, Brimhall and colleagues (2016) found that high quality LMX relations between supervisor and employee were associated with increased feelings of inclusion six and twelve months later. Supplementing this finding, climate SMEs suggested that inclusive climate emerges when there are high levels of LMX with followers across diverse demographics, with little differentiation among members of a work group or team (Creary et al., Personal Communication, April 23–24, 2018; see also Nishii & Mayer, 2009).

> **Proposition 5:** High levels of LMX with followers across diverse demographics will invite bi-directional feedback and input from all group members, thus fostering a climate for inclusion.

Leader Alignment with Inclusive Practices. An additional challenge associated with inclusive leadership is the need for leaders to align their actions and words to develop focused climates. Alignment refers to congruence between words and actions within individual leaders (i.e., the leader walks and talks inclusion), as well as between leader teams across levels of the organization (Creary et al., Personal Communication, April 23–24, 2018). Congruent alignment ensures that followers perceive consistent reinforcing messages that inclusion is valued by the organization (Aarons, Ehrhart, Farahnak, & Sklar, 2014). It is important to note that leaders in organizations comprised of multi-team systems often experience competing goals, motivations, and objectives (e.g., superior outcome expectations and subordinate work realities), which can impede alignment between leaders (Way, Simons, Leroy, & Tuleja, 2018). Therefore, leader alignment is an important antecedent for organizations to examine for assessment and potential intervention.

> **Proposition 6:** Alignment of leader's actions and words—both across leader levels, and within the leaders themselves—will influence the strength and direction of a focused climate.

Group Antecedents. The attributes and processes of the group are perhaps the most proximal antecedents influencing organizational climates (Ostroff, Kinicki, & Muhammed, 2012; Schneider et al., 2013). Because climate emerges from shared perceptions developed from interactions with other group members (Ehrhart et al., 2014), how people interact, and the factors that shape these interactions are important for climate development. Based on our findings, characteristics of the group (e.g., composition, goal and task interdependence, and shared clarity and goals) and social norms that govern group member interactions (See Table 9.2) are primary group antecedents that influence the emergence of climate for inclusion.

Group Attributes. Group attributes are factors that describe the compositional makeup of the group as well as the structures which govern how the group functions on a regular basis (e.g., the scheduled frequency by which group members interact, collaborate, and meet regarding goals, projects, and tasks). These group characteristics influence a leader's capacity to foster inclusive climates in specific ways, as described in propositions 7–9.

TABLE 9.2. Specific Group-Level Antecedents Proposed to Influence the Development of Climates for Inclusion

Group Antecedent	Example
Composition	The degree and types of diversity present within a group
Goal and task interdependence	The amount of collaboration and participation among team members who share a common goal
Shared clarity and goals	The degree to which team members understand the specific objectives to be accomplished and how they can achieve them as a team
Group interaction norms	Interactions within the group are characterized by open, respectful, task- and social-communication

Composition (to include tenure within the work unit). The composition of a team can be described as the configuration of member attributes within a team including surface-level characteristics that are readily apparent (e.g., age, race, gender), as well as less visible, deeper-level characteristics (e.g., work-group tenure, education, personality). Both surface- and deep-level diversity have been shown to influence group processes and outcomes (Thatcher & Patel, 2011; van Knippenberg & Schippers, 2007). Given this, we propose that the composition of member traits will influence the ability of the leader to build a climate for inclusion.

Although greater team diversity has been hypothesized to contribute to perceptions of inclusion (Boekhorst, 2015), we assert that these differences are more likely to contribute to divisions within the group (i.e., faultlines). Faultlines emerge within the group when there are sufficient combinations of differences among group members (e.g. African American females within a predominantly Caucasian male work-group), such that subgroups become salient, leading members to identify more with the activated subgroup than the superordinate workgroup (Lau & Murnighan, 1998; van Knippenberg, Dawson, West, & Homan, 2011)[4]. Strong faultlines, when activated, are likely to produce sub-optimal outcomes, to the possible detriment of the climate. In contrast, when subgroup faultlines are less apparent (for a review, see Thatcher & Patel, 2011) and the superordinate group identity is predominant (van Knippenberg & Schippers, 2007), then members are likely to perceive themselves and others as members of a cohesive whole whose individual contributions and perspectives are vital to group functioning.

Although climate for inclusion is more difficult to achieve when faultlines exist, once reached, existing inclusive climates can also mitigate potential negative effects of increased group diversity. Research demonstrating a moderating effect of inclusion on the relationship between increased diversity and individual and organizational outcomes supports this assertion. Specifically, a climate for inclusion has been shown to enhance information sharing and employee information

---

[4] This is sometimes referred to as faultline distance: "the extent to which subgroups diverge as a result of accumulated differences between subgroups." (Thatcher & Patel, 2012, p. 978).

elaboration (Li, Lin, Tien, & Chen, 2017), as well as reduce task and relationship conflict (Nishii, 2013) in units with higher levels of diversity. Our assertion also aligns with the integration and learning paradigm which maintains that organizations will experience better outcomes in terms of group functioning if they embrace diversity as a means to accomplish work processes, tasks, and strategies (Ely & Thomas, 2001 as cited in Boekhorst, 2015).

Proposition 7: Increased group diversity that activates faultlines may impede the initial development of inclusive climates. Once in place, existing inclusive climates will mitigate the potential negative effects of increased diversity.

1. *Goal & Task Interdependence.* According to the contact hypothesis or Intergroup Contact Theory, attitudes and behaviors toward a particular social category will become more positive after interpersonal interaction with people from that social category (Miller & Brewer, 1984). Decades of research on this subject have shown this relationship to be robust across multiple cultures, groups, and forms of diversity (Pettigrew & Tropp, 2006; Pettigrew, Tropp, Wagner, & Christ, 2011). However, not all contact results in positive change, thus much research has been devoted to understanding the necessary conditions under which positive change occurs. One such condition is the presence of a mutually interdependent relationships, or the necessity of cooperation in the achievement of joint goals (Sherif, 1966). Given this, we assert that both goal and task interdependences are important antecedents to inclusive climates, particularly in situations where it is necessary to overcome social distance or dislike among subgroups. In particular, goal interdependence, or the degree to which a leader and follower's goals align with one another, has been hypothesized to foster inclusive climates (Boekhorst, 2015). This alignment likely facilitates vicarious learning of inclusive behaviors and feelings of belongingness by (a) maximizing incentives to cooperative while minimizing incentives to compete (Boekhorst, 2015) as well as (b) connecting each member's contributions to the broader team goals, thus fostering a sense of feeling valued and integrated within the team (Hogg & Abrams, 1999). According to climate experts, goal interdependence precludes passive participation of group members, and ensures that members actively leverage the unique talents of their team (Creary et al., Personal Communication, April 23–24, 2018).

Proposition 8: Alignment of goals among group members will facilitate vicarious learning of inclusive behaviors by group members, as well as perceptions of belongingness, leading to the development of inclusive climates.

Shared Clarity and Goals. In addition to an interdependence of goals, we also propose that a shared understanding of the group's roles, tasks, and goals facilitates a climate for inclusion. Tasks and goals must be clear so that members can successfully align the unique perspectives and capabilities of personnel with group needs (Dickson, Resick, & Hanges, 2006; Kuenzi & Schminke, 2009; Ostroff et al., 2012). Similarly, the roles of group members must be clear so that members know who is best suited for a given task to ensure efficiency in achieving group goals (e.g., Chen & Bliese, 2002). When members clearly understand the duties and roles of group members, and how it all comes together to achieve group goals, they better understand how they and others can play a unique yet integral part in the success of the group. Within such an environment, followers are more likely to know how to leverage each other's unique expertise without prompting from leaders (Lee, Gillespie, Mann, & Wearing, 2010), resulting in a unique contribution by followers to shared perceptions of inclusion.

> **Proposition 9:** Shared clarity regarding duties and roles of group members will enable leaders and followers to collaboratively align group member capabilities with given tasks, further fostering the development of inclusive climates.

Group Interaction Norms. Although leaders are generally seen as the architects of climate, group members also contribute to the development of climate through their actions and words. Over time, group member interactions and meaning-making, guided by group interaction norms[5], can foster, sustain, and strengthen shared perceptions of the organizational environment. We propose that group interaction norms will facilitate perceptions of inclusion when these norms are grounded in openness and respect of others. Mirroring behaviors modeled by the leader, and transmitted through LMX (see Brimhall et al., 2016), inclusion is likely to be fostered when members are open to new ideas and allow others to express their perspectives, grievances, and identity without reproach (Carmeli et al., 2010; Edmondson, 1999; Nembhard & Edmondson, 2006; Martins, Schilpzand, Kirkman, Ivanaj, & Ivanaj, 2013; Singh, Winkel, & Selvarajan, 2013). Furthermore, an inclusive climate is likely to emerge when group members socialize newcomers to inclusive standards for behavior, and when guidelines for social interaction enable group members to fully get to know one another (Feldman & O'Neill, 2014; Schneider, Personal Communication, July 18–19, 2017; Creary et al., Personal Communication, April 23–24, 2018). These norms are hypothesized to impact inclusion by increasing awareness of the unique perspectives and capabilities of other group members, allowing for individuals to leverage and trust one another in the execution of tasks (Lee et al., 2010).

> **Proposition 10:** The strong relationship between group factors and a climate for inclusion is reflected in their proximity to one another (see Figure 9.1). In particular, group member interactions, driven by well-articulated norms, mediates the effect of leader actions on climate perceptions.

---

[5] The traditions, behavioral standards, and unwritten rules that govern how members function as a group are codified into a set of group norms. Group norms have the potential override individual proclivities and encourage deference to the team (Terry & Hogg, 1996).

Outcomes

Although diversity has been linked with both beneficial and adverse outcomes, a climate for inclusion has been consistently associated with positive outcomes (Mor Barak et al., 2016), suggesting that fostering inclusive climates is an effective strategy to manage diversity. Climates for inclusion have been linked to outcomes such as job satisfaction, organizational commitment, OCBs, job performance, creativity, psychological safety, turnover intentions, and well-being, among others (for a review and meta-analysis, see Mor Barak et al., 2016). Thus climate for inclusion has a sphere of influence broader than just the individuals within the workgroup, enabling improved outcomes for teams and organizations as well. This paper focuses on a subset of these outcomes that we believe are associated with inclusion through its relationship to psychological safety.

Psychological Safety. The climate-related construct of team psychological safety is defined as "a shared belief that the team is safe for interpersonal risk taking," and is characterized by "interpersonal trust and mutual respect in which people are comfortable being themselves" (Edmondson, 1999, p. 354). Although there is significant overlap between inclusion and psychological safety (Creary et al., Personal Communication, April 23–24, 2018; Shore et al., 2018), we believe the focus of these two constructs is somewhat distinct (i.e., feeling safe to contribute, versus being invited to contribute and have influence). Research supports this distinction, as inclusive practices have been shown to contribute to employee perceptions that it is safe to take risks and to speak up in the work environment without fear of negative interpersonal consequences (Nembhard & Edmondson, 2006). Further, psychological safety has been shown to mediate the relationship between inclusive leadership and employee creativity (Carmeli et al., 2010), and to influence the relationship between leader inclusiveness, learning from failure, and subsequent work unit performance (Hirak, Peng, Carmeli & Schaubroeck, 2012).

Proposition 11: The outcome that is most directly, and strongly, influenced by climate for inclusion is psychological safety. Psychological safety then mediates other, more distal outcomes (e.g., creativity and performance).

Job Satisfaction, Organizational Commitment, and Turnover Intentions. Evidence of a relationship between perceptions of inclusion and higher levels of organizational commitment, job satisfaction, and lower turnover intentions, has emerged in recent years. In a study of child welfare workers, Hwang and Hopkins (2015) demonstrated that higher perceptions of inclusion resulted in significantly higher levels of job satisfaction and organizational commitment, the latter of which was associated with reduced intention to leave. Similarly, Nishii's (2013) study of over 1,300 employees at a biomedical company revealed that climate for inclusion significantly increased satisfaction and commitment, and reduced turnover intentions [intentions to quit]. Finally, studies examining elements of

Mor Barak's model of inclusion (2000, p. 344) reveal the robustness of the relationship between inclusion to increased job satisfaction, organizational commitment, as well as decreased turnover intentions, among other factors (Brimhall et al., 2016; Findler, Wind, & Mor Barak, 2007; Hopkins, Cohen-Callow, Kim, & Hwang., 2010; Hwang & Hopkins, 2012; Mor Barak, Levin, Nissly, & Lane, 2006). Although more research is needed to determine how inclusion fosters these beneficial outcomes, we hypothesize that inclusive climates reduce work related anxiety by fostering perceptions of psychological safety resulting in a more enjoyable work experience. For more information about the relationship between psychological safety and beneficial attitudinal outcomes, see Frazier, Fainshmidt, Klinger, Pezeshkan, & Vracheva (2017).

> **Proposition 12:** By eliciting a shared sense of psychological safety, higher levels of inclusion will increase job satisfaction and organizational commitment, as well as reduce intentions to leave the organization. These effects will be most prominent for individuals who otherwise would have felt marginalized by the dominant attitudes of the workforce and afraid to be themselves without negative repercussions.

Creativity, Innovation, and Unit Performance. Empirical studies also support a relationship between inclusion, creativity, innovation, and unit performance. For example, Li, Lin, Tien, and Chen (2017) examined culturally diverse teams and found that a high inclusion climate enhanced team information sharing, which was associated with team creativity. Mitchell et al. (2015) found that inclusive leadership increased identification with the team and reduced perceptions of status differences, which were associated with enhanced team performance. We propose that inclusive climates foster team-based outcomes via the outgrowth of perceived psychological safety that allows employees to feel safe to voice novel ideas and engage experimentation (Brimhall & Mor Barak, 2018; Carmeli et al., 2010). Results of Carmeli and colleagues' (2010) study support this assertion; they found that inclusive leadership is positively related to psychological safety, which, in turn, was related to employee involvement in creative work.

> **Proposition 13:** Higher levels of inclusion will yield greater levels of psychological safety. Individuals who believe they are in safe work environment will take more risks and generate more ideas, leading to increased creativity, innovation, and improved performance.

The Recursive Nature of Climate

A climate's strength refers to the degree to which climate perceptions are similarly shared across all group members (Kuenzi & Schminke, 2009). We propose that strong inclusive climates emerge from a cyclical process involving the previously described antecedents and outcomes (see Figure 9.1). As an example, the perceptions of the organizational context that develop from leader and group member interactions, when shared amongst members, serve to reinforce future leader and group actions and subsequent climate emergence (James et al., 2008; Ostroff et al., 2012; Weick, 1995; Zohar & Hofmann, 2012). Stated more simply, an inclusive current climate will facilitate the emergence of a stronger, more inclusive future climate in downstream measurements of the organizational environment (Creary et al., Personal Communication, April 23–24, 2018).

> **Proposition 14:** There is a co-evolution of climate and group behavior over time where the leader and group member behaviors, along with leader and group member perceptions, increasingly converge, yielding a stronger, and more highly inclusive organizational climate.

DISCUSSION

Theoretical Implications

A wide-reaching review of the literature and input from climate experts reinforces the role of important theoretical constructs underlying a climate for inclusion. These include insights from literatures related to social learning (i.e., role modeling, vicarious learning); social exchange [i.e., LMX, organizational support theory, and positive organizational support (POS)]; and social identity theory (i.e., ODT, superordinate group identities).

Similar to prior theoretical conceptualizations of climate for inclusion, our model draws on social learning theory (Bandura, 1999) to describe how inclusive behaviors, when role-modelled by leaders and group members, give rise to a climate for inclusion. Extending work on inclusive leadership (Boekhorst, 2015; Gotsis & Grimani, 2016), we posit that climate is co-created by leaders and followers through daily interactions, and reinforced by the emerging climate itself. As the behavioral and attitudinal alignment between the leader and group members increases, so does the strength of the emergent climate, contributing to the cyclical development of collective perceptions of the work environment.

Our model also draws from social exchange theory to propose that strong exchange relationships between leaders and group members (i.e., LMX), as well as members and organizations (i.e., POS) are essential to the development of organizational climate. In the case of inclusive climates, we assert the importance of strong exchange relationships across group members, with little differentiation among members of a work group or team. We further suggest that these strong and equitable exchange relationships will lead to increased effort (e.g., unit performance) and loyalty (e.g., commitment) from unit members (see also Kurtessis et al., 2017).

Finally, our model is grounded in optimal distinctiveness theory (Brewer 1991), an extension of social identity theory which posits that perceptions of inclusion rely on satisfaction of competing needs for belongingness and uniqueness. According to the social identity literature, individuals contribute and commit more fully to groups where they feel admired or respected (De Cremer & Tyler, 2005; Sleebos, Ellemers, & De Gilder, 2006; Tyler & Blader, 2002). Given this, we posit that inclusive climates will foster mutual respect and enhanced feelings of psychological safety, which will result in increased organizational commitment, satisfaction, and performance.

Practical Implications

After identifying factors related to inclusive climates, we identified tangible and malleable antecedents to inform potential intervention targets to shape and sustain a climate for inclusion. Group norms, leader actions, and organizational narratives were seen by SMEs as high-value targets for intervention and training (Creary et al., Personal Communication, April 23–24, 2018). According to SMEs, interventions and trainings should encourage both leaders and group members to take personal responsibility for climate creation/engineering, and should foster a shared understanding of norms and expectations. SMEs argued that persistent interventions, delivered and reinforced over multiple iterations and integrated into employees' daily tasks and roles, could be an effective strategy for leaders to build a shared understanding of their desired climate (Creary et al., Personal Communication, April 23–24, 2018).

Leader Actions. Leaders are a primary vehicle through which an organization's policies, practices, and procedures are conveyed to groups of employees (Kozlowski & Doherty, 1989; Walumbwa et al., 2010). More specifically, leaders shape climates by role-modeling and reinforcing desired behaviors via rewards and recognition. Leaders also shape climate by communicating the importance of specific initiatives through the prioritization of specific goals, as well as through direct and frequent communication of the leader's strategic vision for a particular climate type (Barling et al., 2002; Ehrhart et al., 2014; Hong et al., 2013; Schein, 2010; Schneider et al., 2013; Zohar & Luria, 2004, 2005). Given this, leaders are a logical first-line target for intervention and training, and our model provides guidance on specific inclusive leader actions with the greatest potential to shape inclusive climates.

Group Norms. Interventions targeting group norm formation may be one method to quickly influence inclusion perceptions, particularly if these interventions target both leaders and group members. Co-creation of group norms via team-based communication ensures there is agreement among team members on how the group will function, leading to greater ownership and accountability for upholding group standards (Ferdman, 2014). Fostering norms for open, respectful communication is relevant to developing and maintaining inclusive climates (Andersson & Pearson, 1999; Nishii, 2013; Porath, Gerbasi, & Schorch, 2015). We propose that social interaction norms which highlight the competencies everyone brings to the group, is another intervention target likely to foster perceptions of inclusion.

Organizational Narratives. During analysis of the model, SMEs highlighted the degree of influence organizational context exerts on the group, and affirmed the necessity of an organizational culture that values inclusion to foster and sustain inclusive climates (Schneider, Personal Communication, July 18–19, 2017; Creary et al., Personal Communication, April 23–24, 2018). However, when this alignment is not explicit, SMEs recommended leaders frame inclusion goals in a manner that is consistent with an organization's history, values, and existing narrative. This communication strategy was seen as a potential organizational intervention in support of a climate for inclusion.

Research Implications

Research into the antecedents of climate for inclusion is in a nascent state, leading researchers to infer relevant factors and their relationships from the limited research on inclusive climates, or from research on other climate types. Based on feedback and input from SMEs, the final model depicted in Figure 9.1 is not only an accurate reflection of the current state of the literature, but also adds to existing theory regarding how a climate for inclusion emerges from organizational, leader, and group characteristics and processes. Research is needed to empirically test the relationships identified in the model, and to further examine the links between antecedents, climate for inclusion, and individual and organizational outcomes. Additional research questions relevant to climate for inclusion are identified below.

Exploration of Moderators and Mediators. The present model does not fully illustrate the moderators and mediators that influence the development of inclusive climates. Instead we depict higher-order relationships between a limited set of antecedents believed to be crucial to the formation of inclusive climates. Although this decision was intentional, and informed by input from organizational climate SMEs and the intended purpose of the model (i.e., to inform interventions), it is likely that this model simplifies the true relationships between antecedents, outcomes, and climates for inclusion. In general, more research on the moderators and mediators that influence the development of inclusive climates—and their impact on associated outcomes—is warranted.

Evaluation of the Relationship Between Climate and Culture. Also requiring more research is the association between organizational culture and climate. Apart from a few seminal works exploring these constructs and their relationships, this area is largely unexplored (Schneider et al., 2013). We propose that absent an organizational culture that emphasizes the value of inclusion, any attempts to foster a climate for inclusion could not be sustained. Additionally, based on our findings, the development of inclusive climates will be influenced by the degree to which espoused organizational policies and procedures (a potential linking mechanism between climate and culture) align with enacted leader and group practices (Zohar & Hofmann, 2012). Both are areas for further study.

Examination of Workgroup Assimilation Versus Inclusion. Similar to the balance of uniqueness and belongingness faced by individuals in ODT (cf. Brewer, 1991; Shore et al., 2011), groups also must balance the competing goals of individual expression and belongingness to shared group ideals (i.e. balancing assimilation and inclusion needs of the group/organization). If fundamental aspects of the group are not assimilated by individual members (e.g., standards for professional behavior and dress), the group may have difficulty coalescing together. By contrast, if there is too much assimilation enshrined in group policies, optimal organizational functioning may not be achieved (e.g., group becomes less innovative, faultlines become clear for those who diverge from the "standard"). Understanding the proper balance for assimilation and inclusion at the workgroup and organizational level is an area where more research is needed.

Exploration of Relationships Between Similar Climate Types. It has been recognized that multiple climates may exist at the same time and that these climates may act in a collaborative or competitive manner (Ehrhart et al., 2014). Currently, there is a shortage of research into the interplay of simultaneous climates (Kuenzi & Schminke, 2009; Zohar & Hofmann, 2012). Given this, more research is required to determine the specific relationships between climate types similar to a climate for inclusion. In particular, the relationship between conceptually-related climates (e.g., trust, respect, and psychological safety, and inclusion) and potentially conflicting climates (e.g., safety versus performance) should be explored in order to better understand factors that support or impede climate development.

Evaluation of Interventions to Sustain or Enhance Climate for Inclusion. Research is needed on the types of interventions that affect the development of a climate for inclusion, especially given inconsistent evidence as to the effectiveness of traditional diversity training in bias reduction (Broockman & Kalla, 2016; Lai et al., 2014; 2016; Paluck, 2006). Due to the predominance of correlational evidence in the literature, more systematic research is needed on specific climate interventions, particularly those targeting organizational antecedents, leader actions, and group attributes and interaction norms that foster climates for inclusion.

Examination of Selection for Inclusive Predispositions. Finally, workshop participants discussed the importance of leader selection and promotion as a key reinforcing element for fostering inclusive leader behaviors (Creary et al., Personal Communication, April 23–24, 2018). Given that individual dispositions and attitudes are difficult to influence (Staw & Ross, 1985), additional research is warranted on the selection of leaders with dispositions conducive to fostering and sustaining climates for inclusion[6]. This should include consideration of current organizational selection processes of leaders, and explore whether organizations inadvertently select for characteristics that undermine inclusion (Creary et al., Personal Communication, April 23–24, 2018).

---

[6] Findings from the present research suggest that openness, humility, empathy, self-awareness, conscientiousness, emotional stability, and agreeableness are individual dispositions likely related to the development of inclusive environments.

CONCLUSIONS

The development of a conceptual model of climate for inclusion, informed by evidence from the broader climate literature and feedback from experts, adds to the nascent body of literature on this focused climate. The proposed model provides a starting point for future empirical research on the nature of relationships among factors that foster, maintain, and improve a climate for inclusion, and is intended to help organizations identify targets for intervention that could impact climates for inclusion. Encouraging the development of inclusive climates is especially prudent in an increasingly diverse workforce and is anticipated to improve outcomes for individuals, teams, and organizations.

AUTHORS' NOTE

The authors declare that there are no potential conflicts of interest with respect to the research, authorship, and/or publication of this article. The research described herein was sponsored by the U.S. Army Research Institute for the Behavioral and Social Sciences, Department of the Army. The views expressed in this paper are those of the authors and do not reflect the official policy or position of the Department of the Army, DoD, or the U.S. Government.

ACKNOWLEDGEMENTS

We thank the many people who provided input as this effort progressed from the initial development of the hypothesized model to the completion of the final conceptual model. This includes the Institute for Defense Analyses for their input on the large-scale literature review, and from the many incredible subject matter experts who provided valuable insight into key factors and relationships that impact the development of climates for inclusion: Dr. Stephanie J. Creary; Dr. Pamela Hopkins; Dr. Daan van Knippenberg; Dr. Michàlle E. Mor Barak; Dr. Lisa Nishii; Dr. John M. Schaubroeck; Dr. Benjamin Schneider; and Dr. Lynn M. Shore. We appreciate the time and effort dedicated to this project.

REFERENCES

Aarons, G. A., Ehrhart, M. G., Farahnak, L. R., & Sklar, M. (2014). Aligning leadership across systems and organizations to develop a strategic climate for evidence-based practice implementation. *Annual Review of Public Health, 35,* 255–274.

Andersson, L. M., & Pearson, C. M. (1999). Tit for tat? The spiraling effect of incivility in the workplace. *Academy of Management Review, 24,* 452–471.

Bambale, A. J. A. (2014). Relationship between servant leadership and organizational citizenship behaviors: Review of literature and future research directions. *Journal of Marketing and Management, 5,* 1–16.

Bandura, A. (1999). Social cognitive theory of personality. In L. Pervin & O. John (Eds.), *Handbook of personality* (pp. 154–196, 2nd ed.). New York, NY: Guilford Publications.

Barling, J., Loughlin, C., & Kelloway, K. E. (2002). Development and test of a model linking safety-specific transformational leadership and occupational safety. *Journal of Applied Psychology, 87,* 488–496. doi:10.1037//0021-9010.87.3.488

Bartol, K. M., & Srivastava, A. (2002). Encouraging knowledge sharing: The role of organizational reward systems. *Journal of Leadership & Organizational Studies, 9*(1), 64–76.

Boehm, C., & Flack, J. C. (2010). The emergence of simple and complex power structures through social niche construction. In A. Guinote & T. K. Vescio (Eds.), *The social psychology of power* (pp. 46–86). New York, NY: Guilford Press.

Boekhorst, J. A. (2015). The role of authentic leadership in fostering workplace inclusion: A social information processing perspective. *Human Resource Management, 54,* 241–264. doi:10.1002/hrm.21669

Brewer, M. B. (1991). The social self: On being the same and different at the same time. *Personality and Social Psychology Bulletin, 17*(5), 475–482.

Brimhall, K. C., & Mor Barak, M. E. (2018). The critical role of workplace inclusion in fostering innovation, job satisfaction, and quality of care in a diverse human service organization. *Human Service Organizations, Management, Leadership & Governance, 42*(5), 474–492. Retrieved from: https://dx.doi.org/10.1080/23303131.2018.1526151

Brimhall, K. C., Mor Barak, M. E., Hurlburt, M., McArdle, J. J., Palinkas, L., & Henwood, B. (2016). Increasing workplace inclusion: The promise of leader-member exchange. *Human Service Organizations: Management, Leadership & Governance, 41*(3), 222–239.

Broockman, D., & Kalla, J. (2016). Durably reducing transphobia: A field experiment on door-to-door canvassing. *Science, 352,* 220–224.

Carmeli, A., Reiter-Palmon, R., & Ziv, E. (2010). Inclusive leadership and employee involvement in creative tasks in the workplace: The mediating role of psychological safety. *Creativity Research Journal, 22,* 250–260. doi:10.1080/10400419.2010.504654

Chen, G., & Bliese, P. D. (2002). The role of different levels of leadership in predicting self-and collective efficacy: Evidence for discontinuity. *Journal of Applied Psychology, 87*(3), 549.

Cox, T. H., & Blake, S. (1991). Managing cultural diversity: Implications for organizational competitiveness. *The Academy of Management Executive, 5,* 45–56. doi:10.2307/4165021

Creary, S. J., Hopkins, P., van Knippenberg, D., Mor Barak, M. E., Nishii, L., Schaubroeck, J. M., & Shore, L. M. (2018, April 23–24). *Workshop on fostering inclusive climates.* Presented at U.S. Army Research Institute for Behavioral and Social Sciences, Alexandria, VA.

Dickson, M. W., Resick, C. J., & Hanges, P. J. (2006). When organizational climate is unambiguous, it is also strong. *Journal of Applied Psychology, 91*(2), 351.

De Cremer, D., & Tyler, T. R. (2005). Managing group behavior: The interplay between procedural justice, sense of self, and cooperation. *Advances in Experimental Social Psychology, 37,* 151–218.

Edmondson, A. C. (1999). Psychological safety and learning behavior in work teams. *Administrative Science Quarterly, 44,* 350–383. doi:10.2307/2666999

Ehrhart, M. G., Schneider, B., & Macey, W. H. (2014). *Organizational climate and culture: An introduction to theory, research, and practice*. New York, NY: Routledge.

Ely, R. J., & Thomas, D. A. (2001). Cultural diversity at work: The effects of diversity perspectives on work group processes and outcomes. *Administrative Science Quarterly, 46*(2), 229–273.

Feldman, D. C., & O'Neill, O. A. (2014). The role of socialization, orientation, and training programs in transmitting culture and climate and enhancing performance. In B. Schneider & K. M. Barbera (Eds.), *The Oxford handbook of organizational climate and culture* (pp. 44–64). New York, NY: Oxford University Press.

Ferdman, B. M. (2014). The practice of inclusion in diverse organizations: Toward a systematic and inclusive framework. In B. M. Ferdman & B. R. Deane (Eds.), *Diversity at work: The practice of inclusion* (pp. 3–55). San Francisco, CA: Jossey-Bass.

Ferdman, B. M. (2017). Paradoxes of inclusion: Understanding and managing the tensions of diversity and multiculturalism. *The Journal of Applied Behavioral Science, 53*(2), 235–263.

Ferrin, D. L., & Dirks, K. T. (2003). The use of rewards to increase and decrease trust: Mediating processes and differential effects. *Organization Science, 14*(1), 18–31.

Findler, L., Wind, L. H., & Mor Barak, M. E. (2007). The challenge of workforce management in a global society: Modeling the relationship between diversity, inclusion, organizational culture, and employee well-being, job satisfaction and organizational commitment. *Administration in Social Work, 31*(3), 63–94.

Frazier, M. L., Fainshmidt, S., Klinger, R. L., Pezeshkan, A., & Vracheva, V. (2017). Psychological safety: A meta-analytic review and extension. *Personnel Psychology, 70*(1), 113–165.

Good, D. J., Lyddy, C. J., Glomb, T. M., Bono, J. E., Brown, K. W., Duffy, M. K., ... & Lazar, S. W. (2016). Contemplating mindfulness at work: An integrative review. *Journal of Management, 42*(1), 114–142.

Gotsis, G., & Grimani, K. (2016). Diversity as an aspect of effective leadership: Integrating and moving forward. *Leadership & Organization Development Journal, 37*(2), 241–264.

Graen, G. B., & Uhl-Bien, M. (1995). Relationship-based approach to leadership: Development of leader-member exchange (LMX) theory of leadership over 25 years: Applying a multi-level multi-domain perspective. *The Leadership Quarterly, 6*(2), 219–247.

Hannum, K., McFeeters, B. B., & Booysen, L. (Eds.). (2010). *Leading across differences: Cases and perspectives*. San Francisco, CA: Pfeiffer.

Hirak, R., Peng, A. C., Carmeli, A., & Schaubroeck, J. M. (2012). Linking leader inclusiveness to work unit performance: The importance of psychological safety and learning from failures. *The Leadership Quarterly, 23*, 107–117.

Hogg, M. A., & Abrams, D. (1999). *Social identity and social cognition: Historical background and current trends*. Malden, MA: Wiley.

Homan, A. C., van Knippenberg, D., van Kleef, G. A., & De Dreu, C. K. W. (2007). Bridging faultlines by valuing diversity: Diversity beliefs, information elaboration, and performance in diverse work groups. *Journal of Applied Psychology, 92*, 1189–1199. doi:10.1037/0021-9010.92.5.1189

Hong, Y., Liao, H., & Jiang, K. (2013). Missing link in the service profit chain: A meta-analytic review of the antecedents, consequences, and moderators of service climate. *Journal of Applied Psychology, 98*, 237–267. doi:10.1037/a0031666

Hopkins, K. M., Cohen-Callow, A., Kim, H. J., & Hwang, J. (2010). Beyond intent to leave: Using multiple outcome measures for assessing turnover in child welfare. *Children and Youth Services Review, 32*(10), 1380–1387.

Hwang, J., & Hopkins, K. (2012). Organizational inclusion, commitment, and turnover among child welfare workers: A multilevel mediation analysis. *Administration in Social Work, 36*(1), 23–39.

Hwang, J., & Hopkins, K. M. (2015). A structural equation model of the effects of diversity characteristics and inclusion on organizational outcomes in the child welfare workforce. *Children and Youth Services Review, 50*, 44–52.

James, L. R., Choi, C. C., Ko, C. E., McNeil, P. K., Minton, M. K., Wright, M. A., & Kim, K. (2008). Organizational and psychological climate: A review of theory and research. *European Journal of Work and Organizational Psychology, 17*, 5–32. doi:10.1080/13594320701662550

Kearney, E., & Gebert, D. (2009). Managing diversity and enhancing team outcomes: The promise of transformational leadership. *Journal of Applied Psychology, 94*, 77–89.

Keltner, D., Gruenfeld, D. H., & Anderson, C. (2003). Power, approach, and inhibition. *Psychological Review, 110*, 265–284. doi:10.1037/0033-295X.110.2.265

Keltner, D., Gruenfeld, D. H., Galinsky, A., & Kraus, M. W. (2010). Paradoxes of power: Dynamics of the acquisition, experience, and social regulation of social power. In A. Guinote & T. K. Vescio (Eds.), *The social psychology of power* (pp. 177–208). New York, NY: Guilford Press.

Kernis, M. H., & Goldman, B. M. (2006). A multicomponent conceptualization of authenticity: Theory and research. *Advances in Experimental Social Psychology, 38*, 283–357.

Kossek, E. E., & Zonia, S. C. (1993). Assessing diversity climate: A field study of reactions to employer efforts to promote diversity. *Journal of Organizational Behavior, 14*(1), 61–81.

Kozlowski, S. W., & Doherty, M. L. (1989). Integration of climate and leadership: Examination of a neglected issue. *Journal of Applied Psychology, 74*, 546–556.

Kuenzi, M., & Schminke, M. (2009). Assembling fragments into a lens: A review, critique, and proposed research agenda for the organizational work climate literature. *Journal of Management, 35*, 634–717. doi:10.1177/0149206308330559

Kurtessis, J. N., Eisenberger, R., Ford, M. T., Buffardi, L. C., Stewart, K. A., & Adis, C. S. (2017). Perceived organizational support: A meta-analytic evaluation of organizational support theory. *Journal of Management, 43*(6), 1854–1884. Retrieved from: https://doi.org/10.1177/0149206315575554

Lai, C. K., Marini, M., Lehr, S. A., Cerruti, C., Shin, J.-E. L., Joy-Gaba, J. A., . . .& Koleva, S. P. (2014). Reducing implicit racial preferences: I. A comparative investigation of 17 interventions. *Journal of Experimental Psychology: General, 143*, 1765–1785.

Lai, C. K., Skinner, A. L., Cooley, E., Murrar, S., Brauer, M., Devos, T., . . . Nosek, B. A. (2016). Reducing implicit racial preferences: II. Intervention effectiveness across time. *Journal of Experimental Psychology: General, 145*, 1001–1016.

Lau, D. C., & Murnighan, J. K. (1998). Demographic diversity and faultlines: The compositional dynamics of organizational groups. *Academy of Management Review, 23*(2), 325–340.

Lee, P., Gillespie, N., Mann, L., & Wearing, A. (2010). Leadership and trust: Their effect on knowledge sharing and team performance. *Management Learning, 41*(4), 473–491.

Li, C. R., Lin, C. J., Tien, Y. H., & Chen, C. M. (2017). A multilevel model of team cultural diversity and creativity: The role of climate for inclusion. *The Journal of Creative Behavior, 51*(2), 163–179.

Liden, R. C., Wayne, S. J., Zhao, H., & Henderson, D. (2008). Servant leadership: Development of a multidimensional measure and multi-level assessment. *The Leadership Quarterly, 19*(2), 161–177.

Lynn, B., & Ratcliff, N. (2018). *Organizational climate annotated bibliography and literature synthesis* (Technical Report 2018–1365). Fort Belvoir, VA: U.S. Army Research Institute for the Behavioral and Social Sciences.

Maner, J. K., & Mead, N. L. (2010). The essential tension between leadership and power: When leaders sacrifice group goals for the sake of self-interest. *Journal of Personality and Social Psychology, 99*(3), 482.

Martins, L. L., Schilpzand, M. C., Kirkman, B. L., Ivanaj, S., & Ivanaj, V. (2013). A contingency view of the effects of cognitive diversity on team performance: The moderating roles of team psychological safety and relationship conflict. *Small Group Research, 44*(2), 96–126.

Mello, A. L., & Rentsch, J. R. (2015). Cognitive diversity in teams: A multidisciplinary review. *Small Group Research, 46*, 623–658.

Meyer, B., Shemla, M., Li, J., & Wegge, J. (2015). On the same side of the fault line: Inclusion in the leader's subgroup and employee performance. *Journal of Management Studies, 52*, 354–380.

Miller, N., & Brewer, M. B. (Eds.). (1984). *Groups in contact: The psychology of desegregation.* Orlando, FL: Academic Press.

Mitchell, R., Boyle, B., Parker, V., Giles, M., & Chiang, V. (2015). Managing inclusiveness and diversity in teams: How leader inclusiveness affects performance through status and team identity. *Human Resource Management, 54*, 217–239. doi:10.1002/hrm.21658

Mor Barak, M. E. (2000). The inclusive workplace: An ecosystems approach to diversity management. *Social Work, 45*(4), 339–353. Retrieved from: https://dx.doi.org/10.1093/sw/45.4.339

Mor Barak, M. E. (2008). Social psychological perspectives of workforce diversity and inclusion in national and global contexts. In R. Patti (Ed.), *Handbook of human service management* (pp. 239–254). Thousand Oaks, CA: Sage Publications.

Mor Barak, M. E. (2015). Inclusion is the key to diversity management, but what is inclusion? *Human Service Organizations: Management, Leadership & Governance, 39*(2), 83–88.

Mor Barak, M. E., & Daya, P. (2014). Fostering inclusion from the inside out to create an inclusive workplace. In G. M. Ferdman, & B.R. Deane (Eds.), *Diversity at work: The practice of inclusion* (pp. 391–412). San Francisco, CA: Jossey-Bass.

Mor Barak, M. E., Levin, A., Nissly, J. A., & Lane, C. J. (2006). Why do they leave? Modeling child welfare workers' turnover intentions. *Children and Youth Services Review, 28*(5), 548–577.

Mor Barak, M. E., Lizano, E. L., Kim, A., Duan, L., Rhee, M., Hsiao, H., & Brimhall, K. C. (2016). The promise of diversity management for climate of inclusion: A state-of-the art review and meta-analysis. *Human Service Organizations: Management, Leadership, & Governance, 40*, 305–333. doi:10.1080/23303131.2016.1138915

Morrison, E. W., & Milliken, F. J. (2000). Organizational silence: A barrier to change and development in a pluralistic world. *The Academy of Management Review, 25*(4), 706–725. Retrieved from: https://dx.doi.org/10.5465/amr.2000.3707697

Nembhard, I. M., & Edmondson, A. C. (2006). Making it safe: The effects of leader inclusiveness and professional status on psychological safety and improvement efforts in health care teams. *Journal of Organizational Behavior, 27*, 941–966. doi:10.1002/job.413

Nishii, L. H. (2013). The benefits of climate for inclusion for gender-diverse groups. *Academy of Management Journal, 56*, 1754–1774. doi:10.5465/amj.2009.0823

Nishii, L. H., & Mayer, D. M. (2009). Do inclusive leaders help to reduce turnover in diverse groups? The moderating role of leader–member exchange in the diversity to turnover relationship. *Journal of Applied Psychology, 94*, 1412–1426.

Ostroff, C., Kinicki, A. J., & Muhammad, R. S. (2012). Organizational culture and climate. In I. B. Weiner, N. W. Schmitt, & S. Highhouse (Eds.), *Handbook of psychology: Industrial and organizational psychology* (vol. 12, pp. 643–676). Hoboken, NJ: John Wiley & Sons.

Paluck, E. L. (2006). Diversity training and intergroup contact: A call to action research. *Journal of Social Issues, 62*, 577–595.

Pelled, L. H., Eisenhardt, K. M., & Xin, K. R. (1999). Exploring the black box: An analysis of work group diversity, conflict, and performance. *Administrative Science Quarterly, 44*(1), 1–28. Retrieved from: https://dx.doi.org/10.2307/2667029

Peterson, S. J., Walumbwa, F. O., Byron, K., & Myrowitz, J. (2009). CEO positive psychological traits, transformational leadership, and firm performance in high-technology start-up and established firms. *Journal of Management, 35*(2), 348–368.

Pettigrew, T. F., & Tropp, L. R. (2006). A meta-analytic test of intergroup contact theory. *Journal of Personality and Social Psychology, 90*(5), 751.

Pettigrew, T. F., Tropp, L. R., Wagner, U., & Christ, O. (2011). Recent advances in intergroup contact theory. *International Journal of Intercultural Relations, 35*(3), 271–280.

Podsakoff, N. P., Podsakoff, P. M., & Kuskova, V. V. (2010). Dispelling misconceptions and providing guidelines for leader reward and punishment behavior. *Business Horizons, 53*(3), 291–303.

Porath, C. L., Gerbasi, A., & Schorch, S. L. (2015). The effects of civility on advice, leadership, and performance. *Journal of Applied Psychology, 100*, 1527–1541.

Reagans, R., Zuckerman, E., & McEvily, B. (2004). How to make the team: Social networks vs. demography as criteria for designing effective teams. *Administrative Science Quarterly, 49*, 101–133. doi:10.2307/4131457

Schein, E. H. (2010). *Organizational culture and leadership* (4th Ed.). San Francisco, CA: Jossey-Bass.

Schneider, B. (1975). Organizational climates: An essay. *Personnel Psychology, 28*, 447–479. doi:10.1111/j.1744-6570.1975.tb01386

Schneider, B. (2017, July 18–19). *Workshop on fostering inclusive climates.* Presented at U.S. Army Research Institute for Behavioral and Social Sciences, Fort Leavenworth, KS.

Schneider, B., Ehrhart, M. G., & Macey, W. H. (2013). Organizational climate and culture. *Annual Review of Psychology, 64,* 361–388. doi:10.1146/annurevpsych-113011-143809

Schneider, B., González-Romá, V., Ostroff, C., & West, M. A. (2017). Organizational climate and culture: Reflections on the history of the constructs in the *Journal of Applied Psychology. Journal of Applied Psychology, 102*(3), 468.

Sherif, M. (1966). *In common predicament: Social psychology of intergroup conflict and cooperation.* Boston, MA: Houghton Mifflin.

Shore, L. M., Cleveland, J. N., & Sanchez, D. (2018). Inclusive workplaces: A review and model. *Human Resource Management Review, 28*(2), 176–189.

Shore, L. M., Randel, A. E., Chung, B. G., Dean, M. A., Ehrhart, K. H., & Singh, G. (2011). Inclusion and diversity in work groups: A review and model for future research. *Journal of Management, 37,* 1262–1289. doi:10.1177/0149206310385943

Singh, B., Winkel, D. E., & Selvarajan, T. T. (2013). Managing diversity at work: Does psychological safety hold the key to racial differences in employee performance?. *Journal of Occupational and Organizational Psychology, 86*(2), 242–263.

Sleebos, E., Ellemers, N., & de Gilder, D. (2006). The paradox of the disrespected: Disrespected group members' engagement in group-serving efforts. *Journal of Experimental Social Psychology, 42*(4), 413–427.

Stahl, G. K., Mäkelä, K., Zander, L., & Maznevski, M. L. (2010). A look at the bright side of multicultural team diversity. *Scandinavian Journal of Management, 26,* 439–447. doi:10.1016/j.scaman.2010.09.009

Stamper, C. L., & Masterson, S. S. (2002). Insider or outsider? How employee perceptions of insider status affect their work behavior. *Journal of Organizational Behavior: The International Journal of Industrial, Occupational and Organizational Psychology and Behavior, 23*(8), 875–894.

Staw, B. M., & Ross, J. (1985). Stability in the midst of change: A dispositional approach to job attitudes. *Journal of Applied psychology, 70*(3), 469–480.

Terry, D. J., & Hogg, M. A. (1996). Group norms and the attitude-behavior relationship: A role for group identification. *Personality and Social Psychology Bulletin, 22*(8), 776–793.

Thatcher, S. M. B., & Patel, P. C. (2011). Demographic faultlines: A meta-analysis of the literature. *Journal of Applied Psychology, 96,* 1119–1139. doi:10.1037/a0024167

Thatcher, S. M. B., & Patel, P. C. (2012). Group faultlines: A review, integration, and guide to future research. *Journal of Management, 38*(4), 969–1009. Retrieved from: https://dx.doi.org/10.1177/0149206311426187

Tyler, T. R., & Blader, S. L. (2002). Autonomous vs. comparative status: Must we be better than others to feel good about ourselves?. *Organizational Behavior and Human Decision Processes, 89*(1), 813–838.

U.S. Office of Personnel Management, Office of Diversity and Inclusion. (2011). *Government-Wide Diversity and Inclusion Strategic Plan 2011.* Retrieved from https://www.energy.gov/sites/prod/files/OPM%20Government-wide%20Diversity%20and%20Inclusion%20Strategic%20Plan%202011.pdf van Knippenberg, D., Dawson, J. F., West, M. A., & Homan, A. C. (2011). Diversity fault-lines, shared objectives, and top management team performance. *Human Relations, 64*(3), 307–336.

van Knippenberg, D., & Schippers, M. C. (2007). Work group diversity. *Annual Review of Psychology, 58,* 515–541. doi:10.1146/annurev.psych.58.110405.085546

van Vugt, M. (2006). Evolutionary origins of leadership and followership. *Personality and Social Psychology Review, 10,* 354–371. doi:10.1207/s15327957pspr1004_5

Wallace, J. C., Popp, E., & Mondore, S. (2006). Safety climate as a mediator between foundation climates and occupational accidents: A group-level investigation. *Journal of Applied Psychology, 91*(3), 681.

Walumbwa, F. O., Avolio, B. J., Gardner, W. L., Wernsing, T. S., & Peterson, S. J. (2008). Authentic leadership: Development and validation of a theory-based measure. *Journal of Management, 34*(1), 89–126.

Walumbwa, F. O., Hartnell, C. A., & Oke, A. (2010). Servant leadership, procedural justice climate, service climate, employee attitudes, and organizational citizenship behavior: A cross-level investigation. *Journal of Applied Psychology, 95,* 517–529.

Walumbwa, F. O., Mayer, D. M., Wang, P., Wang, H., Workman, K., & Christensen, A. L. (2011). Linking ethical leadership to employee performance: The roles of leader–member exchange, self-efficacy, and organizational identification. *Organizational Behavior and Human Decision Processes, 115*(2), 204–213.

Walumbwa, F. O., & Schaubroeck, J. (2009). Leader personality traits and employee voice behavior: Mediating roles of ethical leadership and work group psychological safety. *Journal of Applied Psychology, 94*(5), 1275.

Wasserman, I. C., Gallegos, P. V., & Ferdman, B. M. (2008). Dancing with resistance: Leadership challenges in fostering a culture of inclusion. In K. M. Thomas (Ed.), *Diversity resistance in organizations* (pp. 175–200). New York, NY: Lawrence Erlbaum.

Way, S. A., Simons, T., Leroy, H., & Tuleja, E. A. (2018). What is in it for me? Middle manager behavior integrity and performance. *Journal of Business Ethics, 150*(3), 765–777.

Weick, K. E. (1995). *Sensemaking in organizations.* Thousand Oaks, CA: Sage.

Williams, K. Y., & O'Reilly, C. A., III. (1998). Demography and diversity in organizations: A review of 40 years of research. In B. M. Staw & L. L. Cummings (Eds.), *Research in organizational behavior* (Vol. 20, pp. 77–140). Greenwich, CT: JAI.

Yuengling, A. R., Parks, K. M., & McDonald, D. P. (2011). *Foundation for diversity training: Competency model and learning objectives* (Report No. 06-12). Patrick Air Force Base, FL, Defense Equal Opportunity Management Institute.

Zaccaro, S. J., Rittman, A. L., & Marks, M. A. (2001). Team leadership. *The Leadership Quarterly, 12,* 451–483. doi:10.1177/0149206309347376

Zohar, D., & Hofmann, D. (2012). Organizational culture and climate. In S. Kozlowski (Ed.), *Oxford handbook of I/O psychology.* Oxford, UK: Oxford University Press.

Zohar, D., & Luria, G. (2004). Climate as a social-cognitive construction of supervisory safety practices: scripts as proxy of behavior patterns. *Journal of Applied Psychology, 89,* 322–333.

Zohar, D., & Luria, G. (2005). A multilevel model of safety climate: Cross-level relationships between organization and group-level climates. *Journal of Applied Psychology, 90,* 616–628. doi:10.1037/0021-9010.90.4.616

CHAPTER 10

IDENTIFYING AND MEASURING RESPONSES TO PERCEIVED DISCRIMINATION FROM SUPERVISORS

M. Fernanda Wagstaff, María del Carmen Triana,
Abby N. Peters, and Eric Mark Arredondo

The purpose of this study was to develop and validate a measure of employees' responses to perceived discrimination from supervisors regardless of reasons for discrimination. A review of the literature indicates that looking at responses to discrimination irrespective of reasons for discrimination is warranted. We found that responses to discriminatory treatment at work by a supervisor are conceptualized in four different ways and that the responses to sexual harassment proposed by Knapp et al. (1997) could be generalized across reasons for discrimination. In Study 1, we generated the items of the scale. In Study 2, we used the items generated to gather additional data in order to evaluate a four-factor structure of responses to discrimination: compensation, social coping, confrontation, and advocacy seeking. In Study 3, we assessed the convergent, discriminant, and criterion-related validity of the scale. The scale offers good reliability, satisfactory loadings, good fit indices, and evidence in support of convergent, discriminant, and criterion-related validity. Results suggest that the scale of responses to perceived discrimination from supervisors is a promising tool for conducting research in an era in which discrimination

Diversity and Inclusion in Organizations, pages 251–284.

is surrounded by both attributional and situational ambiguity. We contribute to the literature by taking the theoretical framework elaborated by Knapp et al. (1997) for responses to sexual harassment and applying it to discrimination more generally. As subtle discrimination leads to more ambiguity surrounding the reason(s) for discrimination, we focus on responses to discrimination from supervisors irrespective of reason(s), and we develop a measure that captures these responses. Having such a measure is valuable at a time when discrimination often unfolds as hidden and multidetermined.

Keywords: perceived discrimination, responses to discrimination, compensation, avoidance/denial, social coping, confrontation, advocacy-seeking

The study of perceived discrimination is of great importance not only to lower employment discrimination but also to provide all employees with fair employment opportunities (Colella, Hebl, & King, 2017). The importance of this topic becomes evident when focusing on responses to discrimination, or responses to perceptions that differential treatment is occurring because of one's group membership (Sanchez & Brock, 1996). In particular, responses to discrimination have been linked to many harmful individual outcomes, including self-reported poor health, psychological distress, depressive symptoms, anxiety, emotional exhaustion, and drug use as well as reduced life satisfaction, job satisfaction, and retention (Barnes & Lightsey, 2005; Hudson et al., 2016; Taylor & Aspinwall, 1996, Tepper, Moos, Lockhart, & Carr, 2007; Terpstra & Baker, 1986). Conversely, responses to discrimination are also associated with positive outcomes such as the ability to hold positive attitudes toward the self, the ability to be creative and productive in one's work, and the creation of safe spaces (Shrivastava, 2015; Taylor & Armor, 1996). Interpersonal outcomes, too, are associated with negative responses to discrimination such as retaliation and public humiliation (Knapp, Faley, Ekeberg, & Dubois, 1997) as well as positive ones such as improved interpersonal relationships between the parties involved (Elligan & Utsey, 1999). Because so many outcomes are associated with responses to discrimination, it is important for researchers to have a measurement instrument that is valid, reliable, and relevant to measure such responses.

It is precisely in the area of measurement that researchers examining responses to discrimination have both a problem and an opportunity for research. The problem is that current measures of responses to discrimination do not match how discrimination is increasingly unfolding in our society. Current research assumes that the reasons for discrimination (e.g., race) are important in understanding responses to discrimination. Although this research has been significant in understanding how people deal with mistreatment, we propose instead to examine responses to perceived discrimination irrespective of reasons. Our rationale is based on the fact that discrimination often unfolds as hidden and multidetermined (Benokraitis, 1997; Dipboye & Colella, 2005; King & Ahmad, 2010; King, Shapiro, Hebl, Singletary, & Turner, 2006; Monteith, Voils, & Ashbur-

Nardo, 2001; Singletary & Hebl, 2009). Related to this reasoning, a victim of perceived discrimination stated: *"It is so hard to tell which one it is. It might have been because I was Muslim but it also may have been because I was African American. So I really never know. All I know is that I'm being discriminated against and I don't quite know why. I know that it could be because I'm a woman. Maybe because I am all three"* (Byng 1998, pp. 477–478). Thus, the victim may be unsure about the perpetrator's reason(s) for discrimination, which may require the victim to aggregate several (ambiguous) events to infer discrimination (Crocker, Major, & Steele, 1998; Deitch et al., 2003; Major & Crocker 1993). Although it may be clear to the victim that the treatment is discriminatory, there is ambiguity surrounding the reasons for discrimination (Crocker et al., 1998). We argue that if the victim is unable to clearly label the perpetrator's motives for discrimination or forced to aggregate events to infer discrimination, then responses to discriminatory treatment may not have a one-to-one correspondence with the reason(s) for discrimination.

Furthermore, despite their merits, current measures of responses to perceived discrimination also possess one of two additional characteristics that limit their use. The first limitation is that some measures do not allow the researcher to single out the perpetrator when perpetrators, especially supervisors, play a major role in theoretical frameworks of responses to discrimination (e.g., Knapp et al., 1997). In this paper, we research the supervisor as a key factor in responses to perceived discrimination.

The second limitation of current measures of responses to discrimination is that they are mostly based on single events or incidents (e.g., Malamut & Offermann, 2001; Wasti & Cortina, 2002). Although this approach has merit, it is problematic because when discrimination is subtle or multidetermined, victims of discrimination may need to aggregate multiple events before they can infer that discrimination related to a specific reason exists. Given how discrimination sometimes unfolds, there is a need to focus on how people *generally* respond to discrimination from supervisors.

The purpose of this study is to develop and validate a scale of responses to perceived discrimination from supervisors that will be usable in future research on antecedents and consequences of responses to supervisor discrimination. The measure captures cases in which victims are certain that they were discriminated against, yet they may or may not know the reason for that discrimination. In conducting this research, we draw from Knapp et al. (1997), who examined four responses to sexual harassment: avoidance/denial, social coping, confrontation, and advocacy seeking. Across three studies, we adopt this framework to examine responses to discrimination regardless of the reason for discrimination. Our goal is to contribute to research on responses to discrimination from supervisors by presenting an instrument that matches the way in which discrimination manifests in today's society: as subtle and multidetermined.

THEORY OF RESPONSES TO DISCRIMINATION

Knapp et al.'s (1997) theory was originally developed to explain responses to sexual harassment. We adopt this theory to examine responses to perceived discrimination more generally because Knapp et al.'s theory of responses to sexual harassment represents a form of discrimination based on a specific reason for discrimination (i.e., sex; Goldman, Gutek, Stein, & Lewis, 2006). The present study represents an effort to develop Knapp et al.'s theory and to apply it more generally from sexual harassment to different reasons of discrimination.

We adopt Knapp et al.'s framework for three reasons. First, the four abovementioned responses have been examined in various studies related to a range of reasons for discrimination. We discuss this in the next pages. Second, Knapp et al.'s (1997) framework focuses on individuals, and we are interested in this level of analysis as opposed to the group level because responses to discriminatory treatment reside mostly in individuals (Lalonde, Majumder, & Parris, 1995; Major, Quinton, McCoy, & Schmader, 2000). Third, this framework is based on behaviors, and research indicates that behaviors are one of the predominant ways of responding to discrimination (Moos & Schaefer, 1993).

Knapp et al. (1997) proposed that responses to sexual harassment are a function of the focus and mode of the response. The focus of the response involves whether the perpetrator is confronted or avoided. The mode of response involves the presence (or absence) of support from others. The juxtaposition of the focus and mode of response may be depicted in a two-by-two matrix with four modes of response: avoidance/denial, confrontation, social coping, and advocacy seeking. Knapp et al.'s first quadrant, avoidance/denial, represents self-focus (i.e., a response that does not involve the perpetrator) and self-response (i.e., the target does not use outside resources to address the discrimination). This strategy involves doing nothing, ignoring, or minimizing the behavior. It can also involve working harder to avoid problems with the supervisor (Holahan, Moos, & Schaefer, 1996; Oyserman & Swim, 2001; Simpson & Yinger, 1985). Knapp et al.'s second quadrant, social coping, refers to seeking support from others, not the perpetrator. The third quadrant, confrontation, is an initiator-focused strategy in which the target addresses the perpetrator directly. The fourth quadrant, advocacy seeking, is the use of individual or organizational support that focuses the response on the perpetrator (e.g., reporting the behavior to the human resources department). Importantly, these responses are not mutually exclusive (i.e., if an individual implements one, that person may still pursue one or more of the others). In fact, research shows that individuals are likely to pursue multiple strategies not only across but also within events (Bingham & Scherer, 1993; Folkman & Lazarus, 1980).

Knapp et al.'s (1997) four responses have received empirical support using measures designed to assess responses to sexual harassment (Cortina & Wasti, 2005; Malamut & Offermann, 2001; Wasti & Cortina, 2002; for an exception see Magley, 2002). We believe that these four responses can generalize across various reasons for discrimination (e.g., Puhl, 2005; Terpstra & Baker, 1986). To partially evaluate this belief, we reviewed the literature on responses to discriminatory treatment at work by using *PsycINFO*, *Sociological Abstracts*, and *Business Source Complete*. The criteria for selecting articles for our literature review were as follows: the article had to have been published in a peer-reviewed journal, and the topic had to be related to discriminatory treatment in work settings (e.g., experiments with students only were dropped). Moreover, the responses examined had to be behavioral. Beyond this search, we also implemented the cascade method of including articles cited in the articles obtained and read through these three databases. Table 10.1 shows the results of our literature review, including the reasons for discrimination, the article citation, and the responses to discriminatory treatment at work as reported in each article.

Upon close inspection of Table 10.1, we identified Knapp et al.'s (1997) four responses across reasons for discrimination. Avoidance/denial seems to be a response associated with immigration status (Beiser, Noh, Hou, Kaspar, & Rummens, 2001; Verwiebe, Seewann, Wolf, & Hacioglu, 2016), chronic illness (McGonagle & Hamblin, 2014), disability (Stone & Colella, 1996), race (Feagin & Sikes, 1994; Fleming, Lamont, & Welburn, 2012; Grijalva & Coombs, 1997; McNeilly et al., 1996; Pettigrew, 1964), sex (Haslett & Lipman, 1997; Livingston, 1982; McDonald & Korabik, 1991; Shrivastava, 2015), weight (Puhl, 2005), and sexual orientation discrimination (Singletary & Hebl, 2009). This response is also reported in studies involving more than one reason for discrimination, particularly sex and race (Haar & Morash, 2013; Shorter-Gooden (2004), sex, race, age, family obligation, and sexual orientation (Volpone & Avery, 2013), as well as sex and sexual orientation (Wilson & Yoshikawa, 2004).

Social coping appears to be a response to perceived discrimination based on age (Grima, 2011), immigration status (Hagey et al., 2001), race (Feagin & Sikes, 1994; Grijalva & Coombs, 1997; Hudson et al., 2016; Plumer and Slane, 1996), sex (Bingham & Scherer, 1993), sexual orientation (Chung, 2001; Chung et al., 2009; Singletary & Hebl, 2009), and weight (Puhl & Brownell, 2003). It also emerges when discrimination based on race and color (Clark, Anderson, Clark, & Williams, 1999) as well as sex and sexual orientation (Wilson & Yoshikawa, 2004) coexist.

Confrontation appears to be a response associated with discrimination based on ethnicity (Torres et al, 2011), race (Feagin & Sikes, 1994; Fleming et al., 2012; Grijalva & Coombs, 1997; Plummer & Slane, 1996), sex (Shrivastava, 2015; Terpstra & Baker, 1986), sexual orientation (Chung, 2001, 2009), and weight (Puhl & Brownell, 2003). It also appears in studies involving more than one reason for discrimination, particularly race and ethnicity (Feagin, 1991), sex, race, and sexual orientation (Hyers, 2007), and sex and sexual orientation (Wilson & Yoshikawa, 2004). Finally, advocacy seeking also seems to manifest across reasons for discrimination, particularly in relation to race (Feagin & Sikes, 1994; Lalonde et al., 1995), immigration status (Hagey et al., 2001), and sex (Livingston, 1982).

TABLE 10.1. Empirical Evidence of Responses to Discriminatory Treatment Across Types of Discrimination

Reasons for Discrimination	Citation	Response Reported
Age	Armenta (2017)	Adopting a younger subjective age and increasing group identification.
Age	Grima (2011)	Standing back (positive reappraisal, overvalue personal future, reversal of the stigmatization); facing up to events (struggle, withdrawal and adaptation—denunciation of the situation, resignation and withdrawal, continuing commitment); absence of constraint (discrimination put into perspective/minimized, social support—emotional and instrumental).
Chronic illness	McGonagle & Hamblin (2014)	Proactive coping: compensatory behaviors and concealment.
Disability	Colella (1996)	Acts to confirm/disconfirm the self-fulfilling prophecy. Displaying increased initiative, seeking challenging opportunities and goals.
Disability	Stone & Colella (1996)	Withdrawal, grievances, requesting help, acknowledging the disability (disclosure), concealment, exerting extraordinarily high levels of effort and performance on the job, action groups.
Disability	Wan (2003)	The defiant, the activists, the serenes, the internalizers, the talkers, the hiders, the flamboyants, the positivists.
Ethnicity	Contrada et al. (2000)	Assertive reactions (i.e., confrontation); less assertive (placate the perpetrator).
Ethnicity	Torres et al. (2011)	Ethnic identity exploration and ethnic identity commitment.
Immigration Status	Beiser et al. (2001)	Passive acceptance, avoidance, confrontation, discussion of problem with others, advocacy seeking.
Immigration Status	Hagey et al. (2001)	Support from family, church, close friends, and others. Seek legal counsel.
Immigration Status	Noor & Shaker (2017)	Problem-oriented coping and emotion/avoidance coping.
Immigration Status	Verkuyten & Nekuee (2001)	Emotion-focused coping, action-focused coping.
Immigration Status	Verwiebe et al. (2016)	Emphasis on performance, distancing and avoidance, resistance, ignoring and ironizing

Race	Feagin & Sikes (1994)	Careful assessment, withdrawal, avoidance, resigned acceptance, adaptation, verbal confrontation, physical confrontation, seek out social support from friends and family, advocacy seeking, legal action, retaliation, education of perpetrator, psychological defense.
Race	Fleming et al. (2012)	Confronting (speaking out, using violence, insulting, suing, lodging a formal complaint, intimidating) and deflating (observing, adopting strategic silence, walking away, ignoring, absence of reaction, and finding comfort, focusing on professional and other goals, manage the self to avoid confirming stereotypes, and surprise), and mix strategy ('pick my battles').
Race	Grijalva & Coombs (1997)	Use of social network support, speak out against or confront the perpetrator, educate the perpetrator, ignore the behavior.
Race	Hudson et al. (2016)	Do nothing, physical activity, smoking, drinking, drug use, social coping, spirituality, and religiosity.
Race	Mallet & Swim (2009)	Proactive coping: self-focused coping; situation-focused coping: physical avoidance.
Race	Kuo (1995)	Emotion-focused coping: problem focused coping.
Race	Lalonde et al. (1995)	Inform, seek advice, file a complaint, consult, take legal action, become active, help, inform media, forget, and organize others.
Race	McNeilly et al. (1996)	Speaking up, accepting, ignoring, trying to change things, keeping it to myself, working harder, praying, avoiding getting violent, forgetting.
Race	Pettigrew (1964)	Moving toward (i.e., seeking full acceptance), moving against (i.e., aggressive reactions), and moving away (i.e., avoidance reactions).
Race	Plummer & Slane (1996)	Problem focused coping: accepting responsibility, confrontive coping, planful problem solving, seeking social support.
Sex	Bingham & Scherer (1993)	Formal reports; informal reports (external authority, internal authority); social support (talked to co-workers, talked to friends or family; talked to the harasser; communication strategies (indirect, assertive, aggressive, facework).
Sex	Haslett & Lipman (1997)	Frustration, stress, anger, withdrawal, ignoring, repressing, depression, open hostility (e.g., confrontation).
Sex	Livingston (1982)	Ignoring the behavior, objecting directly to the harasser's behavior, avoiding the harasser, taking formal action, reporting to a higher authority, joking about the incident, quitting the job.

(continues)

TABLE 10.1. Continued

Reasons for Discrimination	Citation	Response Reported
Sex	McDonald & Korabik (1991)	Direct action, preparatory action, other (e.g., sought revenge, passivity, humor, anger), talked to others, actions taken geared to problem resolution, avoidance/withdrawal, cognitive coping efforts.
Sex	Schneider et al. (1997)	Stayed away from him, told myself it wasn't important, told him I didn't like what he was doing, talked with someone about it, assumed he meant well, made an excuse so he would leave me alone, blamed myself, talked with a supervisor or union rep, tried to forget about it, made a formal complaint, just put up with it.
Sex	Terpstra & Baker (1986)	Respond positively, ignore the incident, avoid the offender, employ indirect means of stopping the behavior, verbally or nonverbally confront the perpetrator, physically retaliate, report the incident, transfer or quit.
Sex	Shrivastava (2015)	Creating a face of assertiveness, creating safe spaces, reliance on informal sisterhood ties, avoiding confrontation with male officers, asserting gender identity, acting male, acting female, role-flexing.
Sexual Orientation	Birt & Dion (1987)	Militancy.
Sexual Orientation	Chung (2001)	Vocational choice: self-employment, job tracking, risk taking; Work adjustment: identity management (acting, passing, covering, implicitly out, explicitly out), discrimination management (quitting, silence, social support, confrontation).
Sexual Orientation	Chung et al. (2009)	Responses to potential discrimination: vocational choice (self-employment, job tracking, risk taking), identity management (acting, passing, covering, implicitly out, explicitly out); responses to encountered discrimination (nonassertive, social support, and confrontation).
Sexual Orientation	Randall et al. (2017)	Partner problem-focused supportive dyadic coping, emotion-focused supportive dyadic coping, partner delegated dyadic coping, and negative dyadic coping.
Sexual Orientation	Ragins & Cornwell (2001)	Passing, disclosure.
Sexual Orientation	Singletary & Hebl (2009)	Compensation (acknowledgment, individuating information, and increased positivity).
Sexual Orientation	Sparkes (1994)	Passing, covering, implicitly coming out, explicitly coming out, seeking social support.
Weight	Puhl (2005)	Confrontation, self-protection, compensation, social activism, avoidance, losing weight.

Weight	Puhl & Brownell (2003)	Confrontation, social support, assertive coping, aggressive, anti-social coping.
Color, Nationality	Wheeler et al. (2014)	Rely on personal values; excuse the behavior; confront; change units, shifts, or leave the position; work harder.
Race, Color	Clark et al. (1999)	John Henryism, social support, religious participation.
Race, Ethnicity	Feagin (1991)	Careful assessment, withdrawal, resigned acceptance, confrontation.
Race, Immigration	Hametner (2014)	Retreating and pragmatically reducing ambitions, trivializing racist experiences and assimilating to the mainstream, naming facts and aiming to improve the situation by communication, delegitimizing and ironically transcending racism.
Sex, Race	Christian et al. (2000)	Compensation, vigilance, caution, social coping, religiosity.
Sex, Race	Haar & Morash (2013)	Straight talk; hard work and good work; putting up with the stressful work environment; mentor assistance; accepting help and protection from male coworkers; avoid and disengage; self-define and assess; formal action, seeing a psychologist, refusing to do certain tasks, hiding emotions.
Sex, Race	Lykes (1983)	Direct and indirect instrument coping, purposeful indirect coping, and passive or non-instrumental.
Sex, Race	Shorter-Gooden (2004)	Internal resources (resting on faith, standing on shoulders, valuing oneself), external resources (leaning on shoulders), specific strategies (role flexing, avoiding, standing up and fighting back).
Sex, Race	St. Jean & Feagin (1997)	Compensation: Over-attention ("to cover all the bases"), social coping.
Sex, Race, Age, Family Obligation, Sexual Orientation	Volpone & Avery (2013)	Changing the situation, avoidance.
Sex, Race, Sexual Orientation	Hyers (2007)	Assertive responses: questioning the perpetrator, direct nonverbal, direct verbal; Non-assertive responses: general non-assertive (joking or laughing), doing nothing.

(continues)

TABLE 10.1. Continued

Reasons for Discrimination	Citation	Response Reported
Sex, Race, Religion	Kim et al. (2011)	Proactive coping; external support; personal resources; spiritual coping.
Sex, Sexual Orientation, Race, Immigration status	Wilson & Yoshikawa (2004)	Confrontation, self-attribution, external attribution, social network responses, avoidance.
Sex, Socioeconomic Status	Ngo et al. (2002)	No action, resignation, internal voice, external voice, and litigation.
General	Deaux & Ethier (1998)	Identity negation (elimination, denial, lowered identification) and identity enhancement (reaffirmation, remooring, intensified group contact, social change).
General	Miller & Kaiser (2001)	Disengagement coping: avoidance, denial; engagement coping: compensation, seeking social support.
General	Miller & Major (2000)	Problem solving, coping that targets others, the self, the interaction (eliminate the stigmatizing condition, conceal, compensate, assertiveness, careful attention, bicultural skills, code switching, avoidance).
General	Wagstaff et al. (2015)	Social support seeking.

Table 10.1 also shows behavioral responses that are unique to specific types of discrimination. For example, losing weight is a strategy that can be useful for overweight individuals but not for those who are discriminated against because of their race. However, unique responses to specific types of discrimination are not relevant to this study because we focus on general responses across different reasons for discrimination.

Additional evidence further supports the claim that Knapp et al.'s responses can be applied to understanding responses to discrimination irrespective of reason. For example, there is evidence in the stigma and legal claiming literatures that regardless of reason(s) for discrimination, people's responses to discrimination are similar. Miller and Major (2000) recognized that although stigmas differ in various ways (e.g., visibility), which will eventually lead to different responses, there are also similarities across stigmas in how people cope with them. In their study of antecedents of legal claiming commitment, Groth, Goldman, Gilliland, and Bies (2002) found that there were no significant differences in legal claiming when broken down by alleged reason for discrimination. Overall, our review indicates that looking at responses to discrimination irrespective of reasons is warranted and that the responses proposed by Knapp et al. (1997) for sexual harassment could be generalized across reasons for discrimination.

VALIDITY OF RESPONSES TO PERCEIVED DISCRIMINATION

In the following pages, we report a series of studies that ultimately allow the validation of responses to perceived discrimination from supervisors. Following Hinkin's (1998) recommendations, in Study 1, we focus on item generation and content validation of our proposed measure. In Study 2, we conduct a confirmatory factor analysis. In Study 3, we evaluate the convergent, discriminant, and criterion-related validity of our measure. Finally, in Study 3, we also focus on studying the relationship between our new validated measure and other related variables with the goal of developing a nomological network (Hinkin, 1998).

Nomological Network

Figure 10.1 depicts the nomological network of responses to perceived discrimination considering the four responses theorized by Knapp et al. (1997). Our review of the literature showed individual, interpersonal, group, organizational, and environmental antecedents as well as individual, interpersonal, and organizational outcomes of responses to perceived discrimination. We present the nomological network with the following caveats. First, although we focus on responses to perceived discrimination from supervisors when the causes for discrimination are ambiguous, many of the authors we reviewed do not explicitly address either ambiguity or the perpetrator. Second, many authors discuss the issue of responses to perceived discrimination in general terms (e.g., active or passive response). Thus, in some cases we draw from general (e.g., active response) as opposed to

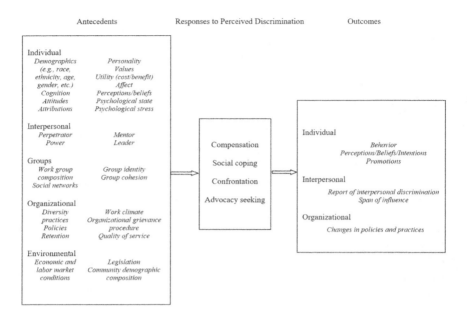

FIGURE 10.1.   Nomological Network of Responses to Perceived Discrimination

specific responses (e.g., confrontation). Third, we focus on results that either seem the most robust or strongly suggest relationships between responses and other related variables. Finally, Figure 10.1 does not pretend to depict a theoretical model with mediators and moderators, or relationships between the four responses. Instead, we exclusively focus on building the nomological network.

Figure 10.1 illustrates several individual-level antecedents of responses to perceived discrimination. One of them is demographic characteristics. Across reasons for discrimination, education positively relates to active coping, such as confrontation (Beiser et al., 2001; Kuo, 1995; Lalonde et al. 1995; Ngo, Tang, Au, 2002). Other research suggests that females are more likely to complain to management (Ngo et al., 2002). The type of occupation (e.g., professionals versus non-professionals) and the age of the target of discrimination appear to relate to more active responses (Volpone & Avery, 2013). Minority status is associated with more active coping, such as social support (Kim, Willingham, Lewis Hall, & Anderson, 2011). In the case of immigration status and the use of English as a second language, evidence points to the use of confrontation and compensation (e.g., working harder; Wheeler, Foster, & Hepburn, 2014). Social status relates to more active, compared to less active, forms of responses, such as social support and confrontation, although results are mixed (Haar & Morash, 2013; Kuo, 1995). Although findings are also mixed (Bingham & Scherer, 1993; Christian,

Al-Mateen, Webb, & Donatelli, 2000; Puhl & Brownell, 2003), females seem more likely than males to use social support coping.

Cognition in the form of expectancies, sensitivity to discrimination, and awareness of the law also relates to various responses to perceived discrimination. Negative mood expectancies seem to be associated with more active forms of coping (see Puhl & Brownell, 2003), anticipated discrimination relates to compensatory behaviors (McGonagle & Hamblin, 2014), and sensitivity to discrimination and knowledge of the law correlate significantly with complaining, which is one way for confrontation to manifest (Ngo et al., 2002). Meanwhile, low performance expectations may relate to less active responses to perceived discrimination (Stone & Colella, 1996; Grijalva & Coombs, 1997).

Attitudes, attributions, perceptions, and beliefs are other key antecedents of responses to perceived discrimination. Positive attitudes contribute to adopting more active responses (Wan, 2003), whereas negative attributions seem to relate to compensatory behaviors (Verwiebe et al., 2016). Perceived controllability of situations in which perceived discrimination occurs is an important determinant of coping (Clark et al. 1999; Puhl & Brownell, 2003). However, results are mixed. Perceived controllability may lead to more active (Miller & Major, 2000; Puhl & Brownell, 2003) or more passive responses (Beiser et al. 2001).

Several personality traits associate with responses to perceived discrimination, among them self-esteem, self-efficacy, optimism, trait anxiety, Type A behavior, neuroticism, proactive personality, and hardiness (Clark et al., 1999; Puhl & Brownell, 2003; Verkuyten & Nekee, 2001). For example, self-esteem is associated with active coping (Verkuyten & Nekuee, 2001). Those high in neuroticism engage in more social coping than those low in this trait (Bolger & Zuckerman, 1995). Low self-efficacy and trait anxiety may lead to less active responses, whereas optimism and proactive personality lead to more active responses (Kim et al. 2011; Mallet & Swim, 2009; Puhl & Brownell, 2003).

Affect and values may also influence responses to perceived discrimination. Valuing employment security may lead to passive responses (Grima, 2011), whereas valuing uniqueness may lead to more active responses (Wan, 2003). In terms of affect, Christian et al. (2000) suggest that guilt is associated with compensation.

Cost-benefit calculations relate to the decision either to respond to perceived discrimination or to not respond (Contrada et al., 2000; Hyers, 2007; Lalonde et al. 1995; Livingston, 1982; Puhl & Brownell, 2003). Stereotype threat, a psychological state induced by situational cues, may lead individuals to respond in passive ways to perceived discrimination (Contrada et al. 2000). Research also suggests that psychological stress may be associated with passive responses to perceived discrimination and diminished social support (Puhl, 2005).

We know significantly less about interpersonal, group, organizational, and environmental antecedents of responses to perceived discrimination. The type of perpetrator (e.g., supervisor, coworker, or client) and the differential power between perpetrator and victim may affect the type of response and the decision to adopt a more active or a more passive response (Bingham & Scherer, 1993; Hyers, 2007; Hudson et al., 2016; Livingston, 1982). Other interpersonal antecedents can include the presence of mentors at work and the presence of fair treatment from key organizational leaders (Grijalva & Coombs, 1997; Stone & Colella, 1996).

In terms of groups, social networks and group identity may facilitate active responses to perceived discrimination, such as advocacy seeking (Puhl & Brownell, 2003). Work group cohesion may also facilitate the selection of responses to perceived discrimination, but researchers need to examine types of responses (Terpstra & Baker, 1986). In addition, we can only speculate that work group composition may facilitate active responses to perceived discrimination (Ragins & Cornwell, 2001).

In terms of organizational antecedents, the adoption of policies against discrimination may relate to active responses, such as confrontation and advocacy seeking (Ragins & Cornwell, 2001; Terpstra & Baker, 1986). Employees who perceive a climate unsupportive of discriminatory treatment may be more likely to confront the perpetrator (Bingham & Scherer, 1993). In addition, evidence suggests that organizational size correlates with more active responses such as confrontation and advocacy seeking (Ngo et al. 2002).

Lastly, the overall environment in which organizations operate may exert influence on the type of response an individual may select. For example, economic and labor market conditions may lead to passive responses when unemployment is high. Legislation may relate to actively reporting perceptions of discriminatory treatment (Ragins & Cornwell, 2001). Culture may explain the selection of certain coping responses, such as social coping (Christian et al., 2000). Finally, the media have been capturing massive amounts of evidence of the #metoo movement, revealing the relationship between social networks and advocacy seeking.

We know significantly less about outcomes of responses to perceive discrimination than about antecedents of these responses. St. Jean and Feagin (1997) argue that compensation relates to performance loss. Wagstaff, Triana, Kim, & Al-Riyami (2015) found that social coping interacting with self-evaluations lowers employee withdrawal behaviors. Active forms of coping, such as confrontation and advocacy seeking, negatively relate to perceptions of psychological stress (Kaiser & Miller, 2004; Noor & Shaker, 2017). Compensation may also relate to perceived career success and reduce anxiety, although it may also increase negative affect and lower authenticity (Singletary & Hebl, 2009; Seibert et al., 1999), and social coping may increase turnover intentions (Munson et al., 2000). Finally, confrontation increases the likelihood of moving up the organizational ladder (Haar & Morash, 2013).

Of all the outcomes of responses to perceived discrimination, we know far less about interpersonal and organizational outcomes. In terms of interpersonal outcomes, monetary compensation relates to reporting less interpersonal discrimination (Singletary & Hebl, 2009). Confrontation in the form of straight talk as a way to stop discrimination increases the span of influence (Haar & Morash, 2013). As for organizational outcomes, we join others in suggesting that advocacy seeking may result in changes to policies and practices regarding selection systems, evaluation procedures, or reward systems (Stone & Colella, 1996).

STUDY 1: ITEM GENERATION AND CONTENT VALIDATION

In this study, we seek to generate an initial set of items to measure responses to perceived discriminatory treatment at work as well as to content validate these items. In doing so, we draw primarily from Knapp et al. (1997) and from our literature review to theoretically derive the items in our scale. We also follow an inductive approach to generate the items (Hinkin, 1998). This approach involves asking adults with work experience about their reactions to discrimination at work so that we can understand how the average person conceptualizes his/her responses to discriminatory treatment at work.

Sample and Procedure

For the item generation, participants included 43 MBA students from a southwestern university and 32 adults contacted in the downtown plaza of a southwestern city in the United States. Participants answered a survey asking them if they had ever been discriminated against at work by a supervisor. If the answer was "no," they only answered demographic questions and were finished with the survey. If the answer was "yes," one of the questions asked was: "What did you do in response to that treatment?"

Of the 75 respondents, 34 reported having been discriminated against by their supervisor. A total of 20% of the cases were related to racial/ethnic background, 25% to gender, 13% to age, 13% to national origin, and 30% to other reasons for discrimination. Of these final participants, 44% were female. The average age was 29 for the MBA students and between 20 and 30 for the adults contacted at the plaza. A total of 73% were Hispanic, 18% White, 3% African American, 3% Asian American, and 3% Other.

Analyses and Results

In order to generate the items, two graduate students blind to the purpose of the study content analyzed the responses provided by the participants in the study (Aronson, Ellsworth, Carlsmith, & Gonzalez, 1990; Krippendorff, 2004). Following Knapp et al. (1997), we established categorical distinctions and their definitions (i.e., avoidance/denial, confrontation, social coping, and advocacy seeking), and these categories were used to classify the answers. We obtained Kappa, a coefficient of agreement for nominal scales (Cohen, 1960). A total of 90% of the judgments made by the two graduate students were agreements (with chance excluded). Next, we analyzed the disagreements case by case. After understanding the sources of these disagreements, the graduate students reached complete agreement. This exercise confirmed that reactions to discriminatory treatment from a supervisor could easily be categorized within Knapp et al.'s four-factor framework. Therefore, we proceeded to generate items for our scale based on Knapp et al.'s framework, our literature review, and the examples collected in the sample of adults with work experience.

The items reflected targets' behaviors in response to discriminatory treatment at work (e.g., "I confront my supervisor directly"). One Ph.D. and one graduate student generated items independently from each other. These items were reviewed following the guidelines suggested by DeVellis (1991) and Spector (1992). As a result, we discarded several items and added new items, retaining a total of 34 items.

For the content validity analysis, eight Ph.D. students participated in the study. We provided definitions of the four responses to discriminatory treatment at work. Then we asked the students to match each item with the corresponding response following the guidelines given by Hinkin (1998). In order for an item to be retained, 75% of respondents had to correctly classify the item in the expected response. Results indicated that of the 34 items, 32 were classified in the expected category by 75% or more of the students. This resulted in 32 items representing avoidance/denial, social coping, confrontation, and advocacy seeking.

STUDY 2: CONFIRMATORY FACTOR ANALYSIS

The purpose of this study was to validate our scale through confirmatory factor analysis (CFA). A CFA was used because we hypothesized a four-factor model a priori based on Knapp et al. (1997).

Sample and Procedures

Participants were recruited through StudyResponse.org to answer a survey on the Internet. StudyResponse is a service with more than 95,000 registered individuals who agree to receive solicitations to answer scholarly research surveys in exchange for prizes such as gift certificates. Research conducted by Stanton (1998) supports the validity of data collected through the Internet. A condition for participating in the study was that participants had to be currently working U.S. residents. A total of 4,883 randomly selected persons from the StudyResponse database were invited to participate, of which 678 answered the survey, representing a 13.9% response rate. This response rate is similar to other data collections on the Internet (Piccolo & Colquitt, 2006). Participants were asked if they had ever experienced discrimination from their supervisor. A total of 104 answered "yes" and were retained for further analysis. In this sub-sample, most participants were females (76%) and 40 years old on average. The racial/ethnic background was as follows: 83.8% Caucasian, 3.8% African American, 3.8% Asian American, 2.9% Hispanic, 2.9% Native American, and 2.8% Other.

Measures

Responses to Discrimination from Supervisors. "I become the best worker possible" and "I confront the supervisor about the mistreatment" are examples of items. Drawing from Carver, Scheier, & Weintraub (1989), we selected the following response options: 1. (I usually don't do this at all), 2. (I usually do this a little bit), 3. (I usually do this a medium amount), and 4. (I usually do this a lot). The reliability was $\alpha = .89$ for confrontation, $\alpha = .79$ for avoidance/denial, $\alpha = .77$ for social coping, and $\alpha = .87$ for advocacy seeking.

Analyses and Results

Before running the CFA, we reduced the number of items in the scale to make it user-friendly (i.e., not too long) following Netemeyer, Bearden, and Sharma (2003). For the item reduction, we used two different samples (labeled here A and B for clarity) not reported in this paper (available from the first author). First, we conducted an exploratory factor (EFA) analysis with sample A. Then, we examined the item-correlations, the item-to-total correlations, and the reliabilities of the factors in the scale with the items loaded in the EFA. As a result of this analysis, we decided to re-labeled avoidance/denial as compensation. Of the eight original items that loaded on the EFA, the best three items measuring the self-focus and self-response strategy were mainly related to compensation to achieve goals despite the existence of discrimination (Miller & Major, 2000; Singletary & Hebl, 2009). Only one of the three items was related to avoidance; the other two items represented working harder. None of the three items was related to denial. Therefore, we named this factor "Compensation." Next, still working with sample A, we ran a CFA and analyzed the modification indices and the standardized residuals. We then cross-validated the findings with sample B. As a result of these analyses, we reduced the number of items in the scale from 32 to 12. The sample reported in Study 2 of this paper was used to run the CFA with a total of 12 items (see Table 10.2).

We ran a CFA using LISREL 8.72. We used maximum likelihood to estimate the model. The standardized loadings for the lambda matrix are shown in Table 10.2. The overall fit of the model was good, $\chi^2(48) = 72.08$, $p < .05$, NNFI = .95, CFI = .95, SRMR = .06, RMSEA < .05. We compared the four-factor solution to a three-, two-, or one-factor solution. The four-factor solution had a better fit than any of the simpler models, and the change in chi-square was significantly different for all comparisons. We found that responses to discriminatory treatment at work by a supervisor were conceptualized in four different ways. Therefore, Knapp et al.'s (1997) framework was generally supported, with the exception that instead of avoidance/denial, one of the four factors of the scale was better represented as compensation. The scale offers good reliability, satisfactory loadings, and acceptable fit indices.

TABLE 10.2. Standardized Loadings of Responses to Perceived Discriminatory Treatment at Work

Items	Confrontation		Compensation		Advocacy Seeking		Social Coping	
	Study 2	Study 3	Study 2	Study 3	Study 2	Study 3	Study 2	Study 3
1. I confront the supervisor about the mistreatment.*a	.90	.83						
2. I bring up the problem with my supervisor.	.94	.86						
3. I let my supervisor know that I am uncomfortable.	.73	.75						
4. I become the best worker possible.*			.71	.79				
5. I make sure I do everything right at work.			.86	.83				
6. I avoid doing anything wrong at work.			.69	.53				
7. I file a formal report.*					.71	.79		
8. I file a report with my human resource department.					.94	.83		
9. I contact the human resource office to see if this treatment is appropriate					.84	.53		
10. I ask my coworkers why my supervisor treats me that way.*							.53	.55
11. I complain about the mistreatment with my intimate friends at work.							.89	.74
12. I talk about my supervisor's mistreatment of me with my coworkers.							.77	.92

a Items with asterisks were set to 1 for identification purposes in running the CFA.

STUDY 3: CONVERGENT, DISCRIMINANT,
AND CRITERION-RELATED VALIDITY

To further analyze the validity of the scale, we examined the convergent, discriminant, and criterion-related validity. For the convergent and discriminant validity of the scale we drew from: a) the multitrait-multimethod (MTMM) technique (Campbell & Fiske, 1959) by using two different approaches: self-responses and observers' responses to discriminatory treatment at work, and b) the technique proposed by Anderson and Gerbing (1988). In performing Anderson and Gerbing's test, we examined if the items of the scale fell on their predicted constructs. Items with high loadings on a predicted construct would be evidence of convergent validity. To examine the discriminant validity, we constrained the estimated correlation parameter between two constructs (factors of the scale) to 1.0 and then ran the same analysis. However, at this point, the model was unconstrained. A significantly lower chi-square value for the unconstrained model would indicate that the constructs are different. We ran this analysis for every pair of factors in the scale.

We further analyzed the discriminant validity by assessing correlations between the four responses to discrimination and other relevant variables. In particular, we drew from the literature on complaining, which is defined as a behavioral expression of dissatisfaction when expectations are not met (Kowalski, 1996). Given that complaining is mainly an interpersonal process (Kowalski, 1996), we expect that complaining will be positively related to the responses involving others (social coping, confrontation, and advocacy seeking) and negatively related to the self-focused response (compensation). We also examined the correlation between the four responses to discrimination and social desirability, the tendency for people to give socially correct answers. This analysis is common practice in scale development for scales that measure discrimination and other sensitive topics. Ideally, the factors in the scale should not be highly and positively correlated with social desirability.

The responses to discriminatory treatment at work should also relate to other personality traits. We reason that compensation is positively related to proactive personality, or the extent to which people take action to influence their environments (Crant, 2000). Individuals who are high on proactive personality take action, show initiative, and persevere. With increased compensation, victims face the environment and change it to overcome discrimination at work.

We also reason that social coping is positively related to neuroticism, a personality trait that relates to being anxious, insecure, emotional, fearful, depressed, and moody (Judge & Bono, 2000; Salgado, 1997). In examining different forms of interpersonal conflict, Bolger and Zuckerman (1995) found that those high in neuroticism engaged in significantly more social coping than those low in neuroticism.

To examine the criterion-related validity (Spector, 1992), we analyzed the main effects of the four responses to perceived discriminatory treatment at work and three outcomes: perceived career success, perceived stress, and turnover intentions. Career success, or the real or perceived achievements individuals have accumulated as a result of their work experiences (Judge et al. 1999), is positively related to compensation. Theory and empirical evidence show that the use of increased positivity by trying to change one's current circumstances relates to both objective and subjective career success (Seibert et al., 1999). We also expect that social coping, confrontation, and advocacy seeking are related to stress, an unpleasant emotional experience associated with fear, dread, anxiety, irritation, annoyance, anger, sadness, grief, and depression (Motowidlo, Pakcard, & Maning, 1986). Active or approach coping, such as confrontation and advocacy seeking, relates to efforts to influence the stressful event or situation and change the situation of being the target of discrimination (Kaiser & Miller, 2004). Therefore, confrontation and advocacy seeking will be negatively associated with stress. Finally, we also hypothesize that stress and turnover intentions are positively associated with social coping because there are many personal and social costs attached to the seeking of social support (Munson et al., 2000).

Sample and Procedures

Study 3's participants completed all measures in one survey. They were recruited through StudyResponse, but the participants from Study 2 were excluded. A total of 9,739 employed U.S. residents were invited to participate, of which 894 answered the survey, representing a 9.18% response rate. Of the 894 participants, 164 answered our survey, and declared that they were discriminated against by their supervisor and were currently working. Of the 164 participants, approximately 71% were females, and the average age was about 42. The majority were Caucasian (81.4%), followed by African American (6.6%), Asian/Asian American (4.8%), Hispanic (3%), and Other (3.3%). In addition, 126 out of the 164 participants also declared that they had an observer who could take part in a survey for us in which the observer would answer questions about the participants in our study. StudyResponse contacted these 126 participants to request the name and e-mail address of the observer. In the end, we obtained 80 participant/observer pairs. Over 88% of the observers reported that they knew the StudyResponse participant very or extremely well.

Measures

Unless otherwise indicated, responses to the measures were in a Likert format from 1 (strongly disagree) to 6 (strongly agree).

Responses to Discrimination from Supervisors. Study 3's internal coefficient reliabilities for compensation, social coping, confrontation, and advocacy seeking were: $\alpha = .75$, $\alpha = .76$, $\alpha = .86$, and $\alpha = .88$ for participants and $\alpha = .71$, $\alpha = .65$, $\alpha = .86$, and $\alpha = .85$ for observers, respectively.

Complaining. We used three items from Kowalski (2003). A sample item was "Whenever I am dissatisfied, I readily express it to other people." The reliability was α = .70.

Turnover Intentions. We used one item from Netemeyer, Bolen, and McMurrian (1996) and one from Seashore, Lawler, Mirvis, and Cammann (1982). One of the items for this measure was "I intend to quit my present job." The reliability was α = .78.

Social Desirability. We used the M-C 1(10) of Strahan and Gerbasi (1972). "I'm always willing to admit it when I make a mistake" is a sample item. The reliability was α = .79.

Proactive Personality. We used six items (Seibert et al. 1999). For example, one item stated: "If I see something that I do not like, I fix it." The reliability was α = .87.

Neuroticism: We measured neuroticism with 10 items (Goldberg 1990, 1992). "I get stressed out easily" is an example of one of the items. Participants responded on a 6-point scale ranging from 1 (extremely inaccurate) to 6 (extremely accurate). The Cronbach's alpha reliability for this measure was .94.

Perceived Career Success. We used three items (Turban & Dougherty, 1994). "How successful has your career been?" is an example of one of the items. Responses were from 1 (very unsuccessful) to 6 (very successful). The Cronbach's alpha reliability was α = .93.

Perceived Stress. We wrote one item for this study: "I often feel very stressed at work." Several studies show that single-item measures can be both valid and reliable (Robins, Hendin, & Trzesniewski, 2001; Wanous & Hudy, 2001; Wanous, Reichers, & Hudy, 1997).

Analyses and Results

We found evidence in support of convergent validity (see Table 10.2). All estimated coefficients were significant on their expected underlying constructs (Anderson & Gerbing, 1988). We also found support for the discriminant validity of all the possible pairs of factors in the scale using Anderson and Gerbing's technique. A significantly lower chi-square value for the unconstrained model, which indicates a better model fit, shows that the constructs were different from each other for all pairs of constructs (results available from the first author).

In addition, evidence of Study 3's discriminant validity was as expected. The four-factor structure (i.e., compensation, social coping, confrontation, and advocacy seeking) had better fit indices, than a three-, two-, or one-factor solution. Moreover, the ΔX^2 indicated that the four-factor structure was better when compared to a three-, two-, and one-factor structure.

We found further evidence of discriminant validity. As expected, complaining had a positive correlation with social coping ($r = .33$, $p < .001$), confrontation ($r = .38$, $p < .001$), and advocacy seeking ($r = .30$, $p < .001$), and a negative correlation with compensation ($r = -.36$, $p < .01$; see Table 10.3). The correlations between ad-

TABLE 10.3. Means, Standard Deviations, and Correlations for Discriminant and Criterion-Related Validity

Variables	Mean	SD	1	2	3	4	5	6	7	8	9	10	11
1. Compensation	3.20	.80	—										
2. Social coping	2.22	.82	-.24**	—									
3. Confrontation	1.93	.89	-.12	.17*	—								
4. Advocacy seeking	1.51	.77	-.09	.08	.53**	—							
5. Social desirability	4.02	.79	.34**	-.24**	-.08	-.12	—						
6. Complaining	3.23	1.10	-.36**	.33**	.38**	.30**	-.37**	—					
7. Proactive personality	4.68	.78	.33**	-.09	.06	-.03	.11	.11	—				
8. Neuroticism	3.19	1.16	-.14	.33**	-.06	.02	-.46**	.43**	-.22**	—			
9. Perceived stress	3.90	1.56	.14	.13	-.17*	-.10	-.03	.14	-.07	.48**	—		
10. Perceived career success	4.22	1.04	.26**	-.11	.04	.01	.05	-.06	.41**	-.20**	-.05	—	
11. Turnover intentions	3.13	1.49	-.15	.29**	-.01	-.10	-.09	.25**	-.11	.41**	.33**	-.21**	—

Note. N = 163, Cronbach's alpha reliabilities are given on the diagonals.
* p < .05, **p < .01 (two-tailed test).

vocacy seeking and social desirability and between confrontation and social desirability were not significant ($r = -.12$, $p = ns$ for advocacy seeking and $r = -.08$, $p = ns$ for confrontation). Furthermore, the correlation between social coping and social desirability was negative and significant ($r = -.24$, $p < .01$). The only positive and significant correlation was between social desirability and compensation ($r = .34$, $p < .01$). However, the magnitude of the correlation indicates that the two constructs are not redundant. Moreover, no particular item was responsible for this correlation. Each of the three items correlated at a level lower than .30. As expected, the correlation between compensation and proactive personality was $r = .33$, $p < .001$. Social coping correlated positively with neuroticism, $r = .33$, $p < .001$.

In addition, we followed Podsakoff, MacKenzie, Lee, and Podsakoff's (2003) recommendation and used the social desirability scale as a fifth method-effect factor. To run the CFA, we parceled the measure of social desirability because the number of parameters to be estimated required a greater sample size than the one obtained, using the guideline to have at least five data points per parameter (Bentler & Chou, 1987). A five-factor solution provided a better fit to the data ($\chi^2 = 91.69$, df = 80, RMSEA = .03, NNFI = .99, CFI = .99, SRMR = .05) compared to various four-factor solutions. Overall, results suggest that socially desirable responses are not a threat to measuring responses to perceived supervisor discrimination.

The correlations for the multitrait-multimethod matrix are shown in Table 10.3. Correlations were broken down by source (self versus observer report). As shown in Table 10.4, the correlations among self reports and observer reports of the four responses ranged from $r = .35$, $p < .01$ to $r = .44$, $p < .01$. Overall, re-

TABLE 10.4. Multitrait-Multimethod Matrix of Responses to Discrimination from Supervisors in Study 3

Variables	Self-report				Observer			
	1	2	3	4	1	2	3	4
Self-report								
1. Compensation	.70							
2. Social coping	-.18	.76						
3. Confrontation	-.04	.06	.89					
4. Advocacy seeking	-.23*	.02	.63**	.89				
Observer								
1. Compensation	.35**	-.12	-.16	-.18	.71			
2. Social coping	-.07	.37**	-.01	-.02	.05	.65		
3. Confrontation	.26*	-.16	.35**	.23*	.17	.26*	.86	
4. Advocacy seeking	.01	-.04	.15	.44**	-.11	.24*	.48**	.85

Note. N = 80, Cronbach's alpha reliabilities are given on the diagonals.
* p < .05, ** p < .01 (two-tailed test).

TABLE 10.5.   Criterion-Related Validity

Variable	Perceived Career Success	Perceived Stress	Turnover Intentions
Social coping	-.06[a]	.20**	.27***
Confrontation	.09	-.18*	.01
Advocacy seeking	-.00	-.00	-.13
Compensation	.26***	.17*	-.09
F	3.33**	3.46**	4.58**
R^2	.08	.08	.11
N = 163.			

a = Standardized coefficients are reported.
* $p \leq .05$, ** $p \leq .01$, *** $p \leq .001$ (two-tailed test).

sults indicate that the monotrait-heteromethod correlations (e.g., observer reports of the participant's compensation and self-reported compensation) were stronger than the heterotrait-heteromethod correlations (e.g., observer reports of participant's compensation and self-reported social coping). Moreover, the correlations between self and observer reports for the same response to discrimination (e.g., self-report of confrontation and observer reports of confrontation) were higher than the correlations between self-reports of different responses to discrimination (e.g., self-report of compensation and self-report of social coping) except for the correlation between the self-report of advocacy seeking and confrontation. Overall, results provide support for the convergent and discriminant validity of the measure of responses to perceived discrimination from supervisors.

Next, we conducted a multiple regression analysis to test the criterion-related validity. Correlations, means, and standard deviations for the criterion-related validity analysis are shown in Table 10.3. We regressed perceived stress, perceived career success, and turnover intentions on the four responses to perceived discriminatory treatment at work (see Table 10.5). As expected, perceived stress was associated with confrontation, $\beta = -.18, p \leq .05$, and social coping, $\beta = .20, p \leq .01$, but it was not associated with advocacy seeking. Also, perceived career success was associated with compensation, $\beta = .26, p \leq .001$. Finally, turnover intentions were positively associated with social coping, $\beta = .27, p \leq .001$.

Discussion

Overall, results show evidence of the convergent and discriminant validity of the responses to discriminatory treatment at work. Advocacy seeking, confrontation, social coping, and compensation are different from each other and, as expected, they relate to other constructs. However, advocacy seeking was not associated with perceived stress as expected. One alternative explanation of this result is the low variance for this measure, which is the lowest of the four responses to perceived discrimination.

GENERAL DISCUSSION

Contributions

As subtle discrimination leads to more ambiguity surrounding the reason(s) for discrimination, we focus our attention on responses to perceived discrimination from supervisors irrespective of reason(s), and we develop a measure that captures these responses. We contribute to the literature on responses to discriminatory treatment at work by taking the theoretical framework elaborated by Knapp et al. (1997) for responses to sexual harassment and applying it to discrimination more generally. Folkman and Lazarus (1980, p. 229) recognized the need for such an approach when they argued that "It may be that to identify coping styles that transcend situation contexts, we must look at another level of abstraction." In this study, we examined responses given by victims who are certain that they were discriminated against, yet may not be able to single out the reason for discrimination. We also re-assessed one of the four dimensions (i.e., avoidance/denial) and labeled it "compensation." We provide theoretical and empirical evidence of the relationship between the four responses to discriminatory treatment at work and individual differences, emotions, and work attitudes.

Implications

Our results imply that in spite of the existence of idiosyncratic responses due to specific reasons for discrimination, some responses are common across reasons. Our study facilitates and integrates research conducted by scholars from many different theoretical perspectives, who all embarked on examining responses to various reasons for discrimination.

We found that confrontation is negatively associated with perceived stress. This finding is important because it implies that a situation that may be seen as negative (i.e., an employee confronting a supervisor) may be a warning sign and an opportunity to mitigate perceived mistreatment and remove stressors. However, current knowledge suggests that situations such as this may not be properly managed by everyone. Goldman et al. (2004) showed that 26% of their participants reported receiving no reply at all when they complained. The management of that confrontation episode by the supervisor could have set the stage for either an escalation or a mitigation of this problem.

Limitations and Future Research

One theoretical limitation of our research is that we focus on responses to discrimination when victims explicitly state that they have been discriminated against. However, in many cases, victims may respond to situations they do not recognize as discrimination. In future research, scholars may devise a measure that encompasses situations in which victims are not sure if they have been discriminated against. In addition, we paid less attention to situation-specific responses (e.g., losing weight in response to weight discrimination) in favor of general responses to discrimination. Although this approach has limitations, we proceeded in this manner in order to reduce the complexity inherent in responses to discrimination under circumstances of ambiguity. However, in no way do we wish to disregard research conducted on responses to discriminatory treatment for specific reasons for discrimination. This research is important in its own way and should continue whenever possible.

Our study also had limitations in our samples. First, we had to discard data from many participants because the majority reported that they had never been discriminated against at work by their supervisor. In part, this could be a function of the participants not having had that experience. Alternatively, victims may not be able to label the experience as discrimination because of the subtleness of discrimination in today's society. However, there is another potential explanation for the high number of respondents reporting that they had never been discriminated against. The theory of personal/group discrimination discrepancy (and empirical evidence based on this theory) indicates that individuals tend to notice discrimination toward their in-group members but not toward themselves (Taylor, Wright, Moghaddam, & Lalonde, 1990). The fact that we had to discard many participants also explains why we did not compare how targets respond to discriminatory treatment when the perpetrator is the supervisor as opposed to a coworker (or other perpetrators). We chose to focus on supervisors because they have legitimate authority over the employee. However, future research may examine responses to discriminatory treatment with different types of perpetrators, including coworkers.

Second, Study's 1 sample was mainly Hispanic. We tried to offset this limitation by collecting more diverse samples in the other two studies (McGrath, 1981). Empirically, it is important to note that racial or ethnic background is not related to any of the four responses to perceived discriminatory treatment at work in any of the samples we collected for this research.

Third, as a result of the attrition, we had small sample sizes. Nevertheless, our empirical evidence suggests that our samples were sufficient for us to run the analyses. For example, although the samples used to run the confirmatory factor analyses were small, the loadings and fit indices provided evidence of the validity of our measure. We also experienced attrition from participants who were invited to answer our surveys compared to those who actually answered. Consequently, our final responses and findings may generalize best to the demographic groups that ultimately answered our survey instruments. Still, non-representative samples can advance our understanding of sensitive topics where data are difficult to collect (Goldman et al., 2006). Future research may cross-validate the results of this study with other demographic groups.

Related to small sample sizes, response rates were very low. Although this represents an empirical limitation, it is important to note that we replicated the four-factor structure in four different samples, only two of which are reported in this paper due to length limitations. According to Tsang and Kwan (1999), replicated findings provide evidence of the validity and reliability of the measurement instrument used.

Finally, we had limitations in our measures. We limited our examination of the validity of our measures to self-reported measures and those of significant others. Future research may validate the instrument with experimental research in which a discrimination manipulation is used and responses are observed and coded by independent raters.

The use of our measurement instrument should enable future research on antecedents and consequences of responses to supervisor discrimination. As shown in Figure 10.1, we know much more about individual-level antecedents of responses to perceived discrimination than about interpersonal, group, organizational, and environmental antecedents. Particularly at the individual level of analysis, more research is needed to examine which victims of perceived discrimination respond to mistreatment as well as why, when, and how they do so. For example, those with high self-efficacy may be better equipped to address mistreatment and confront the perpetrator (Puhl & Brownell, 2003). As for outcomes, Figure 10,1 illustrates how little we know at all levels of analysis and thus points to a need for more research on both antecedents and outcomes of responses to discrimination, particularly for the purpose of identifying best practices and to lessen the impact of perceived discrimination. More importantly, Figure 10.1 calls for an overarching theoretical model of antecedents and outcomes of responses to perceived discrimination considering key mediators of these relationships. In addition, some of the evidence we shared in reviewing the literature also suggests the presence of moderators. In terms of measurement, future research may focus on developing measures of responses to perceived discrimination with other perpetrators, such as coworkers, customers, or suppliers. The measure of responses to perceived discrimination developed and validated in this article will facilitate this important future research.

By better understanding how targets generally respond to perceived discrimination from supervisors, we will be better able to mitigate potentially negative effects of discrimination. This could be achieved by devising interventions capable of solving the problems associated with these types of responses. With this information in hand, we can proactively respond in effective ways that will help prevent further harm to both the victim of alleged discrimination and the organization.

REFERENCES[1]

Anderson, J. C., & Gerbing, D. W. (1988). Structural equation modelling in practice: A review and recommended two-step approach. *Psychological Bulletin, 103,* 411–423.

---

[1]References with * refer to articles included in Table 10.1.

*Armenta, B. M., Stroebe, K., Scheibe, S., Postmes, T., & Van Yperen, N. W. (2017). Feeling younger and identifying with older adults: Testing two routes to maintaining well-being in the face of age discrimination. *PLoS ONE, 12*, 1–21.

Aronson, E., Ellsworth, P. C., Carlsmith, J. M., & Gonzalez, M. H. (1990). *Methods of research in social psychology*. Boston, MA: McGraw-Hill.

Barnes, P. W., & Lightsey, O. R. (2005). Perceived racist discrimination, coping, stress, and life satisfaction. *Journal of Multicultural Counseling and Development, 33*, 48–61.

*Beiser, M., Noh, S., Hou, F., Kaspar, V., & Rummens, J. (2001). Southeast Asian refugees' perceptions of racial discrimination in Canada. *Canadian Ethnic Studies, 33*, 46–70.

Benokraitis, N. V. (1997). *Subtle sexism: Current practices and prospects for change*. Thousand Oaks, CA: Sage Publications.

Bentler, P. M., & Chou, C. (1987). Practical issues in structural modeling. *Sociological Methods and Research, 16*, 78–117.

*Bingham, S. G., & Scherer, L. L. (1993). Factors associated with responses to sexual harassment and satisfaction with outcome. *Sex Roles, 29*, 239–269.

*Birt, C. M., & Dion, K. L. (1987). Relative deprivation theory and responses to discrimination in a gay male and lesbian sample. *British Journal of Social Psychology, 26*, 139–145.

Bolger, N., & Zuckerman, A. (1995). A framework for studying personality in the stress process. *Journal of Personality and Social Psychology, 69*, 890–902.

Byng, M. D. (1998). Mediating discrimination: Resisting oppression among African American Muslim women. *Social Problems, 45*, 473–487.

Campbell, D. T., & Fiske, D. W. (1959). Convergent and discriminant validation by the multitrait-multimethod matrix. *Psychological Bulletin, 56*, 81–105.

Carver, C. S., Scheier, M. F., & Weintraub, J. K. (1989). Assessing coping strategies: A theoretically based approach. *Journal of Personality and Social Psychology, 56*, 267–283.

*Christian, F. M., Al-Mateen, C. S., Webb, C. T., & Donatelli, L. S. (2000). Stress, coping, and the mental health of African American women. In N. J. Burgess, & E. Brown (Eds.), *African American woman: An ecological perspective* (pp. 135–159). New York, NY: Falmer Press.

*Chung, Y. B. (2001). Work discrimination and coping strategies: Conceptual frameworks for counseling lesbian, gay, and bisexual clients. *The Career Development Quarterly, 50*, 33–44.

*Chung, Y. B., Williams, W., & Dispenza, F. (2009). Validating work discrimination and coping strategy models for sexual minorities. *The Career Development Quarterly, 58*, 162–170.

*Clark, R., Anderson, N. B., Clark, V. R., & Williams, D. R. (1999). Racism as a stressor for African Americans: A biopsychosocial model. *American Psychologist, 54*, 805–816.

Cohen, J. (1960). A coefficient of agreement for nominal scales. *Educational and Psychological Measurement, 20*, 37–46.

*Colella, A. (1996). Organizational socialization of newcomers with disabilities: A framework for future research. *Research in Personnel and Human Resources Management, 14*, 351–417.

Colella, A., Hebl, M., & King, E. (2017). One hundred years of discrimination research in the *Journal of Applied Psychology*: A sobering synopsis. *Journal of Applied Psychology, 102*(3), 500–513.

*Contrada, R. J., Ashmore, R. D., Gary, M. L., Coups, E., Egeth, J. D., Sewell, A., Ewell, K., Goyal, T. M., & Chasse, V. (2000). Ethnicity-related sources of stress and their effects on well-being. *Current Directions in Psychological Science, 9,* 136–139.

Cortina, L. M. & Wasti, S. A. (2005). Profiles in coping: Responses to sexual harassment across persons, organizations, and cultures. *Journal of Applied Psychology, 90,* 182–192.

Crant, J. M. (2000). Proactive behavior in organizations. *Journal of Management, 26,* 435–462.

Crocker, J., Major, B., & Steele, C. (1998). Social stigma. In D. T. Gilbert, S. T. Fiske, & G. Lindzey (Eds.), *The handbook of social psychology* (Vols. 1 and 2, pp. 504–553). New York, NY: McGraw-Hill.

*Deaux, K., & Ethier, K. A. (1998). Negotiating social identity. In J. K. Swim, & C. Stangor (Eds.), *Prejudice: The target's perspective* (pp. 301–323). San Diego, CA: Academic Press.

Deitch, E. A., Barsky, A., Butz, R. M., Chan, S., Brief, A. P., & Bradley, J. C. (2003). Subtle yet significant: The existence and impact of everyday racial discrimination in the workplace. *Human Relations, 56,* 1299–1324.

DeVellis, R. F. (1991). *Scale development: Theory and applications.* London, UK: Sage Publications.

Dipboye, R. L., & Colella, A. (2005). *Discrimination at work: The psychological and organizational bases.* Mahwah, NJ: Lawrence Erlbaum Associates.

Elligan, D., & Utsey, S. O. (1999). Utility of an African-centered support group for African American men confronting societal racism and oppression. *Cultural Diversity and Ethnic Minority Psychology, 5,* 156–165.

*Feagin, J. R. (1991). The continuing significance of race: Antiblack discrimination in public places. *American Sociological Review, 56,* 101–116.

*Feagin, J. R., & Sikes, M. P. (1994). *Living with racism: The Black middle class experience.* Boston, MA: Beacon Press.

*Fleming, C. M., Lamont, M., & Welburn, J. A. (2012). African Americans respond to stigmatization: The meanings and salience of confronting, deflecting conflict, educating the ignorant and 'managing the self.' *Ethnic and Racial Studies, 35,* 400–417.

Folkman, S., & Lazarus, R. S. (1980). An analysis of coping in a middle-aged community sample. *Journal of Health and Social Behavior, 21,* 219–239.

Goldberg, L. R. (1990). An alternative "description of personality": The Big-Five factor structure. *Journal of Personality and Social Psychology, 59,* 1216–1229.

Goldberg, L. R. (1992). The development of markers for the Big-Five factor structure. *Psychological Assessment, 4,* 26–42.

Goldman, B. M., Gutek, B. A., Stein, J. H., & Lewis, K. (2006). Employment discrimination in organizations: Antecedents and consequences. *Journal of Management, 32,* 786–830.

Goldman, B. M., Paddock, E. L., & Cropanzano, R. (2004). A transformational model of legal claiming. *Journal of Managerial Issues, 16*(4), 417–441.

*Grijalva, C. A., & Holman Coombs, R. (1997). Latinas in medicine: Stressors, survival skills, and strengths. *Aztlán, 22,* 67–88.

*Grima, F. (2011). The influence of age management policies on older employee work relationships with their company. *The International Journal of Human Resource Management, 22,* 1312–1332.

Groth, M., Goldman, B. M., Gilliland, S. W., & Bies, R. J. (2002). Commitment to legal claiming: Influences of attributions, social guidance, and organizational tenure. *Journal of Applied Psychology*, *87*, 781–788.

*Haarr, R. N., & Morash, M. (2013). The effect of rank on police women coping with discrimination and harassment. *Police Quarterly*, *16*, 395–419.

*Hagey, R., Choudhry, U., Guruge, S., Turrittin, J., Collins, E., & Lee, R. (2001). Immigrant nurses' experience of racism. *Journal of Nursing Scholarship*, *33*, 389–394.

*Hametner, K. (2012). From retreating to resisting: How Austrian-Turkish women deal with experiences of racism. *Migration Letters*, *11*, 288–299.

Hametner, K. (2014). From retreating to resisting: How Austrian-Turkish women deal with experiences of racism. *Migration Letters*, *11*(3), 288–299.

*Haslett, B. B., & Lipman, S. (1997). Micro inequities: Up close and personal. In N. V. Benokraitis (Ed.), *Subtle sexism: Current practices and prospects for change* (pp. 34–53). Thousand Oaks, CA: Sage Publications.

Hinkin, T. R. (1998). A brief tutorial on the development of measures for use in survey questionnaires. *Organizational Research Methods*, *1*, 104–121.

Holahan, C. J., Moos, R. H., & Schaefer, J. A. (1996). Coping, stress resistance, and growth: Conceptualizing adaptive functioning. In M. Zeidner, & N. S. Endler (Ed.), *Handbook of coping. Theory, research, applications* (pp. 24–43). Oxford, UK: John Wiley & Sons.

*Hudson, D. L., Eaton, J., Lewis, P., Grant, P., Sewell, W., & Gilbert, K. (2016). "Racism?!? … Just look at our neighborhoods": Views on racial discrimination and coping among African American Men in Saint Louis. *Journal of Men's Studies*, *24*, 130–150.

*Hyers, L. L. (2007). Resisting prejudice every day: Exploring women's assertive responses to anti-black racism, anti-semitism, heterosexism, and sexism. *Sex Roles*, *56*, 1–12.

Judge, T. A. & Bono, J. E. (2000). Five-factor model of personality and transformational leadership. *Journal of Applied Psychology*, *85*, 751–765.

Judge, T. A., Higgins, C. A., Thoresen, C. J., & Barrick, M. R. (1999). The Big Five personality traits, general mental ability, and career success across the life span. *Personnel Psychology*, *52*, 621–652.

Kaiser, C. R., & Miller, C. T. (2004). A stress and coping perspective on confronting sexism. *Psychology of Women Quarterly*, *28*, 168–178.

Knapp, D. E., Faley, R. H., Ekeberg, S. E., & Dubois, C. L. Z. (1997). Determinants of target responses to sexual harassment: A conceptual framework. *Academy of Management Review*, *22*, 687–729.

*Kim, C. L., Willingham, M. M., Lewis Hall, M. E., & Anderson, T. L. (2011). Coping with discrimination in academia: Asian-American and Christian perspectives. *Asian American Journal of Psychology*, *2*, 291–305.

King, E. B., Shapiro, J. R., Hebl, M. R., Singletary, S. L., & Turner, S. (2006). The stigma of obesity in customer service: A mechanism for remediation on bottom-line consequences of interpersonal discrimination. *Journal of Applied Psychology*, *91*, 579–593.

King, E. B., & Ahmad, A. S. (2010). An experimental field study of interpersonal discrimination toward Muslim job applicants. *Personnel Psychology*, *63*, 881–906.

Kowalski, R. M. (1996). Complaints and complaining: Functions, antecedents, and consequences. *Psychological Bulletin, 119,* 179–196.

Kowalski, R. M. (2003). *Complaining, teasing, and other annoying behaviors.* New Haven, CT: Yale University Press.

Krippendorff, K. (2004). *Content analysis: An introduction to its methodology.* Thousand Oaks, CA: Sage Publications.

*Kuo, W. H. (1995). Coping with racial discrimination: The case of Asian Americans. *Ethnic and Racial Studies, 18,* 109–127.

*Lalonde, R. N., Majumder, S., & Parris, R. D. (1995). Preferred responses to situations of housing and employment discrimination. *Journal of Applied Social Psychology, 25,* 1105–1119.

*Livingston, J. A. (1982). Responses to sexual harassment on the job: Legal, organizational, and individual actions. *Journal of Social Issues, 38,* 5–22.

*Lykes, M. B. (1983). Discrimination and coping in the lives of Black women: Analyses of oral history data. *Journal of Social Issues, 39,* 79–100.

Magley, V. J. (2002). Coping with sexual harassment: Reconceptualizing women's resistance. *Journal of Personality and Social Psychology, 83,* 930–946.

Major, B., & Crocker, J. (1993). Social stigma: The consequences of attributional ambiguity. In D. M. Mackie & D. L. Hamilton (Eds.), *Affect, cognition, and stereotyping. Interactive processes in group perception* (pp. 345–370). New York, NY: Academic Press.

Major, B., Quinton, W. J., McCoy, S. K., & Schmader, T. (2000). Reducing prejudice: The target's perspective. In S. Oskamp (Ed.), *Reducing prejudice and discrimination*: 211–237. Mahwah, NJ: Lawrence Erlbaum Associates.

Malamut, A. B., & Offermann, L. R. (2001). Coping with sexual harassment: Personal, environmental, and cognitive determinants. *Journal of Applied Psychology, 86,* 1152–1166.

*Mallet, R. K., & Swim, J. K. (2009). Making the best of a bad situation: Proactive coping with racial discrimination. *Basic and Applied Social Psychology, 31,* 304–316.

*McDonald, L. M., & Korabik, K. (1991). Sources of stress and ways of coping among male and female managers. *Journal of Social Behavior and Personality, 6,* 185–198.

*McGonagle, A. K., & Hamblin, L. E. (2014). Proactive responding to anticipated discrimination based on chronic illness: Double-edged sword? *Journal of Business and Psychology, 29,* 427–442.

McGrath, J. E. (1981). Dilemmatics: The study of research choices and dilemmas. *The American Behavioral Scientist, 25,* 179–210.

*McNeilly, M. D., Anderson, N. B., Armstead, A., Clark, R., Corbett, M., Robinson, E. L., Pieper, C. F., & Lepisto, E. M. (1996). The perceived racism scale: A multidimensional assessment of the experience of White racism among African Americans. *Ethnicity & Disease, 6,* 154–166.

*Miller, C. T., & Kaiser, C. R. (2001). A theoretical perspective on coping with stigma. *Journal of Social Issues, 57,* 73–92.

*Miller, C. T., & Major, B. (2000). Coping with stigma and prejudice. In T. Heatherton, R. E. Kleck, M. Heble, & J. Hull (Eds.), *The social psychology of stigma* (pp. 243–272). New York, NY: The Guilford Press.

Monteith, M. J., Voils, C. I., & Ashburn-Nardo, L. (2001). Taking a look underground: Detecting, interpreting, and reacting to implicit racial biases. *Social Cognition, 19,* 395–417.

Moos, R. H., & Schaefer, J. A. (1993). Coping resources and processes: Current concepts and measures. In L. Goldberg, & S. Breznitz (Eds.), *Handbook of stress: Theoretical and clinical aspects* (2nd ed., pp. 234–257). New York, NY: The Free Press.

Motowidlo, S. J., Pakcard, J. S., & Maning, M. R. (1986). Occupational stress: Its cause and consequences for job performance. *Journal of Applied Psychology, 71,* 618–629.

Munson, L. J., Hulin, C., & Drasgow, F. (2000). Longitudinal analysis of dispositional influences and sexual harassment: Effects on job and psychological outcomes. *Personnel Psychology, 53,* 21–46.

Netemeyer, R. G., Bearden, W. O., & Sharma, S. (2003). *Scaling procedures: Issues and applications.* Thousand Oaks, CA: Sage Publications.

Netemeyer, R. G., Bolen, J. S., & McMurrian, R. (1996). Development and validation of work-family conflict and family-work conflict scales. *Journal of Applied Psychology, 81,* 400–410.

*Ngo, H. Y., Tang, C., & Au, W. (2002). Behavioral responses to employment discrimination: A study of Hong Kong workers. *International Journal of Human Resource Management, 13,* 1206–1223.

*Noor, N. M., & Shaker, M. N. (2017). Perceived workplace discrimination, coping and psychological distress among unskilled Indonesian migrant workers in Malaysia. *International Journal of Intercultural Relations, 57,* 19–29.

Oyserman, D., & Swim, J. K. (2001). Stigma: An insider's view. *Journal of Social Issues, 57,* 1–14.

*Pettigrew, T. F. (1964). *A profile of the American Negro.* Princeton, NJ: Van Nostrand.

Piccolo, R. F., & Colquitt, J. A. (2006). Transformational leadership and job behaviors: The mediating role of core job characteristics. *Academy of Management Journal, 49,* 327–340.

*Plummer, D. L., & Slane, S. (1996). Patterns of coping in racially stressful situations. *Journal of Black Psychology, 22,* 302–315.

Podsakoff, P. M., MacKenzie, S. B., Lee, J., & Podsakoff, N. P. (2003). Common method biases in behavioral research: A critical review of the literature and recommended remedies. *Journal of Applied Psychology, 88,* 879–903.

*Puhl, R. M. (2005). Coping with weight stigma. In K. D. Brownell, R. M. Puhl, M. B. Schwartz, & L. Rudd (Eds.), *Weight bias: Nature, consequences, and remedies* (pp. 275–293). New York, NY: The Guilford Press.

*Puhl, R. M., & Brownell, K. D. (2003). Ways of coping with obesity stigma: Review and conceptual analysis. *Eating Behaviors, 4,* 53–78.

*Ragins, B. R., & Cornwell, J. M. (2001). Pink triangles: Antecedents and consequences of perceived workplace discrimination against gay and lesbian employees. *Journal of Applied Psychology, 86,* 1244–1261.

*Randall, A. K., Totenhagen, C. J., Walsh, K. J., Adams, C., & Tao, C. (2017). Coping with workplace minority stress: Associations between dyadic coping and anxiety among women in same-sex relationships. *Journal of Lesbian Studies, 21,* 70–87.

Robins, R. W., Hendin, H. M., & Trzesniewski, K. H. (2001). Measuring global self-esteem: Construct validation of a single-item measure and the Rosenberg self-esteem scale. *Personality and Social Psychology Bulletin, 27,* 151–161.

Salgado, J. F. (1997). The five factor model of personality and job performance in the European community. *Journal of Applied Psychology, 82,* 30–43.

Sanchez, J. I., & Brock, P. (1996). Outcomes of perceived discrimination among Hispanic employees: Is diversity management a luxury or a necessity? *Academy of Management Journal, 39,* 704–719.

*Schneider, K. T., Swan, S., & Fitzgerald, L. F. (1997). Job-related and psychological effects of sexual harassment in the workplace: Empirical evidence from two organizations. *Journal of Applied Psychology, 82,* 401–415.

Seashore, S. E., Lawler, E. E., Mirvis, P., & Cammann, C. (1982). *Observing and measuring organizational change: A guide to field practice.* New York, NY: John Wiley.

Seibert, S. E., Crant, M., & Kraimer, M. L. (1999). Proactive personality and career success. *Journal of Applied Psychology, 84,* 416–427.

*Shorter-Gooden, K. (2004). Multiple resistance strategies: How African American women cope with racism and sexism. *Journal of Black Psychology, 30,* 406–425.

*Shrivastava, H. (2015). Harassment at the workplace, powerlessness and identity: Experiences of women civil servants in India. *Indian Journal of Gender Studies, 22,* 437–457.

Simpson, G. E., & Yinger, J. M. (1985). *Racial and cultural minorities. An analysis of prejudice and discrimination.* New York, NY: The Plenum Press.

*Singletary, S. L., & Hebl, M. F. (2009). Compensatory strategies for reducing interpersonal discrimination: The effectiveness of acknowledgments, increased positivity, and individuating information. *Journal of Applied Psychology, 94,* 797–805.

*Sparkes, A. C. (1994). Self, silence, and invisibility as a beginning teacher: A life history of lesbian experience. *British Journal of Sociology of Education, 15,* 93–118.

Spector, P. E. (1992). *Summated rating scale construction. An introduction.* London, UK: Sage Publications.

Stanton, J. M. (1998). An empirical assessment of data collection using the Internet. *Personnel Psychology, 51,* 709–725.

*St. Jean, Y., & Feagin, J. R. (1997). Racial masques: Black women and subtle gendered racism. In N. Benokraitis (Ed.), *Subtle sexism: Current practices and prospects for change* (pp. 179–201). Thousand Oaks, CA: Sage Publications.

*Stone, D. L., & Colella, A. (1996). A model of factors affecting the treatment of disabled individuals in organizations. *Academy of Management Review, 21,* 352–401.

Strahan, R., & Gerbasi, K. C. (1972). Short, homogeneous versions of the Marlowe-Crowne social desirability scale. *Journal of Clinical Psychology, 28,* 191–193.

Taylor, D. M., Wright, S. C. Moghaddam, F. M., & Lalonde, R. N. (1990). The personal/group discrimination discrepancy: Perceiving my group, but not myself, to be a target of discrimination. *Personality and Social Psychology Bulletin, 16,* 254–262.

Taylor, S. E., & Armor, D. A. (1996). Positive illusions and coping with adversity. *Journal of Personality, 64,* 873–898.

Taylor, S. E., & Aspinwall, L. G. (1996). Mediating and moderating processes in psychosocial stress. In H. B. Kaplan (Ed.), *Psychosocial stress: Perspectives on structure, theory, life-course, and methods* (pp. 71–110). San Diego, CA: Academic Press.

Tepper, B. J., Moss, S. E., Lockhart, D. E., & Carr, J. C. (2007). Abusive supervision, upward maintenance communication, and subordinates' psychological distress. *Academy of Management Journal, 50,* 1169–1180.

*Terpstra, D. E., & Baker, D. D. (1986). A framework for the study of sexual harassment. *Basic and Applied Social Psychology, 7,* 17–34.

*Torres, L., Yznaga, S. D., & Moore, K. M. (2011). Discrimination and Latino psychological distress: The moderating role of ethnic identity exploration and commitment. *American Journal of Orthopsychiatry, 81,* 526–534.

Tsang, E. W., & Kwan, K. (1999). Replication and theory development in organizational science: A critical realist perspective. *Academy of Management Review, 24,* 759–780.

Turban, D. B., & Dougherty, T. W. (1994). Role of protégé personality in receipt of mentoring and career success. *Academy of Management Journal, 37,* 688–702.

*Verkuyten, M., & Nekuee, S. (2001). Self-esteem, discrimination, and coping among refugees: The moderating role of self-categorization. *Journal of Applied Social Psychology, 31,* 1058–1075.

*Verwiebe, R., Seewann, L., Wolf, M., & Hacioglu, M. (2016). 'I have to be very good in what I do.' Marginalisation and discrimination in the career-entry phase—experiences and coping strategies among university graduates with a migrant background in Austria. *Journal of Ethnic and Migration Studies, 42,* 1468–2490.

*Volpone, S. D., & Avery, D. R. (2013). It's self defense: How perceived discrimination promotes employee withdrawal. *Journal of Occupational Health Psychology, 18,* 430–448.

*Wagstaff, M. F., Triana, M. C., Kim, S., & Al-Riyami, S. (2015). Responses to perceived discrimination: Relationships between social support seeking, core self-evaluations, and withdrawal behaviors. *Human Resource Management, 54,* 673–687.

*Wan, N. (2003). Orange in a world of apples: The voices of albinism. *Disability and Society, 18,* 277–296.

Wanous, J. P., & Hudy, M. J. (2001). Single-item reliability: A replication and extension. *Organizational Research Methods, 4,* 361–375.

Wasti, S. A., & Cortina, L. M. (2002). Coping in context: Sociocultural determinants of responses to sexual harassment. *Journal of Personality and Social Psychology, 83,* 394–405.

*Wheeler, R. M., Foster, J. W., & Hepburn, K. W. (2014). The experience of discrimination by US and internationally educated nurses in hospital practice in the USA: A qualitative study. *JAN, 70,* 350–358.

*Wilson, P. A., & Yoshikawa, H. (2004). Experiences of and responses to social discrimination among Asian and Pacific Islander gay men: Their relationship to HIV risk. *AIDS Education and Prevention, 16,* 68–83.

CHAPTER 11

THE SOCIALIZATION-STRESS MODEL OF WORKPLACE RACIAL HARASSMENT

Antecedents, Consequences, and Implications

Mary Inman, Phanikiran Radhakrishnan, and Kayla Liggett

We present a socialization-stressor model of racial harassment (SSMR) to explain why racial harassment occurs despite laws against it. It extends prior models and explains how socialization, categorization, and social identity can result in racial harassment. We predict that certain types of organizational climates for diversity, work-group compositions, and employee attitudes perpetrate harassment. Our model explains why some employees perpetrate racial harassment, while others observe it. Our model elaborates on how victims and bystanders use culturally socialized prototypes about racism to interpret which types of ambiguous experiences are racially harassing. We argue that workplace racial harassment is an interpersonal injustice that can be perpetrated by *anyone* in the organization. It is distinct from workplace racial discrimination, a distributive and procedural injustice that can only be perpetrated by those who have supervisory power over the employee. Thus, our model predicts that harassment and discrimination should be related to different outcomes. We then draw on models of stress to explain why, upon experiencing racial harassment, victims and bystanders report poor job attitudes, poor mental health,

Diversity and Inclusion in Organizations, pages 285–329.

and poor physical health which causes them to disengage from their jobs and with-draw from the organization. Our model predicts that because of the derogatory and exclusionary nature of racial harassment, victims' opportunities for advancing with-in the organization start to dwindle, leading to their lowered performance, which in turn, leads to their racial discrimination in evaluations, pay, and promotions. Thus, harassment can predict discrimination. Our comprehensive model has clear direc-tions for future research, implications for theory development, and practical sugges-tions for organizations.

Racial harassment is still very prevalent in the American workplace. Harassment presents itself overtly as racial slurs, derogatory comments, and racially derogato-ry symbols. For example, Black employees at a shipyard in Alabama saw nooses hanging in their break room (Jameel & Yerardi, 2019), while those in Chicago saw a stuffed monkey with a rope around its neck at their workplace (Rothschild, 2014). Some people report hearing White supervisors refer to Black subordinates as "monkeys" (Jameel & Yerardi, 2019) or "ass monkeys" (Rothschild, 2014). Still others at a furniture store in Ohio were told by their White manager to "clear the room" so that manager could give his Black subordinate her "lynching" — a word he used to refer to her performance appraisal (US Equal Employment Op-portunity Commission, EEOC, 2014). Even a brand-name company like Gen-eral Motors is being sued for allowing nooses and "whites-only" signs to be dis-played at its sites, and permitting its employees to wear t-shirts with Nazi symbols (Griffith, 2019).

Racial harassment can also be subtle and may not always involve slurs and racist comments (Dovidio & Gaertner, 2008; Jones, Peddie, Gilraine, King, & Gray, 2016; Wong, Derthick, David, Saw, & Okazaki, 2014). For example, it can take the form of excluding employees because of their race or ethnicity by not sharing job-relevant information with them (Schneider, Hitlan & Radhakrishnan, 2000), by telling them to "go back to where they came from" (Schneider et al., 2000), or by telling them that their performance is expected to be inferior (Jones et al., 2016). These types of behaviors are harder to detect, require more detailed cognitive appraisals, and hence, are more stressful. However, they are more fre-quent (Jones et al., 2016) even if they are difficult to document and litigate against (Jameel & Yerardi, 2019).

Nevertheless, racially harassing experiences take their toll on victims in the workplace. Lowered psychological and physical health, negative work-related at-titudes and withdrawal behaviors are *all* related to both overt and subtle racial harassment (Jones et al., 2016; Schneider et al., 2000), with larger effect sizes for ambiguous than for overt forms of racial harassment (Jones et al., 2016, p. 1603). Further, victims who report it, suffer. Of those who filed reports of racial harass-ment to the EEOC between 2010 to 2017, 40 percent experienced retaliation for reporting it (Jameel & Yerardi, 2019).

At the same time, the US population is rapidly diversifying (Fry & Parker, 2018). Blacks, Asian, Hispanics, and other racial minorities are predicted to make up the majority of the American population by the year 2050 (U.S. Census, 1996). Yet 50% of Americans say that this shift will lead to *more* conflicts between members of different racial and ethnic groups (Parker, Morin, & Horowitz, 2019). American workplaces have a long way to go toward truly including its societal members into their workforces. Workplaces with high incidents of *racial* harassment not only engender a culture of exclusion (cf. Shore, Cleveland, & Sanchez, 2018), but, like the #metoo movement shows, they will ultimately suffer numerous ramifications.

Such disturbing trends offer compelling reasons for scientists to better understand the complexities of workplace racial harassment and how it relates to racial discrimination. In contrast to harassment, discrimination is easier to measure: It manifests itself in terms of racial inequities in hiring, pay, promotions, or advancement opportunities on the job. Often, researchers measure the two together or do not distinguish between them. Such studies show that Black men reported the highest incidents of racial harassment *and* discrimination (25%), followed by women of color (15%), with White men and women reporting the least frequent experiences (11%, 11%, Krieger et al., 2006). While another study found that 71% of Black respondents, 52% of Hispanics and 30% of Whites said they "regularly or occasionally" experienced discrimination or had been treated unfairly due to their race or ethnicity (Pew, 2016). Thus, reports of harassment and discrimination seem to show similar patterns.

Racial harassment could precede discrimination, however. For example, the continued derogation of African-Americans in the American workplace (Pew, 2016) could explain why biases against hiring African-Americans have not declined in the past 25 years (see Quillian, Pager, Hexel, & Midtboen, 2017). However, many models assume that racial discrimination and harassment are similar (Bergman, Palmieri, Drasgow, & Ormerod, 2007; Bergman, Palmieri, Drasgow, & Ormerod, 2012; Gelfand, Nishii, Raver & Schneider, 2005; Stone-Romero & Stone, 2005). We have relatively few empirical studies that distinguish between racial harassment and discrimination (Hitlan & Radhakrishnan, 1999) or that examine the unique correlates of racial harassment (Berdahl & Moore, 2006; Low, Radhakrishnan, Schneider & Rounds, 2007; Raver & Nishii, 2010; Schneider et al., 2000). Therefore, one goal of our paper is to fill this void. We propose a model that explicates the subtle and overt aspects of racial harassment in the workplace and elaborates on both, the unique, and the common, antecedents and consequences that racial harassment shares with racial discrimination.

PRIOR MODELS ABOUT RACIAL HARASSMENT

Like others (Stone-Romero & Stone, 2005), we believe it is important to understand the issues that organizations face when they employ workers from different races, ethnicities, cultures, and subcultures. This is because employees bring their ethnic/racial identities, their cultural values, and worldviews to the workplace (Cox, 1994; Harro; 2013; Trice & Breyer, 1993; Weigel & Howes, 1985). When encountering others who hold different worldviews and values, employees can feel that their racial group's status, their own status, and their self esteem are threatened (Solomon, Greenberg, & Pyszczynski, 1991; Stone & Stone-Romero, 2004). For example, European-Americans value independence, individualism, competitive achievement, goals for the future, time pressure. In contrast, African-Americans value collectivism, families, low-power distance, and a relaxed view of time (Trice & Beyer, 1993). One reason why European-Americans (Whites) derogate African-Americans is that African-Americans do not share the former group's values (Stone-Romero & Stone, 2005; Trice & Beyer, 1993).

To deal with threats to power and values, employees can encourage employees with different values to leave the company, by harassing them with derogatory comments or by excluding them (see Schneider, 1987). Supporting this notion, empirical research shows that non-White employees (i.e., African-Americans, Latino Americans, etc.) often have higher turnover rates and experience greater stress in American workplaces than do White employees (Cox, 1994, Stone & Stone-Romero, 2004). Further, given the subtle forms that racial harassment can take, coupled with the ambiguity of a perpetrator's motives that victims must judge when interpreting such harassment (Crocker & Major, 1989), a model that explains how employees interpret and react to racially harassing events in the workplace is needed. A note about terminology: We use the term "perpetrator" to designate the person doing the harassing, "victim" to designate the direct target or recipient of such behaviors, and "bystander" to describe employees who observe or know of such harassing events and can be indirectly affected by them.

Our proposed model (shown in Figure 11.1) explains why *perpetrators* racially harass certain victims, how *victims* experience harassment, and how *bystanders* interpret, or come to know about racial harassment in the organization and are affected by it. The current literature lacks a model that 1) examines the unique and common antecedents and consequences of racial harassment *and* discrimination, 2) explains why perpetrators harass, and 3) explains the processes that victims and bystanders go through when perceiving and experiencing workplace racial harassment.

We integrate different types of prior models of discrimination into our model of racial harassment *and* discrimination. One type explains racial discrimination at the macro-level, either by emphasizing the role of societal culture on organizational culture (Gelfand et al., 2005) or the role of the cultural context inside the company (Stone & Stone-Romero, 2004; Stone-Romero & Stone, 2005). Another type explains discrimination at the micro-behavioral-level, by elaborating on how culturally-based stereotypes or cognitions (Tajfel, 1978) and motivations (Tajfel & Turner, 1986; Stone-Romero & Stone, 2005) can cause racial discrimination (Stone & Stone-Romero, 2004; Stone-Romero & Stone, 2005). A third type elaborates on the consequences of these experiences for victims and bystanders: It relies on the notion that racial harassment and discrimination are stressors (Bergman et al., 2012; Low et al., 2007; Schneider et al., 2000) that have negative out-

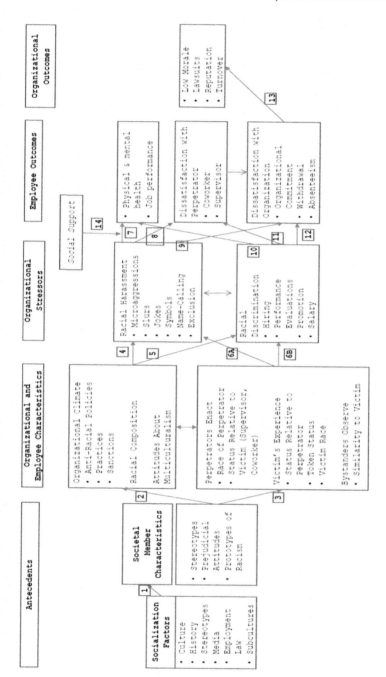

FIGURE 11.1. The Socialization-Stressor Model of Racial Harassment and Discrimination

comes for employees' health, their work-related attitudes, and engagement with their jobs and their organizations (Dhanani, Beus, & Joseph, 2018).

CONTRIBUTIONS OF OUR MODEL

Our model explains the causes and effects of workplace racial harassment. It explains how people perceive and categorize racially harassing events. It recognizes the ambiguity of perpetrator's motives and predicts that victims and bystander/ observers rely on situational features (i.e., the race and status of the perpetrator and victim) and their past experiences to decide if a specific event reflects racial harassment. Our model also predicts that because workplace racial harassment and discrimination are stressors, these experiences can lead victims to *compartmentalize* their experiences and react accordingly. As we explain later, racial harassment can *come from anyone* in the workplace (i.e., supervisors, coworkers, subordinates, clients, etc.) and can lead to negative associations with that perpetrator (e.g., lowered coworker satisfaction). Racial discrimination, by definition can only be perpetrated *by the company and its representatives* (e.g., supervisors). Thus, our model predicts that racial discrimination will be associated with negative attitudes toward the company (e.g., lowered organizational commitment) and its representatives (e.g., supervisor dissatisfaction), whereas racial harassment will additionally be associated with negative attitudes toward the perpetrator (e.g., lowered satisfaction with coworker for perpetrating it) and lowered satisfaction with one's supervisor for allowing the perpetrator to harass). Furthermore, because our model considers the perspective of the bystander and incorporates the contaminating effects of racial harassment on bystanders, it also explains how bystanders come to judge events as racially harassing and are affected by it.

The primary purpose of this paper is to propose and explain our Socialization-Stress Model of Racism shown in Figure 11.1 and to support its claims with relevant empirical research. The subsequent sections of our paper will (a) define key terms, (b) describe prior models about the cultural socialization of harassment and discrimination as it relates to societal members and organizations; (c) present our model and explain how cultural stereotypes can carryover into organizations and cause employees within it to perpetrate racial harassment, (e) explain what factors affect perceptions of racial harassment, (f) explain how victims and bystanders are affected by the stress of racial harassment at work, (g) discuss areas for future research and, (h) discuss the practical implications of our model.

DEFINING KEY TERMS

Race versus Ethnicity

Race is a word used to describe human differences in physical attributes such as skin color, facial features, and hair, presumed to be originally caused by the geographical isolation of populations, resulting in their categorization into one of the three "races": Caucasoid, Negroid, and Mongoloid (Betancourt & Lopez,

1993, p. 631). Ethnicity is defined as values, norms, and beliefs due to one's cultural background that are tied to one's national origin (Betancourt & Lopez, 1993), shared kinship and history (Valdez & Golash-Boza, 2017), or to one's racial group (Betancourt & Lopez, 1993). Although the subject of controversy, we use the word race because, like ethnicity, race can be a vital part of one's identity. Further, race and ethnicity serve as a basis for categorizing people at work into ingroups and outgroups (Tajfel & Turner, 1986). Therefore, we use the word "race" and the term "ethnicity" interchangeably in our model.

In addition, the racial history of the USA (described later) has been such that European- Americans (hereafter referred to as Whites or Anglos) have been the dominant *racial and ethnic* group within societal institutions and workplaces (Harro, 2013; Kerbo, 1983). We use the terms White and Anglo interchangeably. The history of dominance by Whites in the US has resulted in the creation of legislation that reinforces their higher social status and ensures Whites' ability to maximize their own outcomes in employment contexts (Kerbo, 1983; Stone-Romero & Stone, 2005). The systematic exclusion of members of all other racial and ethnic groups from societal institutions and workplaces strengthens positive stereotypes about Whites' abilities. In contrast, ethnic and racial categories other than the White category prime negative cultural stereotypes leading to inferences about employees in non-White groups (Weigel & Howes, 1985). This results in the harassment of people based on their ethnicity and/or race which are inextricably linked in the minds of victims, bystanders, and perpetrators. Further, researchers themselves who are often residents of the American society have typically combined the terms "race" and "ethnicity" when asking employees about their harassment experiences at work (*e.g., to what extent have you received unfair negative treatment due to your race/ethnicity compared to others*). We follow the terminology used by recent meta-analytic reviews of the research on workplace discrimination in US (Dhanani et al., 2018, p. 162; Triana, Jayasinghe, & Pieper, 2015, p. 493) and use the term "race" to encompass race *and* ethnicity.

Racial Harassment versus Discrimination

We define racial and/or ethnic *harassment* as unwelcome, severe, or pervasive conduct toward a person based on his/her race or ethnic origin that interferes with that person's job performance. It involves racial slurs, jokes, derogatory comments, intimidation, name-calling, ridiculing, insults, or the use of offensive objects or images (Chinn, 2018; Schneider, et al., 2000; U.S. EEOC, 1993). It can include anonymous messages left in bathrooms and workspaces, comments made face-to-face, and threats sent on email or social media. It can also involve covert behaviors such as microaggressions (e.g., asking a racial minority, "No, where are you *really* from," implying they are not American) or exclusionary behaviors such as not sharing work-related information that can hinder an employee's performance. Some have labelled such subtle behaviors as "implicit harassment" because people would experience ambivalence for labeling these behaviors as racism (Jones et al., 2016). Others have called racial harassment *informal* discrimination (Dhanani et al., 2018). We consider racial harassment akin to *interpersonal injustice.*

Racial and/or ethnic *discrimination* is defined as behaviors that hinder one's opportunities for employment and to advance on the job due to one's racial/ethnic group membership (Hitlan & Radhakrishnan, 1999; Jones et al., 2016) resulting in biases in screening, hiring, testing, placement, training, performance evaluations, task assignments, promotions, compensation, and/or benefits (U.S. EEOC, 1993). The workplace discrimination literature calls this *formal or institutional* discrimination (Dhanani et al., 2018). We consider racial discrimination to be acts of *procedural* and *distributive injustice.*

Both racial harassment and racial discrimination are rooted in the cultural socialization of stereotypes and prejudicial attitudes, as explained later. Harassment and discrimination reflect ways in which employees of minority racial groups are prevented from advancing in organizations. Both reflect the *injustices* that occur at work, given the legal mandate that employees are to be treated fairly at work. Employees' *expect* to be treated fairly at work. Employees who are racially harassed and discriminated against are being "relatively deprived" compared to others because of their race (Crosby, 1984).

However, harassment and discrimination differ in the *forms* of the injustice they perpetrate. The organizational literature describes three types of injustices: interactional (or interpersonal), distributive, and procedural (Stone-Romero & Stone, 2005). Racial harassment is a form of *interactional injustice,* or unfair interpersonal treatment. Such negative interpersonal treatment can be perpetrated by the employee's supervisor and perpetrated by others in the workplace (like coworkers and subordinates) who can derogate or exclude others. Victims and employees react similarly, regardless of whether the derogatory racial comments came from supervisors or coworkers (Jameel & Yerardi, 2019) because such experiences violate their expectations of interactional justice in the workplace.

Racial discrimination, on the other hand, violates employees' expectations of distributive and procedural justice in the workplace (Stone-Romero & Stone, 2005). *Distributive justice* pertains to the fairness of *outcomes* allocated to individuals relative to their contributions (Leventhal, 1980), whereas *procedural justice* involves the fairness of the *procedures* used to allocate these outcomes (Leventhal, 1980; Lind & Tyler, 1988). We argue that *employees who have the power to allocate opportunities and rewards* (e.g., supervisors) can set up systems and procedures for allocating rewards and opportunities to favor members of their own racial group leading to unfair outcomes, (i.e., discrimination) for employees not in those racial groups. Like others (Stone-Romero & Stone, 2005, p. 445), we propose that racial discrimination occurs because employees who have the power to allocate resources 1) value being part of their own racial group because of the status it affords them, and 2) perceive employees of their own racial group as having more inputs, and so are more deserving of rewards, than employees not in their racial group.

To summarize, our model proposes that racial harassment, a form of interpersonal injustice can be perpetrated by *anyone* in the organization whereas racial discrimination, a form of distributive and procedural injustice, can only be perpetrated by employees with supervisory power over the victim or the power to allocate rewards and opportunities to the victim. Victims, in turn, can differentially react to, and are differentially affected by, racial harassment versus racial discrimination, leading them to compartmentalize these experiences, as we will explain later.

Our model proposes that racial harassment (RH) can lead to racial discrimination (RD, see bidirectional arrow between RH and RD in Figure 11.1). Consider the following example of an employee's progress within an organization. Because racial harassment can take the form of derogatory comments based on negative racial stereotypes, it can characterize that minority employee as incompetent and/or lazy in the minds of supervisors who have the power to allocate resources like challenging assignments to that employee. Continued racial derogation of the employee in the workplace by coworkers and subordinates in the organization can also bias supervisors. Multiple sources of harassment can result in lower-than-expected performance appraisals of these minority employees by their supervisors, and subsequently, lower-than-expected pay. Further, because racial harassment involves exclusion, it can take the form of behaviors like not sharing work-relevant information with subordinates or coworkers of the minority racial group (Schneider et al., 2000). Not sharing work-relevant information can hinder minority employees from doing their jobs well, which can also result in a lower-than-expected performance evaluation, which in turn, can be used to justify why minority employees are not given challenging assignments to enable them to demonstrate their skills and abilities for jobs beyond their current role (a classic example of the Pygmalion effect, Rosenthal & Jacobson, 1968). Thus, both derogation and exclusion can result in minority employees not being evaluated appropriately, not being paid fairly, and not being given opportunities to demonstrate their skills for higher-level roles, preventing their advancement in the company.

Similarly, acts of racial discrimination can lead to acts of racial harassment. For example, when racial minority employees are not given challenging assignment, it lowers their chances for promotion to leadership positions, thus not giving them opportunities to disconfirm negative stereotypes that supervisors or coworkers may have about them or their group. Such professional neglect can cause self-doubt within the minority employee and lower performance of that racial minority employee. This continues to associate low performance with that racial minority employee and his/her racial group, reinforcing the negative stereotype, which, in turn, may then evoke derogation and exclusion (i.e., racial harassment) from coworkers, subordinates or supervisors who belong to dominant race, thus perpetuating the cycle.

Direct versus Observed Harassment. Our model also addresses the causes and effects of harassment that is *directly* experienced, versus harassment that is *observed*, and/or *indirectly* experienced (or *ambient*). We propose that bystanders who witness and/or know about racial harassment in their workplaces (Low et al., 2007), who surmise that the perpetrator's intent was racially motivated, and/ or those who belong to the same status and/or racial group as the victim would readily be thinking, "*Am I next?*" This worry creates stress for bystanders. Further, bystanders may fear retaliation when they speak out or act against harassment (Crosby, 2015).

Legal Definitions versus Research Definitions

Psychological researchers have broader definitions for racial harassment and discrimination than does the American legal system. When measuring racial *harassment,* researchers ask employees to indicate how often they are subject to demeaning verbal slurs, jokes, derogatory comments, subtle put-downs (i.e., microaggressions, Wong et al., 2014), stereotypical characterizations, and social or informational exclusions that hinder their progress in the workplace (see Figure 11.1 "Racial Harassment" box). All these actions are perceived as unwelcome by the victim and trigger rumination and coping strategies in victims (Bergman et al., 2007; Harrick & Sullivan, 1995; Schneider et al., 2000). For example, consider the case of informational exclusion, a form of racial harassment. Failing to tell a coworker of a different race about an opportunity for advancement in the workplace or keeping job-relevant information from that coworker can result in stress in that employee which lowers his/her job performance and other work-related behaviors (Dhanani et al., 2018). Experienced over time, racial harassing behaviors were negatively related to employees' job-attitudes and their psychological and physical well-being (Jones et al., 2016, Schneider et al., 2000).

In contrast, the American legal system not only has a much narrower definition of racial harassment but also has subcultural/geographic differences in how it applies that definition. Petty slights, annoyances, and isolated instances often do not usually rise to the level of litigation in the US (US EEOC, 2018). Judges in the US often make "summary judgments" to decide if a victim's case contains frequent, severe, physically threatening, humiliating, demeaning, and/or unreasonable interference with one's performance on the job to allow a case of racial harassment to proceed to trial. It appears that judges who reside in different subcultures of the USA have different thresholds of what constitutes a racially hostile environment. A lawyer in Alabama with 20 years of litigatory experience notes that cases in Philadelphia involving a supervisor using a slur on a subordinate even once would be deemed as having sufficient evidence for legal proceedings to commence. Not so in Alabama. Frequent and egregious acts in Alabamian workplaces did not proceed legally because they were not deemed viable at the "summary judgment" phase (Jameel & Yerardi, 2019). For example, a judge in Alabama ruled that a shipyard worker who encountered 20 harassing incidents over his 2,261 days at that workplace (one incident for every 113 days worked) was not pervasive enough for a viable claim. Between 2016 and 2017, 89 percent of cases that Alabamian employers requested summary judgments on, were fully or partially dismissed (Jameel & Yerardi, 2019). Perceptions of racial harassment seemed to vary by geographic region.

PRIOR MODELS

This section describes five relevant literatures as they pertain to our Socialization Stressor Model of Racial Harassment and Discrimination (SSMR) shown in Figure 11.1. Two *macro-level* models that explain how cultural socialization processes operate that are relevant are (a) group dominance and the socialization of racism (Jones, 1997; Harro, 2013; Kerbo, 1983) and (b) the culture of dominance as it relates to organizations (Cox, 1994; Gelfand et al., 2005, Stone & Stone-Romero, 2004; Stone-Romero & Stone, 2005). *Micro*-level models explain the causes and consequences of harassment *within* organizations. When elaborating on these micro-level models, we explain how harassment works by (a) categorizing employees, (b) protecting social identity (Tajfel & Turner, 1986), and by (c) creating a significant stressor (Dhanani et al., 2018) resulting in negative psychological, physical and job-related outcomes. We then fully explain our model which adopts several premises from prior models in these five literatures. Last, we elaborate on each link to explain (a) why and how perpetrators enact harassment (b) how victims and bystanders interpret racial harassment, and (c) how victims differentially respond to, and are affected by, racial harassment *versus* racial discrimination.

Macro-level Models: Antecedents—How Socialization Promotes Racism at Work

The Cultural Socialization of Racism. We, like others (Cox,1994; Jones, 1997), adopt the premise that harassing and discriminatory behaviors are taught. People are born into social structures with mechanisms of oppression toward certain racial groups already in place (Cycle-of-Socialization model, Harro, 2013; Jones, 1997; Kerbo, 1983; Weigel & Howes, 1985). Such mechanisms are sustained by cultural institutions within society (e.g., government, businesses) which reinforce which racial groups have power and which ones do not. Societal members can easily internalize these beliefs, act on their misperceptions of different racial groups, and begin to accept and perpetuate social inequalities between groups. Some notable examples of racialized socialization in the US follow (see Box 1 of the model).

Racism in the United States. Like others, we propose that this cycle started when Western-Europeans used force to dominate over the indigenous population of the US and African-American slaves, resulting in a long history of biased treatment towards members of these groups (Dovidio & Gaertner, 1986; Stone-

Romero & Stone, 2005). Later, these now European-Americans (White Anglos) mobilized resources to gain capital, status, and power to dominate over multiple racial groups, while perpetuating negative stereotypes about ethnic groups who threatened their power. For example, negative racial stereotypes (e.g., "savages," "violent," "dumb," "lazy" etc.) were used to justify denying Blacks and Latinos resources like employment, health-care, education, or employment opportunities, thus preventing their economic and social progress (Jones, 1997). Further, anti-Black voting laws, housing laws, and segregation of schools by race (McEneaney, 1996; U.S. Commission on Civil Rights, 1979) resulted in the marginalization, lynching, imprisonment, institutionalization, and genocide of members of out-groups who were perceived as a threat to the supremacy of Whites and their values (Acrey, 1992; Blalock, 1967; Sniderman & Hagen, 1985; Wilson, 1973).

Although the expression of overt harassment has decreased in the workplace (Jameel & Yerardi, 2019), until the 1960s, it was common to hear Whites use racial slurs such as the "n" word. Contemporary expression of covert racial harassment in the workplace is believed to be subtle and caused by "aversive racism" (Dovidio & Gaertner, 1986) which predicts the preferential treatment of Whites over Blacks to be revealed in ambiguous settings, when those settings mask Whites' subtle racial attitudes. Recall that racial groups vary in their beliefs and values (e.g., Whites value individualism more than do Blacks). Whites can legitimize their discriminatory behaviors against Blacks by using job-related criteria (e.g., high need for achievement) that favor European-American values and strivings (Trice & Beyer, 1993; Weigel & Howes, 1985). Whites then rationalize their negative treatment of Blacks to sources other than race (e.g., his low drive for personal achievement, his not belonging to the right country club, Dovidio & Gaertner, 1986, 2008) which then helps them preserve their image to themselves and to others as egalitarian (Crosby, Bromley, & Saxe, 1980).

As shown in Box 1 of the model, another way the culture in the US emphasizes norms for White supremacy is by racial stereotyping (e.g., using "White" to denote good and "Black" to denote undesirable things) seen in life and in the media. For example, consider colloquial usages of the English language in the US. The words Black are paired with bad (e.g., black sheep, black cloud, blackmailed) and White with good (e.g., White lie, white washed). Similarly, movies have portrayed Black-as-bad (e.g., villains are dressed in black, black symbolizing death and evil) and White-as-good (e.g., protagonists in movies wearing White cowboy hats, the portrayal of purity as White, role models in media are often White). These cultural symbols continually reinforce a *cognitive* association between White skin color and goodness in the minds of the members of that society. Negative pairings for other racial groups (e.g., movies showing Latinos as "lazy" and Native Americans as "savages") work similarly.

Our SSMR model predicts that members of the US society come to internalize negative stereotypes and hold prejudiced attitudes against members of minority racial groups (arrow 1). In support of this process, consider the results of the

Implicit Associations Test (IAT) which measures how strongly and automatically a person associates evaluations like "good" and "bad" with faces of people of different races. Since its development, the test has been administered to over 1.5 million Americans (Banaji & Greenwald, 2013) and it finds that a majority of White-Americans more quickly associated negative words like "evil" and "bad" with Black faces than with White faces (Banaji & Greenwald, 2013; Mooney, 2014). Further, media portrayals can affect stereotyping, breed prejudicial attitudes, and result in racial harassment and discrimination of minority employees (arrow 1). For example, the prevalence of news media clips showing Muslim as terrorists were related to increased beliefs about Muslims as aggressive, increased support for US military action in Muslim territories, and increased support for policies harming Muslims (Saleem, Prot, Anderson, & Lemieux, 2017). Similarly, media reports of anti-Latino and anti-immigrant comments made by powerful leaders (e.g., the president of the US) can promote anti-immigration sentiments, biased attitudes, and actions.

Similarly, anti-racism employment law (see Box 1) also set norms that workplace racism is unjust and to be reprimanded. If norms affect perceptions, passing of federal anti-racist employment laws should increase awareness of racism, increase formal reports of workplace racism, and be more strongly related to negative job outcomes (arrows 7–12). Triana et al. (2015) conducted a meta-analysis of studies to test some of these ideas. They examined the strength of relationships between perceived workplace racial discrimination, and its health and work correlates (arrows 10–12, in our model). These relations were compared *prior* to, and *after,* 1991—when the amended Civil Rights Act was passed (forbidding employment discrimination based on race, color, sex, religion, and national origin). Triana et al. (2015) found that the negative relation between reports of racial discrimination and outcomes (such job attitudes, health, and organizational citizenship behaviors) were *stronger* after 1991 than before, supporting our model.

Finally, in Box 1, subcultural differences also influence societal members (see arrow 1). Subcultures provide the context for discussions about race, allow for differences in worldviews to be expressed (especially those different from the worldviews of the dominant racial group), and can result in differences in the interpretation of race-related experiences. For example, as noted, judges in different geographic regions of the US (Alabama vs. Philadelphia) differed in their interpretation of what constitutes "sufficient" racial harassment before they allow for alleged claims of racial harassment to proceed to trial (Jameel & Yerardi, 2019).

The SSMR model predicts that subcultures (e.g., the racial composition of the city, important reference groups) affect people's thoughts (prototypes) about racism and experiences with racism (arrow 1). Research suggests that subcultural differences can predict differences in experiences of racial harassment. For example, in geographic regions where racial minorities were in the numerical *majority,* as in the Southwestern regions of the United States, Hispanic employees from a variety of organizations did not differ from their non-Hispanic counterparts in their reports of direct and observed workplace racial harassment (Schneider et al., 2000; Low et al., 2007), whereas many studies have shown that when racial minorities were the numeric *minority* in the workgroup, company, and/or surrounding community, racial minorities reported experiencing workplace racial harassment more frequently than Whites (Bergman et al., 2012; Raver & Nishii, 2010). The SSMR predicts that subcultures can change the prevalence of racial harassment via their influence on organizational climates.

Subcultures include the differential experiences with past racism. The SSMR predicts members of marginalized racial groups will more readily detect racism and more strongly respond to racism than racially privileged groups. For example, Dhanani et al. (2018) found that the effect sizes reports of workplace discrimination and outcomes were stronger when there were women and minorities in the sample (p. 491) than when they were not. More generally, social movements like the #LivingWhileBlack campaign and Black Lives Matter increase awareness of everyday racism and resistance to it. The long and continued history of discrimination against members of oppressed racial groups by members privileged racial groups creates inequitable living and working conditions between them (e.g., living near waste dumps). Such racial inequities are expressed via many pathways. For example, social toxins like workplace racial harassment and racial discrimination produce biological reactions like hypertension resulting in racial health disparities seen in US workers (see Krieger, 2012, ecosocial theory).

Influence of Culture on Organizations. A second line of macro-level research emphasizes the effect of the national culture on organizations (Cox, 1994; Hofstede, 1991). The ideology of the dominant culture, within which organizations operate in, has a direct impact on organizational factors such as their structure, design, use of technology, their procedures and policies for hiring and promotion, and their pay and reward systems (Cox, 1994; Gelfand et al., 2005; Stone & Stone-Romero, 2004). Dominant groups have ethnocentrism and spur intergroup conflict, which, in turn, affects employee satisfaction, commitment, and organizational effectiveness (Interactional Model of Cultural Diversity, Cox, 1994). Our SSMR also spans across these dimensions. As mentioned, many organizations in the US espouse Western European (now European-American) values and ideologies like independence, individualism, competitive achievement, time pressure, separation of job and life/family that dictate an organization's structures and practices (Cox, 1994; Trice & Beyer, 1993) and have pay structures related to these values. Moreover, Anglos use their own values to set role expectations for workers and can cause role conflict and ambiguity in workers who are not from Anglo backgrounds (Stone & Stone-Romero, 2004, p. 93). Non-Anglo ethnic groups are then expected to conform to values and roles that are not inherent to their socialized racial group.

Micro-level Processes: How Racial Harassment Operates

Empirical and theoretical research in social psychology proposes that many micro-level processes can cause racial harassment. These processes are (1) using race as a way to define and classify oneself (2) using racial categories to group people who are similar to each other (Categorization Theory, Tajfel 1978, 1981), forming ingroups and outgroups based on race, and forming stereotypes (beliefs) about people in different racial groups, with stereotypes about outgroups often being overgeneralized and invalid (Ashmore & Del Boca, 1981), (3) liking ingroups more than outgroups (Brewer, 1999) and having positive stereotypes about ingroups and beliefs that members of ingroups deserve more than members of outgroups, (4) enhancing one's identity as a member of a racial group (i.e., social identity) and protecting that group's status (Social Identity Theory, Tajfel & Turner, 1986), and (5) feeling anxious and uncomfortable when working with members of the outgroup (Dovidio, Gaertner, Kawakami, & Hodson, 2002; Stephan & Stephan, 1985). Organizational theorists extend these social identity processes to explain why interpersonal, distributive, and procedural injustices in organizations occur (Stone-Romero & Stone, 2005). The SSMR draws on this literature which we briefly explain next.

Self-Identities and Categorization. Employees have social identities that they and others use. A perceiver's belief of what a *person should be like* on a host of dimensions like race, appearance, accent, intelligence is called a perceived social identity is. It generally reflects what the perceiver assumes to be normal, acceptable, or desirable (Stone-Romero & Stone, 2007). Members of racial minority groups are stigmatized (i.e., bear marks) to the extent that there is a discrepancy between their perceived and their actual social identity (cf. virtual vs. actual social identity, Goffman, 1963; Jones et al., 1984). Culturally sanctioned, pro-White stereotypes can dictate that the ideal job applicant is one that has "White attributes" (e.g., competitive, hardworking, individualistic), so applicants of a different race (e.g., a *Black* newscaster) are notable, perceived to be negative, and assumed to not possess these attributes (Weigel & Howes, 1985) and, therefore, discredited. Research shows that people who bear various types of stigma are often victims of unfair discrimination in workplaces in the US (Stone, Stone, & Dipboye, 1992). Race is a highly distinctive identity marker that has been subjected to many stereotypes (Fiske & Taylor, 2008).

Kanter (1977) proposed three processes that lead people to form stereotypes about ethnic minorities. The distinctiveness of ethnic minorities among White workers captures attention because they are highly visible. This disproportionate attention can lead observers to attend to characteristics that distinguish members of ethnic minority groups from Whites. Observers then perceive members of ethnic groups they don't belong to in stereotypical ways (ingroup and outgroup identity processes; Tajfel & Turner, 1986). For example, Jamal is the only African-American accountant among White peers at a firm. Workers see the solo — Jamal, categorize him on his unique feature—race, and form inferences about Jamal and about other African Americans.

Stone-Romero and Stone (2005) further explain how categorizations can lead to workplace injustices, including racial bias, in their Group-Based Differential Justice Model (GBDJM). In short, observers automatically make cursory judgments of a target person's salient attributes, like race, unless some other motive entices them to engage in controlled processing like getting to know the target's idiosyncratic features (Fiske & Taylor, 2008, p. 45). Situational constraints (punishments) for injustice, the supervisor's cultural background, and his/her power will all affect the distribution of outcomes (distributive), the procedures used for allocating these outcomes (procedural), and how one interacts with that victim (i.e., interpersonal justice), leading to harassment and/or discriminatory treatment which, in turn will affect the victim's job-attitudes and behaviors (Stone-Romero & Stone, 2005). For example, supervisors recognize the skin color in a victim (e.g., Black), categorize the victim (as African-American), activate the cultural stereotype about the victim's racial group (e.g., defiant, lazy), make inferences about this particular victim based on those stereotypes, can set up reward systems on criteria that disadvantage that victim (e.g., obedient, top-seller), and allocate positive outcomes to members their own racial group because they believe such members are rightfully deserving of those outcomes (Stone-Romero & Stone, 2005, p. 452). In short, *racial discrimination* occurs when supervisors use race-based criteria and positive stereotyping to favor ingroups, when hiring and evaluating employees (see Stone-Romero & Stone, 2005). Outgroups are at a disadvantage.

Extending this, we propose that *racial harassment* can also stem from Whites employees' negative stereotypes of other racial groups, their perceived dissimilarity with members of such groups, and their discomfort when interacting with employees of other racial groups. For example, racial harassment can happen when naïve White employees make comments about race-related topics (like hair or accents), use terms like "*ghetto*" to mean "*dirty*," make comments like "*I'm surprised, you speak English so well!*" or attempt to use racial humor (like "*brother*" or "*homey*"). This interpersonal awkwardness (termed intergroup anxiety, Stephan & Stephan, 1985) is due to a history of infrequent interracial contact which can perpetuate stereotyping and hurt race relations unless trained. Supporting this idea, researchers found that Whites were more uncomfortable talking to Blacks than to other Whites, unless White subjects were given a script to guide their behavior (Avery, Richeson, Hebl, & Ambady, 2009).

The SSMR predicts racial harassment can lead to racial discrimination when such behaviors infect the processes by which important organizational resources are allocated. White interviewers felt more comfortable with White applicants than Black ones by having more eye- contact with them, asking them more open- versus closed-ended questions and by conducting longer interviews with Whites than with Blacks, which led Black applicants to underperform. Such White interviewers then felt justified in using applicants' interview performance to base their hiring decisions and ultimately selected White applicants (Dovidio et al., 2002; Word, Zanna, & Cooper, 1974).

Motivational Basis of Racial Harassment. Many experiments have shown that ingroup members tend to treat outgroup members in a biased fashion (Tajfel, 1970, 1981). Like others (Stone-Romero & Stone, 2005), we think that *Social Identity Theory* (Tajfel & Turner, 1986) explains why ingroup members behave this way. The theory's premises explain why Whites would favor other *Whites* over individuals of other racial groups. The theory's key premises are that people (a) identify with social groups that they belong to (i.e., have social identities); (b) distinguish between groups they belong and don't belong to (i.e., categorize others as ingroup and outgroup members); (c) want to maintain and enhance their self-esteem; (d) enhance the status of their ingroup as a way to elevate their self-esteem; and, (e) in many situations, allow their social identities to guide their behavior. In short, members of powerful groups want to maintain or increase disparities between groups to preserve the higher status of their positions. They use racial stereotypes to justify existing power differentials and keep the status quo. For example, in the US, members of different racial groups have different values (e.g., views about eye-contact, directness of communication, punctuality) but social structures (like performance appraisal systems) are built and based on members of the dominant group's values (Anglo's). Anglos then see these values as "traditionally American" and "normal" and use these structures to legitimize racism (Trice & Beyer, 1993; Weigel & Howes, 1985). These protective motives can stimulate racial harassment and lead to discrimination. Thus, in a company with mostly White employees, the *race* of the non-White employee is salient, that employee's relative status is noted, stereotypes are likely to be activated and applied, resulting in racial harassment.

Relatedly, feelings of frustration, ego-protection, and anxiety along with competition for limited resources can all stimulate racial harassment. For example, in the US, concerns about immigrants taking jobs are greatest among people with the lowest incomes (Pew, 2006). Competition at work for promotions, merit raises, or clients creates frustration and anxiety leading to hostility and the sabotaging of coworkers' performance. Similarly, the motive to protect one's ego predicts stereotyping and subsequent aggression. Studies have shown that when Whites were economically frustrated, they were more prejudiced against Blacks. When the US had poor economic conditions between 1964 and 2012, White Americans felt less warmly towards Blacks, held more negative attitudes towards Blacks, were more likely to condone the use of stereotypes, and regarded racial inequality among the races as natural and acceptable. During poor economic conditions in the US, Black musicians were less likely to secure a musical hit and Black politicians were less likely to win a congressional election (Bianchi, Hall, & Lee, 2018). Similarly experiments show that when threatened, subjects were less willing to hire an outgroup (Jewish) applicant and use these discriminatory methods as a way to affirm themselves (Fein & Spencer, 2008). When threatened, supervisors took out their anger out on subordinates (Fast & Chen, 2009), employees put down their coworkers and were argumentative with them (Anicich, Fast, Halevy, & Galinsky, 2016; Fast, Halevy, & Galinsky, 2012).

These emotions could explain why Americans are racially divided on the impact of having a majority non-white US population (i.e., Blacks, Asians, Latinos) by the year 2050. More Whites said that this non-White majority would be *bad* (28%) than did Blacks (13%) and Latinos (12%). In contrast, a greater percentage of Blacks (53%) and Hispanics (55%) said that having a majority of non-Whites in the US was *good,* whereas only 26% of Whites said this (Parker et al., 2019). In sum, multiple social, cognitive, and motivational factors cause workplace racial harassment. Our model adopts these assumptions and explains the consequences of workplace racial harassment and discrimination.

A SOCIALIZATION-STRESS MODEL OF RACIAL HARASSMENT

Figure 11.1 provides our SSMR model of the factors that lead to racial harassment and discrimination. The model is grounded in the previously described empirical and theoretical research in social and organizational psychology. The purpose of the SSMR is to explain how racial harassment operates for perpetrators, victims, and bystanders. We now describe the elements of the model and the links between them, while integrating relevant theory and research. Afterwards, we discuss future research and practical implications.

Cultural Influence on Societal Members (Arrow 1)

As arrow 1 shows, the national culture and the subculture that one lives in influences how people form stereotypes and develop attitudes biases favoring certain racial groups (e.g., Whites in the US, Banaji & Greenwald, 2013), how they perceive racism, and how they develop (or resist) their own and others' negative racial attitudes. For example, SSMR predicts that (sub)cultures that promote multiculturalism and humanistic values are likely to create members who are aware of racial prejudice, to develop an internal motivation to not be racist, and to resist when they observe racism. Recall that Alabama courts needed more pervasive workplace racial harassment in order to continue legal proceedings than did Philadelphia (Jameel & Yerardi, 2019). Some argue that racial prejudice against Black Americans is so infused in American institutions that current practices will continue to keep the status quo unless societal members become actively aware of the biases in these institutions and act against these biases (Tatum, 1997).

Empirical research also supports these ideas. Anti-Black racial stereotypes are automatically activated, and unless challenged, are automatically applied (Devine, Brodish, & Vance, 2005). The challenge comes from an internal motivation to not be prejudiced (Devine et al., 2005) which can be taught. Several randomized experiments testing the efficacy of interventions to reduce implicit bias and increase awareness on college students show significant improvements for those in the experimental than those in the control group (Devin, Forscher, Austin, & Cox, 2012; Forscher, Mitamura, Dix, Cox, & Devine, 2017; Lai et al., 2014, 2016).

Culture Affects Perceptions *about* **Racism (arrows 3 & 6A).** SSMR also predicts that, just as people categorize each other into ingroups and outgroups (Tajfel & Turner, 1986), they also categorize *behaviors* into "*racial harassment*" or not. Because contemporary forms of racial harassment can take subtle forms (Dovidio & Gaertner, 2008; Wong et al., 2014), victims and bystanders at workplaces often face ambiguous racial comments like "*you people*" that must be classified as racial harassment (or not). People form prototypes (best examples) about racism. They then use these prototypes to compare and classify whether novel, ambiguous, yet racially-charged behaviors are "racist" or not (Inman & Baron, 1996). For example, the media in the US repeatedly showed blatant of Whites derogating Blacks (e.g., the lynching of Blacks by Whites while using the "n" word) which creates the prototype of racism as Whites oppressing Blacks in the minds of societal members. Comments made by White perpetrators to Black victims were labeled as discrimination more readily than identical comments made between all other perpetrator-victim race combinations (i.e., White perpetrator—White victim, Black perpetrator-White victim, Black perpetrator-Black victim, Inman & Baron, 1996). Whites making prejudiced comments such as, "*Our team lost the game because the other team had more Black players than us.*" were perceived as more offensive than similar comments made by Blacks (Cunningham, Ferreira, & Fink, 2009). Thus, prototypes —which involve the races of the perpetrator and victim—-inform perceptions of harassment.

The status of the perpetrator in the context matters too (Inman, Huerta, & Oh, 1998). These authors showed that people more readily saw the perpetrator's actions as racist when his race matched the group that historically had power in that context. For example, the rap music industry has been heavily dominated by African Americans. Inman et al. (1998) varied the race of the perpetrator and examined how Black, Latino, or White supervisors who denied a rising musician a chance to succeed were perceived. They found that people more readily judged the Black supervisor to be the perpetrator of racism than a White and Latino one in this context. Similarly, several other studies have found support for the prototype-matching hypothesis of perceiving racism (Buccianeri & Corning, 2013; Flournoy, Prentice-Dunn, & Klinger, 2002; Marti, Bobier, & Baron, 2000; Simon, Kinias, O'Brien, Major, & Bivolaru, 2013).

Incorporating this research, the SSMR predicts that racial slurs directed at members of racial minority groups would signal racial harassment, especially if the perpetrator was White. For example, making remarks about an Asian-American employee's accent or telling a Latinx employee to "*Go back to where you came from*" would likely be interpreted as racial harassment.

Three additional factors can affect perceptions of racial harassment. We rely on research on sexism to make this prediction. This research suggests that the amount of harm the victim experienced, the intent of the perpetrator, and beliefs about meritocracy and fairness can all play a role. Swim, Scott, Sechrist, Campbell, and Stangor (2003) found that bystanders perceived ambiguous negative comments as sexist when the victim was greatly harmed and the perpetrator's intentions were judged to be malicious. In addition, bystanders' beliefs about meritocracy reduced the degree to which they judged negative evaluations of a minority group member as discriminatory (Major, Kaiser, O'Brien, & McCoy, 2007). These findings have implications for companies, as bystanders' interpretations are often used when conducting internal or external investigations of harassment.

Finally, the SSMR posits that past experiences with racism (predicted from one's subculture) affects perceptions of novel or ambiguous racial events (arrows 1, 3, 6A, 6B). Recall that the SSMR proposes that societal members bring their stereotypes, attitudes, prototypes, and experiences into organizations (arrow 3) and that the race and status of the victim and the perpetrator inform perceptions of racial harassment (arrow 6A & 6B). This suggests that members of ethnic minority groups should perceive racism more readily than Whites given their greater exposure to, and awareness of, harassment. Many studies support this hypothesis. For example, African-American participants more readily perceived discrimination in the prototype studies described above than Whites (Flournoy et al., 2002). Black employees were more aware of harassment and discrimination aimed at people of color than were Whites working in that same company (Chrobot-Mason, Ragins, & Linnehan, 2013).

Organizational Characteristics and Racial Harassment (Arrows 2 and 3)

The SSMR adopts the Interactional Model of Cultural Diversity (IMCD, Cox, 1994) that proposes that the climate of an organization (Box 3) is determined by the national culture (arrow 1). Like others (Cox, 1994; Harro, 2013), we posit in our SSMR that societal members move into organizations (arrow 2) with their stereotypes and prejudicial attitudes and as leaders and founders can create a climate with policies and practices and create characteristics (like the racial composition of work-groups) and human resource systems that hire and promote White employees with race-relevant attitudes. Further, SSMR proposes that the employee's race and status predicts whether or not s/he perpetrates racial harassment. In addition, it also explains why the victim and observer's race and status and the content of workers' race-related comments will predict which behaviors are likely to be interpreted as harassing and whether observers facilitate, denounce, or remain silent about workplace racial harassment. .

Organizational Characteristics. As shown in Box 3 of Figure 11.1, we propose that organizational-level variables like organizational climate (i.e., practices and policies against harassment), the racial composition of the employees within the organization, and White employees' multicultural attitudes can all affect whether perpetrators harass, victims endure (or leave) and whether observers within the company act against it. Victims, perpetrators, and bystanders can also affect these organizational-level variables. Therefore, we propose a bidirectional influence between organizational and employee characteristics (see bidirectional arrow). For example, employees in power can have a vested interest in rewarding their ingroup (maintaining group power). Such supervisors can create the company's policies and procedures which are racially discriminatory (arrow 5, Stone & Stone-Romero, 2004). Further, within an organization with a poor climate for diversity, employees can use racial humor or aggression to tease and ridicule, to enforce or set social norms facilitating harassment, and to undermine collegial interracial relationships. By hiring people with similar worldviews, *both* supervisors and coworkers can perpetrate racial harassment (arrow 6A). The SSMR proposes that three organizational factors, namely the organizational climate for diversity (i.e., policies, practices, and sanctions), the racial composition of the company, and Whites' attitudes would increase the likelihood of racial harassment (arrow 4) and discrimination (arrow 5).

Policies and Practices. Workplaces develop a climate for racial diversity to the extent to which they endorse anti-racial policies, have fair and timely practices when dealing with such complaints, and sanctions against racism and retaliation to either side (perpetrators or victims). Reports of racial harassment and discrimination should increase when such practices are lacking. Several studies find positive relations between poor organizational climate and reports of racial harassment and discrimination. For example, Triana et al. (2015), who examined five studies across a variety of jobs and types of employees, found that a poorer climate for diversity was reliably related to higher reports of workplace racial harassment and racial discrimination. Similarly, in a sample of nearly 4,000 US military personnel, Bergman et al. (2012) found that perceptions of the organizational climate as anti-racist were related to reports of racial harassment and discrimination (see also Radhakrishnan 1998; Reid & Radhakrishnan, 2003).

When perpetrators are not made aware of the inappropriate nature of their behavior, or are not punished for engaging in racial harassment, their behavior continues. Leaders who use language to reinforce the negative stereotypes of non-White racial/ethnic groups or who make jokes about racism undermine anti-harassment policies and set norms that harassment is tolerated in the organization. Bergman et al. (2012) found that leaderships' efforts to implement and enforce anti-harassment and discrimination policies most strongly predicted experiences of racial harassment and discrimination. They found that providing training and providing resources for anti-racism were not sufficient. Efforts by leaders to convey to victims that they have an ally in the company and to show the company's commitment against racism reduced reports of racism.

The SSMR predicts that employee reactions to racial harassment can change these organizational features over time. For example, minority employees can have discussions about racial plurality, file grievances about harassment and discrimination, make petitions to change company policy, or leave the company, thus changing the company's racial composition.

Racial Composition of the Company. According to Kanter (1977) because people are more comfortable with and promote people like themselves the demographic composition of the organization tends to perpetuate itself, leading to less diversity within organization. Thus, the racial composition of the organization also matters for reports of harassment and discrimination. Employees' status as a token in their work-groups predicted their experiences of racial harassment and discrimination (RHD). Tokens (i.e., being the racial minority in one's workgroup) reported more RHD than did non-tokens, suggesting that tokens are more susceptible to racial harassment (Bergman et al., 2012).

Further, when members of underrepresented racial groups hold leadership positions (that were previously held by Whites in the company), they help create new schemas in the minds of employees. Thus, the positive attributes of leadership and competence start to become associated with members of ethnic minorities and not just White men (Nishii, Gotte, & Raver, 2007). Demographic diversity within the organization not only allows for solving problems from various viewpoints, but that it also increases awareness of biased systems, and allows employees of the racial majority group to get to know the employee from the minority racial group as an individual (Brewer & Miller, 1984). Multiple examples of ethnic minorities in leadership positions and/or counter stereotypical roles are needed to change these schemas. The SSMR posits that the greater the diversity in the racial composition of the company, the lower the reports of racial harassment, if, over time, schemas change. Thus, White employees are not surprised when members of underrepresented groups are automatically judged to be competent in leadership or in counter-stereotypical roles (like Black engineer).

Whites' Attitudes about Multiculturalism. Finally, the SSMR predicts that when the majority of White employees' adopt attitudes of multiculturalism, instances of racial harassment and discrimination will be lower (arrows 4 and 5). Organizations and their representatives (i.e., supervisors) can select employees who adopt multiculturalism or ones with colorblind attitudes. Employees with colorblind attitudes prefer homogeneity within the organization and prefer that minority employees assimilate to the dominant culture or be excluded (e.g., declare that Latinx employees can only speak English at the workplace, or that African-Americans employees not wear their hair in its natural form). Such colorblind attitudes amongst White employees can, in turn, predict whether they derogate or exclude racial minority workers and affect the job outcomes of those workers. This hypothesis was supported by a field study of over 4,900 employees in a health-care system by Plaut, Thomas, and Goren (2009) who tested whether Anglo workers' adoption of multicultural versus colorblind attitudes were associated with a climate of valuing diversity and whether that climate, in turn, affected ethnic minority workers' engagement. Adopting a colorblind approach suggests that minority group members assimilate their behaviors to fit the status quo set by the majority group members, whereas adopting a multicultural attitude suggests an appreciation and affirmation of different ethnic groups. Because ethnic minority workers value their ethnicity, a colorblind approach can minimize an important aspect of their identities, adding yet another set of expectations for them (e.g., suppress discussions about race at work). As expected, Plaut et al. (2009) found that, when their Anglo coworkers endorsed multiculturalism, racial minority employees reported placing more importance in succeeding at their jobs and felt more pride in working for the organization.

Perpetrators, Victims, and Bystanders (arrows 6A and 6B).

This section explains how employees perpetrate racial harassment, and how victims and observers/bystanders interpret it when they encounter it. We then discuss the impact of experiencing harassment and discrimination for both, victims and observers. Given the definitions of harassment, discrimination, and the way human resource systems work within organizations, the SSMR predicts that only employees who have the power to provide opportunities and allocate resources to the victim (e.g., supervisors, leaders) can perpetrate racial discrimination, (arrow 6B) but that *anyone* in the organization (supervisors, coworkers, subordinates) can perpetrate racial harassment (arrow 6A).

Perpetrators' Characteristics. The SSMR recognizes that employees vary in their status within society (e.g., Whites have more status than other racial groups) and their status within the company (supervisors vs. not). However, not all Whites and not all employees in high-status supervisory roles are likely to perpetuate racial harassment. People vary in their implicit bias favoring Whites, their motivations to protect the status they acquired based on their race, and in their internal motivations to avoid being prejudiced. The SSMR predicts, given the socialization of racism within the American society, and the cognitive and motivational forces for ingroup favoritism, employees with high social and organizational status (i.e., Whites, supervisors) can easily commit racial harassment especially when cognitively overloaded (Fiske & Taylor, 2008) unless internal restraints or organizational sanctions against harassment are enforced (cf. organizational sanctions were an important mechanism for reducing sexual harassment, Fitzgerald, Hulin, & Drasgow, 1994).

Would most White employees in American organizations be expected to commit racial harassment and discrimination? To answer this question, we review the research on aversive racism (Dovidio & Gaertner, 2008) and apply it to the context of human-resource judgments and decisions (selection decisions, performance evaluations) which are rife with multiple criteria and attributional ambiguity.

Aversive racists are Whites who favor Whites over Blacks on *implicit* attitudes tests (Banaji & Greenwald; 2013; Devine et al., 2012) but endorse egalitarian and humanitarian values on *explicit* attitude surveys (Dovidio & Gaertner, 2008). Pro-White/Anti-Black stereotyping is the *default way of thinking* for White aversive racists (Dovidio & Gaertner, 1986; 2008) given the social, cognitive, and motivational factors we reviewed earlier. According to the theory, White aversive racists will (1) suppress or hide their preferences for Whites in situations where their preferences can be attributed to racism, and (2) will favor Whites in ambiguous situations, when their anti-Black behaviors can be attributed to things other than race. For example, Whites were more willing to discriminate if they can justify not hiring Black applicants due to such applicants lacking racially biased credentials such as being a member of a certain country club (Dovidio & Gaertner, 2008; Dovidio et al., 2002). Moreover, many aversive racists are unaware of their own pro-White/Anti-Black bias. To illustrate, Dovidio et al. (2002) manipulated the credentials of White and Black applicants and asked Whites to recommend applicants for a position. When candidates' qualifications for the job were *less obvious and the decision was ambiguous*, White aversive racists recommended the Black candidate significantly less often than the White one (45% vs. 76%, Dovidio et al., 2002, p. 62).

More importantly, White aversive racists who worked with Black coworkers had the most detrimental effects in the workplace — they sent mixed messages when interacting with Black co-workers (e.g., friendly verbal messages with unfriendly body language). This discrepancy led Black participants to distrust White aversive-racists (Dovidio et al., 2002). This distrust infected the climate in the workplace and led to lower performance of Blacks. That is, team performance was the worst when Blacks worked with an aversive-racist than when they worked with a non-racist or a blatantly racist person (Dovidio et al., 2002). Similarly, another study showed that holding attitudes that favored Whites created negative interpersonal interactions (McConnell & Leibold, 2001) and predicted the lower likelihood of hiring Black over White applicants of similar qualifications (Bertrand & Mullainathan, 2004). In short, negative stereotyping can create cold nonverbal behaviors (exclusion, distancing) that can manifest into overt racial harassment and result in decisions that hinder the progress of racial minorities in the workplace leading to racial discrimination.

Victim's Characteristics That Can Elicit Harassment. We first discuss the factors that lead victims and bystanders to decide whether racial harassment occurred (arrows 6A and 6B). We then discuss the impact of racial harassment and discrimination for victims, observers, and the company.

The SSMR model predicts that when people feel threatened, they will aggress against those who are least likely to retaliate against them. We posit they will look for low-status, tokens, and/or employees in ethnic minority groups who they perceive as having received preferential treatment at hiring. As explained before, being a token *and* being an ethnic minority in a organization dominated by Whites makes race salient, promotes racial stereotyping, and the opportunity for racial harassment. This is because in such situations, racial stereotypes are automatically activated, and unless challenged, automatically applied (Devine et al., 2005). Supporting this prediction, Bergman et al. (2012) found that employees who were in the numerical minority (e.g., female soldiers, Black and Latinx solos in the military) were more likely to experience racial harassment and discrimination than were those who were in the numerical majority. Being a token results in negative experiences even for members of socially privileged groups (e.g., Whites, men). Nevertheless, members of socially disadvantaged groups (i.e., women, Blacks) reported *many more* negative work experiences when they were tokens than those of socially dominant groups (see Thompson & Sekaquaptewa, 2002).

Bystanders' Experience with Racism (arrows 6A and 6B). Bystanders play an important role—they can promote racial tensions, remain indifferent, provide another view of the situation, or be activists. We discussed earlier the SSMR's prediction that factors such as prototypes of racism, cultural and subcultural differences, and the observer's past experiences with racism can all affect victims' and observers' interpretations of whether a certain action reflects harassment (arrows 1, 3 and 6A, Inman & Baron, 1996). For example, an employee who is unaware of America's racial history and who hears a coworker refer to a dark-skinned coworker as "boy" is less likely to see this comment as racial harassment.

Further, the SSMR posits that bystanders' similarity to the victim matters. The more similar the bystander is to the victim (in terms of race, organizational status), the similar the perceptual lens and the similar the interpretation that the event in question reflects harassment. Supporting this notion, we find that bystanders and victims were similar in their interpretations of ambiguous feedback as discriminatory when the bystander's gender matched that of the victim than when it did not (Inman, 2001). Further, Black employees were more aware of harassment and discrimination aimed at *other* people of color in their workplace than were Whites working in the same company (Chrobot-Mason et al., 2013).

Furthermore, SSMR posits that observers can also be affected by the harassment of victims which in turn has important outcomes for the organization as well (arrows 7 through 12). This is supported by empirical research by Low et al. (2007). Similarly, meta-analyses consistently show that indirect exposure to racial harassment and discrimination (RHD) was negatively related to job outcomes (Dhanani et al., 2018).

ORGANIZATIONAL STRESSORS: RACIAL HARASSMENT AND DISCRIMINATION

Like many others, we also propose that experiences of workplace racism (i.e., harassment and discrimination) are stressful (Bergman et al., 2012; Dhanani et al., 2018; Fitzgerald, et al., 1994; Richardson & Taylor, 2009; Richman, Flaherty, & Rospenda, 1996; Rospenda, Richman, & Shannon, 2009; Sanchez & Brock, 1996; Triana et al., 2015; Volpone & Avery, 2013). When being racially harassed and/or discriminated, the worker is being deprived of the company's resources (Crosby, 1984) and/or is subject to unfair practices compared to others. Racial harassment and racial discrimination are stressors in that they are negative experiences that trigger a cognitive appraisal and a response (Lazarus & Folkman,

1984). When the appraisal is negative, the victim can act or remain silent, feel exhausted from facing the stressor or attempting to avoid it, all of which can lead to negative mental and physical health outcomes. The victim also has to appraise the organization's response if s/he makes a complaint about it (e.g., whether the complaint was dealt with sufficiently and swiftly). Richardson and Taylor (2009) noted that women of color who faced *both* sexual and racial harassment underwent similar processes that our SSMR proposes (e.g., perceiving the act, making sense and deciding what to do, resisting it by voicing it or by being silent, and interpreting the company's reaction).

When employees are using their resources to cope with the stressors of racial harassment and/or racial discrimination, it can lead them to psychologically disengage from the job and physically withdraw from the company (Volpone & Avery, 2013). Several studies have supported this idea. Reports of workplace racism showed it was related to negative feelings at work, anxiety, guilt, rumination, hypervigilance and triggered coping strategies (Carter & Forsyth, 2010; Low et al., 2007). Victims of workplace racism attempted to cope (Triana et al., 2015) and were overwhelmed (Dhanani et al., 2018; Volpone & Avery, 2013). Results from three national samples showed that workers experiencing racism at work reported burnout and organizational disengagement (Volpone & Avery, 2013). In a military sample, Bergman et al. (2012) found that experiences of workplace racism predicted supervisor, coworker and job dissatisfaction, which in turn predicted organizationally relevant outcomes such as intentions to quit. A meta-analysis of 79 studies and nearly 84,000 employees showed that those experiencing workplace racism reported poorer mental health and experienced physical distress (22 studies), were more dissatisfied with their job and with their organization (25 studies), exhibited fewer organizational citizenship behaviors, (4 studies), and had stronger intentions to quit the organization (Triana et al., 2015). Workplace racism explained up to 14 percent of the unique variation in work outcomes, beyond negative affectivity (Dhanani et al., 2018).

More importantly, the *nature* of the harassment and discriminatory *experience* is similar for victims of all racial groups who experienced it—all were stressed (Bergman et al., 2007). Typically employees of ethnic minority groups (Blacks, Latinos) experienced more workplace racism than did Whites (Bergman et al., 2007; Berdahl & Moore, 2006). However, in geographic regions where ethnic minorities were in the numerical majority, there were no racial differences in frequency reports of workplace racial harassment (Schneider et al., 2000; Low et al., 2007).

Direct and ambient exposure to workplace racism was related to negative job outcomes for Latino-Americans (Lee & Ahn, 2012), for African-Americans (Lee & Ahn, 2013), and for Asian-Americans (Lee & Ahn, 2011). Finally, two meta-analyses with over 144,000 participants examined perceptions of racism in mental health indicators such as self-esteem, anxiety and depression (Schmitt, Branscombe, Postmes, & Garcia, 2012). Perceived racism was related to poorer mental health with larger effects sizes for members of disadvantaged groups (d=- .24) than for those of advantaged groups (d = .10).

Our lab has also examined the separate effects of *direct* and *observed* harassment on psychological and job outcomes (Low et al, 2007). We found that (1) witnessing racial harassment was just as stressful as directly experiencing it in that it was negatively related to employee satisfaction and health, (2) observing it was commonplace, (3) witnessing it, but not directly experiencing it, was related to poor well-being to the same level as directly experiencing it, and (4) employees reporting the worst job and health outcomes were ones who reported *both* directly experiencing and observing others' racial harassment (Low et al., 2007).

Incorporating these findings then, the SSMR predicts that racial harassment (direct or observed) and racial discrimination (direct or observed) are all stressors that impact employees' physical and mental health, their job performance and their job attitudes (see arrows 7 and 12). Ultimately, such experiences also impact the organization (arrow 13) through their effects on employee job attitudes and lowered job performance.

Furthermore, when the stressors of harassment and discrimination are multiple, severe, and frequent, the reactions should be stronger. Supporting this argument, Dhanani et al. (2018) found that experience of workplace discrimination of *all* kinds (i.e., racism, sexism, heterosexism, ageism, etc.) predicted reports of stress and perceptions of injustice. Stress and perceptions of injustice, in turn, predicted health, job satisfaction, and organizational commitment which then predicted turnover intentions and organizational citizenship behaviors (arrows 7, 9, 10, and 12 in our model). Our SSMR adds that the company's response to harassment and discrimination will be interpreted by victims and observers (as either sufficient or insufficient in addressing the problem) which in turn will affect morale (arrow 13) and subsequently perceptions of organizational climate (see also Radhakrishnan,1998; Richardson & Taylor, 2009).

STRESSORS AT WORK:
RACIAL HARASSMENT *VERSUS* DISCRIMINATION

Our SSMR conceptualizes racial harassment and discrimination as separate experiences because their nature and frequency differ. It is important to note that the majority of empirical studies we reviewed combined measures of racial harassment and discrimination (Bergman et al., 2012; Krieger et al., 2006) even though the concepts differ. Researchers often ask about employees about their experiences of discrimination *and* harassment in the same item (see Krieger et al, 2006; Dhanani et al., 2018). However there are a growing number of studies that assess racial harassment and examine its correlates (Berdahl & Moore, 2006, Low et al. 2007; Raver & Nishii, 2010; Schneider et al. 2000). In a seminal study, our lab measured *harassment* due to race and/or ethnicity and found that it was related to negative job attitudes and withdrawal behaviors (Schneider et al., 2000). We (Hitlan & Radhakrishnan, 1999) also developed a separate and reliable measure of reports of workplace discrimination which we used, along with the Schneider et al (2000) measure to assess harassment and discrimination separately. We found reports of racial harassment were only weakly related to reports of racial discrimination, (rs =.25 to .36, Inman & Radhakrishnan, 2009). Thus, harassment and discrimination differ.

Further, we argue that harassment can be a more frequent experience than discrimination. This is because anyone in the organization can be a perpetrator of harassment, whereas only those with power to allocate job-opportunities and resources to the victim can discriminate. Thus, our SSMR makes two unique predictions compared to past models. It predicts that, though related, racial harassment and racial discrimination, reflect *different* types of injustices: Racial harassment reflects interpersonal injustices involving all employees whereas racial discrimination reflects distributive and procedural injustices involving the company and its representatives (e.g., those with supervisory power). Given these differences, we predict that workers will compartmentalize their reactions to these experiences. Thus, racial harassment and racial discrimination and will have different work-related outcomes. This compartmentalization hypothesis stimulates more research questions which we elaborate on next.

Compartmentalizing Work Experiences (Arrows 7–13)

As explained earlier, racial discrimination (RD) reflects distributive and procedural injustices by the organization or its representatives (i.e., supervisors) whereas racial harassment (RH) reflects interpersonal injustices that can be perpetrated by anyone (supervisors, coworkers subordinates). This is because RD involves the denial of resources and opportunities, only those who have authority over the employee's position within the organization (i.e., supervisors) can perpetrate it. RD results in the employee feeling "relatively deprived" of resources compared to other employees (Crosby, 1984). In contrast, RH is defined as verbal assaults and exclusionary behaviors—those that are *interpersonal* in nature. Employees have more interpersonal contact with coworkers than they do with supervisors: Coworkers are more likely to see the employee's behaviors throughout the day (Borman, 1991). This suggests that coworkers may have more opportunities than supervisors to racially harass, but, because of their power to allocate resources, supervisors can also racially discriminate against employees.

Furthermore, research shows that people remember others' behaviors toward them (Carlston, 1994), so victims of harassment should remember the identity of their harasser, and react accordingly. Experiences of RH and RD violate employees' expectations of how people and the organization should treat them. Employees expect the companies they work for, and the people they work with, to treat them fairly and to prevent RD and RH. This argument is based in part on Social Exchange Theory (Kelley & Thibaut, 1978), which proposes that the relationship between the employee and the company is characterized by interdependence. Employees expect to do their jobs in exchange for a fair distribution of rewards, a fair procedure for distributing those rewards, and for a fair interpersonal interaction with others in the workplace. Such norms of reciprocity and mutual obligation (Cropanzano & Mitchell, 2005) are violated when workplace racial harassment and discrimination occur (Dhanani et al., 2018; Triana et al., 2015).

Relatedly, employees expect organizations (and supervisors) they work for to be held *accountable*—to provide a workplace free of RH and RD (Larsen, Nye, Ormerod, Ziebro, & Siebert, 2013). Thus, employees expect supervisors to punish perpetrators of RH and RD. Therefore, harassment by *anyone* in the organization should be related to lower job satisfaction with the *supervisor,* because the supervisor acts as a proxy for the company and is perceived to be *responsible* for providing a discrimination- and harassment-free workplace.

Racial Discrimination (RD). Additionally, Social Exchange Theory (Kelley & Thibaut, 1978) suggests that employees weigh the costs versus benefits of staying with the company (Cropanzano & Mitchell, 2005), just as people do when deciding to stay or leave a personal relationship (Rusbult & Van Lange,1996). This suggests that the relative costs of RH and RD contribute to employees' decisions to quit the organization. Because RD by definition has relatively higher costs for the employee in terms of their pay and promotional opportunities, SSMR predicts that RD will be more strongly related (or directly related) to organizational withdrawal behaviors (arrow 12) than will experiences of RH (arrow 9). Figure 11.1 shows the outcomes of racial discrimination for the victim and for the organization (arrow 13). Based on the theories described earlier, racial discrimination (RD) should be associated with poorer health and poorer job performance (arrow 10), dissatisfaction with specifically the organizational representative who perpetrated it (arrow 11), dissatisfaction, withdrawal, and disengagement with the company (arrow 12), which can all result in negative organizational outcomes (arrow 13) such as lowered employee morale, increased grievances, high turnover, and a tarnished company reputation.

Racial Harassment (RH). In contrast, direct experiences and observations of racial harassment will result in different outcomes for employees (see arrows 7–9) than will discrimination. Consider the example, in which Juan, a Latino and legal US citizen is repeatedly told by his White coworker Jim to "*Watch out! Or I will call immigration on you!*" and sees the comment "*Go back to where you came from*" sprayed on his locker. The SSMR predicts that faced with such forms racial harassment, Juan and bystanders who are members of Juan's racial group (and/or employees of other disadvantaged groups) will enact coping strategies to deal with this stressor, resulting in their lower physical health (arrow 7). Similar bystanders may further worry that they will be the next target for harassment. In this way, some types of racial harassment (e.g., racial slurs) can be perceived to be directed to all members of that racial group and/or all minority racial groups. Juan/Others will notice *who* the perpetrator is (e.g., a coworker), become dissatisfied with that specific perpetrator (arrow 8) *and* dissatisfied with his supervisor because the supervisor did not prevent, or sufficiently redress, the harassment.

Juan may disengage from the company (via lowered organizational commitment, increased withdrawal, increased absenteeism) because the company failed to provide a harassment-free workplace (arrow 9). The SSMR predicts that depending on the chronic and severe nature of the harassment, both observed *and* experienced racial harassment could eventually yield negative organizational outcomes (arrow 13) such as lowered employee morale, grievances and lawsuits, employee turnover and a tarnished company reputation, (Gelfand et al., 2005).

Status of the Harasser: Compartmentalization. Our SSMR predicts that racial harassment (RH) *by supervisors* result in more severe reactions in employees when compared to racial harassment *by coworkers or subordinates*. Racial harassment by supervisors adds to the fear and worry of additional negative outcomes (poor mental health, arrow 7). Supervisors who harass can also discriminate (bidirectional arrow between RH and RD) given their power to evaluate and to offer advancement opportunities to employees. Racial harassment can lead to employees' negative attitudes toward the supervisor (arrow 8) and to the company (i.e., lowered organizational commitment, arrow 9), which can lead to negative, organizationally-relevant outcomes (i.e., low morale, lawsuits, etc., arrow 13). Supporting this hypothesis, Frone (2000) found that workers who had conflicts with supervisors were more likely to display organizational withdrawal behaviors such as turnover intentions, whereas conflicts with coworkers were associated with lower self-esteem, increased depression, and more headaches. Similarly, Bruk-Lee and Spector (2006) found that conflicts with supervisors predicted counterproductive behaviors toward the organization (e.g., stealing company supplies), whereas conflicts with coworkers predicted counterproductive interpersonal behaviors (e.g., belittling a coworker). These findings suggest that employees *compartmentalize* the outcomes of the relationships they have with different types of employees and react accordingly.

Two empirical studies support our compartmentalization hypothesis that employees are more likely to be harassed by coworkers and that harassed workers are dissatisfied with specific perpetrators who harassed them and with the organization. In a field survey of ethnically diverse workers from different organizations and geographical locations, we assessed the frequency of racial harassment from various type of perpetrators (supervisors, coworkers, others), the amount of racial discrimination experienced, job attitudes, and withdrawal behaviors (Inman & Radhakrishnan, 2009). As predicted by SSMR, employees reported that coworkers were more likely to racially harass them than were supervisors or others in the workplace. And, as expected, supervisors were more likely to racially discriminate when compared to coworkers and others. In addition, reports of racial harassment incrementally predicted dissatisfaction with coworkers, beyond reports of racial discrimination. Reports of racial discrimination incrementally predicted dissatisfaction with supervisors, beyond reports of racial harassment. Finally, as expected, reports of racial discrimination predicted organizational withdrawal behaviors (arrow 12).

Social Support: Moderating the Effects of Harassment and Discrimination (Arrow 14)

Our SSMR predicts that, if the stress model is supported, having social support to cope with workplace racism (RD and RH) should weaken its effects on outcomes by giving emotional aid, tangible help, affirming the employee, and boosting self-efficacy. For brevity, Figure 11.1 shows only one moderating arrow (14). However, we expect social support to moderate the relationship between RH and RD to dissatisfaction with coworkers and dissatisfaction with the company (arrow 14 moderates all arrows 7—12). This section reviews four moderators that have been studied empirically that we propose can be conceptualized as venues for social support. The results from these empirical studies suggest that social support for victims weakened relationships between workplace racism and outcomes (arrows 7, 9, 10, 12).

The Role of Allies. Two of the four empirical studies showed that experiencing incivility (i.e., disrespect, condescending behaviors) at work was related to job dissatisfaction and distress. In contrast, for employees who reported receiving emotional support from others at work via affirmations such as *"I'm here for you"* or from the organization, incivility was no longer related to distress (Miner, Settles, Pratt-Hyatt, & Brady, 2012).

Victim's Ethnic Identity. Perceiving racism can lead to poorer mental health (arrows 7 and 10) for *some* members of racial minority groups than for others in those same groups. This is because some members can personalize the negative treatment they encounter. However, when victims cope with racism by rejecting the negative treatment, by not personalizing it, and by bolstering their ethnic identity, they can maintain positive mental health (Giamo, Schmitt, & Outten, 2012). In several field studies of multi-racial employees, Giamo et al. (2012) found that amongst those who experienced racism, ethnic minorities who identified with their ethnic group reported higher well-being relative to those who did not. Specifically, self-stereotyping (e.g., *"I have a lot in common with the average multiracial person"*) was the protective element of ethnic identity that mediated the relationship between perceived discrimination and well-being (Giamo et al., 2012). When the victim perceived themselves to be part of a larger racial group, it buffered the effects of discrimination.

The Role of Mentoring. The SSMR adopts Relations System Theory (Kahn, 2001) which emphasizes the important role that relationships play in the workplace. Perpetrators of racial harassment may often not be representative of all employees in the organizations. Research suggests that high-quality mentoring may attenuate the relationship between workplace racism and job-outcomes (Ragins, Ehrhardt, Lyness, Murphy, & Capman, 2017). Mentors can offer a safe place for targets of harassment and discrimination to cognitively process events, provide an ally, provide information, and disabuse the idea that no one at the company cares about the treatment to the victim. Mentors can provide stable relationships by anchoring employees to their organizations and help them maintain their organizational commitment in the face of anxiety-producing events like racial harassment and discrimination. In three studies with over 3,000 workers, Ragins, et al. (2017) showed that having a high-quality mentor *who was not a coworker or supervisor* weakened the relationship between *observed/ambient* workplace racism and a variety of outcomes like attendance, sleep quality, and organizational commitment (arrows 10 and 12 in our model).

Enabling Bystanders to Respond. Our model uses Crosby's (2015) review of the empirical and theoretical research to predict that like mentors, active and responsive bystanders can mitigate the negative effects of stress of experiencing workplace racism (i.e., weaken relations 7 through 12). Bystanders may often fail to perceive, respond to, and act against racism when they observe or know about it (Crosby, 2015). This is because bystanders who are typically Whites in the US, experience workplace racism less frequently and so may feel that they may not be accurate in assessing if a certain event reflected harassment or discrimination. Bystanders may also believe that *direct* targets are the only ones who can legitimately make complaints of workplace racism. Even if bystanders perceive workplace racism, the organization they are part of may not have procedures for reporting it. Bystanders also fear retaliation for reporting and/or acting against workplace racism. Finally, bystanders may be motivated to avoid perceiving events as racism because of their own stereotypes, prejudiced attitudes, and the worldviews of the dominant racial group (which may prevail in the organization as well, as explained earlier). Therefore, our model predicts that educating bystanders on how to respond, providing them with the tools for reporting and preventing workplace racism, training them to overcome their own stereotypes/prejudices can all be mechanisms of social support that can help mitigate the effects of harassment.

DIRECTIONS FOR FUTURE RESEARCH

Comprehensive Model Testing. Our SSMR is based on theories and research in social and organizational psychology. The research we review provides substantial, albeit indirect, support for the model, but there has not been a comprehensive, empirical test of the entire model. This might be in assessed in a company spread across different geographic locations across the United States by using separate and distinct measures of harassment (Schneider et al. 2000; Low et al., 2007) and discrimination (Hitlan & Radhakrishnan, 1999; Inman & Radhakrishnan, 2009), measures of organizational climate for diversity, (e.g., Radhakrishnan, 1998), validated measures of stereotypes and attitudes (see Oswald, Mitchell, Blanton, Jaccard, & Tetlock, 2013 for examples), employee attitudes, employee withdrawal behaviors and organizational indicators.

Multiple and separate empirical studies that have tested the different links of the model have been published (as cited throughout this paper) or presented at conferences (e.g., Hitlan & Radhakrishnan, 1999; Radhakrishnan, 1998; Inman & Radhakrishnan, 2009). We rely heavily on one meta-analysis by Dhanani et al. (2018) that has pieced together several of the SSMR's hypothesized relations. In general, their findings support the predictions made by SSMR. However, Dhanani et al. (2018) combined measures of racial harassment and racial discrimination with other measures of discrimination due to gender, age and found that experiences with any kind of work discrimination (sexism, ageism, racism, etc.) predicted employee health, job satisfaction, and organizational commitment, which, in turn, predicted turnover intentions and citizenship behaviors (arrows 7, 9, 10, 12, and 13 in our model).

Identifying Mechanisms via Longitudinal Studies. Longitudinal studies that test assumptions about how racial harassment and discrimination unfold over time are needed. As our model predicts, repeated experiences of racial harassment (e.g., derogation and exclusion) can predict experiences of racial discrimination (i.e., in terms of task assignments, performance appraisals, pay, and promotions). However, much of the empirical research we reviewed not only measured harassment and discrimination in the same item but they also were cross-sectional correlational studies that did not allow for causal conclusions. Longitudinal field studies that utilize daily logs and/or archival records can determine how stereotypes and prejudicial attitudes can infect employee interactions (i.e., harassment) and subsequent personnel decisions (i.e., discrimination) For example, we propose that a supervisor's prejudicial attitudes will not only affect that supervisor's behaviors in the hiring context (e.g., while interviewing applicants, while negotiating salaries with applicants) but also that supervisor's behaviors after hiring (e.g., the sharing information with new recruits, giving new recruits opportunities to improve skills by assigning challenging projects to them, or recommending them for training). Measuring these behaviors can illuminate how racial harassment and racial discrimination unfold over time in organizations. For example, Hernandez, Avery, Volpone, and Kaiser's (2018) paper of the role of race in salary negotiations with three different community samples is a good example of such research. They found that Black job applicants were expected to negotiate for less pay when compared to White applicants. When Black applicants violated this expectation, evaluators (especially biased ones) awarded them lower starting salaries (Study 2). This bias occurred because evaluators became more resistant to making concessions to Black than to White job applicants (Study 3).

Testing the Efficacy of Interventions. Experimental field studies with employed adults are needed to test the efficacy of interventions designed to reduce implicit racial biases. Current attempts to reduce implicit racial biases in potential perpetrators, raise awareness of racism, and raise activism against racism are typically conducted with undergraduate students. Such research shows that theory-based, multi-faceted interventions that contain (1) vivid counter-stereotypical situations (e.g., Black hero saving a White victim), (2) providing personalizing information for successful Black role models, and (3) providing strategies to overcome initial negative stereotyping are all are successful (Forscher et al., 2017; Lai et al, 2014, 2016). For example, compared to the control group (which did a filler task), undergraduates in the experimental condition were more likely to be aware of racism and to publicly object to an essay that endorsed racial stereotyping when they encountered it two years after the intervention. Such research must now be conducted in organizational settings with employees. A meta-analysis of the impact of diversity training initiatives the workplace showed modest gains in learning about other cultures but attitudinal changes were short-lived (Bezrukova, Spell, Perry, & Jehn, 2016).

IMPLICATIONS

Theoretical Implications

By explaining how employees with supervisory power come to perpetrate harassment, how victims *and* bystanders come to interpret events as racial harassment, and how they react to it, we can study racial harassment vis-à-vis other forms of stigma-based discrimination, thus more deeply examining the extent to which employees compartmentalize their negative experiences at work. By measuring different forms of harassment (e.g., ethnic harassment, gender harassment, general workplace harassment), researchers can elaborate on how the harassment-stress link operates. For example, Berdahl & Moore (2006) found that ethnic minority women were doubly jeopardized because they were subject to racial *and* sexual harassment. Similarly, Buchanan and Fitzgerald (2008) found that when African American women reported sexual harassment, racial harassment was often present too. Both studies found increased dissatisfaction with reports of racial harassment. However, the latter study found support for a stress-threshold model rather than an additive one. Similarly, Raver and Nishii (2010) found that although *all* forms of harassment were related to poor well-being and job satisfaction, combining different forms of harassment only minimally increased the prediction of strain over any *one* type of harassment, presumably because victims were depleted of psychological resources with such stressors. Given the prediction of increasing diversity in the workforce (Fry & Parker, 2018), we can expect that employees will bring multiple identities to the workplace. Empirical studies that examine the stress of harassment arising from multiple identities (see for example, Dhanani et al. 2018) and ways to help mitigate the effects of such types of harassment (e.g., via affirming multiple identities) are needed. Ragins et al. (2017) found that mentors effectively buffered the negative effects of observed harassment. Future studies are needed to test whether mentoring helped buffer the negative effects of *direct experiences* of harassment. Studies also need to identify and assess the mechanisms (e.g., increased self-efficacy, reappraisal) through which social support in general (and mentors in particular) can lower negative outcomes for harassed employees.

Our SSMR argues for the separate conceptualization and measurement of racial harassment and discrimination. From this, we can better understand how each operates, test the extent to which workers compartmentalize their experiences, and predict the differential outcomes of these experiences for workers and for the company. Preliminary tests of our model look promising. For instance, we (Inman & Radhakrishna, 2009) find that racial harassment was related to job dissatisfaction, whereas reports of racial discrimination were related to organizational withdrawal. Also, Ragins et al. (2017) found that only certain kinds of mentors (employees who were not coworkers or supervisors) buffered the effects of workplace harassment and discrimination. Taken together, these patterns lend support to the idea that workers compartmentalize their work experiences. Future research could use our model to identify the specific mechanisms that social support uses to be effective (e.g., what mitigates against stress: active listening, information gathering, making the complaint, talking to the perpetrator, etc.).

Prognosis for the Near Future

Although awareness of racism has been increasing due to social movements like Black Lives Matter, we think, on the one hand, racial tensions inside contemporary US organizations will persist for several reasons. The self-protective motives for members of dominant groups to deny power and resources to members of oppressed racial groups may still be powerful according the predictions of social identity theory and the group-based justice model. Employees get defensive when their worldviews are challenged (Stone-Romero & Stone, 2005). The increasing ethnic diversity of the US workforce brings with it a clash of worldviews (Stone & Stone-Romero, 2004) in the workplace. For example, the Anglo worldview of being "direct" while communicating and rewarding individual achievement are not the default values in non-Anglo cultures. Though some organizations are encouraging employees to adopt a multicultural attitude of affirming the worth of employees of different cultural backgrounds, it is not clear that organizational climates, employees' stereotypes about, and/or prejudicial attitudes toward members of disadvantaged groups can change easily. For example a White employee can welcome the celebration of Martin Luther King Day and yet he/she may still show microaggressions and/or exclude minority employees by not sharing information with them, hurting that employee's chances for advancement.

Our SSMR predicts that when a company 1) adopts policies against harassment and discrimination and enforces them, 2) changes its racial composition, and when 3) its employees begin to adopt multicultural attitudes, bystanders should begin to notice when racial harassment occurs and become more effective allies to victims (e.g., by lending advice, sanctioning perpetrators, preventing retaliation from the perpetrator, aiding in the grievance process etc.). Such bystander behaviors, in turn, should enable the company's climate for diversity to become more pervasive, and over time, result in lower levels of harassment and discrimination. To increase the likelihood that bystanders will report incidents of workplace racism, organizations need to convey to *all* employees that the norm of responsibility of reporting workplace racism is on *all* members of the organization, not just direct victims (Crosby, 2015). Organizational interventions should show how workplace racism is a violation of one's core moral values and should attempt to move the focus of *all* employees from one of self-preservation to that of helping others in the organization thrive (Crosby, 2015, p. 546).

There is reason for optimism, however, because millennials who are entering the American workforce are the most culturally diverse group compared to their past cohorts (Fry & Parker, 2018). According to the SSMR, as the company has more employees with multicultural attitudes, reports of racial harassment should first rise due to increased awareness on the part of victims and bystanders, but then fall, due to organizational sanctions and the internalization of multicultural attitudes within all employees of the company.

Implications for Organizations

We think organizations in the US need to take three actions to truly include their racial and ethnic minority employees. First, they need to embrace multi-culturalism, so every employee can see his/her worth in the company. This starts with recruiting, supporting, promoting, and retaining members of different racial and ethnic groups, including promoting them to leadership positions so that they have the resources and power to challenge the existing structures that perpetuate harassment and discrimination. Second, companies need to communicate to their employees about being inclusive to minority employees clearly and often. Anti-racism policies and procedures need to be explicitly explained and enforced. Employees need to be able to articulate the benefits of working with a racially differ-ent other (i.e., in terms of their own growth and the betterment of the company). Such discussions about race and interracial interactions are difficult, especially for White Americans who fear they may discover some uncomfortable truths about themselves and may be perceived as prejudiced (Sue, 2015). Education about race, identity, and the causes, experiences, and outcomes of racism through diver-sity workshops with genuine humility and courage can help people get to know their minority coworkers on a personal level (Brewer & Miller, 1984) and respect each other. Third, companies should focus on inclusion (rather than on "manag-ing" diversity, see Shore et al., 2018 for a full discussion) by developing a pipeline to recruit employees of underrepresented groups, seeking their input in product design, customer service, and community relations. Doing so should enable such employees to truly contribute their skills to the organization and be perceived as deserving of advancement opportunities within it.

Implications for Legislation

The United States government has repeatedly denounced racism via its leg-islations of the Civil Rights Act of 1964 and 1991. Unfortunately, the resources allocated to the EEOC (the enforcement agency) are gravely inadequate (Jameel & Yerardi, 2019). The EEOC "does not have the resources for [the] ... mammoth task (of investigating racial complaints). It has a smaller budget [in 2019] than it did in 1980..[after adjusting] for inflation, and 42 percent less staff [while] ...

the country's labor force has increased by 50 percent to ... 160 million" (Jameel & Yerardi, 2019, p. 5). Because it takes more time and resources to investigate cases of discrimination, Black workers are hurt disproportionately because over a quarter of all EEOC complaints came from them (p. 5). Further, such victims experience retaliation for filing complaints. Thus, it is critical that the government provide the resources to the EEOC, so it can take legal action against companies that perpetrate racial harassment. Without the EEOC, victims have little recourse.

It is imperative to understand the causes and mechanisms by which stereotypes and attitudes manifest in the workplace so as to eliminate workplace racial harassment and discrimination. We think our Socialization-Stress Model of Racism will prove useful for researchers and practitioners. Researchers can study the mechanisms in the model and practitioners can revise their policies and procedures to prevent racial harassment at work.

REFERENCES

Acrey, B.P. (1992). *Navajo history: The land and the people.* Shiprock, NM: Department of Curriculum Materials Development, Central Consolidated School District N. 22, 1978.

Anicich, E. M., Fast, N. J., Halevy, N., & Galinsky, A. D. (2016). When the basis of social hierarchy collide: Power without status drives interpersonal conflict. *Organization Science, 27,* 123–140. Retrieved from: http://dx.doi.org/10.1287/orsc.2015.1019

Ashmore, R. D., & Del Boca, F. K. (1981). Psychological approaches to understanding intergroup conflicts. In P.A. Katz (Ed.), *Towards the elimination of racism* (pp. 73–123). NY: Pergamon.

Avery, D., Richeson, J., Hebl, M., & Ambady, N. (2009). It does not have to be uncomfortable: The role of behavioral scripts in Black-White interracial interactions. *Journal of Applied Psychology, 94,* 1382–1393.

Banaji, M. R., & Greenwald, A. G. (2013). *Blindspot: Hidden biases of good people.* New York, NY: Delacorte Press.

Berdahl, J. L., & Moore, C. (2006). Workplace harassment: Double jeopardy for minority women. *Journal of Applied Psychology, 91,* 426–436.

Bergman, M. E., Palmieri, P. A., Drasgow, F., & Ormerod, A. J. (2007). Racial and ethnic harassment and discrimination: In the eye of the beholder? *Journal of Occupational Health Psychology, 12,* 144–160. doi:http://dx.doi.org/10.1037/1076-8998.12.2.144

Bergman, M. E., Palmieri, P. A., Drasgow, F., & Ormerod, A. J. (2012). Racial/ethnic harassment and discrimination, its antecedents, and its effect on job-related outcomes. *Journal of Occupational Health Psychology, 17,* 65–78. doi:http://dx.doi.org/10.1037/a0026430

Bertrand, M., & Mullainathan, S. (2004). Are Emily and Greg more employable than Lakisha and Jamal? A field experiment on labor market discrimination. *American Economic Review, 94,* 991–1013. Retrieved from: http://dx.doi.org/10.1257/0002828042002561.

Betancourt, H., & Lopez, S. R. (1993). The study of culture, ethnicity, and race in America. *American Psychologist, 48,* 629–637.

Bezrukova, K., Spell, C. S. Perry, J. L., & Jehn, K. A. (2016). A meta-analytical integration of over 40 years of research on diversity. *Psychological Bulletin, 142*(11), 1227–1274.

Bianchi, E. C., Hall, E. V., & Lee, S. (2018). Reexamining the link between economic downturns and racial antipathy: Evidence that prejudice against Blacks rises during recessions. *Psychological science, 29*(10), 1584–1597.

Blalock, H. M. (1967). *Toward a theory of minority-group relations.* New York, NY: Wiley.

Borman, W. C. (1991). Job behavior, performance, and effectiveness. In M. D. Dunnette & L. M. Hough (Eds.), *Handbook of industrial and organizational psychology* (2nd ed., Vol. 2, pp. 271–326). Palo Alto, CA: Consulting Psychologists Press.

Brewer, M. B. (1999). The psychology of prejudice: Ingroup love or outgroup hate. *Journal of Social Issues, 55,* 429–444.

Brewer, M. B., & Miller, N. (1984). Beyond the contact hypothesis: Theoretical perspectives on desegregation. In N. Miller & M. Brewer (Eds.), *Groups in contact: The psychology of desegregation* (pp. 281–302). New York: NY: Academic Press.

Bruk-Lee, V., & Spector, P. E. (2006). The social stressors-counterproductive work behaviors link: Are conflicts with supervisors and coworkers the same? *Journal of Occupational Health Psychology, 11*(2), 145–156.

Bucchianeri, M. M., & Corning, A. F. (2013). Disambiguating discriminatory acts of typical versus atypical perpetrators: The moderating role of need for cognitive closure. *Journal of Applied Social Psychology, 43,* 293–306.

Buchanan, N. T., & Fitzgerald, L. F. (2008). Effects of racial and sexual harassment on work and the psychological well-being of African American women. *Journal of Occupational Health Psychology, 13 (2),* 137–151.

Carlston, D. E. (1994). Associated systems theory: A systematic approach to cognitive representations of persons. In R. S. Wyer Jr. *Advances in social cognition* (Vol. 7, pp. 1–78). Hillsdale, NJ, England: Lawrence Erlbaum.

Carter, R. T., & Forsyth, J. (2010). Reactions to racial discrimination: Emotional stress and help-seeking behaviors. *Psychological Trauma: Theory, Research, Practice, and Policy, 2,* 183–191. doi:http://dx.doi.org/10.1037/a0020102

Chinn, D. (2018).(2018). *What is the consequence of racial harassment in the workplace?* Retrieved January 9, 2019 from: https://smallbusiness.chron.com/consequence-racial-harassment-workplace-19016.html).

Chrobot-Mason, D., Ragins, B. R, & Linnehan, F. (2013). Second-hand smoke: Ambient racial harassment at work. *Journal of Managerial Psychology, 28,* 470–491. Doi:10.1108/JMP-02-2012-0064

Cox, T. (1994). *Cultural diversity in organizations: Theory, research, & practice.* San Francisco, CA: Berrett-Koehler.

Crocker, J., & Major, B. (1989). Social stigma and self-esteem: The self-protective properties of stigma. *Psychological Review, 96,* 608–630.

Cropanzano, R., & Mitchell. M. S. (2005). Social exchange theory: An interdisciplinary review. *Journal of Management, 31,* 874–900. Retrieved from: https://doi.org/10.1177/0149206305279602

Crosby, F. J. (1984). Relative deprivation in organizational settings. *Research in Organizational Behavior, 6,* 51–93.

Crosby, F., Bromley, S., & Saxe, L. (1980). Recent unobtrusive studies of black and white discrimination and prejudice: A literature review. *Psychological Bulletin, 87*, 546–563.

Crosby, J. R. (2015). The silent majority: Understanding and increasing majority group responses to discrimination. *Social and Personality Psychology Compass, 9*(10), 539–550. Doi: 10.11111/spc3.12196

Cunningham, G. B., Ferreira, M., & Fink, J.S. (2009). Reactions to prejudiced statements: The influence of statement content and characteristics of the commenter. *Group Dynamics: Theory, Research, and Practice, 13*, 59–73.

Devine, P., Brodish, A., & Vance, S. (2005). Self-regulatory processes in interracial interactions: The role of internal and external motivation to respond without prejudice. In J. Forgas, K. Williams, & S. Laham (Eds.), *Social motivation: Conscious and unconscious processes.* New York, NY: Cambridge University Press.

Devine, P. G., Forscher, P. S., Austin, A. J., & Cox, W. T. (2012). Long-term reduction in implicit race bias: A prejudice habit-breaking intervention. *Journal of Experimental Social Psychology, 48*, 1267–1278.

Dhanani L. Y., Beus J. M., & Joseph D. L. (2018). Workplace discrimination: A meta-analytic extension, critique, and future research agenda. *Personnel Psychology, 71*, 147–179. Retrieved from: https://doi.org/10.1111/peps.12254

Dovidio, J. F., & Gaertner, S. L. (1986). *Prejudice, discrimination, and racism.* San Diego, CA: Academic.

Dovidio, J., & Gaertner, S. L. (2008). New directions in aversive racism research: Persistence and pervasiveness. In C. Willis-Esqueda (Ed.), *Motivational aspects of prejudice and racism: Nebraska symposium on motivation* (pp. 43–67). New York, NY: Springer.

Dovidio, J. F., Gaertner, S. L., Kawakami, K., & Hodson, G. (2002). Why can't we just get along? Interpersonal biases and interracial distrust. *Cultural Diversity and Ethnic Minority Psychology, 8*, 88–102.

Fast, N. J. & Chen, S. (2009). When the boss feels inadequate: Power, incompetence, and aggression. *Psychological Science, 20*, 1406–1413.

Fast, N.J., Halevy, N., & Galinsky, A.D. (2012). The destructive nature of power without status. *Journal of Experimental Social Psychology, 48*, 391–394.

Fein, S., & Spencer, S. J. (2008). Prejudice as self-image maintenance: Affirming the self through derogating others. In R. H. Fazio, & R. E. Petty (Eds.), *Attitudes: Their structure, function, and consequences* (pp. 261–281). New York, NY ;Psychology Press.

Fiske, S. T., & Taylor, S. E. (2008). *Social cognition: From brains to culture.* New York, NY: McGraw-Hill.

Fitzgerald, L., Hulin, C. & Drasgow, F. (1994). The antecedents and consequences of sexual harassment in organizations: An integrated model. In G. P. Keita & J. J Hurrell, Jr. (Eds.). *Job stress in a changing workforce: Investigating gender diversity and family issues* (pp. 55–73). Washington, DC: American Psychological Association.

Flournoy, J. M., Prentice-Dunn, S., & Klinger, M. R. (2002). The role of prototypical situations in the perceptions of prejudice of African Americans, *Journal of Applied Social Psychology, 32*, 406–423.

Forscher, P., Mitamura, C. Dix, E., Cox, W., & Devine, P. (2017). Breaking the prejudice habit: Mechanisms, time course, and longevity. *Journal of Experimental Social Psychology, 72,* 133–146.

Frone, M. R. (2000). Interpersonal conflict at work and psychological outcomes: Testing a model among young workers. *Journal of Occupational Health Psychology, 5*(2), 246–255.

Fry, R., & Parker, K. (2018). *Early benchmarks show 'post-millennials' on track to be most diverse, best-educated generation yet: A demographic portrait of today's 6- to 21-year-olds.* Retrieved 2018/11/15 from https://www.pewsocialtrends.org/.

Gelfand, M. J., Nishi, L. H., Raver, J. L., & Schneider, B. (2005). Discrimination in organizations: An organizational-level systems perspective. In R. Dipboye & A. Collella (Eds.), *Discrimination at work: The psychological and organizational bases* (pp. 89–118). Mahwah, NY: Lawrence Erlbaum Associates.

Giamo, L. S., Schmitt, M. T., & Outten, H. R. (2012). Perceived discrimination: Group identification, and life satisfaction among multiracial people: A test of the Rejection-Identification Model. *Cultural Diversity and Ethnic Minority Psychology, 18*(4), 319–328.

Goffman, E. (1963). *Stigma: Notes on the management of spoiled identity.* Englewood Cliffs, NJ: Prentice-Hall.

Griffith, J. (2019, Jan. 17). *Black workers at GM plant where nooses were found allege racial harassment is ongoing.* Retrieved from https://www.nbcnews.com/news/us-news/black-workers-gm-plant-where-nooses-were-found-allege-racial-n959956.

Harrick, E. J., & Sullivan, G. M. (1995). Racial harassment: Case characteristics and employer responsibilities. *Employee Responsibilities and Rights Journal, 8,* 81–95.

Harro, B. (2013). The cycle of socialization. In Adams, M., Blumenfeld, W. J., Castaneda, C., Hackman, H. W., Peters, M. L., & Zuniga, X. (Eds). *Readings for diversity and social justice* (3rd ed., pp. 45–51). New York, NY: Routledge.

Hernandez, M., Avery, D. R., Volpone, S. D., & Kaiser, C. R. (2018). Bargaining while Black: The role of race in salary negotiations. *Journal of Applied Psychology.* Advance online publication. Retrieved from: http://dx.doi.org/10.1037/apl0000363.

Hitlan, R. T., & Radhakrishnan, P. (1999). *Development of a context-specific scale of ethnic discrimination.* Presented at the Western Psychological Society. Albuquerque, NM.

Hofstede, G. (1991). *Cultures and organizations: Software of the mind.* London, UK: McGraw-Hill.

Inman, M. L., & Baron, R. S. (1996). Influence of prototypes on perceptions of prejudice. *Journal of Personality and Social Psychology, 70*(4), 727–739.

Inman, M. L. (2001). Do you see what I see: Similarities and differences in victims' and observers' perceptions of discrimination. *Social Cognition, 19,* 521–546.

Inman, M. L., Huerta, J., Oh, S. (1998). Perceiving discrimination: The role of prototypes and norm violation. *Social Cognition, 16*(4), 418–450.

Inman, M., & Radhakrishnan, P. (2009). *Who is doing what? Compartmentalizing experiences of ethnic harassment & discrimination at work.* Presented at the Society for Personality and Social Psychology. Tampa, FL.

Jameel, M., & Yerardi, J. (2019, Feb. 28). *Workplace discrimination is illegal. But our data shows it's still a huge problem.* Retrieved from https://www.vox.com/policy-and-politics/2019/2/28/18241973/workplace-discrimination-cpi-investigation-eeoc

Jones, J. M. (1997). *Prejudice and racism* (2nd ed.). New York, NY: McGraw Hill.

Jones, K., Peddie, C., Gilrane, V., King, E., & Gray, A. (2016). Not so subtle: A meta-analytic investigation of the correlates of subtle and overt discrimination. *Journal of Management, 42,* 1588–1613.

Kanter, R. M. (1977). *Men and women of the corporation.* New York, NY: Basic Books.

Kahn, W. A. (2001). Holding environments at work. *Journal of Applied Behavioral Science, 37,* 260–279. Doi: 10.1177/00218863011373001

Kelley, H. H., & Thibaut, J. W. (1978). *Interpersonal relations: A theory of interdependence.* New York, NY: Wiley.

Kerbo, H. R. (1983). *Social stratification and inequality: Class-conflict in the United States.* New York, NY: McGraw-Hill.

Krieger, N., Waterman, P. D., Hartman, C., Bates, L. M., Stoddard, A. M., Quinn, M. M., Sorensen, G., & Barbeau, E. M. (2006). Social hazards on the job: Workplace abuse, sexual harassment, and racial discrimination—A study of Black, Latino, and White low-income women and men workers in the United States. *International Journal of Health Services, 36*(1), 51–85.

Krieger, N. (2012). Methods for the scientific study of discrimination and health: An eco-social approach. *American Journal of Public Health, 102*(5), 936–945.

Larsen, S. E., Nye, C. D., Ormerod, A. J., Ziebro, M., & Siebert, J. E. (2013). Do actions speak louder than words? A comparison of three organizational practices for reducing racial/ethnic harassment and discrimination. *Military Psychology, 25,* 602–614. doi:http://dx.doi.org/10.1037/mil0000024

Lai, C., Marini, M., Lehr, S., Curruti, C., Shin, J., Joy-Gaba, J., et al. (2014). Reducing implicit racial preferences: I. A comparative investigation of 17 interventions, *Journal of Experimental Psychology: General, 143,* 1765–1785.

Lai, C., Skinner, A., Cooley, E., Murrar, S., Brauer, M., DeVos, T., et al. (2016). Reducing implicit racial preferences: II. Intervention effectiveness across time. *Journal of Experimental Psychology: General, 145,* 1001–1016.

Lazarus, R. S., & Folkman, S. (1984). *Stress, appraisal, and coping.* New York, NY: Singer.

Lee, D. L., & Ahn, S. (2011). Racial discrimination an Asian mental health: A meta-analysis. *The Counseling Psychologist, 39,* 463–489.

Lee, D., & Ahn, S. (2012). Discrimination against Latina/os: A meta-analysis of individual-level resources and outcomes. *The Counseling Psychologist, 40,* 28–65.

Lee, D. L., & Ahn, S. (2013). The relation of racial identity, ethnic identity, and racial socialization to discrimination-distress: A meta-analysis of Black Americans. *Journal of Counseling Psychology, 60,* 1–14.

Leventhal, G. (1980). What should be done with equity theory? New approaches to studying fairness in social relationships. In K. Gergen, M. Greenberg, & H. Willis (Eds.), *Social exchange: Advances in theory and research* (pp. 27–55). New York, NY: Plenum Press.

Lind, E.A., & Tyler, T. R. (1988). *The social psychology of procedural justice.* New York, NY: Plenum Press.

Low, K. S. D., Radhakrishnan, P., Schneider, K. T., & Rounds, J. (2007). The experiences of bystanders of workplace ethnic harassment. *Journal of Applied Social Psychology, 37,* 2261–2297.

Major, B., Kaiser, C. R., O'Brien, L. T., & McCoy, S. K. (2007). Perceived discrimination as worldview threat or worldview confirmation: Implications for self-esteem.

Journal of Personality and Social Psychology, 92(6), 1068–1086. doi:http://dx.doi.org/10.1037/0022-3514.92.6.1068

Marti, M., Bobier, D., & Baron, R. S. (2000). Right before our eyes: The failure to recognize non-prototypical forms of prejudice. *Group Processes and Intergroup Relations, 3,* 403–418.

McConnell, A., & Leibold, J. (2001). Relations among the implicit association test, discriminatory behavior, and explicit measures of racial attitudes. *Journal of Experimental Social Psychology, 37,* 435–442.

McEneaney, E. H. (1996). Poverty, segregation, and race riots: 1960 to 1993. *American Sociological Review, 61,* 590–613.

Miner, K. N., Settles, I., Pratt-Hyatt, J., & Brady, C. (2012). Experiencing incivility in organizations: The buffering effects of emotional and organizational support. *Journal of Applied Social Psychology, 42,* 340–372.

Mooney, C. (2014). *Across America, whites are biased and they don't even know it.* Retrieved from https://www.washingtonpost.com/news/wonk/wp/2014/12/08.

Nishii, L. H., Gotte, A., & Raver, J. L. (2007). *Upper echelon theory revisited: The relationship between upper echelon diversity, the adoption of diversity practices, and organizational performance* (CAHRS Working Paper #07-04). Ithaca, NY: Cornell University, School of Industrial and Labor Relations, Center for Advanced Human Resource Studies. Retrieved from: http://digitalcommons.ilr.cornell.edu/cahrswp/461.

Oswald, F. L., Mitchell, G., Blanton, H., Jaccard, J., & Tetlock, P. E. (2013). Predicting ethnic and racial discrimination: A meta-analysis of IAT criterion studies. *Journal of Personality and Social Psychology, 105*(2), 171–192. doi:http://dx.doi.org.ezproxy.hope.edu/10.1037/a0032734.

Parker, K., Morin, R., & Horowitz, J. M. (2019). *Looking to the future, public sees an America in decline on many fronts: Majorities predict a weaker economy, a growing income divide, a degraded environment, and a broken political system.* Retrieved from https://www.pewsocialtrends.org/2019/03/21.

Pew Research Center. (2006, March 30). *America's immigration quandary.* Retrieved January 26, 2020 from: https://www.pewresearch.org/hispaic/2006/03/30/americas-immigration-quandary

Pew Research Center (2016). *On views of race and inequality, Blacks and Whites are worlds apart.* Retrieved on January 26, 2020 from: https://www.pewsocialtrends.org/2016/06/27/on-views-of-race-and-inequality-blacks-and-whites-are-worlds-apart

Plaut, V. C., Thomas, K. M., & Goren, M. J. (2009). Is multiculturalism or color blindness better for minorities? *Psychological Science, 20*(4), 444–446.

Quillian, L., Pager, D., Hexel, O., & Midtboen, A. (2017). Meta-analysis of field experiments shows no change in racial discrimination in hiring over time. *Proceedings of the National Academy of Sciences, 114*(41), 10870–10875; DOI:10.1073/pnas.1706255114

Radhakrishnan, P. (1998, April). *Racial discrimination and harassment: Mediators or antecedents to the relation between organizational climate and health outcomes.* Paper presented at the Annual Meetings of the Society for Industrial and Organizational Psychology, Dallas, TX

Ragins, B. R., Ehrhardt, K., Lyness, K. S., Murphy, D. D., & Capman, J. F. (2017). Anchoring relationships at work: High quality menors and other supportive work relationships as buffers to ambient racial discrimination. *Personnel Psychology, 70,* 211–256.

Raver, J. L., & Nishii, L. H. (2010). Once, twice, or three times as harmful? Ethnic harassment, gender harassment, and generalized workplace harassment. *Journal of Applied Psychology, 95*(2), 236–254. doi:http://dx.doi.org/10.1037/a0018377

Reid, L. D., & Radhakrishnan, P. (2003). How race still matters: The relation between race and general campus climate. *Cultural Diversity and Ethnic Minority Psychology, 9,* 263–275.

Richman, J. A., Flaherty, J. A., & Rospenda, K. M. (1996). Perceived workplace harassment experiences and problem drinking among physicians: Broadening the stress/ alienation paradigm. *Addiction, 91,* 391–403.

Richardson, B. K., & Taylor, J. (2009). Sexual harassment at the intersection of race and gender: A theoretical model of the sexual harassment experiences of women of color, *Western Journal of Communication, 73*(3), 248–272.

Rosenthal, R., & Jacobson, L. (1968). *Pygmalion in the classroom: Teacher expectation and pupils' intellectual development.* New York, NY: Holt, Rinehart, & Winston.

Rospenda, K. M., Richman, J. A., & Shannon, C. A. (2009). Prevalence and mental health correlates of harassment and discrimination in the workplace. *Journal of Interpersonal Violence, 24,* 819–843).

Rothschild, F. (2014). *Racial slurs and nooses bring forth another EEOC lawsuit.* Retrieved from: https://employmentdiscrimination.foxrothschild.com

Rusbult, C. E., & Van Lange, P. A. (1996). Interdependence processes. In E. T. Higgins & A. W. Kruglanski (Eds.), *Social psychology: Handbook of basic principles* (pp. 564–596). New York, NY: Guilford Press.

Saleem, M, Prot, S., Anderson, C. A., & Lemieux, A. (2017). Exposure to Muslims in media and support for public policies harming Muslims. *Communication Research, 44,* 841–869.

Sanchez, J., & Brock, P. (1996). Outcomes of perceived discrimination among Hispanic employees: Is diversity management a luxury or a necessity? *Academy of Management Journal, 39,* 704–719.

Schmitt, M. T., Branscombe, N. R., Postmes, T., & Garcia, A. (2012). The consequences of perceived discrimination on psychological well-being: A meta-analytic review. *Psychological Review, 140*(4), 921–948.

Schneider, B. (1987). The people make the place. *Personnel Psychology, 40,* 437–453.

Schneider, K. T., Hitlan, R. T., & Radhakrishnan, P. (2000). An examination of the nature and correlates of ethnic harassment experiences in multiple contexts. *Journal of Applied Psychology, 8,* 3–12.

Shore, L. M., Cleveland, J. N., & Sanchez, D. (2018). Inclusive workplaces: A review and model. *Human Resources Management Review, 28,* 176–189.

Simon, S., Kinias, Z., O'Brien, L. T., Major, B., & Bivolaru, E. (2013). Prototypes of discrimination: How status asymmetry and stereotype asymmetry affect judgments of racial discrimination. *Basic and Applied Social Psychology, 35,* 525–533.

Sniderman, P. M., & Hagen, M. G. (1985). *Race and inequality: A study in American values.* Chatham, NJ: Chatham House.

Solomon, S., Greenberg, J., & Pyszczynski,T. (1991). A terror management theory of social behavior: The psychological functions of self-esteem and cultural worldviews. In M. P. Zanna (Ed.), *Advances in experimental social psychology* (Vol. 24, pp. 93–159). San Francisco, CA: Academic Press.

Stephan, W., & Stephan, C. (1985). Intergroup anxiety. *Journal of Social Issues, 41*, 157–175.

Stone, D. L., & Stone-Romero, E. F. (2004). The influence of culture on role-taking in culturally diverse organizations. In M. S. Stockdale & F. J. Crosby (Eds.), *The psychology and management of workplace diversity* (pp. 78–99). Blackwell Publishing.

Stone-Romero, E. F., & Stone, D. L. (2005). How do organizational justice concepts relate to discrimination and prejudice? In J. Greenberg & J. A. Colquitt (Eds.), *Handbook of organizational justice* (pp. 439–467). Oxford: Taylor & Francis Group.

Stone-Romero, E. F., & Stone, D. (2007). Cognitive, affective, and cultural influences on stigmatization: Impact on human resource management processes and practices. In J. J. Martocchio (Ed.), *Research in personnel and human resource management* (pp. 111–161). Amsterdam: Elsevier.

Stone, E. F., Stone, D. L., & Dipboye, R. L. (1992). Stigmas in organizations: Race, handicaps, and physical attractiveness. In K. Kelley (Ed.), *Issues, theory, and research in industrial/organizational psychology* (pp. 385–457). Amsterdam: Elsevier.

Sue, D. W. (2015). *Race talk and the conspiracy of silence: Understanding and facilitating difficult dialogues on race.* Hoboken, NJ: Wiley.

Swim, J. K., Scott, E. D., Sechrist, G. B., Campbell, B., & Stangor, C. (2003). The role of intent and harm in judgments of prejudice and discrimination. *Journal of Personality and Social Psychology, 84*(5), 944–959. doi:http://dx.doi.org/10.1037/0022-3514.84.5.944

Tajfel, H. (1970). Experiments in intergroup discrimination. *Scientific American, 223*, 96–102.

Tajfel, H. (1978). *Differentiation between social groups: Studies in the social psychology of intergroup relations.* London, UK: Academic.

Tajfel, H. (1981). *Human groups and social categories.* Cambridge, UK: Cambridge University Press.

Tajfel, H., & Turner, J. C. (1986). The social identity theory of intergroup behavior. In S. Worchel & W. Austin (Eds.), *Psychology of intergroup relations.* Chicago, IL. Nelson-Hall.

Tatum, B. D. (1997). *"Why are all the black kids sitting together in the cafeteria?"* New York, NY: Basic Books.

Thompson, M., & Sekaquaptewa, D. (2002). When being different is detrimental: Solo status and the performance of women and racial minorities. *Analyses of Social Issues and Public Policy, 2*(1), 183–203.

Triana, M. C., Jayasinghe, M., & Pieper, J. R. (2015). Perceived workplace racial discrimination and its correlates: A meta-analysis. *Journal of Organizational Behavior, 36*, 491–513.

Trice, H., & Beyer, J. (1993). *The cultures of work organizations.* Englewood Cliffs, NJ: Prentice-Hall.

U.S. Census. (1996). *Population projections of the United States by age, sex, race, and Hispanic origin: 1995 to 2050, U.S. Bureau of the Census, current population reports* (pp. 25–1130). Washington, D.C: U.S. Government Printing Office. Retrieved from www.census.gov/content/dam/Census/library/publications/1996/demo/p25-1130.pdf

U.S. Commission on Civil Rights. (1979). *Desegregation of the nation's public schools: A status report.* Washington, DC: U.S. Government Printing Office.

US Equal Employment Opportunity Commission. (1993). Notice of proposed rulemaking: Guidelines on harassment based on race, color, religion, gender, national origin, age, or disability. *Federal Register, 58,* 51266–51269.

US Equal Employment Opportunity Commission. (2014). *Race-based charges FY 1997 through 2013.* Retrieved from http://www.eeoc.gov/eeoc/statistics/enforcement/race.cfm.

Valdez, Z., & Golash-Boza, T. (2017). U.S. racial and ethnic relations in the twenty-first century. *Ethnic and Racial Studies, 40*(13), 2181–2209. doi:http://dx.doi.org.myaccess.library.utoronto.ca/10.1080/01419870.2016.1262052

Volpone, S. D., & Avery, D. R. (2013). It's self defense: How perceived discrimination promotes employee withdrawal. *Journal of Occupational Health Psychology, 18,* 430–448.

Weigel, R. H., & Howes, P. W. (1985). Conceptions of racial prejudice: Symbolic racism reconsidered. *Journal of Social Issues, 41,* 117–138.

Wilson, W. J. (1973). *Power, racism, and privilege.* New York, NY: Macmillan.

Wong, G., Derthick, A. O., David, E. J. R., Saw, A., & Okazaki, S. (2014). The what, the why, and the how: A review of racial microaggressions research in psychology. *Race and Social Problems, 6*(2), 181–200. doi:http://dx.doi.org/10.1007/s12552-013-9107-9

Word, C., Zanna, M., & Cooper, J. (1974). The nonverbal mediation of self-fulfilling prophecies in interracial interaction. *Journal of Experimental Social Psychology, 10*(2), 109–120.

CHAPTER 12

A MODEL OF FACTORS THOUGHT TO INFLUENCE UNFAIR DISCRIMINATION AGAINST IMMIGRANTS IN ORGANIZATIONS

Dianna L. Stone, Kimberly M. Lukaszewski,
Dianna Contreras Krueger, and Julio C. Canedo

Many industrialized countries (e.g., Europe, Japan, US) need immigrants today because they have low population growth, and face shortages of workers for specialized and non-specialized jobs. In spite of these needs, immigrants experience unfair discrimination in the employment process, and have difficulty gaining or maintaining jobs. Thus, we present a model of the factors thought to affect unfair discrimination against immigrants to ensure that individuals have fair employment opportunities. Our model is based on an integration of the Social Cognition Framework (Miller & Brewer, 1984), and the Theory of Intergroup Conflict (Stephan & Stephan, 1995). It predicts that immigrants are typically assigned to a category, and this categorization elicits stereotypes, perceptions of threat, anxiety, negative job expectancies and unfavorable employment decisions. It also argues that three factors affect the categorization process including the (a) attributes of immigrants, (b) attributes of raters, and the (c) nature of the job, and these factors interact to influence

Diversity and Inclusion in Organizations, pages 331–359.

331

employment decisions. Based on our model, we offer hypotheses to guide future research on unfair discrimination against immigrants, and present several strategies that organizations might use to overcome biases against them.

The United States (US) has long been considered a nation of immigrants, and estimates indicate that 98% of the population have parents or ancestors who migrated from other nations (US Census Bureau, 2016) or were brought to the country by the transatlantic slave trade. Only 2% of the population are Native Americans and are indigenous to the land area labeled the US (US Census Bureau, 2016). Given that most people in the US are descendants of immigrants, it is interesting that they have vacillated between viewing immigrants as a harmful burden or a valuable resource for the country. One reason for the concern about immigrants is that analysts have argued that immigrants (a) take jobs from natives, (b) drain social service systems, (c) decrease wage rates, and (d) increase crime levels (Bier, 2018). However, others maintained that immigrants offer a number of important benefits by (a) filling critical job vacancies created by low population growth and shortages of highly specialized workers, (b) enhancing creativity and productivity in organizations, and (c) creating new businesses that meet the changing demands for products and services (Kelly, 2014).

Although many believe that immigrants add value to the nation's workforce, concerns about them often create biases and stigmas that have a negative influence on employment decisions about them. There are approximately 28 million immigrants in the US labor force, and they are, on average, more likely than natives to experience (a) unfair discrimination in the employment process, (b) lower wage rates, (c) assignment to low level dead-end jobs, or (d) underemployment in organizations (Bureau of Labor Statistics, 2018). For instance, foreign born workers in the US, earn, on average, $11,000 less than natives annually (Radford & Budiman 2018). They are also more likely to be employed in low level jobs in agriculture, service, maintenance, and construction occupations than natives, and less likely to hold managerial, professional, and other high-level positions (Bureau of Labor Statistics, 2018). However, not all immigrants are relegated to low level jobs, and 44% are employed in medical science, 34% in software engineering, and 27% in positions in the sciences (Camarota & Zeigler, 2009). Thus, immigrants' job assignments may depend on the level of their education, specialized expertise, or nation of origin. In recent years, the average educational and skill level of immigrants has increased, and approximately 30% of immigrants hold bachelors' degrees or higher compared to 31.6% of natives (Manuel-Krogstad & Radford, 2018).

Even though many of today's immigrants have high levels of education, decision makers may not always hire them because they do not always view foreign degrees or credentials as comparable to those in the US (Bureau of Labor Statistics, 2018). Thus, immigrants may experience unfair discrimination in wage rates and assignment to low level jobs that are not commensurate with their education or skill levels (e.g., underemployment) (Migration Policy Institute, 2019). We believe that underemployment may be influenced by their country of origin (e.g., Latin America), skin color, or raters' perceptions about foreign credentials, etc. Therefore, we consider these and other factors thought to affect unfair discrimination against immigrants in the sections below.

It is clear from our brief review above, that some immigrants experience more unfair discrimination in the workplace than others, and we are not always utilizing the many talents and skills that they bring to the US workforce. Thus, a better understanding is needed of the employment experiences and unfair discrimination experienced by immigrants in organizations. To date, relatively little research in Human Resource Management, Organizational Behavior or related fields has addressed these issues (e.g., Dietz, 2010; Hosoda & Stone-Romero, 2010; Krings & Olivares, 2007), and we know of no comprehensive model of unfair discrimination toward immigrants in these fields. Thus, the primary purposes of this paper are (a) to develop a model to increase our understanding of the factors thought to affect unfair discrimination toward immigrants in work contexts, (b) review the existing research on these factors, (c) offer directions for future research on the topic, and (d) identify strategies that can be used to overcome biases against immigrants in organizations.

It merits emphasis that it is beyond the scope of this paper to provide a comprehensive review of all the literature on the topic, but we do include research from a variety of disciplines (e.g., Management, Psychology, Sociology, and Political Science). Whenever possible, we also review results of research from various regions of the world (e.g., Europe, Pacific Region) to determine if research results generalize across national boundaries. Prior to presenting our model, it is important to define the terms immigrant and unfair discrimination in the workplace. The term immigrants refers to "those foreign born people who migrate to a county, but have the right to reside in their host country irrespective of whether they have or do not have host country citizenship" (Dietz, 2010, p. 104). It merits noting that we limit our discussion to immigrants that are authorized to reside in the US. Unfair discrimination can be defined as "unfair behavioral biases" against members of a group based on their group identity, social category, stigma, or ascribed characteristics" (Dipboye & Colella, 2005, p. 2).

MODEL OF UNFAIR DISCRIMINATION TOWARD IMMIGRANTS

Our model is based on an integration of Social Psychological models of Social Cognition (Miller & Brewer, 1984) and Intergroup Threat developed by Stephan and Stephan (1985). It also considers theory and research from sociology and political science (e.g., Berg, 2010; Hainmueller & Hiscox, 2010; Helbling & Kriesi, 2014). The model predicts that when employers encounter immigrant job applicants or employees they will assign them to a category, and this categorization will elicit stereotypes about them. The stereotypes then evoke perceptions of threat and anxiety, and these perceptions will have a negative impact on job expectancies, job ratings, and employment decisions. The model also indicates that

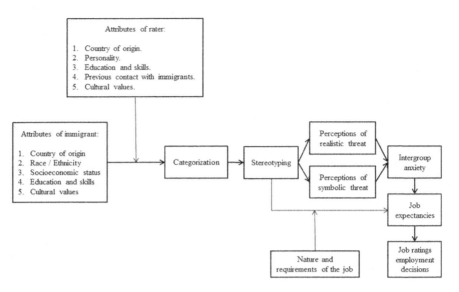

FIGURE 12.1.   Model of Factors Affecting Unfair Discrimination Against Immigrants in Organizations

three factors influence the categorization process including the (a) attributes of the immigrants, (b) attributes of the rater, and (c) nature of the job. In the sections below, we describe our model and present hypotheses stemming from it. A graph of the model is noted in Figure 12.1.

Based on the social cognition framework, our model predicts that when raters encounter immigrants, they often assign them to a category (e.g., Latin American immigrant), and the categorization elicits stereotypes about the person. Stereotypes are often defined as "largely false, overgeneralized" beliefs about members of a category that are typically negative (Ashmore & Del Boca, 1981). For example, if a job applicant is categorized as an immigrant from Latin America, then raters or decision makers may use extant stereotypes (e.g., person is lazy, unintelligent, untrustworthy, and dangerous) to make inferences about the person's suitability for the job (Timberlake & Williams, 2012).

Our model also suggests, based on Intergroup Threat Theory, that negative stereotypes evoke perceptions of realistic and symbolic threats (Stephan & Stephan, 1985). Realistic threats pose a threat to the very existence of ingroups including threats to economic power, and the well-being of members (Stephan, Ybarra & Bachman, 1999). For example, immigrants are likely to prompt realistic threats when raters perceive that they will take jobs from natives, or when they are perceived to pose danger to the safety and security of natives. Symbolic threats refer to the differences in values, beliefs, morals, and norms between natives and immigrants (Stephan et al., 1999). For example, symbolic threats may occur when natives value gender equity and immigrants do not. These types of threats stem from the belief that an ingroup's (herein after refer to as natives) values are morally right, and immigrants who have different values or morals serve as threats to native's worldviews (Stephan et al., 1999). Symbolic threats are also based on the belief that immigrants will undermine or supplant the values of an ingroup (natives) and make them the outsider.

Apart from the process described above, our model predicts that perceived threats will interact with stereotypes of immigrants to create intergroup anxiety. This anxiety stems from negative emotions associated with intergroup interaction (e.g., fear, angst, vulnerability) (Stephan & Stephan, 1985). For instance, if raters perceive that Latin American immigrants are immoral criminals, they may experience fear or danger when interacting with them. These emotional reactions, along with stereotypes of immigrants, are likely to have an extremely negative impact on job expectancies, job ratings, and employment decisions. As a result, immigrants may not be hired for jobs or given job opportunities that are commensurate with their education or skill levels.

In support of our model, researchers in Social Psychology have argued that the theory of Social Cognition has been the dominant framework used to explain prejudice and unfair discrimination in social and work-related settings for the last twenty years (e.g., Devine, 1989; Park & Judd, 2005). For example, the model has been used to explain discrimination based on race/ethnicity (e.g., Hamilton, 1979), gender (Eagly & Steffen, 1984); age (Finkelstein & Burke, 1998), disability (Stone & Colella, 1996), and immigrant status (Baltes & Rudolph, 2010; Lee & Fiske, 2006). Further, a number of studies have provided support for the Intergroup Threat Model (Stephan & Stephan, 1995), and have examined the relations between realistic and symbolic threats and negative attitudes toward immigrants in North America (e.g., Alboim, Finnie, & Meng, 2005; Hitlan, Carrillo, Zarate, & Aikman, 2007). These studies found that perceptions of realistic and symbolic threat led to negative attitudes and prejudice toward immigrants (Hitlan et al., 2007). Still other research used a meta-analysis to examine the relations between various types of intergroup threats (e.g., realistic threats, symbolic threats) and attitudes toward outgroup members (e.g., immigrants) (Riek, Mania, & Gaertner, 2006). The study reviewed results of 95 different studies and found that the types of threats just mentioned were related to negative attitudes toward immigrants (Riek et al., 2006).

Finally, our model indicates that stereotypes and perceptions of threat lead to negative job expectancies which are anticipatory beliefs about the degree to which the immigrant will be successful on the job (Higgins & Bargh, 1987). For example, if raters believe that immigrants are lazy, unintelligent, or untrustworthy, and they are perceived as a threat, then they are likely to expect that they will not perform successfully on the job. Based on these job expectancies, the rater would also be expected to rate the immigrants as unsuitable for the job, and not hire them. To date, relatively little research has examined the impact of categorization, stereotyping, and perceptions of threat on employment decisions about immigrants (e.g., Baltes & Rudolph, 2010; Derous, Nguyen, & Ryan, 2009; Oreopolous 2011). Therefore, we consider the factors thought to affect biases against immigrants below.

ATTRIBUTES OF IMMIGRANTS

As noted above, our model suggests that three factors affect the categorization and stereotyping process including the (a) attributes of the immigrants, (b) attributions of immigrants, and (c) the nature of the job. These factors will be discussed in the sections that follow.

Our model predicts that when organizational decision makers encounter immigrants, they typically assign them to a category, and their category assignment influences stereotypes, perceptions of threat, anxiety, and employment-related decisions about them. Further, the model indicates that a number of attributes of immigrants are likely to affect their assignment to a specific category, and elicit stereotypes about them. For example, immigrants' (a) race or skin color, (b) country of origin, (c) education and skill levels, (d) socioeconomic status, and (e) cultural and religious values are likely to influence the categorization and employment decision-making process. Although we present each of the factors individually in the sections below, we want to emphasize that employment decisions about immigrants are influenced by complex interactions of these factors.

Immigrants' Race, Ethnicity, and Skin Color

One major set of factors that is expected to influence the categorization and stereotyping of immigrants is their race, ethnicity, or skin color. Race is typically defined in terms of physical characteristics such as skin color, facial features, and hair type (Betancourt & Lopez, 1993), and the term ethnicity is used to refer to groups that are characterized in terms of a common nationality, culture or language (Betancourt & Lopez, 1993). We believe, as do others, that immigrants' race, ethnicity, or skin color are likely to influence raters' categorization and stereotypes about them (Lee & Fiske, 2006). One reason for this is that racial minorities or those with a non-white skin color are often stereotyped more negatively in the US, and viewed as less competent, less motivated, more untrustworthy, and more dangerous than those with white skin color (Stone, Stone, & Dipboye, 1992). As a result of these negative stereotypes, raters often feel threatened by immigrants who are racial minorities, and may experience interpersonal anxiety when interacting with them (Stephan & Stephan, 1995). Raters' stereotypes and interpersonal anxiety then have a negative impact on job expectancies, job ratings, and employment decisions.

Given these arguments, immigrants from some racial groups that have a dark skin color (e.g., some immigrants from Africa or Latin American) may be categorized or stereotyped more negatively than those with light skin color. For example, considerable research has found that blacks are more likely to be stereotyped as lazy, unintelligent, violent, irresponsible, aggressive, slovenly, unreliable, physically dirty, and criminals than whites (e.g., Dovidio & Gaertner, 1986; Maddox & Gray, 2002; Peffley & Hurwitz, 1998). Similarly, research by Ortiz and Telles (2012) found that immigrants who had darker skin color were more likely to be perceived as Mexican, stereotyped more negatively and experienced more unfair discrimination than those with lighter skin color. Interestingly, the same study revealed that men with dark skin color were more likely to experience unfair discrimination than women with the same skin color. However, women with dark and light skin color did not differ in terms of unfair discrimination, but a number of individuals with dark skin color indicated that they were not hired because of their racial appearance (Ortiz & Telles, 2012).

Further research by Timberlake and Williams (2012) indicated that Latin American and African immigrants were more likely to be perceived as violent criminals than those from Europe or Asia. One potential reason for these findings is that Latin American and African immigrants typically have darker skin color than those from Europe or Asia. Further, a study by Fairchild and Cozens (1981) revealed that Hispanics were more likely to be stereotyped as aggressive, lazy, ignorant, and cruel than members of other groups. A study by Lee and Fiske (2006) also indicated that Latin American and African immigrants were viewed as having lower competence levels than those from Europe or Asia. Research by Hersch (2011) found that immigrants with darker skin color received lower wage levels, and were more likely to be assigned to lower level jobs than those with lighter skin color.

Research in Canada also provided support for these arguments (Shields, 2011). Results of a longitudinal study of immigrants in Canada found that those who were non-white were more than twice as likely as white immigrants to experience discrimination even when other factors were comparable (e.g., educational level, language fluency) (Shields, 2011). Another survey in Canada found that African immigrants who had dark skin color reported that they experienced higher levels of unfair discrimination (55%) than those who had light skin color (e.g., Chinese or Indian immigrants) (Ray & Preston, 2009).

Research in Europe also found that race or skin color had a negative impact on reactions to immigrants (Zschirnt & Ruedin, 2016). A meta-analysis of hiring decisions found evidence of racial discrimination based on skin color in Europe and North America (Zschirnt & Ruedin, 2016). Another meta-analysis in the Netherlands revealed that non-white and non-Western immigrants were more likely to experience unfair discrimination than white immigrants from Western nations (van den Berg, 2012). A study by Dustmann and Preston (2007) also found that racial prejudice had a negative impact on attitudes toward non-white immigrants in Europe, and a study in Sweden by Rooth (2001) found that immigrants with dark skin color experienced higher levels of unfair discrimination than those with light skin color.

Taken together, these studies suggest that immigrants with dark skin color are stereotyped more negatively and experience higher levels of unfair discrimination than those who have a light skin color. Research findings were consistent across North America, Canada, and Europe, but they focused primarily on social rather than employment contexts. However, we believe that many of the negative reactions to immigrants found in social situations may be exacerbated in employment contexts because individuals may not always be able to choose their coworkers in these settings, but they may be able to choose companions in social contexts. Thus, additional research is needed to determine if immigrants' skin color biases employment decisions about them. Thus, we offer the following hypothesis to guide future research.

H1: Immigrants with dark skin color will be (a) categorized more negatively, (b) stereotyped more unfavorably, and (c) viewed as more threatening than their light skin counterparts.

H2: Immigrants' with dark skin color will experience more negative (a) job expectancies, (b) job ratings, and (c) employment decisions than when immigrants who have a light skin color.

Immigrants' Country of Origin

Another one of the key factors that should influence the categorization of immigrants and employment decisions about them is their country of origin (Lee & Fiske, 2006). We believe, as do others (Lee & Fiske, 2006) that an immigrant's country of origin influences the categorization, stereotyping, and perceived threat associated with immigrants, and these stereotypes coupled with anxiety have a negative impact on job expectancies and employment decisions about them.

In support of these arguments, research by Lee and Fiske (2006) found that raters often develop shared stereotypes of immigrants from particular countries based on social interactions, knowledge of religious beliefs, the economy, and media portrayals of individuals from specific countries. As a result, raters often categorize and stereotype immigrants from some countries more negatively than others. For example, research by Lee and Fiske (2006) found that immigrants who were poor and from Latin America, Africa, India, or Canada were more likely to be stereotyped as low in competence, but higher in interpersonal warmth than those from some other nations. Their results also revealed that Irish and Italian immigrants were rated as low in competence, but higher in warmth than those from Latin America, Africa, or India. Immigrants from France, Germany, Russia, the Middle East, and Vietnam were more likely to be perceived as having moderate competence and low levels of interpersonal warmth than others (Lee & Fiske, 2006). However, immigrants from China, Japan, and Korea who were rich professionals were viewed as having higher levels of competence, but lower levels of warmth than those from other countries (Lee & Fiske, 2006). Although these findings suggest that immigrants' country of origin influences ratings about their competence and warmth, the results are problematic because the study confounded socio-economic status and occupation with the immigrants' nation of origin. Thus, it is difficult to determine if the ratings were due to country of origin or other factors.

Apart from the research by Lee and Fiske (2006), surveys in the US found that Latin American immigrants were viewed more negatively than others, and were more likely to be assigned to low-level dead-end jobs than those from other nations (Pew Research, 2017). Still other studies revealed that raters developed shared stereotypes of immigrants from particular countries, and these shared stereotypes had a negative impact on reactions to them (Stangor & Schaller, 2000). For example, many citizens in the US are aware of the negative stereotypes attributed to Mexican immigrants (e.g., they are unintelligent, violent, untrustworthy, criminals) (Timberlake & Williams, 2012), and research showed that these shared stereotypes have a negative impact on job expectancies and employment decisions about them (Krings & Olivares, 2007). Consistent with these findings, results of a study by Stone-Romero, Stone, Hartman and Hosoda (2020) found that those who traced their ancestry to Mexico were stereotyped more negatively than those who descended from African, Chinese, Indian, or European ancestors.

Results of another study in Germany by Baltes and Rudolph (2010) found that when raters reported negative stereotypes about Turkish job applicants, they were more likely to rate them as unsuitable for jobs than when they did not report negative stereotypes about them. A study by Derous et al. (2009) also found that when applicants' resumes included Arab sounding names, and Dutch raters' were prejudiced toward Arabs, the applicants were rated as less suitable for jobs than when the raters' had low levels of prejudice toward them. Research by Krings and Olivares (2006), in Switzerland, revealed that raters were more likely to discriminate against immigrants who were members of disliked national groups (e.g., those from Kosovo or Albania) than a well-liked group (immigrants from Spain). Further, unfair discrimination against these immigrants was only apparent when raters were prejudiced toward the disliked immigrant groups, and they applied for a job requiring interpersonal skills rather than technical skills.

Other studies in Europe showed that Europeans develop shared negative stereotypes about immigrants from particular nations (e.g., immigrants from Islamic Middle Eastern countries) more than those from other countries (e.g., Ecuador, China) (Stephan & Stephan, 1996). For example, a study in Spain found that Moroccans were perceived as less competent, adaptive, and more threatening than immigrants from Romania and Ecuador (Lopez-Rodriguez, Zagefka, Navas, & Cuadrado, 2014). Similarly, Hitlan et al. (2007) found that immigrants from Middle Eastern countries engendered greater levels of symbolic threat and prejudice among raters than Mexican immigrants, and perceptions of threat predicted negative attitudes toward both Middle Eastern and Mexican immigrants. One reason for these findings is that, on average, individuals from Western nations are more likely to stress values associated with freedom, autonomy, and gender equality than immigrants from some Islamic Middle Eastern nations (Hitlan et al., 2007). Therefore, cultural value differences may explain negative reactions to immigrants, and these issues will be considered in more detail below.

Although the results of the existing research on the influence of immigrants' country of origin on raters' reactions are interesting, they do not clearly indicate if immigrants' country of origin alone affects ratings of immigrants. Thus, we believe that additional research is needed to determine the main and interactive effects of country of origin and other factors (e.g., cultural values, SES) on employment decisions about immigrants. To guide this research, we present the hypotheses below.

H3: Immigrants' country of origin will influence (a) categorization, (b) stereotyping, (c) perceived threat, (d) job expectancies, and (e) employment decisions about them.

H4: Immigrants' country of origin will interact with other factors including (a) race/ skin color, (b) education and skill level, (c) cultural and religious values, and (d) SES to influence (e) categorization, (f) stereotyping, (g) perceived threat, (h) job expectancies, and (i) employment decisions about them.

Immigrants' Education and Skill Levels

Our model also predicts that immigrants' education and skill levels should affect their assignment to a category and employment decisions about them. However, the issues associated with immigrants' educational level are quite complex. For instance, when immigrants have low education and skill levels, they are typically assigned to low-level jobs because they are more likely to confirm the negative stereotypes about them (e.g., they are unintelligent or not motivated) (Helbling & Kriesi, 2014). However, immigrants with high levels of education are more likely to disconfirm stereotypes about them and are viewed as highly motivated, deserving of a high-level job, and more likely to make contributions to the host country than those with low educational levels (Hainmueller & Hiscox, 2010).

Even though many immigrants with high educational levels are hired and assigned to high level jobs, some of them are assigned to low-level jobs because employers do not always view the education or credentials acquired in other nations as comparable to those obtained in the US (Batalova, Fix, & Bachmeier, 2016; International Migration Report, 2017). As a result, research indicated that over two million immigrants with college degrees are unemployed or employed in low skill jobs in the US (Batalova et al., 2016; International Migration Report, 2017). Thus, organizations are not utilizing the broad range of skills and abilities that many immigrants bring to the workforce and some analysts refer to this phenomenon as the "Brain Waste" (Batalova et al., 2016). The lack of recognition of foreign education and credentials is especially problematic today because there is a shortage of professional engineers, scientists, mathematicians, and medical doctors in the US. For example, surveys revealed that there are over 10,000 international medical school graduates who are not able to practice medicine in the US because they are not viewed as qualified until they pass US exams and complete a residency. Only 40% of immigrants who apply for medical residency programs are accepted so these individuals do not always have an opportunity to practice medicine or achieve their full potential in the US (Giovanelli, 2011).

Interestingly, recent research indicated that the recognition of non-US education and credentials may depend on the country where the individuals were trained (Batalova et al., 2016). Results of this research revealed that organizations were less likely to accept the educational credentials of immigrants from Mexico, Latin America, Africa, and the Caribbean than those who were from India and China (Batalova et al., 2016). Thus, the acceptance of immigrants' education and credentials may depend on the location of their educational programs. Apart from these factors, we also believe that immigrants' English fluency and proficiency levels may affect the recognition of their education levels and employment decisions about them. However, only a few studies have examined the effects of English proficiency on hiring decisions, and results of that research indicated that immigrants who struggled with English proficiency were less likely to gain access to jobs than those who were proficient in the language (Oreopoulos, 2011). Similarly, research found that Chinese immigrants were more likely to experience unfair discrimination in the US than European immigrants because they lacked English proficiency and did not understand the social norms in the country (Huynh, Devos, & Smarlarz, 2011). Likewise, research on foreign accents in the workplace showed that qualified immigrants with Mexican-Spanish or Japanese accents were rated more negatively in the hiring process than English speaking applicants (Hosoda, Nuygen, & Stone-Romero, 2012; Hosoda & Stone-Romero, 2010).

Even though some research has examined the extent to which immigrants' educational levels influence their employment opportunities, we believe that more research is needed to determine the degree to which their educational levels, place of education, and English proficiency level interact to influence employment decisions about them. Thus, we posit that:

H5: Immigrants with low levels of education and skills will be (a) assigned to a more negative category, (b) stereotyped more negatively, and will receive more negative (c) job expectancies, (d) job ratings, and (e) employment decisions than those with high levels of education and skills.

H6: Immigrants' (a) level of education, (b) place of education, and (c) English proficiency level will interact to determine (d) their assignment to a category, (e) type of stereotypes elicited, (f) perceived threat, (g) job expectancies, and (h) employment decisions about them.

Immigrants' Socio-Economic Status

We also believe that immigrants' socio-economic status (SES) will influence their category assignment, stereotyping, and employment decisions about them. For instance, those who have high SES should be assigned to a more favorable high-status category and stereotyped more positively than those who have low SES (Lee & Fiske, 2006). Many of the recent migrants to the US have high levels of SES and college degrees. As a result, they are more likely to be accepted by natives in the mainstream US culture than their low SES counterparts (Timberlake & Williams, 2012). Further, research revealed that one reason Latin American immigrants are often viewed negatively in the US is that many of them are poor, and raters perceive that they will drain the social service system (Timberlake & Williams, 2012). One survey revealed that Latin American immigrants in the US were perceived as the poorest of all immigrant groups, the most violent, and least self-sufficient compared to immigrants from Asia or Europe (Timberlake & Williams, 2012). Further, research by Lee and Fiske (2006) found that immigrants who were poor were viewed as less competent and less warm than those who were wealthy.

Research in Europe also revealed that natives believed that low SES immigrants steal jobs, bring low skill levels to jobs, undermine welfare systems, hamper the capacity to innovate, and threaten economic and social systems (Fargues, 2014). Even though research showed that the stereotypes about many low SES immigrants are unfounded, they still influence attitudes and employment decisions about them (Fargues, 2014). Despite these findings, few studies have examined the effects of immigrants' SES levels on employment decisions (Timberlake & Williams, 2012). Thus, we offer the following hypothesis to guide research.

> **H7:** Immigrants with low socio-economic status will more likely be (a) categorized negatively, (b) stereotyped unfavorably, (c) perceived as more threating, and (d) receive more negative job expectancies, ratings, and employment decisions than those with high socio-economic status.

Immigrants' Cultural Values Differences

Another factor that should influence the categorization process and employment decisions about immigrants is the degree to which their cultural and religious values [hereinafter referred to as cultural values] are different from the dominant values in a host nation. Quite simply, interpersonal attraction theory (Byrne, 1971) argues that when individuals have similar cultural values and beliefs, raters will be more likely to hold more positive attitudes toward them than when they have values that are dissimilar. Based on these predictions, we argue, as do others (Stephan & Stephan, 1985), that when immigrants' cultural values are different than the dominant values in the host country, raters will develop more negative attitudes toward them than when their values are similar. One reason for this is that natives in a country often believe that their cultural values are morally right, and immigrants with different cultural values threaten their worldviews (Stephan & Stephan, 1985). For example, individuals in many Western countries value freedom, autonomy, egalitarianism, gender equity, individual achievement, and low power distance (Trice & Beyer, 1993). As a result, they may fear that immigrants who do not share these values will dilute or supplant the dominant culture, and natives will become outsiders (Stephan & Stephan, 1985). Natives may also believe that immigrants with different cultural value systems will not be motivated to achieve economic self-sufficiency or assimilate to the norms in the dominant culture (Stephan & Stephan, 1985).

In support of these arguments, research in the US has indicated that raters react more negatively to Latin American immigrants than others because they view them as having very different cultural values (e.g., they stress collectivism, familism, gender and authority-based hierarchies) than those in the US (Stone-Romero, Stone, & Salas, 2003). Research also revealed that immigrants who do not integrate into the mainstream culture were viewed more negatively in the US than those who do assimilate to the culture (Timberlake & Williams, 2012). Other studies indicated that Latin American and Chinese immigrants are often perceived as the perpetual foreigner, and are viewed as disinterested in assimilating to the dominant culture or learning English (Huynh et al., 2011). As a result, immigrants who are viewed as perpetual foreigners are often assigned to a more negative category, stereotyped unfavorably, and perceived as more threatening than those who are not.

Apart from the studies in the US, research in Europe indicated that negative attitudes toward immigrants were often based on the fact that they endorsed religious values and social practices that were antithetical to the dominant European values (e.g., gender equality, freedom, autonomy, and individual choice) (Pedersen & Hartley, 2012). In particular, studies in Europe revealed that Muslims were viewed more negatively than many other immigrant groups (e.g., Romanians, Ecuadorians) because their cultural values were not consistent with European values, and they were not motivated to assimilate to the dominant culture (Lopez-Rodriguez et al., 2014; Stephan et al., 1999).

Previous theory and research on intergroup threat by Stephan and Stephan (1985) also argued that three social factors affect reactions to immigrants and anxiety toward them including (a) prior relations between groups, (b) intergroup cognitions, and (c) personal experiences with outgroup members. In support of these factors, research by Fang, Friedlander and Pieterse (2016) indicated that immigrants with lower levels of acculturation elicited greater levels of anxiety than those with higher levels of acculturation. Another study found that exposure to threatening news stories about immigrants resulted in greater levels of anxiety, and more negative attitudes toward them than non-threatening stories (Schemer, 2012). Research also revealed that raters experienced greater anxiety when interacting with unauthorized immigrants than authorized immigrants and this anxiety was related to prejudice toward immigrants (Murray & Marx, 2013).

Overall, the research just reviewed suggests that cultural value differences between immigrants and raters in host countries are likely to affect reactions to immigrants. However, it merits noting that most of this research was conducted in social contexts, so we believe that more research is needed to examine these issues in employment settings. Therefore, we propose the following hypothesis to guide research.

H8: When immigrants' cultural values are different than the dominant values in a host country, raters will be more likely to (a) assign them to a negative category, (b) stereotype them negatively, and ascribe them more negative (c) job expectancies, (d) job ratings and (e) employment decisions to them more than when their cultural values are similar to the dominant values in a host nation.

ATTRIBUTES OF THE RATERS

Our model also predicts that the attributes of raters are likely to influence the degree to which immigrants are categorized, stereotyped, perceived as a threat, or experience unfavorable employment decisions. In particular, we believe that the following factors are likely to affect raters' reactions to immigrants including raters' country of origin, personality, demographic characteristics, and previous contact with immigrants, and cultural values.

Rater's Country of Origin

Our model suggests that the rater's country of origin will affect employment decisions about immigrants. One potential reason for this that people in a nation often develop shared or consensual stereotypes about outgroup members based on information provided by their parents, peers, teachers, political leaders, and mass media (Stangor, 2000). Consensual stereotypes are developed because individuals who identify with a social group are often motivated to distinguish their group from other relevant groups in order to enhance the standing of their social group (Brown, 1995; Tajfel & Turner, 1979). When members of native groups are motivated to enhance their own social standing, they often attribute negative traits or behaviors to immigrants (Tajfel & Turner, 1979). For instance, when individuals identify themselves as Americans, they may be motivated to boost their own group's standing by denigrating immigrants (e.g., immigrants take jobs away from natives, depress wages, or engage in criminal activities). This example has been labeled the social identify process.

There are a number of negative consequences associated with the social identity process, and raters who are motivated to heighten their own group's status by disparaging immigrants may be less likely to employ them or more likely assign them to low level jobs that are not commensurate with their skill levels. As a result, organizations and societies may not utilize the many talents and skills that immigrants bring to the workforce, and they may be denied fair employment opportunities in their new countries. We know of at least one study that has examined the degree to which raters disparage immigrants in order to promote their own groups' prominence (Dietz, Joshi, Esses, Hamilton, & Gabarrot, 2015), but we believe that more research is needed on this issue. Therefore, we offer the following hypothesis to guide research.

H9: Raters' country of origin and social identity will influence the degree to which immigrants from other nations will be (a) assigned to an unfavorable category, (b) stereotyped negatively, (c) viewed as a threat, and receive negative (d) job expectancies, (e) job ratings, and (f) employment decisions.

Rater's Personality

Our model also suggests that a rater's personality should have an impact on how immigrants are categorized and stereotyped in the employment process. In particular, two personality variables have been shown to influence prejudice toward immigrants including authoritarianism and social dominance. Authoritarianism refers to the degree to which people defer to authority, accept conventional and conservative rules and norms, and show hostility to outsiders who break social norms (Adorno, Frenkel-Brunswick, Levinson, & Sanford, 1950). Altemeyer (1998) extended this definition and noted that right-wing authoritarianism is the willingness to submit to authorities who are perceived to be legitimate and who have hostile and punitive attitudes toward others. Social dominance orientation (SDO) refers to the extent to which one desires that one's in-group dominate or be superior to out-groups (Pratto, Sidanius, Stallworth & Malle, 1994). People who are high in social dominance also believe in hierarchies of authority, and group based hierarchies (Pratto et al., 1994).

Not surprisingly, research has revealed consistently that raters who are high in authoritarianism express negative attitudes or evaluations of immigrants (Fisher, Deason, Borgida, & Oyamot, 2011; Oyamot, Borgida, & Fisher, 2006; Oyamot, Fisher, Deaso, & Borgida, 2012). However, one study found that the relation between authoritarianism and negative attitudes toward immigrants may depend on social norms and humanitarian values (Oyamot et al., 2012). More specifically, when Americans expressed positive social norms toward immigrants and culturally endorsed humanitarian values then authoritarians were more tolerant of immigrants (Oyamot et al., 2012).

Similarly, research in the US showed that those high in SDO, political conservatism, and authoritarianism had more negative attitudes toward immigrants than their counterparts (Bassett, 2010). A study in France also found that participants who were high in social dominance and inequality were more prejudiced toward immigrants than those low in social dominance and equality (Guimond, De Olveria, Kamiesjki, & Sidanius, 2010). Even though some research has examined the relations between raters' authoritarian and social dominance personalities, we believe that much more research is needed to examine these relations in employment settings. Thus, we propose the following hypothesis:

H10: Raters high in (a) social dominance and (b) authoritarian orientations will be more likely to (c) categorize immigrants unfavorably, (d) stereotype them negatively (e) perceive that they are threatening, and report more negative (f) job expectancies, (g) job ratings and (h) employment decisions than those who are low on these traits.

Raters' Education and Skill Levels

Our model predicts that raters' education and skill levels will influence the categorization, stereotyping, and employment decision-making about immigrants. In particular, we believe that raters with high levels of education and skill levels will have more positive attitudes toward immigrants than raters with low educational or skill levels. One reason for this is that those with high levels of education and skills may be less likely to perceive that immigrants will compete with them for jobs. Another reason is that educational level is often associated with greater tolerance toward outgroup members (Cote & Erickson, 2009). In support of these arguments, research found that tolerance for immigrants is higher among those who are more educated, older, and individuals who live in metropolitan rather than rural areas (Cote, & Erickson, 2009). Similarly, research found that educational level was negatively related to anti-immigrant attitudes (Chandler & Tsai, 2001), and raters with low education and skill levels were more likely to prefer limiting the number of immigrants in the US (Scheve & Slaughter, 2001; Wilkes, Guppy, & Farris, 2008). Other research revealed that both low and high skilled raters preferred immigrants with high skills level over those with low skill levels (Hainmueller & Hiscox, 2010).

Even though there has been some research on raters' education level and their reactions to immigrants, there are only a few studies on the issue. Thus, we believe that additional research is needed, and we propose the following hypothesis to guide that research.

> **H11:** Raters' educational or skill levels will be positively related to (a) the categorization of immigrants, (b) stereotypes about them, (c) threats about them, (d) job expectancies, (e) job ratings, and (f) employment decisions.

Raters' Previous Contact with Immigrants

Our model suggests that increased contact with immigrants should have a positive influence on the categorization process and employment decisions about them. The primary reason for this is that increased contact with immigrants will allow raters to see them as individuals and not members of a stereotyped group (Pettigrew, Tropp, Wagner, & Christ, 2011), and increased contact will enhance their views of immigrants as long as the contact is positive. Stated differently, raters increased contact with immigrants should provide them with individuating information that can be used to disconfirm negative stereotypes about immigrants (Brewer & Miller, 1984), and have a positive influence on employment decisions about them. In support of this prediction, several studies in the US and Europe found that when raters had more frequent contact with immigrants, they experienced less anxiety, and had more positive attitudes toward them than when they did not (e.g., Leong, 2008; Ward & Masgoret, 2006). Other studies revealed that contact with Latino Immigrants increased positive attitudes toward them and resulted in less punitive views about immigration policies (Ellison, Shin, & Leal, 2011). Still other research indicated that white US citizens who were embedded in diverse educational networks (nonwhite) had more positive attitudes toward immigrants than those who were embedded in white homogeneous networks (Berg, 2010).

In addition to research in the US, a number of studies in Europe focused on the influence of interpersonal contact on prejudice toward immigrants, and found that interpersonal contact reduces prejudice (Capozza, Trifiletti, Vezzali, & Favara, 2013). For example, studies in Italy and Belgium found that contact with immigrants increased empathy, reduced intergroup anxiety, and improved attitudes toward them (Capozza et al., 2013; Dhont, Roets, & Van Hiel, 2011; Pagotto, Voci, & Maculan, 2010; Vezzali & Giovanni, 2010; Vezzali, Giovanni, & Capozza, 2010; Visintin, Voci, Pagotto, & Hewstone, 2017; Voci & Hewstone, 2003).

A few other studies have examined the antecedents and outcomes of raters' anxiety on attitudes toward immigrants in other world regions (Bizman & Yinon, 2001). First, a study in Israel found that intergroup anxiety was positively related to prejudice toward immigrants (Bizman & Yinon, 2001). However, research in New Zealand found that more frequent contact with immigrants led to decreased anxiety, and more positive attitudes toward them (Ward & Masgoret, 2006). Another study in Africa indicated that interpersonal contact and perceptions about the consequences of interacting with immigrants were positively related to pro-immigrant sentiments (Gordon, 2016).

Taken together, the results of research suggested that increased contact with immigrants allows raters to gather individuating information, disconfirms stereotypes, decreases anxiety, enhances positive attitudes, and increases positive job expectancies toward them (Pettigrew et al., 2011). Despite this research, we believe that increased contact may be more effective with immigrants from some countries than others. For instance, increased contact with immigrants from countries that are "liked by raters" (e.g., Europe) may increase positive attitudes, but increased contact with immigrants from "disliked or threatening nations" (e.g., Middle Eastern countries) may not. One potential reason for this is that increased contact may not overcome the negative affect stemming from perceptions of threat or differences in cultural values between immigrants and natives. We know of no research on this issue so we offer the following hypothesis to foster research on the topic.

> **H12:** Raters' increased contact with immigrants will interact with the immigrants' country of origin to influence (a) categorization, (b) stereotyping, (c) perceived threat, (d) job expectancies, (e) job ratings, and (f) employment decisions about them.

Cultural Values Differences

Our model also maintains that differences between raters' and immigrants' cultural values will influence the categorization process and employment decisions about immigrants. The rationale for this argument is similar to the one noted above on cultural value differences between immigrants and raters so we will not go into detail on this factor. Quite simply, we predict that when raters and immigrants' share values then raters will view them more positively than when they do not share values. Until recently, the US was a predominantly Protestant nation, and most of the immigrants were from Europe so there were shared value systems. However, the increase in the numbers of Hispanic, Asian, Middle Eastern, and African immigrants has resulted in the influx of different religions (e.g., Muslim, Buddhism, and Hinduism) and cultural value systems so that there are now greater differences in value systems in the country. These differences have threatened some natives, and sparked negative reactions toward immigrants (Stephan et al., 1999).

Research on the effects of raters' cultural value differences on reactions to immigrants found when raters were evangelical Protestants they were less tolerant and held more negative attitudes toward immigrants than when they were members of other religious groups (Moore & Ovadia, 2006). Similar research found that members of Christian fundamentalists were more likely to hold anti-immigration views than others (McDaniel, Nooruddin, & Shortle, 2011). In contrast, however, research indicated that raters who were members of some minority religions (e.g., Jews, members of the Church of Jesus Christ and Latter-Day Saints) were more likely to empathize with the plight of undocumented immigrants, and support liberal immigration policies (Knoll, 2009) than others. One reason for this is that members of these religions know what it feels like to be a minority. Given that the research findings are mixed, we believe that raters' reactions to immigrants with different value systems may be influenced by their empathy or their own experiences with unfair discrimination. Thus, we present the following hypotheses to foster research on this issue.

> **H13:** Cultural value differences between raters and immigrants will interact with raters' (a) empathy and (b) experiences with unfair discrimination to determine the (c) categorization, (d) stereotyping, (e) perceived threat, and negative (f) job expectancies, (g) job ratings, and (h) employment decisions about immigrants.

In summary, our review revealed that a number of raters' attributes are likely to influence the categorization process and employment decisions about immigrants. For instance, we predicted that raters' (a) country of origin, (b) personality, (c) education and skill levels, (d) previous contact with immigrants, and (e) differences in cultural values are likely to affect how immigrants are perceived and treated. There may be other raters' attributes that are related to employment decisions about immigrants (e.g., raters' gender, age, SES) (Stone, Lukaszewski, Krueger, & Canedo, 2019), but space limitations precluded a complete review of these factors. As noted above, our model also predicts that the attributes of immigrants, attributes of raters, and the nature of the job will interact to affect the categorization process and employment decisions about immigrants so we consider factors associated with the nature of the job below.

NATURE OF THE JOB

Our model predicts that the nature and requirements of the job should interact with the stereotyped attributes of immigrants to influence employment decisions about them. Each job has a set of skill requirements (Lofquist & Dawis, 1969), and we believe that the degree to which immigrants are perceived to fit those requirements depends on raters' perceptions of their skill and ability levels. This argument is based on Heilman's (1983) stereotype-job fit model, and our model applied Heilman's framework to predict that raters use two primary sources of information to make employment decisions about immigrants including the: (a) nature of the job requirements (e.g., actual skill or ability requirements, and prototype of ideal candidate), and (b) immigrants' stereotyped skill and ability levels. For instance, raters determine perceived immigrant-job fit by comparing the actual requirements of jobs to perceptions about immigrants' qualifications. Although employment decisions should be relatively straightforward, perceptions of fit are often biased by unfounded stereotypes and job expectancies about immigrants. These biases lead decision makers to perceive that immigrants are not qualified for jobs even though they have the education and skill level needed to perform them (Esses, Deaux, Lalonde, & Brown, 2010; Guerrero & Rothstein, 2012). It merits noting that in the US, the Immigration and Naturalization Act (1952) protects legal aliens from unfair discrimination in the employment process based on citizenship status and nationality (Sec. 274B. [8 U.S.C. 1324b]), but biases exist in spite of this law.

In the past, many immigrants to the US had low education and skill levels, and were assigned to low-level jobs primarily in the fields of agriculture, construction, or personal services (Pew Research, 2017). However, in recent years a large number of immigrants have college degrees, but despite their high educational levels they are often assigned to low level jobs or underemployed. Underemployment is defined as the degree to which individuals' educational and skill levels are underutilized in their current job (e.g., immigrants with doctoral degrees are driving taxis or cleaning offices), and it creates problems for individuals, organizations, and society as a whole (Guerrero & Rothstein, 2012). For instance, when immigrants' are underemployed then organizations do not utilize the many talents and abilities that they bring to the workplace, and there may low levels of innovation and economic growth in society.

In support of these arguments, research revealed that immigrants' stereotyped skill levels interacted with the requirements of the job to influence job suitability ratings (Matoo, Neagu, & Özden, 2008). For instance, an immigrant from Latin America with a bachelor's degree may be categorized by his or her country of origin, and the category assignment elicits stereotypes about the typical Latin American immigrant (e.g., person is unintelligent, lazy, lacks motivation). As a result, the individual is viewed as unqualified for high level jobs and only suitable for low level positions in spite of his or her educational level (Matoo et al., 2008).

Results of studies also revealed that the high levels of education of some immigrants served to disconfirm stereotypes, and make them distinct from the stereotyped group (Yum & Park, 1990). This disconfirming information modified negative stereotypes about immigrants, and had a positive impact on job ratings and employment decisions. As a result, some immigrants with high educational levels were hired for high skilled jobs (e.g., 35% of the software engineering jobs in the US are filled with immigrants) (Guerrero & Rothstein, 2012).

However, other studies revealed that highly educated immigrants from Latin America and Eastern Europe were rated as less suitable for high skilled jobs than those with the same education and skills from Asia or Western Europe (Mattoo et al., 2008). Thus, immigrants' educational level may not always disconfirm negative stereotypes about those from Latin America or Eastern Europe. The results of this study supported the stereotype-job fit predictions that immigrants from disfavored countries (e.g., Latin America) are stereotyped more negatively and more likely to be assigned to low level jobs than those from favored countries (e.g., Europe, Asia). In contrast to these findings, research in Spain found that immigrants were not rated lower in job suitability for skilled jobs than Spanish natives (Bernardi, Garrido, & Miyar, 2011).

Taken together, most of the research just reviewed provided support for our predictions about immigrant stereotype job-fit, and revealed that immigrant stereotypes interacted with the nature of the job to affect job suitability ratings and hiring decisions. Research also revealed that perceived job fit may be determined by the attributes of immigrants (e.g., non-English sounding, country of origin), and attributes of raters including their level of education and skills. Even though some research has examined the degree to which stereotypes about immigrants influence perceived job-fit, we believe that additional research is needed to expand our understanding of this process. Thus, we offer the following hypotheses to guide future research.

H14: Stereotypes of immigrants will interact with the requirements of the job to influence (a) job expectancies, (b) job suitability ratings, and (c) employment decisions. More specifically, when immigrants are stereotyped as unintelligent, lazy, untrustworthy, uneducated, and the job requires high levels of skills or cognitive demands immigrants will be rated as less qualified than when the job requires low skill levels of cognitive demand.

H15: There will be an interaction between raters' attributes (e.g., skill level) and the attributes of immigrants (e.g., foreign sounding names, foreign education) to affect the degree to which immigrants are viewed to fit the requirements of high-level jobs.

OVERALL SUMMARY OF MODEL

In the sections above, we presented a model of the factors that are thought to affect unfair discrimination against immigrants in organizations. Our model predicted that when immigrants apply for job opportunities, raters will assign them to a category and this categorization will elicit negative stereotypes, perceived threat, job expectancies and employment decisions about them. We also argued that three factors are likely to influence the categorization process including the (a) attributes of immigrants, (b) attributes of raters, and (c) nature of the job. Although there has been some research on biases against immigrants in social contexts (Esses et al., 2010; Lee & Fiske, 2006) much less research has examined the extent to which the categorization and stereotyping process influences employment decisions about immigrants. Thus, we hope that our model will foster additional research on unfair discrimination toward immigrants in work-related settings.

We also believe that our model has important implications for overcoming biases against immigrants in organizations, and ensuring that companies utilize the many talents and skills that they bring to the workplace. We also hope that the model will enhance fair employment opportunities for immigrants in their host countries. Thus, we consider several strategies for overcoming biases against immigrants below.

IMPLICATIONS FOR ORGANIZATIONS

Given that immigrants experience unfair discrimination in the employment process, and many nations need immigrants to fill critical job vacancies, we believe that organizations need to develop strategies to overcome biases and increase the inclusion of immigrants in the workplace. In the following sections, we consider some strategies that organizations might use to increase the inclusion of these individuals.

Strategy 1: Decreasing Negative Stereotypes

Our model suggests that immigrants are often categorized and stereotyped negatively in the employment process, and these beliefs have a detrimental impact on employment decisions about them. Thus, we believe that organizations should develop strategies for overcoming unfounded stereotypes about immigrants, and ensure that decision makers have an accurate perception of their job-related skills and abilities.

Consistent with models of organizational change (Porter, Lawler, & Hackman, 1975), we believe that organizations might use a variety of methods to modify inaccurate stereotypes about immigrants and substitute them with their actual skills and abilities. First, they might use training programs to make decision makers aware of their stereotypes and show them that their stereotypes are unfounded. Second, they might use employment tests or work samples to uncover the actual skills and abilities of immigrants rather than rely on perceptions to make inferences about their skill levels. Another strategy that might be used to change stereotypes about immigrants is to increase interpersonal contact with them. For example, immigrants might be hired as interns or apprentices and assigned to key work groups or informal activities that allow decision makers to gather individuating information about them. A fourth method for changing stereotypes about immigrants is to publicize their key contributions and successes in organizations. Even though we expect that these strategies may alter negative beliefs about immigrants, additional research is needed to assess their effectiveness.

Strategy 2: Decreasing Perceptions of Realistic and Symbolic Threat

Our model also predicts that stereotypes influence perceptions of realistic and symbolic threat about immigrants, and these threats are likely to have a negative impact on job ratings and employment decisions. Given that realistic threats often come from misguided perceptions that immigrants will take jobs from natives, we believe that organizations might reduce this threat by informing all employees that Immigration and Naturalization Law (1952) indicates that "US citizens should be given preference in jobs over legal aliens." In addition, organizations might dispel realistic threats by codifying these issues in organizational policies and employee handbooks.

Symbolic threats typically stem from differences in immigrants' norms and values, and natives' beliefs that immigrants will change the existing culture. Given these threats, organizations might decrease perceptions of symbolic threats by ensuring workers that current organizational policies and culture will not change when immigrants are hired. Further, organizations might increase contact between immigrants and natives (e.g., assign to same work team) so that employees come to understand that many immigrants share the same values as natives in a host country. Although these strategies seem plausible, we believe that research is needed to examine their success rates.

Strategy 3: Overcoming Intergroup Anxiety toward Immigrants

Our model also indicates that immigrants may elicit anxiety on the part of natives, and this anxiety often biases employment decisions about them. Much of the anxiety associated with immigrants is based on stereotypes or inaccurate perceptions about them (e.g., they are criminals, drug dealers). As a result, the methods used to decrease negative stereotypes described above may also help reduce the fear associated with working with them. Thus, organizations might use training designed to show employees that anxiety-evoking stereotypes about immigrants are unfounded. They could also increase the interpersonal contact (e.g., social events, work teams) between immigrants and employees so that employees can see immigrants as individuals rather than as members of a stigmatized group. The increased contact with immigrants should reduce employees' anxiety associated with working with them, and should reduce the anxiety associated with working with them. Despite these arguments, research is needed to examine the extent to which these methods reduce anxiety toward immigrants in organizations.

Strategy 4: Overcoming Raters' Biases against Immigrants

Our model suggests that raters' personality, country of origin, and educational levels may bias employment decisions about immigrants. As a result, we believe that all raters should be trained in fair employment practices, and held accountable for the types of decisions that they make about applicants or employees (Cox,

1994). For example, managers could examine the types of decisions made about immigrants and other minorities to ensure that raters are not using stereotypes rather than objective information to make employment decisions. Then, these evaluations could be used to evaluate the performance of raters and determine their outcomes. We also believe that organizations might hire decision makers who value diversity and inclusion, and would work to overcome biases about immigrants and other minority group members. Although these strategies seem possible, research is needed to assess their effectiveness.

CONCLUSION

Many industrialized countries (e.g., Europe, Japan, and US) need immigrants today because of low population growth and a shortage of workers necessary to fill critical job vacancies. In spite of these needs, immigrants experience unfair discrimination in the employment process, and have difficulty gaining or maintaining jobs. For instance, even though many recent immigrants to the US have a college degree, they are not always hired or may be assigned to low level jobs because of existing stereotypes about them. Thus, we presented a model of the factors thought to affect unfair discrimination against immigrants in order to overcome these problems, and ensure that individuals have fair employment opportunities. We also want to make sure that employers utilize the many talents and skills that immigrants bring to the workforce because underutilization of their skills has a negative impact on the overall economy. Based on our model, we also offer hypotheses to guide future research on unfair discrimination against immigrants, and present several strategies that organizations might use to overcome biases against them. We hope that our model will help ameliorate many of the problems experienced by immigrants in work organizations, and enable them to enjoy a fulfilling and satisfying work life in their new countries.

REFERENCES

Adorno, T. W., Frenkel-Brunswik, E., Levinson, D. J., & Sanford, R. N. (1950). *The authoritarian personality.* New York, NY: Harper.

Alboim, N., Finnie, R., & Meng, R. (2005). The discounting of immigrants' skills in Canada: Evidence and policy recommendations. *Institute for Research & Public Policy, 11*(2), 1–26.

Altemeyer, R. A. (1998). The other "authoritarian personality." In M. P. Zanna (Ed.), *Advances in experimental social psychology* (Vol. 30, pp. 47–91). New York, NY: Academic Press.

Ashmore, R. D., & Del Boca, F. K. (1981). Conceptual approaches to stereotypes and stereotyping. In D. L. Hamilton (Ed.), *Cognitive processes in stereotyping and intergroup behavior* (pp. 1–35). Hillsdale, NJ: Erlbaum.

Baltes, B. B., & Rudolph, C. W. (2010). Examining the effect of negative Turkish stereotypes on evaluative workplace outcomes in Germany. *Journal of Managerial Psychology, 25*(2), 148–158.

Bassett, J. F. (2010). The effects of mortality salience and social dominance orientation on attitudes toward illegal immigrants. *Social Psychology, 41*, 52–55.

Batalova, J., Fix, M., & Bachmeier, J. D., (2016). *Untapped talent: The costs of brain waste among highly skilled immigrants in the United States.* Retrieved October 9, 2017 from http://www.migrationpolicy.org/research/untapped-talent-costs-brain-wasteamong-highly-skilled-immigrants-united-states

Berg, J. A. (2010). Race, class, gender, and social space: Using an intersectional approach to study immigration attitudes. *The Sociological Quarterly, 51*(2), 278–302.

Bernardi, F., Garrido, L., & Miyar, M. (2011). The recent fast upsurge of immigrants in Spain and their employment patterns and occupational attainment. *International Migration, 49*(1), 148–187.

Betancourt, H., & López, S. R. (1993). The study of culture, ethnicity, and race in American psychology. *American Psychologist, 48*(6), 629–637.

Bier, D. (2018). *New US immigrants are as educated as new Canadian immigrants.* Retrieved from: https://www.cato.org/blog/new-us-immigrants-are-educated-new-canadian-immigrants

Bizman, A., & Yinon, Y. (2001). Intergroup and interpersonal threats as determinants of prejudice: The moderating role of in group identification. *Basic and Applied Social Psychology, 23*(3), 191–196.

Brewer, M. B., & Miller. N. (1984). Beyond the contact hypothesis: Theoretical perspectives on desegregation. In N. Miller & M. Brewer (Eds.), *Groups in conflict: A psychology of desegregation* (pp. 281–302). San Diego, CA: Academic.

Brown, R. (1995). *Prejudice in social psychology.* Malden, MA: Blackwell Publishing.

Bureau of Labor Statistics (2018). *Foreign-born workers: Labor characteristics.* Retrieved from: https://www.bls.gov/news.release/pdf/forbrn.pdf

Byrne, D. (1971). *The attraction paradigm.* New York, NY: Academic Press.

Cammarota, S. A., & Zeigler, K. (2009). *Jobs Americans won't do? A detailed look at immigrant employment by occupation.* Retrieved from https://cis.org/Memorandum/Jobs-Americans-Wont-Do-Detailed-Look-Immigrant-Employment-Occupation.

Capozza, D., Trifiletti, E., Vezzali, L., & Favara, I. (2013). Can intergroup contact improve humanity attributions? *International Journal of Psychology, 48*(4), 527–541.

Chandler, C. R., & Tsai, Y. M. (2001). Social factors influencing immigration attitudes: An analysis of data from the General Social Survey. *The Social Science Journal, 38*(2), 177–188.

Cote, R. R., & Erickson, B. H. (2009). Untangling the roots of tolerance: How forms of social capital shape attitudes toward ethnic minorities and immigrants. *American Behavioral Scientist, 52*(12), 1664–1689.

Cox, T. (1994). *Diversity in organizations: Theory, research, and practice.* Oakland, CA: Berrett-Koehler.

Derous, E., Nguyen, H. H., & Ryan, A. M. (2009). Hiring discrimination against Arab minorities: Interactions between prejudice and job characteristics. *Human Performance, 22*(4), 297–320.

Devine, P. G. (1989). Stereotypes and prejudice: Their automatic and controlled components. *Journal of Personality and Social Psychology, 56*, 5–18.

Dhont, K., Roets, A., & Van Hiel, A. (2011). Opening closed minds: The combined effects of intergroup contact and need for closure on prejudice. *Personality and Social Psychology Bulletin, 37*(4), 514–528.

Dietz, J. (2010). Introduction to the special issue on employment discrimination against immigrants. *Journal of Managerial Psychology, 25*(2), 104–112.

Dietz, J., Joshi, C., Esses, V. M., Hamilton, L. K., & Gabarrot, F. (2015). The skill paradox: Explaining and reducing employment discrimination against skilled immigrants. *The International Journal of Human Resource Management, 26*(10), 1318–1334.

Dipboye, R. L., & Colella, A. (2005). The dilemmas of workplace discrimination. In R. Dipboye & A. Colella (Eds.), *Discrimination at work: The psychological and organizational bases* (pp. 425–462). Mahwah, NJ: Erlbaum.

Dovidio, J. F., & Gaertner, S. L. (1986). *Prejudice, discrimination, and racism.* New York, NY: Academic Press.

Dustmann, C., & Preston, I. P. (2007). Racial and economic factors in attitudes to immigration. *The BE Journal of Economic Analysis & Policy, 7*(1), 1–41.

Eagly, A. H., & Steffen, V. J. (1984). Gender stereotypes stem from the distribution of women and men into social roles. *Journal of Personality and Social Psychology, 46*(4), 735.

Ellison, C. G., Shin, H., & Leal, D. L. (2011). The contact hypothesis and attitudes toward Latinos in the United States. *Social Science Quarterly, 92*(4), 938–958.

Esses, V. M., Deaux, K., Lalonde, R. N., & Brown, R. (2010). Psychological perspectives on immigration. *Journal of Social Issues, 66,* 635–647.

Fairchild, H. H., & Cozens, J. A. (1981). Chicano, Hispanic, or Mexican American: What's in a name? *Hispanic Journal of Behavioral Sciences, 3*(2), 191–198.

Fang, K., Friedlander, M., & Pieterse, A. L. (2016). Contributions of acculturation, enculturation, discrimination, and personality traits to social anxiety among Chinese immigrants: A context-specific assessment. *Cultural Diversity and Ethnic Minority Psychology, 22*(1), 1–11.

Fargues, P. (2014). *Why pro-immigration policies must be part of an adaptation to predictable demographic changes in Europe?* EUI Forum, European University Institute, Florence, Italy.

Finkelstein, L. M., & Burke, M. J. (1998). Age stereotyping at work: The role of rater and contextual factors on evaluations of job applicants. *The Journal of General Psychology, 125*(4), 317–345.

Fisher, E. L., Deason, G., Borgida, E., & Oyamot, C. M. (2011), "A model of authoritarianism, social norms, and personal values: Implications for Arizona law enforcement and immigration policy," *Analyses of Social Issues and Public Policy, 11*(1), 285–299.

Giovanelli, M. (2011). *Foreign trained doctors kept out of practice in U.S.* Retrieved from https://www.pri.org/stories/2011-04-14/foreign-trained-doctors-kept-out-practice-us.

Gordon, S. L. (2016). Welcoming refugees in the rainbow nation: contemporary attitudes towards refugees in South Africa. *African Geographical Review, 35*(1), 1–17.

Guerrero, L., & Rothstein, M. G. (2012). Antecedents of underemployment: Job search of skilled immigrants in Canada. *Applied Psychology, 61*(2), 323–346.

Guimond, S., De Oliveria, P., Kamiesjki, R., & Sidanius, J. (2010). The trouble with assimilation: Social dominance and the emergence of hostility against immigrants. *International Journal of Intercultural Relations, 34*(6), 642–650.

Hainmueller, J., & Hiscox, M. J. (2010). Attitudes toward highly skilled and low-skilled immigration: Evidence from a survey experiment. *American Political Science Review*, *104*(1), 61–84.

Hamilton, D. L. (1979). A cognitive-attributional analysis of stereotyping. In L. Berkowitz (Ed.), *Advances in experimental social psychology*, (Vol. 12, pp 53–84.). New York, NY: Academic Press.

Heilman, M. E. (1983). Sex bias in work settings: The lack-of-fit model. *Research in Organizational Behavior, 5,* 269–298.

Helbling, M., & Kriesi, H. (2014). Why citizens prefer high-over low-skilled immigrants. labor market competition, welfare state, and deservingness. *European Sociological Review*, *30*(5), 595–614.

Hersch, J. (2011). The persistence of skin color discrimination for immigrants. *Social Science Research, 40*(5), 1337–1349.

Higgins, E. T., & Bargh, J. A. (1987). Social cognition and social perception. *Annual Review of Psychology*, *38*(1), 369–425.

Hitlan, R. T., Carrillo, K., Zárate, M. A., & Aikman, S. N. (2007). Attitudes toward immigrant groups and the effects of the 9/11 terrorist attacks. *Peace and Conflict: Journal of Peace Psychology*, *13*(2), 1–18.

Hosoda, M., Nguyen, L. T., & Stone-Romero, E. F. (2012). The effect of Hispanic accents on employment decisions. *Journal of Managerial Psychology*, *27*(4), 347–364.

Hosoda, M., & Stone-Romero, E. F. (2010). The effects of foreign accents on employment-related decisions. *Journal of Managerial Psychology*, *25*(2), 113–132.

Huynh, Q. L., Devos, T., & Smalarz, L. (2011). Perpetual foreigner in one's own land: Potential implications for identity and psychological adjustment. *Journal of Social and Clinical Psychology*, *30*(2), 133.

Immigration and Naturalization Act. (1952). *Immigration and Naturalization Act*. Retrieved from https://www.uscis.gov/laws/immigration-and-nationality-act

International Migration Report. (2017). *The international migration report*. Retrieved from https://www.un.org/development/desa/publications/international-migration-report-2017.html

Kelly, P. (2014). Understanding intergenerational social mobility: Filipino youth in Canada. *IRPP Study 45*, 1–12.

Knoll, B. R. (2009). "And who is my neighbor?" Religion and immigration policy attitudes. *Journal for the Scientific Study of Religion*, *48*(2), 313–331.

Krings, F., & Olivares, J. (2007). At the doorstep to employment: Discrimination against immigrants as a function of applicant ethnicity, job type, and raters' prejudice. *International Journal of Psychology*, *42*(6), 406–417.

Lee, T. L., & Fiske, S. T. (2006). Not an outgroup, not yet an ingroup: Immigrants in the stereotype content model. *International Journal of Intercultural Relations*, *30*(6), 751–768.

Leong, C. H. (2008). A multilevel research framework for the analyses of attitudes toward immigrants. *International Journal of Intercultural Relations*, *32*(2), 115–129.

Loftquist, L. H., & Dawis, R. V. (1969). *Adjustments to work*. New York, NY: Appleton-Century-Crofts.

López-Rodríguez, L., Zagefka, H., Navas, M., & Cuadrado, I. (2014). Explaining majority members' acculturation preferences for minority members: A mediation model. *International Journal of Intercultural Relations, 38,* 36–46.

Maddox, K. B., & Gray, S. A. (2002). Cognitive representations of Black Americans: Re-exploring the role of skin tone. *Personality and Social Psychological Bulletin, 28,* 250–259

Manuel-Krogstad, J., & Radford, J. (2018). *Education levels of US immigrants are on the rise.* Retrieved from: https://www.pewresearch.org/fact-tank/2018/09/14/education-levels-of-u-s-immigrants-are-on-the-rise/

Mattoo, A., Neagu, I. C., & Özden, Ç. (2008). Brain waste? Educated immigrants in the US labor market. *Journal of Development Economics, 87*(2), 255–269.

McDaniel, E., Nooruddin, I., & Shortle, A. (2011), "Divine boundaries: How religion shapes citizens' attitudes toward immigrants," *American Politics Research, 39*(1), 205–233.

Migration Policy Institute. (2019). *Frequently requested statistics on immigrants and immigration in the United States.* Retrieved from: https://www.migrationpolicy.org/?gclid=Cj0KCQjwyoHlBRCNARIsAFjKJ6CloYJ719XcvtHNgbrqhGKmnwShv96bTPw4z1z7CAFcio_7k05d2gkaAinqEALw_wcB

Miller N., & Brewer, M. B., (Eds). (1984). *Groups in contact: The psychology of desegregation.* Orlando, FL: Academic Press.

Moore, L. M., & Ovadia, S. (2006). Accounting for spatial variation in tolerance: The effects of education and religion. *Social Forces,* 84(4), 2205–2222.

Murray, K. E., & Marx, D. M. (2013). Attitudes toward unauthorized immigrants, authorized immigrants, and refugees. *Cultural Diversity and Ethnic Minority Psychology, 62,* 739–757.

Oreopoulos, P. (2011). Why do skilled immigrants struggle in the labor market? A field experiment with thirteen thousand resumes. *American Economic Journal: Economic Policy, 3*(4), 148–71.

Ortiz, V., & Telles, E. (2012). Racial identity and racial treatment of Mexican Americans. *Race and Social Problems, 4*(1), 41–56.

Oyamot Jr, C. M., Borgida, E., & Fisher, E. L. (2006). Can values moderate the attitudes of right-wing authoritarians? *Personality and Social Psychology Bulletin, 32*(4), 486–500.

Oyamot Jr., C. M., Fisher, E. L., Deason, G., & Borgida, E. (2012). Attitudes toward immigrants: The interactive role of the authoritarian predisposition, social norms, and humanitarian values. *Journal of Experimental Social Psychology, 48*(1), 97–105.

Pagotto, L., Voci, A., & Maculan, V. (2010). The effectiveness of intergroup contact at work: Mediators and moderators of hospital workers' prejudice towards immigrants. *Journal of Community & Applied Social Psychology, 20*(4), 317–330.

Park, B., & Judd, C. M. (2005). Rethinking the link between categorization and prejudice within the social cognition perspective. *Personality and Social Psychology Review, 9*(2), 108–130.

Pedersen, A., & Hartley, L. K. (2012). Prejudice against Muslim Australians: The role of values, gender and consensus. *Journal of Community & Applied Social Psychology, 22*(3), 239–255.

Peffley, M., & Hurwitz, J. (1998). Whites' stereotypes of Blacks: Sources and political consequences. In J. Hurwitz & M. Peffley (Eds.), *Perception and prejudice: Race and politics in the United States* (pp. 58–99) New Haven, CT: Yale University Press.

Pettigrew, T. F., Tropp, L. R., Wagner, U., & Christ, O. (2011). Recent advances in intergroup contact theory. *International Journal of Intercultural Relations, 35*(3), 271–280.

Pew Research (2017). *Race, immigration and discrimination.* Retrieved from http://www.people-press.org/2017/10/05/4-race-immigration-and-discrimination/.

Porter, L. W., Lawler, E. E., & Hackman, J. R. (1975). *Behavior in organizations.* New York, NY: McGraw-Hill.

Pratto, F., Sidanius, J., Stallworth, L. M., & Malle, B. F. (1994). Social dominance orientation: A personality variable predicting social and political attitudes. *Journal of Personality and Social Psychology, 67*(4), 741.

Radford, J., & Budiman, A. (2018, September 14). Facts on U.S. immigrants 2016. Retrieved on January 22, 2019, from http://www.pewhispanic.org/2018/09/14/facts-on-u-s-immigrants-previous-years-data/

Ray, B., & Preston, V. (2009). Geographies of discrimination: Variations in perceived discomfort and discrimination in Canada's gateway cities. *Journal of Immigrant & Refugee Studies, 7*(3), 228–249.

Riek, B. M., Mania, E. W., & Gaertner, S. L. (2006). Intergroup threat and outgroup attitudes: A meta-analytic review. *Personality and Social Psychology Review, 10*(4), 336–353.

Rooth, D. O. (2001). Ethnic discrimination and 'Swedish-specific' knowledge: What we can learn from studies of adoptees and second-generation migrants. *Ekonomisk Debatt, 29*(8), 535–546.

Schemer, C. (2012). The influence of news media on stereotypic attitudes toward immigrants in a political campaign. *Journal of Communication, 19,* 332–341.

Scheve, K. F., & Slaughter, M. J. (2001). Labor market competition and individual preferences over immigration policy. *Review of Economics and Statistics, 83*(1), 133–145.

Shields, J. (2011, February). *Entering the labour market: The association of immigrant class, gender, and country of birth with employment outcomes.* Paper presented at annual meeting at Local Immigrant Partnership (LIP) Conference, Toroa*y readings in social psychology*) (pp. 64—82). Philadelphia, PA: Psychology Press and Taylor & Francis.

Stephan, W. G., & Stephan, C. W. (1985). Intergroup anxiety. *Journal of Social Issues, 41*(3), 157–175.

Stephan, W. G., & Stephan, C. W. (1996). Predicting prejudice. *International Journal of Intercultural Relations, 20*(3–4), 409–426.

Stephan, W. G., Ybarra, O., & Bachman, G. (1999). Prejudice toward immigrants. *Journal of Applied Social Psychology, 29*(11), 2221–2237.

Stone, D. L., & Colella, A. (1996). A model of factors affecting the treatment of disabled individuals in organizations. *Academy of Management Review, 21*(2), 352–401.

Stone, D. L., Lukaszewski, K. M., Krueger, D. C., & Canedo, J. C. (2019). Influence of immigrant's attributes on unfair discrimination in organizations. In A. Georgiadou, M. Gonzalez-Perez, & M. Olivas-Lujan (Eds.), *Diversity within diversity management: Types of diversity in organizations* (pp. 79–93). New York, NY: Emerald Publishers.

Stone, E. F., Stone, D. L., & Dipboye, R. L. (1992). Stigmas in organizations: Race, handicaps, and physical unattractiveness. In K. Kelley (Ed.), *Issues, theory, and research in industrial/organizational psychology* (pp. 385–457). Oxford, UK: North-Holland.

Stone-Romero, E. F., Stone, D. L., Hartman, M., & Hosoda, M. (2020). Stereotypes of ethnic groups in terms of attributes relevant to work organizations: An experimental study. In D. L. Stone, J. H. Dulebohn, & K. M. Lukaszewski (Eds.), *Diversity and Inclusion*. Charlotte, NC: Information Age Publishing.

Stone-Romero, E. F., Stone, D. L., & Salas, E. (2003). The influence of culture on role conceptions and role behavior in organizations. *Applied Psychology, 52*(3), 328–362.

Tajfel, H., & Turner, J. C. (1979). An integrative theory of intergroup conflict. In W. Austin & S. Worchel (Eds), *The social psychology of intergroup relations* (pp. 33–47). Monterey, CA: Brooks/Cole.

Timberlake, J. M., & Williams, R. H. (2012). Stereotypes of U S immigrants from four global regions. *Social Science Quarterly, 93*(4), 867–890.

Trice, H. M., & Beyer, J. M. (1993). *The cultures of work organizations*. New York, NY: Prentice-Hall, Inc.

US Census Bureau (2016). *The foreign-born population in the United States*. Retrieved from https://www.census.gov/newsroom/pdf/cspan_fb_slides.pdf

van den Berg, M. (2012). *Attitudes toward non-Western immigrants in the Netherlands* (unpublished master's theses). Tilburg University, Tilburg, Netherlands.

Vezzali, L., & Giovanni, D. (2010). Social Dominance Orientation, realistic and symbolic threat: Effects on Italians' acculturation orientations, intergroup attitudes and emotions towards immigrants. *TPM-Testing, Psychometrics, Methodology in Applied Psychology, 17*(3), 141–159.

Vezzali, L., Giovanni, D., & Capozza, D. (2010). Longitudinal effects of contact on intergroup relations: The role of majority and minority group membership and intergroup emotions. *Journal of Community & Applied Social Psychology, 20,* 462–479.

Visintin, E. P., Voci, A., Pagotto, L., & Hewstone, M. (2017). Direct, extended, and mass-mediated contact with immigrants in Italy: their associations with emotions, prejudice, and humanity perceptions. *Journal of Applied Social Psychology, 47*(4), 175–194.

Voci, A., & Hewstone, M. (2003). Intergroup contact and prejudice toward immigrants in Italy: The mediational role of anxiety and the moderational role of group salience. *Group Processes & Intergroup Relations, 6*(1), 37–54.

Ward, C., & Masgoret, A. (2006). An integrative model of attitudes toward immigrants. *International Journal of Intercultural Relations, 30*(6), 671–682.

Wilkes, R., Guppy, N., & Farris, L. (2008). "No thanks, we're full": Individual characteristics, national context, and changing attitudes toward immigration. *International Migration Review, 42*(2), 302–329.

Yum, J. O., & Park, H. W. (1990). The effects of disconfirming information on stereotype change. *Howard Journal of Communications, 2*(4), 357–367.

Zschirnt, E., & Ruedin, D. (2016). Ethnic discrimination in hiring decisions: a meta-analysis of correspondence tests 1990–2015. *Journal of Ethnic and Migration Studies, 42*(7), 1115–1134.

AUTHOR BIOGRAPHIES

Brittney Amber is a doctoral candidate studying Applied Social and Organizational Psychology at Indiana University—Purdue University Indianapolis where she also received her master's degree in Industrial Organizational Psychology. Brittney works as a research and teaching assistant in the Kelley School of Business. Her primary goals center around improving employees' work lives through action research and interdisciplinary partnerships. She is interested in topics such as diversity and inclusion in the workplace, professional and leadership development, and teamwork. She also seeks to address negative attitudes and behaviors in the workplace, such as incivility, harassment, microaggressions, and discrimination.

Eric Mark Arredondo is a licensed attorney and currently works in the Contracts and Legal Department at Environmental Systems Research Institute, Inc. in Redlands, California. He earned a JD from Northwestern University School of Law where he was a Senior Articles Editor for the *Journal of Criminal Law and Criminology*. He also earned a MBA and BA in Criminal Justice and Political Science from The University of Texas at El Paso.

Sara E. Barth, M. S. is a doctoral student in the Social, Decision, and Organizational Sciences program at the University of Maryland, College Park. Her research focuses on diversity, discrimination, and inclusion issues in the workplace

Diversity and Inclusion in Organizations, pages 361–371.
Copyright © 2020 by Information Age Publishing
All rights of reproduction in any form reserved.

and investigates how employees manage their diverse identities at work and how these identities are discussed.

Katherine N. Brown is a Ph.D. student in Industrial-Organizational Psychology at Clemson University, where her research is primarily concerned with diversity and inclusion issues. She has conducted research on the perceptions and treatment of women in STEM fields and in leadership positions, and she is also interested in LGBTQ issues in the workplace. Katherine has also conducted research on the relationship between working memory capacity and mental rotation ability. This research appears in the *Journal of Scientific Psychology*. Katherine is a member of the Society for Industrial and Organizational Psychology and the Southeastern Psychological Association.

Courtney M. Bryant, M. A. is a doctoral candidate in the Organizational Psychology program at Michigan State University. As a member of the Diversity Lab at MSU under the advisement of Dr. Ann Marie Ryan, her overall research program uses the lens of authenticity to examine topics such as minority experiences, identity, diversity and discrimination, and coworker relationships in the workplace. She is an NSF Graduate Research Fellow and recipient of the Ford Blue Oval Scholarship.

Julio C. Canedo (Ph.D., University of Texas, San Antonio) is an Assistant Professor at the Marilyn Davies College of Business of the University of Houston Downtown. He is certified in coaching, human resource management (HRM), and ethics. Dr. Canedo is a member of academic and professional organizations like the Society for Industrial and Organizational Psychology, the Academy of Management, and the Houston Hispanic Chamber of Commerce. His research has been published in such outlets as *Research in Human Resource Management,* the *Journal of Managerial Psychology, AIS Transactions on Human-Computer Interaction, Organizational Dynamics*, the *Journal of Business and Entrepreneurship, Oxford University Press,* and *TIP The Industrial-Organizational Psychologist.* Dr. Canedo's research interests include HRM, e-HRM, strategic HRM, leadership, and cross-cultural issues at work. He has presented his work in national and regional conferences of the *Academy of Management* and in sponsored corporate events in Latin America.

Abby Corrington graduated from Rice University with a B.A. in Psychology in 2013 and worked in organizational change management consulting for two years before returning to academia. Currently, Abby is pursuing a Ph.D. in Industrial/Organizational Psychology at Rice University, where she also received her M.A. in Industrial/Organizational Psychology. Broadly, her research is centered on diversity and inclusion in the workplace, in contexts ranging from informal social interactions to the hiring process. Specifically, she is interested in the experiences and perceptions of stigmatized groups in terms of gender, race, sexual orientation, age, religion, culture, and other identities. Her hope is that her research will help provide employees, organizations, and society as a whole with information and strategies for improving workplace experiences.

Thomas Dougherty received his PhD in Industrial/Organizational Psychology from the University of Houston. He joined the Management faculty of the University of Missouri-Columbia in 1979 where he served for 36 years, including the Hibbs/Brown Chair of Business & Economics from 2003–2015, when he transitioned to emeritus professor. His recent research has focused on mentoring and networking processes as they relate to careers and career success. He has published widely in management and psychology journals and edited volumes.

George Dreher initiated his career as an Industrial Psychologist with Southern California Edison Company. He then Joined the faculty in the School of Business at the University of Kansas. Finally, he joined the faculty in the Department of Management and Entrepreneurship at Indiana University-Bloomington, where he is now an emeritus professor. His current research interests focus on opportunity and career attainment, with a particular interest in the late-career competition to reach senior management. Throughout his career he has studied how race and gender influence career success and currently is working on a paper about the interactive role of potential and gender in accounting for the gender pay gap. He is widely published in psychology journals ranging from the Journal of Applied Psychology to Personnel Psychology and in management journals ranging from the Academy of Management Journal to the Journal of Management.

James H. Dulebohn is a Professor of Human Resource Management at the School of Human Resource Management and Labor Relations at Michigan State University. He received his Ph. D. in Human Resource Management and Organizational Behavior from the University of Illinois. His research focuses on leadership in organizations, virtual teams, HR metrics, electronic-human resource management, and other related issues. Results of his research have been published in the *Journal of Management, Human Resource Management Review, Journal of Applied Psychology*, *Personnel Psychology*, and the *Academy of Management*. He is currently the Co-Editor of the *Research in Human Resource Management* series, and serves on the editorial boards of the *Journal of Management, Human Resource Management Review, Group and Organizational Management*, and the *Journal of Managerial Psychology*. He and his co-authors won the best paper award for their research on authentic and servant leadership in the *Journal of Management*.

Jamie M. Fynes works for the Department of Defense. She graduated from Clemson University in 2018 with a Ph.D. in Industrial-Organizational Psychology. Through her research assistantship, she provided support in the development, administration, and analysis of a faculty climate survey for a grant from the National Science Foundation ADVANCE Program, Clemson TIGERS ADVANCE: Transforming the Institution through Gender Equity, Retention, and Support. Dr. Fynes' applied work has been centered around research and analytics consultation and organizational surveys. She is a member of the Society for Industrial and Organizational Psychology.

Mark Hartman received his Master's degree in Industrial and Organizational Psychology at the University of Central Florida. He has conducted research on stereotypes of ethnic minorities, and Hispanic job choice factors. His research on HIspanic job choice factors was published in Management Research. He is now the Director of Global Initiatives at the University of Central Florida.

Mikki Hebl is the Martha and Henry Malcolm Lovett Professor of Psychology and Professor of Management at Rice University. She is an applied psychologist whose research focuses on workplace discrimination and remediation. Her particular area of expertise is in the area of gender discrimination. She has published approximately 150 papers, received 20 teaching awards, been awarded major NIH and NSF funded grants, and recently received both the lifetime award for Gender and Diversity in Organizations at the Academy of Management (2014), the national Cherry Professor of the Year Award (2016), and the Women Researcher Award (2018) from the University of Lausanne.

Megumi Hosoda is a Professor of Psychology at San José State University. She received her PhD in Industrial and Organizational Psychology form the University at Albany, New York State University. Her main research area is diversity in the workplace. She studies various types of diversity in the workplace, including sex, race/ethnicity, immigrants, and disability. Her current research emphasizes issues related to immigrant workers. The results of her research have appeared in such journals as *Personnel Psychology, Journal of Managerial Psychology, Journal of Applied Social Psychology, Journal of Organizational Psychology, College Student Journal, Human Resource Management Review, Disability Studies Quarterly, and Journal of Social Psychology.* She can be reached at megumi. hosoda@sjsu.edu.

Mary Inman is a social psychologist who has been teaching and doing research since 1992. She has taught at Trinity University and then Hope College. She teaches courses in Social Psychology and Industrial-Organizational Psychology, with a focus on understanding prejudice and power. Her research has examined factors affecting perceptions of discrimination, understanding group differences in those perceptions, and testing factors that change perceptions of discrimination. She has over 30 publications in peer-reviewed journals and over 60 presentations at peer-reviewed conferences. She earned her PhD in Social Psychology from the University of Iowa

Melinda Key-Roberts (Ph. D.) is a Senior Research Psychologist and Team Lead at the U.S. Army Research Institute for the Behavioral and Social Sciences. There, she manages several programs of research aimed at conducting innovative and rigorous research to identify and develop core competencies for senior military leaders. As lead for a program of research on climate for inclusion in the military, Melinda oversees senior civilian researchers and research fellows working to develop methods and measures for assessing and improving organizational climate within the Army.

Eden King (Ph. D.) is an Associate Professor of Industrial-Organizational Psychology at Rice University. She is pursuing a program of research– which has yielded over 100 scholarly products and has been featured in outlets such as the New York Times, Good Morning America, and Harvard Business Review– that addresses the challenges that women, LGBT people, religious and racio-ethnic minorities, mothers and pregnant women, and older workers face in the workplace. In addition, this work identifies, develops, and assesses theory-grounded interventions to overcome these obstacles and provide evidence to make work better for everyone. In addition to her scholarship, Dr. King has partnered with organizations to improve diversity climate, increase fairness in selection systems, and to design and implement diversity training programs. She is currently a Senior Associate Editor for the *Journal of Management* and an Associate Editor for the *Journal of Business and Psychology*.

Dianna Contreras Krueger received a Ph.D. in Business Administration, Organizational and Management studies attending The University of Texas at San Antonio and an M.A. in Psychology attending Stephen F. Austin State University. Her research focuses on selection and diversity in organizations. She is currently an assistant professor of management at Tarleton State University. Results of her research have been published in the Journal of Applied Psychology, the Journal of Business and Entrepreneurship, the Business Journal of Hispanic Research, and The Wiley Blackwell Handbook of the Psychology of the Internet at Work.

David Lane is an associate professor in the departments of psychological science, statistics, and administration. He received a BA in psychology from Clark University in 1971, an MA in child study from Tufts University in 1973, and a PhD in psychology in 1977. He has published articles in many fields including cognitive development, statistics, attention. decision ,making, human-computer interaction, gender differences, critical thinking, perception, memory, expertise, educational technology, autism, ADHD, design of scientific graphics, and ecological validity. He is the primary developer of the public domain teaching resource "An Interactive Multimedia Course of Study" which includes an introductory book, interactive simulations and demonstrations, real-world applications, and video versions of the material. He also developed the associated interactive e-book "Introduction to Statistics: An Interactive e-Book." The website won the MERLOT Classic Award in statistics education in 2007. Dr. Lane has taught courses in developmental psychology, statistics, research methods, attention, evolutionary psychology, and human-computer interaction

Kayla Liggett is a recent graduate from Hope College, where she obtained her undergraduate degree in Psychology.

Alex Lindsey is an Assistant Professor of Management in the Fogelman College of Business and Economics at The University of Memphis. He earned his Ph.D. in Industrial and Organizational Psychology from George Mason University in 2016. Dr. Lindsey's program of research investigates fair and equitable solutions to mitigate diversity-related challenges such as prejudice and discrimination in the workplace. Because seemingly trivial instances of disadvantage can create substantial inequity over time in the workplace, it represents a ripe context in which to study manifestations of disadvantage and potential solutions to these serious problems. His research seeks to generate effective strategies that targets of prejudice, their allies, and organizations can use to reduce inequality and promote inclusion in the workplace. Specifically, Dr. Lindsey's work has addressed diversity training effectiveness, impression and identity management strategies, and diverse team dynamics. This work has been published in quality outlets such as *Journal of Applied Psychology* and *Journal of Business and Psychology*.

Kimberly M. Lukaszewski received her Ph.D. from the University at Albany, State University of New York. She is currently an Associate Professor of Management at Wright State University. Her research is focused on electronic human resources and diversity issues. Her work has been published in journals such as the Human Resource Management Review, the Journal of Managerial Psychology, Journal of Business and Psychology, the Journal of Business Issues, the Journal of the Academy of Business Education, *AIS Transaction in Human-Computer Interactions* and *Communications of the Association for Information Systems.* She serves on the editorial boards of *Journal of Managerial Psychology, Research in Human Resource Management, Journal of Human Resource Education*, and served as a guest editor of a special issue of *Journal Managerial Psychology* on social issues, for three special issues of *AIS Transactions Human Computer Interactions* on HRIS and e-HRM, and a research series in *Research in Human Resource Management.*

Brigid Lynn (Ph. D.) is a Senior Evaluation Analyst at VentureWell where she designs and implements systematic methods for collecting, analyzing, and interpreting information to strengthen program effectiveness and efficiency. Brigid strives to understand organizational trends, and tracks and disseminates innovation and entrepreneurial insights. Previously, she was a Senior Research Psychologist at the U.S. Army Research Institute working to establish and maintain climates for inclusion that provide an environment for Soldiers to fully contribute their strengths to mission accomplishment.

Justin Marcus is an assistant professor of Management and Strategy at the College of Administrative Sciences and Economics of Koç University, in Istanbul, Turkey. He received a BA and a BS from the University of Nebraska-Lincoln, and an MS and Ph.D. from the University of Central Florida. His research interests include substantive topics in diversity and prejudice at work and cross-cultural management, and quantitative research methodologies such as meta-analysis, experimentation, and measurement and validation.

James Nye is a Post-Doctoral Research Fellow at the Consortium of Universities of the Washington Metropolitan Area, working with the U.S. Army Research Institute for the Behavioral and Social Sciences. There, James conducts research examining core competencies of senior leaders by exploring methodological alternatives to surveys and focus groups. Additionally, he collaborates with civilian research psychologists in projects aimed to measure and foster climates for inclusion within the military context. James obtained his Ph.D. in Experimental Psychology at the University of South Carolina and then proceeded to his current position as a Post-Doctoral Research Fellow.

Abby Peters is an Assistant Professor of Business at Nevada State College in Henderson, Nevada, where she teaches courses in management and economics. Abby received her MBA with a concentration in Economics and her PhD in International Business with a concentration in Management from the University of Texas at El Paso. Through research in human resource management, teaching, and community partnerships in the Las Vegas metropolitan area, she pursues her mission to improve the lives of workers.

Phani Radhakrishnan has been teaching and doing research since 1991. She has taught at the University of Illinois, Texas, and Windsor before she came to the University of Toronto in 2000.

She teaches courses in Negotiation, Team Building, Leadership Development, and Human Resources at the University of Toronto. Her pedagogical research is focused on how students develop their critical thinking skills with experiential learning activities. Her research on the impact of racial harassment was funded by the National Institutes of Mental Health in the United States. She has over 20 publications in top tier, peer-reviewed, journals and over 60 presentations at peer-reviewed conferences. She obtained her PhD in Industrial/Organizational Psychology from the University of Illinois, Urbana-Champaign and also worked for the US Army Environmental Research Laboratories and for Catalyst (a not-for-profit research and consulting firm on the advancement of women in the workplace).

Aarti Ramaswami is Deputy Dean ESSEC Business School Asia-Pacific, Academic Director of the ESSEC Global MBA program in France and Singapore, and Professor in the Management Department. Her work focuses on systems used to identify, select, and develop managerial and executive talent, with a particular interest in career success, diversity and inclusion, expatriation, and cross-cultural management. Her research has appeared in top international peer-reviewed journals. She teaches various leadership and management topics to MBA, Executive Education, and Doctoral program participants. She graduated with a PhD in Organizational Behavior and Human Resource Management from the Kelley School of Business at Indiana University Bloomington. She has a highly international profile, having lived and worked in India, USA, France, UAE, and now in Singapore.

Nathaniel Ratcliff is a Research Assistant Professor at the University of Virginia working within the Biocomplexity Institute and Initiative's Social and Decision Analytic Division. There, Nathaniel conducts research using the science of all data to answer questions in the interest of the public good. Nathaniel obtained his Ph.D. at the Pennsylvania State University in social psychology and completed a post-doctoral fellowship at the U.S. Army Research Institute.

Patrick J. Rosopa (Ph. D.) is an Associate Professor in the Department of Psychology at Clemson University. His substantive research interests are in personality and cognitive ability, stereotypes and fairness in the workplace, and cross-cultural issues in organizational research. He also has quantitative research interests in applied statistical modeling including applications of machine learning in organizational research and the use of computer-intensive approaches to evaluate statistical procedures. Dr. Rosopa's work has been supported by $4.1 million in grants from various organizations including Alcon, BMW, and the National Science Foundation. Dr. Rosopa's research has been published in various peer-reviewed journals including *Psychological Methods, Organizational Research Methods, Journal of Modern Applied Statistical Methods, Human Resource Management Review, Journal of Managerial Psychology, Journal of Vocational Behavior, Human Performance*, and *Personality and Individual Differences*. In addition, he has co-authored a statistics textbook titled *Statistical Reasoning in the Behavioral Sciences*, published by Wiley in 2010 and 2018. Dr. Rosopa serves on the editorial board of *Human Resource Management Review* and *Organizational Research Methods*. He also serves as Associate Editor-Methodology for *Journal of Managerial Psychology*. Dr. Rosopa is a member of the American Psychological Association, Association for Psychological Science, and Society for Industrial and Organizational Psychology.

Cort W. Rudolph is an assistant professor of Industrial & Organizational Psychology at Saint Louis University. He received a BA from DePaul University, and a MA and Ph.D. from Wayne State University. Cort's research focuses on a variety of issues related to the aging workforce, including applications of lifespan development theories, wellbeing and work-longevity, and ageism/generationalism.

Dianna L. Stone received her Ph. D. from Purdue University, and is now a Research Professor at the University of New Mexico, a Visiting Professor at the University of Albany, and an Affiliate Professor at Virginia Tech. Her research focuses on diversity in organizations, electronic human resource management, privacy in organizations, and cross-cultural issues. Results of her research have been published in the *Journal of Applied Psychology, Personnel Psychology, the Academy of Management Review, Organizational Behavior and Human Decision Processes,* and *Human Resource Management Review.* She is currently the Co-Editor of *Research in Human Resource Management,* a research series in human resource management and related fields. She is also the Associate Editor of *Human Resource Management Review,* and the former Editor of the *Journal of Managerial Psychology.* She is a Fellow of the Society for industrial and Organizational Psychology, the American Psychological Association, and the Association of Psychological Sciences. She has been awarded the Scholarly Achievement Award and the Sage Service Award in the Gender and Diversity Division of the Academy of Management. She also won the Trailblazer Award in the Ph. D. Project.

Eugene F. Stone-Romero (Ph. D., University of California, Irvine) is a Research Professor in the Department of Organizational Studies at the Anderson School of Management, University of New Mexico. He is a Fellow of the Society of Industrial and Organizational Psychology, the Association of Psychological Sciences, and the American Psychological Association. He served as an Associate Editor of the *Journal of Applied Psychology* and as a member of numerous editorial boards. Stone-Romero received (a) the Distinguished Career Award from the Research Methods Division of the Academy of Management, (b) the Thomas Mahoney Career Mentoring Award from the Human Resource Division of the Academy of Management, and (c) the Kenneth and Mamie Clark Award from the American Psychological Association of Graduate Students. He is the author of over 125 journal articles and edited book chapters. His journal articles have appeared in such outlets as the *Journal of Applied Psychology, Organizational Behavior and Human Performance, Personnel Psychology,* the *Journal of Vocational Behavior,* the *Academy of Management Journal,* and *Research in Personnel and Human Resources Management.* His book chapters have dealt with such issues as research methods, statistical methods, human resources management, industrial and organizational psychology, and organizational behavior.

Maria Triana is an Associate Professor at the University of Wisconsin—Madison in the Management and Human Resources Department. She earned a PhD in Organizational Behavior with a minor in Industrial/Organizational Psychology from Texas A&M University. Maria's research interests include diversity and discrimination in the workplace and organizational justice. Maria holds the Kuechenmeister-Bascom Professorship in Business and is a past recipient of the Cynthia and Jay Ihlenfeld Inspired Learning Chair. She is the author of *Managing Diversity in Organizations: A Global Perspective* (Routledge, 1st Ed.) as well as *Organizational Behavior* (Wiley, 5th Ed.). She teaches courses on diversity in organizations as well as team dynamics. She also serves as the Academic Director of the Center for Strategic Human Resource Management in the Wisconsin MBA program. Prior to joining academia, Maria was a systems analyst and project manager for Intel Corporation. She holds professional certifications in both project management and human resource management.

Rachel Trump-Steele is just months away from graduating from Rice University with her Ph.D. Broadly, she studies diversity, discrimination, and inclusion in the workplace. Much of her current work focuses on the role that male allies can play in helping to create gender equity in the workplace. Her work in this area has been presented to academic and applied audiences.

M. Fernanda Wagstaff is an Associate Professor in the Department of Marketing and Management at The University of Texas at El Paso. She received her PhD from Texas A&M University. Her current research interests include diversity issues at work and international human resource management. She is currently the Director of the Center for Multicultural Management and Ethics and the recipient of the Robert E. and Jacqueline Skov Professorship in Business Ethics.

Jennifer L. Wessel, Ph.D. is an Assistant Professor of Psychology in the Social, Decision, and Organizational Sciences program at the University of Maryland, College Park. Dr. Wessel received her Ph.D. from Michigan State University in 2012. Her research focuses on diversity, identity, and authenticity. Dr. Wessel has been published in journals such as *Academy of Management Review, Human Resource Management Review, Journal of Applied Psychology, Psychology of Women Quarterly,* and *Social Psychological and Personality Science.* Her work has been funded by the Social Science Research Council and the Society for Human Resource Management. More information at her website: imglab.umd.edu.

Phoebe Xoxakos is a graduate student and teaching assistant in the Department of Psychology at Clemson University. She is pursuing a Ph.D. in Industrial-Organizational Psychology. Her research interests relate to diversity including ways to enhance diversity climate; the effects of oppressive systems such as sexism, ageism, and racism; and quantitative methods. She is a member of the Society for Industrial and Organizational Psychology.

Hannes Zacher is a professor of work and organizational psychology at the Institute of Psychology, Leipzig University, Germany. He received his Ph.D. from the University of Giessen in 2009. In his research program, he investigates aging at work, career development, and occupational well-being; proactivity, innovation, leadership, and entrepreneurship; and pro-environmental employee behavior.

Made in the USA
Monee, IL
06 January 2021

56612538R00208